TODAY'S MORAL ISSUES

Classic and Contemporary Perspectives

Daniel Bonevac

The University of Texas at Austin

Mayfield Publishing Company
Mountain View, California
London · Toronto

For Alan Gribben and Irene Wong
Courage proves itself in difficulties.
—Swahili proverb

Library of Congress Cataloging-in-Publication Data
Today's moral issues : classic and contemporary perspectives / [edited
  by] Daniel Bonevac.
        p.   cm.
    Includes index.
    ISBN 0-87484-855-5
    1. Moral conditions.   2. Social ethics.   3. Political science—philosophy
  4. Social justice.   I. Bonevac, Daniel A., 1955–
  HM216.T59 1991
  303.3′72—dc20   91-33101
                                                        CIP

Manufactured in the United States of America
10 9 8 7 6 5 4 3 2

Mayfield Publishing Company
1240 Villa Street
Mountain View, California 94041

Sponsoring editor, James Bull; managing editor, Linda Toy; production editor, April Wells;
copy editor, Sally Peyrefitte; text and cover designer, Donna Davis; art director, Jeanne M.
Schreiber; manufacturing manager, Martha Branch. Cover image: Paul Klee, "Separation
at Evening," © Estate of Paul Klee/VAGA, New York 1991. The text was set in 10/12 ITC
Berkeley Oldstyle Book and Berkeley Oldstyle Medium and printed on 50# Finch Opaque
by the Maple-Vail Book Manufacturing Group.

Contents

PART III. Rights 219

Preface

I have designed this book as a text for courses on contemporary moral issues. Like most other texts designed for this purpose, it consists of writings relevant to controversial problems such as censorship, abortion, capital punishment, and affirmative action. The writings collected fall into two categories. Some are excerpts from philosophical classics—Mill's *On Liberty*, for example, or Locke's *Second Treatise of Government*—while others are current discussions of problems in contemporary society.

I have taught classes on contemporary moral issues repeatedly over the past few years and have become increasingly dissatisfied with standard approaches to such courses. Most collections tilt heavily toward contemporary discussions of particular, controversial moral problems, with only a few brief theoretical readings from historical figures. This approach has some obvious pedagogical advantages, but it also creates serious problems.

First, students find it very difficult to abstract general principles and methods of reasoning from discussions of particular problems. Instructors thus face a dilemma. If they rely on students to abstract general principles and methods, they leave most students with only the vaguest sense of what ethical thinking is. If the instructors themselves supply principles and methods, they find their course splitting into two parts—one practical, one theoretical—that are very hard to unify.

Second, collections often draw their readings on contemporary issues from philosophical journals. The articles they include are written by and for professional philosophers. They often presuppose acquaintance with philosophical jargon and strategy that students lack. Moreover, they relate specific points to quite specific philosophical concerns, not to broad, overarching themes of the kind introductory courses should emphasize. Only rarely, therefore, have I found these articles suited for introducing students to an issue.

Third, most collections focus on issues that are largely political in nature. Like the issues mentioned above, they involve problems not only of individual moral choice but also of government policy. Yet, to the extent that the books treat theoretical issues at all, they concentrate on individual choice, saying very little about political theory. This leaves both student and instructor unarmed in confronting issues, such as capital punishment, that turn on conceptions of the bounds of permissible state action.

This collection differs from others, therefore, in several important respects. First, it devotes a large amount of space to theoretical discussions drawn from classics of the Western philosophical tradition. (Another volume, *Beyond the Western Tradition: Readings in Moral and Political Philosophy*, includes readings from non-Western sources that mesh readily with texts included here.) I have found that students feel much more at home, and learn much more, if theoretical issues are directly confronted rather than left unarticulated. Each of the four major divisions of the book begins by introducing concrete moral and political issues and showing how they lead directly to the philosophical questions raised in the theoretical readings. Questions to spur students' reflections and to organize their thoughts in reading the philosophical texts appear at the beginning of each excerpt.

Second, the contemporary readings on particular moral problems are most often from authors prominent in public debate. Some are philosophers, but more are not. The authors whose arguments appear here include economists, politicians, environmental scientists, sociologists, lawyers, journalists, and essayists. I have chosen the selections for their power, clarity, and relation to broader philosophical themes. In every case, I have sought to find the best, most accessible articulations of a given position toward an issue.

Finally, I have included readings on political theory—from Hobbes, Locke, and Rousseau, for example—not usually found in collections of this kind. I have used these in the classroom for several years and have found them very helpful for introducing students to fundamental questions of political theory. Far from leading away from the topics usually treated in contemporary moral issues courses, they offer a perspective for understanding how such issues hang together and how a view on one issue may have ramifications for views on other issues as well. Students emerge with an appreciation, not just for the intricacies of certain specific problems, but for basic approaches to the relation between people and government.

I thank the following people for their thoughtful comments: L. E. Andrade, Illinois State University; Linda Bomstad, California State University, Sacramento; Karen Hanson, Indiana University; and Anita Silvers, San Francisco State University.

PART I   # Liberty

The central problem of political philosophy is the relation between people and their governments—between the rulers and the ruled. When rulers acquire power through force or inheritance, there is little need to take the interests of the people into account. In a democracy, however, the rulers acquire power through elections and therefore must consider the interests of the people to some degree. But even if the rulers follow the will of the majority perfectly, the possibility of conflict remains. Rule by the people, as John Stuart Mill points out, is really rule of each by all the rest. Nothing in the concept of democracy itself protects the minority from the majority's power. Edmund Burke therefore warned of the "oppression of the minority"; Alexis de Tocqueville similarly foresaw "the tyranny of the majority."

Two kinds of issues arise here. First, certain distinct and unpopular or disadvantaged groups may consistently lose elections to a more powerful majority. Democracy, unembellished, does little to protect their rights. Usually, factions shift from issue to issue; a group on the losing side of one issue often comes out on the winning side on the next. Groups may have interests that vary so greatly, however, that the electoral balance of power is stable. Some may consistently win while others consistently lose. Second, individuals have little protection from the majority's power. Voters out of step with the majority may find themselves without any rights at all.

The American Bill of Rights—the first ten amendments to the United States Constitution—attempts to protect people from the unfettered power of undemocratic minorities and democratic majorities. By delineating people's rights, it carves out a sphere of individual liberty that government may not transgress. Philosophers such as John Stuart Mill seek to distinguish a sphere of personal liberty in a different way. A law is *paternalistic* if it restricts a person's liberty for his or her own good. Mill argues, with some important qualifications, that such laws are illegitimate. Mill's *harm principle* asserts that government may restrict a person's liberty only to prevent harm to others. To restrict liberty to prevent people from harming themselves or to promote their own good, Mill contends, goes beyond the proper bounds of government authority.

Many countries have a wide variety of paternalistic laws. They tend to fall into three categories:

1. *Laws promoting morality:* Laws regulating religious practices, diet, and various forms of sexual behavior—adultery, polygamy, polyandry, sodomy, prostitution, premarital sex, pornography, and miscegenation (interracial marriage).
2. *Laws promoting health and safety:* Laws regulating alcohol, drugs (both medical and recreational), suicide, self-mutilation, voluntary euthanasia, working conditions, and the use of motorcycle helmets and seat belts.
3. *Laws promoting economic welfare:* Laws regulating wages, working hours, shopping hours (for example, "blue laws"), gambling, investments, and retirement (for example, Social Security).

Few people would accept all laws of this kind as legitimate, but just as few would find all objectionable. How can we distinguish legitimate from illegitimate paternalistic laws?

One way incorporates Mill's distinction between *self-regarding* and *other-regarding* actions. Roughly, a self-regarding action affects only the agent or agents of the action; an other-regarding action affects others. Mill's harm principle, in these terms, rules out government restriction of self-regarding actions.

There are several complications. Some self-regarding actions involve only a single agent—taking a drug or failing to wear a seat belt, for example. Others involve a group of agents; it takes at least two agents to indulge in prostitution, sodomy, gambling, or employment, for example. In either case, Mill says, we can consider the act self-regarding only if several conditions are satisfied. First, every agent must be acting freely; there must be no coercion. Everyone involved must consent to the action. We can treat ordinary, consensual sexual activity as self-regarding, but rape is clearly other-regarding. Second, every agent must be acting voluntarily. If any participant is in any way incapable of choosing—if he or she is a child, for example, or mentally incapacitated, drugged, or insane—then the action is other-regarding. Third, every agent must be reasonably well-informed about the action. There must be no ignorance or deception about any important and relevant matters. Someone taking a dangerous drug while believing it to be aspirin is not exercising liberty in any meaningful sense. If any participant is ignorant or deceived about an important feature of the action, then, it counts as other-regarding. The harm principle protects from government intrusion only those actions that are undertaken freely and voluntarily by informed agents and that affect nobody but themselves.

Mill's harm principle has met with wide acceptance in certain realms, but it has also met serious objections. Aristotle, for example, holds a completely opposed view of liberty. He contends that the best government is that which produces the best citizens. The chief task of government, in his view, is to promote the good of its citizens by helping to educate and guide them. Edmund Burke and others take a more moderate view. They maintain that individual liberty is only one among many important and competing values. A society should value the individual liberty of its citizens, these philosophers charge, but it should also value harmony, order, justice, and equality, among others. These various values often come into conflict, both in our individual lives and in the political arena. The harm principle tries to resolve all such conflicts in favor of liberty. But, Burke holds, it is not obvious that any value wins out all of the time. Politics, in his view, is an art of balancing values, reconciling them when possible, seeking compromises between them when possible, and, if all else fails, resolving conflicts between them by appeal to analogy and the wisdom we have accumulated from the past.

The Supreme Court and various political philosophers of the twentieth century have responded to Mill's principle by distinguishing civil from economic liberties. Civil liberties—in the original sense of the term, liberties granted by society—have been interpreted as liberties relating in some way to a person's sense of identity or to the political process. It is not clear whether this distinction makes sense. In what category, for example, is the freedom to place an advertisement or produce a commercial in favor of a certain political position? Whatever the answer, Mill means his principle to apply to both civil and economic liberties. Some twentieth-century thinkers, however, have sought to apply it only to civil liberties, contending that liberty does take precedence over other values in such matters, whereas justice, equality, and other concerns often take precedence over liberty in economic matters.

Questions concerning freedom of speech, as Alexis de Tocqueville points out, have a central place in democratic societies. Democracies depend on informed and involved citizens. Citizens can be informed, however, only if they have access to information. Political argument and the supporting information it requires therefore need protection. Types of speech that have little in common with political discussion and debate, however, provoke greater controversy. Some issues concerning freedom of speech—pornography, for example—fall under the general topic of paternalism, for both speaker and listener are voluntary, informed, consenting adults. Other kinds of speech do not. Racial harassment, for example, consists by definition in harm to others.

John Milton advances an early and sophisticated argument for freedom of the press. In brief, he contends that restrictions on publishing

and printing interfere with the search for truth, inevitably fail to restrict
what they are meant to restrict because of practical difficulties, insult
citizens and prevent them from developing their own powers of judgment, and are in any case unnecessary, for truth will conquer falsehood
in a free contest of ideas. John Stuart Mill adds to the arguments of
Milton and Tocqueville. An opinion may be true or contain some elements of truth. Even if it is false, only by battling such falsehoods can
the truth remain vibrant and meaningful. Mill thus concludes that the
content of an opinion can never justify suppressing it. Nor, he contends,
can its manner of expression. Only circumstances in which an utterance might cause serious harm (for example, start a riot) can justify
prohibiting it in those circumstances.

ARISTOTLE

from *Nicomachean Ethics*

Aristotle (384–322 B.C.E.), born in Stagira, was the son of Nicomachus, the court physician to Amyntas II, the king of Macedon. Nicomachus died when Aristotle was a boy. After training in medicine, Aristotle entered Plato's Academy in Athens at the age of seventeen. He stayed twenty years, until Plato's death. In 342, he became the tutor of Alexander the Great, Amyntas's grandson, who was thirteen; Aristotle stayed at the Macedonian court as Alexander's teacher for three years, until Alexander was appointed regent. In 335, Aristotle returned to Athens to establish his own school, the Lyceum. When Alexander died in 323, Athenians became suspicious of Aristotle's links to Macedonia. Fearing that he might be executed, as Socrates had been, he fled Athens, "lest the Athenians sin twice against philosophy." He died a year later in Chalcis of chronic indigestion brought about by overwork.

Aristotle's influence on intellectual history has been immense. He wrote treatises on physics, biology, astronomy, psychology, logic, metaphysics, poetry, rhetoric, ethics, and politics. Through the Middle Ages, in Europe and the Islamic world, Aristotle was known simply as "the philosopher." His philosophy is still important; most Western and Islamic thought is to some degree
Aristotelian. His scientific work, though now chiefly of historical interest, was remarkably sophisticated. It was not superseded for more than fifteen hundred years.

The Nicomachean Ethics addresses the basic questions of moral philosophy: What is the good? What is virtue? What is happiness? Aristotle believes that the good, for human beings—what humans properly desire for its own sake—is happiness, which he thinks has its highest form in contemplative activity. Aristotle holds that people can attain virtue and happiness, however, only in the context of a good state governed in the proper way. Aristotle thus believes that ethics and politics are intertwined. (Source: Reprinted from Aristotle's Nichomachean Ethics, translated by W. D. Ross. [1925], by permission of Oxford University Press.)

QUESTIONS FOR REFLECTION

1. Paternalistic laws restrict a person's freedom for that person's own good. What justification does Aristotle present for paternalistic laws?

2. What is it to be a good person, according to Aristotle? What does this mean for legislation?

BOOK X

9. . . . Surely, as the saying goes, where there are things to be done the end is not to survey and recognize the various things, but rather to do them; with regard to virtue, then, it is not enough to know, but we must try to have and use it, or try any other way
there may be of becoming good. Now if arguments were in themselves enough to make men good, they would justly, as Theognis says, have won very great rewards, and such rewards should have been provided; but as things are, while they seem to have power to encourage and stimulate the generous-minded among our youth, and to make a character

which is gently born, and a true lover of what is noble, ready to be possessed by virtue, they are not able to encourage the many to nobility and goodness. For these do not by nature obey the sense of shame, but only fear, and do not abstain from bad acts because of their baseness but through fear of punishment; living by passion they pursue their own pleasures and the means to them, and avoid the opposite pains, and have not even a conception of what is noble and truly pleasant, since they have never tasted it. What argument would remould such people? It is hard, if not impossible, to remove by argument the traits that have long since been incorporated in the character; and perhaps we must be content if, when all the influences by which we are thought to become good are present, we get some tincture of virtue.

Now some think that we are made good by nature, others by habituation, others by teaching. Nature's part evidently does not depend on us, but as a result of some divine causes is present in those who are truly fortunate; while argument and teaching, we may suspect, are not powerful with all men, but the soul of the student must first have been cultivated by means of habits for noble joy and noble hatred, like earth which is to nourish the seed. For he who lives as passion directs will not hear argument that dissuades him, nor understand it if he does; and how can we persuade one in such a state to change his ways? And in general passion seems to yield not to argument but to force. The character, then, must somehow be there already with a kinship to virtue, loving what is noble and hating what is base.

But it is difficult to get from youth up a right training for virtue if one has not been brought up under right laws; for to live temperately and hardily is not pleasant to most people, especially when they are young. For this reason their nurture and occupations should be fixed by law; for they will not be painful when they have become customary. But it is surely not enough that when they are young they should get the right nurture and attention; since they must, even when they are grown up, practise and be habituated to them, we shall need laws for this as well, and generally speaking to cover the whole of life; for most people obey necessity rather than argument, and punishments rather than the sense of what is noble.

This is why some think that legislators ought to stimulate men to virtue and urge them forward by the motive of the noble, on the assumption that those who have been well advanced by the formation of habits will attend to such influences; and that punishments and penalties should be imposed on those who disobey and are of inferior nature, while the incurably bad should be completely banished. A good man (they think), since he lives with his mind fixed on what is noble, will submit to argument, while a bad man, whose desire is for pleasure, is corrected by pain like a beast of burden. This is, too, why they say the pains inflicted should be those that are most opposed to the pleasures such men love.

However that may be, if (as we have said) the man who is to be good must be well trained and habituated, and go on to spend his time in worthy occupations and neither willingly nor unwillingly do bad actions, and if this can be brought about if men live in accordance with a sort of reason and right order, provided this has force—if this be so, the paternal command indeed has not the required force or compulsive power (nor in general has the command of one man, unless he be a king or something similar), but the law *has* compulsive power, while it is at the same time a rule proceeding from a sort of practical wisdom and reason. And while people hate *men* who oppose their impulses, even if they oppose them rightly, the law in its ordaining of what is good is not burdensome.

In the Spartan state alone, or almost alone, the legislator seems to have paid attention to questions of nurture and occupations; in most states such matters have been neglected, and each man lives as he pleases, Cyclops-fashion, "to his own wife and children dealing law." Now it is best that there should be a public and proper care for such matters; but if they are neglected by the community it would seem right for each man to help his children and friends towards virtue, and that they should have the power, or at least the will, to do this.

It would seem from what has been said that he can do this better if he makes himself capable of legislating. For public control is plainly effected by laws, and good control by good laws; whether written or unwritten would seem to make no difference, nor whether they are laws providing for the education of individuals or of groups—any more than it does in the case of music or gymnastics and other such pursuits. For as in cities laws and prevailing types of character have force, so in households do the injunctions and the habits of the father, and these have even more because of the tie of blood and the benefits he confers; for the children start with a natural affection and disposition to obey. Further, private education has an advantage over public, as private medical treatment has; for while in general rest and abstinence from food are good for a man in a fever, for a particular man they may not be; and a boxer presumably does not prescribe the same style of fighting to all his pupils. It would seem, then, that the detail is worked out with more precision if the control is private; for each person is more likely to get what suits his case.

But the details can be best looked after, one by one, by a doctor or gymnastic instructor or any one else who has the general knowledge of what is good for every one or for people of a certain kind (for the sciences both are said to be, and are, concerned with what is universal); not but what some particular detail may perhaps be well looked after by an unscientific person, if he has studied accurately in the light of experience what happens in each case, just as some people seem to be their own best doctors, though they could give no help to any one else. None the less, it will perhaps be agreed that if a man does wish to become master of an art or science he must go to the universal, and come to know it as well as possible; for, as we have said, it is with this that the sciences are concerned.

And surely he who wants to make men, whether many or few, better by his care must try to become capable of legislating, if it is through laws that we can become good. For to get any one whatever—any one who is put before us—into the right condition is not for the first chance comer; if any one can do it, it is the man who knows, just as in medicine and all other matters which give scope for care and prudence. . . .

JOHN MILTON

from *Areopagitica* (1644)

John Milton (1608–1674) is one of the great figures of English literature. Born in London, the son of a prosperous scribe, he was educated at St. Paul's School in London and at Christ's College, Cambridge, where he received an M.A. in 1632. He traveled widely after receiving his degree, meeting Galileo in Italy in 1638–1639. Many of Milton's early writings are political tracts. He published Areopagitica, *a ringing defense of freedom of the press, when he was thirty-six.*

A year earlier, Parliament had passed an order complaining of the "many false . . . scandalous, seditious, and libellous" works that were being published in England "to the great defamation of Religion and government." It required that all books printed or sold must first be "approved of and licensed by" censors appointed by Parliament. The order moreover gave police the right to search for unlicensed presses and destroy them; to search for unlicensed books and confiscate them; and to arrest authors, publishers, and others involved in publishing unlicensed books. Areopagitica *was Milton's eloquent response.*

In 1652, at the age of forty-four, Milton became totally blind. He nevertheless continued writing, producing Paradise Lost *in 1667 and both* Paradise Regained *and* Samson Agonistes *in 1671. (Source: Oxford, Clarendon Press, 1898.)*

QUESTIONS FOR REFLECTION

1. Milton contends that people should be trusted to distinguish good from harmful publications; if people are not trusted, he says, they cannot develop certain virtues. What virtues does Milton have in mind? Why would they remain undeveloped?

2. Milton argues that "this Order avails nothing to the suppressing of scandalous, seditious, and libellous books"; in other words, that Parliament's action would not succeed in banning harmful works. Why does he believe that censorship will be ineffective? What are his arguments? Do they apply to any act of censorship, or are they limited to this case? If you were an advocate of censorship, could you devise a scheme that would overcome any of Milton's arguments?

3. Milton believes that Parliament's action will discourage learning and make truth harder to attain. Why? Do you find his arguments persuasive?

4. Milton bases several arguments on the observation that censorship requires censors. Who will decide what should be licensed? Milton denies that this question has any adequate answer. Why?

A Speech for the Liberty of Unlicensed Printing, to the Parliament of England (1644)

. . . that . . . clause of Licensing Books . . . I shall now attend with such a homily, as shall lay before ye, first the inventors of it to be those whom ye will be loth to own; next what is to be thought in general of reading, whatever sort the books be; and that this Order avails nothing to the suppressing of scandalous, seditious, and libellous books, which were mainly intended to be suppressed. Last, that it will be primely to the discouragement of all learning, and the stop of Truth, not only of disexercising and blunting our abilities in what we know already, but by hindering and cropping the discovery that might be yet further made both in religious and civil Wisdom.

I deny not, but that it is of greatest concernment in the Church and Commonwealth, to have a vigilant eye how books demean themselves as well as men; and thereafter to confine, imprison, and do sharpest justice on them as malefactors. For books are not absolutely dead things, but do contain a potency of life in them to be as active as that soul was whose progeny they are; nay, they do preserve as in a vial the purest efficacy and extraction of that living intellect that bred them. I know they are as lively, and as vigorously productive, as those fabulous dragon's teeth; and being sown up and down, may chance to spring up armed men. And yet, on the other hand, unless wariness be used, as good almost kill a man as kill a good book. Who kills a man kills a reasonable creature, God's image; but he who destroys a good book, kills reason itself, kills the image of God, as it were in the eye. Many a man lives a burden to the earth; but a good book is the precious life-blood of a master spirit, embalmed and treasured up on purpose to a life beyond life. 'Tis true, no age can restore a life, whereof perhaps there is no great loss; and revolutions of ages do not oft recover the loss of a rejected truth, for the want of which whole nations fare the worse.

We should be wary therefore what persecution we raise against the living labours of public men, how we spill that seasoned life of man, preserved and stored up in books; since we see a kind of homicide may be thus committed, sometimes a martyrdom, and if it extend to the whole impression, a kind of massacre; whereof the execution ends not in the slaying of an elemental life, but strikes at that ethereal and fifth essence, the breath of reason itself, slays an immortality rather than a life. . . .

Good and evil we know in the field of this world grow up together almost inseparably; and the knowledge of good is so involved and interwoven with the knowledge of evil, and in so many cunning resemblances hardly to be discerned, that those confused seeds which were imposed upon Psyche as an incessant labour to cull out, and sort asunder, were not more intermixed. It was from out the rind of one apple tasted, that the knowledge of good and evil, as two twins cleaving together, leaped forth into the world. And perhaps this is that doom which Adam fell into of knowing good and evil, that is to say of knowing good by evil. As therefore the state of man now is; what wisdom can there be to choose, what continence to forbear without the knowledge of evil? He that can apprehend and consider vice with all her baits and seeming pleasures, and yet abstain, and yet distinguish, and yet prefer that which is truly better, he is the true wayfaring Christian.

I cannot praise a fugitive and cloistered virtue, unexercised and unbreathed, that never sallies out and sees her adversary, but slinks out of the race, where that immortal garland is to be run for, not without dust and heat. Assuredly we bring not innocence into the world, we bring impurity much rather; that which purifies us is trial, and trial is by what is contrary. That virtue therefore which is but a youngling in the contemplation of evil, and knows not the utmost that vice promises to her followers, and rejects it, is but a blank virtue, not a pure; her whiteness is but an excremental whiteness. Which was the reason why our sage and serious poet Spenser, whom I dare be known to think a better teacher than Scotus or Aquinas, describing true temperance under the person of Guion, brings him in with his palmer through the cave of Mammon, and the bower of earthly bliss, that he might see and know, and yet abstain. Since therefore the knowledge and survey of vice is in this world so necessary to the constituting of human virtue, and the scanning of error to the confirmation of truth, how can we more safely, and with less danger, scout into the regions of sin and falsity than by reading all manner of tractates and hearing all manner of reason? And this is the benefit which may be had of books promiscuously read.

But of the harm that may result hence three kinds are usually reckoned. First, is feared the infection that may spread; but then all human learning and controversy in religious points must remove out of the world, yea the Bible itself; for that ofttimes relates blasphemy not nicely, it describes the carnal sense of wicked men not unelegantly, it brings in holiest men passionately murmuring against

Providence through all the arguments of Epicurus: in other great disputes it answers dubiously and darkly to the common reader. . . .

Seeing, therefore, that those books, and those in great abundance, which are likeliest to taint both life and doctrine, cannot be suppressed without the fall of learning and of all ability in disputation, and that these books of either sort are most and soonest catching to the learned, from whom to the common people whatever is heretical or dissolute may quickly be conveyed, and that evil manners are as perfectly learnt without books a thousand other ways which cannot be stopped, and evil doctrine not with books can propagate, except a teacher guide, which he might also do without writing, and so beyond prohibiting, I am not able to unfold, how this cautelous [cunning] enterprise of licensing can be exempted from the number of vain and impossible attempts. And he who were pleasantly disposed could not well avoid to liken it to the exploit of that gallant man who thought to pound up the crows by shutting his park gate.

Besides another inconvenience, if learned men be the first receivers out of books and dispreaders both of vice and error, how shall the licensers themselves be confided in, unless we can confer upon them, or they assume to themselves above all others in the land, the grace of infallibility and uncorruptedness? And again, if it be true that a wise man, like a good refiner, can gather gold out of the drossiest volume, and that a fool will be a fool with the best book, yea or without book; there is no reason that we should deprive a wise man of any advantage to his wisdom, while we seek to restrain from a fool, that which being restrained will be no hindrance to his folly. For if there should be so much exactness always used to keep that from him which is unfit for his reading, we should in the judgment of Aristotle not only, but of Solomon and of our Saviour, not vouchsafe him good precepts, and by consequence not willingly admit him to good books; as being certain that a wise man will make better use of an idle pamphlet, than a fool will do of sacred Scripture.

'Tis next alleged we must not expose ourselves to temptations without necessity, and next to that, not employ our time in vain things. To both these objections one answer will serve, out of the grounds already laid, that to all men such books are not temptations, nor vanities, but useful drugs and materials wherewith to temper and compose effective and strong medicines, which man's life cannot want. The rest, as children and childish men, who have not the art to qualify and prepare these working minerals, well may be exhorted to forbear, but hindered forcibly they cannot be by all the licensing that Sainted Inquisition could ever yet contrive. Which is what I promised to deliver next, That this order of licensing conduces nothing to the end for which it was framed; and hath almost prevented me by being clear already while thus much hath been explaining. See the ingenuity of Truth, who, when she gets a free and willing hand, opens herself faster than the pace of method and discourse can overtake her. . . .

. . . For if they fell upon one kind of strictness, unless their care were equal to regulate all other things of like aptness to corrupt the mind, that single endeavour they knew would be but a fond labour; to shut and fortify one gate against corruption, and be necessitated to leave others round about wide open.

If we think to regulate printing, thereby to rectify manners, we must regulate all recreations and pastimes, all that is delightful to man. No music must be heard, no song be set or sung, but what is grave and Doric. There must be licensing dancers, that no gesture, motion, or deportment be taught our youth but what by their allowance shall be thought honest; for such Plato was provided of; it will ask more than the work of twenty licensers to examine all the lutes, the violins, and the guitars in every house; they must not be suffered to prattle as they do, but must be licensed what they may say. And who shall silence all the airs and madrigals that whisper softness in chambers? The windows also, and the balconies must be thought on; there are shrewd books, with dangerous frontispieces, set to sale; who shall prohibit them, shall twenty licensers? The villages also must have their visitors to inquire what lectures the bagpipe and the rebeck reads, even to the ballatry and the gamut of every municipal fiddler, for these are the countryman's Arcadias, and his Monte Mayors.

Next, what more national corruption, for which England hears ill abroad, than household gluttony: who shall be the rectors of our daily rioting? And what shall be done to inhibit the multitudes that frequent those houses where drunkenness is sold and harboured? Our garments also should be referred to the licensing of some more sober workmasters to see them cut into a less wanton garb. Who shall regulate all the mixed conversation of our youth, male and female together, as is the fashion of this country? Who shall still appoint what shall be discoursed, what presumed, and no further? Lastly, who shall forbid and separate all idle resort, all evil company? These things will be, and must be; but how they shall be least hurtful, how least enticing, herein consists the grave and governing wisdom of a state.

To sequester out of the world into Atlantic and Utopian polities which never can be drawn into use, will not mend our condition; but to ordain wisely as in this world of evil, in the midst whereof God hath placed us unavoidably. Nor is it Plato's licensing of books will do this, which necessarily pulls along with it so many other kinds of licensing, as will make us all both ridiculous and weary, and yet frustrate; but those unwritten, or at least unconstraining, laws of virtuous education, religious and civil nurture, which Plato there mentions as the bonds and ligaments of the commonwealth, the pillars and the sustainers of every written statute; these they be which will bear chief sway in such matters as these, when all licensing will be easily eluded. Impunity and remissness, for certain, are the bane of a commonwealth; but here the great art lies, to discern in what the law is to bid restraint and punishment, and in what things persuasion only is to work.

If every action, which is good or evil in man at ripe years, were to be under pittance and prescription and compulsion, what were virtue but a name, what praise could be then due to well-doing, what gramercy to be sober, just, or continent? Many there be that complain of Divine Providence for suffering Adam to transgress; foolish tongues! When God gave him reason, He gave him freedom to choose, for reason is but choosing; he had been else a mere artificial Adam, such an Adam as he is in the motions. We ourselves esteem not of that obedience, or love, or gift, which is of force: God therefore left him free, set before him a provoking object, ever almost in his eyes; herein consisted his merit, herein the right of his reward, the praise of his abstinence. Wherefore

did He create passions within us, pleasures round about us, but that these rightly tempered are the very ingredients of virtue?

They are not skilful considerers of human things, who imagine to remove sin by removing the matter of sin; for, besides that it is a huge heap increasing under the very act of diminishing, though some part of it may for a time be withdrawn from some persons, it cannot from all, in such a universal thing as books are; and when this is done, yet the sin remains entire. Though ye take from a covetous man all his treasure, he has yet one jewel left, ye cannot bereave him of his covetousness. Banish all objects of lust, shut up all youth into the severest discipline that can be exercised in any hermitage, ye cannot make them chaste, that came not thither so: such great care and wisdom is required to the right managing of this point. Suppose we could expel sin by this means; look how much we thus expel of sin, so much we expel of virtue: for the matter of them both is the same; remove that, and ye remove them both alike.

This justifies the high providence of God, who, though He commands us temperance, justice, continence, yet pours out before us, even to a profuseness, all desirable things, and gives us minds that can wander beyond all limit and satiety. Why should we then affect a rigour contrary to the manner of God and of nature, by abridging or scanting those means, which books freely permitted are, both to the trial of virtue and the exercise of truth? It would be better done, to learn that the law must needs be frivolous, which goes to restrain things, uncertainly and yet equally working to good and to evil. And were I the chooser, a dram of well-doing should be preferred before many times as much the forcible hindrance of evil-doing. For God sure esteems the growth and completing of one virtuous person more than the restraint of ten vicious.

And albeit whatever thing we hear or see, sitting, walking, travelling, or conversing, may be fitly called our book, and is of the same effect that writings are, yet grant the thing to be prohibited were only books, it appears that this order hitherto is far insufficient to the end which it intends. Do we not see, not once or oftener, but weekly, that continued court-libel against the Parliament and City, printed, as the wet sheets can witness, and dispersed among us, for all that licensing can do? yet this is the prime service a man would think, wherein this Order should give proof of itself. If it were executed, you'll say. But certain, if execution be remiss or blindfold now, and in this particular, what will it be hereafter and in other books? If then the Order shall not be vain and frustrate, behold a new labour, Lords and Commons, ye must repeal and proscribe all scandalous and unlicensed books already printed and divulged; after ye have drawn them up into a list, that all may know which are condemned, and which not; and ordain that no foreign books be delivered out of custody, till they have been read over. This office will require the whole time of not a few overseers, and those no vulgar men. There be also books which are partly useful and excellent, partly culpable and pernicious; this work will ask as many more officials, to make expurgations and expunctions, that the Commonwealth of Learning be not damnified. In fine, when the multitude of books increase upon their hands, ye must be fain to catalogue all those printers who are found frequently offending, and forbid the importation of their whole suspected typography. In a word, that this your Order may be exact and not deficient, ye must reform it perfectly according to the model of Trent and Seville, which I know ye abhor to do.

Yet though ye should condescend to this, which God forbid, the Order still would be but fruitless and defective to that end whereto ye meant it. If to prevent sects and schisms, who is so unread or so uncatechised in story, that hath not heard of many sects refusing books as a hindrance, and preserving their doctrine unmixed for many ages, only by unwritten traditions? The Christian faith, for that was once a schism, is not unknown to have spread all over Asia, ere any Gospel or Epistle was seen in writing. If the amendment of manners be aimed at, look into Italy and Spain, whether these places be one scruple the better, the honester, the wiser, the chaster, since all the inquisitional rigour that hath been executed upon books.

Another reason, whereby to make it plain that this Order will miss the end it seeks, consider by the quality which ought to be in every licenser. It cannot be denied but that he who is made judge to sit upon the birth or death of books, whether they may be

wafted into this world or not, had need to be a man above the common measure, both studious, learned, and judicious; there may be else no mean mistakes in the censure of what is passable or not; which is also no mean injury. If he be of such worth as behoves him, there cannot be a more tedious and unpleasing journey-work, a greater loss of time levied upon his head, than to be made the perpetual reader of unchosen books and pamphlets, ofttimes huge volumes. There is no book that is acceptable unless at certain seasons; but to be enjoined the reading of that at all times, and in a hand scarce legible, whereof three pages would not down at any time in the fairest print, is an imposition which I cannot believe how he that values time and his own studies, or is but of a sensible nostril, should be able to endure. In this one thing I crave leave of the present licensers to be pardoned for so thinking; who doubtless took this office up, looking on it through their obedience to the Parliament, whose command perhaps made all things seem easy and unlaborious to them; but that this short trial hath wearied them out already, their own expressions and excuses to them who make so many journeys to solicit their licence are testimony enough. Seeing therefore those who now possess the employment by all evident signs wish themselves well rid of it; and that no man of worth, none that is not a plain unthrift of his own hours is ever likely to succeed them, except he mean to put himself to the salary of a press corrector; we may easily foresee what kind of licensers we are to expect hereafter, either ignorant, imperious, and remiss, or basely pecuniary. This is what I had to show, wherein this Order cannot conduce to that end whereof it bears the intention.

I lastly proceed from the no good it can do, to the manifest hurt it causes, in being first the greatest discouragement and affront that can be offered to learning, and to learned men.

It was the complaint and lamentation of prelates, upon every least breath of a motion to remove pluralities, and distribute more equally Church revenues, that then all learning would be for ever dashed and discouraged. But as for that opinion, I never found cause to think that the tenth part of learning stood or fell with the clergy: nor could I ever but hold it for a sordid and unworthy speech of any churchman who had a competency left him. If therefore ye be loth to dishearten heartily and discontent, not the mercenary crew of false pretenders to learning, but the free and ingenuous sort of such as evidently were born to study, and love learning for itself, not for lucre or any other end but the service of God and of truth, and perhaps that lasting fame and perpetuity of praise which God and good men have consented shall be the reward of those whose published labours advance the good of mankind, then know that, so far to distrust the judgment and the honesty of one who hath but a common repute in learning, and never yet offended, as not to count him fit to print his mind without a tutor and examiner, lest he should drop a schism, or something of corruption, is the greatest displeasure and indignity to a free and knowing spirit that can be put upon him.

What advantage is it to be a man over it is to be a boy at school, if we have only escaped the ferula to come under the fescue of an Imprimatur, if serious and elaborate writings, as if they were no more than the theme of a grammar-lad under his pedagogue, must not be uttered without the cursory eyes of a temporising and extemporising licenser? He who is not trusted with his own actions, his drift not being known to be evil, and standing to the hazard of law and penalty, has no great argument to think himself reputed in the Commonwealth, wherein he was born, for other than a fool or a foreigner. When a man writes to the world, he summons up all his reason and deliberation to assist him; he searches, meditates, is industrious, and likely consults and confers with his judicious friends; after all which done he takes himself to be informed in what he writes, as well as any that writ before him. If, in this the most consummate act of his fidelity and ripeness, no years, no industry, no former proof of his abilities can bring him to that state of maturity, as not to be still mistrusted and suspected, unless he carry all his considerate diligence, all his midnight watchings and expense of Palladian oil, to the hasty view of an unleisured licenser, perhaps much his younger, perhaps far his inferior in judgment, perhaps one who never knew the labour of bookwriting, and if he be not repulsed or slighted, must appear in print like a puny with his guardian, and

his censor's hand on the back of his title to be his bail and surety that he is no idiot or seducer, it cannot be but a dishonour and derogation to the author, to the book, to the privilege and dignity of Learning.

And what if the author shall be one so copious of fancy, as to have many things well worth the adding come into his mind after licensing, while the book is yet under the press, which not seldom happens to the best and diligentest writers; and that perhaps a dozen times in one book? The printer dares not go beyond his licensed copy; so often then must the author trudge to his leave-giver, that those his new insertions may be reviewed; and many a jaunt will be made, ere that licenser, for it must be the same man, can either be found, or found at leisure; meanwhile either the press must stand still, which is no small damage, or the author lose his accuratest thoughts, and send the book forth worse than he had made it, which to a diligent writer is the greatest melancholy and vexation that can befall.

And how can a man teach with authority, which is the life of teaching, how can he be a doctor in his book as he ought to be, or else had better be silent, whenas all he teaches, all he delivers, is but under the tuition, under the correction of his patriarchal licensor to blot or alter what precisely accords not with the hidebound humour which he calls his judgment? When every acute reader, upon the first sight of a pedantic licence, will be ready with these like words to ding the book a quoit's distance from him: I hate a pupil teacher, I endure not an instructor that comes to me under the wardship of an overseeing fist. I know nothing of the licenser, but that I have his own hand here for his arrogance; who shall warrant me his judgment? The State, sir, replies the stationer, but has a quick return: The State shall be my governors, but not my critics; they may be mistaken in the choice of a licenser, as easily as this licenser may be mistaken in an author; this is some common stuff; and he might add from Sir Francis Bacon, That such authorised books are but the language of the times. For though a licenser should happen to be judicious more than ordinary, which will be a great jeopardy of the next succession, yet his very office and his commission enjoins him to let pass nothing but what is vulgarly received already.

Nay, which is more lamentable, if the work of any deceased author, though never so famous in his lifetime and even to this day, come to their hands for licence to be printed, or reprinted, if there be found in his book one sentence of a venturous edge, uttered in the height of zeal and who knows whether it might not be the dictate of a divine spirit, yet not suiting with every low decrepit humour of their own, though it were Knox himself, the Reformer of a Kingdom, that spake it, they will not pardon him their dash: the sense of that great man shall to all posterity be lost, for the fearfulness or the presumptuous rashness of a perfunctory licenser. And to what an author this violence hath been lately done, and in what book of greatest consequence to be faithfully published, I could now instance, but shall forbear till a more convenient season.

Yet if these things be not resented seriously and timely by them who have the remedy in their power, but that such iron-moulds as these shall have authority to gnaw out the choicest periods of exquisitest books, and to commit such a treacherous fraud against the orphan remainders of worthiest men after death, the more sorrow will belong to that hapless race of men, whose misfortune it is to have understanding. Henceforth let no man care to learn, or care to be more than worldly-wise; for certainly in higher matters to be ignorant and slothful, to be a common steadfast dunce, will be the only pleasant life, and only in request.

And as it is a particular disesteem of every knowing person alive, and most injurious to the written labours and monuments of the dead, so to me it seems an undervaluing and vilifying of the whole Nation. I cannot set so light by all the invention, the art, the wit, the grave and solid judgment which is in England, as that it can be comprehended in any twenty capacities how good soever, much less that it should not pass except their superintendence be over it, except it be sifted and strained with their strainers, that it should be uncurrent without their manual stamp. Truth and understanding are not such wares as to be monopolised and traded in by tickets and statutes and standards. We must not think to make a staple commodity of all the knowledge in the land, to mark and licence it like our broadcloth and our woolpacks. . . .

. . . this obstructing violence meets for the most part with an event utterly opposite to the end which it drives at: instead of suppressing sects and schisms, it raises them and invests them with a reputation. "The punishing of wits enhances their authority," said the Viscount St. Albans; "and a forbidden writing is thought to be a certain spark of truth that flies up in the faces of them who seek to tread it out." This Order, therefore, may prove a nursing-mother to sects, but I shall easily show how it will be a step-dame to Truth: and first by disenabling us to the maintenance of what is known already.

Well knows he who uses to consider, that our faith and knowledge thrives by exercise, as well as our limbs and complexion. Truth is compared in Scripture to a streaming fountain; if her waters flow not in a perpetual progression, they sicken into a muddy pool of conformity and tradition. A man may be a heretic in the truth; and if he believe things only because his Pastor says so, or the Assembly so determines, without knowing other reason, though his belief be true, yet the very truth he holds becomes his heresy. . . .

There is yet behind of what I proposed to lay open, the incredible loss and detriment that this plot of incensing puts us to; more than if some enemy at sea should stop up all our havens and ports and creeks, it hinders and retards the importation of our richest Merchandise, Truth; nay, it was first established and put in practice by Antichristian malice and mystery on set purpose to extinguish, if it were possible, the light of Reformation, and to settle falsehood; little differing from that policy wherewith the Turk upholds his Alcoran, by the prohibition of Printing. 'Tis not denied, but gladly confessed, we are to send our thanks and vows to Heaven louder than most of nations, for that great measure of truth which we enjoy, especially in those main points between us and the Pope, with his appurtenances the Prelates: but he who thinks we are to pitch our tent here, and have attained the utmost prospect of reformation that the mortal glass wherein we contemplate can show us, till we come to beautific vision, that man by this very opinion declares that he is yet far short of Truth.

Truth indeed came once into the world with her

Divine Master, and was a perfect shape most glorious to look on: but when He ascended, and His Apostles after Him were laid asleep, then straight arose a wicked race of deceivers, who, as that story goes of the Egyptian Typhon with his conspirators, how they dealt with the good Osiris, took the virgin Truth, hewed her lovely form into a thousand pieces, and scattered them to the four winds. From that time ever since, the sad friends of Truth, such as durst appear, imitating the careful search that Isis made for the mangled body of Osiris, went up and down gathering up limb by limb, still as they could find them. We have not yet found them all, Lords and Commons, nor ever shall do, till her Master's second coming; He shall bring together every joint and member, and shall mould them into an immortal feature of loveliness and perfection. Suffer not these licensing prohibitions to stand at every place of opportunity, forbidding and disturbing them that continue seeking, that continue to do our obsequies to the torn body of our martyred saint.

We boast our light; but if we look not wisely on the Sun itself, it smites us into darkness. Who can discern those planets that are oft combust, and those stars of brightest magnitude that rise and set with the Sun, until the opposite motion of their orbs bring them to such a place in the firmament, where they may be seen evening or morning? The light which we have gained was given us, not to be ever staring on, but by it to discover onward things more remote from our knowledge. It is not the unfrocking of a priest, the unmitring of a bishop, and the removing him from off the presbyterian shoulders, that will make us a happy Nation. No, if other things as great in the Church, and in the rule of life both economical and political, be not looked into and reformed, we have looked so long upon the blaze the Zuinglius and Calvin hath beaconed up to us, that we are stark blind. There be who perpetually complain of schisms and sects, and make it such a calamity that any man dissents from their maxims. 'Tis their own pride and ignorance which causes the disturbing, who neither will hear with meekness, nor can convince; yet all must be suppressed which is not found in their Syntagma.* They are the trou-

blers, they are the dividers of unity, who neglect and permit not others to unite those dissevered pieces which are yet wanting to the body of Truth. To be still searching what we know not by what we know, still closing up truth to truth as we find it (for all her body is homogeneal and proportional), this is the golden rule in theology as well as in arithmetic, and makes up the best harmony in a Church; not the forced and outward union of cold and neutral, and inwardly divided minds. . . .

Where there is much desire to learn, there of necessity will be much arguing, much writing, many opinions; for opinion in good men is but knowledge in the making. . . .

What would ye do then? should ye suppress all this flowery crop of knowledge and new light sprung up and yet springing daily in this city? should ye set an oligarchy of twenty engrossers over it, to bring a famine upon our minds again, when we shall know nothing but what is measured to us by their bushel? Believe it, Lords and Commons, they who counsel ye to such a suppressing do as good as bid ye suppress yourselves; and I will soon show how. If it be desired to know the immediate cause of all this free writing and free speaking, there cannot be assigned a truer than your own mild and free and humane government. It is the liberty, Lords and Commons, which your own valorous and happy counsels have purchased us, liberty which is the nurse of all great wits; this is that which hath rarefied and enlightened our spirits like the influence of heaven; this is that which hath enfranchised, enlarged and lifted up our apprehensions degrees above themselves.

Ye cannot make us now less capable, less knowing, less eagerly pursuing of the truth, unless ye first make yourselves, that made us so, less the lovers, less the founders of our true liberty. We can grow ignorant again, brutish, formal and slavish, as ye found us; but you then must first become that which ye cannot be, oppressive, arbitrary and tyrannous, as they were from whom ye have freed us. That our hearts are now more capacious, our thoughts more erected to the search and expectation of greatest and exactest things, is the issue of your own virtue propagated in us; ye cannot suppress that, unless ye reinforce an abrogated and merciless law, that fathers may despatch at will their own children. And

* Systematically arranged treatise. —ED.

who shall then stick closest to ye, and excite others? not he who takes up arms for coat and conduct, and his four nobles of Danegelt.* Although I dispraise not the defence of just immunities, yet love my peace better, if that were all. Give me the liberty to know, to utter, and to argue freely according to conscience, above all liberties. . . .

And now the time in special is, by privilege to write and speak what may help to the further discussing of matters in agitation. The temple of Janus with his two controversial faces might now not unsignificantly be set upon. And though all the winds of doctrine were let loose to play upon the earth, so Truth be in the field, we do injuriously, by licensing and prohibiting, to misdoubt her strength. Let her and Falsehood grapple; who ever knew Truth put to the worse, in a free and open encounter? Her confuting is the best and surest suppressing. He who hears what praying there is for light and clearer knowledge to be sent down among us, would think of other matters to be constituted beyond the discipline of Geneva, framed and fabricked already to our hands. Yet when the new light which we beg for shines in upon us, there be who envy and oppose, if it come not first in at their casements. What a collusion is this, whenas we are exhorted by the wise man to use diligence, to seek for wisdom as for hidden treasures early and late, that another order shall enjoin us to know nothing but by statute? When a man hath been labouring the hardest labour in the deep mines of knowledge; hath furnished out his findings in all their equipage; drawn forth his reasons as it were a battle ranged; scattered and defeated all objections in his way; calls out his adversary into the plain, offers him the advantage of wind and sun, if he please, only that he may try the matter by dint of argument: for his opponents then to skulk, to lay ambushments, to keep a narrow bridge of licensing where the challenger should pass, though it be valour enough in soldiership, is but weakness and cowardice in the wars of Truth.

For who knows not that Truth is strong, next to the Almighty? She needs no policies, nor stratagems, nor licensings to make her victorious; those are the shifts and the defences that error uses against her power. Give her but room, and do not bind her when she sleeps, for then she speaks not true, as the old Proteus did who spake oracles only when he was caught and bound, but then rather she turns herself into all shapes, except her own, and perhaps tunes her voice according to the time, as Micaiah did before Ahab, until she be adjured into her own likeness. Yet is it not impossible that she may have more shapes than one. What else is all that rank of things indifferent, wherein Truth may be on this side or on the other, without being unlike herself? What but a vain shadow else is the abolition of those ordinances, that hand-writing nailed to the cross? What great purchase is this Christian liberty which Paul so often boasts of? His doctrine is, that he who eats or eats not, regards a day or regards it not, may do either to the Lord. How many other things might be tolerated in peace, and left to conscience, had we but charity, and were it not the chief stronghold of our hypocrisy to be ever judging one another? . . .

. . . if it come to prohibiting, there is not aught more likely to be prohibited than truth itself; whose first appearance to our eyes, bleared and dimmed with prejudice and custom, is more unsightly and unplausible than many errors, even as the person is of many a great man slight and contemptible to see to. . . .

---

* An annual tax imposed around 1000 C.E. to protect England from the Danes and continued thereafter. —ED.

EDMUND BURKE

from *Reflections on the Revolution in France* (1790)

Edmund Burke (1729–1797) was born in Ireland to a Protestant family of modest means that had recently converted from Catholicism. Educated at a Quaker school and at Trinity College, Dublin, he took a first-class honors degree in classics, and proceeded to study law in London. He did not, however, practice law. Instead, he became a "man of letters": he edited the Annual Register (a political journal) and belonged to Samuel Johnson's literary club. Burke's first two books appeared when he was twenty-seven; at thirty-seven, he became a member of the House of Commons. Eventually, he became paymaster-general.

Burke was sixty when the French Revolution began in 1789. King Louis XVI, an absolute monarch, had summoned the largely advisory States General, had lost control of it, and had seen it transform itself into the National Assembly. That body had abolished feudalism, seized the lands of the French church, and inspired the capture and imprisonment of the royal family. A young Frenchman, Charles-François Depont, wrote Burke to ask his opinion of the Revolution. His response was Reflections on the Revolution in France, which has become a classic of European political thought. The book is sharply critical of the Revolution. Burke's worries about the extremism of the revolutionaries were soon justified. The Reign of Terror led to the execution of thousands, including the king, his family, and much of the French aristocracy.

Burke is a thoroughly practical thinker. He rejects the Enlightenment view that a change in the social or political order can perfect human nature and society. More fundamentally, he rejects all attempts to analyze human problems in terms of a few basic principles.

Profoundly skeptical of philosophical theorizing, Burke stresses the complexity of real ethical problems. Solving a moral or political problem, he believes, involves balancing various moral considerations—various kinds of goods and evils—in light of features of the particular situation giving rise to it. Liberty, in Burke's view, is one kind of good, but there are many others; liberty does not always take precedence. There is no theory, method, or set of rules for achieving a proper balance between liberty and other goods. Instead, Burke urges, we should reason by analogy, clinging to social mechanisms that have stood the test of time.

QUESTIONS FOR REFLECTION

1. What does Burke mean by a "manly, moral, regulated liberty"?

2. Burke is a pluralist—he believes that there are fundamentally different kinds of moral value. What are some of these kinds? What kind of value is liberty? Is it unequivocally good?

3. Burke points out that "liberty, when men act in bodies, is *power*." What does he deduce from this? What, in your view, does Burke's observation imply about liberty?

4. Burke thinks that it is very important "to derive all we possess as *an inheritance from our forefathers*." Why does Burke place such an emphasis on tradition?

5. Burke worries that democracy allows the "oppression of the minority." Why? What can be done to guard against it?

... I flatter myself that I love a manly, moral, regulated liberty as well as any gentleman of that society, be he who he will; and perhaps I have given as good proofs of my attachment to that cause in the whole course of my public conduct. I think I envy liberty as little as they do to any other nation. But I cannot stand forward and give praise or blame to anything which relates to human actions, and human concerns, on a simple view of the object, as it stands stripped of every relation, in all the nakedness and solitude of metaphysical abstraction. Circumstances (which with some gentlemen pass for nothing) give in reality to every political principle its distinguishing color and discriminating effect. The circumstances are what render every civil and political scheme beneficial or noxious to mankind. Abstractedly speaking, government, as well as liberty, is good; yet could I, in common sense, ten years ago, have felicitated France on her enjoyment of a government (for she then had a government) without inquiry what the nature of that government was, or how it was administered? Can I now congratulate the same nation upon its freedom? Is it because liberty in the abstract may be classed amongst the blessings of mankind, that I am seriously to felicitate a madman, who has escaped from the protecting restraint and wholesome darkness of his cell, on his restoration to the enjoyment of light and liberty? Am I to congratulate a highwayman and murderer who has broke prison upon the recovery of his natural rights? This would be to act over again the scene of the criminals condemned to the galleys, and their heroic deliverer, the metaphysic Knight of the Sorrowful Countenance.*

When I see the spirit of liberty in action, I see a strong principle at work; and this, for a while, is all I can possibly know of it. The wild *gas,* the fixed air, is plainly broke loose; but we ought to suspend our judgment until the first effervescence is a little subsided, till the liquor is cleared, and until we see something deeper than the agitation of a troubled and frothy surface. I must be tolerably sure, before I venture publicly to congratulate men upon a blessing, that they have really received one. Flattery corrupts both the receiver and the giver, and adulation is not of more service to the people than to kings.

I should, therefore, suspend my congratulations on the new liberty of France until I was informed how it had been combined with government, with public force, with the discipline and obedience of armies, with the collection of an effective and well-distributed revenue, with morality and religion, with the solidity of property, with peace and order, with civil and social manners. All these (in their way) are good things, too, and without them liberty is not a benefit whilst it lasts, and is not likely to continue long. The effect of liberty to individuals is that they may do what they please; we ought to see what it will please them to do, before we risk congratulations which may be soon turned into complaints. Prudence would dictate this in the case of separate, insulated, private men, but liberty, when men act in bodies, is *power.* Considerate people, before they declare themselves, will observe the use which is made of *power,* and particularly of so trying a thing as *new* power in *new* persons of whose principles, tempers, and dispositions they have little or no experience, and in situations where those who appear the most stirring in the scene may possibly not be the real movers.

. . . .

... The Revolution was made to preserve our *ancient,* indisputable laws and liberties and that *ancient* constitution of government which is our only security for law and liberty. If you are desirous of knowing the spirit of our constitution and the policy which predominated in that great period which has secured it to this hour, pray look for both in our histories, in our records, in our acts of parliament, and journals of parliament, and not in the sermons of the Old Jewry and the after-dinner toasts of the Revolution Society. In the former you will find other ideas and another language. Such a claim is as ill-suited to our temper and wishes as it is unsupported by any appearance of authority. The very idea of the fabrication of a new government is enough to fill us with disgust and horror. We wished at the period of the Revolution, and do now wish, to derive all we possess as *an inheritance from our forefathers.* Upon that body and stock of inheritance we have taken care not to inoculate any cyon* alien to the nature of the original plant. All the reformations we

---

* A reference to Don Quixote, who set criminals free only to be beaten by them. —Ed.

* A shoot, twig, or graft; old form of *scion.* —Ed.

have hitherto made have proceeded upon the principle of reverence to antiquity; and I hope, nay, I am persuaded, that all those which possibly may be made hereafter will be carefully formed upon analogical precedent, authority, and example. . . .

You will observe that from Magna Charta to the Declaration of Right it has been the uniform policy of our constitution to claim and assert our liberties as an *entailed inheritance* derived to us from our forefathers, and to be transmitted to our posterity—as an estate specially belonging to the people of this kingdom, without any reference whatever to any other more general or prior right. By this means our constitution preserves a unity in so great a diversity of its parts. We have an inheritable crown, an inheritable peerage, and a House of Commons and a people inheriting privileges, franchises, and liberties from a long line of ancestors.

This policy appears to me to be the result of profound reflection, or rather the happy effect of following nature, which is wisdom without reflection, and above it. A spirit of innovation is generally the result of a selfish temper and confined views. People will not look forward to posterity, who never look backward to their ancestors. Besides, the people of England well know that the idea of inheritance furnishes a sure principle of conservation and a sure principle of transmission, without at all excluding a principle of improvement. It leaves acquisition free, but it secures what it acquires. Whatever advantages are obtained by a state proceeding on these maxims are locked fast as in a sort of family settlement, grasped as in a kind of mortmain* forever. By a constitutional policy, working after the pattern of nature, we receive, we hold, we transmit our government and our privileges in the same manner in which we enjoy and transmit our property and our lives. The institutions of policy, the goods of fortune, the gifts of providence are handed down to us, and from us, in the same course and order. Our political system is placed in a just correspondence and symmetry with the order of the world and with the mode of existence decreed to a permanent body composed of transitory parts, wherein, by the disposition of a stupendous wisdom, molding together the great mysterious incorporation

of the human race, the whole, at one time, is never old or middle-aged or young, but, in a condition of unchangeable constancy, moves on through the varied tenor of perpetual decay, fall, renovation, and progression. Thus, by preserving the method of nature in the conduct of the state, in what we improve we are never wholly new; in what we retain we are never wholly obsolete. By adhering in this manner and on those principles to our forefathers, we are guided not by the superstition of antiquarians, but by the spirit of philosophic analogy. In this choice of inheritance we have given to our frame of polity the image of a relation in blood, binding up the constitution of our country with our dearest domestic ties, adopting our fundamental laws into the bosom of our family affections, keeping inseparable and cherishing with the warmth of all their combined and mutually reflected charities our state, our hearths, our sepulchres, and our altars.

Through the same plan of a conformity to nature in our artificial institutions, and by calling in the aid of her unerring and powerful instincts to fortify the fallible and feeble contrivances of our reason, we have derived several other, and those no small, benefits from considering our liberties in the light of an inheritance. Always acting as if in the presence of canonized forefathers, the spirit of freedom, leading in itself to misrule and excess, is tempered with an awful gravity. This idea of a liberal descent inspires us with a sense of habitual native dignity which prevents that upstart insolence almost inevitably adhering to and disgracing those who are the first acquirers of any distinction. By this means our liberty becomes a noble freedom. It carries an imposing and majestic aspect. It has a pedigree and illustrating ancestors. It has its bearings and its ensigns armorial. It has its gallery of portraits, its monumental inscriptions, its records, evidences, and titles. We procure reverence to our civil institutions on the principle upon which nature teaches us to revere individual men: on account of their age and on account of those from whom they are descended. All your sophisters cannot produce anything better adapted to preserve a rational and manly freedom than the course that we have pursued, who have chosen our nature rather than our speculations, our breasts rather than our inventions, for the great conservatories and magazines of our rights and privileges.

---

* Literally "dead hand," a legal device to make a corporation possess something in perpetuity; or, the condition of lands held in perpetuity. —ED.

You might, if you pleased, have profited of our example and have given to your recovered freedom a correspondent dignity. Your privileges, though discontinued, were not lost to memory. Your constitution, it is true, whilst you were out of possession, suffered waste and dilapidation; but you possessed in some parts the walls and in all the foundations of a noble and venerable castle. You might have repaired those walls; you might have built on those old foundations. Your constitution was suspended before it was perfected, but you had the elements of a constitution very nearly as good as could be wished. In your old states you possessed that variety of parts corresponding with the various descriptions of which your community was happily composed; you had all that combination and all that opposition of interests; you had that action and counteraction which, in the natural and in the political world, from the reciprocal struggle of discordant powers, draws out the harmony of the universe. These opposed and conflicting interests which you considered as so great a blemish in your old and in our present constitution interpose a salutary check to all precipitate resolutions. They render deliberation a matter, not of choice, but of necessity; they make all change a subject of *compromise,* which naturally begets moderation; they produce *temperaments* preventing the sore evil of harsh, crude, unqualified reformations, and rendering all the headlong exertions of arbitrary power, in the few or in the many, for ever impracticable. Through that diversity of members and interests, general liberty had as many securities as there were separate views in the several orders, whilst, by pressing down the whole by the weight of a real monarchy, the separate parts would have been prevented from warping and starting from their allotted places.

You had all these advantages in your ancient states, but you chose to act as if you had never been molded into civil society and had everything to begin anew. You began ill, because you began by despising everything that belonged to you.

. . . .

. . . I reprobate no form of government merely upon abstract principles. There may be situations in which the purely democratic form will become necessary. There may be some (very few, and very particularly circumstanced) where it would be clearly desirable. This I do not take to be the case of France

or of any other great country. Until now, we have seen no examples of considerable democracies. The ancients were better acquainted with them. Not being wholly unread in the authors who had seen the most of those constitutions, and who best understood them, I cannot help concurring with their opinion that an absolute democracy, no more than absolute monarchy, is to be reckoned among the legitimate forms of government. They think it rather the corruption and degeneracy than the sound constitution of a republic. If I recollect rightly, Aristotle observes that a democracy has many striking points of resemblance with a tyranny. Of this I am certain, that in a democracy the majority of the citizens is capable of exercising the most cruel oppressions upon the minority whenever strong divisions prevail in that kind of polity, as they often must; and that oppression of the minority will extend to far greater numbers and will be carried on with much greater fury than can almost ever be apprehended from the dominion of a single scepter. In such a popular persecution, individual sufferers are in a much more deplorable condition than in any other. Under a cruel prince they have the balmy compassion of mankind to assuage the smart of their wounds; they have the plaudits of the people to animate their generous constancy under their sufferings; but those who are subjected to wrong under multitudes are deprived of all external consolation. They seem deserted by mankind, overpowered by a conspiracy of their whole species.

. . . .

. . . A brave people will certainly prefer liberty accompanied with a virtuous poverty to a depraved and wealthy servitude. But before the price of comfort and opulence is paid, one ought to be pretty sure it is real liberty which is purchased, and that she is to be purchased at no other price. I shall always, however, consider that liberty as very equivocal in her appearance which has not wisdom and justice for her companions and does not lead prosperity and plenty in her train.

. . . .

The effects of the incapacity shown by the popular leaders in all the great members of the commonwealth are to be covered with the "all-atoning name" of liberty. In some people I see great liberty indeed;

in many, if not in the most, an oppressive, degrading servitude. But what is liberty without wisdom and without virtue? It is the greatest of all possible evils; for it is folly, vice, and madness, without tuition or restraint. Those who know what virtuous liberty is cannot bear to see it disgraced by incapable heads on account of their having high-sounding words in their mouths. Grand, swelling sentiments of liberty I am sure I do not despise. They warm the heart; they enlarge and liberalize our minds; they animate our courage in time of conflict. Old as I am, I read the fine raptures of Lucan and Corneille with pleasure. Neither do I wholly condemn the little arts and devices of popularity. They facilitate the carrying of many points of moment; they keep the people together; they refresh the mind in its exertions; and they diffuse occasional gaiety over the severe brow of moral freedom. Every politician ought to sacrifice to the graces, and to join compliance with reason. But in such an undertaking as that in France, all these subsidiary sentiments and artifices are of little avail. To make a government requires no great prudence. Settle the seat of power, teach obedience, and the work is done. To give freedom is still more easy. It is not necessary to guide; it only requires to let go the rein. But to form a *free government,* that is, to temper together these opposite elements of liberty and restraint in one consistent work, requires much thought, deep reflection, a sagacious, powerful, and combining mind. This I do not find in those who take the lead in the National Assembly. Perhaps they are not so miserably deficient as they appear. I rather believe it. It would put them below the common level of human understanding. But when the leaders choose to make themselves bidders at an auction of popularity, their talents, in the construction of the state, will be of no service. They will become flatterers instead of legislators, the instruments, not the guides, of the people. If any of them should happen to propose a scheme of liberty, soberly limited and defined with proper qualifications, he will be immediately outbid by his competitors who will produce something more splendidly popular. Suspicions will be raised of his fidelity to his cause. Moderation will be stigmatized as the virtue of cowards, and compromise as the prudence of traitors, until, in hopes of preserving the credit which may enable him to temper and moderate, on some occasions, the popular leader is obliged to become active in propagating doctrines and establishing powers that will afterwards defeat any sober purpose at which he ultimately might have aimed....

... I wish my countrymen rather to recommend to our neighbors the example of the British constitution than to take models from them for the improvement of our own. In the former, they have got an invaluable treasure. They are not, I think, without some causes of apprehension and complaint, but these they do not owe to their constitution but to their own conduct. I think our happy situation owing to our constitution, but owing to the whole of it, and not to any part singly, owing in a great measure to what we have left standing in our several reviews and reformations as well as to what we have altered or superadded. Our people will find employment enough for a truly patriotic, free, and independent spirit in guarding what they possess from violation. I would not exclude alteration neither, but even when I changed, it should be to preserve. I should be led to my remedy by a great grievance. In what I did, I should follow the example of our ancestors. I would make the reparation as nearly as possible in the style of the building. A politic caution, a guarded circumspection, a moral rather than a complexional timidity were among the ruling principles of our forefathers in their most decided conduct. Not being illuminated with the light of which the gentlemen of France tell us they have got so abundant a share, they acted under a strong impression of the ignorance and fallibility of mankind. He that had made them thus fallible rewarded them for having in their conduct attended to their nature. Let us imitate their caution if we wish to deserve their fortune or to retain their bequests. Let us add, if we please, but let us preserve what they have left; and, standing on the firm ground of the British constitution, let us be satisfied to admire rather than attempt to follow in their desperate flights the aeronauts of France....

ALEXIS DE TOCQUEVILLE

from *Democracy in America* (1835)

Alexis Charles Henri Clérel de Tocqueville (1805–1859) was born in Paris to an aristocratic Catholic family. His parents had been imprisoned during the French Revolution; his grandfather, great-grandfather, and aunt had been guillotined. Tocqueville was educated at home until he was fifteen, when he went to the Lycée in Metz. At eighteen, he went to Paris to study law. At twenty-two, he was appointed apprentice magistrate at Versailles.

In July 1830, Charles X, a Bourbon, was overthrown in favor of Louis Phillippe. Tocqueville swore allegiance to the new regime, but his service to Charles X and his family's Bourbon connections made him suspect in the eyes of the new government. He and a friend, Gustave de Beaumont, asked for permission to go to the United States to study prison reform. Their request was granted, and they arrived in New York in 1831.

Tocqueville's study of the United States was hardly scientific. He spent most of his time with prominent Americans he met and befriended; six of his eight months in the United States he spent in the Northeast. Still, Tocqueville's observations were acute, and they continue to inspire political thinkers reflecting on the nature of democracy.

His two volumes of Democracy in America *made Tocqueville famous on both sides of the Atlantic. At thirty-six, he was elected to the Académie Française, a very high honor. He served in the Chamber of Deputies and the Constituent Assembly, belonging to a committee that drafted the Second Republic's constitution. After Louis Napoleon's takeover in 1851, Tocqueville retired from politics and wrote one volume of what was to be a three-volume work on the French Revolution.*

Tocqueville's chief concern in Democracy in America *is to understand the consequences of democracy. In a democratic society, he believes, all political power flows upward from the people; the political system rests on and promotes equality. While these features are democracy's great strengths, they also create problems. Tocqueville fears that democracy, by putting power into the hands of the majority, will enable it to oppress the minority. His concern for the possible "tyranny of the majority" leads him to be especially interested in the implications of democracy for individual liberty. (Source: Reprinted from Alexis de Tocqueville,* Democracy in America, *translated by Henry Reeve (New York: J. & H. G. Langley, 1841).*

QUESTIONS FOR REFLECTION

1. Tocqueville finds the laws of New England towns admirable in some ways but oppressive in others. What are their admirable features? In what ways are the laws oppressive? What sort of connection does Tocqueville find between these features?

2. What, for Tocqueville, are the chief differences between the moral world and the political world? How can their very different tendencies "advance together, and mutually support each other"?

3. Tocqueville contrasts two ways of "diminishing the force of authority in a nation." What are they? Give an example of each method.

4. What conception of liberty does Tocqueville find in America? To what extent is it legitimate to restrain people from acting freely, even when their acts concern themselves alone?

5. Outline Tocqueville's arguments for freedom of the press.

6. What is the "tyranny of the majority" that Tocqueville fears? Why does democracy give rise to this danger? What might be done to protect against it?

7. What branch of government, in Tocqueville's view, is most likely to act tyrannically? Why?

CHAPTER II / ORIGIN OF THE ANGLO-AMERICANS, AND IMPORTANCE OF THIS ORIGIN IN RELATION TO THEIR FUTURE CONDITION

The chief care of the legislators, in this body of penal laws,* was the maintenance of orderly conduct and good morals in the community: they constantly invaded the domain of conscience, and there was scarcely a sin which they did not subject to magisterial censure. The reader is aware of the rigor with which these laws punished rape and adultery; intercourse between unmarried persons was likewise severely repressed. The judge was empowered to inflict a pecuniary penalty, a whipping, or marriage, on the misdemeanants; and if the records of the old courts of New Haven may be believed, prosecutions of this kind were not infrequent. We find a sentence bearing date the first of May, 1660, inflicting a fine and a reprimand on a young woman who was accused of using improper language, and of allowing herself to be kissed. The code of 1650 abounds in preventive measures. It punishes idleness and drunkenness with severity. Innkeepers are forbidden to furnish more than a certain quantity of liquor to each consumer; and simple lying, whenever it may be injurious, is checked by a fine or a flogging. In other places, the legislator, entirely forgetting the great principles of religious toleration which he had himself upheld in Europe, renders attendance on divine service compulsory, and goes so far as to visit with severe punishment, and even with death, the Christians who chose to worship God according to a ritual differing from his own. Sometimes indeed, the zeal of his enactments induces him to descend to the most frivolous particulars: thus a law is to be found in the same code which prohibits the use of tobacco. It must not be forgotten that these fantastical and vexatious laws were not imposed by authority, but that they were freely voted by all the persons interested, and that the manners of the community were even more austere and more puritanical than the laws. In 1649 a solemn association was formed in Boston to check the worldly luxury of long hair.

* Tocqueville is referring to the Connecticut Code of 1650. —ED.

These errors are no doubt discreditable to the human reason; they attest the inferiority of our nature, which is incapable of laying firm hold upon what is true and just, and is often reduced to the alternative of two excesses. In strict connexion with this penal legislation, which bears such striking marks of a narrow sectarian spirit, and of those religious passions which had been warmed by persecution, and were still fermenting among the people, a body of political laws is to be found, which, though written two hundred years ago, is still ahead of the liberties of our age.

The general principles which are the groundwork of modern constitutions—principles which were imperfectly known in Europe, and not completely triumphant even in Great Britain, in the seventeenth century—were all recognised and determined by the laws of New England: the intervention of the people in public affairs, the free voting of taxes, the responsibility of authorities, personal liberty, and trial by jury, were all positively established without discussion. . . .

In the laws of Connecticut, as well as in all those of New England, we find the germ and gradual development of that township independence, which is the life and mainspring of American liberty at the present day. The political existence of the majority of the nations of Europe commenced in the superior ranks of society, and was gradually and always imperfectly communicated to the different members of the social body. In America, on the other hand, it may be said that the township was organized before the county, the county before the state, the state before the Union. . . .

But it is by the attention it pays to public education that the original character of American civilization is at once placed in the clearest light. "It being," says the law, "one chief project of Satan to keep men from the knowledge of the Scripture by persuading from the use of tongues, to the end that learning may not be buried in the graves of our forefathers, in church and commonwealth, the Lord assisting our endeavours, . . . " Here follow clauses establishing schools in every township, and obliging the inhabitants, under pain of heavy fines, to support them. Schools of a superior kind were founded in the same manner in the more populous districts. The municipal authorities were bound to enforce the sending of children to school by their parents; they were empowered to inflict fines upon all who refused compliance; and in cases of continued resistance, society assumed the place of the parent, took possession of the child, and deprived the father of those natural rights which he used to so bad a purpose. The reader will undoubtedly have remarked the preamble of these enactments: in America, religion is the road to knowledge, and the observance of the divine laws leads man to civil freedom. . . .

The remarks I have made will suffice to display the character of Anglo-American civilization in its true light. It is the result (and this should be constantly present to the mind) of two distinct elements, which in other places have been in frequent hostility, but which in America have been admirably incorporated and combined with one another. I allude to the spirit of religion and the spirit of liberty.

The settlers of New England were at the same time ardent sectarians and daring innovators. Narrow as the limits of some of their religious opinions were, they were entirely free from political prejudices.

Hence arose two tendencies, distinct but not opposite, which are constantly discernible in the manners as well as in the laws of the country.

It might be imagined that men who sacrificed their friends, their family, and their native land, to a religious conviction, were absorbed in the pursuit of the intellectual advantages which they purchased at so dear a rate. The energy, however, with which they strove for the acquirements of wealth, moral enjoyment, and the comforts as well as the liberties of the world, was scarcely inferior to that with which they devoted themselves to Heaven.

Political principles, and all human laws and institutions were moulded and altered at their pleasure; the barriers of the society in which they were born were broken down before them; the old principles which had governed the world for ages were no more; a path without a turn, and a field without a horizon, were opened to the exploring and ardent curiosity of man: but at the limits of the political world he checks his researches, he discreetly lays aside the use of his most formidable faculties, he no longer consents to doubt or to innovate, but carefully abstaining from raising the curtain of the sanctuary, he yields with submissive respect to truths which he will not discuss.

Thus in the moral world, everything is classed, adapted, decided, and foreseen; in the political world everything is agitated, uncertain, and disputed: in the one is a passive, though a voluntary obedience; in the other an independence, scornful of experience and jealous of authority.

These two tendencies, apparently so discrepant, are far from conflicting; they advance together, and mutually support each other.

Religion perceives that civil liberty affords a noble exercise to the faculties of man, and that the political world is a field prepared by the Creator for the efforts of the intelligence. Contented with the freedom and the power which it enjoys in its own sphere, and with the place which it occupies, the empire of religion is never more surely established than when it reigns in the hearts of men unsupported by aught beside its native strength.

Religion is no less the companion of liberty in all its battles and its triumphs; the cradle of its infancy, and the divine source of its claims. The safeguard of morality is religion, and morality is the best security of law as well as the surest pledge of freedom. . . .

CHAPTER V / NECESSITY OF EXAMINING THE CONDITION OF THE STATES BEFORE THAT OF THE UNION AT LARGE

Administration in New England

Nothing is more striking to a European traveller in the United States than the absence of what we term government, or the administration. Written laws exist in America, and one sees that they are daily executed; but although everything is in motion, the hand which gives the impulse to the social machine can nowhere be discovered. Nevertheless, as all people are obliged to have recourse to certain grammatical forms, which are the foundation of human language, in order to express their thoughts; so all communities are obliged to secure their existence by submitting to a certain portion of authority, without which they fall a prey to anarchy. This authority may be distributed in several ways, but it must always exist somewhere.

There are two methods of diminishing the force of authority in a nation.

The first is to weaken the supreme power in its very principle, by forbidding or preventing society from acting in its own defence under certain circumstances. To weaken authority in this manner is what is generally termed in Europe to lay the foundations of freedom.

The second manner of diminishing the influence of authority does not consist in stripping society of any of its rights, nor in paralysing its efforts, but in distributing the exercise of its privileges among various hands, and in multiplying functionaries, to each of whom the degree of power necessary for him to perform his duty is intrusted. There may be nations whom this distribution of social powers might lead to anarchy; but in itself it is not anarchical. The action of authority is indeed thus rendered less irresistible, and less perilous, but it is not totally suppressed.

The revolution of the United States was the result of a mature and deliberate taste for freedom, not of a vague or ill-defined craving for independence. It contracted no alliance with the turbulent passions of anarchy; but its course was marked, on the contrary, by an attachment to whatever was lawful and orderly.

It was never assumed in the United States that the citizen of a free country has a right to do whatever he pleases: on the contrary, social obligations were there imposed upon him more various than anywhere else; no idea was every entertained of attacking the principles, or of contesting the rights of society; but the exercise of its authority was divided, to the end that the office might be powerful and the officer insignificant, and that the community should be at once regulated and free. In no country in the world does the law hold so absolute a language as in America; and in no country is the right of applying it vested in so many hands. The administrative power in the United States presents nothing either central or hierarchical in its constitution, which accounts for its passing unperceived. The power exists, but its representative is not to be discerned.

We have already seen that the independent townships of New England protect their own private interests; and the municipal magistrates are the persons to whom the execution of the laws of the state is most frequently entrusted. Beside the general laws, the state sometimes passes general police regulations; but more commonly the townships and town officers, conjointly with the justices of the peace, regulate the minor details of social life, according to the necessities of the different localities, and promulgate such enactments as concern the health of the community, and the peace as well as morality of the citizens. Lastly, these municipal magistrates provide of their own accord and without any delegated powers, for those unforeseen emergencies which frequently occur in society. . . .

. . . If the township and the county are not everywhere constituted in the same manner, it is at least true that in the United States the county and the township are always based upon the same principle, namely, that every one is the best judge of what concerns himself alone, and the person most able to supply his private wants. The township and the county are therefore bound to take care of their special interests: the state governs, but it does not interfere with their administration. Exceptions to this rule may be met with, but not a contrary principle. . . .

CHAPTER X / LIBERTY OF THE PRESS IN THE UNITED STATES

. . . But in the countries in which the doctrine of the sovereignty of the people ostensibly prevails, the censorship of the press is not only dangerous, but it is absurd. When the right of every citizen to co-operate in the government of society is acknowledged, every citizen must be presumed to possess the power of discriminating between the different opinions of his contemporaries, and of appreciating the different facts from which inferences may be drawn. The sovereignty of the people and the liberty of the press may therefore be looked upon as correlative institutions; just as the censorship of the press and universal suffrage are two things which are irreconcileably opposed, and which cannot long be retained among the institutions of the same people. Not a single individual of the twelve millions who inhabit the territory of the United States has as yet dared to propose any restrictions to the liberty of the press. . . .

America is perhaps, at this moment, the country of the whole world which contains the fewest germs of revolution; but the press is not less destructive in its principles than in France, and it displays the same violence without the same reasons for indignation. In America, as in France, it constitutes a singular power, so strangely composed of mingled good and evil, that it is at the same time indispensable to the existence of freedom, and nearly incompatible with the maintenance of public order. Its power is certainly much greater in France than in the United States; though nothing is more rare in the latter country than to hear of a prosecution having been instituted against it. The reason of this is perfectly simple; the Americans having once admitted the doctrine of sovereignty of the people, apply it with perfect consistency. It was never their intention to found a permanent state of things with elements which undergo daily modifications; and there is consequently nothing criminal in an attack upon the existing laws, provided it be not attended with a violent infraction of them. They are moreover of opinion that courts of justice are unable to check the abuses of the press; and that as the subtlety of human language perpetually eludes the severity of judicial analysis, offences of this nature are apt to escape the hand which attempts to apprehend them. They hold that to act with efficacy upon the press, it would be necessary to find a tribunal, not only devoted to the existing order of things, but capable of surmounting the influence of public opinion; a tribunal which should conduct its proceedings without publicity, which should pronounce its decrees without assigning its motives, and punish the intentions even more than the language of an author. Whosoever should have the power of creating and maintaining a tribunal of this kind, would waste his time in prosecuting the liberty of the press; for he would be the supreme master of the whole community, and he would be as free to rid himself of the authors as of their writings. In this question, therefore, there is no medium between servitude and extreme license; in order to enjoy the inestimable benefits which the liberty of the press ensures, it is necessary to submit to the inevitable evils which it engenders. To expect to acquire the former, and to escape the latter, is to cherish one of those illusions which commonly mislead nations in their times of sickness, when, tired with faction and exhausted by effort, they attempt to combine hostile opinions and contrary principles upon the same soil. . . .

The number of periodical and occasional publications which appear in the United States actually surpasses belief. The most enlightened Americans attribute the subordinate influence of the press to this excessive dissemination; and it is adopted as an axiom of political science in that country, that the only way to neutralize the effect of public journals is to multiply them indefinitely. . . .

. . . It cannot be denied that the effects of this extreme license of the press tend indirectly to the maintenance of public order. The individuals who are already in possession of a high station in the esteem of their fellow-citizens, are afraid to write in the newspapers, and they are thus deprived of the most powerful instrument which they can use to excite the passions of the multitude to their own advantage.

The personal opinions of the editors have no kind of weight in the eyes of the public: the only use of a journal is, that it imparts the knowledge of certain facts, and it is only by altering or distorting those facts, that a journalist can contribute to the support of his own views.

But although the press is limited to these resources, its influence in America is immense. It is the power which impels the circulation of political life through all the districts of that vast territory. Its eye is constantly open to detect the secret springs of political designs, and to summon the leaders of all parties to the bar of public opinion. It rallies the interests of the community round certain principles, and it draws up the creed which factions adopt; for it affords a means of intercourse between parties which hear, and which address each other, without ever having been in immediate contact. When a great number of the organs of the press adopt the same line of conduct, their influence becomes irresistible; and public opinion, when it is perpetually assailed from the same side, eventually yields to the attack. In the United States each separate journal exercises but little authority: but the power of the periodical press is only second to that of the people.

In the United States the democracy perpetually raises fresh individuals to the conduct of public affairs; and the measures of the administration are consequently seldom regulated by the strict rules of consistency or of order. But the general principles of the government are more stable, and the opinions most prevalent in society are generally more durable than in many other countries. When once the Americans have taken up an idea, whether it be well or ill-founded, nothing is more difficult than to eradicate it from their minds. The same tenacity of opinion has been observed in England, where, for the last century, greater freedom of conscience, and more invincible prejudices have existed, than in all the other countries of Europe. I attribute this consequence to a cause which may at first sight appear to have a very opposite tendency, namely, to the liberty of the press. The nations among which this liberty exists are as apt to cling to their opinions from pride as from conviction. They cherish them because they hold them to be just, and because they exercised their own free will in choosing them; and they maintain them, not only because they are true, but because they are their own. . . .

CHAPTER XI / POLITICAL ASSOCIATIONS IN THE UNITED STATES

. . . The more we consider the independence of the press in its principal consequences, the more are we convinced that it is the chief, and, so to speak, the constitutive element of freedom in the modern world. A nation which is determined to remain free, is therefore right in demanding the unrestrained exercise of this independence. But the *unrestrained* liberty of political association cannot be entirely assimilated to the liberty of the press. The one is at the same time less necessary and more dangerous than the other. A nation may confine it within certain limits without forfeiting any part of its self-control; and it may sometimes be obliged to do so in order to maintain its own authority. . . .

It must be acknowledged that the unrestrained liberty of political association has not hitherto produced, in the United States, those fatal consequences which might perhaps be expected from it elsewhere. The right of association was imported from England, and it has always existed in America. So that the exercise of this privilege is now amalgamated with the manners and customs of the people. At the present time, the liberty of association is become a necessary guarantee against the tyranny of the majority. In the United States, as soon as a party has become preponderant, all the public authority passes under its control; its private supporters occupy all the places, and have all the force of the administration at their disposal. As the most distinguished partisans of the other side of the question are unable to surmount the obstacles which exclude them from power, they require some means of establishing themselves upon their own basis, and of opposing the moral authority of the minority to the physical power which domineers over it. Thus, a dangerous expedient is used to obviate a still more formidable danger.

The omnipotence of the majority appears to me to present such extreme perils to the American republics, that the dangerous measure which is used to repress it, seems to be more advantageous than prejudicial. And here I am about to advance a proposition which may remind the reader of what I said before in speaking of municipal freedom. There are no countries in which associations are more needed, to prevent the despotism of faction, or the arbitrary power of a prince, than those which are democratically constituted. In aristocratic nations, the body of the nobles and the more opulent part of the community are in themselves natural associations, which act as checks upon the abuses of power. In countries in which those associations do not exist, if private individuals are unable to create an artificial and a temporary substitute for them, I can imagine no permanent protection against the most galling tyranny; and a great people may be oppressed by a small faction, or by a single individual, with impunity. . . .

It cannot be denied that the unrestrained liberty of association for political purposes, is the privilege which a people is longest in learning how to exercise. If it does not throw the nation into anarchy, it perpetually augments the chances of that calamity. On one point, however, this perilous liberty offers a security against dangers of another kind; in countries where associations are free, secret societies are unknown. In America there are numerous factions, but no conspiracies.

The most natural privilege of man, next to the right of acting for himself, is that of combining his exertions with those of his fellow-creatures, and of acting in common with them. I am therefore led to conclude, that the right of association is almost as inalienable as the right of personal liberty. No legislator can attack it without impairing the very foundations of society. . . .

CHAPTER XV / UNLIMITED POWER OF THE MAJORITY IN THE UNITED STATES, AND ITS CONSEQUENCES

The very essence of democratic government consists in the absolute sovereignty of the majority: for there is nothing in democratic states which is capable of resisting it. Most of the American constitutions have sought to increase this natural strength of the majority by artificial means.

The legislature is, of all political institutions, the one which is most easily swayed by the wishes of the majority. The Americans determined that the members of the legislature should be elected by the people immediately, and for a very brief term, in order to subject them, not only to the general convictions, but even to the daily passions of their constituents. The members of both houses are taken from the same class in society, and are nominated in the same manner; so that the modifications of the legislative bodies are almost as rapid and quite as irresistible as those of a single assembly. It is to a legislature thus constituted, that almost all the authority of the government has been entrusted. . . .

Tyranny of the Majority

I hold it to be an impious and an execrable maxim that, politically speaking, a people has a right to do whatsoever it pleases; and yet I have asserted that all

authority originates in the will of the majority. Am I, then, in contradiction with myself?

A general law—which bears the name of justice—has been made and sanctioned, not only by a majority of this or that people, but by a majority of mankind. The rights of every people are consequently confined within the limits of what is just. A nation may be considered in the light of a jury which is empowered to represent society at large, and to apply the great and general law of justice. Ought such a jury, which represents society, to have more power than the society in which the laws it applies originate?

When I refuse to obey an unjust law, I do not contest the right which the majority has of commanding, but I simply appeal from the sovereignty of the people to the sovereignty of mankind. It has been asserted that a people can never entirely outstep the boundaries of justice and of reason in those affairs which are more peculiarly its own; and that consequently full power may fearlessly be given to the majority by which it is represented. But this language is that of a slave.

A majority taken collectively may be regarded as a being whose opinions, and most frequently whose interests, are opposed to those of another being, which is styled a minority. If it be admitted that a man, possessing absolute power, may misuse that power by wronging his adversaries, why should a majority not be liable to the same reproach? Men are not apt to change their characters by agglomeration; nor does their patience in the presence of obstacles increase with the consciousness of their strength. And for these reasons I can never willingly invest any number of my fellow-creatures with that unlimited authority which I should refuse to any one of them. . . .

I am therefore of opinion that some one social power must always be made to predominate over the others; but I think that liberty is endangered when this power is checked by no obstacles which may retard its course, and force it to moderate its own vehemence.

Unlimited power is in itself a bad and dangerous thing; human beings are not competent to exercise it with discretion; and God alone can be omnipotent, because his wisdom and his justice are always equal to his power. But no power upon earth is so worthy of honor for itself, or of reverential obedience to the rights which it represents, that I would consent to admit its uncontrolled and all-predominant authority. When I see that the right and the means of absolute command are conferred on a people or upon a king, upon an aristocracy or a democracy, a monarchy or a republic, I recognise the germ of tyranny, and I journey onward to a land of more hopeful institutions.

In my opinion the main evil of the present democratic institutions of the United States does not arise, as is often asserted in Europe, from their weakness, but from their overpowering strength; and I am not so much alarmed at the excessive liberty which reigns in that country, as at the very inadequate securities which exist against tyranny.

When an individual or a party is wronged in the United States, to whom can he apply for redress? If to public opinion, public opinion constitutes the majority; if to the legislature, it represents the majority, and implicitly obeys its instructions; if to the executive power, it is appointed by the majority and is a passive tool in its hands; the public troops consist of the majority under arms; the jury is the majority invested with the right of hearing judicial cases; and in certain states even the judges are elected by the majority. However iniquitous or absurd the evil of which you complain may be, you must submit to it as well as you can. . . .

Power Exercised by the Majority in America upon Opinion

It is in the examination of the display of public opinion in the United States, that we clearly perceive how far the power of the majority surpasses all the powers with which we are acquainted in Europe. Intellectual principles exercise an influence which is so invisible and often so inappreciable, that they baffle the toils of oppression. . . .

I know no country in which there is so little true independence of mind and freedom of discussion as in America. In any constitutional state in Europe every sort of religious and political theory may be advocated and propagated abroad; for there is no country in Europe so subdued by any single authority, as not to contain citizens who are ready to protect the man who raises his voice in the cause of truth, from the consequences of his hardihood. If he is unfortunate enough to live under an absolute government, the people is upon his side; if he inhabits a free country, he may find a shelter behind the authority of the throne, if he require one. The aristocratic part of society supports him in some countries, and the democracy in others. But in a nation where democratic institutions exist, organized like those of the United States, there is but one sole authority, one single element of strength and of success, with nothing beyond it.

In America, the majority raises very formidable barriers to the liberty of opinion: within these barriers an author may write whatever he pleases, but he will repent it if he ever step beyond them. Not that he is exposed to the terrors of an auto-da-fé, but he is tormented by the slights and persecutions of daily obloquy. His political career is closed for ever, since he has offended the only authority which is able to promote his success. Every sort of compensation, even that of celebrity, is refused to him. Before he published his opinions, he imagined that he held them in common with many others; but no sooner has he declared them openly, than he is loudly censured by his overbearing opponents, while those who think, without having the courage to speak, like him, abandon him in silence. He yields at length, oppressed by the daily efforts he has been making, and he subsides into silence as if he was tormented by remorse for having spoken the truth.

Fetters and headsmen were the coarse instruments which tyranny formerly employed; but the civilization of our age has refined the arts of despotism, which seemed however to have been sufficiently perfected before. The excesses of monarchical power had devised a variety of physical means of oppression; the democratic republics of the present day have rendered it as entirely an affair of the mind, as that will which it is intended to coerce. Under the absolute sway of an individual despot, the body was attacked in order to subdue the soul; and the soul escaped the blows which were directed against it, and rose superior to the attempt; but such is not the course adopted by tyranny in democratic republics; there the body is left free, and the soul is enslaved. The sovereign can no longer say, "You shall think as I do on pain of death;" but he says, "You are free to think differently from me, and to retain your life, your property, and all that you possess; but if such be your determination, you are henceforth an alien among your people. You may retain your civil rights, but they will be useless to you, for you will never be chosen by your fellow-citizens, if you solicit their suffrages; and they will affect to scorn you, if you solicit their esteem. You will remain among men, but you will be deprived of the rights of mankind. Your fellow-creatures will shun you like an impure being; and those who are most persuaded of your innocence will abandon you too, lest they should be shunned in their turn. Go in peace! I have given you your life, but it is an existence incomparably worse than death." . . .

If great writers have not at present existed in America, the reason is very simply given in these facts; there can be no literary genius without freedom of opinion, and freedom of opinion does not exist in America. The inquisition has never been able to prevent a vast number of anti-religious books from circulating in Spain. The empire of the majority succeeds much better in the United States, since it actually removes the wish of publishing them. Unbelievers are to be met with in America, but, to say the truth, there is no public organ of infidelity. Attempts have been made by some governments to protect the morality of nations by prohibiting licentious books. In the United States no one is punished for this sort of works, but no one is induced to write them; not because all the citizens are immaculate in their manners, but because the majority of the community is decent and orderly.

In these cases the advantages derived from the exercise of this power are unquestionable; and I am simply discussing the nature of the power itself. This irresistible authority is a constant fact, and its beneficent exercise is an accidental occurrence.

Effects of the Tyranny of the Majority upon the National Character of the Americans

The tendencies which I have just alluded to are as yet very slightly perceptible in political society; but

they already begin to exercise an unfavourable influence upon the national character of the Americans. I am inclined to attribute the singular paucity of distinguished political characters to the ever-increasing activity of the despotism of the majority in the United States. . . .

The Greatest Dangers of the American Republics Proceed from the Unlimited Power of the Majority

. . . If ever the free institutions of America are destroyed, that event may be attributed to the unlimited authority of the majority, which may at some future time urge the minorities to desperation, and oblige them to have recourse to physical force. Anarchy will then be the result, but it will have been brought about by despotism.

Mr. Hamilton expresses the same opinion in the Federalist, No. 51. "It is of great importance in a republic not only to guard the society against the oppression of its rulers, but to guard one part of the society against the injustice of the other part. Justice is the end of government. It is the end of civil society. It ever has been, and ever will be pursued until it be obtained, or until liberty be lost in the pursuit. In a society, under the forms of which the stronger faction can readily unite and oppress the weaker, anarchy may as truly be said to reign as in a state of nature, where the weaker individual is not secured against the violence of the stronger: and as in the latter state even the stronger individuals are prompted by the uncertainty of their condition to submit to a government which may protect the weak as well as themselves, so in the former state will the more powerful factions be gradually induced by a like motive to wish for a government which will protect all parties, the weaker as well as the more powerful. It can be little doubted, that if the state of Rhode Island was separated from the confederacy and left to itself, the insecurity of rights under the popular form of government within such narrow limits, would be displayed by such reiterated oppressions of the factious majorities, that some power altogether independent of the people would soon be called for by the voice of the very factions whose misrule had proved the necessity of it."

Jefferson has also thus expressed himself in a letter to Madison: "The executive power in our government is not the only, perhaps not even the principal object of my solicitude. The tyranny of the legislature is really the danger most to be feared, and will continue to be so for many years to come. The tyranny of the executive power will come in its turn, but at a more distant period." . . .

JOHN STUART MILL

from *On Liberty* (1859)

John Stuart Mill (1806–1873), born in London, was the most influential philosopher of the English-speaking world during the nineteenth century. His father, James Mill (1773–1836), was the son of a Scottish shoemaker who had become a prominent supporter of philosophical radicalism, a school of thought that advocated representative democracy, universal suffrage, and a scientific approach to philosophy. The elder Mill had a highly unusual and ambitious plan for educating his son at home. Consequently, John Stuart Mill never attended any school or college. He learned to read Greek at three and Latin just a few years later; he was well-read in classical literature and history by eight and studied philosophy, mathematics, and economics before reaching his teens. At seventeen, he became a clerk in the East India Company, which governed India under charter from the British government. He eventually became chief of his department and worked at the company until 1858. In that year, Harriet Taylor, Mill's wife of six years—whom in the dedication of On Liberty *he calls "the inspirer, and in part the author, of all that is best in my writings"—died while they were traveling together in France. Mill decided to devote his time fully to writing the works they had discussed together. The next few years saw the publication of Mill's most influential ethical works:* On Liberty *(1859), Utilitar-ianism (1861), and* On the Subjection of Women *(1869). In 1865, Mill won election to Parliament, despite his refusal to campaign or defend his views.*

On Liberty is a classic statement of the importance of individual liberty. Its chapter "Of the Liberty of Thought and Discussion" is probably the most famous and influential defense of freedom of speech ever written. Mill was a staunch advocate of democracy but saw that majority rule, in itself, could allow the oppression of the minority. Mill wrote On Liberty *to outline a realm of freedom that not even democratic majorities may transgress. (Source: London: Parker, 1859.)*

QUESTIONS FOR REFLECTION

1. What is the "one very simple principle"—usually called the *harm principle*—that Mill's essay aims to assert? What does it mean? What conditions and qualifications does Mill place on it? How does it counteract the "tyranny of the majority"?

2. Later philosophers have often stated Mill's harm principle in terms of a distinction between self-regarding and other-regarding actions. How might this distinction be drawn? How can Mill's principle be stated in terms of that distinction?

CHAPTER I / INTRODUCTORY

. . . .The object of this essay is to assert one very simple principle, as entitled to govern absolutely the dealings of society with the individual in the way of compulsion and control, whether the means used be physical force in the form of legal penalties or the moral coercion of public opinion. That principle is that the sole end for which mankind are warranted, individually or collectively, in interfering with the liberty of action of any of their number is self-protection. That the only purpose for which power can be rightfully exercised over any member of a civilized community, against his will, is to prevent harm to others. His own good, either physical or moral, is not a sufficient warrant. He cannot rightfully be compelled to do or forbear because it will be better for him to do so, because it will make him happier, because, in the opinions of others, to do so would be wise or even right. These are good reasons for remonstrating with him, or reasoning with him, or persuading him, or entreating him, but not for compelling him or visiting him with any evil in case he do otherwise. To justify that, the conduct from which it is desired to deter him must be calculated to produce evil to someone else. The only part of the conduct of anyone for which he is amenable to society is that which concerns others. In the part which merely concerns himself, his independence is, of right, absolute. Over himself, over his own body and mind, the individual is sovereign.

It is, perhaps, hardly necessary to say that this doctrine is meant to apply only to human beings in the maturity of their faculties. We are not speaking of children or of young persons below the age which the law may fix as that of manhood or womanhood. Those who are still in a state to require being taken care of by others must be protected against their own actions as well as against external injury. . . . But as soon as mankind have attained the capacity of being guided to their own improvement by conviction or persuasion (a period long since reached in all nations with whom we need here concern ourselves), compulsion, either in the direct form or in that of pains and penalties for noncompliance, is no longer admissible as a means to their own good, and justifiable only for the security of others.

It is proper to state that I forego any advantage which could be derived to my argument from the idea of abstract right as a thing independent of utility. I regard utility as the ultimate appeal on all ethical questions; but it must be utility in the largest sense, grounded on the permanent interests of man as a progressive being. Those interests, I contend, authorize the subjection of individual spontaneity to external control only in respect to those actions of each which concern the interest of other people. If anyone does an act hurtful to others, there is a *prima facie* case for punishing him by law or, where legal penalties are not safely applicable, by general disapprobation. There are also many positive acts for the benefit of others which he may rightfully be compelled to perform, such as to give evidence in a court of justice, to bear his fair share in the common defense or in any other joint work necessary to the interest of the society of which he enjoys the protection, and to perform certain acts of individual beneficence, such as saving a fellow creature's life or interposing to protect the defenseless against ill usage—things which whenever it is obviously a man's duty to do he may rightfully be made responsible to society for not doing. A person may cause evil to others not only by his actions but by his inaction, and in either case he is justly accountable to them for the injury. The latter case, it is true, requires a much more cautious exercise of compulsion than the former. To make anyone answerable for doing evil to others is the rule; to make him answerable for not preventing evil is, comparatively speaking, the exception. Yet there are many cases clear enough and grave enough to justify that exception. In all things which regard the external relations of the individual, he is *de jure* amenable to those whose interests are concerned, and, if need be, to society as their protector. There are often good reasons for not holding him to the responsibility; but these reasons must arise from the special expediencies of the case: either because it is a kind of case in which he is on the whole likely to act better when left to his own discretion than when controlled in any way in which society have it in their power to control him; or because the attempt to exercise control would produce other evils, greater than those which it would prevent. When such reasons as these preclude the enforcement of responsibility, the conscience of the agent himself should step into the vacant judgment seat and protect those interests of others which have no external protection; judging himself all the more rigidly, because the case does not admit of his being made accountable to the judgment of his fellow creatures.

But there is a sphere of action in which society, as distinguished from the individual, has, if any, only an indirect interest: comprehending all that portion of a person's life and conduct which affects only himself or, if it also affects others, only with their free, voluntary, and undeceived consent and participation. When I say only himself, I mean directly and in the first instance; for whatever affects himself may affect others through himself: and the objection which may be grounded on this contingency will receive consideration in the sequel. This, then, is the appropriate region of human liberty. It comprises, first, the inward domain of consciousness, demanding liberty of conscience in the most comprehensive sense, liberty of thought and feeling, absolute freedom of opinion and sentiment on all subjects, practical or speculative, scientific, moral, or theological. The liberty of expressing and publishing opinions may seem to fall under a different principle, since it belongs to that part of the conduct of an individual which concerns other people, but, being almost of as much importance as the liberty of thought itself and resting in great part on the same reasons, is practically inseparable from it. Secondly, the principle requires liberty of tastes and pursuits, of framing the plan of our life to suit our own character, of doing as we like, subject to such consequences as may follow, without impediment from our fellow creatures, so long as what we do does not harm them, even though they should think our conduct foolish, perverse, or wrong. Thirdly, from this liberty of each individual follows the liberty, within the same limits, of combination among individuals; freedom to unite for any purpose not involving harm to others: the persons combining being supposed to be of full age and not forced or deceived.

No society in which these liberties are not, on the whole, respected is free, whatever may be its form of government; and none is completely free in which they do not exist absolute and unqualified. The only freedom which deserves the name is that of pursuing our own good in our own way, so long as we do not attempt to deprive others of theirs or impede their efforts to obtain it. Each is the proper guardian of his own health, whether bodily *or* mental and spiritual. Mankind are greater gainers by suffering each other to live as seems good to themselves than by compelling each to live as seems good to the rest. . . .

QUESTIONS FOR REFLECTION

1. How does Mill's defense of freedom of thought and discussion fit into the overall scheme of *On Liberty*? Is speech self-regarding or other-regarding? Is his defense an application of the harm principle or an extension of it?

2. "All silencing of discussion is an assumption of infallibility," Mill contends. How does he argue for this claim? Do you agree?

3. Why does Mill think that the expression even of obviously false opinions should be protected?

4. Some contemporary advocates of controlling certain forms of expression argue that although the government cannot ban the expression of certain views, it can ban certain ways of expressing them—ways involving pornography, say, or the use of racial epithets. What is Mill's view about such restrictions? What arguments does he advance in support of his position? Do you find his arguments persuasive?

5. Mill mentions one exception to freedom of speech: inciting a mob to violence. What general principle lies behind this exception? What other exceptions might Mill be willing to accept?

CHAPTER II / OF THE LIBERTY OF THOUGHT AND DISCUSSION

. . . Let us suppose . . . that the government is entirely at one with the people, and never thinks of exerting any power of coercion unless in agreement with what it conceives to be their voice. But I deny the right of the people to exercise such coercion, either by themselves or by their government. The power itself is illegitimate. The best government has no more title to it than the worst. It is as noxious, or more noxious, when exerted in accordance with public opinion than when in opposition to it. If all mankind minus one were of one opinion, mankind would be no more justified in silencing that one person than he, if he had the power, would be justified in silencing mankind. Were an opinion a personal possession of no value except to the owner, if to be obstructed in the enjoyment of it were simply a private injury, it would make some difference whether the injury was inflicted only on a few persons or on many. But the peculiar evil of silencing the expression of an opinion is that it is robbing the human race, posterity as well as the existing generation—those who dissent from the opinion, still more than those who hold it. If the opinion is right, they are deprived of the opportunity of exchanging error for truth; if wrong, they lose, what is almost as great a benefit, the clearer perception and livelier impression of truth produced by its collision with error.

It is necessary to consider separately these two hypotheses, each of which has a distinct branch of the argument corresponding to it. We can never be sure that the opinion we are endeavoring to stifle is a false opinion; and if we were sure, stifling it would be an evil still.

First, the opinion which it is attempted to suppress by authority may possibly be true. Those who desire to suppress it, of course, deny its truth; but they are not infallible. They have no authority to decide the question for all mankind and exclude every other person from the means of judging. To refuse a hearing to an opinion because they are sure that it is false is to assume that *their* certainty is the same thing as *absolute* certainty. All silencing of discussion is an assumption of infallibility. . . .

The objection likely to be made to this argument would probably take some such form as the following. There is no greater assumption of infallibility in forbidding the propagation of error than in any other thing which is done by public authority on its own judgment and responsibility. Judgment is given to men that they may use it. Because it may be used erroneously, are men to be told that they ought not to use it at all? To prohibit what they think pernicious is not claiming exemption from error, but fulfilling the duty incumbent on them, although fallible, of acting on their conscientious conviction. If we were never to act on our opinions, because those opinions may be wrong, we should leave all our interests uncared for, and all our duties unperformed. An objection which applies to all conduct can be no valid objection to any conduct in particular. It is the duty of governments, and of individuals, to form the truest opinions they can; to form them carefully, and never impose them upon others unless they are quite sure of being right. But when they are sure (such reasoners may say), it is not conscientiousness but cowardice to shrink from acting on their opinions and allow doctrines which they honestly think dangerous to the welfare of mankind,

either in this life or in another, to be scattered abroad without restraint, because other people, in less enlightened times, have persecuted opinions now believed to be true. Let us take care, it may be said, not to make the same mistake; but governments and nations have made mistakes in other things which are not denied to be fit subjects for the exercise of authority: they have laid on bad taxes, made unjust wars. Ought we therefore to lay on no taxes and, under whatever provocation, make no wars? Men and governments must act to the best of their ability. There is no such thing as absolute certainty, but there is assurance sufficient for the purposes of human life. We may, and must, assume our opinion to be true for the guidance of our own conduct; and it is assuming no more when we forbid bad men to pervert society by the propagation of opinions which we regard as false and pernicious.

I answer, that it is assuming very much more. There is the greatest difference between presuming an opinion to be true because, with every opportunity for contesting it, it has not been refuted, and assuming its truth for the purpose of not permitting its refutation. Complete liberty of contradicting and disproving our opinion is the very condition which justifies us in assuming its truth for purposes of action; and on no other terms can a being with human faculties have any rational assurance of being right.

When we consider either the history of opinion or the ordinary conduct of human life, to what is it to be ascribed that the one and the other are no worse than they are? Not certainly to the inherent force of the human understanding, for on any matter not self-evident there are ninety-nine persons totally incapable of judging of it for one who is capable; and the capacity of the hundredth person is only comparative, for the majority of the eminent men of every past generation held many opinions now known to be erroneous, and did or approved numerous things which no one will now justify. Why is it, then, that there is on the whole a preponderance among mankind of rational opinions and rational conduct? If there really is this preponderance—which there must be unless human affairs are, and have always been, in an almost desperate state—it is owing to a quality of the human mind, the source of everything respectable in man either as an intellectual or as a moral being, namely, that his errors are corrigible. He is capable of rectifying his mistakes by discussion and experience. Not by experience alone. There must be discussion to show how experience is to be interpreted. Wrong opinions and practices gradually yield to fact and argument; but facts and arguments, to produce any effect on the mind, must be brought before it. Very few facts are able to tell their own story, without comments to bring out their meaning. The whole strength and value, then, of human judgment depending on the one property, that it can be set right when it is wrong, reliance can be placed on it only when the means of setting it right are kept constantly at hand. In the case of any person whose judgment is really deserving of confidence, how has it become so? Because he has kept his mind open to criticism of his opinions and conduct. Because it has been his practice to listen to all that could be said against him; to profit by as much of it as was just, and to expound to himself, and upon occasion to others, the fallacy of what was fallacious. Because he has felt that the only way in which a human being can make some approach to knowing the whole of a subject is by hearing what can be said about it by persons of every variety of opinion, and studying all modes in which it can be looked at by every character of mind. No wise man ever acquired his wisdom in any mode but this; nor is it in the nature of human intellect to become wise in any other manner. The steady habit of correcting and completing his own opinion by collating it with those of others, so far from causing doubt and hesitation in carrying it into practice, is the only stable foundation for a just reliance on it; for, being cognizant of all that can, at least obviously, be said against him and having taken up his position against all gainsayers —knowing that he has sought for objections and difficulties instead of avoiding them, and has shut out no light which can be thrown upon the subject from any quarter—he has a right to think his judgment better than that of any person, or any multitude, who have not gone through a similar process. . . .

Let us now pass to the second division of the argument, and dismissing the supposition that any of the received opinions may be false, let us assume them to be true and examine into the worth of the manner in which they are likely to be held when their truth is not freely and openly canvassed. However unwillingly a person who has a strong opinion may admit the possibility that his opinion may be false, he ought to be moved by the consideration that, however true it may be, if it is not fully, frequently, and fearlessly discussed, it will be held as a dead dogma, not a living truth.

There is a class of persons (happily not quite so numerous as formerly) who think it enough if a person assents undoubtingly to what they think true, though he has no knowledge whatever of the grounds of the opinion and could not make a tenable defense of it against the most superficial objections. Such persons, if they can once get their creed taught from authority, naturally think that no good, and some harm, comes of its being allowed to be questioned. Where their influence prevails, they make it nearly impossible for the received opinion to be rejected wisely and considerately, though it may still be rejected rashly and ignorantly; for to shut out discussion entirely is seldom possible, and when it once gets in, beliefs not grounded on conviction are apt to give way before the slightest semblance of an argument. Waiving, however, this possibility—assuming that the true opinion abides in the mind, but abides as a prejudice, a belief independent of, and proof against, argument—this is not the way in which truth ought to be held by a rational being. This is not knowing the truth. Truth, thus held, is but one superstition the more, accidentally clinging to the words which enunciate a truth. . . .

If, however, the mischievous operation of the absence of free discussion, when the received opinions are true, were confined to leaving men ignorant of the grounds of those opinions, it might be thought that this, if an intellectual, is no moral evil and does not affect the worth of the opinions, regarded in their influence on the character. The fact, however, is that not only the grounds of the opinion are forgotten in the absence of discussion, but too often the meaning of the opinion itself. The words which convey it cease to suggest ideas, or suggest only a small portion of those they were originally employed to communicate. Instead of a vivid conception and a living belief, there remain only a few phrases retained by rote; or, if any part, the shell and husk only of the meaning is retained, the finer essence being lost. The great chapter in human history which this fact occupies and fills cannot be too earnestly studied and meditated on.

It is illustrated in the experience of almost all ethical doctrines and religious creeds: They are all full of meaning and vitality to those who originate them, and to the direct disciples of the originators. Their meaning continues to be felt in undiminished strength, and is perhaps brought out into even fuller consciousness, so long as the struggle lasts to give the doctrine or creed an ascendancy over other creeds. At last it either prevails and becomes the general opinion, or its progress stops; it keeps possession of the ground it has gained, but ceases to spread further. When either of these results has become apparent, controversy on the subject flags, and gradually dies away. The doctrine has taken its place, if not as a received opinion, as one of the admitted sects or divisions of opinion; those who hold it have generally inherited, not adopted it; and conversion from one of these doctrines to another, being now an exceptional fact, occupies little place in the thoughts of their professors. Instead of being, as at first, constantly on the alert either to defend themselves against the world or to bring the world over to them, they have subsided into acquiescence and neither listen, when they can help it, to arguments against their creed, nor trouble dissentients (if there be such) with arguments in its favor. From this time may usually be dated the decline in the living power of the doctrine. . . .

. . . There are many reasons, doubtless, why doctrines which are the badge of a sect retain more of their vitality than those common to all recognized sects, and why more pains are taken by teachers to keep their meaning alive; but one reason certainly is that the peculiar doctrines are more questioned and have to be oftener defended against open gainsayers. Both teachers and learners go to sleep at their post as soon as there is no enemy in the field. . . .

It still remains to speak of one of the principal causes which make diversity of opinion advantageous, and will continue to do so until mankind shall have entered a stage of intellectual advancement which at present seems at an incalculable distance. We have hitherto considered only two possibilities: that the received opinion may be false, and some other opinion, consequently, true; or that, the received opinion being true, a conflict with the opposite error is essential to a clear apprehension and deep feeling of its truth. But there is a commoner case than either of these: when the conflicting doctrines, instead of being one true and the other false, share the truth between them, and the nonconforming opinion is needed to supply the remainder of the truth of which the received doctrine embodies only a part. Popular opinions, on subjects not palpable to sense, are often true, but seldom or never the whole truth. They are a part of the truth, sometimes a greater, sometimes a smaller part, but exaggerated, distorted, and disjointed from the truths by which they ought to be accompanied and limited. Heretical opinions, on the other hand, are generally some of these suppressed and neglected truths, bursting the bonds which kept them down, and either seeking reconciliation with the truth contained in the common opinion, or fronting it as enemies, and setting themselves up, with similar exclusiveness, as the whole truth. The latter case is hitherto the most frequent, as, in the human mind, one-sidedness has always been the rule, and many-sidedness the exception. Hence, even in revolutions of opinion, one part of the truth usually sets while another rises. Even progress, which ought to superadd, for the most part only substitutes one partial and incomplete truth for another; improvement consisting chiefly in this, that the new fragment of truth is more wanted, more adapted to the needs of the time than that which it displaces. Such being the partial character of prevailing opinions, even when resting on a true foundation, every opinion which embodies somewhat of the portion of truth which the common opinion omits ought to be considered precious, with whatever amount of error and confusion that truth may be blended. No sober judge of human affairs will feel bound to be indignant because those who force on our notice truths which we should otherwise have overlooked, overlook some of those which we see. Rather, he will think that so long as popular truth is one-sided, it is more desirable than otherwise that unpopular truth should have one-sided assertors, too, such being usually the most energetic and the most likely to compel reluctant attention to the fragment of wisdom which they proclaim as if it were the whole. . . .

. . . only through diversity of opinion is there, in the existing state of human intellect, a chance of fair play to all sides of the truth. When there are persons to be found who form an exception to the apparent unanimity of the world on any subject, even if the world is in the right, it is always probable that dissentients have something worth hearing to say for themselves, and that truth would lose something by their silence. . . .

We have now recognized the necessity to the mental well-being of mankind (on which all their other well-being depends) of freedom of opinion, and freedom of the expression of opinion, on four distinct grounds, which we will now briefly recapitulate:

First, if any opinion is compelled to silence, that opinion may, for aught we can certainly know, be true. To deny this is to assume our own infallibility.

Secondly, though the silenced opinion be an error, it may, and very commonly does, contain a portion of truth; and since the general or prevailing opinion on any subject is rarely or never the whole truth, it is only by the collision of adverse opinions that the remainder of the truth has any chance of being supplied.

Thirdly, even if the received opinion be not only true, but the whole truth; unless it is suffered to be, and actually is, vigorously and earnestly contested, it will, by most of those who receive it, be held in the manner of a prejudice, with little comprehension or feeling of its rational grounds. And not only this, but, fourthly, the meaning of the doctrine itself will be in danger of being lost or enfeebled, and deprived of its vital effect on the character and conduct: the dogma becoming a mere formal profession, inefficacious for good, but cumbering the ground and preventing the growth of any real and heartfelt conviction from reason or personal experience. . . .

CHAPTER III / OF INDIVIDUALITY, AS ONE OF THE ELEMENTS OF WELL-BEING

. . . No one pretends that actions should be as free as opinions. On the contrary, even opinions lose their immunity when the circumstances in which they are expressed are such as to constitute their expression a positive instigation to some mischievous act.

An opinion that corn dealers are starvers of the poor, or that private property is robbery, ought to be unmolested when simply circulated through the press, but may justly incur punishment when delivered orally to an excited mob assembled before the house of a corn dealer, or when handed about among the same mob in the form of a placard. Acts of whatever kind, which without justifiable cause do harm to others may be, and in the more important cases absolutely require to be, controlled by the unfavorable sentiments, and, when needful, by the active interference of mankind. The liberty of the individual must be thus far limited; he must not make himself a nuisance to other people. But if he refrains from molesting others in what concerns them, and merely acts according to his own inclination and judgment in things which concern himself, the same reasons which show that opinion should be free prove also that he should be allowed, without molestation, to carry his opinions into practice at his own cost. . . .

QUESTIONS FOR REFLECTION

1. To what extent may people be punished by the opinions or behavior of others, independent of any legal coercion? Is Mill's view compatible with his analysis of the social stigma attending the expression of unpopular opinions?

2. Mill admits that distinguishing self-regarding from other-regarding actions is a matter of degree, for virtually every action affects someone other than the agent who performs it. What is Mill's criterion for determining whether an act affects others enough to count as other-regarding and, so, to be subject to government interference?

3. What arguments does Mill advance in this section in favor of the harm principle?

CHAPTER IV / OF THE LIMITS TO THE AUTHORITY OF SOCIETY OVER THE INDIVIDUAL

What, then, is the rightful limit to the sovereignty of the individual over himself? Where does the authority of society begin? How much of human life should be assigned to individuality, and how much to society?

Each will receive its proper share if each has that which more particularly concerns it. To individuality should belong the part of life in which it is chiefly the individual that is interested; to society, the part which chiefly interests society.

Though society is not founded on a contract, and though no good purpose is answered by inventing a contract in order to deduce social obligations from it, everyone who receives the protection of society owes a return for the benefit, and the fact of living in society renders it indispensable that each should be bound to observe a certain line of conduct toward the rest. This conduct consists, first, in not injuring the interests of one another, or rather certain interests which, either by express legal provision or by tacit understanding, ought to be considered as rights; and secondly, in each person's bearing his share (to be fixed on some equitable principle) of the labors and sacrifices incurred for defending the society or its members from injury and molestation. These conditions society is justified in enforcing at all costs to those who endeavor to withhold fulfillment. Nor is this all that society may do. The acts of an individual may be hurtful to others or wanting in due consideration for their welfare, without going to the length of violating any of their constituted rights. The offender may then be justly punished by opinion, though not by law. As soon as any part of a person's conduct affects prejudicially the interests of others, society has jurisdiction over it, and the question whether the general welfare will or will not be promoted by interfering with it becomes open to discussion. But there is no room for entertaining any such question when a person's conduct affects the interests of no persons besides himself, or needs not affect them unless they like (all the persons concerned being of full age and the ordinary amount of understanding). In all such cases, there should be perfect freedom, legal and social, to do the action and stand the consequences. . . .

The distinction here pointed out between the part of a person's life which concerns only himself and that which concerns others, many persons will refuse to admit. How (it may be asked) can any part of the conduct of a member of society be a matter of

indifference to the other members? No person is an entirely isolated being; it is impossible for a person to do anything seriously or permanently hurtful to himself without mischief reaching at least to his near connections, and often far beyond them. If he injures his property, he does harm to those who directly or indirectly derived support from it, and usually diminishes, by a greater or less amount, the general resources of the community. If he deteriorates his bodily or mental faculties, he not only brings evil upon all who depended upon him for any portion of their happiness, but disqualifies himself for rendering the services which he owes to his fellow creatures generally, perhaps becomes a burden on their affection or benevolence; and if such conduct were very frequent hardly any offense that is committed would detract more from the general sum of good. Finally, if by his vices or follies a person does no direct harm to others, he is nevertheless (it may be said) injurious by his example, and ought to be compelled to control himself for the sake of those whom the sight or knowledge of his conduct might corrupt or mislead.

And even (it will be added) if the consequences of misconduct could be confined to the vicious or thoughtless individual, ought society to abandon to their own guidance those who are manifestly unfit for it? If protection against themselves is confessedly due to children and persons under age, is not society equally bound to afford it to persons of mature years who are equally incapable of self-government? If gambling, or drunkenness, or incontinence, or idleness, or uncleanliness are as injurious to happiness, and as great a hindrance to improvement, as many or most of the acts prohibited by law, why (it may be asked) should not law, so far as is consistent with practicability and social convenience, endeavor to repress these also? And as a supplement to the unavoidable imperfections of law, ought not opinion at least to organize a powerful police against these vices and visit rigidly with social penalties those who are known to practice them? There is no question here (it may be said) about restricting individuality, or impeding the trial of new and original experiments in living. The only things it is sought to prevent are things which have been tried and condemned from the beginning of the world until now—things which experience has shown not to be useful or suitable to any person's individuality. There must be some length of time and amount of experience after which a moral or prudential truth may be regarded as established; and it is merely desired to prevent generation after generation from falling over the same precipice which has been fatal to their predecessors.

I fully admit that the mischief which a person does to himself may seriously affect, both through their sympathies and their interests, those nearly connected with him and, in a minor degree, society at large. When, by conduct of this sort, a person is led to violate a distinct and assignable obligation to any other person or persons, the case is taken out of the self-regarding class and becomes amenable to moral disapprobation in the proper sense of the term. If, for example, a man, through intemperance or extravagance, becomes unable to pay his debts, or, having undertaken the moral responsibility of a family, becomes from the same cause incapable of supporting or educating them, he is deservedly reprobated and might be justly punished; but it is for the breach of duty to his family or creditors, not for the extravagance. If the resources which ought to have been devoted to them had been diverted from them for the most prudent investment, the moral culpability would have been the same. George Barnwell murdered his uncle to get money for his mistress, but if he had done it to set himself up in business, he would equally have been hanged. Again, in the frequent case of a man who causes grief to his family by addiction to bad habits, he deserves reproach for his unkindness or ingratitude; but so he may for cultivating habits not in themselves vicious, if they are painful to those with whom he passes his life, or who from personal ties are dependent on him for their comfort. Whoever fails in the consideration generally due to the interests and feelings of others, not being compelled by some more imperative duty, or justified by allowable self-preference, is a subject of moral disapprobation for that failure, but not for the cause of it, nor for the errors, merely personal to himself, which may have remotely led to it. In like manner, when a person disables himself, by conduct purely self-regarding, from the performance of some definite duty incumbent on him to the public, he is guilty of a social offense. No person ought to be punished simply for being drunk; but a soldier or policeman should be punished for being drunk on duty. Whenever, in short, there is a definite damage, or a definite risk of damage, either to an individual or to the public, the case is taken out of the province of liberty and placed in that of morality or law.

But with regard to the merely contingent or, as it may be called, constructive injury which a person causes to society by conduct which neither violates any specific duty to the public, nor occasions perceptible hurt to any assignable individual except himself, the inconvenience is one which society can afford to bear, for the sake of the greater good of human freedom. . . .

But the strongest of all the arguments against the interference of the public with purely personal conduct is that, when it does interfere, the odds are that it interferes wrongly and in the wrong place. On questions of social morality, of duty to others, the opinion of the public, that is, of an overruling majority, though often wrong, is likely to be still oftener right, because on such questions they are only required to judge of their own interests, of the manner in which some mode of conduct, if allowed to be practiced, would affect themselves. But the opinion of a similar majority, imposed as a law on the minority, on questions of self-regarding conduct is quite as likely to be wrong as right, for in these cases public opinion means, at the best, some people's opinion of what is good or bad for other people, while very often it does not even mean that—the public, with the most perfect indifference, passing over the pleasure or convenience of those whose conduct they censure and considering only their own preference. There are many who consider as an injury to themselves any conduct which they have a distaste for, and resent it as an outrage to their feelings; as a religious bigot, when charged with disregarding the religious feelings of others, has been known to retort that they disregard his feelings by persisting in their abominable worship or creed. But there is no parity between the feeling of a person for his own opinion and the feeling of another who is offended at his holding it, no more than between the desire of a thief to take a purse and the desire of the right owner to keep it. And a person's taste is as much his own peculiar concern as his opinion or his purse. It is easy for anyone to imagine an ideal public which leaves the freedom and choice of individuals in all uncertain matters undisturbed and only requires them to abstain from modes of conduct which universal experience has condemned. But where has there been seen a public which set any such limit to its censorship? Or when does the public trouble itself about universal experience? In its interferences with personal conduct it is seldom thinking of anything but the enormity of acting or feeling differently from itself; and this standard of judgment, thinly disguised, is held up to mankind as the dictate of religion and philosophy by nine-tenths of all moralists and speculative writers. These teach that things are right because they are right; because we feel them to be so. They tell us to search in our own minds and hearts for laws of conduct binding on ourselves and on all others. What can the poor public do but apply these instructions and make their own personal feelings of good and evil, if they are tolerably unanimous in them, obligatory on all the world? . . .

QUESTIONS FOR REFLECTION

1. Between 1905 and 1937, a period known as the *Lochner* era, the U.S. Supreme Court used a form of the harm principle to strike down laws regulating economic activity: laws setting a minimum wage, for example, or regulating working hours and conditions. Does the harm principle, in Mill's view, apply to economic transactions? How does the harm principle relate to what he calls "the doctrine of 'free trade'"?

2. What is the point of Mill's example of someone about to cross an unsafe bridge? What does it indicate about the harm principle?

3. The United States, like many other countries, regulates advertising. Is such regulation compatible with Mill's position in *On Liberty*? What kinds of regulation, if any, might Mill be willing to accept?

4. Many governments impose "sin taxes" on items such as alcohol and cigarettes. What is Mill's

criterion for determining whether such taxes are acceptable?

5. Mill insists that voluntary slavery ought to be prohibited, although it might appear to fall into the realm of individual liberty. Why? Is Mill's support for this prohibition consistent with the harm principle?

CHAPTER V / APPLICATIONS

Again, trade is a social act. Whoever undertakes to sell any description of goods to the public does what affects the interest of other persons, and of society in general; and thus his conduct, in principle, comes within the jurisdiction of society; accordingly, it was once held to be the duty of governments, in all cases which were considered of importance, to fix prices and regulate the process of manufacture. But it is now recognized, though not till after a long struggle, that both the cheapness and the good quality of commodities are most effectually provided for by leaving the producers and sellers perfectly free, under the sole check of equal freedom to the buyers for supplying themselves elsewhere. This is the so-called doctrine of "free trade," which rests on grounds different from, though equally solid with, the principle of individual liberty asserted in this essay. Restrictions on trade, or on production for purposes of trade, are indeed restraints; and all restraint, *qua* restraint, is an evil; but the restraints in question affect only that part of conduct which society is competent to restrain, and are wrong solely because they do not really produce the results which it is desired to produce by them. As the principle of individual liberty is not involved in the doctrine of free trade, so neither is it in most of the questions which arise respecting the limits of that doctrine, as, for example, what amount of public control is admissible for the prevention of fraud by adulteration; how far sanitary precautions, or arrangements to protect workpeople employed in dangerous occupations, should be enforced on employers. Such questions involve considerations of liberty only in so far as leaving people to themselves is better, *caeteris paribus,* than controlling them; but that they may be legitimately controlled for these ends is in principle undeniable. On the other hand, there are questions relating to interference with trade which are essentially questions of liberty, such as the Maine Law, already touched upon: the prohibition of the importation of opium into China; the restriction of the sale of poisons—all cases, in short, where the object of the interference is to make it impossible or difficult to obtain a particular commodity. These interferences are objectionable, not as infringements on the liberty of the producer or seller, but on that of the buyer.

One of these examples, that of the sale of poisons, opens a new question: the proper limits of what may be called the functions of police; how far liberty may legitimately be invaded for the prevention of crime, or of accident. It is one of the undisputed functions of government to take precautions against crime before it has been committed, as well as to detect and punish it afterwards. The preventive function of government, however, is far more liable to be abused, to the prejudice of liberty, than the punitory function; for there is hardly any part of the legitimate freedom of action of a human being which would not admit of being represented, and fairly, too, as increasing the facilities for some form or other of delinquency. Nevertheless, if a public authority, or even a private person, sees anyone evidently preparing to commit a crime, they are not bound to look on inactive until the crime is committed, but may interfere to prevent it. If poisons were never bought or used for any purpose except the commission of murder, it would be right to prohibit their manufacture and sale. They may, however, be wanted not only for innocent but for useful purposes, and restrictions cannot be imposed in the one case without operating in the other. Again, it is a proper office of public authority to guard against accidents. If either a public officer or anyone else saw a person attempting to cross a bridge which had been ascertained to be unsafe, and there were no time to warn him of his danger, they might seize him and turn him back, without any real infringement of his liberty; for liberty consists in doing what one desires, and he does not desire to fall into the river. Nevertheless, when there is not a certainty, but only a danger of mischief, no one but the person himself

can judge of the sufficiency of the motive which may prompt him to incur the risk; in this case, therefore (unless he is a child, or delirious, or in some state of excitement or absorption incompatible with the full use of the reflecting faculty), he ought, I conceive, to be only warned of the danger; not forcibly prevented from exposing himself to it. Similar considerations, applied to such a question as the sale of poisons, may enable us to decide which among the possible modes of regulation are or are not contrary to principle. Such a precaution, for example, as that of labeling the drug with some word expressive of its dangerous character may be enforced without violation of liberty: the buyer cannot wish not to know that the thing he possesses has poisonous qualities. . . .

The right inherent in society to ward off crimes against itself by antecedent precautions suggests the obvious limitations to the maxim that purely self-regarding misconduct cannot properly be meddled with in the way of prevention or punishment. Drunkenness, for example, in ordinary cases, is not a fit subject for legislative interference, but I should deem it perfectly legitimate that a person who had once been convicted of any act of violence to others under the influence of drink should be placed under a special legal restriction, personal to himself; that if he were afterwards found drunk, he should be liable to a penalty, and that if, when in that state, he committed another offense, the punishment to which he would be liable for that other offense should be increased in severity. The making himself drunk, in a person whom drunkenness excites to do harm to others, is a crime against others. So, again, idleness, except in a person receiving support from the public, or except when it constitutes a breach of contract, cannot without tyranny be made a subject of legal punishment; but if, either from idleness or from any other avoidable cause, a man fails to perform his legal duties to others, as for instance to support his children, it is no tyranny to force him to fulfill that obligation by compulsory labor if no other means are available.

Again, there are many acts which, being directly injurious only to the agents themselves, ought not to be legally interdicted, but which, if done publicly, are a violation of good manners and, coming thus within the category of offenses against others, may rightly be prohibited. Of this kind are offenses against decency; on which it is unnecessary to dwell, the rather as they are only connected indirectly with our subject, the objection to publicity being equally strong in the case of many actions not in themselves condemnable, nor supposed to be so. . . .

A further question is whether the State, while it permits, should nevertheless indirectly discourage conduct which it deems contrary to the best interests of the agent; whether, for example, it should take measures to render the means of drunkenness more costly, or add to the difficulty of procuring them by limiting the number of the places of sale. On this, as on most other practical questions, many distinctions require to be made. To tax stimulants for the sole purpose of making them more difficult to be obtained is a measure differing only in degree from their entire prohibition, and would be justifiable only if that were justifiable. Every increase of cost is a prohibition to those whose means do not come up to the augmented price; and to those who do, it is a penalty laid on them for gratifying a particular taste. Their choice of pleasures and their mode of expending their income, after satisfying their legal and moral obligations to the State and to individuals, are their own concern and must rest with their own judgment. These considerations may seem at first sight to condemn the selection of stimulants as special subjects of taxation for purposes of revenue. But it must be remembered that taxation for fiscal purposes is absolutely inevitable; that in most countries it is necessary that a considerable part of that taxation should be indirect; that the State, therefore, cannot help imposing penalties, which to some persons may be prohibitory, on the use of some articles of consumption. It is hence the duty of the State to consider, in the imposition of taxes, what commodities the consumers can best spare; and *a fortiori,* to select in preference those of which it deems the use, beyond a very moderate quantity, to be positively injurious. Taxation, therefore, of stimulants up to the point which produces the largest amount of revenue (supposing that the State needs all the revenue which it yields) is not only admissible, but to be approved of. . . .

It was pointed out in an early part of this essay that the liberty of the individual, in things wherein the individual is alone concerned, implies a cor-

responding liberty in any number of individuals to regulate by mutual agreement such things as regard them jointly, and regard no persons but themselves. This question presents no difficulty so long as the will of all the persons implicated remains unaltered; but since that will may change it is often necessary, even in things in which they alone are concerned, that they should enter into engagements with one another; and when they do, it is fit, as a general rule, that those engagements should be kept. Yet, in the laws, probably, of every country, this general rule has some exceptions. Not only persons are not held to engagements which violate the rights of third parties, but it is sometimes considered a sufficient reason for releasing them from an engagement that it is injurious to themselves. In this and most other civilized countries, for example, an engagement by which a person should sell himself, or allow himself to be sold, as a slave would be null and void, neither enforced by law nor by opinion. The ground for thus limiting his power of voluntarily disposing of his own lot in life is apparent, and is very clearly seen in this extreme case. The reason for not interfering, unless for the sake of others, with a person's voluntary acts is consideration for his liberty. His voluntary choice is evidence that what he so chooses is desirable, or at least endurable, to him, and his good is on the whole best provided for by allowing him to take his own means of pursuing it. But by selling himself for a slave, he abdicates his liberty; he foregoes any future use of it beyond that single act. He therefore defeats, in his own case, the very purpose which is the justification of allowing him to dispose of himself. He is no longer free, but is thenceforth in a position which has no longer the presumption in its favor that would be afforded by his voluntarily remaining in it. The principle of freedom cannot require that he should be free not to be free. It is not freedom to be allowed to alienate his freedom. These reasons, the force of which is so conspicuous in this peculiar case, are evidently of far wider application, yet a limit is everywhere set to them by the necessities of life, which continually require, not indeed that we should resign our freedom, but that we should consent to this and the other limitation of it. The principle, however, which demands uncontrolled freedom of action in all that concerns only the agents themselves requires that those who have become bound to one another, in things which concern no third party, should be able to release one another from the engagement; and even without such voluntary release there are perhaps no contracts or engagements, except those that relate to money or money's worth, of which one can venture to say that there ought to be no liberty whatever of retraction. Baron Wilhelm von Humboldt . . . states it as his conviction that engagements which involve personal relations or services should never be legally binding beyond a limited duration of time; and that the most important of these engagements, marriage, having the peculiarity that its objects are frustrated unless the feelings of both the parties are in harmony with it, should require nothing more than the declared will of either party to dissolve it. This subject is too important and too complicated to be discussed in a parenthesis, and I touch on it only so far as is necessary for purposes of illustration. If the conciseness and generality of Baron Humboldt's dissertation had not obliged him in this instance to content himself with enunciating his conclusion without discussing the premises, he would doubtless have recognized that the question cannot be decided on grounds so simple as those to which he confines himself. When a person, either by express promise or by conduct, has encouraged another to rely on his continuing to act in a certain way—to build expectations and calculations, and

stake any part of his plan of life upon that supposition—a new series of moral obligations arises on his part toward that person, which may possibly be overruled, but cannot be ignored. And again, if the relation between two contracting parties has been followed by consequences to others; if it has placed third parties in any peculiar position, or, as in the case of marriage, has even called third parties into existence, obligations arise on the part of both the contracting parties toward those third persons, the fulfillment of which, or at all events the mode of fulfillment, must be greatly affected by the continuance or disruption of the relation between the original parties to the contract. It does not follow, nor can I admit, that these obligations extend to requiring the fulfillment of the contract at all costs to the happiness of the reluctant party; but they are a necessary element in the question; and, even if, as von Humboldt maintains, they ought to make no difference in the *legal* freedom of the parties to release themselves from the engagement (and I also hold that they ought not to make *much* difference), they necessarily make a great difference in the *moral* freedom. A person is bound to take all these circumstances into account before resolving on a step which may affect such important interests of others; and if he does not allow proper weight to those interests, he is morally responsible for the wrong. . . .

Drug Legalization

Over the past several decades, drug use has grown from a fashion among a small collection of bohemian artists and musicians into a major social problem. The use of illegal and seriously harmful drugs can be found in almost any high school, college, or university in the United States; scores of cities routinely witness drug-related shootings and other forms of violence. Several times, the government has declared a "war on drugs," but the result has seemed, at best, a stalemate. Frustration with this state of affairs has led some to call for the legalization of drugs.

Drug use might appear to be a self-regarding act that may harm the drug user but has little effect on anyone else. Few contemporary advocates of legalization, however, have rested their case solely on Mill's harm principle. Many writers on both sides of the issue have believed that nonusers suffer significant harms that must be taken into account; they have debated whether criminal penalties reduce or add to the harms to nonusers. Moreover, addictive drugs pose problems related to those Mill confronts in discussing voluntary slavery; people may initially choose, freely and voluntarily, to take an addictive drug, but their freedom does not last long. As Mill asks, do people have the freedom to surrender their freedom? Many contemporary writers share Mill's conviction that they do not and thus count harms to users of addictive drugs as morally relevant. This does not mean, however, that philosophical attitudes toward liberty are unrelated to discussions of the drug problem. Some writers clearly presuppose something akin to Mill's harm principle. Others assume the opposed principle of moral paternalism, holding that a government should promote the moral well-being of its citizens. Still others treat harms to users and harms to nonusers as morally equivalent, in effect denying the significance of the distinction between self-regarding and other-regarding actions.

Milton Friedman, a respected economist, argues that the war on drugs has been a costly failure. He urges decriminalization of drugs, that is, removing criminal penalties against their sale and use. He advocates treating drugs much as we now treat alcohol and cigarettes—

as substances that should be regulated and whose users should be treated rather than jailed.

William Bennett, "drug czar" under Presidents Reagan and Bush, maintains that Friedman's proposal is flawed and even reckless. Bennett defends criminal penalties for drug use by arguing that they reduce harms both to drug users and to others. He contends that "government has a responsibility to craft and uphold laws that help educate citizens about right and wrong."

Richard J. Dennis argues Friedman's case in greater detail. He holds that drug legalization would produce significant economic benefits, reduce crime, and revitalize the inner cities. He adopts state-run liquor stores as a model of how government might regulate drugs. James Q. Wilson further articulates Bennett's case, contending that the war on drugs is justifiable and moderately successful. He holds that enforcing criminal penalties has helped to confine the drug problem to a relatively small portion of the population while sheltering most people from harms associated with the drug trade. Legalization, he believes, would greatly increase drug use and the attendant harms to users and nonusers alike.

MILTON FRIEDMAN

An Open Letter to Bill Bennett

Milton Friedman is Senior Research Fellow at the Hoover Institution at Stanford University and Professor Emeritus of Economics at the University of Chicago. He was awarded the Nobel Prize in economics in 1976. (Source: Reprinted from The Wall Street Journal, *September 7, 1989, p. A14. Copyright © 1989 by Dow Jones and Company, Inc.)*

QUESTIONS FOR REFLECTION

1. Asserting that government prohibition of drug use is illegitimate in itself differs from asserting that it is a bad idea in practice. Certainly Friedman asserts the latter. How does he argue for this position? Does he also assert the former?

2. Friedman claims that the drug war undermines "human liberty and individual freedom." What is Friedman's conception of liberty? Is Friedman's argument compatible with Mill's harm principle?

DEAR BILL:

In Oliver Cromwell's eloquent words, "I beseech you, in the bowels of Christ, think it possible you may be mistaken" about the course you and President Bush urge us to adopt to fight drugs. The path you propose of more police, more jails, use of the military in foreign countries, harsh penalties for drug users, and a whole panoply of repressive measures can only make a bad situation worse. The drug war cannot be won by those tactics without undermining the human liberty and individual freedom that you and I cherish.

You are not mistaken in believing that drugs are a scourge that is devastating our society. You are not mistaken in believing that drugs are tearing asunder our social fabric, ruining the lives of many young people, and imposing heavy costs on some of the most disadvantaged among us. You are not mistaken in believing that the majority of the public share your concerns. In short, you are not mistaken in the end you seek to achieve.

Your mistake is failing to recognize that the very measures you favor are a major source of the evils you deplore. Of course the problem is demand, but it is not only demand, it is demand that must operate through repressed and illegal channels. Illegality creates obscene profits that finance the murderous tactics of the drug lords; illegality leads to the corruption of law enforcement officials; illegality monopolizes the efforts of honest law forces so that they are starved for resources to fight the simpler crimes of robbery, theft and assault.

Drugs are a tragedy for addicts. But criminalizing their use converts that tragedy into a disaster for society, for users and non-users alike. Our experience with the prohibition of drugs is a replay of our experience with the prohibition of alcoholic beverages.

I append excerpts from a column that I wrote in 1972 on "Prohibition and Drugs." The major problem then was heroin from Marseilles; today, it is cocaine from Latin America. Today, also, the problem is far more serious than it was 17 years ago: more addicts, more innocent victims; more drug pushers, more law enforcement officials; more money spent to enforce prohibition, more money spent to circumvent prohibition.

Had drugs been decriminalized 17 years ago, "crack" would never have been invented (it was invented because the high cost of illegal drugs made it profitable to provide a cheaper version) and there would today be far fewer addicts. The lives of thousands, perhaps hundreds of thousands of innocent victims would have been saved, and not only in the U.S. The ghettos of our major cities would not be drug-and-crime-infested no-man's lands. Fewer people would be in jails, and fewer jails would have been built.

Colombia, Bolivia and Peru would not be suffering from narco-terror, and we would not be distorting our foreign policy because of narco-terror. Hell would not, in the words with which Billy Sunday welcomed Prohibition, "be forever for rent," but it would be a lot emptier.

Decriminalizing drugs is even more urgent now than in 1972, but we must recognize that the harm done in the interim cannot be wiped out, certainly not immediately. Postponing decriminalization will only make matters worse, and make the problem appear even more intractable.

Alcohol and tobacco cause many more deaths in users than do drugs. Decriminalization would not prevent us from treating drugs as we now treat alcohol and tobacco: prohibiting sales of drugs to minors, outlawing the advertising of drugs and similar measures. Such measures could be enforced, while outright prohibition cannot be. Moreover, if even a small fraction of the money we now spend on trying to enforce drug prohibition were devoted to treatment and rehabilitation, in an atmosphere of compassion not punishment, the reduction in drug usage and in the harm done to the users could be dramatic.

This plea comes from the bottom of my heart. Every friend of freedom, and I know you are one, must be as revolted as I am by the prospect of turning the United States into an armed camp, by the vision of jails filled with casual drug users and of an army of enforcers empowered to invade the liberty of citizens on slight evidence. A country in which shooting down unidentified planes "on suspicion" can be seriously considered as a drug-war tactic is not the kind of United States that either you or I want to hand on to future generations.

Milton Friedman
Senior Research Fellow
Hoover Institution
Stanford University

Flashback

This is a truncated version of a column by Mr. Friedman in Newsweek's *May 1, 1972, issue, as President Nixon was undertaking an earlier "drug war":*

"The reign of tears is over. The slums will soon be only a memory. We will turn our prisons into factories and our jails into storehouses and corncribs. Men will walk upright now, women will smile, and the children will laugh. Hell will be forever for rent."

That is how Billy Sunday, the noted evangelist and leading crusader against Demon Rum, greeted the onset of Prohibition in early 1920.

We know now how tragically his hopes were doomed.

Prohibition is an attempted cure that makes matters worse—for both the addict and the rest of us.

Consider first the addict. Legalizing drugs might increase the number of addicts, but it is not clear that it would. Forbidden fruit is attractive, particularly to the young. More important, many drug addicts are deliberately made by pushers, who give likely prospects that first few doses free. It pays the pusher to do so because, once hooked, the addict is a captive customer. If drugs were legally available, any possible profit from such inhumane activity would disappear, since the addict could buy from the cheapest source.

Whatever happens to the number of addicts, the individual addict would clearly be far better off if drugs were legal. Addicts are driven to associate with criminals to get the drugs, become criminals themselves to finance the habit, and risk constant danger of death and disease.

Consider next the rest of us. The harm to us from the addiction of others arises almost wholly from the fact that drugs are illegal. It is estimated that addicts commit one third to one half of all street crime in the U.S.

Legalize drugs, and street crime would drop dramatically.

Moreover, addicts and pushers are not the only ones corrupted. Immense sums are at stake. It is inevitable that some relatively low-paid police and other government officials—and some high-paid ones as well—will succumb to the temptation to pick up easy money.

Legalizing drugs would simultaneously reduce the amount of crime and raise the quality of law enforcement. Can you conceive of any other measure that would accomplish so much to promote law and order?

In drugs, as in other areas, persuasion and example are likely to be far more effective than the use of force to shape others in our image.

WILLIAM J. BENNETT

A Response to Milton Friedman

William J. Bennett is Research Fellow at the American Enterprise Institute. He has served as director of the Office of National Drug Control Policy and as U.S. secretary of education. (Source: Reprinted from The Wall Street Journal, *September 19, 1989, p. A30. Copyright © 1989 by Dow Jones and Company, Inc.)*

QUESTIONS FOR REFLECTION

1. Bennett contends that legalizing drugs would increase harms to nonusers. How does he argue this position?

2. Part of Bennett's case rests on his view that enforcing criminal penalties against drug use decreases harms done by drugs to drug users themselves. What is his argument? Is Bennett's use of this argument compatible with Mill's harm principle?

3. Friedman claims that the drug war undermines "human liberty and individual freedom." How does Bennett respond to this allegation, if at all? What does this indicate about Bennett's conception of freedom and of the proper bounds of government authority?

DEAR MILTON:

There was little, if anything, new in your open letter to me calling for the legalization of drugs (The Wall Street Journal, Sept. 7). As the excerpt from your 1972 article made clear, the legalization argument is an old and familiar one, which has recently been revived by a small number of journalists and academics who insist that the only solution to the drug problem is no solution at all. What surprises me is that you would continue to advocate so unrealistic a proposal without pausing to consider seriously its consequences.

If the argument for drug legalization has one virtue it is its sheer simplicity. Eliminate laws against drugs, and street crime will disappear. Take the profit out of the black market through decriminalization and regulation, and poor neighborhoods will no longer be victimized by drug dealers. Cut back on drug enforcement, and use the money to wage a public health campaign against drugs, as we do with tobacco and alcohol.

Counting Costs

The basic premise of all these propositions is that using our nation's laws to fight drugs is too costly. To be sure, our attempts to reduce drug use do carry with them enormous costs. But the question that must be asked—and which is totally ignored by the legalization advocates—is what are the costs of *not* enforcing laws against drugs?

In my judgment, and in the judgment of virtually every serious scholar in this field, the potential costs of legalizing drugs would be so large as to make it a public policy disaster.

Of course, no one, including you, can say with certainty what would happen in the U.S. if drugs were suddenly to become a readily purchased product. We do know, however, that wherever drugs have been cheaper and more easily obtained, drug use—and addiction—has skyrocketed. In opium and cocaine producing countries, addiction is rampant among the peasants involved in drug production.

Professor James Q. Wilson tells us that during the years in which heroin could be legally prescribed by doctors in Britain, the number of addicts increased forty-fold. And after the repeal of Prohibition—an analogy favored but misunderstood by legalization advocates—consumption of alcohol soared by 350%.

Could we afford such dramatic increases in drug use? I doubt it. Already the toll of drug use on American society—measured in lost productivity, in rising health insurance costs, in hospitals flooded with drug overdose emergencies, in drug caused accidents, and in premature death—is surely more than we would like to bear.

You seem to believe that by spending just a little more money on treatment and rehabilitation, the costs of increased addiction can be avoided. That hope betrays a basic misunderstanding of the problems facing drug treatment. Most addicts don't suddenly decide to get help. They remain addicts either because treatment isn't available or because they don't seek it out. The National Drug Control Strategy announced by President Bush on Sept. 5 goes a long way in making sure that more treatment slots are available. But the simple fact remains that many drug users won't enter treatment until they are forced to—often by the very criminal justice system you think is the source of the problem.

As for the connection between drugs and crime, your unswerving commitment to a legalization solution prevents you from appreciating the complexity of the drug market. Contrary to your claim, most addicts do not turn to crime to support their habit. Research shows that many of them were involved in criminal activity before they turned to drugs. Many former addicts who have received treatment continue to commit crimes during their recovery. And even if drugs were legal, what evidence do you have that the habitual drug user wouldn't continue to rob and steal to get money for clothes, food or shelter?

Drug addicts always want more drugs than they can afford, and no legalization scheme has yet come up with a way of satisfying that appetite.

The National Drug Control Strategy emphasizes the importance of reclaiming the streets and neighborhoods where drugs have wrought havoc because, I admit, the price of having drug laws is having criminals who will try to subvert them. Your proposal might conceivably reduce the amount of gang- and dealer-related crime, but it is fanciful to suggest that it would make crime vanish. Unless you are willing to distribute drugs freely and widely, there will always be a black market to undercut the regulated one. And as for the potential addicts, for the school children and for the pregnant mothers, all of whom would find drugs more accessible and legally condoned, your proposal would offer nothing at all.

So I advocate a larger criminal justice system to take drug users off the streets and deter new users from becoming more deeply involved in so hazardous an activity. You suggest that such policies would turn the country "into an armed camp." Try telling that to the public housing tenants who enthusiastically support plans to enhance security in their buildings, or to the residents who applaud police when a local crack house is razed. They recognize that drug use is a threat to the individual liberty and domestic tranquility guaranteed by the Constitution.

I remain an ardent defender of our nation's laws against illegal drug use and our attempts to enforce them because I believe drug use is wrong. A true friend of freedom understands that government has a responsibility to craft and uphold laws that help educate citizens about right and wrong. That, at any rate, was the Founders' view of our system of government.

Liberal Ridicule

Today this view is much ridiculed by liberal elites and entirely neglected by you. So while I cannot doubt the sincerity of your opinion on drug legalization, I find it difficult to respect. The moral cost of legalizing drugs is great, but it is a cost that apparently lies outside the narrow scope of libertarian policy prescriptions.

I do not have a simple solution to the drug problem. I doubt that one exists. But I am committed to fighting the problem on several fronts through imaginative policies and hard work over a long period of time. As in the past, some of these efforts will work and some won't. Your response, however, is to surrender and see what happens. To my mind that is irresponsible and reckless public policy. At a time when national intolerance for drug use is rapidly increasing, the legalization argument is a political anachronism. Its recent resurgence is, I trust, only a temporary distraction from the genuine debate on national drug policy.

William J. Bennett
Director
Office of National Drug Control Policy

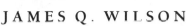

JAMES Q. WILSON

Against the Legalization of Drugs

James Q. Wilson is Collins Professor of Management and Public Policy at the University of California at Los Angeles. (Source: Reprinted from Commentary *[February 1990], by permission; all rights reserved.)*

QUESTIONS FOR REFLECTION

1. Wilson contends that the war on drugs has been successful. What evidence does he adduce in support of this claim?

2. Wilson believes that legalizing drugs would increase drug use significantly, and he supports his view with an economic argument. What is that argument? Do you find it persuasive?

3. Wilson talks about heroin and cocaine, but not marijuana. Which of his arguments would apply to marijuana, in your view? Which would not?

4. Wilson rejects the view that cocaine use is a "victimless crime," that is, a self-regarding act. Why?

5. Wilson does not accept Mill's harm principle; he advocates a rather different conception of individual liberty and societal responsibility. What is Wilson's conception? What role does it play in his argument? Compare Wilson's conception to those of Burke and Tocqueville.

6. Many advocates of legalization recommend treatment over incarceration. Wilson, however, is skeptical of drug treatment, at least in the absence of laws outlawing drug use. Why? Do you find his arguments persuasive?

In 1972, the President appointment me chairman of the National Advisory Council for Drug Abuse Prevention. Created by Congress, the Council was charged with providing guidance on how best to coordinate the national war on drugs. (Yes, we called it a war then, too.) In those days, the drug we were chiefly concerned with was heroin. When I took office, heroin use had been increasing dramatically. Everybody was worried that this increase would continue. Such phrases as "heroin epidemic" were commonplace.

That same year, the eminent economist Milton Friedman published an essay in *Newsweek* in which he called for legalizing heroin. His argument was on two grounds: as a matter of ethics, the government has no right to tell people not to use heroin (or to drink or to commit suicide); as a matter of economics, the prohibition of drug use imposes costs on society that far exceed the benefits. Others, such as the psychoanalyst Thomas Szasz, made the same argument.

We did not take Friedman's advice. (Government commissions rarely do.) I do not recall that we even discussed legalizing heroin, though we did discuss (but did not take action on) legalizing a drug, cocaine, that many people then argued was benign. Our marching orders were to figure out how to win the war on heroin, not to run up the white flag of surrender.

That was 1972. Today, we have the same number of heroin addicts that we had then—half a million, give or take a few thousand. Having that many heroin addicts is no trivial matter; these people deserve our attention. But not having had an increase in that number for over fifteen years is also something that deserves our attention. What happened to the "heroin epidemic" that many people once thought would overwhelm us?

The facts are clear: a more or less stable pool of heroin addicts had been getting older, with relatively few new recruits. In 1976 the average age of heroin users who appeared in hospital emergency rooms was about twenty-seven; ten years later it was thirty-two. More than two-thirds of all heroin users appearing in emergency rooms are now over the age of thirty. Back in the early 1970's, when heroin got onto the national political agenda, the typical heroin addict was much younger, often a teenager. Household surveys show the same thing—the rate of opiate use (which includes heroin) has been flat for the better part of two decades. More fine-grained studies of inner-city neighborhoods confirm this. John Boyle and Ann Brunswick found that the percentage of young blacks in Harlem who used heroin fell from 8 percent in 1970–71 to about 3 percent in 1975–76.

Why did heroin lose its appeal for young people? When the young blacks in Harlem were asked why they stopped, more than half mentioned "trouble with the law" or "high cost" (and high cost is, of course, directly the result of law enforcement). Two-thirds said that heroin hurt their health; nearly all said they had had a bad experience with it. We need not rely, however, simply on what they said. In New York City in 1973–75, the street price of heroin rose dramatically and its purity sharply declined, probably as a result of the heroin shortage caused by the success of the Turkish government in reducing the supply of opium base and of the French government in closing down heroin-processing laboratories located in and around Marseilles. These were short-lived gains for, just as Friedman predicted, alternative sources of supply—mostly in Mexico—quickly emerged. But the three-year heroin shortage interrupted the easy recruitment of new users.

Health and related problems were no doubt part of the reason for the reduced flow of recruits. Over the preceding years, Harlem youth had watched as more and more heroin users died of overdoses, were poisoned by adulterated doses, or acquired hepatitis from dirty needles. The word got around: heroin can kill you. By 1974 new hepatitis cases and drug-overdose deaths had dropped to a fraction of what they had been in 1970.

Alas, treatment did not seem to explain much of the cessation in drug use. Treatment programs can and do help heroin addicts, but treatment did not explain the drop in the number of *new* users (who by definition had never been in treatment) nor even much of the reduction in the number of experienced users.

No one knows how much of the decline to attribute to personal observation as opposed to high prices or reduced supply. But other evidence suggests strongly that price and supply played a large role. In 1972 the National Advisory Council was especially worried by the prospect that U.S. servicemen returning to this country from Vietnam would bring their heroin habits with them. Fortunately, a brilliant study by Lee Robins of Washington University in St. Louis put that fear to rest. She measured drug use of Vietnam veterans shortly after they had returned home. Though many had used heroin regularly while in Southeast Asia, most gave up the habit when back in the United States. The reason: here, heroin was less available and sanctions on its use were more pronounced. Of course, if a veteran had been willing to pay enough—which might have meant traveling to another city and would certainly have meant making an illegal contact with a disreputable dealer in a threatening neighborhood in order to acquire a (possibly) dangerous dose—he could have sustained his drug habit. Most veterans were unwilling to pay this price, and so their drug use declined or disappeared.

Reliving the Past

Suppose we had taken Friedman's advice in 1972. What would have happened? We cannot be entirely certain, but at a minimum we would have placed the young heroin addicts (and, above all, the prospective addicts) in a very different position from the one in which they actually found themselves. Heroin would have been legal. Its price would have been reduced by 95 percent (minus whatever we chose to recover in taxes). Now that it could be sold by the same people who make aspirin, its quality would have been assured—no poisons, no adulterants. Sterile hypodermic needles would have been readily available at the neighborhood drugstore, probably at the same counter where the heroin was sold. No need to travel to big cities or unfamiliar neighborhoods—heroin could have been purchased anywhere, perhaps by mail order.

There would no longer have been any financial or medical reason to avoid heroin use. Anybody could have afforded it. We might have tried to prevent children from buying it, but as we have learned from our efforts to prevent minors from buying alcohol and tobacco, young people have a way of penetrating markets theoretically reserved for adults. Returning Vietnam veterans would have discovered that Omaha and Raleigh had been converted into the pharmaceutical equivalent of Saigon.

Under these circumstances, can we doubt for a moment that heroin use would have grown exponentially? Or that a vastly larger supply of new users would have been recruited? Professor Friedman is a Nobel Prize-winning economist whose understanding of market forces is profound. What did he think would happen to consumption under his legalized regime? Here are his words: "Legalizing drugs might increase the number of addicts, but it is not clear that it would. Forbidden fruit is attractive, particularly to the young."

Really? I suppose that we should expect no increase in Porsche sales if we cut the price by 95 percent, no increase in whiskey sales if we cut the price by a comparable amount—because young people only want fast cars and strong liquor when they are "forbidden." Perhaps Friedman's uncharacteristic lapse from the obvious implications of price theory can be explained by a misunderstanding of how drug users are recruited. In his 1972 essay he said that "drug addicts are deliberately made by pushers, who give likely prospects their first few doses free." If drugs were legal it would not pay anybody to produce addicts, because everybody would buy from the cheapest source. But as every drug expert knows, pushers do not produce addicts. Friends or acquaintances do. In fact, pushers are usually reluctant to deal with non-users because a non-user could be an undercover cop. Drug use spreads in the same way any fad or fashion spreads: somebody who is already a user urges his friends to try, or simply shows already-eager friends how to do it.

But we need not rely on speculation, however plausible, that lowered prices and more abundant supplies would have increased heroin usage. Great Britain once followed such a policy and with almost exactly those results. Until the mid-1960's, British physicians were allowed to prescribe heroin to certain classes of addicts. (Possessing these drugs without a doctor's prescription remained a criminal offense.) For many years this policy worked well enough because the addict patients were typically middle-class people who had become dependent on opiate painkillers while undergoing hospital treatment. There was no drug culture. The British system worked for many years, not because it prevented drug abuse, but because there was no problem of drug abuse that would test the system.

All that changed in the 1960's. A few unscrupulous doctors began passing out heroin in wholesale amounts. One doctor prescribed almost 600,000 heroin tablets—that is, over thirteen pounds—in just one year. A youthful drug culture emerged with a demand for drugs far different from that of the older addicts. As a result, the British government required doctors to refer users to government-run clinics to receive their heroin.

But the shift to clinics did not curtail the growth in heroin use. Throughout the 1960's the number of addicts increased—the late John Kaplan of Stanford estimated by fivefold—in part as a result of the diversion of heroin from clinic patients to new users on the streets. An addict would bargain with the clinic doctor over how big a dose he would receive. The patient wanted as much as he could get, the doctor wanted to give as little as was needed. The patient had an advantage in this conflict because the doctor could not be certain how much was really needed. Many patients would use some of their "maintenance" dose and sell the remaining part to friends, thereby recruiting new addicts. As the clinics learned of this, they began to shift their treatment away from heroin and toward methadone, an addictive drug that, when taken orally, does not produce a "high" but will block the withdrawal pains associated with heroin abstinence.

Whether what happened in England in the 1960's was a mini-epidemic or an epidemic depends on whether one looks at numbers or at rates of change. Compared to the United States, the numbers were small. In 1960 there were 68 heroin addicts known to the British government; by 1968 there were 2,000 in treatment and many more who refused treatment. (They would refuse in part because they did not want to get methadone at a clinic if they could get heroin on the street.) Richard Hartnoll estimates that the actual number of addicts in England is five times the number officially registered. At a minimum, the number of British addicts increased by thirtyfold in ten years; the actual increase may have been much larger.

In the early 1980's the numbers began to rise again, and this time nobody doubted that a real epidemic was at hand. The increase was estimated to be 40 percent a year. By 1982 there were thought to be 20,000 heroin users in London alone. Geoffrey Pearson reports that many cities—Glasgow, Liverpool, Manchester, and Sheffield among them—were now experiencing a drug problem that once had been largely confined to London. The problem, again, was supply. The country was being flooded with cheap, high-quality heroin, first from Iran and then from Southeast Asia.

The United States began the 1960's with a much larger number of heroin addicts and probably a bigger at-risk population than was the case in Great Britain. Even though it would be foolhardy to suppose that the British system, if installed here, would have worked the same way or with the same results, it would be equally foolhardy to suppose that a combination of heroin available from leaky clinics and from street dealers who faced only minimal law-enforcement risks would not have produced a much greater increase in heroin use than we actually experienced. My guess is that if we had allowed either doctors or clinics to prescribe heroin, we would have had far worse results than were produced in Britain, if for no other reason than the vastly larger number of addicts with which we began. We would have had to find some way to police thousands (not scores) of physicians and hundreds (not dozens) of clinics. If the British civil service found it difficult to keep heroin in the hands of addicts and out of the hands of recruits when it was dealing with a few hundred people, how well would the American civil service have accomplished the same tasks when dealing with tens of thousands of people?

Back to the Future

Now cocaine, especially in its potent form, crack, is the focus of attention. Now as in 1972 the government is trying to reduce its use. Now as then some people are advocating legalization. Is there any more reason to yield to those arguments today than there was almost two decades ago?

I think not. If we had yielded in 1972 we almost certainly would have had today a permanent population of several million, not several hundred thousand, heroin addicts. If we yield now we will have a far more serious problem with cocaine.

Crack is worse than heroin by almost any measure. Heroin produces a pleasant drowsiness and, if hygienically administered, has only the physical side effects of constipation and sexual impotence. Regular heroin use incapacitates many users, especially poor ones, for any productive work or social responsibility. They will sit nodding on a street corner, helpless, but at least harmless. By contrast, regular cocaine use leaves the user neither helpless nor harmless. When smoked (as with crack) or injected, cocaine produces instant, intense, and short-lived euphoria. The experience generates a powerful desire to repeat it. If the drug is readily available, repeat use will occur. Those people who progress to "bingeing" on cocaine become devoted to the drug and its effects to the exclusion of almost all other considerations—job, family, children, sleep, food, even sex. Dr. Frank Gawin at Yale and Dr. Everett Ellinwood at Duke report that a substantial percentage of all high-dose, binge users become uninhibited, impulsive, hypersexual, compulsive, irritable, and hyperactive. Their moods vacillate dramatically, leading at times to violence and homicide.

Women are much more likely to use crack than heroin, and if they are pregnant, the effects on their babies are tragic. Douglas Besharov, who has been following the effects of drugs on infants for twenty years, writes that nothing he learned about heroin prepared him for the devastation of cocaine. Cocaine harms the fetus and can lead to physical deformities or neurological damage. Some crack babies have for all practical purposes suffered a disabling stroke while still in the womb. The long-term consequences of this brain damage are lowered cognitive ability and the onset of mood disorders.

Besharov estimates that about 30,000 to 50,000 such babies are born every year, about 7,000 in New York City alone. There may be ways to treat such infants, but from everything we now know the treatment will be long, difficult, and expensive. Worse, the mothers who are most likely to produce crack babies are precisely the ones who, because of poverty or temperament, are least able and willing to obtain such treatment. In fact, anecdotal evidence suggests that crack mothers are likely to abuse their infants.

The notion that abusing drugs such as cocaine is a "victimless crime" is not only absurd but dangerous. Even ignoring the fetal drug syndrome, crack-dependent people are, like heroin addicts, individuals who regularly victimize their children by neglect, their spouses by improvidence, their employers by lethargy, and their coworkers by carelessness. Society is not and could never be a collection of autonomous individuals. We all have a stake in ensuring that each of us displays a minimal level of dignity, responsibility, and empathy. We cannot, of course, coerce people into goodness, but we can and should insist that some standards must be met if society itself—on which the very existence of the human personality depends—is to persist. Drawing the line that defines those standards is difficult and contentious, but if crack and heroin use do not fall below it, what does?

The advocates of legalization will respond by suggesting that my picture is overdrawn. Ethan Nadelmann of Princeton argues that the risk of legalization is less than most people suppose. Over 20 million Americans between the ages of eighteen and twenty-five have tried cocaine (according to a government survey), but only a quarter million use it daily. From this Nadelmann concludes that at most 3 percent of all young people who try cocaine develop a problem with it. The implication is clear: make the drug legal and we only have to worry about 3 percent of our youth.

The implication rests on a logical fallacy and a factual error. The fallacy is this: the percentage of occasional cocaine users who become binge users *when the drug is illegal* (and thus expensive and hard to find) tells us nothing about the percentage who will become dependent when the drug is legal (and thus cheap and abundant). Drs. Gawin and Ellinwood report, in common with several other re-

searchers, that controlled or occasional use of cocaine changes to compulsive and frequent use "when access to the drug increases" or when the user switches from snorting to smoking. More cocaine more potently administered alters, perhaps sharply, the proportion of "controlled" users who become heavy users.

The factual error is this: the federal survey Nadelmann quotes was done in 1985, *before* crack had become common. Thus the probability of becoming dependent on cocaine was derived from the responses of users who snorted the drug. The speed and potency of cocaine's action increases dramatically when it is smoked. We do not yet know how greatly the advent of crack increases the risk of dependency, but all the clinical evidence suggests that the increase is likely to be large.

It is possible that some people will not become heavy users even when the drug is readily available in its most potent form. So far there are no scientific grounds for predicting who will and who will not become dependent. Neither socioeconomic background nor personality traits differentiate between casual and intensive users. Thus, the only way to settle the question of who is correct about the effect of easy availability on drug use, Nadelmann or Gawin and Ellinwood, is to try it and see. But that social experiment is so risky as to be no experiment at all, for if cocaine is legalized and if the rate of its abusive use increases dramatically, there is no way to put the genie back in the bottle, and it is not a kindly genie.

Have We Lost?

Many people who agree that there are risks in legalizing cocaine or heroin still favor it because, they think, we have lost the war on drugs. "Nothing we have done has worked" and the current federal policy is just "more of the same." Whatever the costs of greater drug use, surely they would be less than the costs of our present, failed efforts.

That is exactly what I was told in 1972—and heroin is not quite as bad a drug as cocaine. We did not surrender and we did not lose. We did not win, either. What the nation accomplished then was what most efforts to save people from themselves accomplish: the problem was contained and the number of victims minimized, all at a considerable cost in law enforcement and increased crime. Was the cost worth it? I think so, but others may disagree. What are the lives of would-be addicts worth? I recall some people saying to me then, "Let them kill themselves." I was appalled. Happily, such views did not prevail.

Have we lost today? Not at all. High-rate cocaine use is not commonplace. The National Institute of Drug Abuse (NIDA) reports that less than 5 percent of high-school seniors used cocaine within the last thirty days. Of course this survey misses young people who have dropped out of school and miscounts those who lie on the questionnaire, but even if we inflate the NIDA estimate by some plausible percentage, it is still not much above 5 percent. Medical examiners reported in 1987 that about 1,500 died from cocaine use; hospital emergency rooms reported about 30,000 admissions related to cocaine abuse.

These are not small numbers, but neither are they evidence of a nationwide plague that threatens to engulf us all. Moreover, cities vary greatly in the proportion of people who are involved with cocaine. To get city-level data we need to turn to drug tests carried out on arrested persons, who obviously are more likely to be drug users than the average citizen. The National Institute of Justice, through its Drug Use Forecasting (DUF) project, collects urinalysis data on arrests in 22 cities. As we have already seen, opiate (chiefly heroin) use has been flat or declining in most of these cities over the last decade. Cocaine use has gone up sharply, but with great variation among cities. New York, Philadelphia, and Washington, D.C., all report that two-thirds or more of their arrestees tested positive for cocaine, but in Portland, San Antonio, and Indianapolis the percentage was one-third or less.

In some neighborhoods, of course, matters have reached crisis proportions. Gangs control the streets, shootings terrorize residents, and drug-dealing occurs in plain view. The police seem barely able to contain matters. But in these neighborhoods—unlike at Palo Alto cocktail parties—the people are not calling for legalization, they are calling for help. And often not much help has come. Many cities are will-

ing to do almost anything about the drug problem except spend more money on it. The federal government cannot change that; only local voters and politicians can. It is not clear that they will.

It took about ten years to contain heroin. We have had experience with crack for only about three or four years. Each year we spend perhaps $11 billion on law enforcement (and some of that goes to deal with marijuana) and perhaps $2 billion on treatment. Large sums, but not sums that should lead anyone to say, "We just can't afford this any more."

The illegality of drugs increases crime, partly because some users turn to crime to pay for their habits, partly because some users are stimulated by certain drugs (such as crack or PCP) to act more violently or ruthlessly than they otherwise would, and partly because criminal organizations seeking to control drug supplies use force to manage their markets. These also are serious costs, but no one knows how much they would be reduced if drugs were legalized. Addicts would no longer steal to pay black-market prices for drugs, a real gain. But some, perhaps a great deal, of that gain would be offset by the great increase in the number of addicts. These people, nodding on heroin or living in the delusion-ridden high of cocaine, would hardly be ideal employees. Many would steal simply to support themselves, since snatch-and-grab, opportunistic crime can be managed even by people unable to hold a regular job or plan an elaborate crime. Those British addicts who get their supplies from government clinics are not models of law-abiding decency. Most are in crime, and though their per-capita rate of criminality may be lower thanks to the cheapness of their drugs, the total volume of crime they produce may be quite large. Of course, society could decide to support all unemployable addicts on welfare, but that would mean that gains from lowered rates of crime would have to be offset by large increases in welfare budgets.

Proponents of legalization claim that the costs of having more addicts around would be largely if not entirely offset by having more money available with which to treat and care for them. The money would come from taxes levied on the sale of heroin and cocaine.

To obtain this fiscal dividend, however, legalization's supporters must first solve an economic dilemma. If they want to raise a lot of money to pay for welfare and treatment, the tax rate on the drugs will have to be quite high. Even if they themselves do not want a high rate, the politicians' love of "sin taxes" would probably guarantee that it would be high anyway. But the higher the tax, the higher the price of the drug, and the higher the price the greater the likelihood that addicts will turn to crime to find the money for it and that criminal organizations will be formed to sell tax-free drugs at below-market rates. If we managed to keep taxes (and thus prices) low, we would get that much less money to pay for welfare and treatment and more people could afford to become addicts. There may be an optimal tax rate for drugs that maximizes revenue while minimizing crime, bootlegging, and the recruitment of new addicts, but our experience with alcohol does not suggest that we know how to find it.

The Benefits of Illegality

The advocates of legalization find nothing to be said in favor of the current system except, possibly, that it keeps the number of addicts smaller than it would otherwise be. In fact, the benefits are more substantial than that.

First, treatment. All the talk about providing "treatment on demand" implies that there is a demand for treatment. That is not quite right. There are some drug-dependent people who genuinely want treatment and will remain in it if offered; they should receive it. But there are far more who want only short-term help after a bad crash; once stabilized and bathed, they are back on the street again, hustling. And even many of the addicts who enroll in a program honestly wanting help drop out after a short while when they discover that help takes time and commitment. Drug-dependent people have very short time horizons and a weak capacity for commitment. These two groups—those looking for a quick fix and those unable to stick with a long-term fix—are not easily helped. Even if we increase the number of treatment slots—as we should—we would have to do something to make treatment more effective.

One thing that can often make it more effective is compulsion. Douglas Anglin of UCLA, in common with many other researchers, has found that the longer one stays in a treatment program, the better the chances of a reduction in drug dependency. But he, again like most other researchers, has found that drop-out rates are high. He has also found, however, that patients who enter treatment under legal compulsion stay in the program longer than those not subject to such pressure. His research on the California civil-commitment program, for example, found that heroin users involved with its required drug-testing program had over the long term a lower rate of heroin use than similar addicts who were free of such constraints. If for many addicts compulsion is a useful component of treatment, it is not clear how compulsion could be achieved in a society in which purchasing, possessing, and using the drug were legal. It could be managed, I suppose, but I would not want to have to answer the challenge from the American Civil Liberties Union that it is wrong to compel a person to undergo treatment for consuming a legal commodity.

Next, education. We are now investing substantially in drug-education programs in the schools. Though we do not yet know for certain what will work, there are some promising leads. But I wonder how credible such programs would be if they were aimed at dissuading children from doing something perfectly legal. We could, of course, treat drug education like smoking education: inhaling crack and inhaling tobacco are both legal, but you should not do it because it is bad for you. That tobacco is bad for you is easily shown; the Surgeon General has seen to that. But what do we say about crack? It is pleasurable, but devoting yourself to so much pleasure is not a good idea (though perfectly legal)? Unlike tobacco, cocaine will not give you cancer or emphysema, but it will lead you to neglect your duties to family, job, and neighborhood? Everybody is doing cocaine, but you should not?

Again, it might be possible under a legalized regime to have effective drug-prevention programs, but their effectiveness would depend heavily, I think, on first having decided that cocaine use, like tobacco use, is purely a matter of practical consequences; no fundamental moral significance attaches to either. But if we believe—as I do—that dependency on certain mind-altering drugs *is* a moral issue and that their illegality rests in part on their immorality, then legalizing them undercuts, if it does not eliminate altogether, the moral message.

That message is at the root of the distinction we now make between nicotine and cocaine. Both are highly addictive; both have harmful physical effects. But we treat the two drugs differently, not simply because nicotine is so widely used as to be beyond the reach of effective prohibition, but because its use does not destroy the user's essential humanity. Tobacco shortens one's life, cocaine debases it. Nicotine alters one's habits, cocaine alters one's soul. The heavy use of crack, unlike the heavy use of tobacco, corrodes those natural sentiments of sympathy and duty that constitute our human nature and make possible our social life. To say, as does Nadelmann, that distinguishing morally between tobacco and cocaine is "little more than a transient prejudice" is close to saying that morality itself is but a prejudice.

The Alcohol Problem

Now we have arrived where many arguments about legalizing drugs begin: is there any reason to treat heroin and cocaine differently from the way we treat alcohol?

There is no easy answer to that question because, as with so many human problems, one cannot decide simply on the basis either of moral principles or of individual consequences; one has to temper any policy by a common-sense judgment of what is possible. Alcohol, like heroin, cocaine, PCP, and marijuana, is a drug—that is, a mood-altering substance—and consumed to excess it certainly has harmful consequences: auto accidents, barroom fights, bedroom shootings. It is also, for some people, addictive. We cannot confidently compare the addictive powers of these drugs, but the best evidence suggests that crack and heroin are much more addictive than alcohol.

Many people, Nadelmann included, argue that since the health and financial costs of alcohol abuse are so much higher than those of cocaine or heroin abuse, it is hypocritical folly to devote our efforts to preventing cocaine or drug use. But as

Mark Kleiman of Harvard has pointed out, this comparison is quite misleading. What Nadelmann is doing is showing that a *legalized* drug (alcohol) produces greater social harm than *illegal* ones (cocaine and heroin). But of course. Suppose that in the 1920's we had made heroin and cocaine legal and alcohol illegal. Can anyone doubt that Nadelmann would now be writing that it is folly to continue our ban on alcohol because cocaine and heroin are so much more harmful?

And let there be no doubt about it—widespread heroin and cocaine use are associated with all manner of ills. Thomas Bewley found that the mortality rate of British heroin addicts in 1968 was 28 times as high as the death rate of the same age group of non-addicts, even though in England at the time an addict could obtain free or low-cost heroin and clean needles from British clinics. Perform the following mental experiment: suppose we legalized heroin and cocaine in this country. In what proportion of auto fatalities would the state police report that the driver was nodding off on heroin or recklessly driving on a coke high? In what proportion of spouse-assault and child-abuse cases would the local police report that crack was involved? In what proportion of industrial accidents would safety investigators report that the forklift or drill-press operator was in a drug-induced stupor or frenzy? We do not know exactly what the proportion would be, but anyone who asserts that it would not be much higher than it is now would have to believe that these drugs have little appeal except when they are illegal. And that is nonsense.

An advocate of legalization might concede that social harm—perhaps harm equivalent to that already produced by alcohol—would follow from making cocaine and heroin generally available. But at least, he might add, we would have the problem "out in the open" where it could be treated as a matter of "public health." That is well and good, *if* we knew how to treat—that is, cure—heroin and cocaine abuse. But we do not know how to do it for all the people who would need such help. We are having only limited success in coping with chronic alcoholics. Addictive behavior is immensely difficult to change, and the best methods for changing it—living in drug-free therapeutic communities, becoming faithful members of Alcoholics Anonymous or Narcotics Anonymous—require great personal commitment, a quality that is, alas, in short supply among the very persons—young people, disadvantaged people—who are often most at risk for addiction.

Suppose that today we had, not 15 million alcohol abusers, but half a million. Suppose that we already knew what we have learned from our long experience with the widespread use of alcohol. Would we make whiskey legal? I do not know, but I suspect there would be a lively debate. The Surgeon General would remind us of the risks alcohol poses to pregnant women. The National Highway Traffic Safety Administration would point to the likelihood of more highway fatalities caused by drunk drivers. The Food and Drug Administration might find that there is a non-trivial increase in cancer associated with alcohol consumption. At the same time the police would report great difficulty in keeping illegal whiskey out of our cities, officers being corrupted by bootleggers, and alcohol addicts often resorting to crime to feed their habits. Libertarians, for their part, would argue that every citizen has a right to drink anything he wishes and that drinking is, in any event, a "victimless crime."

However the debate might turn out, the central fact would be that the problem was still, at that point, a small one. The government cannot legislate away the addictive tendencies in all of us, nor can it remove completely even the most dangerous addictive substances. But it can cope with harms when the harms are still manageable.

Science and Addiction

One advantage of containing a problem while it is still containable is that it buys time for science to learn more about it and perhaps to discover a cure. Almost unnoticed in the current debate over legalizing drugs is that basic science has made rapid strides in identifying the underlying neurological processes involved in some forms of addiction. Stimulants such as cocaine and amphetamines alter the way certain brain cells communicate with one another. That alteration is complex and not entirely understood, but in simplified form it involves modi-

fying the way in which a neurotransmitter called dopamine sends signals from one cell to another.

When dopamine crosses the synapse between two cells, it is in effect carrying a message from the first cell to activate the second one. In certain parts of the brain that message is experienced as pleasure. After the message is delivered, the dopamine returns to the first cell. Cocaine apparently blocks this return, or "reuptake," so that the excited cell and others nearby continue to send pleasure messages. When the exaggerated high produced by cocaine-influenced dopamine finally ends, the brain cells may (in ways that are still a matter of dispute) suffer from an extreme lack of dopamine, thereby making the individual unable to experience any pleasure at all. This would explain why cocaine users often feel so depressed after enjoying the drug. Stimulants may also affect the way in which other neurotransmitters, such as serotonin and noradrenaline, operate.

Whatever the exact mechanism may be, once it is identified it becomes possible to use drugs to block either the effect of cocaine or its tendency to produce dependency. There have already been experiments using desipramine, imipramine, bromocriptine, carbamazepine, and other chemicals. There are some promising results.

Tragically, we spend very little on such research, and the agencies funding it have not in the past occupied very influential or visible posts in the federal bureaucracy. If there is one aspect of the "war on drugs" metaphor that I dislike, it is its tendency to focus attention almost exclusively on the troops in the trenches, whether engaged in enforcement or treatment, and away from the research-and-development efforts back on the home front where the war may ultimately be decided.

I believe that the prospects of scientists in controlling addiction will be strongly influenced by the size and character of the problem they face. If the problem is a few hundred thousand chronic, high-dose users of an illegal product, the chances of making a difference at a reasonable cost will be much greater than if the problem is a few million chronic users of legal substances. Once a drug is legal, not only will its use increase but many of those who then use it will prefer the drug to the treatment: they will want the pleasure, whatever the cost to themselves or their families, and they will resist—probably successfully—any effort to wean them away from experiencing the high that comes from inhaling a legal substance.

If I Am Wrong...

No one can know what our society would be like if we changed the law to make access to cocaine, heroin, and PCP easier. I believe, for reasons given, that the result would be a sharp increase in use, a more widespread degradation of the human personality, and a greater rate of accidents and violence.

I may be wrong. If I am, then we will needlessly have incurred heavy costs in law enforcement and some forms of criminality. But if I am right, and the legalizers prevail anyway, then we will have consigned millions of people, hundreds of thousands of infants, and hundreds of neighborhoods to a life of oblivion and disease. To the lives and families destroyed by alcohol we will have added countless more destroyed by cocaine, heroin, PCP, and whatever else a basement scientist can invent.

Human character is formed by society; indeed, human character is inconceivable without society, and good character is less likely in a bad society. Will we, in the name of an abstract doctrine of radical individualism, and with the false comfort of suspect predictions, decide to take the chance that somehow individual decency can survive amid a more general level of deregulation?

I think not. The American people are too wise for that, whatever the academic essayists and cocktail-party pundits may say. But if Americans today are less wise than I suppose, then Americans at some future time will look back on us now and wonder, what kind of people were they that they could have done such a thing?

RICHARD J. DENNIS

The Economics of Legalizing Drugs

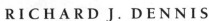

Richard J. Dennis, a commodities trader, is on the editorial board of the New Perspectives Quarterly. *(Source: Copyright © 1990 by Richard J. Dennis, as first published in* The Atlantic.*)*

QUESTIONS FOR REFLECTION

1. Dennis describes the war on drugs as futile and irrational. Why? What are the effects, in his view, of a successful drug raid?

2. Dennis believes that keeping drugs illegal protects the wealthy at the expense of the poor. Why? Do you agree?

3. The drug problem, Dennis says, is not a moral but an economic issue. What role does this contention play in his argument? Does Dennis succeed in being morally neutral, or does his claim presuppose a view about the proper relation between a government and its citizens?

4. Dennis draws distinctions among marijuana, most forms of cocaine, crack, and heroin. Different policies, he believes, are appropriate for each. What are the relevant differences among these drugs? How do these differences relate to the differences among the policies Dennis proposes for them?

Last year federal agents in southern California broke the six-dollar lock on a warehouse and discovered twenty tons of cocaine. The raid was reported to be the largest seizure of illegal narcotics ever. Politicians and law-enforcement officials heralded it as proof not only of the severity of our drug problem but also of the success of our interdiction efforts, and the need for more of the same. However, in reality the California raid was evidence of nothing but the futility and irrationality of our current approach to illegal drugs. It is questionable whether the raid prevented a single person from buying cocaine. Addicts were not driven to seek treatment. No drug lord or street dealer was put out of business. The event had no perceptible impact on the public's attitude toward drug use. People who wanted cocaine still wanted it—and got it.

If the raid had any effect at all, it was perverse. The street price of cocaine in southern California probably rose temporarily, further enriching the criminal network now terrorizing the nation's inner cities. William Bennett, the director of national drug-control policy, and his fellow moral authoritarians were offered another opportunity to alarm an already overwrought public with a fresh gust of rhetoric. New support was given to a Bush Administration plan that is meant to reduce supply but in fact guarantees more money to foreign drug lords, who will soon become the richest private individuals in history.

Indeed, Americans have grown so hysterical about the drug problem that few public figures dare appear soft on drugs or say anything dispassionate about the situation. In a 1989 poll 54 percent of Americans cited drugs as the nation's greatest threat. Four percent named unemployment. It is time, long past time, to take a clear-eyed look at illegal drugs and ask what government and law enforcement can really be expected to do.

Drug illegality has the same effect as a regressive tax: its chief aim is to save relatively wealthy potential users of drugs like marijuana and cocaine from self-destruction, at tremendous cost to the residents of inner cities. For this reason alone, people interested in policies that help America's poor should embrace drug legalization. It would dethrone drug dealers in the ghettos and release inner-city residents from their status as hostages.

Once the drug war is considered in rational terms, the solution becomes obvious: declare peace. Legalize the stuff. Tax it and regulate its distribution, as liquor is now taxed and regulated. Educate those who will listen. Help those who need help.

Arguments for the benefits of drug legalization have appeared frequently in the press, most of them making the point that crime and other social hazards might be reduced as a result. This article presents an economic analysis of the benefits of legalizing drugs.

Some Wrong Ways to Discuss the Drug Problem

In order to make any sort of sane argument about drugs, of course, we have to decide what the problem is. That isn't as simple as it might seem, Bennett's thirty-second sound bites notwithstanding. It's easier to say what the drug problem is not.

The drug problem is not a moral issue. There's a streak of puritanism in the national soul, true, but most Americans are not morally opposed to substances that alter one's mind and mood. That issue was resolved in 1933, with the repeal of Prohibition. There is no question that drugs used to excess are harmful; so is alcohol. Americans seem to have no moral difficulty with the notion that adults should be allowed use alcohol as they see fit, as long as others are not harmed.

The drug problem is not the country's most important health issue. The use of heroin and cocaine can result in addiction and death; so can the use of alcohol and tobacco. In fact, some researchers estimate the yearly per capita mortality rate of tobacco among smokers at more than a hundred times that of cocaine among cocaine users. If the drug-policy director is worried about the effect on public health of substance abuse, he should spend most of his time talking about cigarettes and whiskey.

The drug problem is not entirely a societal issue—at least not in the sense that it is portrayed as one by politicians and the media. Drug dealing is a chance for people without legitimate opportunity. The problem of the underclass will never be solved by attacking it with force of arms.

So what is the problem? The heart of it is money. What most Americans want is less crime and less profit for inner-city thugs and Colombian drug lords. Less self-destruction by drug users would be nice, but what people increasingly demand is an end to the foreign and domestic terrorism—financed by vast amounts of our own money—associated with the illegal drug trade.

This, as it happens, is a problem that can be solved in quick and pragmatic fashion, by legalizing the sale of most drugs to adults. Virtually overnight crime and corruption would be reduced. The drug cartels would be shattered. Public resources could be diverted to meaningful education and treatment programs.

The alternative—driving up drug prices and increasing public costs with an accelerated drug war—inevitably will fail to solve anything. Instead of making holy war on the drug barons, the President's plan subsidizes them.

Laws protecting children should obviously be retained. Some might question the effectiveness of combining legal drug use by adults with harsh penalties for the sale of drugs to minors. But effective statutory-rape laws demonstrate that society can maintain a distinction between the behavior of adults and that of minors when it truly believes such a distinction is warranted.

Legalization would require us to make some critical distinctions among drugs and drug users, of course. The Administration's plan approaches the drug problem as a seamless whole. But in fact crack and heroin are harmful in ways that marijuana is not. This failure to distinguish among different drugs and their consequences serves only to discredit the anti-drug effort, especially among young people. It also disperses law-enforcement efforts, rendering them hopelessly ineffective. Instead of investing immense resources in a vain attempt to control the behavior of adults, we should put our money where the crisis is. Why spend anything to prosecute marijuana users in a college dormitory when the focus should be on the crack pusher in the Bronx schoolyard?

The appropriate standard in deciding if a drug should be made legal for adults ought to be whether it is more likely than alcohol to cause harm to an innocent party. If not, banning it cannot be justified while alcohol remains legal. For example, a sensible legalization plan would allow users of marijuana to buy it legally. Small dealers could sell it legally but would be regulated, as beer dealers are now in states where beer is sold in grocery stores. Their supplies would be licensed and regulated. Selling marijuana to minors would be criminal.

Users of cocaine should be able to buy it through centers akin to state liquor stores. It is critical to remove the black-market profit from cocaine in order to destabilize organized crime and impoverish pushers. Selling cocaine to minors would be criminal, as it is now, but infractions could be better policed if effort were concentrated on them. Any black market that might remain would be in sales of crack or sales to minors, transactions that are now estimated to account for 20 percent of drug sales.

Cocaine runs the spectrum from coca leaf to powder to smokable crack; it's the way people take it that makes the difference. Crack's effects on individual behavior and its addictive potential place it in a category apart from other forms of cocaine. The actual degree of harm it does to those who use it is still to be discovered, but for the sake of argument let's assume that it presents a clear danger to people who come in contact with the users. A crack user, therefore, should be subject to a civil fine, and mandatory treatment after multiple violations. Small dealers should have their supplies seized and be subject to moderate punishment for repeat offenses. Major dealers, however, should be subject to the kinds of sentences that are now given. And any adult convicted of selling crack to children should face the harshest prison sentence our criminal-justice system can mete out.

The same rules should apply to any drug that presents a substantial threat to others.

A serious objection to legalizing cocaine while crack remains illegal is that cocaine could be bought, turned into crack, and sold. But those who now buy powder cocaine could take it home and make it into crack, and very few do so. Moreover,

legal cocaine would most likely be consumed in different settings and under different circumstances than still-illegal crack would be. Researchers believe that more-benign settings reduce the probability of addiction. Legalization could make it less likely that cocaine users will become crack users. In addition, an effective dose of crack is already so cheap that price is not much of a deterrent to those who want to try it. No price reduction as a result of the legalization of cocaine, then, should lead to a significant increase in the numbers of crack users.

As for heroin, the advent of methadone clinics shows that society has realized that addicts require maintenance. But there is little practical difference between methadone and heroin, and methadone clinics don't get people off methadone. Heroin addicts should receive what they require, so that they don't have to steal to support their habit. This would make heroin unprofitable for its pushers. And providing addicts with access to uninfected needles would help stop the spread of AIDS and help lure them into treatment programs.

What the Drug War Costs and What We Could Save

The major argument against legalization, and one that deserves to be taken seriously, is a possible increase in drug use and addiction. But it can be shown that if reasonable costs are assigned to all aspects of the drug problem, the benefits of drug peace would be large enough to offset even a doubling in the number of addicts.

Any numerical cost-benefit analysis of drug legalization versus the current drug war rests on assumptions that are difficult to substantiate. The figures for the costs of drug use must be estimates, and so the following analysis is by necessity illustrative rather than definitive. But the numbers used in the analysis below are at least of the right magnitude; most are based on government data. These assumptions, moreover, give the benefit of the doubt to the drug warriors and shortchange proponents of drug legalization.

The statistical assumptions that form the basis of this cost-benefit analysis are as follows:

- *The social cost of all drug use at all levels can be esti-mated by assuming that America now has two mil-lion illicit-drug addicts.* Slightly more than one million addicts use cocaine (including crack) about four times a week; 500,000 addicts use heroin at about the same rate. This means that there are about 1.5 million hardcore addicts. Some experts argue that the figures for addiction should be higher. An estimate of the social cost of drug use should also take into account casual use, even if the social cost of it is arguable; 10 million people, at most, use cocaine and other dangerous drugs monthly. To ensure a fair esti-mate of social cost, let's assume that America now has two million drug addicts.

- *Legalization would result in an immediate and per-manent 25 percent increase in the number of addicts and the costs associated with them.* This projection is derived by estimating the number of people who would try hard drugs if they were legalized and then estimating how many of them would end up addicted. In past years—during a time when marijuana was more or less decriminalized —approximately 60 million Americans tried marijuana and almost 30 million tried cocaine, America's most popular hard drug. (It is fair to assume that nearly all of those who tried cocaine also tried marijuana and that those who haven't tried marijuana in the past twenty-five years will not decide to try decriminalized cocaine.) This leaves 30 million people who have tried mari-juana but not cocaine, and who might be at risk to try legal, inexpensive cocaine.

  In a 1985 survey of people who voluntarily stopped using cocaine, 21 percent claimed they did so because they feared for their health, 12 percent because they were pressured by friends and family, and 12 percent because the drug was too expensive. The reasons of the other half of those surveyed were unspecified, but for the pur-pose of this exercise we will assume that they stopped for the same reasons in the same propor-tions as the other respondents. (Interestingly, the survey did not mention users who said they had stopped because cocaine is illegal or out of fear of law enforcement.) It seems reasonable to assume that many people would decide not to use legal-

ized drugs for the same reasons that these experi-menters quit. Therefore, of the 30 million people estimated to be at risk of trying legal cocaine, only about a quarter might actually try it—the quarter that is price-sensitive, because the price of cocaine, once the drug was legalized, would plummet. This leaves us with approximately 7.5 million new cocaine users. How many of them could we expect to become cocaine addicts? The estimate that there are now one million cocaine addicts suggests a one-in-thirty chance of addic-tion through experimentation. Thus from the 7.5 million new users we could expect about 250,000 new addicts, or an increase of about 25 percent over the number of cocaine addicts that we now have. We can assume about the same increase in the number of users of other hard drugs.

  Those who argue that wide availability must mean significantly higher usage overlook the fact that there is no economic incentive for dealers to push dirt-cheap drugs. Legalization might thus lead to less rather than more drug use, particu-larly by children and teenagers. Also, the public evinces little interest in trying legalized drugs. Last year, at the direction of this author, the poll-ing firm Targeting Systems Inc., in Arlington, Vir-ginia, asked a nationwide sample of 600 adults, "If cocaine were legalized, would you personally consider purchasing it or not?" Only one percent said they would.

- *The drug war will result in a 25 percent decrease in drug use.* That's the midpoint in William Ben-nett's ten-year plan to cut drug use by 50 percent by the year 2000. Since this figure is based on Bennett's official prediction, we might expect it to be highly optimistic. But to demonstrate the enormous benefits of legalization, let's accept his rosy scenario.

- *The drug war will cost government at all levels $30 billion a year.* Keeping drugs illegal costs state and local law-enforcement agencies approximately $10 billion a year—a conservative figure derived from the costs of arresting, prosecuting, and imprisoning several hundred thousand people a year for drug violations. Bennett recently implied before Congress that state governments will need to spend as much as $10 billion in new money when he was asked about what it will cost to keep in prison a higher proportion of the country's 20 million or more users of hard and soft drugs. The drug war will also cost the federal government about $10 billion a year, mostly in law enforcement—about what Congress has agreed to spend in the next fiscal year.

If marijuana and cocaine were legalized and crack and all drugs for children remained illegal, about 80 percent of current illegal drug use would become legal. This would permit savings of 80 percent—or $8 billion—of the current costs of state and local law enforcement. By rolling back the war on drugs, we could save up to all $20 billion of projected new federal and state expenditures.

• *The current dollar volume of the drug trade is approximately $100 billion a year.* If Bennett's prediction is accurate and drug consumption is cut by half over the next ten years, Colombian drug lords will still receive, on average, $3.75 billion a year, assuming that they net five percent of gross receipts—a conservative estimate. The money reaped by drug lords can be used for weapons, planes, and bombs, which could necessitate U.S. expenditures of at least one dollar to combat every dollar of drug profits if a drug war turned into real fighting.

If legalized, taxed drugs were sold for a seventh or an eighth of their current price—a level low enough for illegal dealing to be financially unattractive—the taxes could bring in at least $10 billion at the current level of usage.

• *The most important—and most loosely defined— variable is the social cost of drug use.* The term "social cost" is used indiscriminately. A narrow definition includes only health costs and taxes lost to the government through loss of income, and a broad definition counts other factors, such as the loss of the personal income itself and the value of stolen property associated with drug use. The Alcohol, Drug Abuse, and Mental Health Administration has estimated that drug and alcohol abuse cost the nation as much as $175 billion a year, of which alcohol abuse alone accounts for at least $115 billion. These figures probably include costs not really related to drug use, as a

result of the Administration's zeal to dramatize the drug crisis. We will assume that $50 billion a year is a realistic estimate of the share for drug use.

Once these usually qualitative factors have been assigned numbers, it is possible to estimate how much the drug war costs in an average year and how much drug peace might save us. Again, this assumes that 25 percent fewer people in a mid-point year will use drugs owing to a successful drug war and 25 percent more people will use drugs with the establishment of drug peace.

If we choose drug peace as opposed to drug war, we'll save $10 billion a year in federal law enforcement, $10 billion a year in new state and local prosecution, about $8 billion a year in other law-enforcement costs (80 percent of the current $10 billion a year), about $6 billion a year in the value of stolen property associated with drug use (80 percent of the current $7.5 billion), and $3.75 billion a year by eliminating the need to match the Colombians' drug profits dollar for dollar. We'll also benefit from taxes of $12.5 billion. These social gains amount to $50.25 billion.

If use rises 25 percent, instead of declining by that amount, it will result in a social cost of $25 billion (50 percent of $50 billion). Therefore, the net social gain of drug peace is $25.25 billion. If legalization resulted in an immediate and permanent increase in use of more than 25 percent, the benefits of drug peace would narrow. But additional tax revenue would partly make up for the shrinkage. For example, if the increase in use was 50 percent instead of 25 percent, that would add another $12.5 billion in social costs per year but would contribute another $2.5 billion in tax revenue.

At the rate at which those numbers converge, almost a 100 percent increase in the number of addicts would be required before the net benefits of drug peace equaled zero. This would seem to be a worst-case scenario. But to the drug warriors, any uncertainty is an opportunity to fan the flames of fear. Last year, Bennett wrote, in *The Wall Street Journal,* "Of course, no one . . . can say with certainty what would happen in the U.S. if drugs were suddenly to become a readily purchased product. We do know, however, that whenever drugs have been cheaper and more easily obtained, drug use—and addiction—have skyrocketed." Bennett cited two examples to prove his thesis: a fortyfold increase in the number of heroin addicts in Great Britain since the drug began to be legally prescribed there, and a 350 percent increase in alcohol consumption in the United States after Prohibition.

In fact experts are far from certain about the outcome of the British experiment. The statistics on the increase in the number of drug abusers are unreliable. All that is known is that a significant rise in the number of addicts seeking treatment took place. Moreover, according to some estimates, Britain has approximately sixty-two addicts or regular users of heroin per 100,000 population (for a total of 30,000 to 35,000), while the United States has 209 heroin addicts or users per 100,000 population, for a total of 500,000. And very few British heroin addicts engage in serious crime, unlike heroin addicts in America. Bennett's criticism notwithstanding, the British apparently have broken the link between heroin addiction and violent crime.

As for Prohibition, its effects were hardly as dramatic as Bennett implied. During 1916–1919 per capita consumption of pure alcohol among the U.S. drinking-age population was 1.96 gallons a year; during Prohibition it dropped to 0.90 gallons; after Repeal, during 1936–1941, it went up about 70 percent, to 1.54 gallons.

And how does Bennett explain the experience of the Netherlands, where the decriminalization of drugs has resulted in decreased use? Does he think that what made all the difference in Holland is the fact that it has a smaller underclass than we do? In essence, the Dutch policy involves vigorous enforcement against dealers of hard drugs, official tolerance of soft drugs such as marijuana and hashish, and decriminalization of all users. The number of marijuana users began decreasing shortly after the Dutch government decriminalized marijuana, in 1976. In 1984 about four percent of Dutch young people age ten to eighteen reported having smoked marijuana—roughly a third of the rate among minors in the United States. In Amsterdam the number of heroin addicts has declined from 9,000 in 1984 to fewer than 6,000 today. Over that same period the average age of addicts has risen from

twenty-six to thirty-one, indicating that few new users have taken up the habit. And there is no evidence that crack has made inroads among Dutch addicts, in contrast to its prevalence in America.

Amsterdam is a capital city close in size (population 695,000), if not in culture and economic demographics, to Washington, D.C. (population 604,000). Amsterdam had forty-six homicides last year, of which perhaps 30 percent were related to the drug trade. Washington had 438 homicides, 60 to 80 percent of which were drug-related. The rate of homicides per 100,000 population was 6.6 in Amsterdam, less than a tenth the rate of 72.5 in Washington.

Holland's strategy is one of only two that have been shown to cause a real decline in drug use. The other is Singapore's, which consists of imposing the death penalty on people caught in possession of as little as fifteen grams of heroin. If this is Bennett's fallback position, perhaps he should say so explicitly.

Some Objections Considered

The fear that legalization would lead to increased drug use and addiction is not, of course, the only basis on which legalization is opposed. We should address other frequently heard objections here.

• *Crack is our No. 1 drug problem. Legalizing other drugs while crack remains illegal won't solve the problem.* Although crack has captured the lion's share of public attention, marijuana has always commanded the bulk of law-enforcement interest. Despite de facto urban decriminalization, more than a third of all drug arrests occur in connection with marijuana—mostly for mere possession. Three fourths of all violations of drug laws relate to marijuana, and two thirds of all people charged with violation of federal marijuana laws are sentenced to prison (state figures are not available).

Crack appears to account for about 10 percent of the total dollar volume of the drug trade, according to National Institute on Drug Abuse estimates of the number of regular crack users. Legalizing other drugs would free up most of the law-enforcement resources currently focused on less dangerous substances and their users. It's true that as long as crack remains illegal, there will be a black market and associated crime. But we would still reap most of the benefits of legalization outlined above.

- *Legalization would result in a huge loss in productivity and in higher health-care costs.* In truth, productivity lost to drugs is minor compared with productivity lost to alcohol and cigarettes, which remain legal. Hundreds of variables affect a person's job performance, ranging from the consumption of whiskey and cigarettes to obesity and family problems. On a purely statistical level it can be demonstrated that marital status affects productivity, yet we do not allow employers to dismiss workers on the basis of that factor.

  If legal drug use resulted in higher social costs, the government could levy a tax on the sale of drugs in some rough proportion to the monetary value of those costs—as it does now for alcohol and cigarettes. This wouldn't provide the government with a financial stake in addiction. Rather, the government would be making sure that users of socially costly items paid those social costs. Funds from the tax on decriminalized drugs could be used for anti-drug advertising, which could be made more effective by a total ban on drug advertising. A government that licenses the sale of drugs must actively educate its citizens about their dangers, as Holland does in discouraging young people from using marijuana.

- *Drug legalization implies approval.* One of the glories of American life is that many things that are not condoned by society at large, such as atheism, offensive speech, and heavy-metal music, are legal. The well-publicized death of Len Bias and other harrowing stories have carried the message far and wide that drugs are dangerous. In arguing that legalization would persuade people that drug use is safe, drug warriors underestimate our intelligence.

- *Any restriction on total legalization would lead to continuing, substantial corruption.* Under the plan proposed here, restrictions would continue on the sale of crack and on the sale of all drugs to children. Even if black-market corruption continued in those areas, we would experience an immediate 80 percent reduction in corruption overall.

- *Legalization is too unpredictable and sweeping an action to be undertaken all at once. It would be better to establish several test areas first, and evaluate the results.* The results of such a trial would probably not further the case of either side. If use went up in the test area, it could be argued that this was caused by an influx of people from areas where drugs were still illegal; if use went down, it could be argued that the area chosen was unrepresentative.

- *Even if current drugs are legalized, much more destructive drugs will be developed in the future.* The most destructive current drug is crack, which would remain illegal. Many analysts believe that the development of crack was a marketing strategy, since powder cocaine was too expensive for many users. If cocaine had been legal, crack might never have been marketed. In any case, if a drug presents a clear danger to bystanders, it should not be legal.

- *No matter how the government distributes drugs, users will continue to seek greater quantities and higher potency on the black market.* If the government restricts the amount of a drug that can be distributed legally, legalization will fail. It must make drugs available at all levels of quantity and potency. The government should regulate the distributors but not the product itself. The model should be the distribution of alcohol through state-regulated liquor stores.

- *Legalizing drugs would ensure that America's inner cities remain places of hopelessness and despair.* If drugs disappeared tomorrow from America's ghettos, the ghettos would remain places of hopelessness and despair. But legalization would put most drug dealers out of business and remove the main source of financing for violent gangs. At the least, legalization would spare the inner cities from drug-driven terrorism.

- *Marijuana in itself may be relatively harmless, but it is a "gateway drug." Legalization would lead its users to more harmful and addictive drugs.* While government studies show some correlation between marijuana use and cocaine addiction, they also show that tobacco and alcohol use correlate with drug addiction. Moreover, keeping marijuana illegal forces buyers into an illegal market, where they are likely to be offered other drugs. Finally, 60 million Americans have tried marijuana, and there are one million cocaine addicts. If marijuana is a gateway drug, the gate is narrow.

- *Legalizing drugs would aggravate the growing problem of "crack babies."* The sale of crack would remain illegal. Even so, it is difficult to believe that anyone ignorant or desperate enough to use crack while pregnant would be deterred by a law. Laws against drug use are more likely to deter users from seeking treatment. Crack babies probably would have a better chance in a less censorious environment, in which their mothers had less to fear from seeking treatment.

Drug use in the United States can be seen as a symptom of recent cultural changes that have led to an erosion of traditional values and an inability to replace them. There are those who are willing to pay the price to try to save people from themselves. But there are surely just as many who would pay to preserve a person's right to be wrong. To the pragmatist, the choice is clear: legalization is the best bet.

Pornography

Most philosophers defend freedom of thought, of speech, and of the press. Some, like Milton, Tocqueville, and Mill, are strongly committed to these freedoms; others, like Burke, acknowledge that they are goods, but believe that they must be balanced against other goods. Nevertheless, virtually no one believes that these freedoms are completely unrestricted. Slander, libel, false advertising, harassment, inciting to riot, and public endangerment—shouting "Fire!" in a crowded theater, for example—have often been held up as exceptions. Thus the problem of determining the proper limits of these freedoms arises.

Pornography raises especially difficult questions about limits on freedom of thought, speech, and the press. The exceptions mentioned above are often thought to be exceptions because they risk or cause harm that outweighs their values as communications. Many people believe pornography to be harmful and base their opposition to it on that ground. But any harms caused by pornography are subtler and harder to detect than those of inciting to riot, for example. Consequently, the question of whether pornography is harmful has become an important focus of debate.

Also, the harm done by a speaker is usually weighed against the value of the communication. It is harder to slander a public official than a private citizen, for example, because the public's need for information about officials of government is much greater than its need for information about you or me; communication about the beliefs and behavior of public officials has greater value than communications about the rest of us. But what does pornography communicate? Often, it is hard to discern any message at all. Is pornography ever communication? These problems make weighing the value of a piece of pornography against its harmful effects very difficult.

Moreover, most of the arguments that Milton, Tocqueville, and Mill advance in favor of free speech rest on the supposition that speech communicates something that might be true or false. Mill argues that an opinion might be true; that, even if false, it might contain part of the truth; and that, even if totally false, its combat with the truth helps keep the truth alive. This argument makes sense for opinions, for propositions or bits of information that might be true or false. But does it make any sense applied to *Sex Orgies Illustrated?* Or *Deep Throat?* Or a *Playboy* centerfold? If not, on what does the case for freedom of pornographic speech rest?

The United States Supreme Court, in *Miller v. California* and *Paris Adult Theater I v. Slaton,* decided that the government may regulate pornographic materials, banning those that are obscene. The Court moreover proposed criteria for determining whether something is obscene: (a) it must, judged by the average person applying contemporary community standards, appeal to a prurient (that is, arousing and unwholesome) interest in sex; (b) it must depict or describe sexual conduct in a patently offensive way; and (c) it must lack serious literary, artistic, political, or scientific value. The first two criteria pertain to harm; the third, to lack of any positive communicative value that might balance the harm.

Dissenters to the decisions have argued that sexual expression deserves protection against government interference. Some hold that such an expression may have positive value for individuals that outweighs any harm it causes; some claim that freedoms of thought, speech, and the press are all forms of freedom of expression, which is what properly defines the limits of government authority. Others believe that there is no fair and accurate way to distinguish obscene from nonobscene materials.

The Attorney General's Commission on Pornography argues at length that certain kinds of pornography, particularly those involving violence, are harmful and ought to be restricted. The Commission argues that these forms of pornography harm not only the "users," the viewers of the material, but also others with whom the users come into contact. The Commission holds, however, that other forms of pornography seem relatively harmless and should escape any government restrictions.

In the final selection, Jeff Rosen points to the difficulties the Court has faced in implementing the *Miller* criteria, which require that police officers, jurors, and judges determine whether works have serious artistic value. Rosen finds such aesthetic issues undecidable and argues that they have no place in a court of law.

Miller v. California (1973)

(*Source:* Miller v. California *413 U.S. [1973]. Most legal references have been omitted.*)

QUESTIONS FOR REFLECTION

1. Explain the obscenity test proposed by the Court.

2. Many critics, including Justice Douglas, have attacked the Court's test for obscenity as vague. What sources of vagueness do you see in the Court's criteria? How might they be eliminated? Should they be eliminated?

3. Justice Brennan complains that it is impossible to distinguish obscene from nonobscene materials accurately. How does the majority defend its view against this complaint?

4. Why does the majority believe that obscenity is not protected by freedom of speech?

5. How does Justice Douglas argue for his contention that "obscenity cases . . . have no business being in the courts"? Do you agree?

6. Offensiveness forms part of the test of obscenity. Justice Douglas contends that offense does not justify government restriction. What are his arguments? How would Mill recommend treating offensive material? What is the difference between offense and harm?

. . . **M**r. Chief Justice Burger delivered the opinion of the Court. . . .

I

This case involves the application of a State's criminal obscenity statute to a situation in which sexually explicit materials have been thrust by aggressive sales action upon unwilling recipients who had in no way indicated any desire to receive such materials. This Court has recognized that the States have a legitimate interest in prohibiting dissemination or exhibition of obscene material when the mode of dissemination carries with it a significant danger of offending the sensibilities of unwilling recipients or of exposure to juveniles. It is in this context that we are called on to define the standards which must be used to identify obscene material that a State may regulate without infringing on the First Amendment as applicable to the States through the Fourteenth Amendment. . . .

Apart from the initial formulation in the *Roth* case, no majority of the Court has at any given time been able to agree on a standard to determine what constitutes obscene, pornographic material subject to regulation under the States' police power. We have seen "a variety of views among the members of the Court unmatched in any other course of constitutional adjudication." This is not remarkable, for in the area of freedom of speech and press the courts must always remain sensitive to any infringement on genuinely serious literary, artistic, political, or scientific expression. This is an area in which there are few eternal verities. . . .

II

This much has been categorically settled by the

Court, that obscene material is unprotected by the First Amendment. We acknowledge, however, the inherent dangers of undertaking to regulate any form of expression. State statutes designed to regulate obscene materials must be carefully limited. As a result, we now confine the permissible scope of such regulation to works which depict or describe sexual conduct. That conduct must be specifically defined by the applicable state law, as written or authoritatively construed. A state offense must also be limited to works which, taken as a whole, appeal to the prurient interest in sex, which portray sexual conduct in a patently offensive way, and which, taken as a whole, do not have serious literary, artistic, political, or scientific value.

The basic guidelines for the trier of fact must be: (a) whether "the average person, applying contemporary community standards" would find that the work, taken as a whole, appeals to the prurient interest; (b) whether the work depicts or describes, in a patently offensive way, sexual conduct specifically defined by the applicable state law; and (c) whether the work, taken as a whole, lacks serious literary, artistic, political, or scientific value. We do not adopt as a constitutional standard the "*utterly* without redeeming social value" test of *Memoirs* v. *Massachusetts;* that concept has never commanded the adherence of more than three Justices at one time.

We emphasize that it is not our function to propose regulatory schemes for the States. That must await their concrete legislative efforts. It is possible, however, to give a few plain examples of what a state statute could define for regulation under part (b) of the standard announced in this opinion:

(a) Patently offensive representations or descriptions of ultimate sexual acts, normal or perverted, actual or simulated.
(b) Patently offensive representations or descriptions of masturbation, excretory functions, and lewd exhibition of the genitals.

Sex and nudity may not be exploited without limit by films or pictures exhibited or sold in places of public accommodation any more than live sex and nudity can be exhibited or sold without limit in such public places. At a minimum, prurient, patently offensive depiction or description of sexual conduct must have serious literary, artistic, political,

or scientific value to merit First Amendment protection. For example, medical books for the education of physicians and related personnel necessarily use graphic illustrations and descriptions of human anatomy. In resolving the inevitably sensitive questions of fact and law, we must continue to rely on the jury system, accompanied by the safeguards that judges, rules of evidence, presumption of innocence, and other protective features provide, as we do with rape, murder, and a host of other offenses against society and its individual members.

Mr. Justice Brennan, author of the opinions of the Court, or the plurality opinions, in *Roth* v. *United States; Jacobellis* v. *Ohio; Ginzburg* v. *United States* (1966); *Mishkin* v. *New York* (1966); and *Memoirs* v. *Massachusetts,* has abandoned his former position and now maintains that no formulation of this Court, the Congress, or the States can adequately distinguish obscene material unprotected by the First Amendment from protected expression. Paradoxically, Mr. Justice Brennan indicates that suppression of unprotected obscene material is permissible to avoid exposure to unconsenting adults, as in this case, and to juveniles, although he gives no indication of how the division between protected and unprotected materials may be drawn with greater precision for these purposes than for regulation of commercial exposure to consenting adults only. Nor does he indicate where in the Constitution he finds the authority to distinguish between a willing "adult" one month past the state law age of majority and a willing "juvenile" one month younger.

Under the holdings announced today, no one will be subject to prosecution for the sale or exposure of obscene materials unless these materials depict or describe patently offensive "hard core" sexual conduct specifically defined by the regulating state law, as written or construed. We are satisfied that these specific prerequisites will provide fair notice to a dealer in such materials that his public and commercial activities may bring prosecution. If the inability to define regulated materials with ultimate, god-like precision altogether removes the power of the States or the Congress to regulate, then "hard core" pornography may be exposed without limit to the juvenile, the passerby, and the consenting adult alike, as, indeed, Mr. Justice Douglas contends. In this belief, however, Mr. Justice Douglas now stands alone.

Mr. Justice Brennan also emphasizes "institutional stress" in justification of his change of view. Noting that "[t]he number of obscenity cases on our docket gives ample testimony to the burden that has been placed upon this Court," he quite rightly remarks that the examination of contested materials "is hardly a source of edification to the members of this Court." He also notes, and we agree, that "uncertainty of the standards creates a continuing source of tension between state and federal courts. . . ." "The problem is . . . that one cannot say with certainty that material is obscene until at least five members of this Court, applying inevitably obscure standards, have pronounced it so." . . .

It is certainly true that the absence, since *Roth,* of a single majority view of this Court as to proper standards for testing obscenity has placed a strain on both state and federal courts. But today, for the first time since *Roth* was decided in 1957, a majority of this Court has agreed on concrete guidelines to isolate "hard core" pornography from expression protected by the First Amendment. . . .

III

Under a National Constitution, fundamental First Amendment limitations on the powers of the States do not vary from community to community, but this does not mean that there are, or should or can be, fixed, uniform national standards of precisely what appeals to the "prurient interest" or is "patently offensive." These are essentially questions of fact, and our Nation is simply too big and too diverse for this Court to reasonably expect that such standards could be articulated for all 50 States in a single formulation, even assuming the prerequisite consensus exists. When triers of fact are asked to decide whether "the average person, applying contemporary community standards" would consider certain materials "prurient," it would be unrealistic to require that the answer be based on some abstract formulation. The adversary system, with lay jurors as the usual ultimate factfinders in criminal prosecutions, has historically permitted triers of fact to draw on the standards of their community, guided

always by limiting instructions on the law. To require a State to structure obscenity proceedings around evidence of a *national* "community standard" would be an exercise in futility. . . .

It is neither realistic nor constitutionally sound to read the First Amendment as requiring that the people of Maine or Mississippi accept public depiction of conduct found tolerable in Las Vegas, or New York City. People in different States vary in their tastes and attitudes, and this diversity is not to be strangled by the absolutism of imposed uniformity. As the Court made clear in *Mishkin* v. *New York,* the primary concern with requiring a jury to apply the standard of "the average person, applying contemporary community standards" is to be certain that, so far as material is not aimed at a deviant group, it will be judged by its impact on an average person, rather than a particularly susceptible or sensitive person—or indeed a totally insensitive one. . . . We hold that the requirement that the jury evaluate the materials with reference to "contemporary standards of the State of California" serves this protective purpose and is constitutionally adequate.

IV

The dissenting Justices sound the alarm of repression. But, in our view, to equate the free and robust exchange of ideas and political debate with commercial exploitation of obscene material demeans the grand conception of the First Amendment and its high purposes in the historic struggle for freedom. It is a "misuse of the great guarantees of free speech and free press. . . . " The First Amendment protects works which, taken as a whole, have serious literary, artistic, political, or scientific value, regardless of whether the government or a majority of the people approve of the ideas these works represent. "The protection given speech and press was fashioned to assure unfettered interchange of *ideas* for the bringing about of political and social changes desired by the people" (emphasis added). But the public portrayal of hard-core sexual conduct for its own sake, and for the ensuing commercial gain, is a different matter.

There is no evidence, empirical or historical, that the stern 19th century American censorship of public distribution and display of material relating to sex in any way limited or affected expression of serious literary, artistic, political, or scientific ideas. On the contrary, it is beyond any question that the era following Thomas Jefferson to Theodore Roosevelt was an "extraordinarily vigorous period," not just in economics and politics, but in *belles lettres* and in "the outlying fields of social and political philosophies." We do not see the harsh hand of censorship of ideas—good or bad, sound or unsound—and "repression" of political liberty lurking in every state regulation of commercial exploitation of human interest in sex.

Mr. Justice Brennan finds "it is hard to see how state-ordered regimentation of our minds can ever be forestalled." These doleful anticipations assume that courts cannot distinguish commerce in ideas, protected by the First Amendment, from commercial exploitation of obscene material. Moreover, state regulation of hard-core pornography so as to make it unavailable to nonadults, a regulation which Mr. Justice Brennan finds constitutionally permissible, has all the elements of "censorship" for adults; indeed even more rigid enforcement techniques may be called for with such dichotomy of regulation. One can concede that the "sexual revolution" of recent years may have had useful byproducts in striking layers of prudery from a subject long irrationally kept from needed ventilation. But it does not follow that no regulation of patently offensive "hard core" materials is needed or permissible; civilized people do not allow unregulated access to heroin because it is a derivative of medicinal morphine.

In sum, we (a) reaffirm the *Roth* holding that obscene material is not protected by the First Amendment; (b) hold that such material can be regulated by the States, subject to the specific safeguards enunciated above, without a showing that the material is "*utterly* without redeeming social value"; and (c) hold that obscenity is to be determined by applying "contemporary community standards," not "national standards." The judgment of the Appellate Department of the Superior Court, Orange County, California, is vacated and the case remanded to that court for further proceedings not inconsistent with the First Amendment standards established by this opinion. . . .

Mr. Justice Douglas, dissenting.

I

Today we leave open the way for California to send a man to prison for distributing brochures that advertise books and a movie under freshly written standards defining obscenity which until today's decision were never the part of any law.

The Court has worked hard to define obscenity and concededly has failed. In *Roth* v. *United States,* it ruled that "[o]bscene material is material which deals with sex in a manner appealing to prurient interest." Obscenity, it was said, was rejected by the First Amendment because it is "utterly without redeeming social importance." The presence of a "prurient interest" was to be determined by "contemporary community standards." That test, it has been said, could not be determined by one standard here and another standard there, but "on the basis of a national standard." My Brother Stewart in *Jacobellis* commented that the difficulty of the Court in giving content to obscenity was that it was "faced with the task of trying to define what may be indefinable."

In *Memoirs* v. *Massachusetts,* the *Roth* test was elaborated to read as follows: "[T]hree elements must coalesce: it must be established that (a) the dominant theme of the material taken as a whole appeals to a prurient interest in sex; (b) the material is patently offensive because it affronts contemporary community standards relating to the description or representation of sexual matters; and (c) the material is utterly without redeeming social value."

In *Ginzburg* v. *United States,* a publisher was sent to prison, not for the kind of books and periodicals he sold, but for the manner in which the publications were advertised. The "leer of the sensualist" was said to permeate the advertisements. The Court said, "Where the purveyor's sole emphasis is on the sexually provocative aspects of his publications, that fact may be decisive in the determination of obscenity." As Mr. Justice Black said in dissent, " . . . Ginzburg . . . is now finally and authoritatively condemned to serve five years in prison for distributing printed matter about sex which neither Ginzburg nor anyone else could possibly have known to be criminal." That observation by Mr.

Justice Black is underlined by the fact that the *Ginzburg* decision was five to four.

A further refinement was added by *Ginzburg* v. *New York,* where the Court held that "it was not irrational for the legislature to find that exposure to material condemned by the statute is harmful to minors."

But even those members of this Court who had created the new and changing standards of "obscenity" could not agree on their application. Some condemn it if its "dominant tendency might be to 'deprave or corrupt' a reader." Others look not to the content of the book but to whether it is advertised "'to appeal to the erotic interests of customers.'" Some condemn only "hard-core pornography"; but even then a true definition is lacking. It has indeed been said of that definition, "I could never succeed in [defining it] intelligibly," but "I know it when I see it."

Today we would add a new three-pronged test: "(a) whether 'the average person, applying contemporary community standards' would find that the work, taken as a whole, appeals to the prurient interest, . . . (b) whether the work depicts or describes, in a patently offensive way, sexual conduct specifically defined by the applicable state law, and (c) whether the work, taken as a whole, lacks serious literary, artistic, political, or scientific value."

Those are the standards we ourselves have written into the Constitution. Yet how under these vague tests can we sustain convictions for the sale of an article prior to the time when some court has declared it to be obscene?

Today the Court retreats from the earlier formulations of the constitutional test and undertakes to make new definitions. This effort, like the earlier ones, is earnest and well intentioned. The difficulty is that we do not deal with constitutional terms, since "obscenity" is not mentioned in the Constitution or Bill of Rights. And the First Amendment makes no such exception from "the press" which it undertakes to protect nor, as I have said on other occasions, in an exception necessarily implied, for there was no recognized exception to the free press at the time the Bill of Rights was adopted which treated "obscene" publications differently from other types of papers, magazines, and books. So there are no constitutional guidelines for deciding what is and what is not "obscene." The Court is at large because we deal with tastes and standards of literature. What shocks me may be sustenance for my neighbor. What causes one person to boil up in rage over one pamphlet or movie may reflect only his neurosis, not shared by others. We deal here with a regime of censorship which, if adopted, should be done by constitutional amendments after full debate by the people.

Obscenity cases usually generate tremendous emotional outbursts. They have no business being in the courts. If a constitutional amendment authorized censorship, the censor would probably be an administrative agency. Then criminal prosecutions could follow as, if, and when publishers defied the censor and sold their literature. Under that regime a publisher would know when he was on dangerous ground. Under the present regime—whether the old standards or the new ones are used—the criminal law becomes a trap. A brand new test would put a publisher behind bars under a new law improvised by the courts after the publication. That was done in *Ginzburg* and has all the evils of an *ex post facto* law.

My contention is that until a civil proceeding has placed a tract beyond the pale, no criminal prosecution should be sustained. For no more vivid illustration of vague and uncertain laws could be designed than those we have fashioned. As Mr. Justice Harlan has said:

> "The upshot of all this divergence in viewpoint is that anyone who undertakes to examine the Court's decisions since *Roth* which have held particular material obscene or not obscene would find himself in utter bewilderment." *Interstate Circuit, Inc.* v. *Dallas.*

. . . In any case—certainly when constitutional rights are concerned—we should not allow men to go to prison or be fined when they had no "fair warning" that what they did was criminal conduct.

[II . . .]

III

While the right to know is the corollary of the right to speak or publish, no one can be forced by government to listen to disclosure that he finds offensive.

That was the basis of my dissent in *Public Utilities Comm'n* v. *Pollak,* where I protested against making streetcar passengers a "captive" audience. There is no "captive audience" problem in these obscenity cases. No one is being compelled to look or to listen. Those who enter newsstands or bookstalls may be offended by what they see. But they are not compelled by the State to frequent those places; and it is only state or governmental action against which the First Amendment, applicable to the States by virtue of the Fourteenth, raises a ban.

The idea that the First Amendment permits government to ban publications that are "offensive" to some people puts an ominous gloss on freedom of the press. That test would make it possible to ban any paper or any journal or magazine in some benighted place. The First Amendment was designed "to invite dispute," to induce "a condition of unrest," to "create dissatisfaction with conditions as they are," and even to stir "people to anger." The idea that the First Amendment permits punishment for ideas that are "offensive" to the particular judge or jury sitting in judgment is astounding. No greater leveler of speech or literature has even been designed. To give the power to the censor, as we do today, is to make a sharp and radical break with the traditions of a free society. The First Amendment was not fashioned as a vehicle for dispensing tranquilizers to the people. Its prime function was to keep debate open to "offensive" as well as to "staid" people. The tendency throughout history has been to subdue the individual and to exalt the power of government. The use of the standard "offensive" gives authority to government that cuts the very vitals out of the First Amendment. As is intimated by the Court's opinion, the materials before us may be garbage. But so is much of what is said in political campaigns, in the daily press, on TV, or over the radio. By reason of the First Amendment—and solely because of it—speakers and publishers have not been threatened or subdued because their thoughts and ideas may be "offensive" to some.

The standard "offensive" is unconstitutional in yet another way. In *Coates* v. *City of Cincinnati,* we had before us a municipal ordinance that made it a crime for three or more persons to assemble on a street and conduct themselves "in a manner annoying to persons passing by." We struck it down, saying: "If three or more people meet together on a sidewalk or street corner, they must conduct themselves so as not to annoy any police officer or other person who should happen to pass by. In our opinion this ordinance is unconstitutionally vague because it subjects the exercise of the right of assembly to an unascertainable standard, and unconstitutionally broad because it authorizes the punishment of constitutionally protected conduct.

"Conduct that annoys some people does not annoy others. Thus, the ordinance is vague, not in the sense that it requires a person to conform his conduct to an imprecise but comprehensive normative standard, but rather in the sense that no standard of conduct is specified at all."

How we can deny Ohio the convenience of punishing people who "annoy" others and allow California power to punish people who publish materials "offensive" to some people is difficult to square with constitutional requirements.

If there are to be restraints on what is obscene, then a constitutional amendment should be the way of achieving the end. There are societies where religion and mathematics are the only free segments. It would be a dark day for America if that were our destiny. But the people can make it such if they choose to write obscenity into the Constitution and define it.

We deal with highly emotional, not rational, questions. To many the Song of Solomon is obscene. I do not think we, the judges, were ever given the constitutional power to make definitions of obscenity. If it is to be defined, let the people debate and decide by a constitutional amendment what they want to ban as obscene and what standards they want the legislatures and the courts to apply. Perhaps the people will decide that the path towards a mature, integrated society requires that all ideas competing for acceptance must have no censor. Perhaps they will decide otherwise. Whatever the choice, the courts will have some guidelines. Now we have none except our own predilections. . . .

Paris Adult Theater I v. Slaton (1973)

(*Source:* Paris Adult Theater I v. Slaton *413 U.S. 49 [1973]. Most legal references have been omitted.*)

QUESTIONS FOR REFLECTION

1. The majority insists that "The States have a long-recognized legitimate interest in regulating the use of obscene material in local commerce and in all places of public accommodation." Why? Which of their arguments are compatible with Mill's harm principle? Which violate it?

2. The majority argues that obscene materials do not communicate ideas and so do not deserve the kind of protection other materials do. Why, according to the majority, is communication of ideas important in determining when to respect or limit freedom of speech? Do you agree? Could something count as obscene by the *Miller* test but still communicate ideas in the sense relevant to freedom of speech?

3. Justice Douglas complains that obscenity is a "matter of taste." How does he argue from this to the conclusion that the government should not restrict obscene materials?

. . . **M**r. Chief Justice Burger delivered the opinion of the Court. . . .

[I . . .]

II

. . . The States have a long-recognized legitimate interest in regulating the use of obscene materials in local commerce and in all places of public accommodation as long as these regulations do not run afoul of specific constitutional prohibitions. . . .

In particular, we hold that there are legitimate state interests at stake in stemming the tide of commercialized obscenity, even assuming it is feasible to enforce effective safeguards against exposure to juveniles and to passersby. Rights and interests "other than those of the advocates are involved."

These include the interest of the public in the quality of life and the total community environment, the tone of commerce in the great city centers, and, possibly, the public safety itself. The Hill-Link Minority Report of the Commission on Obscenity and Pornography indicates that there is at least an arguable correlation between obscene material and crime. Quite apart from sex crimes, however, there remains one problem of large proportions aptly described by Professor Bickel:

> "It concerns the tone of the society, the mode, or to use terms that have perhaps greater currency, the style and quality of life, now and in the future. A man may be entitled to read an obscene book in his room, or expose himself indecently there. . . . We should protect his privacy. But if he demands a right to obtain the books and pictures he wants in the market, and to foregather in public places—discreet, if you will, but accessible to all—with others who share his tastes, *then to grant him his right is to affect the world about the rest*

of us, and to impinge on other privacies. Even supposing that each of us can, if he wishes, effectively avert the eye and stop the ear (which, in truth, we cannot), what is commonly read and seen and heard and done intrudes upon us all, want it or not." (Emphasis added.)

As Mr. Chief Justice Warren stated, there is a "right of the Nation and of the States to maintain a decent society. . . . "

But, it is argued, there are no scientific data which conclusively demonstrate that exposure to obscene material adversely affects men and women or their society. It is urged on behalf of the petitioners that, absent such a demonstration, any kind of state regulation is "impermissible." We reject this argument. It is not for us to resolve empirical uncertainties underlying state legislation, save in the exceptional case where that legislation plainly impinges upon rights protected by the Constitution itself. . . . Although there is no conclusive proof of a connection between antisocial behavior and obscene material, the legislature of Georgia could quite reasonably determine that such a connection does or might exist. In deciding *Roth,* this Court implicitly accepted that a legislature could legitimately act on such a conclusion to protect "*the social interest in order and morality.*"

From the beginning of civilized societies, legislators and judges have acted on various unprovable assumptions. Such assumptions underlie much lawful state regulation of commercial and business affairs. The same is true of the federal securities and antitrust laws and a host of federal regulations. On the basis of these assumptions both Congress and state legislatures have, for example, drastically restricted associational rights by adopting antitrust laws, and have strictly regulated public expression by issuers of and dealers in securities, profit sharing "coupons," and "trading stamps," commanding what they must and must not publish and announce. Understandably those who entertain an absolutist view of the First Amendment find it uncomfortable to explain why rights of association, speech, and press should be severely restrained in the marketplace of goods and money, but not in the marketplace of pornography.

Likewise, when legislatures and administrators act to protect the physical environment from pollu-tion and to preserve our resources of forests, streams, and parks, they must act on such imponderables as the impact of a new highway near or through an existing park or wilderness area. The fact that a congressional directive reflects unprovable assumptions about what is good for the people, including imponderable aesthetic assumptions, is not a sufficient reason to find that statute unconstitutional.

If we accept the unprovable assumption that a complete education requires the reading of certain books and the well nigh universal belief that good books, plays, and art lift the spirit, improve the mind, enrich the human personality, and develop character, can we then say that a state legislature may not act on the corollary assumption that commerce in obscene books, or public exhibitions focused on obscene conduct, have a tendency to exert a corrupting and debasing impact leading to antisocial behavior? "Many of these effects may be intangible and indistinct, but they are nonetheless real." Mr. Justice Cardozo said that all laws in Western civilization are "guided by a robust common sense. . . . " The sum of experience, including that of the past two decades, affords an ample basis for legislatures to conclude that a sensitive, key relationship of human existence, central to family life, community welfare, and the development of human personality, can be debased and distorted by crass commercial exploitation of sex. Nothing in the Constitution prohibits a State from reaching such a conclusion and acting on it legislatively simply because there is no conclusive evidence or empirical data.

It is argued that individual "free will" must govern, even in activities beyond the protection of the First Amendment and other constitutional guarantees of privacy, and that government cannot legitimately impede an individual's desire to see or acquire obscene plays, movies, and books. We do indeed base our society on certain assumptions that people have the capacity for free choice. Most exercises of individual free choice—those in politics, religion, and expression of ideas—are explicitly protected by the Constitution. Totally unlimited play for free will, however, is not allowed in our or any other society. We have just noted, for example, that neither the First Amendment nor "free will" precludes States from having "blue sky" laws to regulate what sellers of securities may write or publish about their wares.

Such laws are to protect the weak, the uninformed, the unsuspecting, and the gullible from the exercise of their own volition. Nor do modern societies leave disposal of garbage and sewage up to the individual "free will," but impose regulation to protect both public health and the appearance of public places. States are told by some that they must await a "laissez-faire" market solution to the obscenity-pornography problem, paradoxically "by people who have never otherwise had a kind word to say for laissez-faire," particularly in solving urban, commercial, and environmental pollution problems.

The States, of course, may follow such a "laissez-faire" policy and drop all controls on commercialized obscenity, if that is what they prefer, just as they can ignore consumer protection in the marketplace, but nothing in the Constitution *compels* the States to do so with regard to matters falling within state jurisdiction.

It is asserted, however, that standards for evaluating state commercial regulations are inapposite in the present context, as state regulation of access by consenting adults to obscene material violates the constitutionally protected right to privacy enjoyed by petitioners' customers. Even assuming that petitioners have vicarious standing to assert potential customers' rights, it is unavailing to compare a theater open to the public for a fee, with the private home of *Stanley* v. *Georgia,* and the marital bedroom of *Griswold* v. *Connecticut.* This Court, has, on numerous occasions, refused to hold that commercial ventures such as a motion-picture house are "private" for the purpose of civil rights litigation and civil rights statutes. The Civil Rights Act of 1964 specifically defines motion-picture houses and theaters as places of "public accommodation" covered by the Act as operations affecting commerce.

Our prior decisions recognizing a right to privacy guaranteed by the Fourteenth Amendment included "only personal rights that can be deemed 'fundamental' or 'implicit in the concept of ordered liberty.'" This privacy right encompasses and protects the personal intimacies of the home, the family, marriage, motherhood, procreation, and child rearing. Nothing, however, in this Court's decisions intimates that there is any "fundamental" privacy right "implicit in the concept of ordered liberty" to watch obscene movies in places of public accommodation.

If obscene material unprotected by the First Amendment in itself carried with it a "penumbra" of constitutionally protected privacy, this Court would not have found it necessary to decide *Stanley* on the narrow basis of the "privacy of the home," which was hardly more than a reaffirmation that "a man's home is his castle." Moreover, we have declined to equate the privacy of the home relied on in *Stanley* with a "zone" of "privacy" that follows a distributor or a consumer of obscene materials wherever he goes. The idea of a "privacy" right and a place of public accommodation are, in this context, mutually exclusive. Conduct or depictions of conduct that the state police power can prohibit on a public street do not become automatically protected by the Constitution merely because the conduct is moved to a bar or a "live" theater stage, any more than a "live" performance of a man and woman locked in a sexual embrace at high noon in Times Square is protected by the Constitution because they simultaneously engage in a valid political dialogue.

It is also argued that the State has no legitimate interest in "control [of] the moral content of a person's thoughts," and we need not quarrel with this. But we reject the claim that the State of Georgia is here attempting to control the minds or thoughts of those who patronize theaters. Preventing unlimited display or distribution of obscene material, which by definition lacks any serious literary, artistic, political, or scientific value as communication, is distinct from a control of reason and the intellect. Where communication of ideas, protected by the First Amendment, is not involved, or the particular privacy of the home protected by *Stanley,* or any of the other "areas or zones" of constitutionally protected privacy, the mere fact that, as a consequence, some human "utterances" or "thoughts" may be incidentally affected does not bar the State from acting to protect legitimate state interests. The fantasies of a drug addict are his own and beyond the reach of government, but government regulation of drug sales is not prohibited by the Constitution.

Finally, petitioners argue that conduct which directly involves "consenting adults" only has, for that sole reason, a special claim to constitutional protection. Our Constitution establishes a broad range of conditions on the exercise of power by the States, but for us to say that our Constitution incorporates the proposition that conduct involving consenting adults only is always beyond state regulation, is a step we are unable to take. Commercial exploitation of depictions, descriptions, or exhibitions of obscene conduct on commercial premises open to the adult public falls within a State's broad power to regulate commerce and protect the public environment. The issue in this context goes beyond whether someone, or even the majority, considers the conduct depicted as "wrong" or "sinful." The States have the power to make a morally neutral judgment that public exhibition of obscene material, or commerce in such material, has a tendency to injure the community as a whole, to endanger the public safety, or to jeopardize, in Mr. Chief Justice Warren's words, the States' "right . . . to maintain a decent society." . . .

Mr. Justice Douglas, dissenting. . . .

. . . Art and literature reflect tastes; and tastes, like musical appreciation, are hardly reducible to precise definitions. That is one reason I have always felt that "obscenity" was not an exception to the First Amendment. For matters of taste, like matters of belief, turn on the idiosyncrasies of individuals. They are too personal to define and too emotional and vague to apply, as witness the prison term for Ralph Ginzburg, not for what he printed but for the sexy manner in which he advertised his creations.

The other reason I could not bring myself to conclude that "obscenity" was not covered by the First Amendment was that prior to the adoption of our Constitution and Bill of Rights the Colonies had no law excluding "obscenity" from the regime of freedom of expression and press that then existed. I could find no such laws; and more important, our leading colonial expert, Julius Goebel, could find none. So I became convinced that the creation of the "obscenity" exception to the First Amendment was a legislative and judicial *tour de force;* that if we were to have such a regime of censorship and punishment, it should be done by constitutional amendment.

People are, of course, offended by many offerings made by merchants in this area. They are also offended by political pronouncements, sociological themes, and by stories of official misconduct. The list of activities and publications and pronouncements that offend someone is endless. Some of it goes on in private; some of it is inescapably public, as when a government official generates crime, becomes a blatant offender of the moral sensibilities of the people, engages in burglary, or breaches the privacy of the telephone, the conference room, or the home. Life in this crowded modern technological world creates many offensive statements and many offensive deeds. There is no protection against offensive ideas, only against offensive conduct.

"Obscenity" at most is the expression of offensive ideas. There are regimes in the world where ideas "offensive" to the majority (or at least to those who control the majority) are suppressed. There life proceeds at a monotonous pace. Most of us would find that world offensive. One of the most offensive experiences of my life was a visit to a nation where bookstalls were filled only with books on mathematics and books on religion.

I am sure I would find offensive most of the books and movies charged with being obscene. But in a life that has not been short, I have yet to be trapped into seeing or reading something that would offend me. I never read or see the materials coming to the Court under charges of "obscenity," because I have thought the First Amendment made it unconstitutional for me to act as a censor. I see ads in bookstores and neon lights over theaters that resemble bait for those who seek vicarious exhilaration. As a parent or a priest or as a teacher I would have no compunction in edging my children or wards away from the books and movies that did no more than excite man's base instincts. But I never supposed that government was permitted to sit in judgment on one's tastes or beliefs—save as they involved action within the reach of the police power of government. . . .

When man was first in the jungle he took care of himself. When he entered a societal group, controls were necessarily imposed. But our society—unlike most in the world—presupposes that freedom and liberty are in a frame of reference that makes the individual, not government, the keeper of his tastes, beliefs, and ideas. That is the philosophy of the First Amendment; and it is the article of faith that sets us apart from most nations in the world. . . .

The Question of Harm

(Source: from the United States Attorney General's Commission on Pornography, Attorney General's Commission on Pornography: Final Report *[Washington: U.S. Department of Justice, 1986].)*

QUESTIONS FOR REFLECTION

1. In answering the question "What is a harm?" the commission distinguishes primary from secondary harm. Explain this distinction. What, according to the commission, is its moral significance?

2. Why does the commission believe that sexually violent material is harmful?

3. The commission holds that nonviolent but degrading material is also harmful. What is "degrading" material? Why is it harmful?

4. What is the commission's opinion of nonviolent, nondegrading pornography? Is it harmful in any way? Should the government attempt to restrict access to such material, according to the commission? Do you agree?

5. Does the test for obscenity in *Miller* correspond to the distinction the commission makes between harmful and (largely) harmless pornography? If not, how might the test be revised to make it correspond?

5.1.2 What Counts as a Harm?

What is a harm? And why focus on harm at all? We do not wish in referring repeatedly to "harm" to burden ourselves with an unduly narrow conception of harm. To emphasize in different words what we said in the previous section, the scope of identifiable harms is broader than the scope of that with which government can or should deal. We refuse to truncate our consideration of the question of harm by defining harms in terms of possible government regulation. And we certainly reject the view that the only noticeable harm is one that causes physical or financial harm to identifiable individuals. An environment, physical, cultural, moral, or aesthetic, can be harmed, and so can a community, organization, or group be harmed independent of identifiable harms to members of that community.

Most importantly, although we have emphasized in our discussion of harms the kinds of harms that can most easily be observed and measured, the idea of harm is broader than that. To a number of us, the most important harms must be seen in moral terms, and the act of moral condemnation of that which is immoral is not merely important but essential. From this perspective there are acts that need be seen not only as causes of immorality but as manifestations of it. Issues of human dignity and human decency, no less real for their lack of scientific measurability, are for many of us central to thinking about the question of harm. And when we think about harm in this way, there are acts that must be condemned not because the evils of the world will thereby be eliminated, but because conscience demands it.

We believe it useful in thinking about harms to note the distinction between harm and offense.

Although the line between the two is hardly clear, most people can nevertheless imagine things that offend them, or offend others, that still would be hard to describe as harms. . . .

In thinking about harms, it is useful to draw a rough distinction between primary and secondary harms. Primary harms are those in which the alleged harm is commonly taken to be intrinsically harmful, even though the precise way in which the harm is harmful might yet be further explored. Nevertheless, murder, rape, assault, and discrimination on the basis of race and gender are all examples of primary harms in this sense. We treat these acts as harms not because of where they will lead, but simply because of what they are.

In other instances, however, the alleged harm is secondary, not in the sense that it is in any way less important, but in the sense that the concern is not with what the act *is,* but where it will lead. Curfews are occasionally imposed not because there is anything wrong with people being out at night, but because in some circumstances it is thought that being out at night in large groups may cause people to commit other crimes. Possession of "burglar tools" is often prohibited because of what those tools may be used for. Thus, when it is urged that pornography is harmful because it causes some people to commit acts of sexual violence, because it causes promiscuity, because it encourages sexual relations outside of marriage, because it promotes so-called "unnatural" sexual practices, or because it leads men to treat women as existing solely for the sexual satisfaction of men, the alleged harms are secondary, again not in any sense suggesting that the harms are less important. The harms are secondary here because the allegation of harm presupposes a causal link between the act and the harm, a causal link that is superfluous if, as in the case of primary harms, the act quite simply *is* the harm.

Thus we think it important, with respect to every area of possible harm, to focus on whether the allegation relates to a harm that comes from the sexually explicit material itself, or whether it occurs *as a result* of something the material does. If it is the former, then the inquiry can focus directly on the nature of the alleged harm. But if it is the latter, then there must be a two-step inquiry. First it is necessary to determine if some hypothesized result is in fact

harmful. In some cases, where the asserted consequent harm is unquestionably a harm, this step of the analysis is easy. With respect to claims that certain sexually explicit material increases the incidence of rape or other sexual violence, for example, no one could plausibly claim that such consequences were not harmful, and the inquiry can then turn to whether the causal link exists. In other cases, however, the harmfulness of the alleged harm is often debated. With respect to claims, for example, that some sexually explicit material causes promiscuity, encourages homosexuality, or legitimizes sexual practices other than vaginal intercourse, there is serious societal debate about whether the consequences themselves are harmful.

Thus, the analysis of the hypothesis that pornography causes harm must start with the identification of hypothesized harms, proceed to the determination of whether those hypothesized harms are indeed harmful, and then conclude with the examination of whether a causal link exists between the material and the harm. When the consequences of exposure to sexually explicit material are not harmful, or when there is no causal relationship between exposure to sexually explicit material and some harmful consequence, then we cannot say that the sexually explicit material is harmful. But if sexually explicit material of some variety is causally related to, or increases the incidence of, some behavior that *is* harmful, then it is safe to conclude that the material is harmful. . . .

5.2.1 Sexually Violent Material

The category of material on which most of the evidence has focused is the category of material featuring actual or unmistakably simulated or unmistakably threatened violence presented in sexually explicit fashion with a predominant focus on the sexually explicit violence. Increasingly, the most prevalent forms of pornography, as well as an increasingly prevalent body of less sexually explicit material, fit this description. Some of this material involves sado-masochistic themes, with the standard accoutrements of the genre, including whips, chains, devices of torture, and so on. But another theme of some of this material is not sado-masochistic, but involves instead the recurrent theme of a man making some sort of sexual advance to a woman, being rebuffed, and then raping the woman or in some other way violently forcing himself on the woman. In almost all of this material, whether in magazine or motion picture form, the woman eventually becomes aroused and ecstatic about the initially forced sexual activity, and usually is portrayed as begging for more. There is also a large body of material, more "mainstream" in its availability, that portrays sexual activity or sexually suggestive nudity coupled with extreme violence, such as disfigurement or murder. The so-called "slasher" films fit this description, as does some material, both in films and in magazines, that is less or more sexually explicit than the prototypical "slasher" film. . . .

When clinical and experimental research has focused particularly on sexually violent material, the conclusions have been virtually unanimous. In both clinical and experimental settings, exposure to sexually violent materials has indicated an increase in the likelihood of aggression. More specifically, the research . . . shows a causal relationship between exposure to material of this type and aggressive behavior towards women.

Finding a link between aggressive behavior towards women and sexual violence, whether lawful or unlawful, requires assumptions not found exclusively in the experimental evidence. We see no reason, however, not to make these assumptions. The assumption that increased aggressive behavior towards women is causally related, for an aggregate population, to increased sexual violence is significantly supported by the clinical evidence, as well as by much of the less scientific evidence. They are also to all of us assumptions that are plainly justified by our own common sense. This is not to say that all people with heightened levels of aggression will commit acts of sexual violence. But it is to say that over a sufficiently large number of cases we are confident in asserting that an increase in aggressive behavior directed at women will cause an increase in the level of sexual violence directed at women.

Thus we reach our conclusions by combining the results of the research with highly justifiable assumptions about the generalizability of more limited research results. Since the clinical and experi-

mental evidence supports the conclusion that there is a causal relationship between exposure to sexually violent materials and an increase in aggressive behavior directed towards women, and since we believe that an increase in aggressive behavior towards women will in a population increase the incidence of sexual violence in that population, we have reached the conclusion, unanimously and confidently, that the available evidence strongly supports the hypothesis that substantial exposure to sexually violent materials as described here bears a causal relationship to antisocial acts of sexual violence and, for some subgroups, possibly to unlawful acts of sexual violence.

Although we rely for this conclusion on significant scientific empirical evidence, we feel it worthwhile to note the underlying logic of the conclusion. The evidence says simply that the images that people are exposed to bears a causal relationship to their behavior. This is hardly surprising. What would be surprising would be to find otherwise, and we have not so found. We have not, of course, found that the images people are exposed to are a greater cause of sexual violence than all or even many other possible causes the investigation of which has been beyond our mandate. Nevertheless, it would be strange indeed if graphic representations of a form of behavior, especially in a form that almost exclusively portrays such behavior as desirable, did not have at least some effect on patterns of behavior.

Sexual violence is not the only negative effect reported in the research to result from substantial exposure to sexually violent materials. The evidence is also strongly supportive of significant attitudinal changes on the part of those with substantial exposure to violent pornography. These attitudinal changes are numerous. Victims of rape and other forms of sexual violence are likely to be perceived by people so exposed as more responsible for the assault, as having suffered less injury, and as having been less degraded as a result of the experience. Similarly, people with a substantial exposure to violent pornography are likely to see the rapist or other sexual offender as less responsible for the act and as deserving of less stringent punishment.

These attitudinal changes have been shown experimentally to include a larger range of attitudes than those just discussed. The evidence also strongly supports the conclusion that substantial exposure to violent sexually explicit material leads to a greater acceptance of the "rape myth" in its broader sense— that women enjoy being coerced into sexual activity, that they enjoy being physically hurt in sexual context, and that as a result a man who forces himself on a woman sexually is in fact merely acceding to the "real" wishes of the woman, regardless of the extent to which she seems to be resisting. The myth is that a woman who says "no" really means "yes," and that men are justified in acting on the assumption that the "no" answer is indeed the "yes" answer. We have little trouble concluding that this attitude is both pervasive and profoundly harmful, and that any stimulus reinforcing or increasing the incidence of this attitude is for that reason alone properly designated as harmful.

Two vitally important features of the evidence supporting the above conclusions must be mentioned here. The first is that all of the harms discussed here, including acceptance of the legitimacy of sexual violence against women but not limited to it, are more pronounced when the sexually violent materials depict the woman as experiencing arousal, orgasm, or other form of enjoyment as the ultimate result of the sexual assault. This theme, unfortunately very common in the materials we have examined, is likely to be the major, albeit not the only, component of what it is in the materials in this category that causes the consequences that have been identified.

The second important clarification of all of the above is that the evidence lends some support to the conclusion that the consequences we have identified here *do not vary with the extent of sexual explicitness so long as the violence is presented in an undeniably sexual context.* Once a threshold is passed at which sex and violence are plainly linked, increasing the sexual explicitness of the material, or the bizarreness of the sexual activity, seems to bear little relationship to the extent of the consequences discussed here. Although it is unclear whether sexually violent material makes a substantially greater causal contribution to sexual violence itself than does material containing violence alone, it appears that increasing the amount of violence after the threshold of connecting sex with violence is more related to increase in the incidence or severity of

harmful consequences than is increasing the amount of sex. As a result, the so-called "slasher" films, which depict a great deal of violence connected with an undeniably sexual theme but less sexual explicitness than materials that are truly pornographic, are likely to produce the consequences discussed here to a greater extent than most of the materials available in "adults only" pornographic outlets.

Although we have based our findings about material in this category primarily on evidence presented by professionals in the behavioral sciences, we are confident that it is supported by the less scientific evidence we have consulted, and we are each personally confident on the basis of our own knowledge and experiences that the conclusions are justified. None of us has the least doubt that sexual violence is harmful, and that general acceptance of the view that "no" means "yes" is a consequence of the most serious proportions. We have found a causal relationship between sexually explicit materials featuring violence and these consequences, and thus conclude that the class of such materials, although not necessarily every individual member of that class, is on the whole harmful to society.

5.2.2 Nonviolent Materials Depicting Degradation, Domination, Subordination, or Humiliation

Current research has rather consistently separated out violent pornography, the class of materials we have just discussed, from other sexually explicit materials. With respect to further subdivision the process has been less consistent. A few researchers have made further distinctions, while most have merely classed everything else as "non-violent." We have concluded that more subdivision than that is necessary. Our examination of the variety of sexually explicit materials convinces us that once again the category of "non-violent" ignores significant distinctions within this category, and thus combines classes of material that are in fact substantially different.

The subdivision we adopt is one that has surfaced in some of the research. And it is also one that might explain a significant amount of what would otherwise seem to be conflicting research results. Some researchers have found negative effects from non-violent material, while others report no such negative effects. But when the stimulus material these researchers have used is considered, there is some suggestion that the presence or absence of negative effects from non-violent material might turn on the non-violent material being considered "degrading," a term we shall explain shortly. It appears that effects similar to although not as extensive as that involved with violent material can be identified with respect to such degrading material, but that these effects are likely absent when neither degradation nor violence is present.

An enormous amount of the most sexually explicit material available, as well as much of the material that is somewhat less sexually explicit, is material that we would characterize as "degrading," the term we use to encompass the undeniably linked characteristics of degradation, domination, subordination, and humiliation. The degradation we refer to is degradation of people, most often women, and here we are referring to material that, although not violent, depicts people, usually women, as existing solely for the sexual satisfaction of others, usually men, or that depicts people, usually women, in decidedly subordinate roles in their sexual relations with others, or that depicts people engaged in sexual practices that would to most people be considered humiliating. Indeed, forms of degradation represent the largely predominant proportion of commercially available pornography.

With respect to material of this variety, our conclusions are substantially similar to those with respect to violent material, although we make them with somewhat less confidence and our making of them requires more in the way of assumption than was the case with respect to violent material. The evidence, scientific and otherwise, is more tentative, but supports the conclusion that the material we describe as degrading bears some causal relationship to the attitudinal changes we have previously identified. That is, substantial exposure to material of this variety is likely to increase the extent to which those exposed will view rape or other forms of sexual violence as less serious than they otherwise would have, will view the victim of rape and

other forms of sexual violence as significantly more responsible, and will view the offenders as significantly less responsible. We also conclude that the evidence supports the conclusion that substantial exposure to material of this type will increase acceptance of the proposition that women like to be forced into sexual practices, and, once again, that the woman who says "no" really means "yes."

With respect to material of this type, there is less evidence causally linking the material with sexual aggression, but this may be because this is a category that has been isolated in only a few studies, albeit an increasing number. The absence of evidence should by no means be taken to deny the existence of the causal link. But because the causal link is less the subject of experimental studies, we have been required to think more carefully here about the assumptions necessary to causally connect increased acceptance of rape myths and other attitudinal changes with increased sexual aggression and sexual violence. And on the basis of all the evidence we have considered, from all sources, and on the basis of our own insights and experiences, we believe we are justified in drawing the following conclusion: Over a large enough sample a population that believes that many women like to be raped, that believes that sexual violence or sexual coercion is often desired or appropriate, and that believes that sex offenders are less responsible for their acts, will commit more acts of sexual violence or sexual coercion than would a population holding these beliefs to a lesser extent.

We should make clear what we have concluded here. We are not saying that everyone exposed to material of this type had his attitude about sexual violence changed. We are saying only that the evidence supports the conclusion that substantial exposure to degrading material increases the likelihood for an individual and the incidence over a large population that these attitudinal changes will occur. And we are not saying that everyone with these attitudes will commit an act of sexual violence or sexual coercion. We are saying that such attitudes will increase the likelihood for an individual and the incidence for a population that acts of sexual violence, sexual coercion, or unwanted sexual aggression will occur. Thus, we conclude that substantial exposure to materials of this type bears some causal relationship to the level of sexual violence, sexual coercion, or unwanted sexual aggression in the population so exposed.

We need mention as well that our focus on these more violent or more coercive forms of actual subordination of women should not diminish what we take to be a necessarily incorporated conclusion: Substantial exposure to materials of this type bears some causal relationship to the incidence of various non-violent forms of discrimination against or subordination of women in our society. To the extent that these materials create or reinforce the view that women's function is disproportionately to satisfy the sexual needs of men, then the materials will have pervasive effects on the treatment of women in society far beyond the incidence of identifiable acts of rape or other sexual violence. We obviously cannot here explore fully all of the forms in which women are discriminated against in contemporary society. Nor can we explore all of the causes of that discrimination against women. But we feel confident in concluding that the view of women as available for sexual domination is one cause of that discrimination, and we feel confident as well in concluding that degrading material bears a causal relationship to the view that women ought to subordinate their own desires and beings to the sexual satisfaction of men.

Although the category of the degrading is one that has only recently been isolated in some research, in the literature generally, and in public discussion of the issue, it is not a small category. If anything, it constitutes somewhere between the predominant and the overwhelming portion of what is currently standard fare heterosexual pornography, and is a significant theme in a broader range of materials not commonly taken to be sexually explicit enough to be pornographic. But as with sexually violent materials, the extent of the effect of these degrading materials may not turn substantially on the amount of sexual explicitness once a threshold of undeniable sexual content is surpassed. The category therefore includes a great deal of what would now be considered to be pornographic, and includes a great deal of what would now be held to be legally obscene, but it includes much more than that. Since we are here identifying harms for a class, rather than identifying harms caused by every member of that class, and since we are here

talking about the identification of harm rather than making recommendations for legal control, we are not reluctant to identify harms for a class of material considerably wider than what is or even should be regulated by law.

5.2.3 Non-Violent and Non-Degrading Materials

Our most controversial category has been the category of sexually explicit materials that are not violent and are not degrading as we have used that term. They are materials in which the participants appear to be fully willing participants occupying substantially equal roles in a setting devoid of actual or apparent violence or pain. This category is in fact quite small in terms of currently available materials. There is some, to be sure, and the amount may increase as the division between the degrading and the non-degrading becomes more accepted, but we are convinced that only a small amount of currently available highly sexually explicit material is neither violent nor degrading. We thus talk about a small category, but one that should not be ignored. . . .

. . . Although the social science evidence is far from conclusive, we are on the current state of the evidence persuaded that material of this type does not bear a causal relationship to rape and other acts of sexual violence. . . .

A larger issue is the very question of promiscuity. Even to the extent that the behavior depicted is not inherently condemned by some or any of us, the manner of presentation almost necessarily suggests that the activities are taking place outside of the context of marriage, love, commitment, or even affection. Again, it is far from implausible to hypothesize that materials depicting sexual activity without marriage, love, commitment, or affection bear some causal relationship to sexual activity without marriage, love, commitment, or affection. There are undoubtedly many causes for what used to be called the "sexual revolution," but it is absurd to suppose that depictions or descriptions of uncommitted sexuality were not among them. Thus, once again our disagreements reflect disagreements in society at large, although not to as great an extent. Although there are many members of this society who can and have made affirmative cases for uncommitted sexuality, none of us believes it to be a good thing. A number of us, however, believe that the level of commitment in sexuality is a matter of choice among those who voluntarily engage in the activity. Others of us believe that uncommitted sexual activity is wrong for the individuals involved and harmful to society to the extent of its prevalence. Our view of the ultimate harmfulness of much of this material, therefore, is reflective of our individual views about the extent to whether sexual commitment is purely a matter of individual choice.

Even insofar as sexually explicit material of the variety being discussed here is not perceived as harmful for the messages it carries or the symbols it represents, the very publicness of what is commonly taken to be private is cause for concern. Even if we hypothesize a sexually explicit motion picture of a loving married couple engaged in mutually pleasurable and procreative vaginal intercourse, the depiction of that act on a screen or in a magazine may constitute a harm in its own right (a "primary harm" in the terminology introduced earlier in this Chapter) solely by virtue of being shown. Here the concern is with the preservation of sex as an essentially private act, in conformity with the basic privateness of sex long recognized by this and all other societies. The alleged harm here, therefore, is that as soon as sex is put on a screen or put in a magazine it changes its character, regardless of what variety of sex is portrayed. And to the extent that the character of sex as public rather than private is the consequence here, then that to many would constitute a harm. . . .

A number of witnesses have testified about the effects on their own sexual relations, usually with their spouses, of the depiction on the screen and in magazines of sexual practices in which they had not previously engaged. A number of these witnesses, *all women,* have testified that men in their lives have used such material to strongly encourage, or coerce, them into engaging in sexual practices in which they do not choose to engage. To the extent that such implicit or explicit coercion takes place as a result of these materials, we all agree that it is a harm. There has been other evidence, however, about the extent to which such material might for some be a way of revitalizing their sex lives, or, more commonly, simply constituting a part of a mutually pleasurable sexual experience for both partners. On this we could not agree. For reasons relating largely to the question of publicness in the first sense discussed above, some saw this kind of use as primarily harmful. Others saw it as harmless and possibly beneficial in contexts such as this. Some professional testimony supported this latter view, but we have little doubt that professional opinion is also divided on the issue. . . .

JEFF ROSEN

"Miller" Time

Jeff Rosen is a journalist and law student at Yale University. (Source: Reprinted by permission of The New Republic, *October 1, 1990, pp. 17–19. Copyright © 1990 by the New Republic, Inc.*)

QUESTIONS FOR REFLECTION

1. How, according to the *Miller* test, should art be distinguished from obscenity? To what extent does the test require jurors, judges, and police officers to make aesthetic judgments about art?

2. Rosen plainly despairs of devising any test for determining whether a work has serious artistic value. What is the rationale for his despair? Do you share it?

3. How might the *Miller* test be revised so that tests of artistic seriousness are unnecessary?

4. Rosen makes several arguments for overturning *Miller* that are independent of his worries about judging serious artistic value. What are they? Do you find them convincing?

This fall a Cincinnati curator is facing a federal judge for having displayed the photographs of Robert Mapplethorpe. Luther Campbell of 2 Live Crew will appeal his Florida conviction for having produced *As Nasty As They Wanna Be*. And Karen Finley may challenge her grant denial from the National Endowment for the Arts. All three will use the Supreme Court's obscenity test to defend their work as "serious" art. But in a perverse betrayal of its purpose, the Supreme Court's test, properly applied, may threaten naughty artists more than it protects them.

When the test was announced in *Miller* v. *California* in 1973, it promised to distinguish art from obscenity by protecting sexually explicit work that had "serious" artistic value. (The more lenient previous test said obscenity had to be "utterly without redeeming social value.") But over the years, art has become more sexually explicit, the line between high art and low has been increasingly blurred, and artists have come to question the idea of artistic "seriousness." Now the *Miller* test measures art by a standard that many artists are unwilling to meet and that jurors are unable to identify. For different reasons, unlikely allies such as William Brennan, Antonin Scalia, and movie czar Jack Valenti agree that it's time to take aesthetic decisions out of the courtrooms.

In *Miller* the Court said that judges and juries should ask themselves three questions when attempting to distinguish between art and obscenity: first, "whether 'the average person, applying contemporary community standards' would find that the work, taken as a whole, appeals to the prurient interest"; second, "whether the work depicts or describes, in a patently offensive way, sexual conduct specifically defined by the applicable state law"; and, third, "whether the work, taken as a whole, lacks serious literary, artistic, political, or scientific value." If the answer to all three questions is yes, then the work can be banned; if not, then the work must be protected.

From the moment it was conceived, the test seemed ambiguous. "To be prurient and offensive, a work has to turn you on and gross you out at the same time," says Kathleen Sullivan of Harvard Law School. But during the 1980s the ambiguous test became unintelligible as changes in art and law eliminated "serious" artistic values as a viable distinction between art and obscenity. First, artistic goals changed. As Amy Adler argues in a student note in a recent issue of *The Yale Law Journal,* postmodernism rebelled against the modernist demand that art should be "serious," or that it should have any traditional "value" at all. "Bad" painters like David Salle juxtaposed images from art history and pornography. Sculptors like Jeff Koons created what *New York Times* critic Michael Brenson called "art that looks like trash and trashes high art," including a porcelain bust of Italian porn star Cicciolina. And rappers like 2 Live Crew mixed scatology with Muddy Waters. As a result, the *Miller* test has come to evaluate postmodern art by the very standard that postmodern art seeks to defy.

Second, the *Miller* test itself changed. Three years ago, in *Pope* v. *Illinois,* the Supreme Court decided that courts should ask whether a "reasonable person" would find serious value in the suspect art. It is hard to imagine a more philistine and less appropriate test for artistic value than the aesthetic sensibility of the "reasonable person." Reasonable people attacked Manet's *Déjeuner Sur L'Herbe* and Beethoven's "Ode to Joy" as indecent. And reasonable people are even less likely to find serious value in artists like Mapplethorpe and Finley, who go out of their way to offend reasonable tastes. When the "reasonable person" standard was announced, liberals like Brennan cringed at the bewildering union of law and aesthetics. But they were joined by the conservative Scalia, who is wary of judicial subjectivity wherever it occurs. "[I]t is quite impossible," wrote Scalia, "to come to an objective assessment of (at least) literary or artistic value. . . . Since ratiocination has little to do with esthetics, the fabled 'reasonable man' is of little help in the inquiry. . . . For the law courts to decide 'What is Beauty' is novelty even by today's standards."

The changes in art and law left artists vulnerable to prosecution when local authorities decided to crack down in 1990. As a result, the artists who face federal judges this fall have no way of predicting with confidence whether they have broken the law. To appreciate their predicament, pretend you are a juror at an obscenity trial and try to apply the *Miller* test to the work of Mapplethorpe, 2 Live Crew, and Finley.

Start with Mapplethorpe's photograph of the man with the bullwhip up his ass. Would an average person in our community find that it appeals to the prurient interest? The Supreme Court complicates matters by defining "prurient" not only as "material having a tendency to excite lustful thoughts," but also as material that shows a "shameful or morbid interest in nudity, sex, or excretion." An expert witness may be helpful. "The male genitals are often presented . . . as surrogates for the face," write the poet Richard Howard in a tribute to Mapplethorpe. Sounds like an interest in nudity, which might even be shameful, depending on what your neighbors are used to. Is the simulation of sodomy patently offensive? Again, your community is the judge. As for the third criterion, wouldn't someone like Dennis Barrie, the director of the Contemporary Arts Center of Cincinnati, know "serious" artistic value when he sees it? Other art experts, though, doubt Mapplethorpe's seriousness. Robert Hughes calls Mapplethorpe an "overrated photographer." And Hilton Kramer of *The New Criterion* detects no serious artistic value. "Are these disputed pictures works of art?" Kramer asks. "Alas, I suppose they are," but they do not "belong to the highest levels of art." Who is a more reasonable person, Barrie or Kramer? Would a reasonable person find either of them reasonable?

Now try the same exercise with 2 Live Crew. Assume, as Judge Jose A. Gonzalez did, that *As Nasty As They Wanna Be* appeals to lustful thoughts (it doesn't; it's boring), and that it is patently offensive in some parts of Florida (Gonzalez justified his knowledge of community standards by noting that he had "attended public functions and events" throughout the community). Scholars and journalists have been properly ridiculed for defending 2 Live Crew by exaggerating their artistic, literary, even scientific seriousness. . . . But the legal test requires no less, refusing to protect pop culture unless it masquerades as high culture.

It is hard to conclude, as Gonzalez did (using the wrong test), that *Nasty* is "utterly without any redeeming social value." You don't have to compare the rappers' braggadocio in the call and response form to duets from Wagner's Siegfried ("The boy is fearless and his sword is sharp") to recognize that boasting about sex in rhyme is part of the black oral tradition. If dirty rap can be banned, suggests Bruce Jackson, an English professor at the State University of New York at Buffalo, then so can hundreds of equally filthy verses dating back to the nineteenth century. And a quick skim of his anthology of black narrative poetry, *Get Your Ass in the Water and Swim Like Me,* proves the point.

But if a nineteenth-century pedigree suggests that scatology in rhyme may have *some* literary or artistic value, how is anyone, reasonable or not, to decide whether the value is "serious"? In a relativistic age, that is a judgment that even the defenders of rap are reluctant to make. To complicate matters, black culture, from novels to jazz, has long rejected the distinction between popular art and serious art. Gonzalez's analysis is embarrassing ("Obscenity? Yes!" his opinion shrieked), but 2 Live Crew leaves the *Miller* test at a loss.

Finally, consider a performance artist like Finley, whose angry, scatological feminism is intended to be *anti*-pornographic. "If a woman can't talk about rape or sexual violence in the language she was abused in," Finley said in 1988, "it's against our First Amendment rights." But it may not be if our First Amendment rights are defined by *Miller.* Prurient interest? Finley says, "There's nothing sexually exciting about my work"; but remember that prurient also means "a shameful or morbid interest in nudity, sex, or excretion." That, suggests Adler, sounds like an apt description of Finley's oeuvre, as she smears food into her genitals, defecates onstage, and describes graphic sex acts with priests and the handicapped. Patently offensive? That's Finley's goal. Which leaves "serious artistic value" as the only way of distinguishing Finley from the pornography she abhors. But performance art was designed to mock the idea of artistic seriousness. "This is work that sends up the notion of art taking itself seriously," says Barbara Tsumagari, executive director of the Kitchen, a performance space in New York where Finley has performed. Does that effort itself have

serious artistic value? "It's a very postmodern question. We need a postmodern test," says Tsumagari.

Until we get one, sexually explicit artists will continue to be suppressed. But that can't be constitutional if the First Amendment protects self-expression regardless of its political value, as the Supreme Court has repeatedly held. In other words, if art can't be cleanly distinguished from obscenity, as more than thirty years of failed Supreme Court tests make clear, then private consumption of obscenity must be endured so that art can be protected.

Justices Brennan and Scalia, who rarely agreed on anything, have said that the *Miller* test should be reconsidered, although they disagree about appropriate alternatives. In a little noticed concurrence last January, Scalia suggested that courts should focus on the intention of the distributors, rather than on the intention of the creators, of sexually explicit material. He would prohibit communities from suppressing particular books or films, but would allow them to close down adult bookstores and theaters that specialize in pandering sex for profit. Scalia's solution has the clear advantage of taking the courts out of aesthetics and guaranteeing that individual works of literature or art (or pornography for that matter) could never be banned in America again. At the same time, Scalia would allow communities to reduce access to soft-core porn, which is constitutionally protected, as well as hardcore porn, which is not. But Mapplethorpe, Campbell, and Finley would be safe.

Justice Brennan's alternative—no obscenity test at all—fell one vote short of a Supreme Court majority in 1973 and is likely to fall shorter today. But it remains the solution of choice for First Amendment absolutists, and it would allow communities to focus their attention on the problem at hand: keeping sexually explicit material away from children and unwilling adults in an increasingly explicit age. Until the *Miller* test exposed itself this year, the most important pornography cases over the past two decades concerned zoning regulations rather than aesthetic decisions. In 1976, and again in 1986, the Supreme Court gave local communities broad discretion to concentrate red light districts or to disperse them in the interest of preserving the "quality of urban life." Liberals like Brennan dissented from the zoning decisions, criticizing them as speech discrimination masquerading as urban renewal. But zoning regulations would seem much less threatening if the states were denied the draconian power to ban obscenity entirely.

In addition to zoning regulations, voluntary self-regulation of movies and records can reduce the need for state regulation. And the recent efforts of Jack Valenti for the Motion Picture Association and Tipper Gore for the Parents' Music Resource Center on behalf of voluntary warning labels have been in precisely the right direction. Valenti has resisted calls for an "A" rating between R and X to distinguish sexually explicit "art" films from soft-core porn. The purpose of ratings, he says, is to warn parents, not to identify art. And he recognizes that ratings boards are no more qualified than judges to specify the mystic point at which an "artistic" portrayal of cannibalism, for example, becomes, for some, obscene.

As for explicit records, 2 Live Crew vindicates Gore as a civil libertarian and a prophet as well. In 1985 she predicted that if liberals didn't embrace voluntary warning labels, "extremists" would resort to bans, which she opposes unequivocally. And her efforts on behalf of voluntary labels helped to preempt legislation requiring labels in twenty-two states.

Reversing *Miller* would also focus the debate over congressional subsidies on aesthetics rather than law. The current debate over reauthorizing the NEA is harping obsessively on the *Miller* test: liberals, having accepted some legal restrictions as inevitable, want to limit them to the language of *Miller;* conservatives want broader restrictions. "I think there is an enormous irony that the artistic community is embracing *Miller* so ardently today," says Floyd Abrams, who is representing the New School in its challenge to NEA chairman John Frohnmayer's loyalty oaths.

The legalistic squabbles, suggests Michael Mc-Connell of Chicago Law School, obscure the distinction between criminalization and refusal to fund. When the NEA is saddled with congressional restrictions, a sensible grant refusal can look like an obscenity charge. By legislating aesthetics, and making heroes out of refuseniks, Congress reduces, rather than enhances, the Endowment's ability to discriminate on the basis of artistic merit. Even if the *Miller* test is not overturned, an NEA reauthorized without *Miller*'s restrictions would have a freer hand to reject art that lacked "serious" value. And artistic value is a more appropriate test for public subsidy than for criminal punishment.

Abandoning *Miller,* finally, would protect our judges from the scourge of pornography. There has been something sordid over the past thirty years about Supreme Court justices peering at skin flicks in the dark basement of the Court. (Justice Harlan, almost blind, asked his clerks to narrate as the action unfolded.) David Souter seems like an ascetic and upright man. For his own sake, he should join Scalia, persuade the liberals, and remove aesthetics from the courts.

Racial Harassment

College campuses across the country have been witnessing an increase in incidents involving racism or other forms of prejudice. The increase has led many colleges and universities to formulate antiharassment codes. Outside the academy, legal scholars have proposed new rules for adjudicating torts—wrongs justifying civil lawsuits—related to racial insults and harassment. Advocates of such policies point to equality and the protection of rights, which have great moral as well as social and legal weight. Critics, however, see restrictions on speech that are difficult to justify.

The freedoms of thought, of speech, and of the press do have well-recognized exceptions. One may not slander another person, incite a mob to riot, or shout "Fire!" in a crowded but fireless theater. In Mill's words, "Acts, of whatever kind, which without justifiable cause do harm to others may be, and in the more important cases absolutely require to be, controlled by the unfavorable sentiments, and, when needful, by the active interference of mankind." In cases of the kinds just mentioned, the harm done to particular people outweighs—by a large margin—any positive value the speech possesses.

Is the same true of racial insults? Like any insult, they cause harm to the insulted. Ordinarily, however, we do not maintain that insults should be grounds for legal action; the harm they cause is not large or important enough. But the specifically racial character of a racial insult makes it especially harmful. Richard Delgado, in "Words That Wound," argues at length that racial insults are harmful enough to justify legal remedies.

Do racial insults have any positive value that might offset harms they cause? Some judges have said that they let people "blow off steam"; otherwise, they seem entirely negative. But two subtler problems arise. First, we cannot easily write off racial insults as having no communicative value at all. Unlike pornography, perhaps, such insults do communicate ideas; that is why they hurt. The ideas communicated may be repugnant, and any assertions communicated may be blatantly false, but ideas and assertions are involved. One can argue that the reasoning of Milton, Tocqueville, and Mill does not apply to pornography, because it communicates nothing, but one cannot advance the same argument about racial harassment. Racial insults belong, perhaps, in Mill's categories of opinions that are obviously false and are expressed in an offensive manner. But Mill thought that such opinions deserved protection nevertheless. Second, weighing harms and positive values is not independent of a definition of harassment. To weigh accurately, we must define racial harassment carefully. A racial epithet has little content; an argument that some racial groups are, on average, more intelligent than others may have a great deal of highly controversial content. The narrower the definition of harassment, in general, the less significant the ideas communicated, and the more likely the harms outweigh them.

The most important court case concerning racial or ethnic harassment is *Collin v. Smith*. It arose when the American Nazi Party asked for a permit to march through Skokie, Illinois, home to many survivors of the Holocaust. The Nazis, with the support of the American Civil Liberties Union, argued that freedom of speech protected their right to march, displaying Nazi uniforms and swastikas, through the Chicago suburb. Skokie refused to grant the permit.

Richard Delgado, a law professor, argues for a new legal rule applying specifically to cases of racial harassment. He points out the substantial harms caused by racial insults and responds to objections that allowing victims of such insults to sue will crimp freedom of speech, generate a flood of frivolous lawsuits, and raise undecidable questions about damages.

Finally, Chester E. Finn, Jr., a professor of education and public policy, discusses cases showing, he thinks, that the cure for racial harassment is worse than the disease. Finn attacks broad definitions of harassment, maintaining that they allow the suppression of legitimate opinion. According to his analysis, antiharassment codes and other campus policies, such as affirmative action, are motivated by a quest for diversity—a goal he alleges, that the policies themselves undermine.

Collin v. Smith (1978)

(*Source:* Collin v. Smith *578 F.2d 1197 [1978]. Most legal references have been omitted.*)

QUESTIONS FOR REFLECTION

1. What were the important provisions of Skokie's ordinances banning the Nazi march? How similar are they to university rules against racist speech?

2. Why does the Court refuse to consider the Nazi march as analogous to "fighting words"? Do you agree with this justification?

3. What is Skokie's fourth argument? Why does the Court reject it? Do you agree?

4. What is Judge Sprecher's basis for dissent? How does Judge Pell respond to the arguments he raises?

PELL, Circuit Judge.

Plaintiff-appellee, the National Socialist Party of America (NSPA) is a political group described by its leader, plaintiff-appellee Frank Collin, as a Nazi party. Among NSPA's more controversial and generally unacceptable beliefs are that black persons are biologically inferior to white persons, and should be expatriated to Africa as soon as possible; that American Jews have "inordinate . . . political and financial power" in the world and are "in the forefront of the international Communist revolution." NSPA members affect a uniform reminiscent of those worn by members of the German Nazi Party during the Third Reich, and display a swastika thereon and on a red, white, and black flag they frequently carry.

The Village of Skokie, Illinois, a defendant-appellant, is a suburb north of Chicago. It has a large Jewish population, including as many as several thousand survivors of the Nazi holocaust in Europe before and during World War II. Other defendants-appellants are Village officials.

When Collin and NSPA announced plans to march in front of the Village Hall in Skokie on May 1, 1977, Village officials responded by obtaining in state court a preliminary injunction against the demonstration. After state courts refused to stay the injunction pending appeal, the United States Supreme Court ordered a stay, *National Socialist Party of America v. Village of Skokie* (1977). The injunction was subsequently reversed first in part, *Village of Skokie v. National Socialist Party of America* (1977), and then in its entirety (1978). On May 2, 1977, the Village enacted three ordinances to prohibit demonstrations such as the one Collin and NSPA had threatened. This lawsuit seeks declaratory and injunctive relief against enforcement of the ordinances.

Village Ordinance No. 77–5–N–994 (hereinafter designated, for convenience of reference, as 994) is a comprehensive permit system for all parades or public assemblies of more than 50 persons. It requires permit applicants to obtain $300,000 in public liability insurance and $50,000 in property damage insurance. One of the prerequisites for a permit is a finding by the appropriate official(s) that the assembly

will not portray criminality, depravity or lack of virtue in, or incite violence, hatred, abuse or hostility toward a person or group of persons by reason of reference to religious, racial, ethnic, national or regional affiliation.

Another is a finding that the permit activity will not be conducted "for an unlawful purpose." None of this ordinance applies to activities by the Village itself or of a governmental agency, and any provision of the ordinance may be waived by unanimous consent of the Board of Trustees of the Village. To parade or assemble without a permit is a crime, punishable by fines from $5 to $500.

Village Ordinance No. 77–5–N–995 (995) prohibits

[t]he dissemination of any materials within the Village of Skokie which promotes and incites hatred against persons by reason of their race, national origin, or religion, and is intended to do so.

"Dissemination of materials" includes

publication or display or distribution of posters, signs, handbills, or writings and public display of markings and clothing of symbolic significance.

Violation is a crime punishable by fine of up to $500, or imprisonment of up to six months. Village Ordinance No. 77–5–N–996 (996) prohibits public demonstrations by members of political parties while wearing "military-style" uniforms, and violation is punishable as in 995.

Collin and NSPA applied for a permit to march on July 4, 1977, which was denied on the ground the application disclosed an intention to violate 996. The Village apparently applies 994 so that an intention to violate 995 or 996 establishes an "unlawful purpose" for the march or assembly. The permit application stated that the march would last about a half hour, and would involve 30 to 50 demonstrators wearing uniforms including swastikas and carrying a party banner with a swastika and placards with statements thereon such as "White Free Speech," "Free Speech for the White Man," and "Free Speech for White America." A single file sidewalk march that would not disrupt traffic was proposed, without speeches or the distribution of handbills or literature. Counsel for the Village advises us that the Village does not maintain that Collin and NSPA will behave other than as described in the permit application(s).

The district court, after considering memoranda, exhibits, depositions, and live testimony, issued a comprehensive and thorough opinion granting re-

relief to Collin and NSPA. The insurance requirements of 994 were invalidated as insuperable obstacles to free speech in Skokie, and [other sections] were adjudged impermissible prior restraints. Ordinance 995 was determined to be fatally vague and overbroad, and 996 was invalidated as overbroad and patently unjustified.

On its appeal, the Village concedes the invalidity of the insurance requirements as applied to these plaintiffs and of the uniform prohibition of 996.

I

The conflict underlying this litigation has commanded substantial public attention, and engendered considerable and understandable emotion. We would hopefully surprise no one by confessing personal views that NSPA's beliefs and goals are repugnant to the core values held generally by residents of this country, and, indeed, to much of what we cherish in civilization. As judges sworn to defend the Constitution, however, we cannot decide this or any case on that basis. Ideological tyranny, no matter how worthy its motivation, is forbidden as much to appointed judges as to elected legislators.

The record in this case contains the testimony of a survivor of the Nazi holocaust in Europe. Shortly before oral argument in this case, a lengthy and highly publicized citizenship revocation trial of an alleged Nazi war criminal was held in a federal court in Chicago, and in the week immediately after argument here, a four-part "docudrama" on the holocaust was nationally televised and widely observed. We cannot then be unmindful of the horrors associated with the Nazi regime of the Third Reich, with which to some real and apparently intentional degree appellees associate themselves. Nor does the record allow us to ignore the certainty that appellees know full well that, in light of their views and the historical associations they would bring with them to Skokie, many people would find their demonstration extremely mentally and emotionally disturbing, or the suspicion that such a result may be relished by appellees.

But our tasks here is to decide whether the First Amendment protects the activity in which appellees wish to engage, not to render moral judgment on their views or tactics. No authorities need be cited to establish the proposition, which the Village does not dispute, that First Amendment rights are truly precious and fundamental to our national life. Nor is this truth without relevance to the saddening historical images this case inevitably arouses. It is, after all, in part the fact that our constitutional system protects minorities unpopular at a particular time or place from governmental harassment and intimidation, that distinguishes life in this country from life under the Third Reich.

Before undertaking specific analysis of the clash between the Village ordinances and appellees' desires to demonstrate in Skokie, it will be helpful to establish some general principles of pertinence to the decision required of us. Putting to one side for the moment the question of whether the content of appellees' views and symbols makes a constitutional difference here, we find we are unable to deny that the activities in which the appellees wish to engage are within the ambit of the First Amendment.

These activities involve the "cognate rights" of free speech and free assembly. "[T]he wearing of an armband for the purpose of expressing certain views is the type of symbolic act that is within the Free Speech Clause of the First Amendment." *Tinker v. Des Moines Independent Community School District* (1969). Standing alone, at least, it is "closely akin to 'pure speech' which, we have repeatedly held, is entitled to comprehensive protection under the First Amendment." The same thing can be said of NSPA's intended display of a party flag and of the messages intended for the placards party members would carry. Likewise, although marching, parading, and picketing, because they involve conduct implicating significant interests in maintaining public order, are less protected than pure speech, they are nonetheless subject to significant First Amendment protection. Indeed, an orderly and peaceful demonstration, with placards, in the vicinity of a seat of government, is "an exercise of [the] basic constitutional rights of [speech, assembly, and petition] in their most pristine and classic form."

No doubt, the Nazi demonstration could be subjected to reasonable regulation of its time, place, and manner. Although much of the permit system of 994 is of that nature, the provisions attacked here are not. No objection is raised by the Village, in ordinances or in their proofs and arguments in this case, to the

suggested time, place, or manner of the demonstration, except the general assertion that in the place of Skokie, in these times, *given the content of appellees' views and symbols,* the demonstration and its symbols and speech should be prohibited. Because the ordinances turn on the content of the demonstration, they are necessarily not time, place, or manner regulations.

Legislating against the content of First Amendment activity, however, launches the government on a slippery and precarious path:

> [A]bove all else, the First Amendment means that government has no power to restrict expression because of its messages, its ideas, its subject matter, or its content. To permit the continued building of our politics and culture, and to assure self-fulfillment for each individual, our people are guaranteed the right to express any thought, free from government censorship. The essence of this forbidden censorship is content control. Any restriction on expressive activity because of its content would completely undercut the "profound national commitment to the principle that debate on public issues should be uninhibited, robust, and wide-open." *New York Times Co. v. Sullivan* [1964]. *Mosley* [1972].

This is not to say, of course, that content legislation is *per se* invalid. Chief Justice Burger concurred in *Mosley* just to point out the established exceptions to such a rule, namely obscenity, fighting words, and, as limited by constitutional requirements, libel. Likewise, in very narrow circumstances, a government may proscribe content on the basis of imminent danger of a grave substantive evil. But analysis of content restrictions must begin with a healthy respect for the truth that they are the most direct threat to the vitality of First Amendment rights.

II

We first consider ordinance 995, prohibiting the dissemination of materials which would promote hatred towards persons on the basis of their heritage. The Village would apparently apply this provision to NSPA's display of swastikas, their uniforms, and, perhaps, to the content of their placards.

The ordinance cannot be sustained on the basis of some of the more obvious exceptions to the rule against content control. While some would no doubt be willing to label appellees' views and symbols obscene, the constitutional rule that obscenity is unprotected applies only to material with erotic content. Furthermore, although the Village introduced evidence in the district court tending to prove that some individuals, at least, might have difficulty restraining their reactions to the Nazi demonstration, the Village tells us that it does not rely on a fear of responsive violence to justify the ordinance, and does not even suggest that there will be any physical violence if the march is held. This confession takes this case out of the scope of *Brandenburg v. Ohio* and *Feiner v. New York* (1951) (intentional "incitement to riot" may be prohibited). The Village does not argue otherwise.

The concession also eliminates any argument based on the fighting words doctrine of *Chaplinsky v. New Hampshire* (1942). The Court in *Chaplinsky* affirmed a conviction under a statute that, as authoritatively construed, applied only to words with a direct tendency to cause violence by the persons to whom, individually, the words were addressed. A conviction for less than words that at least tend to incite an immediate breach of the peace cannot be justified under *Chaplinsky*. The Illinois Supreme Court, in *Village of Skokie v. National Socialist Party of America* has squarely ruled that responsive violence fears and the fighting words doctrine could not support the prohibition of appellees' demonstration. Although that decision was in a prior restraint context, and we are here considering only the post facto criminal aspects of 995, the decision does buttress our conclusion that *Chaplinsky* does not cover this case. Again, the Village does not seriously contest this point.

Four basic arguments are advanced by the Village to justify the content restrictions of 995. First, it is said that the content criminalized by 995 is "totally lacking in social content," and that it consists of "false statements of fact" in which there is "no constitutional value." *Gertz v. Robert Welch, Inc.* (1974). We disagree that, if applied to the proposed demonstration, the ordinance can be said to be limited to "statements of fact," false or otherwise. No handbills are to be distributed; no speeches are planned. To the degree that the symbols in question can be said to assert anything specific, it must be the Nazi ideology, which cannot be treated as a mere false "fact."

We may agree with the district court that

if any philosophy should be regarded as completely unacceptable to civilized society, that of plaintiffs, who, while disavowing on the witness stand any advocacy of genocide, have nevertheless deliberately identified themselves with a regime whose record of brutality and barbarism is unmatched in modern history, would be a good place to start.

But there can be no legitimate start down such a road.

Under the First Amendment there is no such thing as a false idea. However pernicious an opinion may seem, we depend for its correction not on the conscience of judges and juries but on the competition of other ideas.

Gertz. In the words of Justice Jackson, "every person must be his own watchman for truth, because the forefathers did not trust any government to separate the true from the false for us." *Thomas v. Collins* [1945]. The asserted falseness of Nazi dogma, and, indeed, its general repudiation, simply do not justify its suppression.

The Village's second argument, and the one on which principal reliance is placed, centers on *Beauharnais v. Illinois* (1952). There a conviction was upheld under a statute prohibiting, in language substantially (and perhaps not unintentionally) similar to that used in the ordinance here, the dissemination of materials promoting racial or religious hatred. The closely-divided Court stated that the criminal punishment of libel of an *individual* raised no constitutional problems, relying on *Chaplinsky v. New Hampshire*:

There are certain well-defined and narrowly limited classes of speech, the prevention and punishment of which have never been thought to raise any Constitutional problem. These include the lewd and obscene, the profane, the libelous, and the insulting or "fighting" words. . . . [S]uch utterances are no essential part of any exposition of ideas, and are of such slight social value as a step to truth that any benefit that may be derived from them is clearly outweighed by the social interest in order and morality.

That being so, the Court reasoned that the state could constitutionally extend the prohibition to utterances aimed at groups.

In our opinion *Beauharnais* does not support ordinance 995, for two independent reasons. First, the rationale of that decision turns quite plainly on the strong tendency of the prohibited utterances to cause violence and disorder. The Illinois Supreme Court had so limited the statute's application, as the United States Supreme Court noted. The latter Court also pointed out that the tendency to induce breach of the peace was the traditional justification for the criminal libel laws which had always been thought to be immune from the First Amendment. After stating the issue (whether Illinois could extend criminal libel to groups) the Court turned to Illinois' history of racial strife "and its frequent obligato of extreme racial and religious propaganda" and concluded that the Illinois legislature could reasonably connect the strife and the propaganda and criminalize the latter to prevent the former. *Cantwell v. Connecticut* (1940) was quoted:

> The danger in these times from the coercive activities of those who in the delusion of racial or religious conceit *would incite violence and breaches of the peace* in order to deprive others of their equal right to the exercise of their liberties, is emphasized by events familiar to all. These and other transgressions of [the limits to First Amendment rights] the States appropriately may punish. [Emphasis added.]

It may be questioned . . . whether the *tendency to induce violence* approach sanctioned implicitly in *Beauharnais* would pass constitutional muster today. Assuming that it would, however, it does not support ordinance 995, because the Village, as we have indicated, does not assert appellees' possible violence, an audience's possible responsive violence, or possible violence against third parties by those incited by appellees, as justifications for 995. Ordinance 995 would apparently be applied in the absence of any such threat. The rationale of *Beauharnais,* then, simply does not apply here.

Further, when considering the application of *Beauharnais* to the present litigation, we cannot be unmindful of the "package" aspects of the ordinances and that the "insulting" words are to be made public only after a 30-day permit application waiting period. Violence occurring under such a circumstance would have such indicia of premeditation as to seem inconsistent with calling into play any remaining vitality of the *Beauharnais* rationale.

The Village asserts that *Beauharnais* implicitly sanctions prohibiting the use of First Amendment rights to invoke racial or religious hatred *even without reference to fears of violence*. In the light of our discussion of *Beauharnais'* premises, we do not find the case susceptible of this interpretation. Even if it were, however, we agree with the district court that decisions in the quarter-century since *Beauharnais* have abrogated the *Chaplinsky* dictum, made one of the premises of *Beauharnais,* that the punishment of libel "has never been thought to raise any Constitutional problem." *New York Times Co. v. Sullivan* (1964); *Garrison v. Louisiana* (1964) (criminal libel); and *Gertz v. Robert Welch, Inc.* are indisputable evidence that libel does indeed now raise serious and knotty First Amendment problems, sufficient as a matter of constitutional law to require the substantial rewriting of both criminal and civil state libel laws.

The Eighth Circuit and Judge Wright of the District of Columbia Circuit have expressed doubt, which we share, that *Beauharnais* remains good law at all after the constitutional libel cases. We agree at least this far: If 995 is to be sustained, it must be done on the basis of the Village's interest asserted, and the conduct to which 995 applies, not on the basis of blind obeisance to uncertain implications from an opinion issued years before the Supreme Court itself rewrote the rules.

The Villages' third argument is that it has a policy of fair housing, which the dissemination of racially defamatory material could undercut. We reject this argument without extended discussion. That the effective exercise of First Amendment rights may undercut a given government's policy on some issue is, indeed, one of the purposes of those rights. No distinction is constitutionally admissible that turns on the intrinsic justice of the particular policy in issue.

The Village's fourth argument is that the Nazi march, involving as it does the display of uniforms and swastikas, will create a substantive evil that it has a right to prohibit: the infliction of psychic trauma on resident holocaust survivors and other Jewish residents. The Village points out that Illinois recognizes the "new tort" of intentional infliction of severe emotional distress, the coverage of which may well include personally directed racial slurs. Assuming that specific individuals could proceed in tort under this theory to recover damages provably occasioned by the proposed march, and that a First Amendment defense would not bar the action, it is nonetheless quite a different matter to criminalize protected First Amendment conduct in anticipation of such results.

It would be grossly insensitive to deny, as we do not, that the proposed demonstration would seriously disturb, emotionally and mentally, at least some, and probably many of the Village's residents. The problem with engrafting an exception on the First Amendment for such situations is that they are indistinguishable in principle from speech that "invite[s] dispute . . . induces a condition of unrest, creates dissatisfaction with conditions as they are, or even stirs people to anger." *Terminiello v. Chicago* (1949). Yet these are among the "high purposes" of the First Amendment. It is perfectly clear that a state many not "make criminal the peaceful expression of unpopular views." *Edwards v. South Carolina* [1963]. Likewise, "mere public intolerance or animosity cannot be the basis for abridgement of these constitutional freedoms." *Coates v. City of Cincinnati* (1971). Where, as here, a crime is made of a silent march, attended only by symbols and not by extrinsic conduct offensive in itself, we think the words of the Court in *Street v. New York* are very much on point:

> [A]ny shock effect . . . must be attributed to the content of the ideas expressed. It is firmly settled that under our Constitution the public expression of ideas may not be prohibited merely because the ideas are themselves offensive to some of their hearers. [Citations omitted.]

It is said that the proposed march is not speech, or even "speech plus," but rather an invasion, intensely menacing no matter how peacefully conducted. The Village's expert psychiatric witness, in fact, testified that the effect of the march would be much the same regardless of whether uniforms and swastikas were displayed, due to the intrusion of self-proclaimed Nazis into what he characterized as predominately Jewish "turf." There is room under the First Amendment for the government to protect targeted listeners from offensive speech, but only when the speaker intrudes on the privacy of the home, or a captive audience cannot practically avoid exposure.

The Supreme Court has consistently stressed that "we are often 'captives' outside the sanctuary of the home and subject to objectionable speech." The ability of government, consonant with the Constitution, to shut off discourse solely to protect others from hearing it is, in other words, dependent upon a showing that substantial privacy interests are being invaded in an essentially intolerable manner. *Any broader view of this authority would effectively empower a majority to silence dissidents simply as a matter of personal predilections.* [Emphasis added.]

Cohen v. California [1971].

This case does not involve intrusion into people's homes. There *need be* no captive audience, as Village residents may, if they wish, simply avoid the Village Hall for thirty minutes on a Sunday afternoon, which no doubt would be their normal course of conduct on a day when the Village Hall was not open in the regular course of business. Absent such intrusion or captivity, there is no justifiable substantial privacy interest to save 995 from constitutional infirmity, when it attempts, by fiat, to declare the entire Village, at all times, a privacy zone that may be sanitized from the offensiveness of Nazi ideology and symbols.

We conclude that 995 may not be applied to criminalize the conduct of the proposed demonstration. Because it is susceptible to such an application, we also conclude that it suffers from substantial overbreadth, even if some of the purposes 995 is said to serve might constitutionally be protected by an appropriate and narrower ordinance. The latter conclusion is also supported by the fact that the ordinances could conceivably be applied to criminalize dissemination of *The Merchant of Venice* or a vigorous discussion of the merits of reverse racial discrimination in Skokie. Although there is reason to think, as the district court concluded, that the ordinance is fatally vague as well, because it turns in part on subjective reactions to prohibited conduct, we do not deem it necessary to rest our decision on that ground.

III

Our decision that 995 cannot constitutionally be applied to the proposed march necessarily means that a permit for the march may not be denied on the basis of anticipated violations thereof. We turn to the question of whether the similar provision built into 994 by § 27–56(c) can be the basis of a permit denial.

The answer really follows with even greater strength from our conclusion on 995. Because 994 § 27–56(c) gives to Village "officials the power to deny use of a forum in advance of actual expression," *Southeastern Promotions, Ltd. v. Conrad* (1975), it is a prior restraint, which thus "comes to this Court with a 'heavy presumption' against its constitutional validity." *Organization for a Better Austin v. Keefe* (1971).

> The presumption against prior restraints is heavier—and the degree of protection broader—than that against limits on expression imposed by criminal penalties. Behind the distinction is a theory deeply etched in our law: a free society prefers to punish the few who abuse rights of speech *after* they break the law than to throttle them and all others beforehand.

Southeastern Promotions. The slightly more specific language of §27–56(c) than that which 995 contains might cut against finding the former provision unconstitutionally vague, but there is otherwise no meaningful difference between the two provisions except the element of prior restraint. The requested parade permit cannot be denied on the basis of § 27–56(c). . . .

SPRECHER, Circuit Judge, concurring in part and dissenting in part.

The basic situation in this case—the efforts of avowed and uniformed Hitlerian Nazis to demonstrate without municipal regulations in the streets of a predominantly Jewish village housing some 7,000 Jewish survivors of World War II and their families —conjures up a unique amalgam of complex First Amendment concepts such as prior restraint, group libel, fighting words and hostile audiences, incitement to riot, and shouting "fire" in a crowded theater. Seldom before has a federal court been faced with a situation raising such powerful cross-pressures as have been created in this case. For instance, the fact that it now seems to be instilled in Jewish culture to confront threatened oppression with active resistance and aggressive retaliation differentiates this case factually from *Terminiello v. Chicago* (1949).

With a situation that is so unique, it is important to keep in mind Mr. Justice Stevens's admonition from one of the most recent First Amendment cases that "[e]ven within the area of protected speech, a difference in content may require a different governmental response." *Young v. American Mini Theatres, Inc.* (1976). There may very well be a necessity for a new balancing of values in these circumstances as opposed to the immediate governmental paralysis which is supposed to occur when the rubric of "prior restraint" is sounded. . . .

[I . . .]

[II . . .]

III

. . . We must first examine whether plaintiffs' proposed conduct falls within the scope of the First Amendment. We are dealing with a proposed march through a predominantly Jewish community. The plaintiffs would wear nazi-style uniforms and swastika armbands or emblems and carry written signs. No speeches were to be made. Plaintiffs' handbills had been distributed in the Village and a number of Skokie residents with Jewish surnames had received "offensive and threatening telephone calls." The portent of this action and the proposed march could not be lost on anyone familiar with the methods of Hitler's Nazis in Germany.

Under these circumstances, the appearance of plaintiffs' group in Skokie may be so extremely offensive and of such little social utility as to be beyond the protection of the First Amendment. In this sense the present case does not differ greatly from *Chaplinsky v. New Hampshire* (1942), where the Court upheld the conviction of a Jehovah's Witness for calling complainant a "God damned racketeer" and "a damned fascist." The analysis the Court used there applies with equal force here to the activities proposed by plaintiffs:

> Allowing the broadest scope to the language and purpose of the Fourteenth Amendment, it is well under-

stood that the right of free speech is not absolute at all times and under all circumstances. There are certain well-defined and narrowly limited classes of speech, the prevention and punishment of which have never been thought to raise any Constitutional problem. These include . . . "fighting" words—those which by their very utterance inflict injury or tend to incite an immediate breach of the peace. It has been well observed that such utterances are no essential part of any exposition of ideas, and are of such slight social value as a step to truth that any benefit that may be derived from them is clearly outweighed by the social interest in order and morality. "Resort to epithets or personal abuse is not in any proper sense communication of information or opinion safeguarded by the Constitution. . . . "

Another basis on which to conclude that plaintiffs' proposed conduct falls outside the protection of the First Amendment is that under the circumstances it constitutes a pernicious form of group libel. In *Beauharnais v. Illinois* (1952), the Court upheld a statute which is strikingly similar to those attacked here. The Court there declared:

It is not within our competence to confirm or deny claims of social scientists as to the dependence of the individual on the position of his racial or religious group in the community. It would, however, be arrant dogmatism, quite outside the scope of our authority in passing on the powers of a State, for us to deny that the Illinois legislature may warrantably believe that a man's job and his educational opportunities and the dignity accorded him may depend as much on the reputation of the racial and religious group to which he willy-nilly belongs, as on his own merits. This being so, we are precluded from saying that speech concededly punishable when immediately directed at individuals cannot be outlawed if directed at groups with whose position and esteem in society the affiliated individuals may be inextricably involved.

Nor do we need to back away from this analysis merely because the Supreme Court has substantially modified the law of libel insofar as it relates to public officials or public figures as opposed to the minor backtracking concerning libel of private individuals. Moreover, although *Beauharnais* is said to have been scarcely noted since 1952, neither has it been overruled.

It appears to me that plaintiffs' proposed activities, under the circumstances presented here, might reasonably be viewed as not within the area of constitutionally protected activity. At least the question seems close enough to warrant serious concern and analysis within the factual situation presented. Plaintiffs' proposed actions in this case arguably "are no essential part of any exposition of ideas, and are of such slight social value as a step to truth that any benefit that may be derived from them is clearly outweighed by the social interest in order and morality." *Chaplinsky v. New Hampshire.* This conclusion supports a finding at the very least of the validity of the challenged insurance ordinance.

IV

Concerning the assumption that the content of speech or conduct is an impermissible consideration when regulation of those activities are proposed, we note that regulation of First Amendment activities never has been and never can be "content blind." As early as 1919, the Supreme Court in *Schenck v. United States* declared through Mr. Justice Holmes:

The question in every case is whether the words used are used in such circumstances and are of such a nature as to create a clear and present danger that they will bring about the substantive evils that Congress has a right to prevent. It is a question of proximity and degree.

There is no dispute that speech may not be suppressed merely because it offends its listeners. At some point, however, considerations of a neutral desire to maintain the public peace and general welfare come into play in determining whether activities should be allowed. Where the activity is, as here, by its nature and by the circumstances, a threat to a reasonable attempt to maintain the public order, it cannot claim to go unregulated under the auspices that content may not properly be considered. . . .

RICHARD DELGADO

Words That Wound: A Tort Action for Racial Insults, Epithets, and Name Calling

Richard Delgado is Professor of Law at the University of California at Los Angeles. (Source: Reprinted from Richard Delgado, "Words That Wound: A Tort Action for Racial Insults, Epithets, and Name Calling," Harvard Civil Rights–Civil Liberties Law Review 17 [1982]. Copyright © 1982 by the President and Fellows of Harvard College.)

QUESTIONS FOR REFLECTION

1. What, according to Delgado, are the harmful effects of racial harassment? Is a racial insult more harmful than other kinds of insults? How?

2. How, according to Delgado, should courts apportion damages—that is, decide who is responsible for how much harm to a person who has suffered from racial harassment?

3. Delgado believes that allowing victims of racial harassment to sue for redress is consistent with the First Amendment's protection of freedom of speech. How does he try to reconcile the two?

4. Which of the cases mentioned in Finn's article, below, would justify tort action under Delgado's criterion?

[Introduction . . .]

I. Psychological, Sociological, and Political Effects of Racial Insults

American society remains deeply afflicted by racism. Long before slavery became the mainstay of the plantation society of the antebellum South, Anglo-Saxon attitudes of racial superiority left their stamp on the developing culture of colonial America. Today, over a century after the abolition of slavery, many citizens suffer from discriminatory attitudes and practices, infecting our economic system, our cultural and political institutions, and the daily interactions of individuals. The idea that color is a badge of inferiority and a justification for the denial of opportunity and equal treatment is deeply ingrained.

The racial insult remains one of the most pervasive channels through which discriminatory attitudes are imparted. Such language injures the dignity and self-regard of the person to whom it is addressed, communicating the message that distinctions of race are distinctions of merit, dignity, status, and personhood. Not only does the listener learn and internalize the messages contained in racial insults, these messages color our society's institutions and are transmitted to succeeding generations. . . .

[A . . .]

B. The Harms of Racial Insults

Immediate mental or emotional distress is the most obvious direct harm caused by a racial insult. Without question, mere words, whether racial or otherwise, can cause mental, emotional, or even physical harm to their target, especially if delivered in front of others or by a persons in a position of authority. Racial insults, relying as they do on the unalterable fact of the victim's race and on the history of slavery and race discrimination in this country, have an even greater potential for harm than other insults.

Although the emotional damage caused is variable and depends on many factors, only one of which is the outrageousness of the insult, a racial insult is always a dignitary affront, a direct violation of the victim's right to be treated respectfully. Our moral and legal systems recognize the principle that individuals are entitled to treatment that does not denigrate their humanity through disrespect for their privacy or moral worth. This ideal has a high place in our traditions, finding expression in such principles as universal suffrage, the prohibition against cruel and unusual punishment, the protection of the fourth amendment against unreasonable searches, and the abolition of slavery. A racial insult is a serious transgression of this principle because it derogates by race, a characteristic central to one's self-image.

The wrong of this dignitary affront consists of the expression of a judgment that the victim of the racial slur is entitled to less than that to which all other citizens are entitled. Verbal tags provide a convenient means of categorization so that individuals may be treated as members of a class and assumed to share all the negative attitudes imputed to the class. Verbal tags thus make it easier for their users to justify their own superior position with respect to others. Racial insults also serve to keep the victim compliant. Such dignitary affronts are certainly no less harmful than others recognized by the law. Clearly, a society whose public law recognizes harm in the stigma of separate but equal schooling and the potential offensiveness of the required display of a state motto on automobile license plates, and whose private law sees actionable conduct in an unwanted kiss or the forcible removal of a person's hat, should also recognize the dignitary harm inflicted by a racial insult.

The need for legal redress for victims also is underscored by the fact that racial insults are intentional acts. The intentionality of racial insults is obvious: what other purpose could the insult serve? There can be little doubt that the dignitary affront of racial insults, except perhaps those that are over-

heard, is intentional and therefore most reprehensible. Most people today know that certain words are offensive and only calculated to wound. No other use remains for such words as "nigger," "wop," "spick," or "kike."

In addition to the harms of immediate emotional distress and infringement of dignity, racial insults inflict psychological harm upon the victim. Racial slurs may cause long-term emotional pain because they draw upon and intensify the effects of the stigmatization, labeling, and disrespectful treatment that the victim has previously undergone. Social scientists who have studied the effects of racism have found that speech that communicates low regard for an individual because of race "tends to create in the victim those very traits of 'inferiority' that it ascribes to him." Moreover, "even in the absence of more objective forms of discrimination—poor schools, menial jobs, and substandard housing—traditional stereotypes about the low ability and apathy of Negroes and other minorities can operate as 'self-fulfilling prophecies.'" These stereotypes, portraying members of a minority group as stupid, lazy, dirty, or untrustworthy, are often communicated either explicitly or implicitly through racial insults.

Because they constantly hear racist messages, minority children, not surprisingly, come to question their competence, intelligence, and worth. Much of the blame for the formation of these attitudes lies squarely on value-laden words, epithets, and racial names. These are the materials out of which each child "grows his own set of thoughts and feelings about race." If the majority "defines them and their parents as no good, inadequate, dirty, incompetent, and stupid," the child will find it difficult not to accept those judgments. . . .

It is, of course, impossible to predict the degree of deterrence a cause of action in tort would create. However, as Professor van den Berghe has written, "for most people living in racist societies racial prejudice is merely a special kind of convenient rationalization for rewarding behavior." In other words, in racist societies "most members of the dominant group will exhibit both prejudice and discrimination," but only in conforming to social norms. Thus, "[W]hen social pressures and rewards for racism are absent, racial bigotry is more likely to be restricted to people for whom prejudice fulfills a psychological 'need.' In such a tolerant milieu prejudiced persons may even refrain from discriminating behavior to escape social disapproval." Increasing the cost of racial insults thus would certainly decrease their frequency. Laws will never prevent violations altogether, but they will deter "whoever is deterrable."

Because most citizens comply with legal rules, and this compliance in turn "reinforce[s] their own sentiments toward conformity," a tort action for racial insults would discourage such harmful activity through the teaching function of the law. The establishment of a legal norm "creates a public conscience and a standard for expected behavior that check overt signs of prejudice." Legislation aims first at controlling only the acts that express undesired attitudes. But "when expression changes, thoughts too in the long run are likely to fall into line." "Laws . . . restrain the middle range of mortals who need them as a mentor in molding their habits." Thus, "If we create institutional arrangements in which exploitative behaviors are no longer reinforced, we will then succeed in changing attitudes [that underlie these behaviors]." Because racial attitudes of white Americans "typically follow rather than precede actual institutional [or legal] alteration," a tort for racial slurs is a promising vehicle for the eradication of racism.

II. Legal Protection from Racial Insults

[A . . .]

[B . . .]

C. Objections Based on the First Amendment

It is surprising, especially after *Collin,* that the question whether racial insults are protected by the first amendment has not arisen in any case involving a racial insult. Until it does, the extent to which free speech considerations would shape the cause of action must remain an open question. No reported decision is on point; analysis can proceed only by examination of the nature of racial insults and the policies that underlie the first amendment.

Under first amendment doctrine, regulation of expressive activities is scrutinized more closely when directed at content of the speech rather than merely at the time, place, or manner of the speech in question. Because racial insults differ from ordinary, non-actionable insults precisely because they use racial terms for the purpose of demeaning the victim, a tort for racial insults will almost surely be seen as a regulation of content and thus be subject to the more exacting scrutiny afforded in such cases. But regardless of the standard applied, courts ultimately must balance the government's interest against that of the utterer of the infringed speech.

1. The Government Interests

The primary government interest served by a tort action for racial insults is the elimination of the harms of racism and racial insults discussed earlier. Not only the victim of a racial insult but also his or her children, future generations, and our entire society are harmed by racial invective and the tradition of racism which it furthers.

The government also has an interest in regulating the use of words harmful in themselves. In *Chaplinsky v. New Hampshire,* the United States Supreme Court stated that words which "by their very utterance inflict injury or tend to incite an immediate breach of the peace" are not protected by the first amendment. Racial insults, and even some of the words which might be used in a racial insult, inflict injury by their very utterance. Words such as "nigger" and "spick" are badges of degradation even when used between friends; these words have no other connotation.

The Supreme Court also has recognized that in some contexts the government may restrict speech directed at a captive or unwilling audience. These cases have concerned speech both inside and outside the home. However, in *Cohen v. California* the Court overturned a conviction for wearing a jacket with the words "Fuck the Draft" written on it. In meeting the state's argument that the message was thrust upon unwilling listeners, the Court pointed out that viewers could simply avert their eyes.

Racial insults are easily distinguishable from the inscription in *Cohen*. One cannot avert one's ears from an insult. More importantly, a racial insult is directed at a particular victim; it is analogous to the statement "Fuck you," not the statement "Fuck the Draft." Finally, a racial insult, unlike the slogan in *Cohen,* is not political speech; its perpetrator intends not to discover truth or advocate social action but to injure the victim.

2. *The Free Speech Interests*

Examination of the free speech values served by a racial insult is best undertaken within the framework of the categories outlined by Professor Emerson in his seminal article, *Toward a General Theory of the First Amendment.* Four categories of values are suggested by Professor Emerson: individual self-fulfillment; ascertainment of the truth; securing participation by the members of society in social and political decision making; and maintaining the balance between stability and change.

a. **Individual Self-Fulfillment** The values of individual self-fulfillment to be furthered through free expression are based on the rights of individuals to develop their full potentials as members of the human community. But bigotry, and thus the attendant expression of racism, stifles, rather than furthers, the moral and social growth of the individual who harbors it. In addition, a racial insult is only in small part an expression of self: it is primarily an attempt to injure through the use of words. No one would argue that the value of self-fulfillment is not limited by consideration of the effects of one's means of expression on other members of society. Although one may dress in Nazi uniforms and demonstrate before the city hall in Skokie, Illinois, one may not paint swastikas on one's neighbors' doors.

b. **Ascertainment of the Truth** Professor Emerson argued that "[t]hrough the acquisition of new knowledge, the toleration of new ideas, the testing of opinion in open competition, the discipline of re-

thinking its assumptions, a society will be better able to reach common decisions that will meet the needs and aspirations of its members." This function of free speech, to achieve the best decisions on matters of interest to all, has been extremely influential in first amendment literature. Indeed, one theory of the first amendment is that the amendment's protections extend only to speech that can be characterized as "political." In this respect most racial insults are distinguishable from the expressions found protected in *Collin*. The plaintiff in *Collin,* the National Socialist Party of America, was a political party whose race-related beliefs were only a part of a set of ideals. But the characteristic most significant in determining the value of racial insults is that they are not intended to inform or convince the listener. Racial insults invite no discourse, and no speech in response can cure the inflicted harm.

Racial insults may usefully be analogized to obscenity. Although the government may regulate obscenity, it may not prohibit expression of the view that obscenity should be protected or that, for example, adultery may be proper behavior. Similarly, protecting members of racial minorities from injury through racial insults, and society itself from the accumulated harms of racism, is very different from prohibiting espousal of the view that race discrimination is proper.

The reasons the Supreme Court articulated in explaining why obscenity may be regulated are also instructive in analyzing racism and racial insults. In *Paris Adult Theatre I v. Slaton,* the Court pointed to the "at least . . . arguable correlation between obscene material and crime" and the "'right of the Nation and of the States to maintain a decent society.'" Racial insults, through the racism and race discrimination they further, are severely at odds with the goals of antidiscrimination laws and the commands of the thirteenth amendment. A prohibition of such insults would surely further the government's interest in maintaining a "decent society."

c. **Participation in Decision Making** In a democracy, as Professor Emerson argued, all members of society must be permitted to voice their opinions so that the government's authority is derived in fact "from the consent of the governed." Racial insults do not further this goal. On the contrary, they constitute "badges and incidents of slavery" and contribute to a stratified society in which political power is possessed by some and denied to others.

d. The Balance between Stability and Change

Some of the many evils of the suppression of expression also are effects of racism and racial insults. Professor Emerson mentioned the following arguments, among others, under the rubric of maintaining the balance between stability and change: suppression of discussion substitutes force for logic; suppression of speech promotes institutional rigidity and inability to respond to changing circumstances; free expression leads those who lose public controversies to accept the result because they have had an opportunity to convert others to their opinion; and freedom of expression prevents violent upheavals by alerting the government to valid grievances. But racism, in part through racial slurs, furthers all the evils caused by the suppression of speech. Racism dulls the moral and social senses of its perpetrators, while disabling its victims from fully participating in society and leaving unprejudiced members of society demoralized. Bigotry and systems of discrimination continue to exist for no reason other than that the prejudiced are in positions of power or authority. Individuals infected by these ills will be peopled by like-minded individuals and thus will be slow to respond to changing circumstances. Furthermore, racism excludes minorities from participating in the contemplation of public issues because their concerns are discounted by the majority and because they have been demoralized by repeated victimization. And it is painfully clear that this exclusion, not only from political discussion but also from the abundance of our country's wealth, is capable of leading to violent outbreaks.

III. Elements of the Cause of Action

In order to prevail in an action for a racial insult, the plaintiff should be required to prove that

> Language was addressed to him or her by the defendant that was intended to demean through reference to race; that the plaintiff understood as intended to demean through reference to race; and that a reasonable person would recognize as a racial insult.

Thus, it would be expected that an epithet such as "You damn nigger" would almost always be found actionable, as it is highly insulting and highly racial. However, an insult such as "You incompetent fool," directed at a black person by a white, even in a context which made it highly insulting, would not be actionable because it lacks a racial component. "Boy," directed at a young black male, might be actionable, depending on the speaker's intent, the hearer's understanding, and whether a reasonable person would consider it a racial insult in the particular context. "Hey, nigger," spoken affectionately between black persons and used as a greeting, would not be actionable. An insult such as "You dumb honkey," directed at a white person, could be actionable under this formulation of the cause of action, but only in the unusual situations where the plaintiff would suffer harm from such an insult.

The plaintiff may be able to show aggravating circumstances, such as abuse of a position of power or authority or knowledge of the victim's susceptibility to racial insults, which may render punitive damages appropriate. The common law defenses of privilege and mistake may be applicable, and retraction of the insult may mitigate damages. . . .

CHESTER E. FINN, JR.

The Campus: "An Island of Repression in a Sea of Freedom"

Chester E. Finn, Jr., is Professor of Education and Public Policy at Vanderbilt University and Director of the Educational Excellence Network. He served as Assistant Secretary of Education from 1985 to 1988. (Source: Reprinted from Commentary *[September 1989], by permission; all rights reserved.)*

QUESTIONS FOR REFLECTION

1. Finn believes that attempts to restrict discriminatory speech are unjustifiable. He thus rejects the position that the harms inflicted by such speech outweigh any positive value it has. What argument does Finn offer for his rejection of that position?

2. Finn contends that restrictions on racial harassment are themselves harmful. How? How extensive are the harms?

3. Consider Finn's examples of unjustified complaints under antiharassment codes. What features of the codes give rise to these complaints? Would the approaches discussed by Delgado, for example, allow these complaints?

4. Finn links the issue of racial harassment to that of affirmative action. What analogy does he see between these issues?

5. According to Finn, antiharassment codes are likely to aggravate the very problems they are meant to solve. How does he argue for this view? Do you agree?

Two weeks before the Supreme Court held that the First Amendment protects one's right to burn the flag, the regents of the University of Wisconsin decreed that students on their twelve campuses no longer possess the right to say anything ugly to or about one another. Though depicted as an anti-discrimination measure, this revision of the student-conduct code declares that "certain types of expressive behavior directed at individuals and intended to demean and to create a hostile environment for education or other university-authorized activities would be prohibited and made subject to disciplinary sanctions." Penalties range from written warnings to expulsion.

Several months earlier, the University of Michigan adopted a six-page "anti-bias code" that provides for punishment of students who engage in conduct that "stigmatizes or victimizes an individual on the basis of race, ethnicity, religion, sex, sexual orientation, creed, national origin, ancestry, age, marital status, handicap, or Vietnam-era veteran status." (Presumably this last bizarre provision applies whether the "victim" is labeled a war hero or a draft dodger.)

Nor are Wisconsin and Michigan the only state universities to have gone this route. In June, the higher-education regents of Massachusetts prohibited "racism, anti-Semitism, ethnic, cultural, and religious intolerance" on their 27 campuses. A kindred regulation took effect on July 1 at the Chapel Hill campus of the University of North Carolina. And in place for some time at the law school of the State University of New York at Buffalo has been the practice of noting a student's use of racist language on his academic record and alerting prospective employers and the bar association.

Not to be outdone by the huge state schools, a number of private universities, like Emory in Atlanta and Stanford in California, have also made efforts to regulate unpleasant discourse and what the National Education Association terms "ethnoviolence," a comprehensive neologism that includes "acts of insensitivity."

Proponents of such measures are straightforward about their intentions. Says University of Wisconsin President Kenneth Shaw of the new rule: "It can particularly send a message to minority students that the board and its administration do care." Comments Emory's director of equal opportunity: "We just wanted to ensure that at a time when other universities were having problems that we made it clear that we wouldn't tolerate graffiti on walls or comments in classes." And in Massachusetts, the regents concluded that "There must be a unity and cohesion in the diversity which we seek to achieve, thereby creating an atmosphere of pluralism."

This "pluralism" is not to be confused with the version endorsed by the First Amendment. Elsewhere we are expected, like it or not, to attend to what Justice Brennan calls the "bedrock principle . . . that the government may not prohibit the expression of an idea simply because society finds the idea itself offensive or disagreeable." Not so for those running universities. "What we are proposing is not completely in line with the First Amendment," a leader of Stanford's student government has acknowledged to a reporter, but "I'm not sure it should be. We . . . are trying to set a standard different from what society at large is trying to accomplish." Explains the Emory official: "I don't believe freedom of speech on campus was designed to allow people to demean others on campus." And a Stanford law professor contends that "racial epithets and sexually haranguing speech silences rather than furthers discussion."

Disregard the hubris and the sanctimony. Academics and their youthful apprentices have long viewed their own institutions and causes as nobler than the workaday world and humdrum pursuits of ordinary mortals. Forget, too, the manifest evidence of what some of the nation's most esteemed universities are teaching their students about basic civics. Consider only the two large issues that these developments pose, each freighted with a hefty burden of irony.

The first can still evoke a wry smile. We are, after all, seeing students pleading for controls to be imposed on campus behavior in the name of decency and morality. Yet these same students would be outraged if their colleges and universities were once again to function *in loco parentis* by constraining personal liberty in any other way. What is more, faculties, administrators, and trustees are complying with the student demands; they are adopting and— one must assume—enforcing these behavior codes. By and large, these are the same campuses that have long since shrugged off any serious responsibility for student conduct with respect to alcohol, drugs, and promiscuity (indeed, have cheerily collaborated in making the last of these behaviors more heedless by installing condom dispensers in the dorms). These are colleges that do not oblige anyone to attend class regularly, to exercise in the gym, to drive safely, or to eat a balanced diet. A student may do anything he likes with or to his fellow students, it appears, including things that are indisputably illegal, unhealthy, and dangerous for everyone concerned, and the university turns a blind eye. But a student may not, under any circumstances, speak ill of another student's origins, inclinations, or appearance.

The larger—and not the least bit amusing—issue is, of course, the matter of freedom of expression and efforts to limit it. That the emotionally charged flag-burning decision emerged from the Supreme Court the same month as authorities in China shot hundreds of students (and others) demonstrating for democracy in the streets of Beijing is as stark an illustration as one will ever see of the gravity and passion embedded in every aspect of this question.

In the Western world, the university has historically been the locus of the freest expression to be found anywhere. One might say that the precepts embodied in the First Amendment have applied there with exceptional clarity, and long before they were vouchsafed in other areas of society. For while private colleges are not formally bound by the Bill of Rights, they, like their public-sector counterparts, are heirs to an even older tradition. The campus was a sanctuary in which knowledge and truth might be pursued—and imparted—with impunity, no matter how unpopular, distasteful, or politically heterodox the process might sometimes be. That is the essence of academic freedom and it is the only truly significant distinction between the universities of the democracies and those operating under totalitarian regimes. Wretched though the food and lodging are for students on Chinese campuses, these were not the provocations that made martyrs in Tiananmen Square. It was the idea of freedom that stirred China's students and professors (and millions of others, as well). And it was the fear of allowing such ideas to take root that prompted the government's brutal response.

Having enjoyed almost untrammeled freedom of thought and expression for three and a half centuries, and having vigorously and, for the most part, successfully fended off efforts by outsiders (state legislators and congressional subcommittees, big donors, influential alumni, etc.) to constrain that freedom, American colleges and universities are now muzzling themselves. The anti-discrimination and anti-harassment rules being adopted will delimit what can be said and done on campus. Inevitably, this must govern what can be taught and written in lab, library, and lecture hall, as well as the sordid antics of fraternity houses and the crude nastiness of inebriated teenagers. ("The calls for a ban on 'harassment by vilification' reached a peak last fall" at Stanford, explained the New York *Times,* "after two drunken freshmen turned a symphony recruiting poster into a black-face caricature of Beethoven and posted it near a black student's room.")

Constraints on free expression and open inquiry do not, of course, depend on the adoption of a formal code of conduct. Guest speakers with controversial views have for some years now risked being harassed, heckled, even shouted down by hostile campus audiences, just as scholars engaging in certain forms of research, treading into sensitive topics, or reaching unwelcome conclusions have risked calumny from academic "colleagues." More recently, students have begun to monitor their professors and to take action if what is said in class irks or offends them.

Thus, at Harvard Law School this past spring, Bonnie Savage, the aptly-named leader of the Har-

vard Women's Law Association (HWLA), sent professor Ian Macneil a multicount allegation of sexism in his course on contracts. The first offense cited was Macneil's quoting (on page 963 of his textbook) Byron's well-known line, "And whispering, 'I will ne'er consent,'—consented." This, and much else that he had said and written, the HWLA found objectionable. "A professor in any position at any school," Savage pronounced, "has no right or privilege to use the classroom in such a way as to offend, at the very least, 40 percent of the students. . . . "

This was no private communication. Savage dispatched copies to sundry deans and the chairman of the faculty-appointments committee because, she later explained, "We thought he might be considered for tenure." The whole affair, Macneil responded in the *Harvard Law Record,* was "shoddy, unlawyerlike, reminiscent of Senator McCarthy, and entirely consistent with HWLA's prior conduct." As for the Byron passage, it "is in fact a perfect summary of what happens in the Battle of Forms" (a part of the contract-making process).

Macneil is not the only Harvard professor to have been given a hard time in recent years for writing or uttering words that upset students, however well-suited they might be to the lesson at hand. Not long ago, the historian Stephan Thernstrom was accused by a student vigilante of such classroom errors as "read[ing] aloud from white plantation owners' journals 'without also giving the slaves' point of view.'" Episodes of this kind, says Thernstrom, serve to discourage him and other scholars from even teaching courses on topics that bear on race and ethnicity.

Nor is Harvard the only major university where student allegations, unremonstrated by the administration, have produced such a result. At Michigan last fall, the distinguished demographer, Reynolds Farley, was teaching an undergraduate course in "race and cultural contact," as he had done for the previous ten years, when a column appeared in the Michigan *Daily* alleging racial insensitivity on his part, citing—wholly out of context, of course—half a dozen so-called examples, and demanding that the sociology department make amends. Farley was not amused and, rather than invite more unjust attacks, is discontinuing the course. Consequently 50 to 125 Michigan students a year will be deprived of the opportunity to examine issues of ethnicity and the history of race relations in America under the tutelage of this world-class scholar. And to make matters even worse, Farley notes that several faculty colleagues have mentioned that they are dropping any discussion of various important race-related issues from their courses, lest similar treatment befall them.

This might seem perverse, not least from the standpoint of "aggrieved" students and their faculty mentors, because another of their major goals is to oblige everyone to take more courses on precisely these topics. "I would like to see colleges engage all incoming students in mandatory racial-education programs," writes William Damon, professor of psychology and chairman of the education department at Clark University, in the *Chronicle of Higher Education*. And his call is being answered on a growing number of campuses, including the state colleges of Massachusetts, the University of Wisconsin, and the University of California at Berkeley.

Ironies abound here, too, since the faculties and governing boards adopting these course requirements are generally the very bodies that resist any suggestion of a "core curriculum" or tight "distribution requirements" on the ground that diverse student preferences should be accommodated and that, in any case, there are no disciplines, writings, or ideas of such general importance that everyone should be obliged to study them. Curricular relativism can be suspended, though, when "pluralism" is itself the subject to be studied. "It is important to make such programs mandatory," Professor Damon explains, "so that they can reach students who otherwise might not be inclined to participate."

Save for the hypocrisy, this may appear at first glance to be part of an ancient and legitimate function of college faculties: deciding what subjects are of sufficient moment as to require students to examine them. If a particular university has its curricular priorities askew, requiring the study of racism rather than, say, mathematics, one can presumably enroll elsewhere (there being about 3,400 institutions to choose from).

A second glance is in order, however, before conceding legitimacy. What is commonly sought in these required courses, and the non-credit counterparts that abound on campuses where they have not

yet entered the formal curriculum, is not open inquiry but, rather, a form of attitude adjustment, even ideological indoctrination. Thus Professor Damon:

> Such programs should emphasize discussions in which trained instructors explore students' beliefs concerning racial diversity and its societal implications. . . . They should cover, and *provide clear justification for, any racially or ethnically sensitive admissions or hiring criteria* that students may see on campus. [Emphasis added]

Along similar lines, the Massachusetts regents insist that each campus provide "a program of educational activities designed to enlighten faculty, administrators, staff and students with regard to . . . ways in which the dominant society manifests and perpetuates racism." So, too, the Berkeley academic senate last year voted (227 to 194) to begin requiring all undergraduates to sign up for new courses in "American cultures" in which they will explore questions like "How have power relations between groups been manifested in such matters as racism, economics, politics, environmental design, religion, education, law, business, and the arts in the United States?"

In response to Professor Damon's description of the instructional goals of the mandatory course he is urging, Harvard's Thernstrom wrote in a letter to the *Chronicle of Higher Education*:

> Justification? Is that what educators are supposed to provide? For "any" criteria that omniscient administrators choose to adopt? . . . How about a mandatory course providing "a clear justification" for American foreign policy since 1945? Or one justifying the Reagan administration's domestic policies? . . . True, Professor Damon declares that such courses should "avoid preaching and indoctrination," but it seems to me that providing "justification" for highly controversial social programs cannot be anything but indoctrination.

Whether this bleak assessment will prove accurate hinges in large part on who ends up teaching these courses and the intellectual norms to which they hew. With scholars of the stature of Farley and Thernstrom already deterred—coerced into self-censorship—it is likely that colleges will enlist as instructors people who agree that the purpose of these "education" efforts is more political than intellectual. Such individuals are not hard to find in the curricular domain now known as "cultural studies." In this field, acknowledged Professor Donald Lazere at the 1988 conference of the Modern Language Association (MLA), "politics are obviously central." Indeed, the agenda of the field itself was defined by Richard Johnson, an Englishman who is one of its leading figures, as

> a series of critiques of innocent-sounding categories or innocent-sounding practices, obviously culture, and art and literature, but also communication, and consumption, entertainment, education, leisure, style, the family, femininity and masculinity, and sexuality and pleasure, and, of course, the most objective-sounding, neutral-sounding categories of all, knowledge and science.

It is not far from MLA discussions to campus staffing decisions. Here is how the historian Alan C. Kors of the University of Pennsylvania describes the organization of a dorm-based program to educate students at his institution about "racism, sexism, and homophobia":

> [W]hat the administration has done, in fact, is turn this education of the students over to ideologically-conscious groups with ideological and political agendas, namely, the "Women's Center" and the Office of Affirmative Action. . . . These are people who have been granted, in effect, to use a term they like, the "privileged ideological position" on campus. Now the notion that the Penn Women's Center speaks for Penn women is absurd, since it obviously doesn't speak for more than a very small minority of a diverse, individuated female population. . . . But the university's administration has an easy way of buying off certain pressure groups, and it consists of giving those in possession of privileged ideologies the responsibility for reeducating students and faculty with improper attitudes. As a result, you really have the foundations of a University of Beijing in Philadelphia.

These additions to the formal and informal curricula of American colleges and universities, like the behavior codes and anti-harassment policies the institutions are embracing, are invariably promulgated in the name of enhancing "diversity" on campus. That has become the chief purpose of

present-day affirmative-action hiring and admissions policies, too. It has, after all, been a while since one could observe prospective students or instructors turned away in any numbers at the campus gates because they were women or minority-group members or because of their religion or handicap. The one exception in recent years has been Asian students, whose dazzling academic performance led some universities to impose admission quotas lest this group become "overrepresented" in the student body. Asians, in fact, recently won a victory at Berkeley, when the chancellor apologized for admissions policies that had held down their numbers and announced a new one. The changes include raising from 40 to 50 percent the fraction of Berkeley undergraduates who will be admitted on the basis of academic merit alone; the other half must be "underrepresented minorities." (The likely impact of this new policy will be to maintain the enrollment shares of black and Hispanic students, to boost the numbers of Asians admitted, and to cause a drop in white matriculants, who plainly will not make it as a minority and who may be trounced by the Asians in the merit competition.)

With these few exceptions, however, affirmative action in the late 80's has nothing to do with invidious discrimination on grounds of race, gender, etc. Most colleges and universities would kill for more blacks and Hispanics in their student bodies and for more of the same minorities, as well as more women, in their faculties. (The only reason they are not equally eager for additional female *students* is that women today constitute a clear majority of the nation's 12.8 million higher-education enrollees.) "Diversity," then, is now the goal.

That we have generally grown used to this in matters of campus admission and employment does not mean that the academy lacks the capacity to surprise and dismay. These days that capacity usually entails a faculty-hiring decision where the race or gender or ideology of the candidate is entangled with his academic specialty. In recent months, I have run into several outstanding young (white male) political scientists who are finding it impossible to land tenure-track teaching posts at medium- and high-status colleges because, as one of them wryly explained to me, their scholarly strengths lie in the study of "DWEMs." When I confessed ignorance of the acronym, he patiently explained that it stands for "Dead White European Males." Had they specialized in revolutionary ideologies, the politics of feminism and racism, or trendy quantitative social-science methodologies, they could perhaps have transcended their inconvenient gender and mundane color and have a reasonable shot at academic employment. But to spend one's hours with the likes of Aristotle, Machiavelli, Hobbes, and Burke is to have nothing very important to offer a political-science department today, whatever one's intellectual and pedagogical accomplishments.

One can, by contrast, get wooed by the largest and most prestigious of academic departments, no matter how repugnant one's own views, provided that one offers the right blend of personal traits and intellectual enthusiasms. Richard Abowitz recently recounted the efforts by the University of Wisconsin to attract June Jordan, a radical black activist (and poet), from Stony Brook to Madison. After examining her writings and orations spanning the previous fifteen years, Abowitz concluded that if Jordan remained true to form, "her courses at the University of Wisconsin would do nothing more than propagate the crudest forms of social, political, and economic prejudice," exactly the attitudes that the university had dedicated itself to wiping out through such measures as the new student conduct code. Yet with but a single abstention, Madison's English department voted unanimously to offer her a tenured position with a generous salary. (Berkeley's offer must have been even more attractive, for that is where Jordan now teaches.)

Esoteric forms of affirmative action are by no means confined to the professoriate. Last year the editors of the *Columbia Law Review* adopted a new "diversity" program that will reserve special slots on the editorial board for individuals who qualify by virtue of their race, physical handicap, or sexual orientation. Law-review boards, of course, have customarily been meritocracies, with membership gained through outstanding academic achievement. With Columbia in the lead, one must suppose this will no longer be the rule even though, the New York *Post* commented, "No one has yet stepped forward . . . to explain why sexual orientation, for instance, would keep a student from performing well enough

in law school to compete for the law review on the same basis as everyone else."

Diversity and tolerance, evenhandedly applied, are estimable precepts. But that is not how they are construed in the academy today. Nor do the narrowing limits on free expression lead only to penalties for individuals who engage in "biased" talk or "hostile" behavior. They also leave little room for opinion that deviates from campus political norms or for grievances from unexpected directions. During Harvard's race-awareness week last spring, when a white student dared to complain that she had experienced "minority ethnocentrism" on campus—black and Hispanic students, it seems, often ignored her—she was given short shrift and no sympathy by the speaker (who had already suggested that Harvard and Dartmouth were "genocidal" institutions).

More commonly, however, it is rambunctious student newspapers and magazines that get into trouble with academic authorities for printing something that contravenes the conventional wisdom. Given the predominant campus climate, it is not surprising that these are often publications with a moderate or Right-of-Center orientation. Sometimes, clearly, they do mischievous, stupid, and offensive things, but for such things the degree of toleration in higher education seems to vary with the ideology of the perpetrator. (Acts of discrimination and oppression based on political views, it should be observed, are *not* among the categories proscribed in the new codes of behavior.) In addition to a much-reported sequence of events at Dartmouth, there have been recent efforts to censor or suppress student publications, and sometimes to discipline their staff members, at Brown, Berkeley, UCLA, Vassar, and California State University at Northridge.

The last of these prompted one of the most extraordinary media events of 1989, a joint press conference on May 16 featuring—no one could have made this up—former Attorney General Edwin Meese III and the director of the Washington office of the American Civil Liberties Union (ACLU), Morton Halperin. What brought them together was shared outrage over what Halperin termed the "double standard" on campus. "Our position," he reminded the attending journalists, "is that there is an absolute right to express views even if others find those views repugnant." He could cite numerous instances, he said, where campus authorities were making life difficult for outspoken conservative students, yet could find "no cases where universities discipline students for views or opinions on the Left, or for racist comments against non-minorities."

Meese, not surprisingly, concurred, as did James Taranto, the former Northridge student journalist whose lawsuit settlement afforded the specific occasion for the press conference. In 1987, Taranto, then news editor of his campus paper, had written a column faulting UCLA officials for suspending a student editor who had published a cartoon mocking affirmative action. Taranto reproduced the offending cartoon in the Northridge paper, whereupon his faculty adviser suspended *him* from his position for two weeks because he had printed "controversial" material without her permission. The ACLU agreed to represent him in a First Amendment suit—"We were as outraged as he was by the attempt to censor the press," Halperin recalled—and two years later a settlement was reached.

While we are accumulating ironies, let it be noted that the ACLU, the selfsame organization in which Michael Dukakis's "card-carrying membership" yielded George Bush considerable mileage in the 1988 election campaign, has been conspicuously more vigilant and outspoken about campus assaults on free expression in 1989 than has the Bush administration. The Secretary of Education, Lauro Cavazos (himself a former university president), has been silent. The White House has been mute. During an incident at Brown in May, when an art professor canceled a long-planned screening of the classic film, *Birth of a Nation,* because the Providence branch of the NAACP had denounced it, the local ACLU affiliate was the only voice raised in dismay. "University officials," declared its executive director, "have now opened the door to numerous pressure groups who may wish to ban from the campus other films that they too deem 'offensive.'" Indeed. A colleague of mine recently revived a long-lapsed membership in the ACLU on the straightforward ground that no other national entity is resisting the spread of attitude-adjustment, censorship, and behavior codes in higher education.

All this would be worrisome enough even if the academy were doing well with respect to actual education for the minority students whose numbers it is so keen to increase and whose sensibilities campus administrators are so touchy about. But that is simply not the case.

Black and Hispanic students are less likely to enroll in college to begin with. This is not because admission offices turn them away—to the contrary—and not because too little student aid is available to help them defray the costs. (In any event, 80 percent of all students attend state institutions, in which tuitions average about $1,200 per year.) The largest reason more minority students do not matriculate is that so many attended wretched elementary and secondary schools in which they took the wrong courses, were poorly taught, had little expected of them, skipped class a lot, never learned much, and may well have dropped out.

Minority youngsters are not, of course, the only victims of our foundering public-education system, but they are the ones whose life prospects are most blighted by it, the ones for whom a solid basic education can make the biggest difference. Academic leaders know this full well, just as they understand that shoddy schools are major producers of ill-prepared college students. Yet for all its protestations and pieties, and notwithstanding its ardor for enhancing "diversity" on campus, the higher-education system has done essentially nothing to strengthen the schools that serve as its feeder institutions. It has not even taken the straightforward steps that are well within its purview—such as a complete overhaul of the education of teachers and principals. It has not reached down into the schools to begin the "admissions-counseling" process with disadvantaged fifth- and sixth-graders. And it most certainly has not made the tough decisions that over time could have a profound influence on the standards of the entire elementary-secondary system, such as announcing well in advance that beginning in, say, 1998 no student will be admitted to college who has not actually attained a specified level of knowledge and skills.

Such strong medicine is resisted with the argument that it must surely be bad for minority youngsters. That has been precisely the response to the NCAA's attempts to curb exploitation of minority athletes by requiring them to meet minimum academic standards in order to play intercollegiate sports or receive athletic scholarships. Georgetown's basketball coach staged a well-publicized one-man "strike" to protest this, claiming that the rules are discriminatory. The NCAA is expected to recant, heedless of the warning by the black tennis champion Arthur Ashe that "Black America stands to lose another generation of our young men unless they are helped to learn as well as play ball."

Getting more adequately prepared students inside the campus gates might also help to boost the egregiously low proportion of minority matriculants who end up with a degree. The college-dropout rate is a problem for everyone, and has been rising over the past decade, but it is manifestly worse for black and Hispanic students. According to the U.S. Department of Education, among the 1980 high-school graduates who immediately enrolled full-time in college, 50 percent of the Asians and 56 percent of the white students earned their bachelor's degrees within five-and-a-half years, but this was true for only 31 percent of black students, and for 33 percent of Hispanics. (For minority *athletes,* the dropout rate is higher still. "It's no secret," Ashe writes, "that 75 percent of black football and basketball players fail to graduate from college.")

One has got to conclude that if the colleges and universities put as much effort into high-quality instruction, vigorous advising, extra tutoring, summer sessions, and other supplementary academic services as they do to combating naughty campus behavior and unkind words—and maximizing field-house revenues—they could make a big dent in these numbers. But, of course, it is easier to adopt a behavior code for students than to alter faculty-time allocations and administration priorities. Symbolic responses to problems are always quicker and less burdensome, at least in the short run, than hard work.

Completing the degree, regrettably, does not end the matter, either. While possessing a college diploma will indisputably help a person get ahead in life even if he is still ignorant and intellectually inept, for a variety of public and private reasons it is desirable that college graduates also be well-educated. For minority graduates, it may be especially important that any plausible grounds for doubt be erased—from the minds of prospective employers, among others—as to the actual intellectual standards that their degrees represent.

Today, unfortunately, one cannot equate the acquisition of a bachelor's degree with possession of substantial knowledge and skills. When the Department of Education examined literacy levels among young adults in 1985, it accumulated data that enable us to glimpse the cognitive attainments of college graduates, as well as those with less schooling. The good news is that the former had generally attained a higher level than the latter. The bad news is that degree-holders did none too well.

Three scales were used, representing "prose literacy," "document literacy," and "quantitative literacy." At the highest level of the scales, white college graduates were to be found in proportions of 47, 52, and 48 percent, respectively—not really very laudable considering that the intellectual challenges to be mastered at those levels entailed such tasks as discerning the main point of a newspaper column, coping with a bus schedule, and calculating the change due and tip owed on a simple lunch. Among black college graduates, however, these levels were reached by only 18, 11, and 14 percent respectively. (The number of Hispanic college graduates in the sample was too small for statistical reliability.)

The higher-education system, in short, is awarding a great many diplomas to individuals whose intellectual attainments are meager, even at the end of college, and for minority graduates this is happening so often that the academy may be faulted for massive deception. It is giving people degrees which imply that they have accomplished something they have not in fact achieved. Like driving a new car home from the dealer only to discover that it is a lemon, the owners of such degrees are likely one day to think themselves cheated rather than aided by the hypocrisy and erratic quality control of the academic enterprise. The taxpayers who now underwrite most of that enterprise are apt to feel much the same. Over time this can only diminish the support, the respect, and the allure of higher education itself, as well as further depleting its tiny residuum of moral capital.

Some academic leaders understand this. A few also have the gumption to say it. "The alternatives I see ahead for our higher-education system are reform from without or reform from within," Stephen J. Trachtenberg, the new president of George Washington University, predicted in a recent address to the American Association of University Administrators. "The present situation cannot hold because too many Americans are coming to regard it as incompatible with ethics, values, and moral imperatives."

Reform from within would surely be preferable. It nearly always is. But in 1989 the most prominent forms of spontaneous change on many of our high-status college and university campuses are apt instead to exacerbate the gravest problems the academy faces. Creating more complex and onerous rituals as they worship at the altar of "diversity," they concurrently provide the putative beneficiaries of their efforts so feeble an education as to suggest a cynical theology indeed. Meanwhile, in the realms of intellectual inquiry and expression, they permit ever less diversity, turning the campus (in the memorable phrase of civil-rights scholar Abigail Thernstrom) into "an island of repression in a sea of freedom."

PART II   # Utility

Utilitarianism, a moral theory mentioned in Plato's dialogues, first advocated by Francis Hutcheson, and brought to full development by Jeremy Bentham and John Stuart Mill, can be summarized in two words: *Maximize good.* Utilitarians hold that all of ethics and political philosophy reduces to that one maxim, the principle of utility.

The principle seems simple but has a number of far-reaching consequences. First, utilitarians evaluate actions by the extent to which they maximize good. They evaluate actions, therefore, solely by examining their consequences. In determining whether an action or kind of action is right or wrong, we need to ask, Is it for the best? What effect does it have on the amount of good in the universe? Utilitarianism is thus a version of *consequentialism,* the view that the moral value of an action depends completely on its consequences.

Other moral philosophers contend that other features of actions are relevant to their moral value. Killing, for example, is generally a bad thing. But our judgment of a killer depends on other factors. Was the killing purely accidental, or did it result from negligence? Did it stem from a fit of rage, or was it premeditated? The prior actions, motives, intentions, and general state of mind of the agent, we think, make a moral difference. Utilitarians are committed to saying that all these things are irrelevant to evaluating the killing itself—but, they would say, they are highly relevant to evaluating the killer. Utilitarians need not banish motives, intentions, states of mind, and circumstances from ethics. But they must define their moral values ultimately in terms of the moral value of actions. We might say that an intention is good, for example, to the extent that it results in good actions; that a motive is good to the extent that it results in good intentions; that a character trait is good to the extent that it results in good motives; and so on.

Second, utilitarianism is a *universalist* theory: We must judge whether an action or kind of action maximizes the total amount of good in the universe. Thus, we must consider the consequences of the action on everyone it affects. We cannot consider ourselves alone, or just people in our community, or our fellow citizens; we must consider *everyone.* Most actions affect only a few people in any significant, identifiable way. Political decisions, however, often affect millions. In either case, we must be prepared to consider the effects on everyone affected.

Third, utilitarianism requires an independent theory of the good. The principle of utility tells us to maximize good, but it does not tell us what the good is. What, exactly, must we maximize? Bentham and Mill are *hedonists:* they believe that pleasure and pain are the only sources of value. The good, for both, is pleasure and the absence of pain. On the view of these philosophers, then, the principle of utility directs us to maximize the balance of pleasure over pain. Other utilitarians hold other theories of the good. Some, for example, identify the good with the satisfaction of desire. Some maintain that the good is indefinable and cannot be identified with anything else.

Whatever theory of the good a utilitarian holds, however, that theory must treat the good as a quantity to be maximized. The principle requires us to maximize good; good, therefore, must be the kind of thing that can be maximized. Certainly this means that we must be able to judge whether one circumstance contains more good than another. It probably also means that we must be able to quantify the amount of good in any given circumstance; that is, that we be able to say how much good that circumstance contains—ideally, by assigning it a number.

Utilitarians tend to fall into two main varieties. Some, called *act-utilitarians,* take the evaluation of individual actions as primary. They judge an action by the effects it has on the amount of good. Others, *rule-utilitarians,* take the evaluation of kinds of actions as primary. They judge rules by the effects of following them and then judge individual actions by appealing to the recommended rules. Bentham is an act-utilitarian; Mill appears to be a rule-utilitarian, although it is possible to interpret him as an act-utilitarian.

In most cases, act- and rule-utilitarians agree in their moral evaluations of individual actions. They disagree, however, (*a*) when an action maximizes good while violating rules that usually—but not in a particular case—maximize good, and (*b*) when an action does not maximize good in particular case but does follow those rules. Both situations involve a conflict between the principle of utility and a rule designed to maximize good in general. Act-utilitarians consider it bizarre to say that we should follow the rule instead of the principle of utility; according to rule-utilitarianism itself, the rule derives its force solely from the principle in the first place. But rule-utilitarians believe that rules are indispensable to moral thinking. We cannot calculate what to do in every individual case; we must think about kinds of actions, formulate rules that, if followed, maximize good, and then follow those rules.

Rule-utilitarians encounter a special difficulty: the rules justified by the principle of utility may come into conflict with each other. Among the good-maximizing rules, for example, are some commanding us to avoid murder and to save innocent lives. But there may be cases in which we can save lives only by committing a murder. Which rule takes precedence? Mill suggests that in such cases, we appeal to the principle of utility itself. In his theory, then, the principle has two roles. It determines which rules we should adopt and resolves conflicts between them.

JEREMY BENTHAM

from *An Introduction to the Principles of Morals and Legislation* (1789)

Jeremy Bentham (1748–1832), an English utilitarian, was born in Houndsditch, London. He was a prodigious student, entering Queen's College, Oxford, at twelve and graduating at fifteen. He studied law at Lincoln's Inn and was admitted to the bar at nineteen. Bentham was so appalled by English law, however, that he never practiced it, even for a day. Instead, he devoted his life to legal reform.

Bentham wrote many thousands of pages of pamphlets, papers, and books, relatively few of which were published during his lifetime. He founded a group of powerful and ultimately very influential thinkers, the philosophical radicals, which included James Mill, economist David Ricardo, and legal theorist John Austin. Bentham also founded the Westminster Review, *a political journal, and University College, London, where his embalmed body still rests, seated, in a glass case in the library.*

Principles of Morals and Legislation, *the only major theoretical work of his own that Bentham saw in print, appeared in 1789, the year of the French Revolution. Bentham objects strongly to views of morality and politics that stress individual conscience or religious conviction; both, in his view, are little more than prejudice in disguise. Bentham also rejects doctrines of natural rights, such as those invoked by the French revolutionaries, calling them "nonsense on stilts." Instead, he proposes to base ethics and politics on a single principle, the principle of utility. Roughly, Bentham's version of this principle states that a good action increases the balance of pleasure over pain in the community of people affected by it; a bad action decreases the balance. From this principle, taken together with the facts about the effects of actions, Bentham maintains,* all our correct moral and political judgments follow. *(Source: Reprinted from Jeremy Bentham,* An Introduction to the Principles of Morals and Legislation. *London: Printed for T. Payne, 1789.)*

QUESTIONS FOR REFLECTION

1. What is Bentham's principle of utility? What is utility?

2. What does Bentham's principle imply about what ought to be done when (a) only one available option, on balance, augments the happiness of the community; (b) only one available option, on balance, diminishes the happiness of the community; (c) all available options augment, on balance, the happiness of the community; (d) all available options diminish, on balance, the happiness of the community? What, intuitively, ought to be done in such cases, from a utilitarian point of view? What does this indicate about Bentham's principle?

3. Actions that, on balance, augment the happiness of the community "ought to be done" or at least are not ones that "ought not to be done." Explain the difference. Why does Bentham waffle? (Consider the cases mentioned in the previous question.)

4. How does Bentham argue for the principle of utility?

5. What is the principle of sympathy and antipathy? Why does Bentham disapprove of it?

6. In Chapter IV, Bentham details the *moral calculus*, his method for computing the utility of actions. How does it work? What aspects of pleasure and pain does Bentham consider?

CHAPTER 1 / OF THE PRINCIPLE OF UTILITY

1. Nature has placed mankind under the governance of two sovereign masters, *pain* and *pleasure*. It is for them alone to point out what we ought to do, as well as to determine what we shall do. On the one hand the standard of right and wrong, on the other the chain of causes and effects, are fastened to their throne. They govern us in all we do, in all we say, in all we think: every effort we can make to throw off our subjection, will serve but to demonstrate and confirm it. In words a man may pretend to abjure their empire: but in reality he will remain subject to it all the while. The *principle of utility* recognises this subjection, and assumes it for the foundation of that system, the object of which is to rear the fabric of felicity by the hands of reason and of law. Systems which attempt to question it, deal in sounds instead of senses, in caprice instead of reason, in darkness instead of light.

But enough of metaphor and declamation: it is not by such means that moral science is to be improved.

2. The principle of utility is the foundation of the present work: it will be proper therefore at the outset to give an explicit and determinate account of what is meant by it. By the principle of utility is meant that principle which approves or disapproves of every action whatsoever; according to the tendency which it appears to have to augment or diminish the happiness of the party whose interest is in question: or, what is the same thing in other words, to promote or to oppose that happiness. I say of every action whatsoever, and therefore not only of every action of a private individual, but of every measure of government.

3. By utility is meant that property in any object, whereby it tends to produce benefit, advantage, pleasure, good, or happiness, (all this in the present case comes to the same thing) or (what comes again to the same thing) to prevent the happening of mischief, pain, evil, or unhappiness to the party whose interest is considered: if that party be the community in general, then the happiness of the community: if a particular individual, then the happiness of that individual.

4. The interest of the community is one of the most general expressions that can occur in the phraseology of morals: no wonder that the meaning of it is often lost. When it has a meaning, it is this. The community is a fictitious *body*, composed of the individual persons who are considered as constituting as it were its *members*. The interest of the community then is, what?—the sum of the interests of the several members who compose it.

5. It is in vain to talk of the interest of the community, without understanding what is the interest of the individual. A thing is said to promote the interest, or to be *for* the interest, of an individual, when it tends to add to the sum total of his pleasures: or, what comes to the same thing, to diminish the sum total of his pains.

6. An action then may be said to be conformable to the principle of utility, or, for shortness sake, to utility, (meaning with respect to the community at large) when the tendency it has to augment the happiness of the community is greater than any it has to diminish it.

7. A measure of government (which is but a particular kind of action, performed by a particular person or persons) may be said to be conformable to or dictated by the principle of utility, when in like manner the tendency which it has to augment the happiness of the community is greater than any which it has to diminish it.

8. When an action, or in particular a measure of government, is supposed by a man to be conformable to the principle of utility, it may be convenient, for the purposes of discourse, to imagine a kind of law or dictate, called a law or dictate of utility; and to speak of the action in question, as being conformable to such law or dictate.

9. A man may be said to be a partisan of the principle of utility, when the approbation or disapprobation he annexes to any action, or to any measure, is determined by and proportioned to the tendency which he conceives it to have to augment or to diminish the happiness of the community: or in other words, to its conformity or uncomformity to the laws or dictates of utility.

10. Of an action that is conformable to the principle of utility one may always say either that it is one that ought to be done, or at least that it is not

one that ought not to be done. One may say also, that it is right it should be done; at least that it is not wrong it should be done: that it is a right action; at least that it is not a wrong action. When thus interpreted, the words *ought,* and *right* and *wrong,* and others of that stamp, have a meaning: when otherwise, they have none.

11. Has the rectitude of this principle been ever formally contested? It should seem that it had, by those who have not known what they have been meaning. Is it susceptible of any direct proof? it should seem not: for that which is used to prove every thing else, cannot itself be proved: a chain of proofs must have their commencement somewhere. To give such proof is as impossible as it is needless.

12. Not that there is or ever has been that human creature breathing, however stupid or perverse, who has not on many, perhaps on most occasions of his life, deferred to it. By the natural constitution of the human frame, on most occasions of their lives men in general embrace this principle, without thinking of it: if not for the ordering of their own actions, yet for the trying of their own actions, as well as of those of other men. There have been, at the same time, not many, perhaps, even of the most intelligent, who have been disposed to embrace it purely and without reserve. There are even few who have not taken some occasion or other to quarrel with it, either on account of their not understanding always how to apply it, or on account of some prejudice or other which they were afraid to examine into, or could not bear to part with. For such is the stuff that man is made of: in principle and in practice, in a right track and in a wrong one, the rarest of all human qualities is consistency.

13. When a man attempts to combat the principle of utility, it is with reasons drawn, without his being aware of it, from that very principle itself. His arguments, if they prove any thing, prove not that the principle is *wrong,* but that, according to the application he supposes to be made of it, it is *misapplied.* Is it possible for a man to move the earth? Yes; but he must first find out another earth to stand upon.

14. To disprove the propriety of it by arguments is impossible; but, from the causes that have been mentioned, or from some confused or partial view of it, a man may happen to be disposed not to relish it. Where this is the case, if he thinks the settling of his opinions on such a subject worth the trouble, let him take the following steps and at length, perhaps, he may come to reconcile himself to it.

1. Let him settle with himself, whether he would wish to discard this principle altogether; if so, let him consider what it is that all his reasonings (in matters of politics especially) can amount to?

2. If he would, let him settle with himself, whether he would judge and act without any principle, or whether there is any other he would judge and act by?

3. If there be, let him examine and satisfy himself whether the principle he thinks he has found is really any separate intelligible principle; or whether it be not a mere principle in words, a kind of phrase, which at bottom expresses neither more nor less than the mere averment of his own unfounded sentiments; that is, what in another person he might be apt to call caprice?

4. If he is inclined to think that his own approbation or disapprobation, annexed to the idea of an act, without any regard to its consequences, is a sufficient foundation for him to judge and act upon, let him ask himself whether his sentiment is to be a standard of right and wrong, with respect to every other man, or whether every other man's sentiment has the same privilege of being a standard to itself?

5. In the first case, let him ask himself whether his principle is not despotical, and hostile to all the rest of human race?

6. In the second case, whether it is not anarchical, and whether at this rate there are not as many different standards of right and wrong as there are men? and whether even to the sane man, the same thing, which is right to-day, may not (without the least change in its nature) be wrong to-morrow? and whether the same thing is not right and wrong in the same place at the same time? and in either case, whether all argument is not at an end? and whether, when two men have said, "I like this," and "I don't like it," they can (upon such a principle) have any thing more to say?

7. If he should have said to himself, No: for that the sentiment which he proposes as a standard must be grounded on reflection, let him say on what particulars the reflection is to turn? if on particulars having relation to the utility of the act, then let him say whether this is not deserting his own principle, and borrowing assistance from that very one in opposition to which he sets it up: or if not on those particulars, on what other particulars?

8. If he should be for compounding the matter, and adopting his own principle in part, and the prin- ciple of utility in part, let him say how far he will adopt it?

9. When he has settled with himself where he will stop, then let him ask himself how he justifies to himself the adopting it so far? and why he will not adopt it any farther?

10. Admitting any other principle than the principle of utility to be a right principle, a principle that it is right for a man to pursue; admitting (what is not true) that the word *right* can have a meaning without reference to utility, let him say whether there is any such thing as a *motive* that a man can have to pursue the dictates of it: if there is, let him say what that motive is, and how it is to be distinguished from those which enforce the dictates of utility: if not, then lastly let him say what it is this other principle can be good for? . . .

CHAPTER II / OF PRINCIPLES ADVERSE TO THAT OF UTILITY

11. Among principles adverse to that of utility, that which at this day seems to have most influence in matters of government, is what may be called the principle of sympathy and antipathy. By the principle of sympathy and antipathy, I mean that principle which approves or disapproves of certain actions, not on account of their tending to augment the happiness, nor yet on account of their tending to diminish the happiness of the party whose interest is in question, but merely because a man finds himself disposed to approve or disapprove of them: holding up that approbation or disapprobation as a sufficient reason for itself, and disclaiming the necessity of looking out for any extrinsic ground. Thus far in the general department of morals: and in the particular department of politics, measuring out the quantum (as well as determining the ground) of punishment, by the degree of the disapprobation.

12. It is manifest, that this is rather a principle in name than in reality: it is not a positive princi- ple of itself, so much as a term employed to signify the negation of all principle. What one expects to find in a principle is something that points out some external consideration, as a means of warranting and guiding the internal sentiments of approbation and disapprobation: this expectation is but ill fulfilled by a proposition, which does neither more nor less than hold up each of those sentiments as a ground and standard for itself.

13. In looking over the catalogue of human actions (says a partisan of this principle) in order to determine which of them are to be marked with the seal of disapprobation, you need but to take counsel of your own feelings: whatever you find in yourself a propensity to condemn, is wrong for that very reason. For the same reason it is also meet for punishment: in what proportion it is adverse to utility, or whether it be adverse to utility at all, is a matter that makes no difference. In that same *proportion* also is it meet for punishment: if you hate much, punish much: if you hate little, punish little: punish as you hate. If you hate not at all, punish not at all: the fine feelings of the soul are not to be overborne and tyrannised by the harsh and rugged dictates of political utility.

14. The various systems that have been formed concerning the standard of right and wrong, may all be reduced to the principle of sympathy and antipathy. One account may serve for all of them. They consist all of them in so many contrivances for avoiding the obligation of appealing to any external standard, and for prevailing upon the reader to accept of the author's sentiment or opinion as a reason for itself. The phrase is different, but the principle the same.

15. It is manifest, that the dictates of this principle will frequently coincide with those of utility, though perhaps without intending any such thing. Probably more frequently than not: and hence it is

that the business of penal justice is carried on upon that tolerable sort of footing upon which we see it carried on in common at this day. For what more natural or more general ground of hatred to a practice can there be, than the mischievousness of such practice? What all men are exposed to suffer by, all men will be disposed to hate. It is far yet, however, from being a constant ground: for when a man suffers, it is not always that he knows what it is he suffers by. A man may suffer grievously, for instance, by a new tax, without being able to trace up the cause of his sufferings to the injustice of some neighbour, who has eluded the payment of an old one.

16. The principle of sympathy and antipathy is most apt to err on the side of severity. It is for applying punishment in many cases which deserve none: in many cases which deserve some, it is for applying more than they deserve. There is no incident imaginable, be it ever so trivial, and so remote from mischief, from which this principle may not extract a ground of punishment. Any difference in taste: any difference in opinion: upon one subject as well as upon another. No disagreement so trifling which perseverance and altercation will not render serious. Each becomes in the other's eyes an enemy, and if laws permit, a criminal. This is one of the circumstances by which the human race is distinguished (not much indeed to its advantage) from the brute creation.

17. It is not, however, by any means unexampled for this principle to err on the side of lenity. A near and perceptible mischief moves antipathy. A remote and imperceptible mischief, though not less real, has no effect. Instances in proof of this will occur in numbers in the course of the work. It would be breaking in upon the order of it to give them here. . . .

19. There are two things which are very apt to be confounded, but which it imports us carefully to distinguish:—the motive or cause, which, by operating on the mind of an individual, is productive of any act: and the ground or reason which warrants a legislator, or other by-stander, in regarding that act with an eye of approbation. When the act happens, in the particular instance in question, to be productive of effects which we approve of, much more if we happen to observe that the same motive may fre-

quently be productive, in other instances, of the like effects, we are apt to transfer our approbation to the motive itself, and to assume, as the just ground for the approbation we bestow on the act, the circumstance of its originating from that motive. It is in this way that the sentiment of antipathy has often been considered as a just ground of action. Antipathy, for instance, in such or such a case, is the cause of an action which is attended with good effects: but this does not make it a right ground of action in that case, any more than in any other. Still farther. Not only the effects are good, but the agent sees beforehand that they will be so. This may make the action indeed a perfectly right action: but it does not make antipathy a right ground of action. For the same sentiment of antipathy, if implicitly deferred to, may be, and very frequently is, productive of the very worst effects. Antipathy, therefore, can never be a right ground of action. No more, therefore, can resentment, which, as will be seen more particularly hereafter, is but a modification of antipathy. The only right ground of action, that can possibly subsist, is, after all, the consideration of utility, which if it is a right principle of action, and of approbation, in any one case, is so in every other. Other principles in abundance, that is, other motives, may be the reasons why such and such an act *has* been done: that is, the reasons or causes of its being done: but it is this alone that can be the reason why it might or ought to have been done. Antipathy or resentment requires always to be regulated, to prevent its doing mischief: to be regulated by what? always by the principle of utility. The principle of utility neither requires nor admits of any other regulator than itself.

CHAPTER IV / VALUE OF A LOT OF PLEASURE OR PAIN, HOW TO BE MEASURED

1. Pleasures then, and the avoidance of pains, are the *ends* which the legislator has in view: it behooves him therefore to understand their *value*. Pleasures and pains are the *instruments* he has to work with: it behooves him therefore to understand their force, which is again, in other words, their value.

2. To a person considered *by himself,* the value of a pleasure or pain considered *by itself,* will be greater or less, according to the four following circumstances:

1. Its *intensity.*
2. Its *duration.*
3. Its *certainty* or *uncertainty.*
4. Its *propinquity* or *remoteness.*

3. These are the circumstances which are to be considered in estimating a pleasure or a pain considered each of them by itself. But when the value of any pleasure or pain is considered for the purpose of estimating the tendency of any *act* by which it is produced, there are two other circumstances to be taken into account; these are,

5. Its *fecundity,* or the chance it has of being followed by sensations of the *same* kind: that is, pleasures, if it be a pleasure: pain, if it be a pain.

6. Its *purity,* or the chance it has of *not* being followed by sensations of the *opposite* kind: that is, pains, if it be a pleasure: pleasures, if it be a pain.

These two last, however, are in strictness scarcely to be deemed properties of the pleasure or the pain itself; they are not, therefore, in strictness to be taken into the account of the value of that pleasure or that pain. They are in strictness to be deemed properties only of the act, or other event, by which such pleasure or pain has been produced; and accordingly are only to be taken into the account of the tendency of such act or such event.

4. To a *number* of persons, with reference to each of whom the value of a pleasure or a pain is considered, it will be greater or less, according to seven circumstances: to wit, the six preceding ones; *viz.*

1. Its *intensity.*
2. Its *duration.*
3. Its *certainty* or *uncertainty.*
4. Its *propinquity* or *remoteness.*
5. Its *fecundity.*
6. Its *purity.*

And one other; to wit:

7. Its *extent;* that is, the number of persons to whom it *extends;* or (in other words) who are affected by it.

5. To take an exact account then of the general tendency of any act, by which the interests of a community are affected, proceed as follows. Begin with any one person of those whose interests seem most immediately to be affected by it: and take an account,

1. Of the value of each distinguishable *pleasure* which appears to be produced by it in the *first* instance.
2. Of the value of each *pain* which appears to be produced by it in the *first* instance.
3. Of the value of each pleasure which appears to be produced by it *after* the first. This constitutes the *fecundity* of the first *pleasure* and the *impurity* of the first *pain.*
4. Of the value of each *pain* which appears to be produced by it after the first. This constitutes the *fecundity* of the first *pain,* and the *impurity* of the first pleasure.
5. Sum up all the values of all the *pleasures* on the one side, and those of all the pains on the other. The balance, if it be on the side of pleasure, will give the *good* tendency of the act upon the whole, with respect to the interests of that *individual* person; if on the side of pain, the *bad* tendency of it upon the whole.
6. Take an account of the *number* of persons whose interests appear to be concerned; and repeat the above process with respect to each. *Sum up* the numbers expressive of the degrees of *good* tendency, which the act has, with respect to each individual, in regard to whom the tendency of it is *good* upon the whole: do this again with respect to each individual, in regard to whom the tendency of it is *bad* upon the whole. Take the *balance;* which, if on the side of *pleasure,* will give the general *good tendency* of the act, with respect to the total number or community of individuals concerned; if on the side of pain, the general *evil tendency,* with respect to the same community.

6. It is not to be expected that this process should be strictly pursued previously to every moral judgment, or to every legislative or judicial operation. It may, however, be always kept in view: and as near as the process actually pursued on these occasions approaches to it, so near will such process approach to the character of an exact one.

7. The same process is alike applicable to pleasure and pain, in whatever shape they appear: and by whatever denomination they are distinguished: to pleasure, whether it be called *good* (which is properly the cause or instrument of pleasure) or *profit* (which is distant pleasure, or the cause or instrument of distant pleasure,) or *convenience, or advantage, benefit, emolument, happiness,* and so forth: to pain, whether it be called *evil,* (which corresponds to *good*) or *mischief,* or *inconvenience,* or *disadvantage,* or *loss,* or *unhappiness,* and so forth.

8. Nor is this a novel and unwarranted, any more than it is a useless theory. In all this there is nothing but what the practice of mankind, wheresoever they have a clear view of their own interest, is perfectly conformable to. An article of property, an estate in land, for instance, is valuable, on what account? On account of the pleasures of all kinds which it enables a man to produce, and what comes to the same thing the pains of all kinds which it enables him to avert. But the value of such an article of property is universally understood to rise or fall according to the length or shortness of the time which a man has in it: the certainty or uncertainty of its coming into possession: and the nearness or remoteness of the time at which, if at all, it is to come into possession. As to the *intensity* of the pleasures which a man may derive from it, this is never thought of, because it depends upon the use which each particular person may come to make of it; which cannot be estimated till the particular pleasures he may come to derive from it, or the particular pains he may come to exclude by means of it, are brought to view. For the same reason, neither does he think of the *fecundity* or *purity* of those pleasures. . . .

JOHN STUART MILL

from *Utilitarianism* (1861)

(*Source: Reprinted from John Stuart Mill*, Utilitarianism. *London: Longman's, 1907.*)

QUESTIONS FOR REFLECTION

1. What is Mill's principle of utility? What does he mean by "utility"?

2. Mill distinguishes qualities, as well as quantities, of pleasures. Why? How does Mill rank pleasures in terms of quality?

3. People sometimes choose pleasures of lower quality over those of higher quality. How does Mill explain this?

4. Some philosophers have held that Mill's distinction between qualities of pleasures confronts him with a dilemma. Either differences in quality can be measured in terms of differences in quantity, in which case the distinction does not seem very important, or they cannot be, in which case the idea of maximizing the general happiness seems to make little sense. How do you think Mill might respond to this dilemma?

5. What objections against utilitarianism does Mill consider? How does he respond to them?

6. What are the roles of tradition and conscience in Mill's theory?

7. What are secondary principles? What role do they play in Mill's theory? How do we decide which secondary principles to adopt? What happens when these principles conflict?

CHAPTER II / WHAT UTILITARIANISM IS

... The creed which accepts as the foundation of morals "utility" or the "greatest happiness principle" holds that actions are right in proportion as they tend to promote happiness; wrong as they tend to produce the reverse of happiness. By happiness is intended pleasure and the absence of pain; by unhappiness, pain and the privation of pleasure. To give a clear view of the moral standard set up by the theory, much more requires to be said; in particular, what things it includes in the ideas of pain and pleasure, and to what extent this is left an open question. But these supplementary explanations do not affect the theory of life on which this theory of morality is grounded—namely, that pleasure and freedom from pain are the only things desirable as ends; and that all desirable things (which are as numerous in the utilitarian as in any other scheme) are desirable either for pleasure inherent in themselves or as means to the promotion of pleasure and the prevention of pain.

Now such a theory of life excites in many minds, and among them in some of the most estimable in feeling and purpose, inveterate dislike. To suppose that life has (as they express it) no higher end than pleasure—no better and nobler object of desire and pursuit—they designate as utterly mean and groveling, as a doctrine worthy only of swine, to whom the followers of Epicurus were, at a very early period, contemptuously likened; and modern holders of the doctrine are occasionally made the subject of equally polite comparison by its German, French, and English assailants.

When thus attacked, the Epicureans have always answered that it is not they, but their accusers, who represent human nature in a degrading light, since the accusation supposes human beings to be capable of no pleasures except those of which swine are capable. If this supposition were true, the charge could not be gainsaid, but would then be no longer an imputation; for if the sources of pleasure were precisely the same to human beings and to swine, the rule of life which is good enough for the one would be good enough for the other. The comparison of the Epicurean life to that of beasts is felt as degrading, precisely because a beast's pleasures do not satisfy a human being's conceptions of happiness. Human beings have faculties more elevated than the animal appetites and, when once made conscious of them, do not regard anything as happiness which does not include their gratification. I do not indeed, consider the Epicureans to have been by any means faultless in drawing out their scheme of consequences from the utilitarian principle. To do this in any sufficient manner, many Stoic, as well as Christian, elements require to be included. But there is no known Epicurean theory of life which does not assign to the pleasures of the intellect, of the feelings and imagination, and of the moral sentiments a much higher value as pleasures than to those of mere sensation. It must be admitted, however, that utilitarian writers in general have placed the superiority of mental over bodily pleasures chiefly in the greater permanency, safety, uncostliness, etc., of the former—that is, in their circumstantial advantages rather than in their intrinsic nature. And on all these points utilitarians have fully proved their case; but they might have taken the other and, as it may be called, higher ground with entire consistency. It is quite compatible with the principle of utility to recognize the fact that some kinds of pleasure are more desirable and more valuable than others. It would be absurd that, while in estimating all other things quality is considered as well as quantity, the estimation of pleasure should be supposed to depend on quantity alone.

If I am asked what I mean by difference of quality in pleasures, or what makes one pleasure more valuable than another, merely as a pleasure, except its being greater in amount, there is but one possible answer. Of two pleasures, if there be one to which all or almost all who have experience of both give a decided preference, irrespective of any feeling of moral obligation to prefer it, that is the more desirable pleasure. If one of the two is, by those who are competently acquainted with both, placed so far above the other that they prefer it, even though knowing it to be attended with a greater amount of discontent, and would not resign it for any quantity of the other pleasure which their nature is capable of, we are justified in ascribing to the preferred enjoyment a superiority in quality so far outweighing quantity as to render it, in comparison, of small account.

Now it is an unquestionable fact that those who are equally acquainted with and equally capable of appreciating and enjoying both do give a most marked preference to the manner of existence which employs their higher faculties. Few human creatures would consent to be changed into any of the lower animals for a promise of the fullest allowance of a beast's pleasures; no intelligent human being would consent to be a fool, no instructed person would be an ignoramus, no person of feeling and conscience would be selfish and base, even though they should be persuaded that the fool, the dunce, or the rascal is better satisfied with his lot than they are with theirs. They would not resign what they possess more than he for the most complete satisfaction of all the desires which they have in common with him. If they ever fancy they would, it is only in cases of unhappiness so extreme that to escape from it they would exchange their lot for almost any other, however undesirable in their own eyes. A being of higher faculties requires more to make him happy, is capable probably of more acute suffering, and certainly accessible to it at more points, than one of an inferior type; but in spite of these liabilities, he can never really wish to sink into what he feels to be a lower grade of existence. We may give what explanation we please of this unwillingness; we may attribute it to pride, a name which is given indiscriminately to some of the most and to some of the least estimable feelings of which mankind are capable; we may refer it to the love of liberty and personal independence, an appeal to which was with the Stoics one of the most effective means for the inculcation of it; to the love of power or to the love of excitement, both of which do really enter into and contribute to it; but its most appropriate appellation is a sense of dignity, which all human beings possess in one form or other, and in some, though by no means in exact, proportion to their higher faculties, and which is so essential a part of the happiness of those in whom it is strong that nothing which conflicts with it could be otherwise than momentarily an object of desire to them. Whoever supposes that this preference takes place at a sacrifice of happiness—that the superior being, in anything like equal circumstances, is not happier than the inferior—confounds the two very different ideas of happiness and content. It is indisputable that the being whose capacities of enjoyment are low has the greatest chance of having them fully satisfied; and a highly endowed being will always feel that any happiness which he can look for, as the world is constituted, is imperfect. But he can learn to bear its imperfections, if they are at all bearable; and they will not make him envy the being who is indeed unconscious of the imperfections, but only because he feels not at all the good which those imperfections qualify. It is better to be a human being dissatisfied than a pig satisfied; better to be Socrates dissatisfied than a fool satisfied. And if the fool, or the pig, are of a different opinion, it is because they only know their own side of the question. The other party to the comparison knows both sides.

It may be objected that many who are capable of the higher pleasures occasionally, under the influence of temptation, postpone them to the lower. But this is quite compatible with a full appreciation of the intrinsic superiority of the higher. Men often, from infirmity of character, make their election for the nearer good, though they know it to be the less valuable; and this no less when the choice is between two bodily pleasures than when it is between bodily and mental. They pursue sensual indulgence to the injury of health, though perfectly aware that health is the greater good. It may be further objected that many who begin with youthful enthusiasm for everything noble, as they advance in years, sink into indolence and selfishness. But I do not believe that those who undergo this very common change voluntarily choose the lower description of pleasures in preference to the higher. I believe that, before they devote themselves exclusively to the one, they have already become incapable of the other. Capacity for the nobler feelings is in most natures a very tender plant, easily killed, not

only by hostile influences, but by mere want of sustenance; and in the majority of young persons it speedily dies away if the occupations to which their position in life has devoted them, and the society into which it has thrown them, are not favorable to keeping that higher capacity in exercise. Men lose their high aspirations as they lose their intellectual tastes, because they have not time or opportunity for indulging them; and they addict themselves to inferior pleasures, not because they deliberately prefer them, but because they are either the only ones to which they have access or the only ones which they are any longer capable of enjoying. It may be questioned whether anyone who has remained equally susceptible to both classes of pleasures ever knowingly and calmly preferred the lower, though many, in all ages, have broken down in an ineffectual attempt to combine both.

From this verdict of the only competent judges, I apprehend there can be no appeal. On a question which is the best worth having of two pleasures, or which of two modes of existence is the most grateful to the feelings, apart from its moral attributes, and from its consequences, the judgment of these who are qualified by knowledge of both, or, if they differ, that of the majority among them, must be admitted as final. And there needs be the less hesitation to accept this judgment respecting the quality of pleasures, since there is no other tribunal to be referred to even on the question of quantity. What means are there of determining which is the acutest of two pains, or the intensest of two pleasurable sensations, except the general suffrage of those who are familiar with both? Neither pains nor pleasures are homogeneous, and pain is always heterogeneous with pleasure. What is there to decide whether a particular pleasure is worth purchasing at the cost of a particular pain, except the feelings and judgment of the experienced? When, therefore, those feelings and judgment declare the pleasures derived from the higher faculties to be preferable *in kind,* apart from the question of intensity, to those of which the animal nature, disjoined from the higher faculties, is susceptible, they are entitled on this subject to the same regard.

I have dwelt on this point as being part of a perfectly just conception of utility or happiness considered as the directive rule of human conduct. But it is by no means an indispensable condition to the acceptance of the utilitarian standard; for that standard is not the agent's own greatest happiness, but the greatest amount of happiness altogether; and if it may possibly be doubted whether a noble character is always the happier for its nobleness, there can be no doubt that it makes other people happier, and that the world in general is immensely a gainer by it. Utilitarianism, therefore, could only attain its end by the general cultivation of nobleness of character, even if each individual were only benefited by the nobleness of others, and his own, so far as happiness is concerned, were a sheer deduction from the benefit. But the bare enunciation of such an absurdity as this last renders refutation superfluous.

According to the greatest happiness principle, as above explained, the ultimate end, with reference to and for the sake of which all other things are desirable—whether we are considering our own good or that of other people—is an existence exempt as far as possible from pain, and as rich as possible in enjoyments, both in point of quantity and quality; the test of quality and the rule for measuring it against quantity being the preference felt by those who, in their opportunities of experience, to which must be added their habits of self-consciousness and self-observation, are best furnished with the means of comparison. This, being according to the utilitarian opinion the end of human action, is necessarily also the standard of morality, which may accordingly be defined "the rules and precepts for human conduct," by the observance of which an existence such as has been described might be, to the greatest extent possible, secured to all mankind; and not to them only, but, so far as the nature of things admits, to the whole sentient creation. . . .

I must again repeat what the assailants of utilitarianism seldom have the justice to acknowledge, that the happiness which forms the utilitarian standard of what is right in conduct is not the agent's own happiness but that of all concerned. As between his own happiness and that of others, utilitarianism requires him to be as strictly impartial as a disinterested and benevolent spectator. In the golden rule of Jesus of Nazareth, we read the complete spirit of the ethics of utility. "To do as you would be done by," and "to love your neighbor as yourself," constitute the ideal perfection of utilitarian morality. As the

means of making the nearest approach to this ideal, utility would enjoin, first, that laws and social arrangements should place the happiness or (as, speaking practically, it may be called) the interest of every individual as nearly as possible in harmony with the interest of the whole; and, secondly, that education and opinion, which have so vast a power over human character, should so use that power as to establish in the mind of every individual an indissoluble association between his own happiness and the good of the whole, especially between his own happiness and the practice of such modes of conduct, negative and positive, as regard for the universal happiness prescribes; so that not only he may be unable to conceive the possibility of happiness to himself, consistently with conduct opposed to the general good, but also that a direct impulse to promote the general good may be in every individual one of the habitual motives of action, and the sentiments connected therewith may fill a large and prominent place in every human being's sentient existence. If the impugners of the utilitarian morality represented it to their own minds in this its true character, I know not what recommendations possessed by any other morality they could possibly affirm to be wanting to it; what more beautiful or more exalted developments of human nature any other ethical system can be supposed to foster, or what springs of action, not accessible to the utilitarian, such systems rely on for giving effect to their mandates.

The objectors to utilitarianism cannot always be charged with representing it in a discreditable light. On the contrary, those among them who entertain anything like a just idea of its disinterested character sometimes find fault with its standard as being too high for humanity. They say it is exacting too much to require that people shall always act from the inducement of promoting the general interest of society. But this is to mistake the very meaning of a standard of morals and confound the rule of action with the motive of it. It is the business of ethics to tell us what are our duties, or by what test we may know them; but no system of ethics requires that the sole motive of all we do shall be a feeling of duty; on the contrary, ninety-nine hundredths of all our actions are done from other motives, and rightly so done if the rule of duty does not condemn them. It is the more unjust to utilitarianism that this particular misapprehension should be made a ground of objection to it, inasmuch as utilitarian moralists have gone beyond almost all others in affirming that the motive has nothing to do with the morality of the action, though much with the worth of the agent. He who saves a fellow creature from drowning does what is morally right, whether his motive be duty or the hope of being paid for his trouble; he who betrays the friend that trusts him is guilty of a crime, even if his object be to serve another friend to whom he is under great obligations. But to speak only of actions done from the motive of duty, and in direct obedience to principle: it is a misapprehension of the utilitarian mode of thought to conceive it as implying that people should fix their minds upon so wide a generality as the world, or society at large. The great majority of good actions are intended not for the benefit of the world, but for that of individuals, of which the good of the world is made up; and the thoughts of the most virtuous man need not on these occasions travel beyond the particular persons concerned, except so far as is necessary to assure himself that in benefiting them he is not violating the rights, that is, the legitimate and authorized expectations, of anyone else. The multiplication of happiness is, according to the utilitarian ethics, the object of virtue: the occasions on which any person (except one in a thousand) has it in his power to do this on an extended scale—in other words, to be a public benefactor—are but exceptional; and on these occasions alone is he called on to consider public utility; in every other case, private utility, the interest or happiness of some few persons, is all he has to attend to. Those alone the influence of whose actions extends to society in general need concern themselves habitually about so large an object. In the case of abstinences indeed—of things which people forbear to do from moral considerations, though the consequences in the particular case might be beneficial—it would be unworthy of an intelligent agent not to be consciously aware that the action is of a class which, if practiced generally, would be generally injurious, and that this is the ground of the obligation to abstain from it. The amount of regard for the public interest implied in this recognition is no greater than is demanded by every system of morals, for they all enjoin to abstain from whatever is manifestly pernicious to society.

The same considerations dispose of another reproach against the doctrine of utility, founded on a still grosser misconception of the purpose of a standard of morality and of the very meaning of the words "right" and "wrong." It is often affirmed that utilitarianism renders men cold and unsympathizing; that it chills their moral feelings toward individuals; that it makes them regard only the dry and hard consideration of the consequences of actions, not taking into their moral estimate the qualities from which those actions emanate. If the assertion means that they do not allow their judgment respecting the rightness or wrongness of an action to be influenced by their opinion of the qualities of the person who does it, this is a complaint not against utilitarianism, but against any standard or morality at all; for certainly no known ethical standard decides an action to be good or bad because it is done by a good or bad man, still less because done by an amiable, a brave, or a benevolent man, or the contrary. These considerations are relevant, not to the estimation of actions, but of persons; and there is nothing in the utilitarian theory inconsistent with the fact that there are other things which interest us in persons besides the rightness and wrongness of their actions. The Stoics, indeed, with the paradoxical misuse of language which was part of their system, and by which they strove to raise themselves above all concern about anything but virtue, were fond of saying that he who has that has everything; that he, and only he, is rich, is beautiful, is a king. But no claim of this description is made for the virtuous man by the utilitarian doctrine. Utilitarians are quite aware that there are other desirable possessions and qualities besides virtue, and are perfectly willing to allow to all of them their full worth. They are also aware that a right action does not necessarily indicate a virtuous character, and that actions which are blamable often proceed from qualities entitled to praise. When this is apparent in any particular case, it modifies their estimation, not certainly of the act, but of the agent. I grant that they are, notwithstanding, of opinion that in the long run the best proof of a good character is good actions; and resolutely refuse to consider any mental disposition as good of which the predominant tendency is to produce bad conduct. This makes them unpopular with many people, but it is an unpopularity which they must share with everyone who regards the distinction between right and wrong in a serious light; and the reproach is not one which a conscientious utilitarian need be anxious to repel.

If no more be meant by the objection than that many utilitarians look on the morality of actions, as measured by the utilitarian standards, with too exclusive a regard, and do not lay sufficient stress upon the other beauties of character which go toward making a human being lovable or admirable, this may be admitted. Utilitarians who have cultivated their moral feelings, but not their sympathies, nor their artistic perceptions, do fall into this mistake; and so do all other moralists under the same conditions. What can be said in excuse for other moralists is equally available for them, namely, that, if there is to be any error, it is better that it should be on that side. As a matter of fact, we may affirm that among utilitarians, as among adherents of other systems, there is every imaginable degree of rigidity and of laxity in the application of their standard; some are even puritanically rigorous, while others are as indulgent as can possibly be desired by sinner or by sentimentalist. But on the whole, a doctrine which brings prominently forward the interest that mankind have in the repression and prevention of conduct which violates the moral law is likely to be inferior to no other in turning the sanctions of opinion against such violations. It is true, the question "What does violate the moral law?" is one on which those who recognize different standards of morality are likely now and then to differ. But difference of opinion on moral questions was not first introduced into the world by utilitarianism, while that doctrine does supply, if not always an easy, at all events a tangible and intelligible, mode of deciding such differences.

It may not be superfluous to notice a few more of the common misapprehensions of utilitarian ethics, even those which are so obvious and gross that it might appear impossible for any person of candor and intelligence to fall into them; since persons, even of considerable mental endowment, often give themselves so little trouble to understand the bearings of any opinion against which they entertain a prejudice, and men are in general so little conscious of this voluntary ignorance as a defect that the vulgarest misunderstandings of ethical doctrines are continually met with in the deliberate writings of persons of the greatest pretensions both to high principle and to philosophy. We not uncommonly hear the doctrine of utility inveighed against a *godless* doctrine. If it be necessary to say anything at all against so mere an assumption, we may say that the question depends upon what idea we have formed of the moral character of the Deity. If it be a true belief that God desires, above all things, the happiness of his creatures, and that this was his purpose in their creation, utility is not only not a godless doctrine, but more profoundly religious than any other. If it be meant that utilitarianism does not recognize the revealed will of God as the supreme law of morals, I answer that a utilitarian who believes in the perfect goodness and wisdom of *God* necessarily believes that whatever God has thought fit to reveal on the subject of morals must fulfill the requirements of utility in a supreme degree. But others besides utilitarians have been of opinion that the Christian revelation was intended, and is fitted, to inform the hearts and minds of mankind with a spirit which should enable them to find for themselves what is right, and incline them to do it when found, rather than to tell them, except in a very general way, what it is; and that we need a doctrine of ethics, carefully followed out, to *interpret* to us the will of God. Whether this opinion is correct or not, it is superfluous here to discuss; since whatever aid religion, either natural or revealed, can afford to ethical investigation is as open to the utilitarian moralist as to any other. He can use it as the testimony of God to the usefulness or hurtfulness of any given course of action by as good a right as others can use it for the indication of a transcendental law having no connection with usefulness or with happiness.

Again, utility is often summarily stigmatized as an immoral doctrine by giving it the name of "expediency," and taking advantage of the popular use of that term to contrast it with principle. But the expedient, in the sense in which it is opposed to the right, generally means that which is expedient for the particular interest of the agent himself; as when a minister sacrifices the interests of his country to keep himself in place. When it means anything better than this, it means that which is expedient for some immediate object, some temporary purpose, but which violates a rule whose observance is expedient in a much higher degree. The expedient, in this sense, instead of being the same thing with the useful, is a branch of the hurtful. Thus it would often be expedient, for the purpose of getting over some momentary embarrassment, or attaining some object immediately useful to ourselves or others, to tell a lie. But inasmuch as the cultivation in ourselves of a sensitive feeling on the subject of veracity is one of the most useful, and the enfeeblement of that feeling one of the most hurtful, things to which our conduct can be instrumental; and inasmuch as any, even unintentional, deviation from truth does that much toward weakening the trustworthiness of human assertion, which is not only the principal support of all present social well-being, but the insufficiency of which does more than any one thing that can be named to keep back civilization, virtue, everything on which human happiness on the largest scale depends—we feel that the violation, for a present advantage, of a rule of such transcendent expediency is not expedient, and that he who, for the sake of convenience to himself or to some other individual, does what depends on him to deprive mankind of the good, and inflict upon them the evil, involved in the greater or less reliance which they can place in each other's words, acts the part of one of their worst enemies. Yet that even this rule, sacred as it is, admits of possible exceptions is acknowledged by all moralists; the chief of which is when the withholding of some fact (as of information from a malefactor, or of bad news from a person dangerously ill) would save an individual (especially an individual other than oneself) from great and unmerited evil, and when the withholding can only be effected by denial. But in order that the exception may not extend itself beyond the need, and may have the least possible effect in weakening reliance on veracity, it ought to be recognized and, if possible, its limits defined; and, if the principle of utility is good for anything, it must be good for weighing these conflicting utilities against one another and marking out the region within which one or the other preponderates.

Again, defenders of utility often find themselves called upon to reply to such objections as this—that there is not time, previous to action, for calculating and weighing the effects of any line of conduct on the general happiness. This is exactly as if anyone were to say that it is impossible to guide our conduct by Christianity because there is not time, on every occasion on which anything has to be done, to read through the Old and New Testaments. The answer to the objection is that there has been ample time, namely, the whole past duration of the human species. During all that time mankind have been learning by experience the tendencies of actions; on which experience all the prudence as well as all the morality of life are dependent. People talk as if the commencement of this course of experience had hitherto been put off, and as if, at the moment when some man feels tempted to meddle with the property or life of another, he had to begin considering for the first time whether murder and theft are injurious to human happiness. Even then I do not think that he would find the question very puzzling; but, at all events, the matter is now done to his hand. It is truly a whimsical supposition that, if mankind were agreed in considering utility to be the test of morality, they would remain without any agreement as to what *is* useful, and would take no measures for having their notions on the subject taught to the young and enforced by law and opinion. There is no difficulty in proving any ethical standard whatever to work ill if we suppose universal idiocy to be conjoined with it; but on any hypothesis short of that, mankind must by this time have acquired positive beliefs as to the effects of some actions on their happiness; and the beliefs which have thus come down are the rules of morality for the multitude, and for the philosopher until he has succeeded in finding better. That philosophers might easily do this, even now, on many subjects; that the received code of ethics is by no means of divine right; and that mankind have still much to learn as to the effects of actions on the general happiness, I admit or rather earnestly maintain. The corollaries from the principle of utility, like the precepts of every practical art, admit of indefinite improvement, and, in a progressive state of the human mind, their improvement is perpetually going on. But to consider the rules of morality as improvable is one thing; to pass over the intermediate generalization entirely and endeavor to test each individual action directly by the first principle is another. It is a strange notion that the acknowledgment of a first principle is inconsistent with the admission of secondary ones. To inform a traveler respecting the place of his ultimate destination is not to forbid the use of landmarks and direction-posts on the way. The proposition that happiness is the end and aim of morality does not mean that no road ought to be laid down to that goal, or that persons going thither should not be advised to take one direction rather than another. Men really ought to leave off talking a kind of nonsense on this subject, which they would neither talk nor listen to on other matters of practical concernment. Nobody argues that the art of navigation is not founded on astronomy because sailors cannot wait to calculate the Nautical Almanac. Being rational creatures, they go to sea with it ready calculated; and all rational creatures go out upon the sea of life with their minds made up on the common questions of right and wrong, as well as on many of the far more difficult questions of wise and foolish. And this, as long as foresight is a human quality, it is to be presumed they will continue to do. Whatever we adopt as the fundamental principle of morality, we require subordinate principles to apply it by; the impossibility of doing without them, being common to all systems, can afford no argument against any one in particular; but gravely to argue as if no such secondary principles could be had, and as if mankind had remained till now, and always must remain, without drawing any general conclusions from the experience of human life is as high a pitch, I think, as absurdity has ever reached in philosophical controversy.

The remainder of the stock arguments against utilitarianism mostly consist in laying to its charge the common infirmities of human nature, and the general difficulties which embarrass conscientious persons in shaping their course through life. We are told that a utilitarian will be apt to make his own particular case an exception to moral rules, and, when under temptation, will see a utility in the breach of a rule, greater than he will see in its observance. But is utility the only creed which is able to furnish us with excuses for evil-doing and means of cheating our own conscience? They are afforded in abundance by all doctrines which recognize as a fact in morals the existence of conflicting considerations, which all doctrines do that have been believed by sane persons. It is not the fault of any creed, but of the complicated nature of human affairs, that rules of conduct cannot be so framed as to require no exceptions, and that hardly any kind of action can safely be laid down as either always obligatory or always condemnable. There is no ethical creed which does not temper the rigidity of its laws by giving a certain latitude, under the moral responsibility of the agent, for accommodation to peculiarities of circumstances; and under every creed, at the opening thus made, self-deception and dishonest casuistry get in. There exists no moral system under which there do not arise unequivocal cases of conflicting obligation. These are the real difficulties, the knotty points both in the theory of ethics and in the conscientious guidance of personal conduct. They are overcome practically, with greater or with less success, according to the intellect and virtue of the individual; but it can hardly be pretended that anyone will be the less qualified for dealing with them, from possessing an ultimate standard to which conflicting rights and duties can be referred. If utility is the ultimate source of moral obligations, utility may be invoked to decide between them when their demands are incompatible. Though the application of the standard may be difficult, it is better than none at all; while in other systems, the moral laws all claiming independent authority, there is no common umpire entitled to interfere between them; their claims to precedence one over another rest on little better than sophistry, and, unless determined, as they generally are, by the unacknowledged influence of consideration of utility, afford a free scope for the action of personal desires and partialities. We must remember that only in these cases of conflict between secondary principles is it requisite that first principles should be appealed to. There is no case of moral obligation in which some secondary principle is not involved; and if only one, there can seldom be any real doubt which one it is, in the mind of any person by whom the principle itself is recognized.

Education

Utilitarianism is the doctrine that one should act to maximize the happiness of the community. Discussions on public policy often presuppose utilitarianism in the form of cost-benefit analysis. What are the costs of the proposed policy? What benefits is it likely to produce? What are the costs and benefits of competing policies? Even if the principle of utility does not completely characterize morality, it does provide a powerful tool for the analysis of public policy.

This section concentrates on arguments concerning education. Education has recently—indeed, has almost always—been a focus of public debate. In standardized tests, students in the United States finish last among students from industrialized nations and close to last in the world as a whole. Government spending on education has soared during the past decade, and the amount spent per pupil—even adjusted for inflation—has more than tripled in the past thirty years. This increase in spending, accompanied by several rounds of educational reform, has produced little. Test scores continue to decline; fewer students take demanding courses; courses, in turn, become less demanding. The decline of education despite repeated increases in funding led the National Commission on Excellence in Education to pronounce the United States "a nation at risk." Education is important: It is the chief way for students to acquire the knowledge they need to lead productive lives. It is also a society's chief tool for making its work force competitive in a highly interdependent world economy. Finally, it is a society's way of transmitting its knowledge, its values, its culture to a new generation.

The commission, in its report entitled *A Nation at Risk,* outlines the problems facing American education. The commission contends that student performance has suffered because content has been watered down, standards have been lowered, expectations have been dropped, and students have been spending less time on schooling. Minorities particularly suffer from inadequate education.

Bhikhu Parekh argues for a kind of reform known as multicultural education. Maintaining that minority students feel excluded from

education because its content is almost entirely foreign to them and
their cultures, he insists that education, to be effective, must be multicultural. Traditional education, he maintains, alienates minorities by
covertly suggesting that all achievements—and all culture worth
studying—has been produced by white European males. To give
minority students self-esteem and a corresponding chance at success he
recommends revamping the curriculum to represent minority cultures
among course topics and authors read.

Allan Bloom, in an address at Harvard, counters that Western Civilization is more than the product of "Eurocentrism" and oppression. He
critiques the views underlying demands for multiculturalism, which, he
feels, are committed to some form of relativism, and urges that the real
issue "is *not* about Western and non-Western but about the possibility of
philosophy." If philosophy is possible—and if it is possible to make
moral judgments—then, Bloom urges, the relativists are wrong. One cannot speak of oppression and be a relativist at the same time.

Diane Ravitch, in "Multiculturalism," distinguishes two forms of multiculturalism: pluralism and particularism. Pluralism seeks a richer common culture and advocates including women and minorities in a curriculum that has too often excluded them. Particularism, by contrast,
denies that a common culture is possible and maintains that there are
no criteria of intellectual quality that are common to all cultures. Ravitch
argues in favor of pluralism but against particularism. She contends that
there are independent criteria of excellence and, moreover, that many
works by women and minorities meet them. Molefi Kete Asante, in
response, contends that these criteria are far from neutral and independent. Both he and Ravitch agree that their different perspectives on education reflect very different and incompatible visions of the future of the
United States.

NATIONAL COMMISSION ON EXCELLENCE IN EDUCATION

from *A Nation at Risk:*
The Imperative for Educational Reform

(*Source: From the National Commission on Excellence in Education,* A Nation at Risk: The Imperative for Educational Reform *[Washington: U.S. Department of Education, 1983].)*

QUESTIONS FOR REFLECTION

1. Why does the commission believe education to be important? What, exactly is at risk?

2. What evidence does the commission present that there is a crisis in education in the United States? What are the most important bits of evidence, in your view? Do you think that there is a crisis?

3. What are the commission's chief findings?

Our Nation is at risk. Our once unchallenged preeminence in commerce, industry, science, and technological innovation is being overtaken by competitors throughout the world. This report is concerned with only one of the many causes and dimensions of the problem, but it is the one that undergirds American prosperity, security, and civility. We report to the American people that while we can take justifiable pride in what our schools and colleges have historically accomplished and contributed to the United States and the well-being of its people, the educational foundations of our society are presently being eroded by a rising tide of mediocrity that threatens our very future as a Nation and a people. What was unimaginable a generation ago has begun to occur—others are matching and surpassing our educational attainments.

If an unfriendly foreign power had attempted to impose on America the mediocre educational performance that exists today, we might well have viewed it as an act of war. As it stands, we have allowed this to happen to ourselves. We have even squandered the gains in student achievement made in the wake of the Sputnik challenge. Moreover, we have dismantled essential support systems which helped make those gains possible. We have, in effect, been committing an act of unthinking, unilateral educational disarmament.

Our society and its educational institutions seem to have lost sight of the basic purposes of schooling, and of the high expectations and disciplined effort needed to attain them. This report, the result of 18 months of study, seeks to generate reform of our educational system in fundamental ways and to renew the Nation's commitment to schools and colleges of high quality throughout the length and breadth of our land.

That we have compromised this commitment is, upon reflection, hardly surprising, given the multitude of often conflicting demands we have placed on our Nation's schools and colleges. They are routinely called on to provide solutions to personal, social, and political problems that the home and other institutions either will not or cannot resolve. We must understand that these demands on our schools and colleges often exact an educational cost as well as a financial one.

On the occasion of the Commission's first meeting, President Reagan noted the central importance of education in American life when he said: "Certainly there are few areas of American life as important to our society, to our people, and to our families as our schools and colleges." This report, therefore, is as much an open letter to the American people as it is a report to the Secretary of Education. We are confident that the American people, properly informed, will do what is right for their children and for the generations to come.

The Risk

History is not kind to idlers. The time is long past when America's destiny was assured simply by an abundance of natural resources and inexhaustible human enthusiasm, and by our relative isolation from the malignant problems of older civilizations. The world is indeed one global village. We live among determined, well-educated, and strongly motivated competitors. We compete with them for international standing and markets, not only with products but also with the ideas of our laboratories and neighborhood workshops. America's position in the world may once have been reasonably secure with only a few exceptionally well-trained men and women. It is no longer.

The risk is not only that the Japanese make automobiles more efficiently than Americans and have government subsidies for development and export. It is not just that the South Koreans recently built the world's most efficient steel mill, or that American machine tools, once the pride of the world, are being displaced by German products. It is also that these developments signify a redistribution of trained capability throughout the globe. Knowledge, learning, information, and skilled intelligence are the new raw materials of international commerce and are today spreading throughout the world as vigorously as miracle drugs, synthetic fertilizers, and blue jeans did earlier. If only to keep and improve on the slim competitive edge we still retain in world markets, we must dedicate ourselves to the reform of our educational system for the benefit of all—old and young alike, affluent and poor, majority and minority. Learning is the indispensable investment required for success in the "information age" we are entering.

Our concern, however, goes well beyond matters such as industry and commerce. It also includes the intellectual, moral, and spiritual strengths of our people which knit together the very fabric of our society. The people of the United States need to know that individuals in our society who do not possess the levels of skill, literacy, and training essential to this new era will be effectively disenfranchised, not simply from the material rewards that accompany competent performance, but also from the chance to participate fully in our national life. A high level of shared education is essential to a free, democratic society and to the fostering of a common culture, especially in a country that prides itself on pluralism and individual freedom.

For our country to function, citizens must be able to reach some common understandings on complex issues, often on short notice and on the basis of conflicting or incomplete evidence. Education helps form these common understandings, a point Thomas Jefferson made long ago in his justly famous dictum:

> I know no safe depository of the ultimate powers of the society but the people themselves; and if we think them not enlightened enough to exercise their control with a wholesome discretion, the remedy is not to take it from them but to inform their discretion.

Part of what is at risk is the promise first made on this continent: All, regardless of race or class or economic status, are entitled to a fair chance and to the tools for developing their individual powers of mind and spirit to the utmost. This promise means that all children by virtue of their own efforts, competently guided, can hope to attain the mature and informed judgment needed to secure gainful employment and to manage their own lives, thereby serving not only their own interests but also the progress of society itself.

Indicators of the Risk

The educational dimensions of the risk before us have been amply documented in testimony received by the Commission. For example:

- International comparisons of student achievement, completed a decade ago, reveal that on

19 academic tests American students were never first or second and, in comparison with other industrialized nations, were last seven times.

- Some 23 million American adults are functionally illiterate by the simplest tests of everyday reading, writing, and comprehension.

- About 13 percent of all 17-year-olds in the United States can be considered functionally illiterate. Functional illiteracy among minority youth may run as high as 40 percent.

- Average achievement of high school students on most standardized tests is now lower than 26 years ago when Sputnik was launched.

- Over half the population of gifted students do not match their tested ability with comparable achievements in school.

- The College Board's Scholastic Aptitude Tests (SAT) demonstrate a virtually unbroken decline from 1963 to 1980. Average verbal scores fell over 50 points and average mathematics scores dropped nearly 40 points.

- College Board achievement tests also reveal consistent declines in recent years in such subjects as physics and English.

- Both the number and proportion of students demonstrating superior achievement on the SATs (i.e., those with scores of 650 or higher) have also dramatically declined.

- Many 17-year-olds do not possess the "higher order" intellectual skills we should expect of them. Nearly 40 percent cannot draw inferences from written material; only one-fifth can write a persuasive essay; and only one-third can solve a mathematics problem requiring several steps.

- There was a steady decline in science achievement scores of U.S. 17-year-olds as measured by national assessments of science in 1969, 1973, and 1977.

- Between 1975 and 1980, remedial mathematics courses in public 4-year colleges increased by 72 percent and now constitute one-quarter of all mathematics courses taught in those institutions.

- Average tested achievement of students graduating from college is also lower.

- Business and military leaders complain that they are required to spend millions of dollars on costly remedial education and training programs in such basic skills as reading, writing, spelling, and computation. The Department of the Navy, for example, reported to the Commission that one-quarter of its recent recruits cannot read at the ninth grade level, the minimum needed simply to understand written safety instructions. Without remedial work they cannot even begin, much less complete, the sophisticated training essential in much of the modern military.

. . . .

Findings

We conclude that declines in educational performance are in large part the result of disturbing inadequacies in the way the educational process itself is often conducted. The findings that follow, culled from a much more extensive list, reflect four important aspects of the educational process: content, expectations, time, and teaching.

Findings Regarding Content

By content we mean the very "stuff" of education, the curriculum. Because of our concern about the curriculum, the Commission examined patterns of courses high school students took in 1964–69 compared with course patterns in 1976–81. On the basis of these analyses we conclude:

- Secondary school curricula have been homogenized, diluted, and diffused to the point that they no longer have a central purpose. In effect, we have a cafeteria-style curriculum in which the appetizers and desserts can easily be mistaken for the main courses. Students have migrated from vocational and college preparatory programs to "general track" courses in large numbers. The proportion of students taking a general program of study has increased from 12 percent in 1964 to 42 percent in 1979.

- This curricular smorgasbord, combined with extensive student choice, explains a great deal about where we find ourselves today. We offer intermediate algebra, but only 31 percent of our recent high school graduates complete it; we offer French I, but only 13 percent complete it; and we offer geography, but only 16 percent complete it. Calculus is available in schools enrolling about 60 percent of all students, but only 6 percent of all students complete it.

- Twenty-five percent of the credits earned by general track high school students are in physical and health education, work experience outside the school, remedial English and mathematics, and personal service and developmental courses, such as training for adulthood and marriage.

Findings Regarding Expectations

We define expectations in terms of the level of knowledge, abilities, and skills school and college graduates should possess. They also refer to the time, hard work, behavior, self-discipline, and motivation that are essential for high student achievement. Such expectations are expressed to students in several different ways:

- by grades, which reflect the degree to which students demonstrate their mastery of subject matter;

- through high school and college graduation requirements, which tell students which subjects are most important;

- by the presence or absence of rigorous examinations requiring students to demonstrate their mastery of content and skill before receiving a diploma or a degree;

- by college admissions requirements, which reinforce high school standards; and

- by the difficulty of the subject matter students confront in their texts and assigned readings.

Our analyses in each of these areas indicate notable deficiencies:

- The amount of homework for high school seniors has decreased (two-thirds report less than 1 hour a night) and grades have risen as average student achievement has been declining.

- In many other industrialized nations, courses in mathematics (other than arithmetic or general mathematics), biology, chemistry, physics, and geography start in grade 6 and are required of *all* students. The time spent on these subjects, based on class hours, is about three times that spent by even the most science-oriented U.S. students, i.e., those who select 4 years of science and mathematics in secondary school.

- A 1980 State-by-State survey of high school diploma requirements reveals that only eight States require high schools to offer foreign language instruction, but none requires students to take the courses. Thirty-five States require only 1 year of mathematics, and 36 require only 1 year of science for a diploma.

- In 13 States, 50 percent or more of the units required for high school graduation may be electives chosen by the student. Given this freedom to choose the substance of half or more of their education, many students opt for less demanding personal service courses, such as bachelor living.

- "Minimum competency" examinations (now required in 37 States) fall short of what is needed, as the "minimum" tends to become the "maximum," thus lowering educational standards for all.

- One-fifth of all 4-year public colleges in the United States must accept every high school graduate within the State regardless of program followed or grades, thereby serving notice to high school students that they can expect to attend college even if they do not follow a demanding course of study in high school or perform well.

- About 23 percent of our more selective colleges and universities reported that their general level of selectivity declined during the 1970s, and 29 percent reported reducing the number of specific high school courses required for admission (usually by dropping foreign language requirements, which are now specified as a condition for admission by only one-fifth of our institutions of higher education).

- Too few experienced teachers and scholars are involved in writing textbooks. During the past decade or so a large number of texts have been "written down" by their publishers to ever-lower reading levels in response to perceived market demands.

- A recent study by Education Products Information Exchange revealed that a majority of students were able to master 80 percent of the material in some of their subject-matter texts before they had even opened the books. Many books do not challenge the students to whom they are assigned.

- Expenditures for textbooks and other instructional materials have declined by 50 percent over the past 17 years. While some recommend a level of spending on texts of between 5 and 10 percent of the operating costs of schools, the budgets for basal texts and related materials have been dropping during the past decade and a half to only 0.7 percent today.

Findings Regarding Time

Evidence presented to the Commission demonstrates three disturbing facts about the use that American schools and students make of time: (1) compared to other nations, American students spend much less time on school work; (2) time spent in the classroom and on homework is often used ineffectively; and (3) schools are not doing enough to help students develop either the study skills required to use time well or the willingness to spend more time on school work.

- In England and other industrialized countries, it is not unusual for academic high school students to spend 8 hours a day at school, 220 days per year. In the United States, by contrast, the typical school day lasts 6 hours and the school year is 180 days.

- In many schools, the time spent learning how to cook and drive counts as much toward a high school diploma as the time spent studying mathematics, English, chemistry, U.S. history, or biology.

- A study of the school week in the United States found that some schools provided students only 17 hours of academic instruction during the week, and the average school provided about 22.

- A California study of individual classrooms found that because of poor management of classroom time, some elementary students received only one-fifth of the instruction others received in reading comprehension.

- In most schools, the teaching of study skills is haphazard and unplanned. Consequently, many students complete high school and enter college without disciplined and systematic study habits.

Findings Regarding Teaching

The Commission found that not enough of the academically able students are being attracted to teaching; that teacher preparation programs need substantial improvement; that the professional working life of teachers is on the whole unacceptable; and that a serious shortage of teachers exists in key fields.

- Too many teachers are being drawn from the bottom quarter of graduating high school and college students.

- The teacher preparation curriculum is weighted heavily with courses in "educational methods" at the expense of courses in subjects to be taught. A survey of 1,350 institutions training teachers indicated that 41 percent of the time of elementary school teacher candidates is spent in education courses, which reduces the amount of time available for subject matter courses.

- The average salary after 12 years of teaching is only $17,000 per year, and many teachers are required to supplement their income with part-time and summer employment. In addition, individual teachers have little influence in such critical professional decisions as, for example, textbook selection.

- Despite widespread publicity about an overpopulation of teachers, severe shortages of certain kinds of teachers exist: in the fields of mathematics, science, and foreign languages; and among specialists in education for gifted and talented, language minority, and handicapped students.

- The shortage of teachers in mathematics and science is particularly severe. A 1981 survey of 45 States revealed shortages of mathematics teachers in 43 States, critical shortages of earth sciences teachers in 33 States, and of physics teachers everywhere.

- Half of the newly employed mathematics, science, and English teachers are not qualified to teach these subjects; fewer than one-third of U.S. high schools offer physics taught by qualified teachers. . . .

BHIKHU PAREKH

The Concept of Multicultural Education

Bhikhu Parekh is Professor of Political Theory at the University of Hull, United Kingdom, and Deputy Chairman of the Commission for Racial Equality.
(Source: Reprinted by permission of Falmer Press from Sohan Modgil, Gajendra K. Verma, Kanka Mallick, and Celia Modgil [ed.], Multicultural Education: The Interminable Debate. *Copyright © 1986 by S. Modgil, G. Verma, K. Mallick, and C. Modgil.)*

QUESTIONS FOR REFLECTION

1. What does Parekh mean by "multicultural education"?

2. What does Parekh mean when he says, "Education is not culturally neutral"? What argument does he advance for this claim? Do you find it convincing?

3. What is "monocultural education"? Would you describe your own education, up to now, as monocultural?

4. How, in Parekh's view, is monocultural education harmful?

5. Can we, in Parekh's opinion, judge different cultures? What does this imply about education?

The idea of multi-cultural education has gained considerable currency in Britain during the last ten years, and has become a subject of acute controversy. For the conservative critics, it represents an attempt to politicize education in order to pander to minority demands, whereas for some radicals it is the familiar ideological device of perpetuating the reality of racist exploitation of ethnic minorities by pampering their cultural sensitivities. In this paper I propose to do three things: first, to elucidate the meaning and implications of the concept of multi-cultural education; second, to show why it is desirable; and third, to assess the validity of the criticisms made of it.

I

According to the traditional and widely accepted view of education, it seeks to achieve the following objectives. First, it aims to cultivate such basic human capacities as critical reflection, imagination, self-criticism, the ability to reason, argue, weigh up evidence and to form an independent judgment of one's own. It is hoped that as a result of acquiring these and other related capacities, the pupil will one day become capable of self-determination and live a free man's life, that is, a life free from ignorance, prejudices, superstitions and dogmas and one in which he freely chooses his beliefs and plans his pattern of life. Second, it aims to foster such intellectual and moral qualities as the love of truth, openness to the world, objectivity, intellectual curiosity, humility, healthy skepticism about all claims to finality and respect and concern for others. Third, it aims to familiarize the pupil with the great intellectual, moral, religious, literary and other achievements of the human spirit. It is concerned to initiate him not merely into the cultural capital of his own community but of the entire mankind in so far as this is possible, and thus to humanize rather than merely socialize him. He is to be taught the languages, history, geography, culture, social structures, religions and so on of other communities in order that his sympathies and affections are enlarged and he learns to appreciate the unity and diversity of mankind.

While this view of education is intellectually persuasive and more coherent than its rivals, it suffers from a serious defect. It is sociologically naive and does not take account of the way in which its realization in practice is constantly frustrated by the social context in which every educational system exists and functions. As a result its advocates do not generally appreciate the extent to which their practice falls short of it, nor explore how the practice can be improved.

An educational system does not exist in a historical and social vacuum. It is an integral part of a specific social structure by which it is profoundly shaped. A social structure, further, is not a homogeneous whole, but composed of different classes, religions and communities. If it is to endure, it must develop a common public culture, that is, a generally shared body of values, beliefs, attitudes and assumptions about man and society. Of the diverse and even conflicting cultures that obtain in any lively society, one generally acquires dominance. It is presented as *the* culture of that society and is embodied in its legal, moral, political, economic, educational and other institutions and becomes its official or dominant public culture. The educational system disseminates the dominant culture among the young and ensures its preservation and reproduction across the generations. Its structure, organization, ethos, pedagogical techniques, its view of what constitutes knowledge and what is worth teaching are all profoundly shaped by the dominant culture. What is more, it does not merely disseminate but also legitimizes the dominant culture. The school is an authoritarian institution in the sense that the teachers wield both intellectual and legal authority; they know the subject whereas their pupils do not, and they have the power to punish and discipline their pupils. By deciding to teach X rather than Y, they proclaim that X is *worth* studying and Y is not, and throw the full weight of their intellectual and legal authority behind it. Similarly by teaching X in a certain manner, they imply that this is the only correct way of looking at it.

Education then is not culturally neutral. Its intellectual content and orientation is permeated by the world-view characteristic of the dominant culture. Further education is not apolitical either. It cultivates specific attitudes and values. In so far as these assist and conduce to the maintenance of a particular type of social and political order, it is also a political activity and cannot be politically neutral. All this means that although an educational system may avow the ideals of freedom, objectivity, independent thought, universality of knowledge, intellectual curiosity, and so on, in actual practice it often does little more than initiate and even indoctrinate its pupils into the dominant culture. To put it differently, it claims to provide *liberating* or liberal education, that is, education in and for freedom; in reality it only provides *Liberal* education, that is, education into the kind of culture that has become dominant in the West since the eighteenth century. The point can be illustrated by taking the example of the English educational system.

II

Although perhaps less so than the educational systems of many other Western countries, the English educational system has a deep mono-cultural orientation. And although the orientation has diminished during the last few decades, it is still pervasive. This is evident in the organization, personnel, the structure of authority, the curriculum, the pedagogical techniques, the competitive ethos, and so on, of our schools. Our schools have a fair number of Jewish, Indian, Pakistani, Chinese, West Indian, and other ethnic minority children. One would naturally expect, even require, them to adjust to the long-established structure and rules of their schools. Equally it would not be unreasonable to expect the schools to respect their children's sensitivities in areas that matter to them deeply and do not defeat the basic objectives of the school. The school's response, however, has been largely negative.

A large number of Hindu children are vegetarians, and Muslim children do not eat pork. Muslim girls and even some Hindu girls hold certain norms of modesty and are deeply averse to undressing in a common room, or wearing swimming costumes, or wearing shorts in a gymnasium. The Asian and West Indian children spontaneously tend to speak to each other in their own languages on school premises. Nearly all Asian children are non-Christian and find the traditional religious assembly a perplexing and pointless exercise. Many of their parents have poor English and occasionally need their children's help when visiting a hospital or a doctor's surgery. There is no reason why schools cannot accommodate minority sensitivities and needs in these areas by making small adjustments in their rules and organization. In fact, however, many school authorities have shown little willingness to alter the school menu, admit alternative dresses in gymnasiums, offer freedom of choice of sport, condone occasional absence of their pupils or exempt them from their daily assembly or give it a multi-faith orientation. And some even forbid them to speak their own languages on the school premises. In their view, a request for a small adjustment is really a plea for a privileged treatment and poses a mortal threat to their very identity. They cannot understand why anyone should be different, why everyone cannot eat the same food, dress the same way, hold the same ideas of propriety and modesty, speak the same language and profess the same religion as their white children do.

The mono-cultural orientation is evident also in what the schools teach and the way they teach. Our curriculum on religious studies largely concentrates on Christianity, and either ignores other religions or goes over them in a confused and cursory manner. Christianity is presented as the greatest or even the only true religion, and others are dismissed as "primitive" and "quaint" or of inferior quality. Islam is said to be "fanatical" and "dogmatic," whereas the Pope or the Anglican church affirming similar traditional dogmas is held up as a champion of "eternal verities." Little attempt is made to raise the pupil above his own religious beliefs and to get him to enter into the spirit of other religions, appreciate their visions of human predicament, understand their complex symbols and imagery, and respect and enjoy them as diverse and fascinating achievements of the human spirit.

Our history curriculum is little better. It concentrates on the history of Britain and, to some extent, parts of Europe and America, and ignores the great non-Western civilizations. Africa is dismissed as a dark continent whose inhabitants never really rose above animal life, and the Asian societies are all supposed to have been governed by despots who lived by plunder and hardly allowed the development of culture and civilization. There are history textbooks still in use which proclaim the glory of Europe and present other societies as if they had neither history nor culture before the Europeans "discovered" them. Professor Hugh Trevor-Roper writes:

> Perhaps in the future there will be some African history to teach, but at present there is none, or very little; there is only the history of Europeans in Africa, the rest is largely darkness, like the history of pre-European, pre-Columbian America, and darkness is not a subject for history.

Trevor-Roper, who only reiterates here views articulated by Hegel, Marx, J.S. Mill and others, does not care to explain what he means by history, why he defines only certain types of events as historic or even historical, why *his* ignorance of the African history should be taken to imply that the latter does not exist, nor why we should accept his impertinent assumption that what does not exist for *him* does not exist *at all.* A child raised on such a narcissistic diet can hardly be expected to develop sympathetic imagination and acquire much respect for, or even curiosity about, non-European cultures. Mercifully we are becoming increasingly sensitive to the narrow nationalistic bias of our history books. We need to combat Eurocentric and racist bias as well.

Like history, our geography curriculum also heavily concentrates on Britain and some parts of Europe and America, and ignores the rest of the world. When other countries than Britain are discussed, the emphasis is on the locations of towns, cities, rivers, mountains, climate, crops, resources and topography of different parts of the world, and so on. We pay little attention to their people, their culture, their modes of dress, habits of food, arts, and forms of social organization, and explain how their different ways of walking, talking, dressing, eating, treating animals and worshipping mountains and rivers make eminent sense within the context of their climate and natural habitat. We do not locate other societies against their natural background, bring them alive to our pupils, lift the latter out of their prejudices and conventional stereotypes, and stimulate them to participate imaginatively in the vastly diverse forms of life created by intelligent men in other parts of the world.

Other parts of the curriculum are equally narrow in their content and treated in an equally biased manner. The curriculum on social studies rarely steps outside Britain. Home economics includes little more than British and to some extent European styles of food. English literature does not generally include literary works in English by non-Western writers. Art and music taught in our schools are almost wholly European, and those of other cultures are not only not taught but treated as primitive and clumsy. The importance of learning foreign languages has yet to be fully appreciated in our schools. An attitude to a language reflects an attitude to the people who speak it. If one valued and took sympathetic interest in other societies, one would wish to know more about them by learning their languages. Not to encourage a pupil to master another language is not only to shut him off from a different way of understanding and experiencing the world, but also to suggest that he is unlikely to derive much benefit from it.

III

Let us now briefly explore the impact of this type of mono-cultural education (whether in Britain or elsewhere) on the child and how it measures up to the objectives the school claims to achieve.

First, it is unlikely to awaken his curiosity about other societies and cultures either because he is not exposed to them at all or because they are presented in uncomplimentary terms, or both. Thus our curriculum on religious studies is hardly likely to inspire him to enquire how some non-Christian religions manage to do without the idea of God as the creator of the universe, or have very different views of prophets, or conceive human destiny and come to terms with death and suffering in very different ways. A child exposed to no other religion but his own grows up asking only those questions that it encourages him to ask. And since he asks only those questions that his religion answers, he finds its answers satisfactory. In other words, he never gets out of its framework, and never feels disturbed or perplexed enough to explore other religions. What is true of religious studies is equally true of history, geography, literature, social studies and so on, none of which is likely to stimulate his curiosity about other civilizations and societies.

Second, mono-cultural education is unlikely to develop the faculty of imagination. Imagination represents the ability to conceive alternatives; that is, it is the capacity to recognize that things can be done, societies can be organized and activities can be performed in several different ways, of which the most familiar is but one and not necessarily the best. Imagination does not develop in a vacuum. It is only when one is exposed to different societies and cultures that one's imagination is stimulated and the consciousness of alternatives becomes an inseparable part of one's ways of thinking. One cannot then think of anything, be it an activity, a form of enquiry, a culture or a society without at the same time realizing that it can be conceptualized or thought about or conducted in several different ways. And this awareness of alternatives radically alters one's perspective to the way it is organized in one's own environment. One cannot avoid asking *why* it is organized in a particular manner in one's society, and *if* this way of organizing it is better than others. Mono-cultural education blots out the awareness of alternatives and restricts imagination. It cannot avoid encouraging the illusion that the limits of one's world are the limits of the world itself, and that the conventional way of doing things is the only natural way.

Third, mono-cultural education stunts the growth of the critical faculty. A child taught to look at the world from the narrow perspective of his own culture and not exposed to any other is bound to reject all that cannot be accommodated within the narrow categories of his own way of looking at the world. He judges other cultures and societies by the norms and standards derived from his own, and predictably finds them odd and even worthless. And since he judges his society in terms of its own norms, he can never take a genuinely critical attitude to it. Further, as we saw, mono-cultural education blunts imagination, and therefore the child lacks the sharp awareness of alternatives that alone can give a cutting edge to his critical faculties. Unable to criticize his society and unable to appreciate alternatives, he can hardly avoid admiring its "glory" and the "genius" and greatness of his "race," and remains vulnerable to the deadly vice of narcissism.

Fourth, mono-cultural education tends to breed arrogance and insensitivity. The child who is not encouraged to study other cultures and societies or to study them with sympathy and imagination cannot develop a respect for them. Imprisoned within the framework of his own culture, he cannot understand and appreciate differences nor accept diversity of values, beliefs, dress, food, ways of life and views of the world as an integral part of the human condition. He does not welcome, let alone rejoice in, diversity. Naturally he feels threatened by it and does not know how to cope with it. He approaches the world on his own terms, expecting it to adjust to him and seeing no reason why he should adjust to it. This leads to arrogance and double standards and, what is but a converse of it, an attitude of hypocrisy. When he visits other countries, he sees no need to learn their languages and adjust to their customs, whereas he expects others visiting his own to speak his language and accept its customs. If an outsider makes a mistake in speaking his language or pronouncing his name, he is quietly corrected and even mocked. If, on the other hand, he makes similar mistakes, this is "only to be expected" and, indeed, he even expects to be complimented for attempting to learn a foreign language or pronounce a foreign name. In short, he makes demands on others that they are not allowed to make on him, and he judges others by standards they are not supposed to apply to him.

Fifth, mono-cultural education provides a fertile ground for racism. Since a pupil knows very little about other societies and cultures, he can only respond to them in terms of superficial generalizations and stereotypes. These, in turn, are not haphazard products of individual imagination but culturally derived. A culture not informed by a sensitive appreciation of others cannot but judge them

in terms of its own norms. It sets itself up as an absolute, that is, as the only universally valid point of reference, and evaluates others in terms of their approximation to it. The greater the degree to which they resemble it, the more civilized or developed they are supposed to be. And conversely the more they diverge from it, the more uncivilized they are judged to be. This is indeed how the Victorians built up a hierarchy of human societies. They placed the African societies at the bottom, the Asians a little higher, the Mediterranean still higher, and so on until they got to the English whom they regarded as representing the highest stage of human development. When asked why other societies should have remained backward and one's own should be so advanced, the usual tendency was, and is, to give a racist explanation. It is the "genius" of the English "race" that has enabled it to achieve such great heights, and conversely the misfortunes of other societies are due to the inferiority of their "race." Such an attitude, albeit in an attenuated form, is still discernible in our text-books and in the attitudes of some of our teachers. It should hardly surprise us that white children grow up thinking of non-whites as racially and inherently inferior.

We have so far considered the impact of mono-cultural education on white children. We may now briefly consider its impact on their black peers. The latter obviously suffer from the same consequences as the former. In addition they also suffer from other sets of consequences.

The white children raised on a mono-cultural diet look at their black peers through the prism of the stereotypes they have acquired from their education. They find it difficult to accept them as equals, relax in their presence, appreciate their desire to retain their distinct cultural identity, and generally treat them with a mixture of contempt and pity. For their part, the black children either reciprocate the hostility, or bend over backwards to conform to their white peers' expectations and in so doing alienate their parents and less conformist peers. Like the white children, some white teachers have grown up on a mono-cultural diet and share their cultural arrogance and insensitivity. Consciously or unconsciously they approach their black pupils with the familiar stereotypes; they expect little of them, tend not to stretch them to their fullest, and fail to provide them with necessary educational and emotional support and encouragement. Not surprisingly many black children tend to under-achieve, rarely feel relaxed at school, lack trust in their teachers and go through the school with a cartload of frustrations and resentment.

When constantly fed on an ethnocentric curriculum that presents their communities and cultures in a highly biased and unflattering manner, black children can hardly avoid developing a deep sense of inferiority and worthlessness. They feel that they belong to a "race" which is culturally deficient and scarred by grave defects of character and intelligence; and that their ancestors have contributed "nothing" to the growth of human civilization, invented nothing of which others should take note, composed nothing which others could read with profit, built no empires, left behind nothing that is worth preserving or even cherishing, and indeed had lived such a fragile and primitive life that, but for the white colonizers, they would have by now become extinct. The impact of all this on the self-respect and identity of a black child and on his relations with his parents, brothers, elders and indeed with the members of his community in general is shattering. Lacking a sense of worth, he develops self-pity and self-hatred. He resents his parents for what they are and what they have done to him. He feels they have nothing worthwhile to teach or transmit to him; and that diminishes his respect for them, and consequently their authority over him. With their authority diminished, the parents feel compelled to rely on physical force to maintain a modicum of order in the family.

Like his relation with his parents, the black child's relations with other members of his family and community suffer a deep distortion. At one level he feels that he is one of them; at another level he feels like a total stranger. When he is with them, he recalls all that he has read and heard about them and cannot help thinking what his white friends would think and feel if they were there. He knows that they would find his compatriots noisy, loud, talking in funny ways, doing strange things, eating weird food, and so on; and he finds himself saying all this to himself silently and without any outward

sign lest he should hurt those he loves and cares for. At times he gets caught thinking thoughts the others had often suspected him of harbouring and which they had themselves often half-thought. He denies it all or makes a self-righteous confession; in either case, he is full of rage and soon of tears. He wonders how he will cope with it the next time around.

The black child raised on a mono-cultural diet in an English school experiences profound self-alienation. His colour and his affections bind him to his people; the culture he is in the process of acquiring distances him from them. His birth and his destiny, his past and his future, point in wholly different and incompatible directions. His present is nothing but a battleground between his present and his future, and he is not quite sure which will eventually win. He feels suspended between two worlds; he half-wishes to leave one but he cannot, and it would not let go of him either; he half-wishes to embrace the other, but fears that he cannot and that it will not accept him either.

IV

If what we have said so far is not wholly mistaken, the consequences of mono-cultural education are disturbing. It damages and impoverishes all children, black or white. So far as white children are concerned, it restricts the growth of imagination, curiosity and critical self-reflection, and encourages narcissism, moral insensitivity and arrogance. It prevents them from appreciating the great ingenuity with which the human spirit copes with problems of human existence and develops so many different types of cultures, religion, morality, social structure, systems of belief, and so on. It restricts their range of moral sympathy and denies them access to several finer feelings and sentiments that their own culture ignores or underemphasizes. What happens to white children also happens to the black. In addition they suffer from a sense of worthlessness, self-pity, confusion of identity, self-alienation, a self-divided and schizophrenic consciousness and a haunting fear of losing their roots.

If we are worried about these consequences, we should explore ways of releasing our educational system from its mono-cultural prison and opening it up to the liberating influences of other cultural perspectives. No educational system can, of course, be wholly detached from its specific cultural milieu. If it is a lively and self-critical system, it can, however, become receptive to other cultures and endeavor to broaden its perimeters. Instead of resenting and ignoring diversity, it can welcome it and encourage its children to enter into the spirit of and appreciate other cultures, religions, ways of life, civilizations and societies. It can help them to look at the world the way others do and to realize that almost everything in experience can be construed in several different ways, some more partial than others but none wholly impartial, and that partiality can only be reduced by entering into a sympathetic and critical dialogue with others.

What is, perhaps clumsily, called multi-cultural education is ultimately nothing more than this. It is essentially an attempt to release a child from the confines of the ethnocentric straitjacket and to awaken him to the existence of other cultures, societies and ways of life and thought. It is intended to de-condition the child as much as possible in order that he can go out into the world as free from biases and prejudices as possible and able and willing to explore its rich diversity. Multi-cultural education is therefore an education in freedom—freedom *from* inherited biases and narrow feelings and sentiments, as well as freedom *to* explore other cultures and perspectives and make one's own choices in full awareness of available and practicable alternatives. Multi-cultural education is therefore not a departure from, nor incompatible with, but a further refinement of, the liberal idea of education. It does not cut off a child from his own culture; rather it enables him to enrich, refine and take a broader view of it without losing his roots in it.

The inspiring principle of multi-cultural education then is to sensitize the child to the inherent plurality of the world—the plurality of systems, belief, ways of life, cultures, modes of analyzing familiar experiences, ways of looking at historical events and so on. How it can be realized in practice is a difficult question about which a few remarks would be in order.

A school is almost like a little world with its own distinct ethos, form of organization, schedule of work, modes of interpersonal relationship, curriculum and pedagogical methods. Although the principle of multi-cultural education is more directly relevant to some of these than to the others, it has important implications for all of them. For example, the structure of the school could be so broadened as to reflect the different cultures of its pupils. The school could provide a multi-faith assembly, accommodate different dietary requirements, permit variation in dress or choice of sport, celebrate major holidays of its constituent religious communities, and so on, and thereby build plurality and diversity into its day-to-day practice. Similarly its ethos could become multi-cultural if it were to encourage its pupils to speak their languages, talk about their ways of life and customs, come to school in their conventional dress or play their music or decorate their classrooms the way they like on certain days, and so on. In these and other ways the school celebrates diversity and becomes a home for all its pupils, be they white or black, Christian or Muslim.

The area where the principle of multi-cultural education is most relevant is obviously that of the curriculum. A curriculum conceived in a multi-cultural perspective has two features. First, it is not unduly narrow. No curriculum can cover everything in the world and must of necessity be selective. However, selection can be made on various grounds, some more justified than others. Selection based on a multi-cultural perspective would aim to ensure that the child acquires some familiarity with the major representative forms of the subject in question and that, while he would concentrate on some, his curiosity would be sufficiently stimulated to lead him to follow up the rest on his own. Thus the curriculum on religious studies would include the major religions of the world and aim to enable the child to appreciate the different ways in which they conceptualize and respond to basic perplexities of human existence. Similarly the history curriculum would include the major civilizations of the world, including not only the Greco-Roman but also those such as the Chinese, Hindu and the Arab which he is unlikely to encounter in the normal course and were constituted very differently from ones with which he is already familiar.

Second, the curriculum should be taught in a manner that is as little biased and dogmatic as possible. Slavery, for example, can be seen in several different ways and is viewed very differently by the slave-owning and slave-supplying societies. Similarly, colonial rule looks very different, depending on whether one studies it from the standpoint of a metropolitan power or its colony. In other words, the so-called facts are always and necessarily impregnated with interpretations, and although some are more plausible than others, all interpretations are partial and corrigible. The curriculum should therefore be taught in a manner that alerts the pupil to this fact and leaves him free, even encourages him to examine the various interpretations and arrive at a view of his own.

The teacher needs to be equally cautious in teaching other societies, cultures, religions, moral systems and so on. He should elucidate their beliefs and practices with sympathy and sensitivity, and give an account of them as close as possible to one that would be given by someone belonging to them; ideally he should let another culture, religion or society speak for itself. It is only when this is done that evaluation of it has a meaning. However, evaluating another society in terms of the norms of one's own inevitably leads to distortion and is intellectually illegitimate. Instead, a teacher should encourage his pupils to set up a dialogue between their own and another society, exploring each in terms of the other, asking questions about another society that arise from their own and asking questions about the latter that someone from another society would wish to ask. Beyond this a teacher cannot go. He is not an arbiter between different societies; and it is not his business to deliver the final judgment. He owes it to his pupils to let them arrive at their own judgments.

Contrary to what some writers have said, the principle of multi-cultural education does not imply that other cultures *cannot* be judged. Rather that the judgment must be based on the fullest understanding of their character and complexity, and a child is hardly capable of this degree of understanding. Further, if they can be judged, so can one's own, and therefore the latter cannot be treated as sacrosanct. Again, judging a culture is a highly intricate enterprise and one must avoid the mistake of judging it on the basis of the norms and values of one's own culture. Finally, the judgment of a culture cannot be equated with the judgment of the human beings involved in the sense that, if a culture is judged to be defective, it does not follow that the human beings involved are defective and inferior.

Nor does the principle of multi-cultural education imply that different cultures, societies and religions are all *equally* good. Such a judgment presupposes a transcultural standard, and that is simply not available. Even as respect for all men does not commit one to the view that they are all equally good or possess an equal potential; respect for all cultures as implied in the principle of multi-cultural education does not mean that they are all equally good. Rather it means that they make sense in their own contexts, have a right to be understood in their own terms, and need to be explored with sensitivity and sympathy. Respect for a culture is not a *reward* for its achievements. Rather a culture itself is an achievement, and to respect it is to recognize it as the expression of the efforts and aspirations of a group of intelligent fellow human beings.

V

In the light of our discussion, the case for multi-cultural education can easily be made. If education is concerned to develop such basic human capacities as curiosity, self-criticism, capacity for reflection, ability to form an independent judgment, sensitivity, intellectual humility and respect for others, and to open the pupil's mind to the great achievements of mankind, then it *must* be multi-cultural in orientation. Mono-cultural education not only does not fully develop these qualities and capacities, but tends to encourage their opposites. It is simply *not* good education. That it tends to inflict grave psychological and moral damage on the ethnic minority child is a further argument against it.

The case for multi-cultural education does not in any way depend on the presence of ethnic minority children in our schools. Their presence has, no doubt, brought into sharp relief the mono-cultural orientation of our education and highlighted its consequences. However, their presence is *not* the reason for accepting multi-cultural education. As we saw, multi-cultural education is good education, whereas mono-cultural education is not. It is good for *all* children, white or black, and the case for it would be just as strong even if there were to be no ethnic minority children in our schools. Indeed the case for it would then be even stronger for, lacking the physical presence of people of different cultural backgrounds and outlooks, the educational system would have to make a special effort to awaken the white pupil to the diversity and plurality of the world. . . .

ALLAN BLOOM

Western Civ—and Me: An Address at Harvard University

Allan Bloom is Professor of Social Thought at the University of Chicago. (Source: From Giants and Dwarfs *by Allan Bloom. Copyright 1990 by Allan Bloom. Reprinted by permission of Simon & Schuster, Inc.)*

QUESTIONS FOR REFLECTION

1. How does Bloom analyze the attack on "Eurocentrism"? How, in his view, does it lead to thought control?

2. Bloom believes that relativism underlies this attack. Why? What does he mean by "relativism"?

3. What is the issue of the "canon"? Why, according to Bloom, is it essentially a power struggle?

4. To Bloom, the real issue is the possibility of philosophy. Why? How does it relate to issues concerning the canon and the attack on Eurocentrism? If philosophy is impossible, what is the alternative?

FELLOW ELITISTS:

If I were E. D. Hirsch, of "cultural literacy" fame—people do tend to mix us up—I might ask, "What is the literary influence on my salutation?" The answer is Franklin D. Roosevelt's salutation to another select audience, the Daughters of the American Revolution. He began his address, "Fellow Immigrants."

Roosevelt was gently ridiculing those ladies for believing that in America old stock constitutes any title whatsoever to privilege. That notion is a relic of the aristocratic past which this democracy supplanted in favor of equality or of privilege based on merit. Roosevelt was urbane and witty, this century's greatest virtuoso of democratic leadership. We, the immigrants or the children of immigrants, loved his act; he was on our side. Our enjoyment of his joke was enhanced by the acid of vengeance against those who thought they were better than we. F.D.R. knew how to manipulate such sentiments, and his slap at the D.A.R. was not entirely disinterested insofar as there were a lot more of us than there were of them.

Moreover, Roosevelt's enjoyment was quite different from ours. He was really one of them. His family's claims to antiquity, wealth, and distinction were as good as practically anyone's. It was certainly more pleasant to poke fun at his equals or inferiors than to show resentment toward his superiors. His was an aristocratic condescension. He condescended to rule in a democracy, to be, as was often said about him at the time, "a traitor to his class"—a neat mixture of man's perpetual striving to be first and the demands of a society where all are held to be equal. The psychology of democracy is complex and fascinating.

That psychology determined the very unusual intensity of the response to my book, *The Closing of the American Mind,* focusing on my alleged elitism. I was suspect as an enemy of our democratic regime. And the first and loudest voices in this chorus came from the Ivy League, particularly from those with some connection to Harvard. Everybody knows that Harvard is in every respect—its students, its faculty, its library, and its endowment—the best university in the world. Long ago when I, a Middle Westerner, taught for a year at Yale, I was amazed at the little Harvard worm that was eating away at the souls of practically all the professors and students there, except for the ones who had turned down the opportunity to be at Harvard. Elite is not a word I care for very much—it is imprecise and smacks of sociological abstraction—but if any American institution of any kind merits that name, it is Harvard, and it lends that tincture to everyone associated with it.

Why, then, this passion to accuse others of the crime of elitism? One is tempted to attribute it to simple self-protectiveness. "If we say *he* is one, they won't notice *us*." But I suspect some, or many, acted from a more tortuous, more ambiguous motive—guilt. The leading principle of our regime is the equal worth of all persons, and facts or sentiments that appear to contradict that principle are experienced by a democrat as immoral. Bad conscience accompanies the democrat who finds himself part of an elite. He tries to suppress or deny to himself whatever covert feelings he might experience—I am sure that none of you has had them—of delight or superiority in the fact that he has been distinguished by Harvard, that he is much better off than the poor jerks at Kalamazoo College, even that he deserves it, that superior gifts merit superior education, position, and esteem. A few might consciously believe such things, but since they would be at odds with the egalitarian opinions of democracy, they tend to become spiritual outlaws, hypocrites, and cynically indifferent to the only American principle of justice. The rest, to soothe their consciences, have to engage in casuistry, not to say sophistry.

The simple democratic answer would be open admissions, just as there would be if Harvard were located in Europe, where such elitism is less tolerated. But nobody here really considers that. Harvard, I gather, intends to remain adamantly exclusive, implying thereby that there are significant natural differences among human beings. President Derek Bok's way of squaring such elitism with democratic right-thinking has been, apparently, to teach that the Harvard person is a doer of good works for society as a whole. This is in the spirit of Harvard's own political philosopher, John Rawls, who permits people to possess and cultivate superior talents if they can be proved to benefit the most disadvantaged part of society. Whether this solution is reason or rationalization is open to discussion.

All this suggests the intricate psychology of the democrat, which we must be aware of in order to know ourselves and which we are not likely to be aware of without the help of significant thinkers like Tocqueville, Burke, and Plato, who see us from the outside and judge us in terms of serious alternatives to democracy. The charge of elitism reflects the moral temper of our regime, as the charge of atheism would have done in an earlier age. You couldn't get much of a response in a university today by saying that Allan Bloom doesn't believe in God. But you can get a lot of people worked up by saying that Allan Bloom doesn't believe in equality. And this tells us a lot about our times, and explains how tempting a career is offered to egalitarian Tartufferie. "Elitist" is not a very precise charge; yet compared with the Ivy League, I would have at worst to be called a moderate elitist, and by persons other than those who are now making the charge.

But the real disagreement concerns the content of today's and tomorrow's elite education. We are now witnessing in our universities the introduction of a new "non-elitist," "non-exclusionary" curriculum in the humanities and in parts of the social sciences, and with it a program for reforming the human understanding. This is an extremely radical project whose supporters pass it off as mainstream by marching under the colors of all the movements toward a more equal society which almost all Americans endorse. Not recognized for what it is, this radicalism can thus marshal powerful and sometimes angry passions alongside its own fanatic ones. The American Council of Learned Societies—upset by "the disturbing success" of my book, which it attributed to "American anti-intellectualism"—has even issued a report ordering us to believe that there is now a scholarly consensus, nay, a proof, that all classic texts are expressions of the unconscious class, gender, or race prejudices of their authors. The calling of the humanities in our day, it seems, is to liberate us from the sway of those authors and their prejudices—Shakespeare and Milton, among others, are mentioned in the report. This puts humanists at the cutting edge of the battle against "Eurocentrism." (Clearly, the characters who wrote this report were sent by central casting for the movie version of *The Closing of the American Mind*.)

The battle is not primarily, or even at all, scholarly but moral and political, and members of the reactionary rear-guard are the objects of special fury, the enemies of historic destiny. Consequently, *The Closing of the American Mind,* which takes an entirely different view of the classic texts and of the humanities in general—a view fundamentally at odds with the radical reform being imposed on us —has been brought before this Inquisition and condemned to banishment from the land of the learned.

People's angers reveal much about what concerns them. Anger almost always disguises itself as moral indignation and, as Aristotle teaches, is the only one of the passions that requires speech and reason—to provide arguments which justify it and without which it is frustrated and withers. Anger proves man's rationality while it obscures and endangers reason. The arguments it adduces always lead back to a general principle of morality and then issue in blame. Here is an example, as reported by Richard Bernstein in the New York *Times* (September 25, 1988):

> In some respects, the scene in North Carolina last weekend recalled the daily "minute of hatred" in George Orwell's *1984,* when citizens are required to rise and hurl invective at pictures of a man known only as Goldstein, the Great Enemy of the state.
>
> At a conference on the future of liberal education sponsored by Duke University and the University of North Carolina at Chapel Hill, speaker after speaker denounced what they called "the cultural conservatives" who, in the words of a Duke English professor, Stanley Fish, have mounted "dyspeptic attacks on the humanities."
>
> There were no pictures of these "cultural conservatives" on the wall, but they were derided, scorned, laughed at. . . .

Such sentiments—and I appreciate the *Time's* making explicit the resemblance to Stalinist thought control—represent the current establishment in the humanities, literature, and history. These professors are from hot institutions like Stanford and Duke which have most openly dedicated themselves to the new educational dawn called *openness,* a dawn whose rosy fingers are currently wrapped tightly around the throat of the curriculum in most universities.

In *The Closing of the American Mind* I offer a description of the young people of today as they have been affected by the times into which they were born and the failure of liberal education, dominated as it now is by doctrinaire forms of historicism and relativism, to liberate them from the clichés of the age. Contrary to what some have alleged, I feel sorrow or pity, not contempt, for these young people whose horizon has become so dark and narrow that, in this enlightened country, it has begun to resemble a cave. Self-consciousness, self-awareness, the Delphic "know thyself" seems to me to be the serious business of education. It is, I recognize, very difficult even to understand what that means, let alone to achieve it. But one thing is certain. If one's head is crammed with ideas that were once serious but have become clichés, if one does not even know that these clichés are not as natural as the sun and moon, and if one has no notion that there are alternatives to them, one is doomed to be the puppet of other people's ideas. Only the search back to the origins of one's ideas in order to see the real arguments for them, before people became so certain of them that they ceased thinking about them at all, can liberate us.

Our study of history has taught us to laugh at the follies of the whole past, the monarchies, oligarchies, theocracies, and aristocracies with their fanaticism for empire or salvation, once taken so seriously. But we have very few tools for seeing ourselves in the same way, as others will see us. Each age always conspires to makes its own way of thinking appear to be the only possible or just way, and our age has the least resistance to the triumph of its own way. There is less real presence of respectable alternatives and less knowledge of the titanic intellectual figures who founded our way. Moreover, we are also affected by historicism, which tells us one cannot resist one's way, and relativism, which asks, "What's the use, anyway?" All this has the effect of crippling the natural longing to get out.

In the *The Closing of the American Mind* I criticized doctrinaire historicism and relativism as threats to the self-awareness of those who honestly seek it. I pointed to the great sources of those serious ideas which have become dogmas and urged that we turn to the study of them in order to purge ourselves of our dogmatism. For this I have been violently attacked as nostalgic, ideological, and doctrinaire myself. The real meaning is: "Don't touch our belief structure; it hurts."

Yet we ought to recognize, on the basis of historical observation, that what epochs consider their greatest virtue is most often really their greatest temptation, vice, or danger—Roman manliness, Spanish piety, British class, German authenticity. We have to learn to put the scalpel to our virtues. Plato suggests that anyone born in a democracy is likely to be a relativist: it goes with the territory. Relativism may be true, but since we are by birthright inclined to it, we especially had better think it over. Not for the sake of good morals or good social order, at least in any usual sense of those terms, but for the sake of our freedom and our self-awareness.

Since I first addressed the issue of relativism, I have learned with what moral fervor it is protected. For example, the celebrated liberal, Professor Arthur M. Schlesinger, Jr., says that (in contrast to my own alleged absolutism) the authentic American tradition is relativist. To support this latter contention he cites—*mirabile dictu*—the Declaration of Independence's "We hold these truths to be self-evident, that all men are created equal and are endowed by their Creator with certain inalienable rights. . . . " Professor Schlesinger takes this statement of fundamental principle to be evidence of the American Founders' *relativism*. He made this astounding argument in a commencement address at Brown University, where he apparently thinks the students will believe anything.

It is a waste of time to defend myself when the charges allege that I said things I did not say, but it is perhaps useful to instruct Professor Schlesinger about the real question. I never stated, nor do I believe, that man is, or can be, in possession of absolutes. I tried to teach, evidently not very successfully in his case, that there are two threats to reason, the opinion that one knows the truth about the most important things and the opinion that there is no truth about them. Both of these opinions are fatal to philosophy; the first asserts that the quest for the

truth is unnecessary, while the second asserts that it is impossible. The Socratic knowledge of ignorance, which I take to be the beginning point of all philosophy, defines the sensible middle ground between two extremes, the proofs of which demand much more than we know. Pascal's formula about our knowing too little to be dogmatists and too much to be skeptics perfectly describes our human condition as we really experience it, although men have powerful temptations to obscure it and often find it intolerable.

Socrates' way of life is the consequence of his recognition that we can know what it is that we do not know about the most important things and that we are by nature obliged to seek that knowledge. We must remain faithful to the bit of light which pierces through our circumambient darkness.

The fervor with which relativism is protected is matched by the zeal with which its contemporary opposite, "Eurocentrism," is attacked (though in this attack Professor Schlesinger, perhaps a little inconsistently, does not join). This fervor does not propose an investigation but a crusade. The very idea that we ought to look for rational standards by which to judge ourselves is scandalous. One simply has to believe in the current understanding of openness if one is to believe in democracy and be a decent person.

This openness dogma was epitomized by one intellectual who, unencumbered by acquaintance with my book, ridiculed me for not simply accepting that all cultures are equal. He said that this opinion must be standard equipment for all those who expect to cope with "the century of the Pacific" which is upon us.

His formulation set my imagination in motion. I decided it might be interesting to experience a Gulliver's travel to Japan to see whether we really want to set our bark on the great Pacific with a relativist compass and without a "Eurocentric" life jacket. We can weigh anchor at the new, new Stanford, whose slogan has in effect become "Join Stanford and see the world." When we arrive in Japan we shall see a thriving nation. Its success has something to do with its society, which asks much of itself and gets it. It is a real community; its members have roots.

Japanese society is often compared to a family. These characteristics are in tune with much of current liberal thought in America. (Remember Governor Mario Cuomo's keynote speech on this very theme to the Democratic convention in 1984.)

But the family in general is exclusive. There is an iron wall separating insiders from outsiders, and its members feel contrary sentiments toward the two. So it is in Japanese society, which is intransigently homogeneous, barring the diversity which is the great pride of the United States today. To put it brutally, the Japanese seem to be racists. They consider themselves superior; they firmly resist immigration; they exclude even the Koreans who have lived for generations among them. They have difficulty restraining cabinet officers from explaining that America's economic failings are due to blacks.

Should we open ourselves up to this new culture? Sympathize with its tastes? Should we aim for restrictiveness rather than diversity? Should we experiment with a more effective racism? All these things could be understood as part of our interest in keeping up with the Japanese economic miracle. Or they could, in a tonier vein, help us in our search for community and roots.

Of course, we recoil in horror at even having such thoughts. But how can we legitimate our horror? It is only the result of our acculturation, excess baggage brought with us on such voyages of discovery. If there are no transcultural values, our reaction is Eurocentric. And the one thing we know absolutely is that Eurocentrism is bad. So we have painted ourselves into a corner.

Condemning Eurocentrism is frequently a sign of intellectual, although not necessarily moral, progress. But it is only a first step. To recognize that some of the things our culture believes are not true imposes on us the duty of finding out which are true and which are not, a business altogether more difficult than the wholesale jettisoning of all that one thought one knew. Such jettisoning always ends up with the selective and thoughtless return to old Eurocentric ideas on the basis of what one needs right now, of what pleases one, of pure feeling.

This process has been nicely illustrated in recent times by the case of Salman Rushdie, author of the novel *The Satanic Verses,* which insulted the Muslim faith and occasioned the Ayatollah Khomeini's com-

mand to have Rushdie killed. There was general shock throughout the Western world at this, and writers, whose ox was being gored, rushed before the TV cameras to denounce so blatant an attack on the inviolable principle of freedom of speech. All well and good. But the kicker was that most of these very same writers had for many years been teaching that we must respect the integrity of other cultures and that it was arrogant Eurocentrism to judge other cultures according to our standards, themselves merely products of our culture. In this case, however, all such reasonings were forgotten, and the Eurocentric principle of freedom of speech was treated as though its claims to transcultural status, its claims to be valid everywhere and always, were true. A few days earlier such claims had been treated as instruments of American imperialism; miraculously they were transformed into absolutes. By now, however, one can already see a softening on the question of Rushdie's innocence among the more modish radical intellectuals.

Leaving aside the intellectual incoherence here, this floating means to say that we do not know from moment to moment what we will do when there are conflicts, which there inevitably will be, between human rights and the imperatives of the culturally sacred. The serious arguments that established the right of freedom of speech were made by philosophers—most notably Locke, Milton, and John Stuart Mill—but our contemporaries do not return to them to refresh their memories and to see whether the arguments are really good. And this is due not only to laziness but also to the current attack on the very idea of such study.

From the slogans and the arguments echoed so frequently in the universities and the press one can judge the intentions of the "non-elitist" and "non-exclusionary" curriculum now sweeping the country, and what is at stake. The key word is *canon.* What we are witnessing is the Quarrel of the Canons, the 20th century's farcical version of the 17th century's Quarrel Between the Ancients and the Moderns—the greatest document of which is Swift's *Battle of the Books.* Would that he were here to describe ours as he described theirs!

The issue is that food best nourishes the hungers of young souls. The canon is the newly valued, demagogically intended, expression for the books taught and read by students at the core of their formal education. But as soon as one adopts the term, as both sides have done, the nature of the debate has thereby been determined. For canon means what is established by authority, by the powers, hence not by criteria that are rationally defensible. The debate shifts from the content of books to how they become powerful, the motives for which they are used. And since canons are, by definition, instruments of domination, they are there to be overthrown, *deconstructed,* in the name of liberation by those who seek *empowerment.*

Philosophy in the past was about knowing; now it is about power. "Philosophy is the most spiritualized will to power." That is from Nietzsche, as is, more or less, all the current talk about the canon. "It's all about power," as they say, and in a more metaphysical sense than most know. This is the source of the deep drama being played out so frivolously about us. Professor Edward Said of the Columbia English department said at Stanford that the new university reforms were the triumph of post-modernism, meaning, among other things, that the curriculum which taught that the theoretical life is highest has been overcome. Curiously, books are invested with a very great significance in all this. They are the causes, not mere epiphenomena, as Marxism would have it. Change the books, not the ownership of the means of production, and you change the world. "Readers of the world, you have nothing to lose but your canon."

Underlying the tumult over non-Western content, then, is a discussion among Westerners using entirely Western categories about the decline or end of the West. The suicide of the West is, by definition, accomplished by Western hands. The *Times* report of the North Carolina conference gives the flavor of the public discussion:

> . . . the conference's participants denounced what they said was a narrow, outdated interpretation of the humanities and of culture itself, one based, they frequently pointed out, on works written by "dead white European males."

That is *the* slogan. Above all the campaign is against Eurocentrism:

The message of the North Carolina conference was that American society has changed too much for this view to prevail any longer. Blacks, women, Latinos, and homosexuals are demanding recognition for their own canons. "Projects likes those of [William] Bennett, [E.D.] Hirsch, and [Allan] Bloom all look back to the recovery of the earlier vision of American culture, as opposed to the conception of a kind of ethnic carnival or festival of cultures or ways of life or customs," Professor Fish said.

Replace the old, cold Greek temple with an Oriental bazaar. Overthrow the Waspocracy by means of a Rainbow Coalition. This has more or less plausibility as a political "strategy." Whether it should be the polar star in the formation of young minds is another question. It promises continuing wondrous curricular variations as different specialties and groups vie for power.*

This is the popular surface of the movement, the publicly acceptable principle of everyone's getting a piece of the action in a nation that has bought into group politics. But there is a deeper, stronger, and more revealing side:

> The conference buzzed with code words. When the speakers talked about "the hegemonic culture," they meant undemocratic domination by white men. The scholars particularly scorned the idea that certain great works of literature have absolute value or represent some eternal truth. Just about everything, they argued, is an expression of race, class, or gender.

---

* During the question period following the lecture from which this article has been adapted, I discovered that this project has been a roaring success with at least some students. A Chinese, a black, an Armenian, and a person speaking for homosexuals wondered whether they were being "excluded," inasmuch as books by members of their "communities" are not represented in curricula in proportion to their numbers in the population. They seemed to think that Greeks and Italians have been in control of the universities and that now their day is coming. One can imagine a census which would redistribute the representation of books. The premise of these students' concerns is that "where you come from," your culture, is more important than where you are going. They are rather like Plato's noble guardian dogs in the *Republic* who love what is familiar, no matter how bad it is, and hate all that is strange or foreign. This kind of demand is entirely new. You do not go to college to discover for yourself what is good but to be confirmed in your origins.

This is academic jargon, one-third Marxist, two-thirds Nietzschean; but it points toward the metaphysics of the cosmic power struggle in terms of which we interpret everything nowadays. All books have to be reinterpreted to find the conscious or unconscious power motive of their authors. As Nietzsche puts it, "Every philosophy is the author's secret confession."

The other side in this struggle can be found in the words of the black writer and activist W.E.B. Du Bois at the turn of the century:

> I sit with Shakespeare and he winces not. Across the color line I walk arm in arm with Balzac and Dumas, where smiling men and welcoming women glide in gilded halls. From out of the caves of evening that swing between the strong-limbed earth and the tracery of the stars, I summon Aristotle and Aurelius and what soul I will, and they come all graciously with no scorn or condescension. So, wed with Truth, I dwell above the veil.

I confess that this view is most congenial to me. Du Bois found our common transcultural humanity not in a canon, but in certain works from which he learned about himself and gained strength for his lonely journey, beyond the veil. He found community rather than war. He used the books to think about his situation, moving beyond the corrosive of prejudice to the independent and sublime dignity of the fully developed soul. He recapitulates the ever-renewed experience of books by intelligent poor and oppressed people seeking for a way out.

But during the recent Stanford curriculum debate, a leader of the black student group declared that the implicit message of the Western civilization curriculum is "nigger go home." From this perspective Du Bois was suffering from false consciousness, a deceptive faith in theoretical liberation offered by the inventors of practical slavery.

Now, obviously books are being used by nations and religions to support their way and to train the young to it. But that is not the whole story. Many books, perhaps the most important ones, have an independent status and bring us light from outside our cave, without which we would be blind. They are frequently the acid which reveals the outlines of abusive power. This is especially true in a liberal society like our own, where it is hard to find a "canonical" book which truly supports our way unqualifiedly. Further, it is at least plausible that the books which have a continuing good reputation and used to be read in colleges have made it on their intrinsic merits. To be sure, traditions tend to ossify and also to aggregate superfluous matters, to be taught authoritatively by tiresome persons who do not know why they are important and who hold their jobs because they are virtuosos of trivia. But this only means that the traditions have to be renewed from time to time and the professors made to give an account of themselves.

One of the most obvious cases of a writer used as an authority to bolster what might be called a structure of power is Aristotle during the Christian Middle Ages. Scholasticism was a stifling force which had to be rebelled against in order to free the mind. But to take that Will Durant-like interpretation as exhaustive would be naive. In the first place, Aristotle is something on his own. He survived the wreckage of scholasticism quite nicely and needed no power structure prior to that time or afterward to insure the continuing interest in his works.

Secondly, Aristotle's accession to power was a result of a revolution in Christianity brought about by the explosion of Greek philosophy into Christian Europe. That philosophy had been preserved and renewed among the Muslims, and the challenge of reason to revelation presented by the Muslim philosophers precipitated a crisis in Christianity that was appeased but not entirely resolved by Thomas Aquinas. Here we have a truly interesting case of the relation between the allegedly Western and the allegedly non-Western.

But this is by no means the only case which shows what a grave error it is to accept that the books of the dead white Western male canon are essentially Western—or any of those other things. The fact that I am doubtful about the non-Western craze suggests automatically, even to sympathetic critics, that I am promoting Western Civ or the like. Yet the very language used reveals how enslaved we have become to the historicist assertion that all thought is decisively culture-bound. When Averroes and Thomas Aquinas read Aristotle they did not think of him as Greek and put him into his historical context. They had no interest in Greek Civ but treated him as a wise man, hence a contemporary at all times.

We smile at this naiveté, but they understood Aristotle better than do our scholars, as one can see simply by perusing their commentaries. Plato and Kant claim that they speak to all men everywhere and forever, and I see no reason to reject those claims *a priori*. But that is precisely what is done when they are taken to be parts of Western Civ. To the extent they are merely that, the appeals against them are justified, for Western Civ is clearly partial, demanding the supplement of all the other Civs. The strength of these appeals is thus in their demand for wholeness or completeness of understanding.

Hence, the real, underlying quarrel is *not* about Western and non-Western but about the possibility of philosophy. Nobody, or practically nobody, argues that natural science is essentially Western. Some efforts have been made in that direction, just as some feminists have tried to show that science is essentially male, but these efforts, aside from their admirable sense of the need for theoretical consistency, have not proved persuasive. There is that big rock of transcultural knowledge or truth, natural science, standing in our midst while we chatter on about the cultural basis of all knowledge. A serious non-Western *Putsch* would require that students learn 50 percent non-Western math, 50 percent non-Western physics, 50 percent non-Western biology, and so forth for medicine and engineering. The reformers stop there because they know they would smack up against a brick wall and discredit their whole movement. But philosophy, they say, is not like that. Perhaps, but I have yet to see a serious discussion about wherein it differs. Differ it does today. But qualitatively? That question ought to keep us busy for a long time. Science is surely somehow transcultural. Religion seems pretty much limited to cultures, even to define them. Is philosophy like science, or is it like religion? What we are witnessing is an attempt to drag it away definitively to the camp of religion.

The universities have dealt with this problem by ceding the despised historicized humanities to the political activists and extremists, leaving undisturbed their non-historicized scientific disciplines, which is where the meat and the money are. It is a windfall for administrators to be able to turn all the affirmative-action complaints over to the humanities, which act as a lightning rod while their ship continues its stately progress over undisturbed waters. Stanford shows its "concerned," "humane," radical face to its inner community, and its serious technical face to the outside community, particularly to its donors. The humanities radicals will settle for this on the calculation that if they can control the minds of the young, they will ultimately gain political control over the power of science.

The serious scholars in non-Western thought should bring us the powerful *texts* they know of to help us. For the true canon aggregates around the most urgent questions we face. That is the only ground for the study of books. Nietzsche did not seek out Socrates because he was part of the classical canon German boys learned in school. He did so in spite of that fact. Socrates was necessary to him as the profoundest statement of what philosophy is and as the worthiest of rivals. Machiavelli was impelled by real need, not by conformism, when he sought out Xenophon. Male, female, black, white, Greek, barbarian—that was all a matter of indifference, as it should be. Nietzsche reflected on Buddha when he wanted to test the principle of contradiction. That is a model of the way things should be. The last thing we need is a sort of philosophic UN run by bureaucrats for the sake of representation for all peoples.

Each must ultimately judge for himself about the important books, but a good beginning would be to see what other thinkers the thinkers who attract him turn to. That will quickly lead to the top. There are very few who remain there, and they recognize each other. There is no conspiracy; only the desire to know. If we allow ourselves to be seduced by the plausible theses of our day, and turn our backs on the great dialogue, our loss will be irreparable.

In my book I connected this radical historicism with fascism and asserted that the thinking of the European Right had wandered over to the Left in America. This earned me severe and unthinking criticism (with the honorable exception of Richard Rorty). It seems to such critics that I am one of the persons who trivialize unique and terrible phenomena by calling anyone whom I dislike a fascist or a Nazi. But I did not call persons active in the 60's those names. I said that the language of the New Left was no longer truly Marxist and had become imbued with the language of fascism. And anyone with an ear for the speech of the intellectuals in Weimar Germany will hear echoes all around us of the dangerous ideas to which they became accustomed.

Since the publication of *The Closing of the American Mind,* fortuitously there has been fresh attention paid to the Nazism of Martin Heidegger, more and more widely recognized as the most intelligent figure contributing to the post-modernist movement. At the same time the late Paul de Man, who as a professor at Yale introduced deconstructionism into the U.S., was revealed to have written, as a young man in his native Belgium, pro-Nazi articles for a collaborationist newspaper. In reading these articles I was struck by the fact that if one suppresses the references to Hitler and Hitlerism, much of it sounds like what one reads in advanced literary reviews today.

The lively debate around these issues has not been very helpful, for it focuses more on questions of personal guilt than on the possible relation of Heidegger's or de Man's thought to the foulest political extremism. The fact that de Man had become a leftist after settling in America proves not a thing. He never seems to have passed through a stage where he was attracted by reason or liberal democracy. Those who chose culture over civilization, the real opposition, which we have forgotten, were forced to a position beyond good and evil, for to them good and evil were products of cultures.

This, then, is how the contemporary American intellectual scene looks. Much greater events occurring outside the United States, however, demonstrate the urgency of our task. Those events are epitomized by the Statue of Liberty erected by the Chinese students in Tiananmen Square. Apparently, after some discussion about whether it should be altered to have Chinese rather than *Eurocentric* features, there was a consensus that it did not make any difference.

The terror in China continues, and we cannot yet know what will become of those courageous young persons. But we do know the justice of their causes; and although there is no assurance that it will ultimately triumph, their oppressors have won the universal execration of mankind. With Marxist ideology a wretched shambles everywhere, nobody believes any longer in Communist legitimacy. Everywhere in the Communist world what is wanted is rational liberal democracy that recognizes men's natural freedom and equality and the rights dependent on them. The people of that world need and want education in democracy and the institutions that actualize it. Such education is one of the greatest services the democracies can offer to the people who still live or recently have lived under Communist tyrannies and long for liberty. The example of the United States is what has impressed them most, and their rulers have been unable to stem the infection.

Our example, though, requires explanations, the kind the Founders gave to the world. And this is where we are failing: the dominant schools in American universities can tell the Chinese students only that they should avoid Eurocentrism, that rationalism has failed, that they should study non-Western cultures, and that bourgeois liberalism is the most despicable of regimes. Stanford has replaced John Locke, *the* philosopher of liberalism, with Frantz Fanon, an ephemeral writer once promoted by Jean-Paul Sartre because of his murderous hatred of Europeans and his espousal of terrorism. However, this is not what the Chinese need. They have Deng Xiaoping to deconstruct their Statue of Liberty. We owe them something much better.

DIANE RAVITCH

Multiculturalism: E Pluribus Plures

*Diane Ravitch is Adjunct Professor of History and Edu-
cation at the Teacher's College of Columbia University.
(Source: Reprinted from* The American Scholar, *Volume 59, Number 3, Summer 1990. Copyright © 1990
by the author.)*

QUESTIONS FOR REFLECTION

1. What, according to Ravitch, is pluralism? What is
   her attitude toward it?

2. What is particularism? How does it differ from
   pluralism? How does it relate to a sense of community?

3. Why does Ravitch reject particularism? What are
   its supposed advantages? What disadvantages
   does she see?

4. What is universalism? Why is it a crucial issue,
   according to Ravitch?

5. Advocates of multiculturalism have claimed that
   their proposals are needed to give minority students self-esteem. Does Ravitch agree? What are
   her arguments?

6. What are Ravitch's chief criticisms of "A Curriculum of Inclusion"?

7. How, according to Ravitch, should we choose a
   curriculum?

Questions of race, ethnicity, and religion have
been a perennial source of conflict in American
education. The schools have often attracted the
zealous attention of those who wish to influence the
future, as well as those who wish to change the way
we view the past. In our history, the schools have
been not only an institution in which to teach young
people skills and knowledge, but an arena where
interest groups fight to preserve their values, or to
revise the judgments of history, or to bring about
fundamental social change. In the nineteenth century, Protestants and Catholics battled over which
version of the Bible should be used in school, or
whether the Bible should be used at all. In recent
decades, bitter racial disputes—provoked by policies of racial segregation and discrimination—have
generated turmoil in the streets and in the schools.
The secularization of the schools during the past
century has prompted attacks on the curricula
and textbooks and library books by fundamentalist

Christians, who object to whatever challenges their
faith-based views of history, literature, and science.

Given the diversity of American society, it has
been impossible to insulate the schools from pressures that result from differences and tensions
among groups. When people differ about basic values, sooner or later those disagreements turn up in
battles about how schools are organized or what the
schools should teach. Sometimes these battles remove a terrible injustice, like racial segregation.
Sometimes, however, interest groups politicize the
curriculum and attempt to impose their views on
teachers, school officials, and textbook publishers.
Across the country, even now, interest groups are
pressuring local school boards to remove myths and
fables and other imaginative literature from children's readers and to inject the teaching of cre-
ationism in biology. When groups cross the line into
extremism, advancing their own agenda without
regard to reason or to others, they threaten public

education itself, making it difficult to teach any issues honestly and making the entire curriculum vulnerable to political campaigns.

For many years, the public schools attempted to neutralize controversies over race, religion, and ethnicity by ignoring them. Educators believed, or hoped, that the schools could remain outside politics; this was, of course, a vain hope since the schools were pursuing policies based on race, religion, and ethnicity. Nonetheless, such divisive questions were usually excluded from the curriculum. The textbooks minimized problems among groups and taught a sanitized version of history. Race, religion, and ethnicity were presented as minor elements in the American saga; slavery was treated as an episode, immigration as a sidebar, and women were largely absent. The textbooks concentrated on presidents, wars, national politics, and issues of state. An occasional "great black" or "great woman" received mention, but the main narrative paid little attention to minority groups and women.

With the ethnic revival of the 1960s, this approach to the teaching of history came under fire, because the history of national leaders—virtually all of whom were white, Anglo-Saxon, and male—ignored the place in American history of those who were none of the above. The traditional history of elites had been complemented by an assimilationist view of American society, which presumed that everyone in the American melting pot would eventually lose or abandon those ethnic characteristics that distinguished them from mainstream Americans. The ethnic revival demonstrated that many groups did not want to be assimilated or melted. Ethnic studies programs popped up on campuses to teach not only that "black is beautiful," but also that every other variety of ethnicity is "beautiful" as well; everyone who had "roots" began to look for them so that they too could recover that ancestral past of themselves that had not been homogenized.

As ethnicity became an accepted subject for study in the late 1960s, textbooks were assailed for their failure to portray blacks accurately; within a few years, the textbooks in wide use were carefully screened to eliminate bias against minority groups and women. At the same time, new scholarship about the history of women, blacks, and various

ethnic minorities found its way into the textbooks. At first, the multicultural content was awkwardly incorporated as little boxes on the side of the main narrative. Then some of the new social historians (like Stephan Thernstrom, Mary Beth Norton, Gary Nash, Winthrop Jordan, and Leon Litwack) themselves wrote textbooks, and the main narrative itself began to reflect a broadened historical understanding of race, ethnicity, and class in the American past. Consequently, today's history textbooks routinely incorporate the experiences of women, blacks, American Indians, and various immigrant groups.

Although most high school textbooks are deeply unsatisfactory (they still largely neglect religion, they are too long, too encyclopedic, too superficial, and lacking in narrative flow), they are far more sensitive to pluralism than their predecessors. For example, the latest edition of Todd and Curti's *Triumph of the American Nation,* the most popular high school history text, has significantly increased its coverage of blacks in America, including profiles of Phillis Wheatley, the poet; James Armistead, a revolutionary war spy for Lafayette; Benjamin Banneker, a self-taught scientist and mathematician; Hiram Revels, the first black to serve in the Congress; and Ida B. Wells-Barnett, a tireless crusader against lynching and racism. Even better as a textbook treatment is Jordan and Litwack's *The United States,* which skillfully synthesizes the historical experiences of blacks, Indians, immigrants, women, and other groups into the mainstream of American social and political history. The latest generation of textbooks bluntly acknowledges the racism of the past, describing the struggle for equality by racial minorities while identifying individuals who achieved success as political leaders, doctors, lawyers, scholars, entrepreneurs, teachers, and scientists.

As a result of the political and social changes of recent decades, cultural pluralism is now generally recognized as an organizing principle of this society. In contrast to the idea of the melting pot, which promised to erase ethnic and group differences, children now learn that variety is the spice of life. They learn that America has provided a haven for many different groups and has allowed them to maintain their cultural heritage or to assimilate, or—as is often the case—to do both; the choice is theirs, not the state's. They learn that cultural pluralism is one of the norms of a free society; that differences among groups are a national resource rather than a problem to be solved. Indeed, the unique feature of the United States is that its common culture has been formed by the interaction of its subsidiary cultures. It is a culture that has been influenced over time by immigrants, American Indians, Africans (slave and free) and by their descendants. American music, art, literature, language, food, clothing, sports, holidays, and customs all show the effects of the commingling of diverse cultures in one nation. Paradoxical though it may seem, the United States has a common culture that is multicultural.

Our schools and our institutions of higher learning have in recent years begun to embrace what Catherine R. Stimpson of Rutgers University has called "cultural democracy," a recognition that we must listen to a "diversity of voices" in order to understand our culture, past and present. This understanding of the pluralistic nature of American culture has taken a long time to forge. It is based on sound scholarship and has led to major revisions in what children are taught and what they read in school. The new history is—indeed, must be—a warts-and-all history; it demands an unflinching examination of racism and discrimination in our history. Making these changes is difficult, raises tempers, and ignites controversies, but gives a more interesting and accurate account of American history. Accomplishing these changes is valuable, because there is also a useful lesson for the rest of the world in America's relatively successful experience as a pluralistic society. Throughout human history, the clash of different cultures, races, ethnic groups, and religions has often been the cause of bitter hatred, civil conflict, and international war. The ethnic tensions that now are tearing apart Lebanon, Sri Lanka, Kashmir, and various republics of the Soviet Union remind us of the costs of unfettered group rivalry. Thus, it is a matter of more than domestic importance that we closely examine and try to understand that part of our national history in which different groups competed, fought, suffered, but ultimately learned to live together in relative peace and even achieved a sense of common nationhood.

Alas, these painstaking efforts to expand the understanding of American culture into a richer and more varied tapestry have taken a new turn, and not for the better. Almost any idea, carried to its extreme, can be made pernicious, and this is what is happening now to multiculturalism. Today, pluralistic multiculturalism must contend with a new, particularistic multiculturalism. The pluralists seek a richer common culture; the particularists insist that no common culture is possible or desirable. The new particularism is entering the curriculum in a number of school systems across the country. Advocates of particularism propose an ethnocentric curriculum to raise the self-esteem and academic achievement of children from racial and ethnic minority backgrounds. Without any evidence, they claim that children from minority backgrounds will do well in school *only* if they are immersed in a positive, prideful version of their ancestral culture. If children are of, for example, Fredonian ancestry, they must hear that Fredonians were important in mathematics, science, history, and literature. If they learn about great Fredonians and if their studies use Fredonian examples and Fredonian concepts, they will do well in school. If they do not, they will have low self-esteem and will do badly.

At first glance, this appears akin to the celebratory activities associated with Black History Month or Women's History Month, when schoolchildren learn about the achievements of blacks and women. But the point of those celebrations is to demonstrate that neither race nor gender is an obstacle to high achievement. They teach all children that everyone, regardless of their race, religion, gender, ethnicity, or family origin, can achieve self-fulfillment, honor, and dignity in society if they aim high and work hard.

By contrast, the particularistic version of multiculturalism is unabashedly filiopietistic and deterministic. It teaches children that their identity is determined by their "cultural genes." That something in their blood or their race memory or their cultural DNA defines who they are and what they may achieve. That the culture in which they live is not their own culture, even though they were born here. That American culture is "Eurocentric," and therefore hostile to anyone whose ancestors are not European. Perhaps the most invidious implication of particularism is that racial and ethnic minorities are not and should not try to be part of American culture; it implies that American culture belongs only to those who are white and European; it implies that those who are neither white nor European are alienated from American culture by virtue of their race or ethnicity; it implies that the only culture they do belong to or can ever belong to is the culture of their ancestors, even if their families have lived in this country for generations.

The war on so-called Eurocentrism is intended to foster self-esteem among those who are not of European descent. But how, in fact, is self-esteem developed? How is the sense of one's own possibilities, one's potential choices, developed? Certainly, the school curriculum plays a relatively small role as compared to the influence of family, community, mass media, and society. But to the extent that curriculum influences what children think of themselves, it should encourage children of all racial and ethnic groups to believe that they are part of this society and that they should develop their talents and minds to the fullest. It is enormously inspiring, for example, to learn about men and women from diverse backgrounds who overcame poverty, discrimination, physical handicaps, and other obstacles to achieve success in a variety of fields. Behind every such biography of accomplishment is a story of heroism, perseverance, and self-discipline. Learning these stories will encourage a healthy spirit of pluralism, of mutual respect, and of self-respect among children of different backgrounds. The children of American society today will live their lives in a racially and culturally diverse nation, and their education should prepare them to do so.

The pluralist approach to multiculturalism promotes a broader interpretation of the common American culture and seeks due recognition for the ways that the nation's many racial, ethnic, and cultural groups have transformed the national culture. The pluralists say, in effect, "American culture belongs to us, all of us; the U.S. is us, and we remake it in every generation." But particularists have no interest in extending or revising American culture; indeed, they deny that a common culture exists. Particularists reject any accommodation among groups, any interactions that blur the distinct lines between them. The brand of history that they espouse is one in which everyone is either a descendant of victims or oppressors. By doing so, ancient hatreds are fanned and recreated in each new generation. Particularism has its intellectual roots in the ideology of ethnic separatism and in the black nationalist movement. In the particularist analysis, the nation has five cultures: African American, Asian American, European American, Latino/Hispanic, and Native American. The huge cultural, historical, religious, and linguistic differences within these categories are ignored, as is the considerable intermarriage among these groups, as are the linkages (like gender, class, sexual orientation, and religion) that cut across these five groups. No serious scholar would claim that all Europeans and white Americans are part of the same culture, or that all Asians are part of the same culture, or that all people of Latin-American descent are of the same culture, or that all people of African descent are of the same culture. Any categorization this broad is essentially meaningless and useless.

Several districts—including Detroit, Atlanta, and Washington, D.C.—are developing an Afrocentric curriculum. *Afrocentricity* has been described in a book of the same name by Molefi Kete Asante of Temple University. The Afrocentric curriculum puts Africa at the center of the student's universe. African Americans must "move away from an [sic] Eurocentric framework" because "it is difficult to create freely when you use someone else's motifs, styles, images, and perspectives." Because they are not Africans, "white teachers cannot inspire in our children the visions necessary for them to overcome limitations." Asante recommends that African Americans choose an African name (as he did), reject European dress, embrace African religion (not Islam or Christianity) and love "their own" culture. He scorns the idea of universality as a form of Eurocentric arrogance. The Eurocentrist, he says, thinks of Beethoven or Bach as classical, but the Afrocentrist thinks of Ellington or Coltrane as classical; the Eurocentrist lauds Shakespeare or Twain, while the Afrocentrist prefers Baraka, Shange, or Abiola. Asante is critical of black artists like Arthur Mitchell and Alvin Ailey who ignore Afrocentricity. Likewise, he speaks contemptuously of a group of black university students who spurned the Afrocentrism of the local Black Student Union and formed an organization called Inter-race: "Such madness is the direct consequence of self-hatred, obligatory attitudes, false assumptions about society, and stupidity."

The conflict between pluralism and particularism turns on the issue of universalism. Professor Asante warns his readers against the lure of universalism: "Do not be captured by a sense of universality given to you by the Eurocentric viewpoint; such a viewpoint is contradictory to your own ultimate reality." He insists that there is no alternative to Eurocentrism, Afrocentrism, and other ethnocentrisms. In contrast, the pluralist says, with the Roman playwright Terence, "I am a man: nothing human is alien to me." A contemporary Terence would say "I am a person" or might be a woman, but the point remains the same: You don't have to be black to love Zora Neale Hurston's fiction or Langston Hughes's poetry or Duke Ellington's music. In a pluralist curriculum, we expect children to learn a broad and humane culture, to learn about the ideas and art and animating spirit of many cultures. We expect that children, whatever their color, will be inspired by the courage of people like Helen Keller, Vaclav Havel, Harriet Tubman, and Feng Lizhe. We expect that their response to literature will be determined by the ideas and images it evokes, not by the skin color of the writer. But particularists insist that children can learn only from the experiences of people from the same race.

Particularism is a bad idea whose time has come. It is also a fashion spreading like wildfire through the education system, actively promoted by organizations and individuals with a political and professional interest in strengthening ethnic power bases in the university, in the education profession, and in society itself. One can scarcely pick up an educational journal without learning about a school district that is converting to an ethnocentric curriculum in an attempt to give "self-esteem" to children from racial minorities. A state-funded project in a Sacramento high school is teaching young black males to think like Africans and develop the "African Mind Model Technique," in order to free themselves of the racism of American culture. A popular black rap singer, KRS-One, complained in an op-ed

article in the *New York Times* that the schools should be teaching blacks about their cultural heritage, instead of trying to make everyone Americans. "It's like trying to teach a dog to be a cat," he wrote. KRS-One railed about having to learn about Thomas Jefferson and the Civil War, which had nothing to do (he said) with black history.

Pluralism can easily be transformed into particularism, as may be seen in the potential uses in the classroom of the Mayan contribution to mathematics. The Mayan example was popularized in a movie called *Stand and Deliver,* about a charismatic Bolivian-born mathematics teacher in Los Angeles who inspired his students (who are Hispanic) to learn calculus. He told them that their ancestors invented the concept of zero; but that wasn't all he did. He used imagination to put across mathematical concepts. He required them to do homework and to go to school on Saturdays and during the Christmas holidays, so that they might pass the Advanced Placement mathematics examination for college entry. The teacher's reference to the Mayans' mathematical genius was a valid instructional device: It was an attention-getter and would have interested even students who were not Hispanic. But the Mayan example would have had little effect without the teacher's insistence that the class study hard for a difficult examination.

Ethnic educators have seized upon the Mayan contribution to mathematics as the key to simultaneously boosting the ethnic pride of Hispanic children and attacking Eurocentrism. One proposal claims that Mexican-American children will be attracted to science and mathematics if they study Mayan mathematics, the Mayan calendar, and Mayan astronomy. Children in primary grades are to be taught that the Mayans were first to discover the zero and that Europeans learned it long afterwards from the Arabs, who had learned it in India. This will help them see that Europeans were latecomers in the discovery of great ideas. Botany is to be learned by study of the agricultural techniques of the Aztecs, a subject of somewhat limited relevance to children in urban areas. Furthermore, "ethnobotanical" classifications of plants are to be substituted for the Eurocentric Linnaean system. At first glance, it may seem curious that Hispanic children are deemed to have no cultural affinity with Spain; but to acknowledge the cultural tie would confuse the ideological assault on Eurocentrism.

This proposal suggests some questions: Is there any evidence that the teaching of "culturally relevant" science and mathematics will draw Mexican-American children to the study of these subjects? Will Mexican-American children lose interest or self-esteem if they discover that their ancestors were Aztecs or Spaniards, rather than Mayans? Are children who learn in this way prepared to study the science and mathematics that are taught in American colleges and universities and that are needed for advanced study in these fields? Are they even prepared to study the science and mathematics taught in *Mexican* universities? If the class is half Mexican-American and half something else, will only the Mexican-American children study in a Mayan and Aztec mode or will all the children? But shouldn't all children study what is culturally relevant for them? How will we train teachers who have command of so many different systems of mathematics and science?

The efficacy of particularist proposals seems to be less important to their sponsors than their value as ideological weapons with which to criticize existing disciplines for their alleged Eurocentric bias. In a recent article titled "The Ethnocentric Basis of Social Science Knowledge Production" in the *Review of Research in Education,* John Stanfield of Yale University argues that neither social science nor science are objective studies, that both instead are "Euro-American" knowledge systems which reproduce "hegemonic racial domination." The claim that science and reason are somehow superior to magic and witchcraft, he writes, is the product of Euro-American ethnocentrism. According to Stanfield, currents fears about the misuse of science (for instance, "the nuclear arms race, global pollution") and the "the power-plays of Third World nations (the Arab oil boycott and the American-Iranian hostage crisis) have made Western people more aware of nonscientific cognitive styles. These last events are beginning to demonstrate politically that which has begun to be understood in intellectual circles: namely, that modes of social knowledge such as theology, science, and magic are different, not inferior or superior. They represent different ways of perceiving, defining, and organizing knowledge of life

experiences." One wonders: If Professor Stanfield broke his leg, would he go to a theologian, a doctor, or a magician?

Every field of study, it seems, has been tainted by Eurocentrism, which was defined by a professor at Manchester University, George Ghevarughese Joseph, in *Race and Class* in 1987, as "intellectual racism." Professor Joseph argues that the history of science and technology—and in particular, of mathematics—in non-European societies was distorted by racist Europeans who wanted to establish the dominance of European forms of knowledge. The racists, he writes, traditionally traced mathematics to the Greeks, then claimed that it reached its full development in Europe. These are simply Eurocentric myths to sustain an "imperialist/racist ideology," says Professor Joseph, since mathematics was found in Egypt, Babylonia, Mesopotamia, and India long before the Greeks were supposed to have developed it. Professor Joseph points out too that Arab scientists should be credited with major discoveries traditionally attributed to William Harvey, Isaac Newton, Charles Darwin, and Sir Francis Bacon. But he is not concerned only to argue historical issues; his purpose is to bring all of these different mathematical traditions into the school classroom so that children might study, for example, "traditional African designs, Indian *rangoli* patterns and Islamic art" and "the language and counting systems found across the world."

This interesting proposal to teach ethnomathematics comes at a time when American mathematical educators are trying to overhaul present practices, because of the poor performance of American children on national and international assessments. Mathematics educators are attempting to change the teaching of their subject so that children can see its uses in everyday life. There would seem to be an incipient conflict between those who want to introduce real-life applications of mathematics and those who want to teach the mathematical systems used by ancient cultures. I suspect that most mathematics teachers would enjoy doing a bit of both, if there were time or student interest. But any widespread movement to replace modern mathematics with ancient ethnic mathematics runs the risk of disaster in a field that is struggling to update existing curricula. If, as seems likely, ancient mathematics is taught mainly to minority children, the gap between them and middle-class white children is apt to grow. It is worth noting that children in Korea, who score highest in mathematics on international assessments, do not study ancient Korean mathematics.

Particularism is akin to cultural Lysenkoism, for it takes as its premise the spurious notion that cultural traits are inherited. It implies a dubious, dangerous form of cultural predestination. Children are taught that if their ancestors could do it, so could they. But what happens if a child is from a cultural group that made no significant contribution to science or mathematics? Does this mean that children from that background must find a culturally appropriate field in which to strive? How does a teacher find the right cultural buttons for children of mixed heritage? And how in the world will teachers use this technique when the children in their classes are drawn from many different cultures, as is usually the case? By the time that every culture gets its due, there may be no time left to teach the subject itself. This explosion of filiopietism (which, we should remember, comes from adults, not from students) is reminiscent of the period some years ago when the Russians claimed that they had invented everything first; as we now know, this nationalistic braggadocio did little for their self-esteem and nothing for their economic development. We might reflect, too, on how little social prestige has been accorded in this country to immigrants from Greece and Italy, even though the achievements of their ancestors were at the heart of the classical curriculum.

Filiopietism and ethnic boosterism lead to all sorts of odd practices. In New York State, for example, the curriculum guide for eleventh grade American history lists three "foundations" for the United States Constitution, as follows:

A. Foundations
  1. 17th and 18th century Enlightenment thought
  2. Haudenosaunee political system
     a. Influence upon colonial leadership and European intellectuals (Locke, Montesquieu, Voltaire, Rousseau)
     b. Impact on Albany Plan of Union, Articles of Confederation, and U.S. Constitution
  3. Colonial experience

Those who are unfamiliar with the Haudenosaunee political system might wonder what it is, particularly since educational authorities in New York State rank it as equal in importance to the European Enlightenment and suggest that it strongly influenced not only colonial leaders but the leading intellectuals of Europe. The Haudenosaunee political system was the Iroquois confederation of five (later six) Indian tribes in upper New York State, which conducted war and civil affairs through a council of chiefs, each with one vote. In 1754, Benjamin Franklin proposed a colonial union at a conference in Albany; his plan, said to be inspired by the Iroquois Confederation, was rejected by the other colonies. Today, Indian activists believe that the Iroquois Confederation was the model for the American Constitution, and the New York State Department of Education has decided that they are right. That no other state sees fit to give the American Indians equal billing with the European Enlightenment may be owing to the fact that the Indians in New York State (numbering less than forty thousand) have been more politically effective than elsewhere or that other states have not yet learned about this method of reducing "Eurocentrism" in their American history classes.

Particularism can easily be carried to extremes. Students of Fredonian descent must hear that their ancestors were seminal in the development of all human civilization and that without the Fredonian contribution, we would all be living in caves or trees, bereft of art, technology, and culture. To explain why Fredonians today are in modest circumstances, given their historic eminence, children are taught that somewhere, long ago, another culture stole the Fredonians' achievements, palmed them off as their own, and then oppressed the Fredonians.

I first encountered this argument almost twenty years ago, when I was a graduate student. I shared a small office with a young professor, and I listened as she patiently explained to a student why she had given him a D on a term paper. In his paper, he argued that the Arabs had stolen mathematics from the Nubians in the desert long ago (I forget in which century this theft allegedly occurred). She tried to explain to him about the necessity of historical evidence. He was unconvinced, since he believed that he had uncovered a great truth that was beyond proof. The part I couldn't understand was how anyone could lose knowledge by sharing it. After all, cultures are constantly influencing one another, exchanging ideas and art and technology, and the exchange usually is enriching, not depleting.

Today, there are a number of books and articles advancing controversial theories about the origins of civilization. An important work, *The African Origin of Civilization: Myth or Reality,* by Senegalese scholar Cheikh Anta Diop, argues that ancient Egypt was a black civilization, that all races are descended from the black race, and that the achievements of "western" civilization originated in Egypt. The views of Diop and other Africanists have been condensed into an everyman's paperback titled *What They Never Told You in History Class* by Indus Khamit Kush. This latter book claims that Moses, Jesus, Buddha, Mohammed, and Vishnu were Africans; that the first Indians, Chinese, Hebrews, Greeks, Romans, Britains, and Americans were Africans; and that the first mathematicians, scientists, astronomers, and physicians were Africans. A debate currently raging among some classicists is whether the Greeks "stole" the philosophy, art, and religion of the ancient Egyptians and whether the ancient Egyptians were black Africans. George G. M. James's *Stolen Legacy* insists that the Greeks "stole the Legacy of the African Continent and called it their own." James argues that the civilization of Greece, the vaunted foundation of European culture, owed everything it knew and did to its African predecessors. Thus, the roots of western civilization lie not in Greece and Rome, but in Egypt and, ultimately, in black Africa.

Similar speculation was fueled by the publication in 1987 of Martin Bernal's *Black Athena: The Afroasiatic Roots of Classical Civilization,* Volume 1, *The Fabrication of Ancient Greece, 1785–1985,* although the controversy predates Bernal's book. In a fascinating foray into the politics of knowledge, Bernal attributes the preference of Western European scholars for Greece over Egypt as the fount of knowledge to nearly two centuries of racism and "Europocentrism," but he is uncertain about the color of the ancient Egyptians. However, a review of Bernal's book last year in the *Village Voice* began, "What color were the ancient Egyptians? Blacker than Mubarak, baby." The same article claimed that white racist archeologists chiseled the noses off ancient Egyptian statues so that future generations would not see the typically African facial characteristics. The debate reached the pages of the *Biblical Archeology Review* lat year in an article titled "Were the Ancient Egyptians Black or White?" The author, classicist Frank J. Yurco, argues that some Egyptian rulers were black, others were not, and that "the ancient Egyptians did not think in these terms." The issue, wrote Yurco, "is a chimera, cultural baggage from our own society that can only be imposed artificially on ancient Egyptian society."

Most educationists are not even aware of the debate about whether the ancient Egyptians were black or white, but they are very sensitive to charges that the schools' curricula are Eurocentric, and they are eager to rid the schools of the taint of Eurocentrism. It is hardly surprising that America's schools would recognize strong cultural ties with Europe since our nation's political, religious, educational, and economic institutions were created chiefly by people of European descent, our government was shaped by European ideas, and nearly 80 percent of the people who live here are of European descent. The particularists treat all this history as a racist bias toward Europe, rather than as the matter-of-fact consequences of European immigration. Even so, American education is not centered on Europe. American education, if it is centered on anything, is centered on itself. It is "Americentric." Most American students today have never studied any world history; they know very little about Europe, and even less about the rest of the world. Their minds are rooted solidly in the here and now. When the Berlin Wall was opened in the fall of 1989, journalists discovered that most American teenagers had no idea what it was, nor why its opening was such a big deal. Nonetheless, Eurocentrism provides a better target than Americentrism.

In school districts where most children are black and Hispanic, there has been a growing tendency to embrace particularism, rather than pluralism. Many of the children in these districts perform poorly in academic classes and leave school without graduating. They would fare better in school if they had well-educated and well-paid teachers, small classes, good materials, encouragement at home and school, summer academic programs, protection from the drugs and crime that ravage their neighborhoods, and higher expectations of satisfying careers upon graduation. These are expensive and time-consuming remedies that must also engage the larger society beyond the school. The lure of particularism is that it offers a less complicated anodyne, one in which the children's academic deficiencies may be addressed—or set aside—by inflating their racial pride. The danger of this remedy is that it will detract attention from the real needs of schools and the real interests of children, while simultaneously arousing distorted race pride in children of all races, increasing racial antagonism and producing fresh recruits for white and black racist groups.

The particularist critique gained a major forum in New York in 1989, with the release of a report called "A Curriculum of Inclusion," produced by a task force created by the State Commissioner of Education, Thomas Sobol. In 1987, soon after his appointment, Sobol appointed a Task Force on Minorities to review the state's curriculum for instances of bias. He did this not because there had been complaints about bias in the curriculum, but because—as a newly appointed state commissioner whose previous job had been to superintend the public schools of a wealthy suburb, Scarsdale—he wanted to demonstrate his sensitivity to minority concerns. The Sobol task force was composed of representatives of African American, Hispanic, Asian American, and American Indian groups.

The task force engaged four consultants, one from each of the aforementioned racial or ethnic minorities, to review nearly one hundred teachers' guides prepared by the state. These guides define the state's curriculum, usually as a list of facts and concepts to be taught, along with model activities. The primary focus of the consultants, not surprisingly, was the history and social studies curriculum. As it happened, the history curriculum had been extensively revised in 1987 to make it multicultural, in both American and world history. In the 1987 revision the time given to Western Europe was reduced to one-quarter of one year, as part of a two-year global studies sequence in which equal time was allotted to seven major world regions, including Africa and Latin America.

As a result of the 1987 revisions in American and world history, New York State had one of the most advanced multicultural history-social studies curricula in the country. Dozens of social studies teachers and consultants had participated, and the final draft was reviewed by such historians as Eric Foner of Columbia University, the late Hazel Hertzberg of Teachers College, Columbia University, and Christopher Lasch of the University of Rochester. The curriculum was overloaded with facts, almost to the point of numbing students with details and trivia, but it was not insensitive to ethnicity in American history or unduly devoted to European history.

But the Sobol task force decided that this curriculum was biased and Eurocentric. The first sentence of the task force report summarizes its major thesis: "African Americans, Asian Americans, Puerto Ricans/Latinos, and Native Americans have all been the victims of an intellectual and educational oppression that has characterized the culture and institutions of the United States and the European American world for centuries."

The task force report was remarkable in that it vigorously denounced bias without identifying a single instance of bias in the curricular guides under review. Instead, the consultants employed harsh, sometimes inflammatory, rhetoric to treat every difference of opinion or interpretation as an example of racial bias. The African-American consultant, for example, excoriates the curriculum for its "White Anglo-Saxon (WASP) value system and norms," its "deep-seated pathologies of racial hatred" and its "white nationalism"; he decries as bias the fact that children study Egypt as part of the Middle East instead of as part of Africa. Perhaps Egypt should be studied as part of the African unit (geographically, it is located on the African continent); but placing it in one region rather than the other is not what most people think of as racism or bias. The "Latino" consultant criticizes the use of the term "Spanish-American War" instead of "Spanish-Cuban-American War." The Native American consultant complains that tribal languages are classified as "foreign languages."

The report is consistently Europhobic. It repeatedly expresses negative judgments on "European Americans" and on everything Western and European. All people with a white skin are referred to as "Anglo-Saxons" and "WASPs." Europe, says the report, is uniquely responsible for producing aggresive individuals who "were ready to 'discover, invade and conquer' foreign land because of greed, racism and national egoism." All white people are held collectively guilty for the historical crimes of slavery and racism. There is no mention of the "Anglo-Saxons" who opposed slavery and racism. Nor does the report acknowledge that some whites have been victims of discrimination and oppression. The African American consultant writes of the Constitution, "There is something vulgar and revolting in glorifying a process that heaped undeserved rewards on a segment of the population while oppressing the majority."

The New York task force proposal is not merely about the reconstruction of what is taught. It goes a step further to suggest that the history curriculum may be used to ensure that "children from Native American, Puerto Rican/Latino, Asian American, and African American cultures will have higher self-esteem and self-respect, while children from European cultures will have a less arrogant perspective of being part of the group that has 'done it all.'"

In February 1990, Commissioner Sobol asked the New York Board of Regents to endorse a sweeping revision of the history curriculum to make it more multicultural. His recommendations were couched in measured tones, not in the angry rhetoric of his task force. The board supported his request unanimously. It remains to be seen whether New York pursues the particularist path marked out by the Commissioner's advisory group or finds its way to the concept of pluralism within a democratic tradition.

The rising tide of particularism encourages the politicization of all curricula in the schools. If education bureaucrats bend to the political and ideological winds, as is their wont, we can anticipate a generation of struggle over the content of the curriculum in mathematics, science, literature, and history. Demands for "culturally relevant" studies, for ethnostudies of all kinds, will open the classroom to unending battles over whose version is taught, who gets credit for what, and which ethno-interpretation is appropriate. Only recently have districts begun to resist the demands of fundamentalist groups to censor textbooks and library books (and some have not yet begun to do so).

The spread of particularism throws into question the very idea of American public education. Public schools exist to teach children the general skills and knowledge that they need to succeed in American society, and the specific skills and knowledge that they need in order to function as American citizens. They receive public support because they have a public function. Historically, the public schools were known as "common schools" because they were schools for all, even if the children of all the people did not attend them. Over the years, the courts have found that it was unconstitutional to teach religion in the common schools, or to separate children on the basis of their race in the common schools. In their curriculum, their hiring practices, and their general philosophy, the public schools must not discriminate against or give preference to any racial or ethnic group. Yet they are permitted to accommodate cultural diversity by, for example, serving food that is culturally appropriate or providing library collections that emphasize the interests of the local community. However, they should not be expected to teach children to view the world through an ethnocentric perspective that rejects or ignores the common culture. For generations, those groups that wanted to inculcate their religion or their ethnic heritage have instituted private schools—after school, on weekends, or on a full-time basis. There, children learn with others of the same group—Greeks, Poles, Germans, Japanese, Chinese, Jews, Lutherans, Catholics, and so on—and are taught by people from the same group. Valuable as this exclusive experience has been for those who choose it, this has not been the role of public education. One of the primary purposes of public education has been to create a national community, a definition of citizenship and culture that is both expansive and *inclusive*.

The curriculum in public schools must be based on whatever knowledge and practices have been determined to be best by professionals—experienced teachers and scholars—who are competent to make these judgments. Professional societies must be prepared to defend the integrity of their disciplines. When called upon, they should establish review committees to examine disputes over curriculum and to render judgment, in order to help school officials fend off improper political pressure. Where genuine controversies exist, they should be taught and debated in the classroom. Was Egypt a black civilization? Why not raise the question, read the arguments of the different sides in the debate, show slides of Egyptian pharaohs and queens, read books about life in ancient Egypt, invite guest scholars from the local university, and visit museums with Egyptian collections? If scholars disagree, students should know it. One great advantage of this approach is that students will see that history is a lively study, that textbooks are fallible, that historians disagree, that the writing of history is influenced by the historian's politics and ideology, that history is written by people who make choices among alternative facts and interpretations, and that history changes as new facts are uncovered and new interpretations win adherents. They will also learn that cultures and civilizations constantly interact, exchange ideas, and influence one another, and that the idea of racial or ethnic purity is a myth. Another advantage is that students might once again study ancient history, which has all but disappeared from the curricula of American schools. (California recently introduced a required sixth grade course in ancient civilizations, but ancient history is otherwise *terra incognita* in American education.)

The multicultural controversy may do wonders for the study of history, which has been neglected for years in American schools. At this time, only half of our high school graduates ever study any world history. Any serious attempt to broaden students' knowledge of Africa, Europe, Asia, and Latin America will require at least two, and possibly three years of world history (a requirement thus far only in California). American history, too, will need more time than the one-year high-school survey course. Those of us who have insisted for years on the importance of history in the curriculum may not be ready to assent to its redemptive power, but hope that our new allies will ultimately join a constructive dialogue that strengthens the place of history in the schools.

As cultural controversies arise, educators must adhere to the principle of "E Pluribus Unum." That is, they must maintain a balance between the demands of the one—the nation of which we are common citizens—and the many—the varied histories of the American people. It is not necessary to denigrate either the one or the many. Pluralism is a positive value, but it is also important that we preserve a sense of an American community—a society and a culture to which we all belong. If there is no overall community with an agreed-upon vision of liberty and justice, if all we have is a collection of racial and ethnic cultures, lacking any common bonds, then we have no means to mobilize public opinion on behalf of people who are not members of our particular group. We have, for example, no reason to support public education. If there is no larger community, then each group will want to teach its own children in its own way, and public education ceases to exist.

History should not be confused with filiopietism. History gives no grounds for race pride. No race has a monopoly on virtue. If anything, a study of history should inspire humility, rather than pride. People of every racial group have committed terrible crimes, often against others of the same group. Whether one looks at the history of Europe or Africa or Latin America or Asia, every continent offers examples of inhumanity. Slavery has existed in civilizations around the world for centuries. Examples of genocide can be found around the world, throughout history, from ancient times right through to our own day. Governments and cultures, sometimes by edict, sometimes simply following tradition, have practiced not only slavery, but human sacrifice, infanticide, cliterodectomy, and mass murder. If we teach children this, they might recognize how absurd both racial hatred and racial chauvinism are.

What must be preserved in the study of history is the spirit of inquiry, the readiness to open new questions and to pursue new understandings. History, at its best, is a search for truth. The best way to portray this search is through debate and controversy, rather than through imposition of fixed beliefs and immutable facts. Perhaps the most dangerous aspect of school history is its tendency to become Official History, a sanctified version of the Truth taught by the state to captive audiences and embedded in beautiful mass-market textbooks as holy writ. When Official History is written by committees responding to political pressures, rather than by scholars synthesizing the best available research, then the errors of the past are replaced by the politically fashionable errors of the present. It may be difficult to teach children that history is both important and uncertain, and that even the best historians never have all the pieces of the jigsaw puzzle, but it is necessary to do so. If state education departments permit the revision of their history courses and textbooks to become an exercise in power politics, then the entire process of state-level curriculum-making becomes suspect, as does public education itself.

The question of self-esteem is extraordinarily complex, and it goes well beyond the content of the curriculum. Most of what we call self-esteem is formed in the home and in a variety of life experiences, not only in school. Nonetheless, it has been important for blacks—and for other racial groups—to learn about the history of slavery and of the civil rights movement; it has been important for blacks to know that their ancestors actively resisted enslavement and actively pursued equality; and it has been important for blacks and others to learn about black men and women who fought courageously against racism and who provide models of courage, persis-

tence, and intellect. These are instances where the content of the curriculum reflects sound scholarship, and at the same time probably lessens racial prejudice and provides inspiration for those who are descendants of slaves. But knowing about the travails and triumphs of one's forebears does not necessarily translate into either self-esteem or personal accomplishment. For most children, self-esteem—the self-confidence that grows out of having reached a goal—comes not from hearing about the monuments of their ancestors but as a consequence of what they are able to do and accomplish through their own efforts.

As I reflected on these issues, I recalled reading an interview a few years ago with a talented black runner. She said that her model is Mikhail Baryshnikov. She admires him because he is a magnificent athlete. He is not black; he is not female; he is not American-born; he is not even a runner. But he inspires her because of the way he trained and used his body. When I read this, I thought how narrow-minded it is to believe that people can be inspired *only* by those who are exactly like them in race and ethnicity.

MOLEFI KETE ASANTE AND DIANE RAVITCH

Multiculturalism: An Exchange

Molefi Kete Asante is Professor and Chairman of the Department of Afro-American Studies at Temple University and editor of the Journal of Black Studies. *Diane Ravitch is Adjunct Professor of History and Education at the Teacher's College of Columbia University.* (Source: Reprinted from The American Scholar, Volume 60, Number 2, Spring 1991. Copyright © 1991 by the authors.)

QUESTIONS FOR REFLECTION

1. What does Asante mean by saying that "we are all implicated in the positions we hold about society, culture, and education"? Do you agree?

2. Why does Asante say that Ravitch's pluralism is "a new form of Eurocentric hegemonism"?

3. How does Asante argue in favor of multiculturalism? What does he mean by that term?

4. Ravitch claims that Asante's position might better be described as "multiple -centrisms"? How does she criticize that view?

MOLEFI KETE ASANTE

Multiculturalism without Hierarchy:
An Afrocentric Reply to Diane Ravitch

We are all implicated in the positions we hold about society, culture, and education. Although the implications may take quite different forms in some fields and with some scholars, such as the consequences and our methods and inquiry on our systems of values, we are nevertheless captives of the positions we take, that is, if we take those positions honestly.

In a recent article in *The American Scholar* (Summer 1990), Diane Ravitch reveals the tensions between scholarship and ideological perspectives in an exceedingly clear manner. The position taken in her article "Multiculturalism: E Pluribus Plures" accurately demonstrates the thesis that those of us who write are implicated in what we choose to write. This is not a profound announcement since most fields of inquiry recognize that a researcher's presence must be accounted for in research or a historian's relationship to data must be examined in seeking to establish the validity of conclusions. This is not to say that the judgment will be invalid because of the intimacy of the scholar with the information but rather that in accounting for the scholar's or researcher's presence we are likely to know better how to assess the information presented. Just as a researcher may be considered an intrusive presence in an experiment, the biases of a scholar may be just as intrusive in interpreting data or making analysis. The fact that a writer seeks to establish a persona of a non-interested observer means that such a writer wants the reader to assume that an unbiased position is being taken on a subject. However, we know that as soon as a writer states a proposition, the writer is implicated and such implication holds minor or extreme consequences.

The remarkable advantage of stating aims and objectives prior to delivering an argument is that the reader knows precisely to what the author is driving. Unfortunately, too many writers on education either do not know the point they are making or lose sight of their point in the making. Such regrettably is the case with Diane Ravitch's article on multicultural education.

Among writers who have written on educational matters in the last few years, Professor Ravitch of Columbia University's Teacher's College is considered highly quotable and therefore, in the context of American educational policy, influential. This is precisely why her views on multiculturalism must not remain unchallenged. Many of the positions taken by Professor Ravitch are similar to the positions taken against the Freedmen's Bureau's establishment of black schools in the South during the 1860s. Then, the white conservative education policymakers felt that it was necessary to control the content of education so that the recently freed Africans would not become self-assured. An analysis of Ravitch's arguments will reveal what Martin Bernal calls in *Black Athena* "the neo-Aryan" model of history. Her version of multiculturalism is not multiculturalism at all, but rather a new form of Eurocentric hegemonism.

People tend to do the best they can with the information at their disposal. The problem in most cases where intellectual distortions arise is ignorance rather than malice. Unlike in the political arena where oratory goes a long way, in education, sooner or later the truth must come out. The proof of the theory is in the practice. What we have seen in the past twenty-five years is the gradual dismantling of the educational kingdom built to accompany the era of white supremacy. What is being contested is the speed of its dismantling. In many ways, the South African regime is a good parallel to what is going on in American education. No longer can the structure of knowledge which supported white hegemony be defended; whites must take their place, not above or below, but alongside the rest of humanity. This is a significantly different reality than we have experienced in American education and there are several reasons for this turn of events.

The first reason is the accelerating explosion in the world of knowledge about cultures, histories, and events seldom mentioned in American education. Names of individuals and their achievements, views of historiography and alternatives to European perspectives have proliferated due to international interaction, trade, and computer technology. People from other cultures, particularly non-Western people, have added new elements into the educational equation. A second reason is the rather recent intellectual liberation of large numbers of African-descended scholars. While there have always been African scholars in every era, the European hegemony, since the 1480s, in knowledge about the world, including Africa, was fairly complete. The domination of information, the naming of things, the propagation of concepts, and the dissemination of interpretations were, and still are in most cases in the West, a Eurocentric hegemony. During the twentieth century, African scholars led by W. E. B. DuBois began to break from the intellectual shackles of Europe and make independent inquiries into history, science, origins, and Europe itself. For the first time in five hundred years, a cadre of scholars, trained in the West, but largely liberated from the hegemonic European thinking began to expose numerous distortions, often elevated to "truth" in the works of Eurocentric authors. A third reason for the current assault on the misinformation spread by white hegemonic thinkers is the conceptual inadequacy of simply valorizing Europe. Few whites have ever examined their culture critically. Those who have done so have often been severely criticized by their peers: the cases of Sidney Willhelm, Joe Feagin, Michael Bradley, and Basil Davidson are well known.

As part of the Eurocentric tradition, there seems to be silence on questions of hegemony, that is, the inability to admit the mutual conspiracy between race doctrine and educational doctrine in America. Professor Ravitch and others would maintain the facade of reasonableness even in the face of arguments demonstrating the irrationality of both white supremacist ideas on race and white hegemonic ideas in education. They are corollary and both are untenable on genetic and intellectual grounds.

Eurocentric Hegemonism

Let us examine the argument of the defenders of the Eurocentric hegemony in education more closely. The status quo always finds its best defense in territoriality. Thus, it is one of the first weapons used by the defenders of the white hegemonic education. Soon after my book *The Afrocentric Idea* was published, I was interviewed on "The Today Show" along with Herb London, the New York University professor/politician who is one of the founders of the National Association of Professors. When I suggested the possibility of schools weaving information about other cultures into the fabric of the teaching-learning process, Professor London interrupted that "there is not enough *time* in the school year for what Asante wants." Of course there is, if there is enough for the Eurocentric information, there is enough time for cultural information from other groups. Professor Ravitch uses the same argument. Her strategy is to cast serious examinations of the curriculum as pressure groups, much like creationists in biology. Of course, the issue is neither irrational nor sensational; it is pre-eminently a question of racial dominance, the maintenance of which, in any form, I oppose. On the contrary, the status quo defenders, like the South African Boers, believe that it is possible to defend what is fundamentally anti-intellectual and immoral: the dominance and hegemony of the Eurocentric view of reality on a multicultural society. There is space for Eurocentrism in a multicultural enterprise so long as it does not parade as universal. No one wants to banish the Eurocentric view. It is a valid view of reality where it does not force its way. Afrocentricity does not seek to replace Eurocentricity in its arrogant disregard for other cultures.

The Principal Contradictions

A considerable number of white educators and some blacks have paraded in single file and sometimes in concert to take aim at multiculturalism. In her article Professor Ravitch attempts to defend the indefensible. Believing, I suspect, that the best defense of the status quo is to attack, she attacks diversity, and those that support it, with gusto, painting straw fellows along the way. Her claim to support multiculturalism is revealed to be nothing more than an attempt to apologize for white cultural supremacy in the curriculum by using the same logic as white racial supremacists used in trying to defend white racism in previous years. She assumes falsely that there is little to say about the rest of the world, particularly about Africa and African Americans. Indeed, she is willing to assert, as Herbert London has claimed, that the school systems do not have enough time to teach all that Afrocentrists believe ought to be taught. Nevertheless, she assumes that all that is not taught about the European experience is valid and necessary. There are some serious flaws in her line of reasoning. I shall attempt to locate the major flaws and ferret them out.

Lip service is paid to the evolution of American education from the days of racial segregation to the present when "new social historians" routinely incorporate the experiences of other than white males. Nowhere does Professor Ravitch demonstrate an appreciation for the role played by the African American community in overcoming the harshest elements of racial segregation in the educational system. Consequently, she is unable to understand that more fundamental than eliminating racial segregation has to be the removal of racist thinking, assumptions, symbols, and materials in the curriculum.

However, there is no indication that Professor Ravitch is willing to grant an audience to this reasoning because she plods deeper into the same quagmire by attempting to conceptualize multiculturalism, a simple concept in educational jargon. She posits a *pluralist* multiculturalism—a redundancy—then suggests a *particularistic* multiculturalism—an oxymoron—in order to beat a dead horse. The ideas are non-starters because they have no reality in fact. I wrote the first book in this country on trans-racial communication and edited the first handbook on intercultural communication, and I am unaware of the categories Professor Ravitch seeks to forge. She claims that the pluralist multiculturalist believes in pluralism and the particularistic multiculturalist believes in particularism. Well, multiculturalism in education is almost self-defining. It is simply the idea that the educational experience should reflect the diverse cultural heritage of our system of knowledge. I have contended that such is not the case and cannot be the case until teachers know more about the African American, Native American, Latino, and Asian experiences. This position obviously excites Professor Ravitch to the point that she feels obliged to make a case for "mainstream Americans."

The Myth of Mainstream

The idea of "mainstream American" is nothing more than an additional myth meant to maintain Eurocentric hegemony. When Professor Ravitch speaks of mainstream, she does not have Spike Lee, Aretha Franklin, or John Coltrane in mind. Bluntly put, "mainstream" is a code word for "white." When a dean of a college says to a faculty member, as one recently said, "You ought to publish in mainstream journals," the dean is not meaning *Journal of Black Studies* or *Black Scholar*. As a participant in the racist system of education, the dean is merely carrying out the traditional function of enlarging the white hegemony over scholarship. Thus, when the status quo defenders use terms like "mainstream," they normally mean "white." In fact, one merely has to substitute the words "white controlled" to get at the real meaning behind the code.

Misunderstanding Multiculturalism

Misunderstanding the African American struggle for education in the United States, Professor Ravitch thinks that the call to multiculturalism is a matter of anecdotal references to outstanding individuals or descriptions of civil rights. But neither acknowledgement of achievements per se, nor descriptive accounts of the African experience adequately conveys the aims of the Afrocentric restructuring, as we shall see. From the establishment of widespread public education to the current emphasis on massaging the curriculum toward an organic and systemic recognition of cultural pluralism, the African American concept of nationhood has been always central. In terms of Afrocentricity, it is the same. We do not seek segments or modules in the classroom but rather the infusion of African American studies in every segment and in every module. The difference is between "incorporating the experiences" and "infusing the curriculum with an entirely new life." The real unity of the curriculum comes from infusion, not from including African Americans in what Ravitch would like to remain a white contextual hegemony she calls mainstream. No true mainstream can ever exist until there is knowledge, understanding, and acceptance of the role Africans have played in American history. One reason the issue is debated by white scholars such as Ravitch is because they do not believe there is substantial or significant African information to infuse. Thus, ignorance becomes the reason for the strenuous denials of space for the cultural infusion. If she knew or believed that it was possible to have missed something, she would not argue against it. What is at issue is her own educational background. Does she know classical Africa? Did she take courses in African American studies from qualified professors? Those who know do not question the importance of Afrocentric or Latino infusion into the educational process.

The Misuse of Self-Esteem

Professor Ravitch's main critique of the Afrocentric, Latinocentric, or Americentric (Native American) project is that it seeks to raise "self-esteem and self-respect" among Africans, Latinos, and Native Americans. It is important to understand that this is not only a self-serving argument, but a false argument. In the first place, I know of no Afrocentric curriculum planner—Asa Hilliard, Wade Nobles, Leonard Jeffries, Don McNeely being the principal ones—who insist that the primary aim is to raise self-esteem. The argument is a false lead to nowhere because the curriculum planners I am familiar with insist that the fundamental objective is to provide

accurate information. A secondary effect of accuracy and truth might be the adjustment of attitudes by both black and white students. In several surveys of college students, research has demonstrated that new information changes attitudes in both African American and white students. Whites are not so apt to take a superior attitude when they are aware of the achievements of other cultures. They do not lose their self-esteem, they adjust their views. On the other hand, African Americans who are often as ignorant as whites about African achievements adjust their attitudes about themselves once they are exposed to new information. There is no great secret in this type of transformation. Ravitch, writing from the point of view of those whose cultural knowledge is reinforced every hour, not just in the curriculum, but in every media, smugly contends that she cannot see the value of self-esteem. Since truth and accuracy will yield by-products of attitude adjustments, the Afrocentrists have always argued for the accurate representation of information.

Afrocentricity does not seek an ethnocentric curriculum. Unfortunately, Diane Ravitch chose to ignore two books that explain my views on this subject, *The Afrocentric Idea* (1987) and *Kemet, Afrocentricity and Knowledge* (1990) and instead quotes from *Afrocentricity* (1980), which was not about education but about personal and social transformation. Had she read the later works she would have understood that Afrocentricity is not an ethnocentric view in two senses. In the first place, it does not valorize the African view while downgrading others. In this sense, it is unlike the Eurocentric view, which is an ethnocentric view because it valorizes itself and parades as universal. It becomes racist when the rules, customs, and/or authority of law or force dictate it as the proper view. This is what often happens in school curricula. In the second place, as to method, Afrocentricity is not a naive racial theory. It is a systematic approach to presenting the African as subject rather than object. Even Ravitch might be taught the Afrocentric Method!

American Culture

There is no common American culture as is claimed by the defenders of the status quo. There is a hegemonic culture to be sure, pushed as if it were a common culture. Perhaps Ravitch is confusing concepts here. There is a common American *society,* which is quite different from a common American culture. Certain cultural characteristics are shared by those within the society but the meaning of *multicultural* is "many cultures." To believe in multicultural education is to assume that there are many cultures. The reason Ravitch finds confusion is because the only way she can reconcile the "many cultures" is to insist on many "little" cultures under the hegemony of the "big" white culture. Thus, what she means by multiculturalism is precisely what I criticized in *The Afrocentric Idea,* the acceptance of other cultures within a Eurocentric framework.

In the end, the neat separation of pluralist multiculturalists and particularistic multiculturalists breaks down because it is a false, straw separation developed primarily for the sake of argument and not for clarity. The real division on the question of multiculturalism is between those who truly seek to maintain a Eurocentric hegemony over the curriculum and those who truly believe in cultural pluralism without hierarchy. Ravitch defends the former position.

Professor Ravitch's ideological position is implicated in her mis-reading of several scholars' works. When Professor John Stanfield writes that modes of social knowledge such as theology, science, and magic are different, not inferior or superior, Ravitch asks, "If Professor Stanfield broke his leg, would he go to a theologian, a doctor, or a magician?" Clearly she does not understand the simple statement Stanfield is making. He is not writing about *uses* of knowledge, but about *ranking* of knowledge. To confuse the point by providing an answer for a question never raised is the key rhetorical strategy in Ravitch's case. Thus, she implies that because Professor George Ghevarughese Joseph argues that mathematics was developed in Egypt, Babylonia, Mesopotamia, and India long before it came to Europe, he seeks to replace modern math with "ancient ethnic mathematics." This is a deliberate misunderstanding of the professor's point: mathematics in its modern form owes debts to Africans and Asians.

Another attempt to befuddle issues is Ravitch's gratuitous comment that Koreans "do not study ancient mathematics" and yet they have high scores. There are probably several variables for the Koreans making the highest scores "in mathematics on international assessments." Surely one element would have to be the linkage of Korean traditions in mathematics to present mathematical problems. Koreans do not study European theorists prior to their own; indeed they are taught to honor and respect the ancestral mathematicians. This is true for Indians, Chinese, and Japanese. In African traditions, the *European* slave trade broke the linkage, and the work of scholars such as Ahmed Baba and Hypathia remains unknown to the African American and thus does not take its place in the family of world mathematics.

Before Professor Ravitch ends her assault on ethnic cultures, she fires a volley against the Haudenosaunee political system of Native Americans. As a New Yorker, she does not like the fact that the state's curriculum guide lists the Haudenosaunee Confederation as an inspiration to the United States Constitution alongside the Enlightenment. She says readers "might wonder what it is." Bluntly put, a proper education would acquaint students with the Haudenosaunee Confederation, and in that case Professor Ravitch's readers would know the Haudenosaunee as a part of the conceptual discussion that went into the development of the American political systems. Only a commitment to white hegemony would lead a writer to assume that whites could not obtain political ideas from others.

Finally, she raises a "controversy" that is no longer a controversy among reputable scholars: Who were the Egyptians? Most scholars accept a simple answer: They were Africans. The question of whether or not they were black was initially raised by Eurocentric scholars in the nineteenth century seeking to explain the testimony of the ancient Greeks, particularly Herodotus and Diodorus Siculus, who said that Egyptians were "Black with woolly hair." White hegemonic studies that sought to maintain the false notion of white racial supremacy during the nineteenth century fabricated the idea of a European or an Asian Egyptian to deny Africa its classical past and to continue the Aryan myth. It is shocking to see Professor Ravitch raise this issue in the 1990s. It is neither a controversial issue nor should it be to those familiar with the evidence.

The debate over the curriculum is really over a vision of the future of the United States. Keepers of the status quo, such as Professor Ravitch, want to maintain a "white framework" for multiculturalism because they have no faith in cultural pluralism without hierarchy. A common culture does not exist, but this nation is on the path toward it. Granting all the difficulties we face in attaining this common culture, we are more likely to reach it when we allow the full participation of all ethnic groups in a quest for a usable curriculum. In the end, we will find that such a curriculum, like inspiration, will not come from this or that individual model but from integrity and accuracy.

DIANE RAVITCH

Reply to Asante

In responding to Professor Asante's critique of my article, "Multiculturalism: E Pluribus Plures," I had continually to reread what I had written, because I did not recognize my article from his description. His repeated allegations of racism and "neo-Aryanism" are not supported by quotations from the text, because nothing in my article validates his outrageous charges either directly or by inference. His statements associating my views with those who opposed the education of black children after the Civil War and with white South Africans are simply mud-slinging. He acknowledges in passing that my view of multiculturalism is shared by some black educators, but this anomaly does not cause him to pause in his scurrilous allegations of racism.

In the article, I described the major changes that have occurred in the school curriculum over the past generation. I stated that the teaching of American history had long ignored the historical experiences of minority groups and women, and that recent scholarship had made it possible, indeed necessary, to forge historical narratives that accurately represent the diverse nature of our society. The resulting effort to weave together the different strands of our historical experience, I argued, provides a more accurate portrait of the American people than the flawed historical account that it replaced. Children in school now learn, I wrote, "that cultural pluralism is one of the norms of a free society; that differences among groups are a national resource rather than a problem to be solved. Indeed, the unique feature of the United States is that its common culture has been formed by the interaction of its subsidiary cultures. It is a culture that has been influenced over time by immigrants, American Indians, Africans (slave and free) and by their descendants. American music, art, literature, language, food, clothing, sports, holidays, and customs all show the effects of the commingling of diverse cultures in one nation. Paradoxical though it may seem, the United States has a common culture that is multicultural."

I then went on to argue that demands for diversification of the curriculum had in some instances been pressed to the extremes of ethnocentrism; that some educators want not a portrait of the nation that shows how different groups have shaped our history, but immersion of children in the ancestral exploits of their own race or ethnic group. In trying to explain the bifurcation of the multicultural movement, I struggled to find the right nomenclature for the two competing strains of thought, and I used the terms *pluralistic* and *particularistic*. Professor Asante is right that I should not have called one of them "pluralistic multiculturalism" and the other "particularistic multiculturalism." While pluralism *is* multicultural, particularism is not. Pluralism and particularism are opposite in spirit and methods. The demands for ethnocentrism associated with the Afrocentric movement should not be seen as an extreme form of multiculturalism, but as a *rejection* of multiculturalism. Afrocentrism and other kinds of ethnocentrism might better be described as racial fundamentalism. What has confused the matter is the fact that Afrocentrists present their program in public forums as "multicultural," in order to shield from public view their assertions of racial superiority and racial purity, which promote not the racial understanding that our society so desperately needs, but racial antagonism.

Professor Asante and others in the Afrocentric movement like Leonard Jeffries, Jr., Wade Nobles, and Asa Hilliard are inconsistent about whether Afrocentrism is for descendants of Africans only, or for everyone. Their literature sometimes claims that everyone—not only blacks—must learn that all the achievements of civilization originated in Africa; but at other times, Afrocentrists appear to endorse the idea that each racial group should study its own peculiar history (which I call "multiple -centrisms"). The former version of Afrocentrism veers toward racism, with its specious claims about the superiority of those whose skin is darkened by melanin and its attacks on whites as the "ice people." The latter, the "multiple -centrisms" approach, is in its way even more dangerous, because it is insidious. The "multiple -centrisms" position is superficially appealing, because on the surface it gives something to everyone: African Americans may be Afrocentric, Asian Americans may be Asiacentric, Native Americans may be Native Americentric, and Latinos may be Latinocentric, while those who are of European descent must be taught to feel guilt and shame for the alleged misdeeds of their ancestors. This "multiple -centrisms" model is now a hot educational trend, emanating from Portland, Oregon, where the local office of multicultural education has prepared Afrocentric curricular materials and plans to develop similar materials for Asian Americans, Latino Americans, Native Americans, and Pacific Islanders. This was also the organizing principle of Commissioner Thomas Sobol's "task force on minorities" in New York State, whose misnamed "Curriculum of Inclusion" called not for inclusion of minority cultures into a pluralistic mainstream but for "multiple- centrisms."

The "multiple -centrisms" approach is deeply flawed. It confuses race with culture, as though everyone with the same skin color has the same culture and history. It ignores the fact that within every major racial group, there are many different cultural groups, and within each major racial group, there exist serious ethnic and cultural tensions. Furthermore, the "multiple -centrisms" approach denies the *synchretistic* nature of all cultures and civilizations that mingle, and the multiple ways in which they change one another. Neither world history nor American history is the story of five racial groups; such a concept leads to false history and to racial stereotyping. This gross oversimplification of history and culture could be taken seriously only in a society where educators are themselves either intimidated or uneducated.

Professor Asante relentlessly argues against positions that I did not take and attributes to me things that I did not write. For example, Professor Asante quotes Herbert London of New York University to the effect that there is "not enough time in the school year" to teach black history and proceeds to say that I "use the same argument." He does not quote me because he cannot find support for his statement in my article. In fact, I do believe in the importance of teaching black history, drawing on the work of such respected scholars of African American history as John Hope Franklin, Eric Foner, Eugene Genovese, Gary Nash, Leon Litwack, Winthrop Jordan, and Nathan Huggins. It is not possible to teach the history of the United States accurately without teaching black history.

Professor Asante willfully misconstrues a reference that I made to "mainstream Americans." The context was as follows: I wrote about how American history textbooks had for generations ignored race, ethnicity, and religion, and how "the main narrative paid little attention to minority groups and women. With the ethnic revival of the 1960s, this approach to the teaching of history came under fire, because the history of national leaders—virtually all of whom were white, Anglo-Saxon, and male—ignored the place in American history of those who were none of the above. The traditional history of elites had been complemented by an assimilationist view of American society, which presumed that everyone in the American melting pot would eventually lose or abandon those ethnic characteristics that distinguished them from mainstream Americans. The ethnic revival demonstrated that many groups did not want to be assimilated or melted." Professor Asante distorts this to claim that I felt "obliged to make a case for 'mainstream Americans.'" I nowhere made a case for the mainstream, nor did I describe who was included or excluded in this putative "mainstream." I wrote: "The pluralist approach to multiculturalism promotes a broader interpretation of the common American culture and seeks due recognition for the ways that the nation's many racial, ethnic, and cultural groups have transformed the national culture. The pluralists say, in effect, 'American culture belongs to us, all of us; the U.S. is us, and we remake it in every generation.'" By this description, Spike Lee and Aretha Franklin are very much part of the common culture and the American mainstream. So are Duke Ellington, Count Basie, Bill Cosby, Eddie Murphy, Oprah Winfrey, William

Raspberry, Carl Lewis, Marion Barry, Malcolm X, Jackie Robinson, Leontyne Price, Langston Hughes, James Weldon Johnson, Countee Cullen, Alice Walker, Martin Luther King, Jr., Frederick Douglass, Jesse Jackson, Henry Gates, Derrick Bell, Jr., and Kenneth B. Clark. As for publishing in "mainstream" journals, Professor Asante misunderstands the dean. She (or he) does not mean that one must publish in a *white* journal; she means that one gains credibility in the academic world by publishing in a journal that has clear standards of scholarship, where false charges of racism, character assassination, and out-of-context quotations are not permissible.

Professor Asante asserts that the ethnocentric curriculum does not claim to raise the self-esteem of students of the same racial or ethnic group. This is not correct. Professor Wade Nobles, whom he cites, runs a state-funded program in California called the HAWK Federation Youth Development and Training Program which aims to immerse young black males in African and African American culture; its purpose, according to the program's brochure, is to address "simultaneously the problems of substance abuse prevention [sic], gang violence, academic failure and low aspirations and poor self-esteem." The New York State task force report, "A Curriculum of Inclusion," whose chief consultant was Professor Leonard Jeffries, Jr., repeatedly asserts the relationship between the curriculum and the self-esteem of students. The report claims that a rewriting of the curriculum will promote "higher self-esteem and self-respect" among children from racial minorities "while children from European cultures will have a less arrogant perspective of being part of the group that has 'done it all.'"

After stating that the leaders of the Afrocentric movement do not rest their case on building self-esteem, but rather on truth, Professor Asante then claims that Korean students do well in mathematics because "they are taught to honor and respect the ancestral mathematicians. This is true for Indians, Chinese, and Japanese." Here is the full-blown ethnocentric premise: You can do well if you are taught that your ancestors did it before you. Professor Asante offers no evidence for his statements about Asian children, because none exists. According to Professor Harold Stevenson of the University of Michigan, who

has conducted extensive cross-cultural studies of mathematics education in the United States, Japan, and China, children in Japan and China do not study "the ancestral mathematicians." They study mathematics; they learn to solve problems.

Of course, everyone needs to know that they, and people like them, are respected as equals in the society they live in. But to assume that self-esteem is built on reverence for one's ancestors is highly questionable. If this were true, the highest academic achievement in the Western world would be recorded by children of Greek and Italian ancestry, since they are the descendants of ancient Greece and Rome; but this is not the case either in the United States or in international assessments. In fact, according to a recent article in the *New York Times*, Italian-American students—the lineal descendants of Cicero and Julius Caesar—have the lowest achievement and the highest dropout rate of any white ethnic group in New York City schools.

Nor is it clear that self-esteem (in the sense of feeling good about yourself) is a reliable indicator of academic achievement. In the most recent international assessment of mathematics, Korean children had the highest achievement and American children had the lowest achievement. When the students were asked whether they were good in mathematics, the Koreans had the lowest score, and the Americans had the highest score. In other words, the Americans had the highest self-esteem and the lowest achievement; the Koreans had the lowest self-esteem and the highest achievement. Why did Korean students fare so well? Consider the research report that accompanied the assessment results: "Korea's success can be partially attributed to the nation's and parents' strong interest in education, reflected in a 220-day school year. While there is virtually no adult illiteracy in the country, only 13 percent of Korea's parents have completed some post-secondary education. They nonetheless see education as the hope for their children and grandchildren. Everyone recognizes that Korea's job market is very demanding and the scientific and technological areas carry high prestige." Another contributing factor to Korean success is a national curriculum that is two-to-three years more advanced than the mathematics that American children study. Presumably, what Korean children learn is not that they are the greatest, but that those who care about them expect them to work hard and to study, and that if they do, they will succeed.

Professor Asante's appeal to the instructional power of ethnocentrism ignores the fact that Asian children in the United States out-perform children of all other racial and ethnic groups in mathematics; the SAT mathematics scores of Asian students are far above those of other groups. Asian American children study mathematics in the same classrooms, using the same textbooks as their classmates; they do not study their "ancestral mathematicians." But, according to numerous studies, Asian children do more homework, take school more seriously, and study harder than children of other groups. The enormous success of Asian American students in American schools and universities suggests that their hard work pays off in academic achievement.

One of Professor Asante's most remarkable statements is: "Few whites have ever examined their culture critically." As I survey my own bookshelf, I see the works of scores of critics of American culture, of European culture, and of white racism. I see books by John Dewey, Gunnar Myrdal, and Karl Marx, among many others; I see the works of feminists, liberals, conservatives, radicals, Marxists, and other critics. Professor Asante is under the misapprehension that everything written about Europe or the United States by white scholars is celebratory, perhaps because he believes that every writer is irredeemably ethnocentric.

The purpose of historical study is not to glorify one's ancestors, nor anyone else's ancestors, but to understand what happened in the past and to see events in all their complexity. The fascination of historical study is that what we know about the past changes as scholars present new interpretations supported by evidence. The problem with the ethnocentric approach is that it proposes to teach children the greatness of their ancestors, based on claims that have not been validated by reputable scholars. So, in the Afrocentric curriculum, children are taught that the ancient Egyptians were responsible for the origins of mathematics, science, philosophy, religion, art, architecture, and medicine. No other civilization made any noteworthy contribu-

tion to any field, though all learned at the feet of the ancient Egyptians. The ancient Egyptians are shown as the most perfect civilization in all history. They did not enslave the Hebrews; indeed, unlike other ancient civilizations, they held no slaves at all. They were unrelated to today's Arab population, which allegedly did not arrive in Egypt until the seventh or eighth century. Such assertions ought to be reviewed by qualified, reputable scholars before they are taught in compulsory public schools. Nor is the relationship of African American children to the ancient Egyptians altogether clear, since the Africans who were brought in chains to the Western hemisphere were not from Egypt, but from West Africa.

The issue here is not the color of the ancient Egyptians; nor is it a matter of debate that Egypt is on the African continent or that it was a great civilization. What does matter is the claim that a single ancient civilization was responsible for every significant advance in the history of humankind. No civilization can claim credit for every idea, discovery, and forward movement in the history of humanity. Every great civilization grows by exchanging ideas, art, and technology with other civilizations.

Professor Asante is generously willing to permit "Eurocentrism" to survive "so long as it does not parade as universal." But there are elements in every civilization that have universal resonance, and every serious study of world history demonstrates the movement of ideas, art, and technology across the national boundaries and across oceans and continents. Those ideas, those artistic achievements, and those technological advances that are most successful do become truly universal. Aspects of American popular culture, some amalgam of jeans, Coca-Cola, jazz and rock, has become part of the universal culture, as mediated by television and Hollywood. It is not only the West that has produced ideas, art, and technology that are universal; the educated person learns about universal features in all great civilizations. Picasso and other great modern artists freely acknowledged their debt to African art. Whether one is in Tokyo, Paris, Buenos Aires, New York, or any other great cosmopolitan center, the multiple influences of Europe, Asia, Africa, the United States, and Latin America are everywhere apparent.

This is why, for example, in California, the recently adopted history curriculum for the state requires all children to study three years of world history. All children will learn about the art, ideas, religions, and culture of the world's great civilizations. For the first time in American history, American public school children will study not only ancient Greece and Rome, but also the African kingdoms of Mali and Ghana, the Aztecs, Mayans, and Incas, and the ancient civilizations of China and India.

But they also study those elements of the Western democratic ideology that have become universal over time and that provide a standard for human rights activists on every continent today. This is not just a political system based on the consent of the governed (a revolutionary concept in world history), but a philosophy that promotes the ideas of individualism, choice, personal responsibility, the pursuit of happiness, and belief in progress. In the spring of 1989, Chinese students in Tiananmen Square carried signs that quoted Patrick Henry and Thomas Jefferson. In the fall of 1989, Czechoslovakian students sang "We shall overcome" and quoted Martin Luther King, Jr. In the fall of 1990, Gibson Kamau Kuria, a Kenyan human rights lawyer and dissident, went into exile in the United States. Kamau Kuria resisted the undemocratic actions of the Kenyan government and appealed to the democratic standards contained in the Universal Declaration of Human Rights.

Some of Professor Asante's complaints about Eurocentrism in the United States are built upon legitimate grievances against the racism that excluded knowledge of black history and achievements from the curriculum of schools and universities for most of our nation's history. I, too, would banish the Eurocentrism found in the textbooks of earlier generations, because their monocultural perspective led to wild inaccuracies and pervasive bias. If, however, Asante's scorn for Eurocentrism is a reflexive aversion to everything European or white, then his own view leads to wild inaccuracies and pervasive bias. Europe has a unique place in the history of the United States for a variety of reasons. Europe is significant for Americans because our governmental institutions were created by men of British

descent who had been educated in the ideas of the European Enlightenment; they argued their ideas extensively in print, so the sources of their beliefs are not a secret. Europe is important, too, because the language that most Americans speak is English, and throughout American history, there have been close cultural, commercial, and political ties with European nations. And, not least, Europe is important to America as the source of seminal political ideas, including democracy, socialism, capitalism, and Marxism.

Europe, of course, is not the whole story, not of the United States and not of the world. We Americans—coming as we do from every part of the globe—have been significantly influenced, and continue to be influenced, by people who do not trace their origins to Europe. Our openness to ideas and people from all over the world makes our society dynamic. What is most exciting about American culture is that it is a blending of elements of Europe, Africa, Latin America, and Asia. Whether or not we have a melting pot, we do have a cultural mosaic or at the very least a multitextured tapestry of cultures. Whatever our differences, we are all Americans.

Behind this exchange between Professor Asante and me is a disagreement about the meaning of truth and how it is ascertained. The Afrocentrists alternately say that they want to teach the Truth, the lost, stolen, or hidden truths about the origins of all things; or they say that "truth" is defined by who is in power. Take your choice: either there is absolute Truth or all "truth" is a function of power. I make a different choice. I reject the absolute truths of fundamentalists, and I reject the relativistic idea that truth depends on power alone. I claim that what we know must be constantly tested, challenged, and reexamined, and that decisions about knowledge must be based on evidence and subject to revision. Reason and intelligence, not skin color and emotion, must be the ultimate arbiters of disputes over fact.

Professor Asante suggests that we disagree about our vision of the future of the United States. He is right. I fear that Afrocentrism intends to replace the discredited white supremacy of the past with an equally disreputable theory of African supremacy. The theory of white supremacy was wrong and socially disastrous; so is the theory of black supremacy. I fear that the theory of "multiple -centrisms" will promote social fragmentation and ethnocentrism, rather than racial understanding and amity. I think we will all lose if we jettison the notion of the common good and learn to identify only with those people who look just like ourselves. The ethnocentrists believe that children should learn to "think with their blood," as the saying goes. This is the way to unending racial antagonism, as well as disintegration of the sense of mutuality on which social progress depends.

The Environment

We have become increasingly aware that human actions can have initially undreamt-of effects on other humans and on the natural environment. The use of a new drug, a new agricultural product, or a new industrial process can produce immense benefits, but it can also produce deadly side effects. Progress, we have learned, sometimes exacts costs that must be paid by all, whether or not they enjoy its benefits.

Environmental issues lend themselves particularly well to utilitarian arguments. New products and processes may promise benefits but also threaten costs; the utilitarian calculus offers a method for relating costs and benefits and deciding what to do. Not everyone believes that cost-benefit calculations are adequate to environmental problems; extremists on both sides stress one part of the calculation, contending that the other parts do not deserve a hearing. Some corporate officers act as though environmental costs were irrelevant. And some naturalists argue for a quasi-religious respect for nature, or for truly "natural" rights held by inanimate objects. Most people, however, believe that both costs and benefits are morally relevant.

This section contains a variety of readings on environmental issues. Carl Sagan, an astronomer and writer on scientific topics, contends that we are "Pulling the Plug on Mother Earth." He argues that "society is, to put it simply, fouling its nest" and that immediate action is needed if we are to avoid environmental catastrophe.

Barry Commoner, a biologist, argues that environmental issues are often misunderstood. Many people approach environmental calculations by figuring economic benefits on one side and environmental costs on the other. This approach suggests that economic growth and environmental quality are incompatible. Commoner insists that this is not so. He claims that available technology can spur economic growth and solve environmental problems at the same time. He admits, however, that such technology is likely to be implemented only if we change the way industrial decisions are made. Commoner urges that we remove investment decisions from managers, directors, and stockholders and put them in public hands.

William K. Reilly, administrator of the Environmental Protection Agency, argues that capitalism is not a threat to the environment. Instead, he contends, it encourages decisions that respect environmental values. Reilly points out that capitalist democracies tend to be far cleaner and safer than socialist countries. The evidence suggests that the workings of the free market lead to cleaner air and water than the alternative, government control of environmental decisions.

Journalists Gretchen Morgenson and Gale Eisenstodt make a series of proposals for improving the environment. They believe that government policies and programs are usually counterproductive, failing a utilitarian cost-benefit calculation. Nevertheless, they argue, the environment is a public good; we cannot just ignore it. Someone who pollutes the air or water consumes a public good and affects the welfare of many other people. Market mechanisms, they suggest, can take these "external costs" into account without putting environmental decision making under bureaucratic control.

CARL SAGAN

Pulling the Plug on Mother Earth

Carl Sagan is Professor of Astronomy at Cornell University. (Source: Copyright © 1991 The Council of State Governments. Reprinted with permission from State Government News.*)*

QUESTIONS FOR REFLECTION

1. What, according to Sagan, are the principal environmental threats facing us?

2. What solutions does Sagan propose for meeting these threats? Evaluate their likely costs and benefits.

The Earth is experiencing an unprecedented global environmental crisis. Mankind started out a million or so years ago, small in number, weak in technology, wholly unable to change any thing on a global scale.

But as the numbers exponentially increased, society's ability to transform nature through technology greatly improved. Mankind finds itself inadvertently making profound changes in the global life-support system. This requires a degree of responsibility never before needed.

Society is, to put it simply, fouling its nest. Even birds, whose intelligence is sometimes criticized, know better.

The principal threats come from invisible gases or, in the case of radioactivity, physical particles. It's not something that can be seen or heard. It's a little abstract, a little distant. Naturally, if it can't be seen or touched, and especially if responding to it is expensive, a certain degree of skepticism is not only appropriate but inevitable.

Despite this, depletion of the ozone layer and global warming are real and serious and need to be faced quickly. This problem is long-term. What is done today affects the global environment decades and centuries hence, or in the case of radioactivity, thousands of years hence. So society has a new kind of responsibility—not only for this generation, but for the next generation and for generations to follow.

Another unique aspect of this dilemma that transcends national character is the physical state of molecules. Molecules don't have passports. Molecules released in one nation affect the temperature in other nations. There's no barrier or law that keeps the greenhouse gases or the ozone-destroying molecules over a specific territory. What every nation does affects every other nation's environment. No one nation can arrive at a solution to the problem.

This is a different circumstance than society is used to facing. There are no military solutions, and there are no ready technological fixes. It is impossible to simply flush the excess carbon dioxide out of the atmosphere and keep doing business as usual.

The solutions must involve a widespread, broad-based understanding of science and technology, and a transgenerational perspective. It's tempting to only be concerned with the problems of this lifetime, but these solutions must be implemented for future generations.

With regard to the transnational global perspective, mankind is in this greenhouse together. Ideological quarrels between nations do not transcend the mutual responsibility to protect the global environment on which everyone depends. Today's political institutions were not designed and are not yet prepared, much less optimized, to correct the situation.

Ozone and CFCs: Fatal Attraction

Chlorofluorocarbons (CFCs) were devised by industrial chemists to be non-toxic, non-irritating molecules that would do no damage whatsoever. This chemically inert molecule has a wide range of industrial and household uses—in refrigerators, air conditioners, aerosol spray cans and fast food packaging.

But precisely because the CFC molecule is inert and so safe down here, it doesn't chemically combine with anything. So it stays around for a long time until the earth's atmosphere carries it up to the ozone layer. Then, the extremely reactive ozone combines with the extremely inert chlorofluorocarbons and the ozone is destroyed. Chlorine is a catalyst that destroys ozone molecules.

Why should mankind worry that the ozone is being destroyed? The ozone in the upper atmosphere acts as a protective shield against dangerous ultraviolet light from the sun. The total amount of ozone is extremely minute. If it was dropped down into a room, it would be a layer approximately three millimeters thick. Life on earth is exquisitely sensitive to ultraviolet light from the sun.

What would happen if the amount of ozone significantly decreased? The amount of ultraviolet light that gets through the ozone shield would increase. What would happen then?

The most widely advertised consequence is skin cancer, tens of thousands of cases a year. Ultraviolet light also compromises the human immune system —the body's machinery for fighting disease. It is precisely the same system that is attacked by the AIDS virus.

But the most serious aspect, and the one least understood, has to do with global ecology. There is a real danger to the food chain on which our lives

depend. The food chain in the ocean starts with one-celled microscopic plants that live at the surface of the water. These phytoplankton convert sunlight into food and energy. One-celled animals eat the plants. Then shrimplike crustaceans eat the one-celled animals; the fish eat the crustaceans, and on up the food chain.

If the one-celled plant is wiped out, the whole food chain collapses. It's all dependent on phytoplankton, which are preferentially sensitive to ultraviolet light. There are many such food chains, on land and water, and all are vulnerable to ultraviolet light.

It is this challenge to the global ecological web on which all life depends that is the most serious aspect of depletion of the ozone layer.

Yet there is some natural resistance to this idea. For decades, this resistance was largely from the principal manufacturers of chlorofluorocarbons.

Then, in a way, mankind got lucky. A huge hole developed in the ozone layer over the Antarctic, the least inhabited place on the planet, that no one expected, not even the scientists who were predicting that CFCs would produce damage to the ozone layer.

Time's Running Out

That suggested the true seriousness of the situation. Du Pont finally announced in 1988 that it would phase out the manufacture of CFCs. Many of the nations that produce and use CFCs signed an agreement calling for the phasing out of all CFCs by 2000.

That, however, is 11 years away and a lot of damage can be done between now and then. Additionally, CFCs that are put up into the atmosphere now will do their damage over the next 100 years.

Society cannot simply stop releasing these chemicals into the atmosphere, and make everything fine. Rather, society stops now and the ozone layer heals itself a century later. Still, there will be three generations of humans who have to survive that interim.

Who discovered the link between this inert chemical and destruction of the ozone? Was it atmospheric chemists employed by the principal manufacturers? Was it some laboratory associated with the Environmental Protection Agency? No, this danger was first pointed out by two chemists at the Irvine campus of the University of California in 1974. This underscores the importance of pure scientific research.

Global Warming

A little greenhouse is a good thing. Ordinary light from the sun comes in and passes through a large and transparent atmosphere, and strikes the surface of the earth. The earth then radiates light to space—mainly in the infrared part of the spectrum, not the visible.

The temperature on the earth is a balance between the amount of visible light that is absorbed by the earth's surface and the amount of infrared light that the earth radiates away. Those gases that are transparent in the visible but semiopaque in the infrared are called greenhouse gases. They act as a kind of blanket. They pull the heat in and raise the surface temperature of the earth.

If not for that, the earth's temperature would be far below the freezing point of water—the oceans would be solid blocks of ice.

The problem is, that as the amount of greenhouse gases increases, the surface temperature goes up and then even small temperature increases can have serious consequences.

Since the 1950s, the amount of these gases has been rising because of industrial activities such as burning of coal, oil and wood. Carbon dioxide, the most serious greenhouse gas, increases as population and industry increase.

The four hottest years of the 20th Century occurred in the 1980s. Scientists were and still are predicting temperature increases. Some predictions are that in the next century the Midwest might turn into a desert. As the climate warms, glacial ice melts—raising sea levels. Rising temperatures would have drastic implications for the environment—decreased agricultural productivity, unavailability of fresh water, widespread drought and the inundation of coastal cities.

A Time for Action

Faced with the fact that we're not 100 percent sure of these problems, people have the tendency to deal with it later. Denial is human, but in this case it is dangerous. If a bridge is in danger of collapsing, money is required to fix it. The same should be done for the environment. We should raise the issue of environmental taxes. If activities that endanger the environment are not outlawed, they ought to be taxed. Some things can be done.

What is needed is a quick phase-out of all CFCs to protect the ozone layer. To deal with the greenhouse problem, improved energy efficiency is essential. We must learn how to get more energy out of a lump of coal or a gallon of gas; stress renewable energy sources, such as solar energy; encourage the planting of trees; and curb the population explosion.

In the Book of Proverbs, chapter 1, verse 18, it is written: "They set an ambush for their own lives."

That need not be the case.

BARRY COMMONER

Economic Growth and Environmental Quality: How to Have Both

Barry Commoner is Director of the Center for the Biology of Natural Systems at Queens College of the University of New York. (Source: Reprinted from Social Policy, *Summer 1985, pp. 18–26. Copyright © 1985 by the Social Policy Corporation.)*

QUESTIONS FOR REFLECTION

1. What, according to Commoner, has been responsible for environmental problems? What evidence does he give for this conclusion?

2. Energy production, in Commoner's view, is especially important to environmental quality. Why?

What aspects of energy production does Commoner find troublesome? What improvements does he suggest? Analyze their costs and benefits.

3. Measures to improve the environment often meet resistance because their cost, or other restrictions they impose, restrict economic growth. Commoner believes that this problem can be overcome. How? What is his strategy?

4. Commoner believes that reconciling economic and environmental concerns requires sweeping changes in the way economic and political decisions are made. What changes does he propose? What benefits does he believe would result? What costs might the changes impose?

There is a widespread perception that the relation between environmental quality and economic development is governed by unavoidable contradictions. Business people warn that if we insist on rigorous control of industrial pollution, plants will be closed and jobs lost. Ecologically-minded economists insist that out of respect for the inherent limits of the ecosystem, we must give up economic growth. Ecological ideologues, citing the parsimonious principles of ecology, preach against efforts to improve the standard of living.

These are familiar ideas, but I believe that they are wrong. My thesis is the reverse: that properly understood, the principles of ecology show how the economy can grow, the standard of living and jobs can be increased, and, at the same time, environmental quality can be improved. To understand why this constructive course is possible, we must under-

take a *fundamental* analysis of the origin of the environmental problems that have plagued the world in recent years. To see how this goal can be achieved, we must translate this understanding into a new political direction.

The Origins of Environmental Degradation

Ever since the early 1970s, when increasing pollution led to the rediscovery of the environment, there have been serious disagreements about the cause of the problem. A number of ecologists were convinced that human society behaves like any other group of organisms, in which the natural tendency toward geometric growth of the population is held in check by the resultant strains on the ecosystem that supports it. They concluded that the rapid degradation of the environment is caused by unrestrained growth of the population—and by an affluent lifestyle. According to the ecologist, Paul R. Ehrlich, for example:

> The causal chain of the deterioration [of the environment] is easily followed to its source. Too many cars, too many factories, too much detergent, too much pesticide, multiplying contrails, inadequate sewage treatment plants, too little water, too much carbon dioxide —all can be traced easily to *too many people.*

And according to another ecologist, Walter S. Howard:

> The affluent society has become an effluent society. The six percent of the world's population in the United States produces 70 percent or more of the world's solid wastes.

These statements are quoted from *The Closing Circle,* in which I analyzed the actual evidence regarding the role of population and affluence in the sharp increases in environmental pollution that occurred in the United States in the 25 years after World War II. The analysis showed that neither the concurrent increase in population nor in affluence (as measured, for example, by per capita consumption of specific goods) could account for more than a very small part of the five- to ten-fold increase in pollution. Thus, in that period of time, while the United States population increased by about 42 percent, nitrogen oxides emitted by automobiles, which cause smog, increased by 63 percent; the emission of phosphate into surface waters, which causes eutrophication, increased by 700 percent; the production of non-returnable beer bottles, which contributes to trash, rose by 595 percent. Nor did affluence increase appreciably in that period of time. Per capita consumption of food—and for that matter, of beer—remained about constant; per capita consumption of textiles increased by only 9 percent; per capita housing increased by only 6 percent. Clearly, neither the increase in population, nor in affluence, nor both together could account for the very large increase in environmental pollution.

The analyses presented in *The Closing Circle* revealed the real cause of the sharp post-war increase in environmental degradation: *changes in the tech-nology of production.* Thus, U.S. automobile engines produced much more nitrogen oxide than before because they were redesigned, after World War II, to run at high compression and temperature. This caused oxygen and nitrogen in the cylinder air to react and form nitrogen oxides, and therefore smog. The huge increase in phosphate emissions into surface waters coincided exactly with the phosphate content of detergents, which had rapidly replaced soap as cleaning agents. The sharp increase in glass trash from beer bottles resulted from the replacement of returnable bottles, which were used about 40 times before being discarded, with non-returnable ones, which are discarded after only one use.

A dramatic transformation in production technology has occurred in every industrialized country since World War II. A series of natural products— soap, cotton, wool, wood, paper and leather—have been displaced by synthetic petrochemical products: detergents, synthetic fibers and plastics. In agriculture, natural fertilizers have been displaced by chemical ones, and natural methods of pest control such as crop rotation have been displaced by synthetic pesticides. In transportation, rail freight has been displaced by truck freight. In manufacturing, the amount of energy, especially in the form of electricity, used per unit of goods produced has increased sharply. In commerce, reusable goods have been replaced by throw-aways.

These changes have intensified environmental degradation. For the benefits that farmers gain from the heavy use of nitrogen fertilizer, we pay the price of eutrophication of surface waters. Since truck freight uses four times more fuel than rail freight per ton of freight carried per mile, more fuel is burned, worsening air pollution. With the increased use of electricity comes acid rain from coal-burning plants, and radioactive hazards from nuclear plants. Throw-away plastics have sharply increased the burden of trash, which, when incinerated, generate toxic emissions.

When trash was incinerated before 1940, it contained all the components of present-day municipal waste—paper, food waste, discarded metal and glass —*except plastics.* Since then, the introduction of chlorinated plastics into the waste stream has converted incinerators into dioxin and dibenzofuran factories. The incinerator magnifies and disseminates more widely the ecological insults originally inflicted on us by the petrochemical industry's plastics.

The Link Between Ecology and Economics

In sum, then, in the last 40 years there has been a sweeping transformation in the technology of production, which is responsible for nearly all the environmental degradation that has occurred in that period of time. Now we can begin to see the fundamental connection between ecology and economics. The fate of the ecosystem is closely related to the nature of the system of production, which in turn is firmly linked to the economic system. Thus, the link between the economic system and the ecosystem is production.

The nature of the production system is governed almost exclusively by economic considerations. Specifically, the choice of production technology is determined by a single economic consideration—maximization of the rate of profit. In turn, as we have seen, the choice of production technology determines the impact of pollution on the ecosystem. In effect, profit maximization governs the design of the system of production and therefore the fate of the ecosystem.

This explains, I believe, why the post-war transformation of production technology has created serious economic inefficiencies as well as the severe impact on the environment. The efficiency of the overall economy is determined by the efficiencies with which resources, labor, and capital are converted by the production system into economic output. These efficiencies are generally expressed as resource productivity (goods produced per unit of resource used), labor productivity (goods produced per unit of labor used), and capital productivity (goods produced per unit of capital invested).

In the post-war transformation, production technologies with relatively high-capital and resource productivity and low-labor productivity were replaced by technologies with relatively low-capital and resource productivity and high-labor produc-

tivity. When a typical displaced product such as leather is replaced by plastics, as in shoes, the productivity of energy and capital falls, while the productivity of labor increases. In every case the new production process yielded a higher rate of profit than the one that it replaced.

It is perhaps natural to assume a direct relation between the two processes of economic growth and environmental pollution and conclude that the growth in output causes pollution because of a corresponding increase in the demand for resources. An analysis of the actual changes in the production system that have taken place in the post-war transformation invalidates this conclusion. A good example is the transformation in agriculture. It is certainly true that in this period agricultural output has increased and that the technological change responsible for much of the increase—the introduction of chemical fertilizers and pesticides—has generated intense pollution problems. But the quantitative relationship between crop production and the use of agricultural chemicals has changed.

Between 1960 and 1981 crop output in the United States increased by 67 percent, while the use of agricultural chemicals increased by 26 percent. Thus, the efficiency with which chemical inputs are converted to crop output has declined sharply. The economic productivity of agricultural chemicals—the crop output produced per unit of chemical input—has decreased by 50 percent since 1960 and is still falling. For the same reason, the environmental impact of crop production has intensified; there is now a larger environmental impact per unit of crop produced than before.

The decline in the economic efficiency of agricultural chemicals and the intensification of their environmental impact is inherent in the agricultural ecosystem. As increasing amounts of fertilizer are applied to the soil, crop growth reaches a limit, and a considerable part of the excess fertilizer is not incorporated into the crop, but leaches into rivers and lakes. In the same way, continued use of pesticides breeds resistance in the pests, so that progressively more chemicals must be used to achieve the same results. Thus, there is an inherent linkage between increased stress on the environment and reduced economic efficiency.

The manufacturing sector provides another illuminating example. As noted earlier, in this sector the post-war transformation in production technology has been characterized by a substitution of capital, in the form of machinery, for labor. This process also produces the same dual effect noted above: environmental stress increases and, in certain important aspects, economic productivity declines. The chief reason is that increased use of machinery inevitably demands more energy to drive it, so that there is a substitution of energy for labor. This relationship is particularly strong with respect to electricity, which is the preferred energy source for driving machinery. During the post-war transformation in production technology in the United States manufacturing sector, the productivity of labor, expressed as value added per man-hour, doubled, while the productivity of electricity, expressed as value added per kw.hr. of electricity, declined by nearly the same proportion.

Once again this shift is related to environmental impact: as output (in this case expressed as value-added in manufacturing) increased, larger amounts of electricity were consumed per unit of economic gain. Inevitably this was accompanied by intensified environmental impact: sulfur dioxide emissions and acid rain from coal-burning power plants, and radioactive wastes and the danger of accidents from nuclear power plants. Environmental pollution has increased per unit of goods manufactured. Once again we see the linkage between intensified impact on the environment and the declining efficiency with which a major resource, energy, is used.

The role of energy in the economy is particularly illuminating. In an ecologically balanced system, the economic cost of producing the energy needed to drive the system of production must remain in balance with the rest of the system. In most industrialized countries, about 95 percent of the energy is *non-renewable*. As they are consumed, such sources become progressively more difficult to produce, for it becomes necessary to exploit deeper, less accessible deposits of oil, natural gas, coal, and uranium. Consequently, the cost of producing a unit of energy from oil or natural gas rises exponentially with the total amount produced from a given source. In turn, this means that a progressively larger proportion of the available investment capital must be used to produce the energy needed to drive the economic system. Thus, in the United States in 1966, energy production used about 15 percent of the capital available for business investment. Since then, this figure has risen exponentially and it is now well over 30 percent.

In this way, depending on non-renewable sources of energy means that simply to make its necessary contribution to the economy, energy production will demand a progressively larger part of the economic output. In effect, a non-renewable energy system cannibalizes the economic system that it is supposed to support. The overall efficiency of the economy will rapidly decline if it is driven by a system of non-renewable energy. This process appears to be a major factor in the drop in the rate of improvement of economic productivity that has occurred in many countries since the mid-1960s.

In two crucial sectors—electric power production and petrochemicals—there is a special kind of relationship between environmental effects and the pattern of capital investment. In recent years, particularly with the introduction of nuclear power, power plants have become increasingly large, requiring capital investment in very large units, ranging up to billions of dollars per plant. To some degree, such plants have increased in size as a means of minimizing the frequency with which sites need to be chosen—a process that confronts the inherent environmental hazards associated with power production, especially from nuclear plants. In turn, the large plant size means that for a time after the plant begins to operate, there will be a considerable excess in capacity, for demand increases only gradually. This results in an inefficient use of capital, intensifying the drain on investment capital resulting from reliance on non-renewable sources of energy.

Another link between the large capital units characteristic of the new technologies and environmental impact is illustrated by the petrochemical industry. In this case, the installations tend to be large for economic reasons. A large plant capacity reduces the need, relative to output, for the most expensive inputs: labor and process controls. The petrochemical industry's very large capacity impels it to invade very large existing markets—textiles, paper, and soap, for example—and to temporarily cut prices to ensure that sales match the large production capacity. This helps to explain the speed with which synthetic fibers, plastics, and detergents have swept into the market, generating their serious environmental problems so rapidly as to catch us unawares.

Increased Economic Efficiency: An Ecological Imperative

I have sought to delineate a basic fact: that the post-war changes in the technology of production, which are largely responsible for environmental pollution, have also brought about a serious decline in the efficiency with which two major economic inputs— resources (especially energy) and capital—are used. I have argued that these economic and ecological effects are closely linked, for both are consequences of the same changes in the production system. Now it is time to turn our attention from analysis of the problem to what can be done to solve it.

Given the foregoing analysis, what steps should be taken to reduce the assault on the environment? At least in the United States, the conventional approach toward improving the quality of the environment is certainly not based on this analysis—or for that matter on any other cogent analysis of the origin of the problem. The fact that certain production technologies create pollution is simply accepted without asking *why* this should be so. Instead, reducing pollution is simply a matter of "controlling" the emissions: cars are equipped with exhaust devices; sulfur dioxide scrubbers are installed at coal-burning power plants and safety devices at nuclear power plants; toxic wastes are transferred to more secure sites; in extreme cases the offending factory is simply shut down.

It is this approach to environmental improvement that gives rise to the apparent antagonism between ecology and the economy. If cars and power plants must be equipped with environmental controls, the cost of travel and electricity increase; if petrochemical plants must give up their cheap but hazardous toxic dumps, the price of their products will rise; if the owner of a heavily polluting factory

decides that it is more profitable to close the plant than improve it, the workers will lose their jobs. This approach leads to the generalization that there is always an economic cost to environmental improvement, and that the two must somehow be balanced, one against the other, by means of some sort of "cost/benefit" philosophy.

Clearly this approach is superficial; it does not address the problem at its root; it does not attempt to cure the disease but only to relieve its symptoms. This approach avoids the basic issue—the fault in the technology of production—and for that reason falls into the trap of creating a false and unnecessary conflict between ecology and the economy.

If, on the other hand, we confront the problem at its root, it becomes possible to find ways of improving *both* the environment and the economy. To support this assertion, I offer two practical examples, in agriculture and power production.

Agriculture

Like most aspects of the production system, since World War II agriculture has undergone sweeping changes in production technology that have created serious environmental problems. The chemical fertilizers, especially nitrogen, which have replaced natural sources of fertility, have leached into streams, lakes, and oceans, causing serious eutrophication.

At the same time, heavy dependence on increasing inputs of fertilizers and pesticides has become progressively less efficient; the economic return, per unit of chemicals used, has declined. In the United States, this process, together with heavy investments in equipment, has placed many farmers in a precarious economic position. Bankruptcies have become so frequent that a new, militant farmers' movement has begun to form. Thus, the post-war transformation of agriculture has created both serious environmental and economic problems. Given this understanding, it is possible to find ways of changing the technology of agricultural production that accomplish the reverse—that improve the environment *and* economic efficiency.

What are the economic consequences, for example, if, for the sake of improving the environment, farmers give up the use of the new fertilizers and pesticides? A CBNS study of Corn Belt farms provides a surprising answer. A five-year comparison between large-scale conventional farms and organic farms (which used neither chemical fertilizers nor pesticides but were otherwise very similar to conventional farms) showed that the latter's crop output was reduced by about 8.5 percent. But the resultant loss in income was exactly balanced by the savings gained by not buying agricultural chemicals. Consequently, on the average, the organic farms produced the same net income per acre as the conventional farms. In some sense this is even an economic *gain,* for it means that the farmers become less dependent on bank loans and, therefore, less vulnerable to bankruptcy.

One reason for farmers' economic difficulties is their dependence on non-renewable sources of energy, not only for fuel but also as the source of fertilizers such as ammonia and petrochemical pesticides. The price of these agricultural chemicals has risen sharply, along with the price of oil and natural gas, from which they are made. Yet, ecological principles tell us that the farm is itself a source of renewable solar energy. Can this capability be used to decrease the farm's dependence on non-renewable, progressively more costly, oil and natural gas and thereby improve its economic position?

Again, a recent CBNS study provides a surprising answer. We found that the farmers' economic position could be greatly improved, and the depletion of oil reduced, by appropriate changes in production technology. This is achieved by converting part of the farm's crop into ethanol—an excellent replacement of gasoline as a motor fuel—which is thereby a way of operating vehicles and machinery on solar energy.

The economic consequences of introducing this ecologically sound technology depend on how it is integrated into the overall agricultural system. It has often been pointed out that the use of a crop such as corn to produce ethanol will reduce the availability of food. Although the residue from ethanol fermentation can be used to feed animals, it has only 40 percent of the feed value of the original grain. If ethanol fermentation is simply added to the *present* agricultural system (which in the Corn Belt is based largely on corn and soybeans), there is no doubt that

any economic gain to the farmer from selling ethanol would be outweighed by a reduction in the supply of animal feed and an increase in the price of food.

The principles of ecology, which emphasize the importance of *systems,* teach us how to overcome this difficulty. In the CBNS study we used a computer model to ask the following question: What new crop system, for the production of *both* food and ethanol, would maximize the farmers' profit without reducing food production? The answer was surprisingly simple. Recall that ethanol (which contains carbon, hydrogen, oxygen, but no nitrogen) is made from only the crop's carbohydrate. Therefore, to avoid the conflict between food and fuel, we need only increase the total carbohydrate content of the crop. This can readily be done. The study showed that by substituting sugar beets for soybeans, the farm would produce about as much protein as before but nearly twice as much carbohydrate. As a result, the extra carbohydrate could be converted to ethanol, leaving enough carbohydrate and protein to support as much animal production as before. The study showed that by 1995, such a crop system would double the farmers' profit, compared to profit from conventional agriculture. Applied to U.S. agriculture as a whole, this new system of agricultural technology could produce enough ethanol to replace about 20 percent of the national demand for gasoline without reducing the overall supply of food or significantly affecting its price.

Here, then, is a way of both improving the environmental impact of agriculture, and expanding its economic output. This approach could readily be combined with a sharp reduction in the use of fertilizers and pesticides, for any resultant loss in crop output would be far outweighed by the added production of ethanol. In sum, in agriculture it is possible to achieve economic growth *and* improve the environment—by sensibly applying the principles of ecology.

Power Production

In the United States, it is widely recognized that the electric power industry is in an economic crisis; several electric utilities have been threatened with bankruptcy. Last year a cover story in *Business Week* asked whether the industry had become "obsolete." The chief reason is that the present technology of electric power production is highly centralized and, therefore, dependent on very large capital investments. This leads to the economic inefficiencies of overcapacity and vulnerability to technological problems (as in the case of nuclear power). From the social point of view, the present technology is also inefficient because, for inescapable thermodynamic reasons, two-thirds of the energy available from the fuel is discarded into the environment as waste heat. Since the production and use of fuel causes important environmental problems, this means that the industry causes three times as much pollution per unit of useful energy produced as it would if all the wasted energy could be put to use.

The present centralized technology of power production is the source of both its thermodynamic inefficiency and environmental impact. The heat that a central power station ordinarily discards could readily be recaptured and used, for example, to heat homes. However, because heat can be distributed only over relatively short distances, this economically efficient process—cogeneration—cannot be used with the large centralized plants that are now commonly built. No one wants to live that close to a power plant, especially if it is nuclear.

Once again, by changing the technology of production in keeping with sensible, ecological principles, both the environmental and the economic situations can be improved. The basic change is to *decentralize* the production of electricity, building small cogenerator plants just large enough to meet the local energy demand. With the cogenerator supplying both heat and electricity at a high level of thermodynamic efficiency, the amount of fuel needed to meet the demand is reduced; this decreases both environmental impact and the cost of energy. For example, a recent CBNS study shows that the installation of a cogenerator in a typical New York City 50-apartment building reduces energy costs by 36 percent. Clearly, the gradual replacement of large centralized power plants by cogenerators scaled to the local demand would benefit both the environment and the economy.

The function of energy is economic; it generates the work needed to drive the production system that yields economic output. Capital must be invested in the production of energy, and if the entire system is to be stable, the efficiency with which capital yields energy must be kept in balance with the output of the economic system. As long as the economic system is driven by non-renewable energy, this balance is impossible. The very use of non-renewable energy has an influence on the resource itself: As energy is used, what remains becomes less accessible; every barrel of oil taken out of the ground makes the next barrel more costly to produce, requiring more capital investment per unit of energy produced. As indicated earlier, the cost of producing a unit amount of oil or natural gas has been rising exponentially in the United States, as these long-exploited supplies are depleted. This process progressively erodes the overall efficiency of the economy.

Solar energy can support the economy without demanding an ever-increasing investment of capital. Solar energy is derived from an energy source that is totally unaffected by the rate at which its radiation is put to use on the Earth; there is no way that the use of solar energy can influence the sun's output or make it less accessible. For that reason, unlike non-renewable sources, solar energy is not subject to escalating production costs. The transition to solar energy is, therefore, an important way of relieving the present strain of the energy system on the economy. Solar energy is both a means of improving the environment and a major source of economic growth.

The example cited earlier—replacing gasoline with ethanol produced from crops—illustrates the economic power of this transition. This process could greatly increase total agricultural output, eventually doubling agricultural profits, providing it is based on changes in production technology that integrate both food and fuel into a single system. Less is known about the economics of solar production of methane, which can replace natural gas. Exploratory studies suggests that "ocean farming," the production of marine algae in off-shore ocean areas, could produce very significant amounts of methane along with residues that can be used to feed domestic animals. Such an integrated ocean/land agricultural system could be used to significantly increase the production of both food and fuel. It could reduce the strain of natural gas production on the economy, add significantly to the net output of the production system, and at the same time improve the environment.

Structural Implications of the New Opportunities for Economic Development

The preceding discussion shows that it is now possible to undertake a new transformation of the system of production that is designed to remedy both the environmental and economic defects imposed by the post-war transformation of production technology. Of course, this is an enormously difficult, complex task, but it is useful, nevertheless, to delineate the features of such a new transformation, so that the nature of the task can be understood clearly.

A major characteristic of the new transformation is that, as compared with the present, new capital facilities will require a higher proportion of initial capital relative to operating costs. For example, a local photovoltaic installation calls for a large initial investment but very little ongoing costs, since the solar energy input is free and the device is so simple as to require very little maintenance. On the other hand, the new production technologies will require capital investment in very much smaller units than the present technologies that they would replace. In the United States the average current cost of a coal-fired power plant is perhaps $400 million, and for a nuclear plant $3 billion. In contrast, a cogenerator for a 50-apartment building costs about $25,000; a solar collector to supply a family's home with hot water costs several thousand dollars; a photovoltaic installation for a small factory might cost about $1 million. Finally, investments in the new production technologies will represent relatively long-term investments in which returns will be slower than those of current investments.

The economic value of a new ecologically sound production technology depends a great deal on how well it is integrated into the *existing* system of production. For example, the CBNS cogenerator study found that if a cogenerator is used to supply *all* the necessary heat (i.e., meeting the winter maximum in demand), then a good deal of the invest-

ment is wasted in the summer and the savings, over a conventional system, are relatively small—about $6,000 per year. In contrast, by properly matching the cogenerator to the baseline demand for heat and using the existing system to provide additional heat at the appropriate times, the energy savings are increased to about $18,000 per year. Similarly, for the maximum economic gain from ethanol production, it must be integrated into the existing food-producing system, gradually transforming it into a system that produces both food and fuel. It is also necessary to achieve integration among several major economic sectors: agriculture, auto manufacturing, and the oil industry.

Political Implications

The preceding discussion has established, I believe, that there are ways of changing the present technology of production in agriculture, energy production, and transportation (which in turn will affect the types of goods produced in the manufacturing sector) that not only improve the environment but also increase the efficiency of the economic system.

Such a transformation can contribute to economic growth. For example, if, as indicated earlier, it is possible to use the same amount of land to produce, in addition to its present output of food, a very significant output of ethanol, then clearly economic growth has occurred. Similarly, if a central power plant that uses only 35 percent of the energy available from the increasingly expensive fuel that it burns is replaced by cogenerators that use fuel with an overall efficiency of 70 percent, then the net output of the economic system has grown. The same is true of changes that replace a non-renewable source of energy with a solar source, for the economy is thereby relieved of the drain of capital progressively diverted into energy production. The same can be said of a change in production technology that replaces a synthetic product of the petrochemical industry with a natural one, for society is thereby relieved of the economic burden of contending with the inevitable degradation that is inherent in petrochemical production.

Obviously this kind of economic growth cannot continue indefinitely. It takes place only during the course of the change in production technology, which remedies serious economic inefficiencies of the present system of production. The ultimate goal of the transformation is to efficiently integrate every productive process into an overall system based entirely on solar energy and on recycling of materials that is so well decentralized as to avoid the waste of capital associated with overly centralized investments. Achieving that goal will generate considerable economic growth. But when this transformation is complete, the economy may confront the limits inherent in its dependence on the ecosystem.

In the abstract sense there is, of course, an ecological limit to economic growth. The limit results from the fact that natural resources—the ecosystem that occupies the Earth's thin skin and the underlying mineral deposits—are essential to production and are finite. While the limit to the Earth's human population is set by the maximum rate of food production, the limit to economic growth is determined by the availability of minerals and energy. However, since mineral elements are indestructible, they can be recycled indefinitely, providing the necessary energy needed to collect and refine the dispersed minerals is available. (For example, perhaps 80–90 percent of all the gold ever mined remains in use.) As already pointed out, nonrenewable sources of energy cannot be relied on, for they erode the economy. Hence, the ultimate limit on economic growth is imposed by the rate at which renewable solar energy can be captured and used. This in turn is limited (if we ignore the *very* long-term decrease in solar radiation) by the finite surface of the Earth, which determines how much of the energy radiated by the sun is actually intercepted and can be used.

Thus, in very general terms the ecological limit to the growth of production, and therefore the economy, is determined by the rate at which the Earth receives solar energy. How close are we to this limit at the present time? It has been estimated that the solar energy that falls annually on the Earth's land surface is more than a thousand times the amount of energy now being used to support the global economy. So even if we conclude that due to geographic inhomogeneities and unavoidable inefficiencies only one-tenth of this solar energy could be used, it still would be possible to expand our present

rate of using natural resources by perhaps 100-fold before encountering the inherent limits to growth. Even if this figure should turn out to be somewhat optimistic, it seems clear that, at present, we are nowhere near the limit that natural resources will eventually impose on economic growth.

I believe, therefore, that the self-evident fact that the finiteness of the Earth's ecosystem imposes an ultimate limit on the capacity of the global system of production and, therefore, on economic growth is not relevant to current policy decisions. There are immediate opportunities for improving the efficiency of the economic system by introducing ecologically sound production technologies that yield both economic growth and environmental improvement. Once that transition is accomplished and production properly integrates human needs with ecological requirements, that balanced system could still expand very considerably before it approaches the ultimate limit imposed by the amount of solar energy that the Earth can receive. The issue that we face, then, is to determine what policies will facilitate the new transition. Both financial and political policies need to be considered.

Financial Policies

The preceding section summarized some of the financial implications of the transformation. Considerable initial capital is needed, and the overall transition will require a very large total sum of capital. Where can it come from? A useful suggestion is the more than $500 billion per year that we now literally destroy—causing more human harm than all the world's pollutants combined—by devoting it to war and the preparation of war.

Recall also that the capital is needed in relatively small units, in order to create the local decentralized facilities that are characteristic of the new production technologies. Unfortunately, it is usually difficult for relatively small local entities to accumulate the initial capital. Yet they are often the ones that are most in need of the economic returns that can be gained by the new technologies.

This paradox is illustrated by the CBNS experience with energy-conserving measures for low-income families in New York City. In recent years the cost of energy has placed a severe burden on such families. The rising price of energy has unavoidably taken a progressively larger part of the family budget, leaving less for other essential expenditures such as food or taxes; if the winter is severe, some poor families must choose between food and fuel. The remedy is to install several relatively simple but effective energy-conserving measures such as insulation and double-glazed windows. We have found that an investment of about $2,000 for a typical apartment will reduce energy bills by about 30 percent.

Nevertheless, few families can take advantage of this opportunity, simply because they do not have the needed capital. This situation applies as well to the installation of energy-conserving cogenerators in city residential buildings, or the construction of an ethanol plant in a farm community. The fact that such new, economically advantageous measures typically require a relatively large initial investment is a serious hurdle, which people who would benefit most have difficulty in overcoming. Another hurdle is the relatively slow rate of return of some of the new investments. If such an investment, for example, the restoration of impoverished soil, must compete with existing investments that yield profits quickly, it is certain to be ignored.

Obviously, none of these new investments will be made if the decision is governed by the existing "free market," which favors large-scale investments over decentralized ones and short-term over long-term returns. What is required, therefore, is an investment policy that is under social rather than private control. The key to the new transformation is social governance of the choice of production technologies, through democratic control of investment decisions.

Political Policies

The conventional approach to the questions of political policy that govern the relation between the environment and the economy, at least in the United States, is encompassed by the idea of "risk versus benefit." By this is meant the notion that the importance of reducing an environmental risk must be compared with the size of the economic benefits of the production process that creates the risk. In ef-

fect, this approach formalizes the spurious conflict between environmental quality and the economy. It is not surprising, therefore, that the efforts to develop procedures for comparing the risk with the benefit have only amplified the conflict, often to the point of absurdity.

One effort is based on the notion that the risk must be evaluated economically so that it can be compared with the benefit. Since the risk, for example of a toxic pollutant, can usually be converted to some number of human lives that may be lost, one outcome of this approach is an effort to place a dollar value on a human life. This effort leads to politically regressive results. Because this value is customarily based on a person's earning power, it turns out that a man's life is worth much more than a woman's; a black person's life is worth much less than a white's. In effect, the environmental risk is considered small if the people it kills are poor. Since many polluting industries are near neighborhoods occupied by poor people, this approach helps to diminish the importance of environmental improvement.

A more humane approach is to convert the risk into dollars by calculating the cost of the controls needed to reduce the risk. In this case it becomes necessary to decide how far the risk is to be reduced, for the cost of controlling it escalates sharply as the risk is diminished. Another version of this approach, which has become increasingly popular in the United States, is "risk assessment," in which the severity of a new risk is compared with well-established ones. This usually gives rise to a table that shows, for example, that the risk of dying of cancer from exposure to dioxin from a trash-burning incinerator is x-times less than the risk of death from riding a motorcycle or (in the case of a table prepared by the chemical industry) "going over Niagara Falls in a barrel."

In my opinion, such efforts are absurd because they are misdirected. The real problem is not to compare the risk and the benefit of the *same productive process,* but to compare the risks involved in equivalent productive processes that differ in their technology and therefore in their environmental impact. Thus, if there is a certain risk to health from the production of electricity by a nuclear power plant, then what is of interest are the alternative means of producing the same amount of electricity at a lesser risk to health and at a reasonably similar cost. This approach recognizes that the problem arises from the nature of the productive technology and that the social issue relates to the *choice* of a particular technology among the alternative ones that produce the same good.

Obviously the approach that I propose is radical; it calls for social rather than private investment decisions, for social rather than private governance of the means of production. It is curious to note, however, that this same approach is contained in a law that is usually not regarded as radical—the National Environmental Policy Act, which is the basis of all environmental legislation in the United States. According to Section 102(c) of this act, an Environmental Impact Statement must include: "(i) the environmental impact of the proposed action; (ii) any adverse environmental effects which cannot be avoided should the proposal be implemented; (iii) alternatives to the proposed action."

Thus, if the "proposed action" is the construction of a nuclear power plant, and its generation of radioactive waste is an "adverse environmental effect(s) which cannot be avoided," then, according to the law it is necessary to consider alternative, less hazardous, ways of producing electricity. The alternatives include cogenerators, photovoltaic cells, or for that matter, a well-controlled coal-burning plant. Thus, the law calls for an environmental comparison of different technological means of producing the same good; it is literally a means of exercising social control of the means of production.

Needless to say, the law has never been used in this way. Instead, American industry—and often enough, I am sorry to say, American environmental organizations—have uniformly adopted the "risk/benefit" approach or sometimes the "risk assessment" approach, out of a natural interest in avoiding confrontation with so fundamental and far-reaching a political issue.

I want to be very clear about the purpose of social governance of the means of production. It is a policy directed toward the *choice of the actual technology used to produce the goods that society needs*. I re-emphasize this point because technological choices are usually regarded as outside the realm of public policy, determined instead by "objective" scientific considerations. It should be evident from the preceding discussion that this is simply not true. Certainly it is an objective scientific fact that high-compression automobile engines are particularly powerful and generate smog. But there is no objective way to determine whether it is more important to build engines that are powerful or engines that do not produce smog. Such a choice is social, not scientific. When it was decided in the United States to build high-compression engines in place of less powerful low-compression ones, a social policy was established. But the engine was regarded as a value-free piece of technology, and no questions were asked about its other attributes. The social decision was hidden from view until it was revealed, too late, by the blanket of smog that covers our cities.

The failure to deal with a technological decision as a social choice has had much wider effects than to create the false dichotomy between economic progress and environmental quality. It also affects, for example, the question of employment. Not only the decisions that substituted plastics for leather but also decisions that substitute robots for workers reduce the number of available jobs. The number of jobs created or destroyed is as important a reason for social governance of technological decisions as environmental impact. Social control of technological decisions is vital not only for environmental quality but for nearly everything else that determines how people live: employment, working conditions, the cost of transportation, energy and other necessities, and economic growth.

The Historic Transition

The argument put forward here has implications for our understanding of the relation between technology and the great historic transitions with which the world has struggled for nearly a century. Some would argue that technology is a force that develops, autonomously, from the new knowledge that the inevitable progress of science creates. This implies that, while the nature of a given technology will influence society, the reverse relation is very unlikely.

I am convinced that technology is a *social* institution that, like all others, reflects to a very large degree the governing aims of the society in which it develops. I believe that the harm generated by modern post-World War II technology is closely associated with its origin in a historic period dominated by the unresolved transition from capitalism to socialism. The basic science that gave rise to modern technology was developed in the period between World Wars I and II. The world's first socialist state, the USSR, was created at the start of that period; like the capitalist countries it developed systems of scientific research and technology. Yet, despite the fundamental difference between the two societies, after World War II both adopted essentially the same inherently harmful technologies, derived from earlier research especially in physics and chemistry. In both the socialist and capitalist countries there appeared the same dangerous nuclear power plants, the same inherently toxic industrial and agricultural chemicals, the same undegradable plastics, the same polluting cars. And the impact on the environment was the same in both societies. After all, should we expect the cars built in the USSR by an imported Fiat plant to produce less pollution in Moscow than they do in Rome, perhaps out of respect for socialism?

What does this mean? Does it prove that technology is indeed autonomous, independent of social forces? What does it tell us about the difference between the USSR and the capitalist countries? There are no brief answers to these questions, but here are some relevant thoughts.

First, it is a historic fact that nearly all of the troublesome post-war production technologies were developed and first put to commercial use in the capitalist countries, and were only later adopted by the USSR and other socialist countries. Second, the basic features of the capitalist social system in which they originated are heavily imprinted on the very nature of these technologies. For example, in keeping with the capitalist principle of unrestrained competition, petrochemical technologies were deliberately designed to create new and more highly profitable enterprises that could push older, equally (or more) socially useful enterprises out of the market. Clearly there was no concern about the economic and social consequences of these replacements: unemployment; loss of existing productive facilities such as natural rubber plantations; environmental pollution. In effect, the very technical design of the petrochemical industry was created to seize new markets and to maximize profit, regardless of the effect on public welfare.

So, the reason why modern production creates environmental and energy problems is not that there is some general fault with technology as a whole. Rather, the problem is that the particular *kinds* of technologies that are the present basis for the productive systems of *both* socialist and capitalist countries were developed in capitalist societies. And for that reason they are characterized by their ability to enhance what capitalists want—profit maximization and domination of the market— rather than the welfare of the people.

I believe that the fact that both capitalist and socialist societies alike have been burdened by the same damaging and dangerous technologies is a tragic consequence of a basic failure in the course of socialist development, as exemplified by the USSR. It is generally recognized that Soviet society has failed to adequately develop the democratic processes that are essential to the successful operation of a socialist state. What is perhaps less obvious, but equally important, is that Soviet society has also failed to create socialist technologies capable of generating means of production that, because they are deliberately designed for that purpose, serve the national interest and the people's welfare. To put this issue more concretely, the tragedy is that the Soviet Union has failed to undertake the transition to solar energy but instead leads the world in building new nuclear power plants; that it has failed to develop a chemical industry based on natural materials, but instead relies increasingly on the inherently toxic petrochemical industry. Indeed, there is a fundamental connection between the democratic and technological failures. The unwise Soviet decision to rely so heavily on nuclear power plants may be one consequence of the suppression of critics who might challenge it.

Where, then, can we look for the development of the necessary new productive technologies? We can continue to hope that the USSR and the other socialist countries will, in the course of time, learn about not only the necessity of democratic reforms, but also of technological reforms. But perhaps more immediately, I believe that this task should be undertaken by the left in capitalist countries, and especially by political parties that have already accepted the task of creating democratic socialism.

WILLIAM K. REILLY

"The Green Thumb of Capitalism: The Environmental Benefits of Sustainable Growth"

William K. Reilly is Administrator of the United States Environmental Protection Agency. (Source: Reprinted from Policy Review, *Fall 1990, pp. 16–21. Copyright © 1990 by the Heritage Foundation.)*

QUESTIONS FOR REFLECTION

1. Reilly believes that economic growth benefits the environment. How?

2. How does Reilly relate environmental and population issues? What is the connection between population and environmental problems?

3. What conclusion does Reilly draw from the environmental problems of Eastern Europe?

4. What is the "paradox of technology"? How might technology solve the serious environmental problems we face?

5. What proposals does Reilly make for improving the environment? What are their likely costs and benefits?

Murmurs of agreement rippled through the business world last year when the new chairman of Du Pont, Edgar S. Woolard, declared himself to be the company's "chief environmental officer." "Our continued existence as a leading manufacturer," he said, "requires that we excel in environmental performance."

Ed Woolard has plenty of company these days. The sight of CEOs wrapped in green, embracing concepts such as "pollution prevention" and "waste minimization," is becoming almost commonplace. Businessmen increasingly are acknowledging the value, to their profit margins and to the economy as a whole, of environmentally sound business practices—reducing emissions, preventing waste, conserving energy and resources. Government is trying to help by creating market incentives to curb pollution, by encouraging energy efficiency and waste reduction, and by developing flexible, cost-effective regulatory programs. The recognition by business leaders and government that a healthy environment and a healthy economy go together—that in fact, they reinforce each other—reflects a growing awareness throughout society of this profound reality of modern life.

Less has been said or written, however, about the other side of the coin—the environmental benefits of a prosperous, growing economy. Many environmentalists remain ambivalent—and some openly suspicious—about many forms of economic growth and development. Entire industries are viewed as unnecessary or downright illegitimate by a shifting subset of activist, although not mainstream, environmentalist opinion: offshore oil development, animal husbandry, plastics, nuclear energy, surface mining, agribusiness. These skeptics equate growth with pollution, the cavalier depletion of natural resources, the destruction of natural systems, and—more abstractly—the estrangement of humanity from its roots in nature. Studs Terkel's trenchant comment about corporate polluters—"They infect our environment and then make a good buck on the sale of disinfectants"—remains a common attitude among certain activists. At the grass-roots level, conflicts over industrial pollution, waste disposal, and new development tend to erupt with particular intensity and passion. One activist recently put it to me directly: In relation to waste incinerators, he said, "People think we're NIMBYs (Not-In-My-Backyard). But we're not. We're NOPEs (Not-On-Planet-Earth)."

The skepticism of some environmentalists toward growth is grounded in painful experience. Historically, economic expansion has led to the exploitation of natural resources with little or no concern for their renewal. At some levels of population and economic activity the damage from such practices was not readily apparent. But growing populations, demands for higher living standards, and widespread access to the necessities of modern life in economically advanced societies—and even in developing countries that provide raw materials to richer consumers—have created steadily increasing pressures on the environment. These include air and water pollution, urban congestion, the careless disposal of hazardous wastes, the destruction of wildlife, and the degradation of valuable ecosystems. Up to half of the wetlands in the lower 48 states that were here when the first European settlers arrived are gone; and the United States continues to lose 300,000 to 500,000 acres of this ecologically—and economically—productive resource to development every year. Furthermore, the byproducts of rapid industrialization have become so pervasive that they are altering the chemical composition of the planet's atmosphere, depleting stratospheric ozone and adding to atmospheric carbon dioxide.

Economic development based on unsustainable resource use cannot continue indefinitely without endangering the carrying capacity of the planet. Old growth patterns must change—and quickly—if we are to ensure the long-term integrity of the natural systems that sustain life on Earth.

Great Expectations

To achieve *sustainable* growth—growth consistent with the needs and constraints of nature—we need to secure the link between environmental and economic policies at all levels of government and in all sectors of the economy. Harmonizing economic expansion with environmental protection requires a recognition that there are environmental benefits to growth, just as there are economic benefits flowing from healthy natural systems. Most environmentalists realize this, and a growing number are working creatively toward new policies that serve the long-term interests of both the environment and the economy.

How does economic growth benefit the environment?

First, growth raises expectations and creates demands for environmental improvement. As income levels and standards of living rise and people satisfy their basic needs for food, shelter, and clothing, they can afford to pay attention to the quality of their lives and the condition of their habitat. Once the present seems relatively secure, people can focus on the future.

Within our own country, demands for better environmental protection (for example, tighter controls on land development and the creation of new parks) tend to come from property owners, often affluent ones. Homeowners want to guarantee the quality of their surroundings. On the other hand, environmental issues have never ranked high on the agenda of the economically disadvantaged. Even though the urban poor typically experience environmental degradation most directly, the debate proceeds for the most part without their active participation.

The correlation between rising income and environmental concern holds as true among nations as it does among social groups. The industrialized countries with strong economies and high average standards of living tend to spend more time and resources on environmental issues, and thus to be better off environmentally. Between 1973 and 1984, when Japan emerged as a global economic power, it also took significant steps to clean up its historic legacy of pollution; and the energy and raw materials used per unit of Japanese production decreased by an impressive 40 percent. In contrast, the developing nations, mired in poverty and struggling to stay one step ahead of mass starvation, have had little time and even less money to devote to environmental protection. Some of the world's worst and most intractable pollution problems are in the developing world and Eastern Europe.

Recent United Nations data analyzed by the World Resources Institute (WRI) show that the rivers with the highest levels of bacterial contamination, including urban sewage, are in Colombia, India, and Mexico. The WRI also reports consistently higher levels of sulfur dioxide and particulate air pollution in cities in Eastern Europe and the Third World than in most (although not all) of the cities in the developed world. And it is in Third World countries like Brazil, Indonesia, and Colombia that tropical rain forests are being lost at such alarming rates; while in Africa, India, and China, deserts are growing amid ever-worsening water shortages.

Growth Lowers Birth Rates

Economic growth can mitigate these resource and environmental pressures in the developing nations in two closely related ways: by reducing poverty, and by helping to stabilize population growth. Many global environmental problems result less from the activities of those supposed villains, the profit-hungry multinational corporations, than from the incremental, cumulative destruction of nature from the actions of many individuals—often the poor trying desperately to eke out a living. These actions range from the rural poor in Latin America clearing land for title, for cattle, or for subsistence farming; to gold miners, electroplaters, and small factories releasing toxic substances into the air and water; to farmers ruining fields and groundwater with excessive applications of pesticides.

In the developing nations especially, the population explosion of the past few decades (developing countries have more than doubled in population just since 1960) has greatly intensified the accumulating pressures on the environment. Even though the *rate* of increase is starting to fall in most of the Third World, population growth in countries such as Mexico, the Philippines, Kenya, Egypt, Indonesia, and Brazil has contributed and will continue to contribute to global degradation, to loss of natural resources, to poverty, and to hunger. Continued rapid

population growth will cancel our environmental gains, and offset environmental investments.

One widely acceptable strategy that can make an important contribution to lowering fertility rates is education. The World Bank has drawn attention to the close correlation between education of children—specifically, bringing basic literacy to young girls—and reduction in the birth rate. Economic growth also offers hope for some relief. As countries grow economically, their fertility rates tend to decline; in most developed nations the birthrate has dropped below replacement levels, although it is creeping back up in some countries. Stable populations coupled with economic growth mean rising per capita standards of living. Education and economic development are the surest paths to stabilizing population growth.

A Walk on the Supply Side

The benefits of economic growth just described—higher expectations for environmental quality in the industrialized countries, and reduced resource demands and environmental pressures related to poverty and swelling populations in the developing nations—show up on the demand side of the prosperity/progress equation. But economic expansion contributes on the supply side as well—by generating the financial resources that make environmental improvements possible.

In the United States, for example, economic prosperity has contributed to substantial progress in environmental quality. The gains this country has made in reducing air and water pollution since 1970 are measurable, they are significant, and they are indisputable. In most major categories of air pollution, emissions on a national basis have either leveled off or declined since 1970. And the improvements are even more impressive when compared with where we would be without the controls established in the early 1970s.

Air emissions of particulates went down by 63 percent between 1970 and 1988; the EPA estimates that without controls particulate emissions would be 70 percent higher than current levels. Sulfur dioxide emissions are down 27 percent; without controls, they would be 42 percent higher than they are now. Nitrogen oxide, which is up about 7 percent from 1970 levels, would have increased by 28 percent without controls. Volatile organic chemicals are down 26 percent; without controls, they would be 42 percent higher than today's levels. Carbon monoxide is down 40 percent; without controls, it would be 57 percent higher than current levels. And without controls on lead, particularly the phase-in of unleaded gasoline, lead emissions to the air would be fully 97 percent higher than they are today. Instead, atmospheric lead is down 96 percent from 1970 levels.

Similar, although more localized, gains can be cited with respect to water pollution. In the Great Lakes, thanks to municipal sewage treatment programs, fecal coliform is down, nutrients are down, algae are down, biological oxygen demand is down. Twenty years ago pollution in Lake Erie decimated commercial fishing; now Lake Erie is the largest commercial fishery in the Great Lakes. The Potomac River in Washington, D.C., was so polluted that people who came into contact with it were advised to get an inoculation for tetanus. Now on a warm day the Potomac belongs to the windsurfers.

It cost the American taxpayers, consumers, and businessmen a great deal of money to realize these gains. The direct cost of compliance with federal environmental regulations is now estimated at more than $90 billion a year—about 1.7 percent of gross national product (GNP), the highest level among western industrial nations for which data are available. Yet the United States achieved its remarkable environmental progress during a period when GNP increased by more than 70 percent.

We can learn two important lessons from the U.S. experience of the past two decades. First, our environmental commitments were compatible with economic advancement; the United States is now growing in a qualitatively better, healthier way because we made those commitments. And second, it was not just good luck that substantial environmental progress occurred during a period of economic prosperity. Our healthy economy paid for our environmental gains; economic expansion created the capital to finance superior environmental performance.

Eco-Catastrophe in Eastern Europe

The contrast between the U.S. experience and that of the Soviet Union and Eastern Europe over the past two decades is both stark and illuminating. While the United States prospered and made a start on cleaning up, Poland, Hungary, Romania, East Germany, Czechoslovakia, and the Soviet Union were undergoing an environmental catastrophe that will take many years and hundreds of billions of dollars to correct. In Eastern Europe, whole cities are blackened by thick dust. Chemicals make up a substantial percentage of river flows. Nearly two-thirds of the length of the Vistula, Poland's largest river, is unfit even for industrial use. The Oder River, which forms most of Poland's border with East Germany, is useless over 80 percent of its length. Parts of Poland, East Germany, and Romania are literally uninhabitable; zones of ecological disaster cover more than a quarter of Poland's land area. Millions of Soviets live in cities with dangerously polluted air. Military gas masks were issued in 1988 to thousands of Ukrainians to protect them from toxic emissions from a meat-processing plant.

The Soviet Union and its former satellites are plagued by premature deaths, high infant mortality rates, chronic lung disorders and other disabling illnesses, and worker absenteeism. The economic drain from these environmental burdens, in terms of disability benefits, health care, and lost productivity is enormous—15 percent or more of GNP, according to one Eastern European minister with whom I spoke.

The lifting of the Iron Curtain has revealed to the world that authoritarian, centrally planned societies pose much greater threats to the environment than capitalist democracies. Many environmental principles were undefendable in the absence of private property: Both the factory and the nearby farmland contaminated by its pollution were the property of the state. And the state, without elections, was not subject to popular restraints or reform. Equally important, decisions to forgo environmental controls altogether, in order to foster all-out, no-holds-barred economic development, now can be seen to have done nothing for the economy. The same policies that ravaged the environment also wrecked the economy. There is a good reason that no economic benefits have been identified from all the pollution controls these nations avoided: Healthy natural systems are a *sine qua non* for all human activity, including economic activity.

What has happened in the United States and Eastern Europe is convincing evidence that in the modern industrial world prosperity is essential for environmental progress. Sustainable economic growth can and must be the engine of environmental improvement; it must pay for the technologies of protection and cleanup.

Cleaner Technologies

The development of cleaner, more environmentally benign technologies clearly makes up a central element in the transition to sustainable patterns of growth. Technology, like growth, can be a mixed blessing. Technological progress has given many of the Earth's people longer, healthier lives, greater mobility, and higher living standards than most would have thought possible just a century ago. Technology has alerted us to environmental concerns such as stratospheric ozone depletion and the buildup of "greenhouse" gases in the atmosphere.

But the adverse consequences to the environment from new technology, while neither intended nor anticipated, have also been significant. Twentieth-century industrial and transportation technologies, heavily dependent on fossil fuels for their energy and on nonrenewable mineral and other resources for raw materials, have contributed substantially to today's environmental disruptions. So, too, has the widespread use of certain substances—asbestos, chlorofluorocarbons (CFCs), PCBs, a number of synthetic organic chemicals—which have proved to be hazardous to human health or the environment, or both.

But if technological development has caused many of the environmental ills of the past and present, it also has a vital role to play in their cure. This "paradox of technology," as Massachusetts Institute of Technology President Paul Gray calls it, is increasingly accepted by environmentalists and technocrats alike. In fact, some environmentalists and

legislators are more inclined to invest faith in technology even than are the captains of industry. Gus Speth, a co-founder of the Natural Resources Defense Council and now president of World Resources Institute, has called for a "new Industrial Revolution" in which "green" technologies are adopted that "facilitate economic growth while sharply reducing the pressures on the natural environment."

I share this enthusiasm for the promise of technology, especially after observing firsthand the truly encouraging results of bioremediation in cleaning up Alaska's Prince William Sound after the Exxon *Valdez* oil spill. When I first saw the full scale of that disaster, my initial thought was: Where are the exotic new technologies, the products of genetic engineering, that can help us clean this up? It was immediately clear that conventional oil spill response technology was overwhelmed.

Not long after the spill, EPA's research and development staff brought together 30 or so scientists to develop a program of bioremediation. This program does not involve any genetically engineered organisms—just applications of nutrients to feed and accelerate the creation of naturally occurring, oil-eating microbes.

Having been to Alaska several times to check on the progress of the cleanup, I've seen what bioremediation can do to minimize the effects of a massive crude oil spill—especially below the surface of the shoreline. Those areas of shoreline that were treated only by washing or scrubbing still have unacceptably high levels of subsurface oil contamination—much higher than the areas treated with nutrients. The success of bioremediation is, in fact, virtually the only good news to result from that tragic oil spill.

Biotechnology also has great potential for many other environmental applications. Last February, I urged biotechnology companies to give a high priority to locating and developing microorganisms that can safely and inexpensively neutralize harmful chemicals at hazardous waste sites, as well as other pollutants in the air and water.

Other technologies, such as space satellites and sensors, increasingly sophisticated environmental monitoring and modeling capabilities, will give us the information base we need to respond appropriately to global atmospheric changes. The recent international agreement to phase-out ozone-depleting CFCs before the end of this century was greatly facilitated by scientific studies of the Antarctic ozone hole and the rapid development of safe substitutes for CFCs. And continued advancements in medical technology and in our understanding of the role of environmental factors in human health will continue to enhance human life expectancy and freedom from disease.

Commuting by Computer

President Bush recently called attention to the environmental and social benefits of a technological advance known as "telecommuting": working from home or a neighborhood center close to home, sending messages and papers back and forth via fax or computer. By giving Americans an attractive alternative to driving, telecommuting helps reduce harmful auto emissions, from smog precursors to carbon dioxide. It also saves energy, relieves traffic congestion, and according to some studies, can even increase productivity by 20 percent or more.

As a fan of face-to-face communication, who believes also that creativity is often stimulated by the chance encounter, I must confess to a bit of skepticism about some of the virtues attributed to telecommuting. But environmentally and economically, it has incontestable appeal. And as congestion grows in many American cities, the appeal of telecommuting will also increase. Recognizing this, the federal government and several states have tried telecommuting in pilot projects; the EPA is among the federal agencies testing the concept at selected locations.

Many other environmentally beneficial technologies are changing for the better the way humans interact with the environment. Miniaturization, fiber optics, and new materials are easing the demand for natural resources. As older plants and equipment wear out, they are replaced by more efficient, less polluting capital stock. The evolution of energy will continue with clean coal technologies and with the commercialization of economically competitive, non-polluting, renewable energy technologies such as photovoltaic solar cells. New self-enclosed industrial processes will prevent toxic

substances such as lead and cadmium, which are almost impossible to dispose of safely, from entering the ambient environment. The wise manufacturer is already asking new questions about products—not just how will the product be used, but how will it be disposed, and with what effects?

A Resource Saved Is a Resource Earned

Corporations such as Dow, 3M, Monsanto, Du Pont, Hewlett-Packard, Pratt & Whitney, Union Carbide, and others have curtailed emissions and saved resources through a wide variety of successful pollution-prevention techniques. Dow's Louisiana division, for example, recently designed and installed a vent recovery system to recapture hydrocarbon vapors that were being released as liquid hydrocarbons were loaded into barges. The new system recovers 98 percent of the vaporized hydrocarbons, abating hydrocarbon emissions to the atmosphere by more than 100,000 pounds year.

As environmentalists have been pointing out for years, a pollutant is simply a resource out of place. By taking advantage of opportunities for pollution prevention, companies not only can protect the environment, they can save resources and thus enhance productivity and U.S. competitiveness in an increasingly demanding international market.

Accordingly, the EPA has made the encouragement of pollution prevention one of its leading priorities. At the same time, the administration is pursuing an innovative regulatory approach that builds on traditional command-and-control programs with economic incentives to harness the dynamics of the marketplace on behalf of the environment. By engaging the market in environmental protection, we can send the kind of signals to the economy that will encourage cleaner industrial processes and the wise stewardship of natural resources. The Department of Energy is involved as well; DOE is placing heavy emphasis on increasing energy efficiency and the commercialization of renewable energy technologies.

These governmental efforts are badly needed because the development of environmentally and economically beneficial new technology has been slowed by the high cost of capital in the United States—a direct consequence of the immense federal budget deficit. The deficit drives up interest rates, slows the pace of economic expansion, and discourages modernization and other environmentally friendly investments. While there are many reasons to bring the federal deficit under control, the need to free capital for environmental investments is certainly an important one.

Deficit spending is, unfortunately, not the only government policy inhibiting environmental improvements. A wide range of regulatory requirements and subsidies, in the United States and in many other countries, lead to market distortions that encourage inefficiencies while promoting the unsustainable use of timber, water, cropland, and other resources. The Foundation for Research on Economics and the Environment (FREE), a free-market think tank based in Seattle, Washington, and Bozeman, Montana, has done pioneering work in the field of "New Resource Economics"; FREE argues that hundreds of millions of dollars could be saved and much environmental damage avoided every year by discontinuing subsidized clear-cutting in national forests and by curtailing heavily subsidized water development projects. For similar reasons, the Reagan administration opposed development on coast barrier islands, which required heavy subsidies for bridges, flood insurance, and seawalls, and also exposed taxpayers to the costs of disaster relief when the inevitable hurricanes devastated the fragile handiwork of human beings.

Accounting for Pollution

One important step toward achieving greater harmony between economic and environmental policies would be for the government to consider seriously some long-overdue changes in the way the nation's economic health and prosperity are evaluated. As environmentalists and economists at think tanks like Resources for the Future have been pointing out for years, traditional economic accounting systems such as GNP and NNP (net national product) are poor measures of overall national well-being. They ignore or undervalue many nonmarket factors that add immeasurably to our quality of life: clean air and water, unspoiled natural landscapes, wilderness, wildlife in its natural setting. President Bush's Clean Air Act proposals for curtailing sulfur dioxide emissions, which are precursors of acid rain, will significantly improve visibility in the northeastern United States. People literally will be able to see farther. But we have not yet found a way to put a price tag on a scenic vista.

At the same time, GNP and NNP fail to discount from national income accounts the environmental costs of production and disposal, or the depletion of valuable natural capital such as lost cropland and degraded wetlands. The Exxon *Valdez* oil spill, a terrible environmental disaster, shows up as a *gain* in GNP because of all the goods and services expended in the clean-up. Without a realistic measure of national welfare, it is difficult to pursue policies that promote healthy, sustainable growth—growth that draws on the interest on stocks of renewable natural capital—in place of policies that contribute to the depletion of the capital itself.

The effort to develop a more comprehensive measure of national welfare should be just one part of an overall national strategy to achieve environmentally sound, sustainable economic growth. Such a strategy should be based on two fundamental premises:

First, economic growth confers many benefits, environmental and otherwise. Growth provides jobs, economic stability, and the opportunity for environmental and social progress. Only through economic growth can the people of the world, and especially the poor and hungry, realize their legitimate aspirations for security and economic betterment. And second, not all growth is "good" growth. What the world needs is healthy, sustainable, "green" growth: growth informed by the insights of ecology and wise natural resource management, growth guided by what President Bush refers to as an ethic of "global stewardship."

At the recent White House conference on global climate change, the president said, "Strong economies allow nations to fulfill the obligations of stewardship. And environmental stewardship is crucial to sustaining strong economies. . . . True global stewardship will be achieved . . . through more informed, more efficient, and cleaner growth."

A "Good Growth" Strategy

Good growth means greater emphasis on conservation, greater efficiency in resource use, and greater use of renewables and recycling. Good growth unifies environmental, social, and economic concerns, and stresses the responsibility of all individuals to sustain a healthy relationship with nature.

Good growth enhances productivity and international competitiveness and makes possible a rising standard of living for everyone, without damaging the environment. It encourages broader, more integrated, longer-term policy-making. It anticipates environmental problems rather than reacting to the crisis of the moment.

Good growth recognizes that increased production and consumption are not ends in themselves, but means to an end—the end being healthier, more secure, more humane, and more fulfilling lives for all humanity. Good growth is about more than simply refraining from inflicting harm on natural systems. It has an ethical, even spiritual dimension. Having more, using more, does not in the final scheme of things equate to being more.

Good growth can illuminate the path to a sustainable society—a society in which we fulfill our ethical obligations to be good stewards of the planet and responsible trustees of our legacy to future generations.

GRETCHEN MORGENSON WITH GALE EISENSTODT

"Profits Are for Rape and Pillage"

Gretchen Morgenson is a senior editor of Forbes *magazine. Gale Eisenstodt is a* Forbes *reporter. (Source: Reprinted by permission of* Forbes *magazine, March 5, 1990. © Forbes, Inc., 1990.)*

QUESTIONS FOR REFLECTION

1. Environmentalists usually propose government action to solve problems of pollution. Why are Morgenson and Eisenstodt suspicious of governmental solutions?

2. What, according to Morgenson and Eisenstodt, is the proper role of government with respect to the environment?

3. What market-based solutions to environmental problems do Morgenson and Eisenstodt propose? What benefits do they foresee? What costs might these solutions impose?

Against all experience the belief persists: Increased government spending and reams of new regulations are the only solutions to the problems of a polluted planet. Although President Bush, in a speech delivered to the U.N. Environment Program last month, argued in favor of free market approaches to environmental issues, he has nonetheless decided to raise the Environmental Protection Agency to Cabinet level. As EPA's political clout grows, so does its budget. Just five years ago EPA bagged $4.4 billion annually. Gramm-Rudman-Hollings notwithstanding, its yearly budget is now $5 billion and rising.

At the very time when government regulation is discredited and out of favor nearly everywhere, it is making a comeback in the environmental field. Although political and economic arguments for socialism are derided around the world—and the power of the market to allocate resources intelligently is widely acclaimed—environmentalism is being used as an excuse for the government to move back into managing the minutiae of our lives.

Consider what's going on in California. The South Coast Air Quality Management District, a re gional regulatory agency, announced a plan last year that advocates, among other things, banning the sale and manufacture of lighter fluids in outdoor cooking. The California plan has 123 measures that ban or restrict various practices or items, including automobile tires, and would cost buckets of money. Putting just 58 of the measures into effect would cost industry and taxpayers around $3.4 billion a year.

And that's just in California. At the federal level, the costs are higher. Take the disastrous $8.5 billion Superfund. Created with taxpayers' money to clean up toxic waste sites, in ten years the fund has cleaned up just 50 of the thousands of sites it considers dangerous. What's taking the EPA so long to exorcise the toxics? Litigation. Superfund legislation gives the EPA authority to go after polluters and make them pay: Much of Superfund's money has been spent trying to find the deepest pockets around a given waste site and litigating to reap damages. While it looks for someone to whom it can assign liability, the cleanups languish.

Then there's the Resource Conservation & Recovery Act, a 14-year-old bit of legislation administered by the EPA covering the storage, transportation and disposal of hazardous wastes. RCRA has required some companies to clean up and maintain their industrial sites at so-called background levels—that is, levels at which chemicals occur naturally in the surrounding environment. Even if a chemical is found to be nonthreatening to human health, it must be reduced to background levels if the company is to comply with regulations and avoid fines. RCRA recent regulations will cost industry—and ultimately the consumer—tens of billions of dollars for compliance.

Why is the government so woefully bad at creating environmentally responsible legislation that doesn't waste money? A crusading Congress has no incentive to weigh the costs of its laws against the benefits. As Robert Crandall, a senior fellow at Washington's Brookings Institution, says: "When you're carrying out a crusade, you don't ask what's the cost of the religion."

But there's another reason the politically driven approach isn't the best way to clean up the environment. It substitutes the actions of a relatively small number of bureaucrats for the actions of tens of millions of freely acting individuals, and so loses the market's stunning ability to harness a great deal of information. Moreover, if individual consumer choice is circumvented, abuse of the political system grows. The peoples of Eastern Europe have spent half a century learning this. Californians may spend the next half-century learning it.

Examples? A key part of the Clean Air Act of 1977 effectively required new power plants to install expensive scrubbers to cut down on sulfur dioxide emissions from their plants. Cost to the industry: $3 billion, even though a solution such as the use of low-sulfur coal would have achieved the same emission-reduction goal at a fraction of the cost. Why scrubbers? Successful lobbying by high-sulfur-coal producers and the United Mine Workers.

A more recent example of special interests' clout can be found in the Clean Fuels Program, part of the amendment to the Clean Air Act being debated in Congress now. In an attempt to reduce smog, one plan pushes the use of alternative fuels such as methanol and ethanol in nine major U.S. cities by 1997. This plan would also compel automakers to produce up to 1 million alternative-fuel cars per year by 1997.

Will people buy such cars? Will they be efficient? Affordable? These are not questions bureaucrats ask themselves.

Conspicuously absent from the Clean Air Act: nuclear power. Nuclear-generated electricity causes neither the acid rain nor greenhouse gases that coal-fired plants do. Safe methods of storing nuclear waste have been developed and are now being used in France. Nuclear power is the best feasible solution to dependence on other countries for our energy. Yet nuclear power is so politicized in this country that few politicians are courageous enough even to discuss it.

The alternative fuels that are offered by the Clean Air Act, it turns out, are no great alternative. Take ethanol, an alcohol fuel made primarily from corn. Although its use would reduce lead and carbon monoxide emissions, ethanol would also produce four times the aldehyde emissions of gasoline. Aldehyde adds to ozone formation and, unlike gasoline, damages plant life. Other negatives: Ethanol costs between 11 cents and 17 cents more per gallon than gasoline, and widespread production of the fuel would raise food prices between an estimated $6 billion and $9 billion a year, according to the House Energy & Commerce Committee, because corn that could otherwise be used for food would be used for fuel. Of course, if the government phases in ethanol production, as planned, midwestern corn producers would win big. No surprise that Representative Richard Durbin (D-Ill.) introduced a bill mandating production of 5.5 billion gallons of ethanol each year. Result: an estimated windfall of $1.1 billion a year for farmers.

Well-meaning though they may be, government solutions are almost always long on costs and short on benefits. If the amendments to the Clean Air Act now before Congress are passed as is, the legislation will, according to the Business Roundtable in New York, cost consumers and taxpayers some $54 billion a year. This without taking into consideration the cost to the U.S.' international competitiveness.

The politicians, of course, can cite the polls. Several recent polls show that most Americans would pay higher taxes for a cleaner environment. [Such polls are inherently elitist: Were they taken widely in Brazil and other developing countries whose peoples do not enjoy high living standards, the results would be entirely different.] But growth *or* a cleaner environment is not putting the alternatives correctly. The two are not mutually exclusive. The real question is: How should environmental decisions be made? By many millions of consumers acting in their own interests in the marketplace? Or a few thousand powerful political operatives bending and swaying to pressure group lobbying?

Environmentalists, many of them old-time business-bashers, like to blame environmental despoliation on corporate greed. Listen to Roger Featherstone, an independent organizer with the environmental group Earth First: "It's more economically viable in the long run to run a corporation environmentally benignly, but in the short term, profits are better for rape and pillage."

Sadly, governments in Hungary and the U.S.S.R. are showing greater interest today in free market approaches to environmental issues than our own bureaucrats are. Zachary Willey, senior economist at the Environmental Defense Fund, a free market environmental group, is scheduled shortly to speak on market-based solutions to environmental problems at Karl Marx University in Budapest. Sighs Willey: "I wish the EPA was as open to ideas as the Hungarian government is."

Willey will bring this message to the Hungarians: The state should set financial and other incentives that producers and consumers can factor into their decisions about what to make and buy. Once the incentives have been set, the state should step aside and let the market allocate resources. If given the right incentives, the private sector—entrepreneurs, private investors, and nonprofit organizations—can be the environment's best friend.

Note that Willey is not saying the state does not have a positive role to play. The environment is what economists call a "public good": like national defense, education and a sound legal system, "the environment" is not something that can be produced and consumed by self-interested individuals at a profit. Yet society depends upon the production of such goods.

To resolve this paradox, market-oriented economists have long agreed that the state, as Adam Smith wrote in *The Wealth of Nations,* has a "duty of erecting and maintaining certain public institutions,

which it can never be for the interest of any individual, or small number of individuals, to erect and maintain"—but to do so in such ways that the preferences and desires of self-interested individuals will not be trampled by an omnipotent state apparatus. Setting overall standards and then letting the market prevail, said Smith, would free the state from an impossible task: "the duty of superintending the industry of private people, and of directing it towards the employments most suitable to the interest of the society."

In other words, environmental policy can and should work through the market. Only if it does can we hope to leave a healthy globe to our grandchildren without forcing them to go back to riding bicycles and scrubbing diapers on an old-fashioned washboard.

One of the greatest flaws in the current system is that new regulatory standards must be met by the entire nation, even though pollution levels vary from state to state. It would be fairer, in some cases, to set standards that address regional differences: Why should a new-car buyer in Montana pay thousands of dollars more for a car with auto-emissions equipment when pollution from automobiles isn't even an issue where he lives?

Another problem with our setup now: Congress, EPA and other agencies often mandate which technologies must be used to achieve a given pollution-reduction standard. Both House and Senate Clean Air bills, for example, would require installation of special canisters on autos to cut down on emissions, even though these systems pose fire risks. Rather than tell automakers how to reduce air pollution, the government should work with industry to set reasonably achievable standards, then police industry's activities to ensure that standards are met. The tricky business of R&D, however, should be left to those with expertise in it—corporations and entrepreneurs.

The government can also encourage private industry to come up with new solutions to pollution problems by creating markets for environmentally beneficial goods, such as recycled paper. How? If Congress required all the government's paper suppliers to use 25% recycled materials in their products, a powerful market for recycled paper would be created.

Is the benefit commensurate with the cost? The answer really depends on knowing more about environmental costs. Hence the intelligence of the Bush Administration's emphasis on stepped-up environmental research.

If we are to achieve progress on cleanup problems, we must shed the easy belief that pollution is caused solely by corporate greed. It is not. It is caused by us, all of us, because we want convenient products and we want them cheap. We want low jet fares, safe and comfortable cars, we want to toss away our toddlers' diapers, drink soft drinks from lightweight plastic jugs. We live in a world of relative leisure because energy-consuming products do so much work for us. The polluter is not acting out of greed; he is acting out of an imperative to give us the goods we want at a price we are willing to pay.

Events such as the *Exxon Valdez* spill in Alaska and the company's more recent oil seepage in Staten Island's Arthur Kill waterway make big headlines. What doesn't make the news? Most water pollution today isn't a byproduct of manufacturing at all. The greatest volume of pollution comes instead from thousands of farms nationwide that use pesticides which seep into the water table and run off into nearby streams. Easy to abuse Exxon, but down-home farmers make less interesting targets.

Fred Smith Jr., president of the Competitive Enterprise Institute, a public interest group in Washington, points out: "Current policy assigns virtually no responsibility for pollution to the individual. He's viewed as the helpless victim of a willful technology implemented by an immoral market system."

Exxon is forced to pay for the cleanup of the Arthur Kill. Fair enough. So why shouldn't Americans who drive polluting cars have to pay for the damage they do?

How would such an arrangement work? Through economic incentives and disincentives set up to ensure that a product bears its social costs. Offending material—whether it's pesticides, plastics or disposable diapers—imposes cleanup and disposal costs on society. Wouldn't it make sense to tack these cleanup costs onto the original price of the products—through earmarked taxes or user charges?

Take cars, for example. Instead of mandating that manufacturers install expensive pollution-control equipment on all cars, the costs of which would be paid by every car buyer nationwide, why not tax those drivers, old and new, whose cars exceed federally set emission limits? That way, one could still drive one's favorite polluter-on-wheels. Freedom of choice would still exist. But choosing the high-pollution vehicle would cost one more. Making pollution more expensive would also create a vibrant market for new, more efficient pollution-control technologies.

Disposable diapers, one of America's favorite convenience items, are a huge contributor to our nation's burgeoning solid waste problem. Pampers, Luvs, Huggies et al. now account for 2% of the nation's municipal solid waste—in 1988, 18 billion paper and plastic diapers were landfilled in the U.S. That's 3.6 million tons of waste that, researchers believe, will take 500 years to decompose.

What's the solution to this mounting problem? A tax on single-use diapers that will pay the true costs of their disposal. Dumping costs are increasing dramatically, thanks to the fact that most old landfills are glutted and new ones are difficult to site. Tipping fees, costs levied on dumpers by landfill operators, now run an average of about $27 per ton. This means that, on average, parents who use disposable diapers are paying about $50 a year per child to have these diapers dumped, or some 10 cents on every diaper dollar spent. But since tipping fees are expected to cost $100 per ton in ten years, that will jack up the annual cost of disposal to $200 per child.

Cloth diapers are the obvious solution to the Pampers problem: They cost about half of what the single-use variety does and they decompose in six months. To encourage more parents to use cloth diapers, a tax should be slapped on disposables that is roughly equivalent to tipping fees of $100 a ton. The added cost, about 40 cents on very diaper dollar spent, might just convince some mothers to return to cloth. Those who want to continue to use Pampers can, but must pay the full price, including the environmental component.

Pollution taxes like these can be levied on anything—even foam containers and bags of garbage. Where would pollution taxes go? To the town or municipality that handles the waste. Plus, a portion of the revenues could go toward funding private sector development of new ways to recycle or manage the waste. Where such taxes have been tried, results have been good. In 1981 the city of Seattle began charging residents variable rates to cart away their garbage every month. The more refuse you put out, the more you pay. Since the system was implemented, the amount of refuse generated has declined substantially—from 3.5 cans per family to 1.4—and recycling has picked up. Economic incentives work wonders.

What about industrial air pollution? An interesting, and proven, market-based solution to the problem involves trading in Emission-Reduction Credits. So-called tradable permit systems begin with a total allowable level of pollution in a given area—as defined by the EPA. Manufacturers in that area can buy and sell permits among themselves based on how much pollution they generate and how much pollution is allowed.

Here's how it works. Let's say Neon Paint Co., of Louisville, Ky., has retrofitted one of its plants in order to bring its annual pollution emissions to a level further below its legal limit. Neon's emission reduction qualifies it for an Emission Reduction Credit. The company can either hang on to this valuable credit to offset an increase in emissions that occurs at another of its plants or that it may expect in coming years, or sell its emissions credit to another firm in the area.

Who would such a buyer be? It could be Petro Chemical, also in Louisville. Petro is exceeding its air pollution limits and therefore has a debit that must be offset. In buying Neon's credit, Petro would be properly penalized for being an excessive polluter. As long as Petro exceeds pollution limits, the company will be forced to pay for credits—a strong incentive to clean up its act.

Such trading, although on a small scale, is going on now. Corporate giants 3M, Armco, GE, Exxon and Texaco have executed ERC trades. The same type of system, although somewhat more costly, could be used to control water pollution as well. John Palmisano is a broker who trades Emission Reduction Credits at AERX, a firm he started six years ago. According to Palmisano, hydrocarbon emissions, a by-product of dry cleaning processes, plastics manufacturing and painting, are the most commonly traded pollutant. He says: "The going price for a hydrocarbon credit is from $750 to

$2,500 a pound; the price for these credits has been going up about 30% a year since 1984." Futures on the emissions credits can be traded as well.

Trading in ERCs exemplifies a free market approach to pollution. The system is based on the self-interest and intelligence of millions of individuals. It rewards those who should be rewarded, penalizes offenders and, once markets are established, does not require additional government regulation or staffing.

So far, emissions trading has been small in scale, but President Bush's clean air legislation includes a plan to reduce acid rain through the use of such credits. If passed, the law would force electric power plants to cut sulfur dioxide emissions by 10 million tons and nitrogen oxide emissions by 2 million tons. But the Administration's program would allow the utilities to decide for themselves how to meet those goals. If one utility reduced its pollution to levels below its allocation, it could sell its credit to firms exceeding the limits. "This could be the first large-scale demonstration showing that markets can function for environmental goods, just as they do for computers or anything else," says Daniel Dudek, senior economist at the Environmental Defense Fund.

In the ten years or so that Emission Reduction Credits have been traded, the cost savings to industry and government is estimated at $5 billion. Joshua Margolis, director of trading operations at AERX, explains that with ERCs "you can make money on pollution control. Companies no longer look at it as a fixed cost but as an opportunity."

By contrast, the present system tends to make pollution control more of a risk than an opportunity. As Superfund is structured now, almost any party associated with a waste site—even those only remotely linked to it, like a bank that forecloses on the property, or a company that leased equipment for use at the site—can be held liable for the cleanup of toxics found there. Says Roger Feldman, head of project finance at the Washington law firm of McDermott, Will & Emery: "If the government paid more attention to the mitigation of risk—if it didn't leave Superfund liability hanging over everyone's head—new companies would emerge to clean up."

The state of California is beginning to see the wisdom in this. Richard Stroup, senior associate at the Political Economy Research Center in Bozeman, Mont., has been discussing with state officials how to clean up waste dumps through privatization. How does privatization work? Take an orphan toxic waste site, so called because the polluter responsible for the mess has abandoned it. First authorities would decide what must be done to sanitize or seal the site. Then an auction among companies who may be interested in the site is arranged, and it's sold to the highest bidder, who puts money in escrow against future problems at the site. Therefore, the firm with the best technology for cleaning up a given site—maybe a biotech company with a new waste-treatment technique—takes on the risk attendant with cleaning up the site and profits by managing it properly. Says Stroup: "Rather than let the bureaucrats decide what and how to do these cleanups, let's let entrepreneurs figure out how."

Can entrepreneurs do the job? Edwin Hafner, president of Hafner Industries, Inc. in New Haven, Conn., is a career chemicals man who has found a way to recycle polyvinylchloride (PVC) and other plastics. It has taken 20 years for Hafner to perfect his process and attract necessary funding from corporations to build his PVC recycling plants, but his tenacity should pay off. Hafner says: "I can recycle PVC into a quality that's exactly as good as virgin, for 20% of the energy cost of creating new PVC."

To provide funding for such projects, project finance lawyer Feldman suggests that municipalities give partial guarantees—a sort of bridge loan—to environmental facilities that would help finance their construction and startup until cash flow is sufficient to cover the debt. He says: "Fiscal devices to enhance private sector investment must be refined." Is there potential for abuse in such fiscal enhancements? Of course. But the potential is far less than it would be if the state completely elbowed aside the market.

Advocates of let-the-government-do-it have a lot to answer for in our society. Not the least is the mess in land management. The trouble with public, or common, ownership of lands is that because no one really owns the property, no one has a stake in keeping that property from deteriorating. Land that is tended to and cared for generally increases in value, so when property is privately held, incentives to maintain its beauty are strong. When the government is the owner these incentives disappear.

Consider what the Nature Conservancy Hawaiian chapter, an 8,500-member nonprofit organization, has done. Since it was established in 1980, the conservancy has protected more than 43,000 acres in Hawaii. These lands will be aggressively managed by conservancy staffers and protected from introduced species such as pigs, which uproot mosses and trees from the forest floor. The state of Hawaii, which owns 40% of the land on the islands, has only now begun to understand that its increasingly damaged holdings must be managed.

In fact, voluntary conservation organizations like the Nature Conservancy are some of the best land managers around. Some allow oil drilling or other corporate activities to take place on their land, proving that commercial and environmental interests can coexist. The Welder Wildlife Foundation, near Corpus Christi, Tex. is an example. On its 7,800 acres, students learn wildlife ecology and management; also on-site are an active oilfield and a cattle ranch that help pay to maintain the land. James Teer, director of the foundation, says: "If you don't have the constraints of public organizations, you can do things more efficiently. Our land is used profitably, but we also have fantastic wildlife."

Two centuries ago Adam Smith wrote: "It is not from the benevolence of the butcher, the brewer, or the baker, that we expect our dinner, but from their regard to their own interest." He might have said the same thing about the environment. Instead of seeking to curb the profit motive and freedom of individual choice, we would do well to stimulate them both in ways that let the free market reconcile the industrial revolution with the age of environmentalism.

PART III # Rights

We find it hard to talk for very long about ethics or politics without talking about rights. But talk of rights is young by philosophical standards. Rights first made their appearance in Western moral discourse about 340 years ago, in the writings of Thomas Hobbes. Hobbes and many later writers present rights in the context of a general theory of government. To understand their conceptions of rights, therefore, we must consider their overall political theories.

Hobbes revives an ancient idea: that a government is legitimate if people, given a choice, would voluntarily opt to be subject to its dominion. Facing this choice requires us to consider what life would be like without government, in what Hobbes calls the state of nature. Hobbes provides a brief but stunning glimpse of the state of nature where, in his view, life would be "solitary, poor, nasty, brutish, and short." Even the strongest and smartest would be vulnerable to the tricks and physical force of groups of others. No one would be safe; people would routinely fight each other to survive. To gain security, therefore, people would choose to form a government. They would be willing to sacrifice much of their freedom to gain relief from the brutality of the state of nature. The resulting compact among competing individuals underlies the legitimacy of government. Hobbes's account is thus a version of *social contract theory.*

Rights emerge at two levels of Hobbes's theory. First, people have some rights even in the state of nature. There are *natural* rights that do not depend on government. Second, people have rights bestowed by government, which they acquire through the social contract. These are *social,* or *civil,* rights. These kinds of rights rest on different foundations. Hobbes believes that natural rights must underlie civil rights, for civil rights are founded on a contract. That contract can bind the contracting parties only if they already recognize an obligation to keep promises and, correlatively, a right to have promises kept. This kind of right and obligation must be prior to civil rights, depending not on a social contract but on the nature of human beings.

In any version of social contract theory, we can ask two questions that determine much about the theory of government that results: (1) What do the parties hope to gain by entering into the social contract? (2) What are they willing to give up to achieve it? In Hobbes's theory, the parties hope to gain security, which, for them, is a matter of life and death. They are willing to give up much for the protection of government. As a result, in Hobbes's theory, there are few limitations on the government, which Hobbes calls by the name of a monster, *Leviathan*. People are willing to sacrifice even their natural rights in order to survive.

John Locke presents a very different social contract theory. He, too, considers government legitimate only if it would be chosen over the state of nature. But Locke's state of nature is far tamer than Hobbes's. Precisely because everyone is vulnerable to everyone else's revenge, few would commit crimes, and those few would meet severe punishment. In the state of nature, we would have natural rights of life, liberty, and property, which would give us the right to punish anyone who violated those rights. The chief danger Locke sees in this condition is that punishment, often at the hands of the people wronged or those closely associated with them, would tend to be harsh, indiscriminate, and unfair. Consequently, people would feel the need for an impartial judge who could enforce the law of nature. People would therefore contract to form a government to serve as impartial arbitrator of their disputes. What do they hope to gain? Impartiality. This is important, but not a matter of life and death, as in Hobbes, except in extreme cases. What, therefore, are people willing to give up? A limited amount, according to Locke. They would give up their right to enforce the laws of nature by themselves. But they would retain their natural rights to life, liberty, and property, as long as they did not violate the rights of others. And they would gain civil rights to impartial treatment as well. Stemming from Locke's conception of the social contract is a limited view of government, which has little role other than enforcement and arbitration.

Jean-Jacques Rousseau provides a third version of contract theory, in which people are willing to give up everything in order to regain everything. Rousseau sees the state of nature as inconvenient and difficult; people would band together, entering the social contract to overcome these difficulties through cooperation. Because cooperation is their major motivation, they would be willing to surrender everything they have to the community to help others, and also would expect the entire community to help them. For Rousseau, there are no natural rights; all rights—and all questions—arise from the social contract. All rights, for him, are civil rights. Government, according to Rousseau, has only one constraint: that it act in accord with the general will, that is, for the best of the whole community.

Rights are fundamental to our modern conception of ethics and political philosophy. But they give rise to a serious problem. Rights frequently seem to come into conflict. Abortion, capital punishment, and many other public problems can be seen as involving conflicts of rights. How are such conflicts to be resolved? Social contract theory, in itself, provides little help.

Some philosophers have maintained that conflicts cannot arise, because rights stem from a single, underlying moral principle. Immanuel Kant, for example, maintains that all of ethics reduces to a single principle: the categorical imperative. Kant articulates five versions of this principle, but he takes all to be equivalent. In one version, the principle is this: Treat everyone as an end, not merely as a means. The categorical imperative underlies all obligations, as well as all rights. Each of us, according to the imperative, has a right to be treated as an end.

What is the link between obligations and rights? We can see rights as obligations of a certain kind. Philosophers have traditionally called obligations *perfect* if there are corresponding rights. Suppose that A has an obligation to do something for B. B may or may not have a right that A perform that action. If B does have the right, the obligation is perfect, and A treats B unjustly if A fails to perform. If not, the obligation is imperfect, and no question of rights or justice arises. For example, perhaps A ought to help B. Ordinarily, this is an imperfect obligation; B has no right to A's help, and if A does not help, A commits no injustice. But suppose that A ought to keep a specific promise to B. Then B has a right to A's fulfilling the promise and is treated unjustly if A fails to perform. Natural and civil rights both correspond to perfect obligations. Moreover, both raise issues of justice. If a right is violated, an injustice is done; that is, justice requires that rights be respected.

Kant aims to provide a single, unified framework for rights and justice. But it is not clear that such a framework is possible. Burke argues that conflicts among rights cannot be resolved in any systematic way. Ethical and political questions are so complex, he contends, that no principle or even theory can specify accurately what rights people have or what rights take precedence over others. Indeed, Burke maintains, our best guide to action is experience—the wisdom gained from encountering similar situations in the past—rather than any abstract account of rights or justice. Burke doubts whether any theory can envision enough of the complexity of real-life situations to provide a general way of deciding how to respect rights in all circumstances.

THOMAS HOBBES

from *Leviathan* (1651)

Thomas Hobbes (1588–1679) was born prematurely in Malmesbury, Wiltshire, England, when his mother heard of the approach of the Spanish Armada. "Fear and I were born twins," he later quipped. He was raised by an uncle after his father, a vicar, was involved in a fistfight outside the door of his church. Hobbes attended Magdalen Hall, Oxford, at fourteen, completing his degree five years later. He became tutor to an earl's son, a position that provided him a good library and the means to travel. He became a member of an intellectual circle in France that included Mersenne, Gassendi, and Descartes. In 1636, he met Galileo. In 1640, when King Charles I dissolved Parliament, Hobbes fled England for Paris.

Over the next decade, while in his fifties, Hobbes wrote a series of notable works: Human Nature, De Corpore Politico (On the Body Politic), De Cive (On the State), *and several works on optics. In 1646–1647, he tutored the future King Charles II in Paris. In 1651, Hobbes published* Leviathan, *probably his greatest work, in which he argued for absolute and undivided sovereignty in the state. Hobbes there gave the first modern defense of social contract theory, which, despite our contemporary distaste for monarchy, continues to be influential.*

When Charles II was restored to the throne in 1660, Hobbes returned to England. He was seventy-two, but still an avid tennis player. The king, in gratitude for Hobbes's tutoring and for his public defense of monarchy, granted him a government pension. In 1665, however, came the great plague; the great fire of London followed a year later. Parliament, taking these events as signs of divine displeasure, investigated anyone who was suspected of atheism. Hobbes's Leviathan *made him a target; he was forbidden to publish any further writings. Still vigorous, however, Hobbes continued to write, completing several major works while in his eighties. (Source: Reprinted from Thomas Hobbes,* Leviathan. *Oxford: Clarendon Press, 1909.)*

QUESTIONS FOR REFLECTION

1. What is Hobbes's conception of the state of nature? Why would a person's life in that state be "solitary, poor, nasty, brutish, and short"?

2. What, for Hobbes, is liberty? What is a law of nature? How does Hobbes distinguish law from right?

3. What are the first three laws of nature, according to Hobbes? How does he derive them from the state of nature?

4. What motivates us, in the state of nature, to contract to form associations and governments? What are we willing to give up? What do we hope to gain?

5. Why, according to Hobbes, are we obliged to fulfill contracts, even when doing so is not in our best interest?

6. "Whatsoever is done to a man conformable to his own will, signified to the doer, is no injury to him." This is Hobbes's statement of a traditional principle: "To the willing no injustice is done." How does Hobbes argue for this? How does this principle relate to Mill's harm principle?

PART I, CHAPTER XIII / OF THE NATURAL CONDITION OF MANKIND AS CONCERNING THEIR FELICITY AND MISERY

Nature has made men so equal in the faculties of body and mind, as that though there be found one man sometimes manifestly stronger in body, or of quicker mind than another; yet when all is reckoned together, the difference between man and man is not so considerable, as that one man can thereupon claim to himself any benefit to which another may not pretend as well as he. For as to the strength of body, the weakest has strength enough to kill the strongest, either by secret machination or by confederacy with others, that are in the same danger with himself.

And as to the faculties of the mind (setting aside the arts grounded upon words, and especially that skill of proceeding upon general and infallible rules, called science; which very few have, and but in few things; as being not a native faculty, born with us; nor attained, [as prudence] while we look after somewhat else), I find yet a greater equality amongst men than that of strength. For prudence is but experience; which equal time equally bestows on all men in those things they equally apply themselves unto. That which may perhaps make such equality incredible is but a vain conceit of one's own wisdom which almost all men think they have in a greater degree than the vulgar; that is, than all men but themselves and a few others, whom by fame, or for concurring with themselves, they approve. For such is the nature of men, that howsoever they may acknowledge many others to be more witty, or more eloquent, or more learned; Yet they will hardly believe there be many so wise as themselves: For they see their own wit at hand, and other men's at a distance. But this proves rather that men are in that point equal, than unequal. For there is not ordinarily a greater sign of the equal distribution of anything, than that every man is contented with his share.

From this equality of ability, arises equality of hope in the attaining of our ends. And therefore if any two men desire the same thing, which nevertheless they cannot both enjoy, they become enemies; and in the way to their end (which is principally their own conservation, and sometimes their delectation only) endeavour to destroy or subdue one another. And from hence it comes to pass, that where an invader has no more to fear than another man's single power; if one plant, sow, build, or possess a convenient seat, others may probably be expected to come prepared with forces united to dispossess and deprive him not only of the fruit of his labour, but also of his life or liberty. And the invader again is in the like danger of another.

And from this diffidence of one another, there is no way for any man to secure himself, so reasonable, as anticipation; that is, by force or wiles to master the persons of all men he can, so long, till he see no other power great enough to endanger him: And this is no more than his own conservation requires and is generally allowed. Also because there be some, that taking pleasure in contemplating their own power in the acts of conquest, which they pursue farther than their security requires; if others, that otherwise would be glad to be at ease within modest bounds, should not by invasion increase their power, they would not be able, long time, by standing only on their defence, to subsist. And by consequence, such augmentation of dominion over men, being necessary to a man's conservation . . . ought to be allowed him.

Again, men have no pleasure (but on the contrary a great deal of grief) in keeping company where there is no power able to over-awe them all. For every man looks that his companion should value him at the same rate he sets upon himself: And upon all signs of contempt or undervaluing naturally endeavours, as far as he dares (which amongst them that have no common power to keep them in quite is far enough to make them destroy each other) to extort a greater value from his contemners, by dommage; and from others, by the example.

So that in the nature of man, we find three principal causes of quarrel. First, competition; secondly, diffidence; thirdly, glory.

The first makes men invade for gain; the second, for safety; and the third, for reputation. The first use violence to make themselves masters of other men's persons, wives, children, and cattle; the second, to

EDITOR'S NOTE: Spelling and punctuation have been modernized for clarity.

defend them; the third, for trifles, as a word, a smile, a different opinion, and any other sign of under-value, either direct in their persons, or by reflexion in their kindred, their friends, their nation, their profession, or their name.

Hereby it is manifest that during the time men live without a common power to keep them all in awe, they are in that condition which is called war; and such a war as is of every man against every man. For war consists not in battle only, or the act of fighting; but in a tract of time, wherein the will to contend by battle is sufficiently known: and there-fore the notion of *time* is to be considered in the nature of war, as it is in the nature of weather. For as the nature of foul weather lies not in a shower or two of rain, but in an inclination thereto of many days together; So the nature of war consisteth not in actual fighting, but in the known disposition thereto during all the time there is no assurance to the con-trary. All other time is peace.

Whatsoever therefore is consequent to a time of war, where every man is enemy to every man; the same is consequent to the time wherein men live without other security than what their own strength and their own invention shall furnish them withall. In such condition, there is no place for industry; because the fruit thereof is uncertain: and conse-quently no culture of the earth, no navigation, nor use of the commodities that may be imported by sea; no commodious building; no instruments of moving, and removing such things as require much force; no knowledge of the face of the earth; no account of time; no arts; no letters; no society; and which is worst of all, continual fear and danger of violent death; And the life of man, solitary, poor, nasty, brutish, and short.

It may seem strange to some man that has not well weighed these things that nature should thus dissociate and render man apt to invade and destroy one another: and he may therefore, not trusting to this inference made from the passions, desire per-haps to have the same confirmed by experience. Let him therefore consider with himself, when taking a journey, he arms himself and seeks to go well ac-companied; when going to sleep, he locks his doors; when even in his house he locks his chests; and this when he knows there be laws and public officers armed to revenge all injuries shall be done him;

what opinion he has of his fellow subjects, when he rides armed; of his fellow citizens, when he locks his doors; and of his children and servants when he locks his chests. Does he not there as much accuse mankind by his actions, as I do by my words? But neither of us accuse man's nature in it. The desires, and other passions of man, are in themselves no sin. No more are the actions, that proceed from those passions, till they know a law that forbids them: which till laws be made they cannot know: nor can any law be made, till they have agreed upon the per-son that shall make it.

It may peradventure be thought, there was never such a time, nor condition of war as this; and I believe it was never generally so, over all the world; but there are many places, where they live so now. For the savage people in many places of *America,* except the government of small families, that con-cord whereof depends on natural lust, have no gov-ernment at all; and live at this day in that brutish manner, as I said before. Howsoever, it may be per-ceived what manner of life there would be where there were no common power to fear; by the manner of life, which men that have formerly lived under a peaceful government, use to degenerate into, in a civil war.

But though there had never been any time wherein particular men were in a condition of war one against another, yet in all times kings, and per-sons of sovereign authority, because of their Inde-pendence, are in continual jealousies and in the state and posture of gladiators, having their weapons pointing and their eyes fixed on one another; that is, their forts, garrisons, and guns, upon the frontiers of their kingdoms and continual spies upon their neighbours; which is a posture of war. But because they uphold thereby the industry of their subjects, there does not follow it that misery which accompa-nies the liberty of particular men.

To this war of every man against every man, this also is consequent; that nothing can be unjust. The notions of right and wrong, justice and injustice have no place. Where there is no common power, there is no law: where no law, no injustice. Force, and fraud are in war, and two cardinal virtues. Jus-tice and injustice are none of the faculties neither of the body nor mind. If they were, they might be in a man that were alone in the world, as well as his senses and passions. They are qualities that relate to men in society, not in solitude. It is consequent also to the same condition, that there be no propriety, no dominion, no *mine* and *thine* distinct; but only that to be every man's, that he can get; and for so long as he can keep it. And thus much for the ill condition, which man by mere nature is actually placed in; though with a possibility to come out of it, consisting partly in the passions, partly in his reason.

The passions that incline men to peace are fear of death, desire of such things as are necessary to commodious living, and a hope by their industry to obtain them. And reason suggests convenient articles of peace, upon which men may be drawn to agreement. These articles are they, which otherwise are called the laws of nature, whereof I shall speak more particularly in the following chapters.

CHAPTER XIV / OF THE FIRST AND SECOND NATURAL LAWS AND OF CONTRACTS

The right of nature, which writers commonly call *jus naturale,* is the liberty each man has to use his own power, as he wills himself, for the preservation of his own nature; that is to say, of his own life; and consequently, of doing anything which in his own judgment and reasons he shall conceive to be the aptest means thereunto.

By liberty is understood, according to the proper signification of the word, the absence of external impediments: which impediments may oft take away part of a man's power to do what he would but cannot hinder him from using the power left him, according as his judgment and reason shall dictate to him.

A law of nature (*lex naturalis*) is a precept, or general rule, found out by reason, by which a man is forbidden to do that which is destructive of his life or takes away the means of preserving the same and to omit that by which he thinks it may be best preserved. For though they that speak of this subject used to confound *jus,* and *lex, right* and *law;* yet they ought to be distinguished, because right, consists in liberty to do or to forbear, whereas law determines and binds to one of them: so that law and right differ

as much as obligation and liberty, which in one and the same matter are inconsistent.

And because the condition of man (as has been declared in the precedent chapter) is a condition of war of everyone against everyone, in which case everyone is governed by his own reason; and there is nothing he can make use of that may not be a help unto him in preserving his life against his enemies; it follows that in such a condition, every man has a right to everything; even to one another's body. And therefore, as long as this natural right of every man to every thing endures, there can be no security to any man (how strong or wise soever he be) of living out the time which nature ordinarily allows men to live. And consequently it is a precept or general rule of reason, *That every man ought to endeavour peace, as far as he has hope of obtaining it; and when he cannot obtain it, that he may seek, and use, all helps and advantages of war.* The first branch of which rule contains the first and fundamental law of nature; which is *to seek peace and follow it.* The second, the sum of the right of nature, which is by *all means we can, to defend ourselves.*

From this fundamental law of nature, by which men are commanded to endeavour peace, is derived this second law; *That a man be willing, when others are so too, as far-forth, as for peace and defence of himself he shall think it necessary to lay down this right to all things and be contented with so much liberty against other men as he would allow other men against himself.* For as long as every man holds this right of doing any thing he likes, so long are all men in the condition of war. But if other men will not lay down their right, as well as he, then there is no reason for anyone to devest himself of his: For that were to expose himself to prey (which no man is bound to) rather than to dispose himself to peace. This is that law of the gospel: *Whatsoever you require that others should do to you, that do ye to them.* And that law of all men, *Quod tibi fieri non vis, alteri ne feceris.**

To *lay down* a man's *right* to any thing is to divest himself of the *liberty* of hindering another of the benefit of his own right to the same. For he that renounces or passes away his right gives not to any other man a right which he had not before; because

---

* "What you do not want done to yourself, do not do to others." —ED.

there is nothing to which every man had not right by nature; but only stands out of his way, that he may enjoy his own original right without hindrance from him; not without hindrance from another. So that the effect which redounds to one man by another man's defect of right is but so much diminution of impediments to the use of his own right original.

Right is laid aside, either by simply renouncing it or by transferring it to another. By *simply* renouncing when he cares not to whom the benefit thereof redounds. By transferring when he intends the benefit thereof to some certain person or persons. And when a man has in either manner abandoned or granted away his right, then is he said to be obliged, or bound, not to hinder those to whom such right is granted or abandoned from the benefit of it; and that he *ought,* and it is his duty, not to make void that voluntary act of *his* own; and that such hindrance is injustice and injury, as being *sine jure,* the right being before renounced or transferred. So that *injury* or *injustice,* in the controversies of the world, is somewhat like to that which in the disputations of scholars is called *absurdity.* For as it is there called an absurdity to contradict what one maintained in the beginning: so in the world, it is called injustice and injury voluntarily to undo that which from the beginning he had voluntarily done. The way by which a man either simply renounces or transfers his right is a declaration or signification by some voluntary and sufficient sign or signs that he does so renounce or transfer, or has so renounced or transferred the same to him that accepts it. And these signs are either words only, or actions only, or (as it happens most often) both words and actions. And the same are the bonds by which men are bound and obliged: bonds that have their strength, not from their own nature (for nothing is more easily broken than a man's word), but from fear of some evil consequence upon the rupture.

Whensoever a man transfers his right or renounces it, it is either in consideration of some right reciprocally transferred to himself or for some other good he hopes for thereby. For it is a voluntary act: and of the voluntary acts of every man, the object is some *good to himself.* And therefore there be some rights which no man can be understood by any words, or other signs, to have abandoned or trans-

ferred. As first a man cannot lay down the right of resisting them, that assault him by force or take away his life, because he cannot be understood to aim thereby at any good to himself. The same may be said of wounds and chains and imprisonment, both because there is no benefit consequent to such patience, as there is to the patience of suffering another to be wounded or imprisoned, as also because a man cannot tell, when he sees men proceed against him by violence whether they intend his death or not. And lastly the motive, and end for which this renouncing and transferring of Right is introduced, is nothing else but the security of a man's person in his life and in the means of so preserving life as not to be weary of it. And therefore if a man by words, or other signs, seems to despoil himself of the End for which those signs were intended, he is not to be understood as if he meant it or that it was his will, but that he was ignorant of how such words and actions were to be interpreted.

The mutual transferring of right is that which men call contract.

There is difference between transferring of right to the thing and transferring, or tradition, that is, delivery of the thing itself. For the thing may be delivered together with the translation of the right, as in buying and selling with ready money or exchange of goods or lands, and it may be delivered some time after.

Again, one of the contractors may deliver the thing contracted for on his part and leave the other to perform his part at some determinate time after and in the meantime be trusted; and then the contract on his part, is called pact, or covenant: Or both parts may contract now to perform hereafter, in which cases he that is to perform in time to come, being trusted, his performance is called *keeping of promise,* or faith; and the failing of performance (if it be voluntary) *violation of faith.*

When the transferring of right is not mutual, but one of the parties transfers in hope to gain thereby friendship or service from another or from his friends; or in hope to gain the reputation of charity, or magnanimity; or to deliver his mind from the pain of compassion; or in hope of reward in heaven, this is not contract, but gift, free-gift, grace: which words signify one and the same thing.

Signs of contract are either *express* or by *inference.* Express are words spoken with understanding of what they signify: And such words are either of the time *present,* or *past*; as, *I give, I grant, I have given, I have granted, I will that this be yours:* Or of the future; as, *I will give, I will grant:* which words of the future, are called promise.

Signs by inference are sometimes the consequence of words; sometimes the consequence of silence; sometimes the consequence of actions; sometimes the consequence of forbearing an action: and generally a sign by inference, of any contract, is whatsoever sufficiently argues the will of the contractor. . . .

In contracts, the right passes not only where the words are of the time present or past, but also where they are of the future, because all contract is mutual translation, or change of right; and therefore he that promises only because he has already received the benefit for which he promises is to be understood as if he intended the right should pass: for unless he had been content to have his words so understood, the other would not have performed his part first. And for that cause, in buying, and selling, and other acts of contract, a promise is equivalent to a covenant; and therefore obligatory. . . .

If a covenant be made wherein neither of the parties perform presently but trust one another in the condition of mere nature (which is a condition of war of every man against every man) upon any reasonable suspicion, it is void: But if there be a common power set over them both, with right and force sufficient to compel performance, it is not void. For he that performs first has no assurance the other will perform after, because the bonds of words are too weak to bridle men's ambition, avarice, anger, and other passions without the fear of some coercive power; which in the condition of mere nature, where all men are equal and judges of the justness of their own fears, cannot possibly be supposed. And therefore he which performs first does but betray himself to his enemy; contrary to the right (he can never abandon) of defending his life, and means of living.

But in a civil estate, where there is a power set up to constrain those that would otherwise violate their faith, that fear is no more reasonable; and for that

cause, he which by the covenant is to perform first is obliged so to do. . . .

Covenants entered into by fear, in the condition of mere nature, are obligatory. For example, if I covenant to pay a ransom or service for my life to an enemy, I am bound by it. For it is a contract, wherein one receives the benefit of life; the other is to receive money or service for it; and consequently, where no other law (as in the condition, of mere nature) forbids the performance, the covenant is valid. Therefore prisoners of war, if trusted with the payment of their ransom, are obliged to pay it: And if a weaker prince make a disadvantageous peace with a stronger for fear, he is bound to keep it, unless (as has been said before) there arises some new and just cause of fear to renew the war. And even in commonwealths, if I be forced to redeem myself from a thief by promising him money, I am bound to pay it till the civil law discharge me. For whatsoever I may lawfully do without obligation, the same I may lawfully covenant to do through fear: and what I lawfully covenant, I cannot lawfully break.

A former covenant makes void a later. For a man that has passed away his right to one man today has it not to pass tomorrow to another: and therefore the later promise passes no right, but is null.

A covenant not to defend myself from force, by force, is aways void. For (as I have shown before) no man can transfer or lay down his right to save himself from death, wounds, and imprisonment (the avoiding whereof is the only end of laying down any right) and therefore the promise of not resisting force in no covenant transfers any right nor is obliging. For though a man may covenant thus, *Unless I do so, or so, kill me;* he cannot covenant thus, *Unless I do so, or so, I will not resist you, when you come to kill me.* For man by nature chooses the lesser evil, which is danger of death in resisting; rather than the greater, which is certain and present death in not resisting. And this is granted to be true by all men, in that they lead criminals to execution and prison with armed men, notwithstanding that such criminals have consented to the law by which they are condemned.

A covenant to accuse oneself without assurance or pardon is likewise invalid. For in the condition of nature, where every man is judge, there is no place for accusation; and in the civil state, the accusation is followed with punishment, which, being Force, a man is not obliged not to resist. The same is also true of the accusation of those by whose condemnation a man falls into misery; as of a father, wife, or benefactor. For the testimony of such an accuser, if it be not willingly given, is presumed to be corrupted by nature and therefore not to be received: and where a man's testimony is not to be credited, he is not bound to give it. Also accusations upon torture are not to be reputed as testimonies. For torture is to be used but as means of conjecture, and light, in the further examination and search of truth; and what is in that case confessed tends to the ease of him that is tortured, not to the informing of the torturers, and therefore ought not to have the credit of a sufficient testimony; for whether he deliver himself by true or false accusation, he does it by the right of preserving his own life. . . .

JOHN LOCKE

from *Second Treatise of Government* (1690)

John Locke (1632–1704) was born in Wrington, Somer-set, England. The son of an attorney, he was raised in a liberal Puritan family. At the age of fourteen, he entered Westminster School, where he studied the classics, Hebrew, and Arabic. At twenty, he entered Christ's Church, Oxford, where he earned a B.A. in 1656. After receiving an M.A., he was appointed censor of moral philosophy at Oxford.

When his father died in 1661, Locke received a small inheritance. He began studying for a medical degree, and in 1667 became personal physician to the earl of Shaftesbury. Locke received his medical degree in 1674; while completing his studies, he wrote the first two drafts of his Essay Concerning Human Understanding, *was appointed a fellow of the Royal Society, and was named secretary to the Council of Trade and Plantations.*

Locke spent several years in France, returning in 1679. Because of his ties to Shaftesbury, who had been implicated in a plot against the king, Locke was placed under surveillance; he fled to Holland in 1683. There he became an adviser to William of Orange, published a series of works, and wrote the third draft of the Essay. *The revolution of 1688 enabled him to return to England in the company of the future queen, Mary. In 1689 and 1690, Locke published the philosophical work that made him internationally famous: the* Essay *and the* Two Treatises of Government. *He became commissioner of the Board of Trade and Plantations, where he served with great distinction until failing health forced him to retire.*

Locke's Second Treatise *presents a classically liberal theory of government. People in the state of nature would choose to sacrifice a portion of their liberty for the impartial judgment the government can provide. The people nevertheless retain most of their natural rights, which place limits on the power of government. In addition, they receive social rights from the government itself. The government's purpose is the protection of life, liberty, and property; it can act only with the consent of the governed. (Source: Reprinted from John Locke,* Two Treatises of Government. *London: Printed for Awnsham Churchill, 1690.)*

QUESTIONS FOR REFLECTION

1. In what sense is the state of nature a state of equality?

2. How does Locke distinguish liberty from license? Why is the state of nature characterized only by the former?

3. How does Locke argue for capital punishment?

4. What motivates us, in the state of nature, to contract to form a government? What are we willing to give up? What do we hope to gain?

5. Hobbes describes the state of nature as a "war of every man against every man." Locke, however, finds the state of nature different from a state of war. In what ways?

6. What, for Locke, is natural liberty? Liberty in society? Liberty under government?

CHAPTER II / OF THE STATE OF NATURE

§. 4. To understand political power right and derive it from its original, we must consider what state all men are naturally in, and that is a state of perfect freedom to order their actions and dispose of their possessions and persons, as they think fit, within the bounds of the law of nature, without asking leave or depending upon the will of any other man.

A state also of equality, wherein all the power and jurisdiction is reciprocal, no one having more than another; there being nothing more evident than that creatures of the same species and rank, promiscuously born to all the same advantages of nature and the use of the same faculties should also be equal one amongst another without subordination or subjection, unless the lord and master of them all should, by any manifest declaration of his will, set one above another and confer on him, by an evident and clear appointment, an undoubted right to dominion and sovereignty.

§. 5. This equality of men by nature the judicious Hooker* looks upon as so evident in itself and beyond all question that he makes it the foundation of that obligation to mutual love amongst men, on which he builds the duties they owe one another and from whence he derives the great maxims of justice and charity. His words are,

> The like natural inducement has brought men to know that it is no less their duty to love others than themselves; for seeing those things which are equal must needs all have one measure; if I cannot but wish to receive good, even as much at every man's hands as any man can wish unto his own soul, how should I look to have any part of my desire herein satisfied, unless myself be careful to satisfy the like desire, which is undoubtedly in other men, being of one and the same nature? To have anything offered them repugnant to this desire must needs in all respects grieve them as much as me; so that if I do harm, I must look to suffer, there being no reason that others should show greater

EDITOR'S NOTE: Spelling and punctuation have been modernized for clarity.

* Richard Hooker (1553–1600), English theologian and political philosopher, wrote *The Laws of Ecclesiastical Polity*, which focuses on reason and natural law as foundations of the state. —ED.

measure of love to me than they have by me shown unto them: my desire therefore to be loved of my equals in nature, as much as possible may be, imposes upon me a natural duty of bearing to them fully the like affection; from which relation of equality between ourselves and them that are as ourselves, what several rules and canons natural reason has drawn for direction of life no man is ignorant, Eccl. Pol. Lib. 1.

§. 6. But though this be a state of liberty, yet it is not a state of licence: though man in that state have an uncontrollable liberty to dispose of his person or possessions, yet he has not liberty to destroy himself or so much as any creature in his possession, but where some nobler use than its bare preservation calls for it. The state of nature has a law of nature to govern it, which obliges every one: and reason, which is that law, teaches all mankind who will but consult it that being all equal and independent, no one ought to harm another in his life, health, liberty, or possessions: for men being all the workmanship of one omnipotent and infinitely wise maker, all the servants of one sovereign master, sent into the world by his order and about his business; they are his property, whose workmanship they are, made to last during his, not one another's pleasure: and being furnished with like faculties, sharing all in one community of nature, there cannot be supposed any such subordination among us that may authorize us to destroy one another, as if we were made for one another's uses, as the inferior ranks of creatures are for ours. Every one, as he is bound to preserve himself and not to quit his station wilfully, so by the like reason, when his own preservation comes not in competition, ought he as much as he can to preserve the rest of mankind and may not, unless it be to do justice on an offender, take away or impair the life or what tends to the preservation of the life, the liberty, health, limb, or goods of another.

§. 7. And that all men may be restrained from invading others' rights and from doing hurt to one another, and the law of nature be observed which wills the peace and preservation of all mankind, the execution of the law of nature is, in that state, put into every man's hands, whereby everyone has a right to punish the transgressors of that law to such a degree as may hinder its violation: for the law of nature would, as all other laws that concern men in this world, be in vain if there were no body that in the state of nature had a power to execute that law and thereby preserve the innocent and restrain offenders. And if any one in the state of nature may punish another for any evil he has done, every one may do so: for in that state of perfect equality, where naturally there is no superiority or jurisdiction of one over another, what any may do in prosecution of that law everyone must needs have a right to do.

§. 8. And thus, in the state of nature, one man comes by a power over another; but yet no absolute or arbitrary power to use a criminal, when he has got him in his hands, according to the passionate heats, or boundless extravagancy of his own will; but only to retribute to him, so far as calm reason and conscience dictate, what is proportionate to his transgression, which is so much as may serve for reparation and restraint: for these two are the only reasons why one man may lawfully do harm to another, which is that we call punishment. In transgressing the law of nature, the offender declares himself to live by another rule than that of reason and common equity, which is that measure God has set to the actions of men for their mutual security; and so he becomes dangerous to mankind, the tie which is to secure them from injury and violence being slighted and broken by him. Which being a trespass against the whole species and the peace and safety of it provided for by the law of nature, every man upon this score, by the right he has to preserve mankind in general, may restrain or, where it is necessary, destroy things noxious to them and so may bring such evil on anyone who has transgressed that law, as may make him repent the doing of it and thereby deter him, and by his example others, from doing the like mischief. And in the case, and upon this ground, every man has a right to punish the offender and be executioner of the law of nature.

§. 9. I doubt not but this will seem a very strange doctrine to some men: but before they condemn it, I desire them to resolve me, by what right any prince or state can put to death or punish an alien for any crime he commits in their country. It is certain their laws, by virtue of any sanction they receive from the promulgated will of the legislative, reach not a stranger: they speak not to him, nor, if they did, is he bound to hearken to them. The legislative authority, by which they are in force over the subjects of that commonwealth, has no power over him. Those who have the supreme power of making laws in England, France or Holland are to an Indian but like the rest of the world, men without authority: and therefore, if by the law of nature every man has not a power to punish offences against it as he soberly judges the case to require, I see not how the magistrates of any community can punish an alien of another country; since, in reference to him, they can have no more power than what every man naturally may have over another.

§. 10. Besides the crime which consists in violating the law and varying from the right rule of reason, whereby a man so far becomes degenerate and declares himself to quit the principles of human nature and to be a noxious creature, there is commonly injury done to some person or other, and some other man receives damage by his transgression: in which case he who has received any damage has, besides the right of punishment common to him with other men, a particular right to seek reparation from him that has done it: and any other person who finds it just may also join with him that is injured and assist him in recovering from the offender so much as may make satisfaction for the harm he has suffered.

§. 11. From these two distinct rights, the one of punishing the crime for restraint and preventing the like offence, which right of punishing is in everybody; the other of taking reparation, which belongs only to the injured party, comes it to pass that the magistrate, who by being magistrate has the common right of punishing put into his hands, can often, where the public good demands not the execution of the law, remit the punishment of criminal offenses by his own authority, but yet cannot remit the satisfaction due to any private man for the damage he has received. That he who has suffered the damage has a right to demand in his own name, and he alone can remit: the damnified person has this power of appropriating to himself the goods or service of the offender by right of self-preservation, as every man has a power to punish the crime to prevent its being committed again, by the right he has of preserving all mankind and doing all reasonable things he can in order to that end: and thus it is that every man in the state of nature has a power to kill a murderer, both to deter others from doing the like injury, which no reparation can compensate, by the example of the punishment that attends it from everybody, and also to secure men from the attempts of a criminal, who having renounced reason, the common rule and measure God has given to mankind, has by the unjust violence and slaughter he has committed upon one, declared war against all mankind and therefore may be destroyed as a lion or a tiger, one of those wild savage beasts with whom men can have no society nor security: and upon this is grounded that great law of nature, *Whoso sheddeth man's blood, by man shall his blood be shed*. And Cain was so fully convinced that every one had a right to destroy such a criminal that after the murder of his brother, he cries out, *Every one that findeth me, shall slay me;* so plain was it writ in the hearts of all mankind.

§. 12. By the same reason may a man in the state of nature punish the lesser breaches of that law. It will perhaps be demanded, with death? I answer, each transgression may be punished to that degree and with so much severity as will suffice to make it an ill bargain to the offender, give him cause to repent, and terrify others from doing the like. Every offence that can be committed in the state of nature may in the state of nature be also punished equally, and as far forth as it may, in a commonwealth: for though it would be besides my present purpose to enter here into the particulars of the law of nature or its measures of punishment, yet, it is certain there is such a law, and that too as intelligible and plain to a rational creature and a studier of that law as the positive laws of commonwealths; nay, possibly plainer, as much as reason is easier to be understood than the fancies and intricate contrivances of men following contrary and hidden interests put into words; for so truly are a great part of the municipal laws of countries, which are only so far right as they are founded on the law of nature, by which they are to be regulated and interpreted.

§. 13. To this strange doctrine, *viz.* That in the state of nature every one has the executive power of the law of nature, I doubt not but it will be objected that it is unreasonable for men to be judges in their own cases, that self-love will make men partial to themselves and their friends, and, on the other side, that ill nature, passion and revenge will carry them too far in punishing others; and hence nothing but confusion and disorder will follow and that therefore God has certainly appointed government to restrain the partiality and violence of men. I easily grant that civil government is the proper remedy for the inconveniences of the state of nature, which must certainly be great where men may be judges in their own case, since it is easy to be imagined that he who was so unjust as to do his brother an injury will scarce be so just as to condemn himself for it: but I shall desire those who make this objection to remember that absolute monarchs are but men; and if government is to be the remedy of those evils which necessarily follow from men's being judges in their own cases and the state of nature is therefore not to be endured, I desire to know what kind of government that is and how much better it is than the state of nature, where one man commanding a multitude has the liberty to be judge in his own case and may do to all his subjects whatever he pleases, without the least liberty to anyone to question or control those who execute his pleasure? and in whatsoever he does, whether led by reason, mistake or passion, must be submitted to? Much better it is in the state of nature, where men are not bound to submit to the unjust will of another, and if he that judges judges amiss in his own or any other case, he is answerable for it to the rest of mankind.

§. 14. It is often asked as a mighty objection, where are, or ever were there, any men in such a state of nature? To which it may suffice as an answer at present that since all princes and rulers of independent governments all through the world are in a state of nature, it is plain the world never was, nor ever will be, without numbers of men in that state. I have named all governors of independent communities, whether they are or are not in league with others: for it is not every compact that puts an end to the state of nature between men, but only this one of agreeing together mutually to enter into the community and make one body politic; other promises and compacts men may make one with another and yet still be in the state of nature. The promises and bargains for truck, &c. between the two men in the desert island, mentioned by Garcilasso de la Vega in his history of Peru, or between a Swiss and an Indian in the woods of America are binding to them, though they are perfectly in a state of nature in reference to one another: for truth and keeping of faith belongs to men as men and not as members of society.

§. 15. To those that say there were never any men in the state of nature, I will not only oppose the authority of the judicious Hooker, *Eccl. Pol. lib.* i. *sect.* 10. where he says, *The laws which have been hitherto mentioned,* i.e. the laws of nature, *do bind men absolutely, even as they are men, although they have never any settled fellowship, never any solemn agreement amongst themselves what to do, or not to do: but forasmuch as we are not by ourselves sufficient to furnish ourselves with competent store of things, needful for such a life as our nature doth desire, a life fit for the dignity of man; therefore to supply those defects and imperfections which are in us, as living single and solely by ourselves, we are naturally induced to seek communion and fellowship with others: this was the cause of men's uniting themselves at first in politic societies.* But I moreover affirm that all men are naturally in that state and remain so until by their own consents they make themselves members of some politic society; and I doubt not in the sequel of this discourse, to make it very clear.

CHAPTER III / OF THE STATE OF WAR

§. 16. The state of war is a state of enmity and destruction: and therefore declaring by word or action, not a passionate and hasty, but a sedate settled design upon another man's life, puts him in a state of war with him against whom he has declared such an intention, and so has exposed his life to the other's power to be taken away by him or any one that joins with him in his defence and espouses his quarrel; it being reasonable and just, I should have a right to destroy that which threatens me with destruction: for by the fundamental law of nature, man being to be preserved as much as possible, when all cannot be preserved, the safety of the innocent is to be preferred: and one may destroy a man who makes war upon him or has discovered an enmity to his being, for the same reason that he may kill a wolf or a lion; because such men are not under the ties of the common law of reason, have no other rule but

that of force and violence, and so may be treated as beasts of prey those dangerous and noxious creatures that will be sure to destroy him whenever he falls into their power.

§. 17. And hence it is that he who attempts to get another man into his absolute power does thereby put himself into a state of war with him, it being to be understood as a declaration of a design upon his life: for I have reason to conclude that he who would get me into his power without my consent would use me as he pleased when he had got me there and destroy me too when he had a fancy to it; for nobody can desire to have me in his absolute power, unless it be to compel me by force to that which is against the right of my freedom, i.e. make me a slave. To be free from such force is the only security of my preservation, and reason bids me look on him, as an enemy to my preservation, who would take away that freedom which is the fence to it; so that he who makes an attempt to enslave me thereby puts himself into a state of war with me. He that in the state of nature would take away the freedom that belongs to anyone in that state must necessarily be supposed to have a design to take away every thing else, that freedom being the foundation of all the rest; as he that in the state of society would take away the freedom belonging to those of that society or commonwealth must be supposed to design to take away from them everything else and so be looked on as in a state of war.

§. 18. This makes it lawful for a man to kill a thief who has not in the least hurt him nor declared any design upon his life any farther than by the use of force so to get him in his power, as to take away his money, or what he pleases, from him; because using force where he has no right to get me into his power, let his pretence be what it will, I have no reason to suppose that he who would take away my liberty would not, when he had me in his power, take away everything else. And therefore it is lawful for me to treat him as one who has put himself into a state of war with me, i.e. kill him if I can; for to that hazard does he justly expose himself, whoever introduces a state of war and is aggressor in it.

§. 19. And here we have the plain difference between the state of nature and the state of war, which however some men have confounded, are as far distant as a state of peace, good will, mutual assistance and preservation and a state of enmity, malice, violence and mutual destruction are one from another. Men living together according to reason, without a common superior on earth with authority to judge between them, is properly the state of nature. But force, or a declared design of force, upon the person of another, where there is no common superior on earth to appeal to for relief, is the state of war: and it is the want of such an appeal gives a man the right of war even against an aggressor, though he be in society and a fellow subject. Thus a thief, whom I cannot harm but by appeal to the law for having stolen all that I am worth, I may kill when he sets on me to rob me but of my horse or coat; because the law, which was made for my preservation where it cannot interpose to secure my life from present force, which, if lost, is capable of no reparation, permits me my own defence and the right of war, a liberty to kill the aggressor, because the aggressor allows not time to appeal to our common judge nor the decision of the law for remedy in a case where the mischief may be irreparable. Want of a common judge with authority puts all men in a state of nature: force without right upon a man's person makes a state of war, both where there is and is not a common judge.

§. 20. But when the actual force is over, the state of war ceases between those that are in society and are equally on both sides subjected to the fair determination of the law; because then there lies open the remedy of appeal for the past injury and to prevent future harm: but where no such appeal is, as in the state of nature, for want of positive laws and judges with authority to appeal to, the state of war once begun continues, with a right to the innocent party to destroy the other whenever he can until the aggressor offers peace and desires reconciliation on such terms as may repair any wrongs he has already done and secure the innocent for the future; nay, where an appeal to the law and constituted judges lies open, but the remedy is denied by a manifest perverting of justice and a barefaced wresting of the laws to protect or indemnify the violence or injuries of some men or party of men, there it is hard to imagine anything but a state of war: for whereever violence is used and injury done, though by hands appointed to administer justice, it is still violence and injury, however coloured with the name, pretences, or forms of law, the end whereof being to protect and redress the innocent by an unbiased application of it to all who are under it; whereever that is not *bona fide* done, war is made upon the sufferers, who, having no appeal on earth to right them, they are left to the only remedy in such cases, an appeal to heaven.

§. 21. To avoid this state of war (wherein there is no appeal but to heaven, and wherein every the least difference is apt to end where there is no authority to decide between the contenders) is one great reason of men's putting themselves into society and quitting the state of nature: for where there is an authority, a power on earth from which relief can be had by appeal there the continuance of the state of war is excluded, and the controversy is decided by that power. Had there been any such court, any superior jurisdiction on earth, to determine the right between Jephtha and the Ammonities, they had never come to a state of war: but we see he was forced to appeal to heaven. *The Lord the Judge* (says he) *be judge this day between the children of* Israel *and the children of* Ammon, *Judg.* xi. 27. and then prosecuting and relying on his appeal, he leads out his army to battle: and therefore in such controversies, where the question is put, *who shall be judge?* It cannot be meant, who shall decide the controversy; everyone knows what Jephtha here tells us, that the Lord the Judge shall judge. Where there is no judge on earth, the appeal lies to God in heaven. That question then cannot mean, who shall judge whether another has put himself in a state of war with me and whether I may, as Jephtha did, appeal to heaven in it? of that I myself can only be judge in my own conscience, as I will answer it, at the great day, to the supreme judge of all men.

CHAPTER IV / OF SLAVERY

§. 22. The natural liberty of man is to be free from any superior power on earth and not to be under the will or legislative authority of man, but to have only the law of nature for his rule. The liberty of man in society is to be under no other legislative power but that established by consent in the commonwealth, nor under the dominion of any will or restraint of any law but what that legislative shall enact according to the trust put in it. Freedom then is not what Sir Robert Filmer tells us, *Observations, A. 55. a liberty for every one to do what he lists, to live as he pleases, and not to be tied by any laws:* but *freedom of men under government* is to have a standing rule to live by, common to every one of that society and made by the legislative power erected in it; a liberty to follow my own will in all things, where the rule prescribes not; and not to be subject to the inconstant, uncertain, unknown, arbitrary will of another man: as freedom of nature is to be under no other restraint but the law of nature.

§. 23. This freedom from absolute, arbitrary power is so necessary to and closely joined with a man's preservation that he cannot part with it, but by what forfeits his preservation and life together: for a man, not having the power of his own life, cannot by compact or his own consent enslave himself to anyone nor put himself under the absolute, arbitrary power of another to take away his life when he pleases. Nobody can give more power than he has himself; and he that cannot take away his own life cannot give another power over it. Indeed, having by his fault forfeited his own life by some act that deserves death, he to whom he has forfeited it may (when he has him in his power) delay to take it and make use of him to his own service, and he does him no injury by it: for whenever he finds the hardship of his slavery outweigh the value of his life, it is in his power, by resisting the will of his master, to draw on himself the death he desires. . . .

JEAN-JACQUES ROUSSEAU

from *On the Social Contract* (1762)

Jean-Jacques Rousseau (1712–1778), philosopher, essayist, and novelist, was born in Geneva. His mother died a few days after he was born; he was raised by his somewhat unstable father and an aunt. Rousseau had little formal education. He studied for two years with a country minister. He became apprentice to a notary and then to an engraver, who treated him badly. Discouraged, Rousseau left Geneva at the age of sixteen. He went to France, where he met Madame de Warens, a convert to Roman Catholicism. They became friends; Rousseau too converted. He traveled with her and stayed at her estate in Chambéry. In 1740 he became a private tutor in Lyon.

At thirty-one, Rousseau became secretary to the French ambassador at Venice. He lost the post the next year after quarelling with the ambassador. At thirty-three, he began an affair with Thérèse Le Vasseur, by whom he had five illegitimate children—all of whom he sent to an orphanage. Rousseau's intellectual career brought him in contact with the greatest minds of Europe, many of whom he met, befriended, and shortly thereafter alienated.

In 1755, Rousseau published his Discourse on the Origin of Inequality, *which presented an idealized, romantic view of the state of nature, from which humanity fell by inventing the notion of property. In 1762,* On the Social Contract *appeared, which offers an account of the social contract and the power of government. According to that work, people band together to form a government by surrendering everything they have to the community. On balance, they gain from this arrangement, according to Rousseau, for each person receives in turn a share of the entire community and rights that arise from the community. The community has a general will, directed toward what is best for itself as a whole. Individual wills in conflict with the general will are in error. (Source: Reprinted from* The Basic Political Writings of Jean-Jacques Rousseau, *translated and edited by Donald A. Cress. Copyright © 1987 by Hackett Publishing Company Inc., Indianapolis, IN, and Cambridge, MA.)*

QUESTIONS FOR REFLECTION

1. What, for Rousseau, is the foundation of all rights?

2. Why, according to Rousseau, does physical power have no moral force?

3. Why, in Rousseau's view, is slavery—even voluntary slavery—illegitimate?

4. Why, according to Rousseau, do people enter into a social compact? What do they give up? What do they hope to gain?

5. What is Rousseau's analysis of conflicts between an individual will and the general will?

6. Why does Rousseau approve of capital punishment?

Book I

CHAPTER I / SUBJECT OF THE FIRST BOOK

Man is born free, and everywhere he is in chains. He who believes himself the master of others does not escape being more of a slave than they. How did this change take place? I have no idea. What can render it legitimate? I believe I can answer this question.

Were I to consider only force and the effect that flows from it, I would say that so long as a people is constrained to obey and does obey, it does well. As soon as it can shake off the yoke and does shake it off, it does even better. For by recovering its liberty by means of the same right that stole it, either the populace is justified in getting it back or else those who took it away were not justified in their actions. But the social order is a sacred right which serves as a foundation for all other rights. Nevertheless, this right does not come from nature. It is therefore founded upon convention. Before coming to that, I ought to substantiate what I just claimed.

CHAPTER III / ON THE RIGHT OF THE STRONGEST

The strongest is never strong enough to be master all the time, unless he transforms force into right and obedience into duty. Hence the right of the strongest, a right that seems like something intended ironically and is actually established as a basic principle. But will no one explain this word to me? Force is a physical power; I fail to see what morality can result from its effects. To give in to force is an act of necessity, not of will. At most, it is an act of prudence. In what sense could it be a duty?

Let us suppose for a moment that there is such a thing as this alleged right. I maintain that all that results from it is an inexplicable mish-mash. For once force produces the right, the effect changes places with the cause. Every force that is superior to the first succeeds to its right. As soon as one can disobey with impunity, one can do so legitimately; and

since the strongest is always right, the only thing to do is to make oneself the strongest. For what kind of right is it that perishes when the force on which it is based ceases? If one must obey because of force, one need not do so out of duty; and if one is no longer forced to obey one is no longer obliged. Clearly then, this word "right" adds nothing to force. It is utterly meaningless here.

Obey the powers that be. If that means giving in to force, the precept is sound, but superfluous. I reply it will never be violated. All power comes from God—I admit it—but so does every disease. Does this mean that calling in a physician is prohibited? If a brigand takes me by surprise at the edge of a wooded area, is it not only the case that I must surrender my purse, but even that I am in good conscience bound to surrender it, if I were able to withhold it? After all, the pistol he holds is also a power.

Let us then agree that force does not bring about right, and that one is obliged to obey only legitimate powers. Thus my original question keeps returning.

CHAPTER IV / ON SLAVERY

Since no man has a natural authority over his fellow man, and since force does not give rise to any right, conventions therefore remain the basis of all legitimate authority among men.

If, says Grotius,* a private individual can alienate his liberty and turn himself into the slave of a master, why could not an entire people alienate its liberty and turn itself into the subject of a king? There are many equivocal words here which need explanation, but let us confine ourselves to the word *alienate*. To alienate is to give or to sell. A man who makes himself the slave of someone else does not give himself; he sells himself, at least for his subsistence. But why does a people sell itself? Far from furnishing his subjects with their subsistence, a king derives his own from them alone, and, according to

* Hugo Grotius (1583–1645), Dutch jurist, statesman, and political philosopher, wrote *On the Law of War and Peace,* which argues for international law based on natural law and the social contract. —ED.

Rabelais, a king does not live cheaply. Do subjects then give their persons on the condition that their estate will also be taken? I fail to see what remains for them to preserve.

It will be said that the despot assures his subjects of civil tranquility. Very well. But what do they gain, if the wars his ambition drags them into, if his insatiable greed, if the oppressive demands caused by his ministers occasion more grief for his subjects than their own dissensions would have done? What do they gain, if this very tranquility is one of their miseries? A tranquil life is also had in dungeons; is that enough to make them desirable? The Greeks who were locked up in the Cyclops' cave lived a tranquil existence as they awaited their turn to be devoured.

To say that a man gives himself gratuitously is to say something absurd and inconceivable. Such an act is illegitimate and null, if only for the fact that he who commits it does not have his wits about him. To say the same thing of an entire populace is to suppose a populace composed of madmen. Madness does not bring about right.

Even if each person can alienate himself, he cannot alienate his children. They are born men and free. Their liberty belongs to them; they alone have the right to dispose of it. Before they have reached the age of reason, their father can, in their name, stipulate conditions for their maintenance and for their well-being. But he cannot give them irrevocably and unconditionally, for such a gift is contrary to the ends of nature and goes beyond the rights of paternity. For an arbitrary government to be legitimate, it would therefore be necessary in each generation for the people to be master of its acceptance or rejection. But in that event this government would no longer be arbitrary.

Renouncing one's liberty is renouncing one's dignity as a man, the rights of humanity and even its duties. There is no possible compensation for anyone who renounces everything. Such a renunciation is incompatible with the nature of man. Removing all morality from his actions is tantamount to taking away all liberty from his will. Finally, it is a vain and contradictory convention to stipulate absolute authority on one side and a limitless obedience on the other. Is it not clear that no commitments are made to a person from whom one has the right to demand everything? And does this condition alone not bring with it, without equivalent or exchange, the nullity of the act? For what right would my slave have against me, given that all he has belongs to me, and that, since his right is my right, my having a right against myself makes no sense?

Grotius and others derive from war another origin for the alleged right of slavery. Since, according to them, the victor has the right to kill the vanquished, these latter can repurchase their lives at the price of their liberty—a convention all the more legitimate, since it turns a profit for both of them.

But clearly this alleged right to kill the vanquished does not in any way derive from the state of war. Men are not naturally enemies, for the simple reason that men living in their original state of independence do not have sufficiently constant relationships among themselves to bring about either a state of peace or a state of war. It is the relationship between things and not that between men that brings about war. And since this state of war cannot come into existence from simple personal relations, but only from real [proprietary] relations, a private war between one man and another can exist neither in the state of nature, where there is no constant property, nor in the social state, where everything is under the authority of the laws.

Fights between private individuals, duels, encounters are not acts which produce a state. And with regard to private wars, authorized by the ordinances of King Louis IX of France and suspended by the Peace of God, they are abuses of feudal government, an absurd system if there ever was one, contrary to the principles of natural right and to all sound polity.

War is not therefore a relationship between one man and another, but a relationship between one state and another. In war private individuals are enemies only incidentally: not as men or even as citizens, but as soldiers; not as members of the homeland but as its defenders. Finally, each state can have as enemies only other states and not men, since there can be no real relationship between things of disparate natures.

This principle is even in conformity with the established maxims of all times and with the constant practice of all civilized peoples. Declarations of war are warnings not so much to powers as to their subjects. The foreigner (be he king, private individual, or a people) who robs, kills or detains subjects of another prince without declaring war on the prince, is not an enemy but a brigand. Even in the midst of war a just prince rightly appropriates to himself everything in an enemy country belonging to the public, but respects the person and goods of private individuals. He respects the rights upon which his own rights are founded. Since the purpose of war is the destruction of the enemy state, one has the right to kill the defenders of that state so long as they bear arms. But as soon as they lay down their arms and surrender, they cease to be enemies or instruments of the enemy. They return to being simply men; and one no longer has a right to their lives. Sometimes a state can be killed without a single one of its members being killed. For war does not grant a right that is unnecessary to its purpose. These principles are not those of Grotius. They are not based on the authority of poets. Rather they are derived from the nature of things; they are based on reason.

As to the right of conquest, the only basis it has is the law of the strongest. If war does not give the victor the right to massacre the vanquished peoples, this right (which he does not have) cannot be the basis for the right to enslave them. One has the right to kill the enemy only when one cannot enslave him. The right to enslave him does not therefore derive from the right to kill him. Hence it is an iniquitous exchange to make him buy his life, to which no one has any right, at the price of his liberty. In establishing the right of life and death on the right of slavery, and the right of slavery on the right of life and death, is it not clear that one falls into a vicious circle?

Even if we were to suppose that there were this terrible right to kill everyone, I maintain that neither a person enslaved during wartime nor a conquered people bears any obligation whatever toward its master, except to obey him for as long as it is forced to do so. In taking the equivalent of his life, the victor has done him no favor. Instead of killing him unprofitably he kills him usefully. Hence, far from the victor having acquired any authority over him beyond force, the state of war subsists between them

just as before. Their relationship itself is the effect of war, and the usage of the right to war does not suppose any peace treaty. They have made a convention. Fine. But this convention, far from destroying the state of war, presupposes its continuation.

Thus, from every point of view, the right of slavery is null, not simply because it is illegitimate, but because it is absurd and meaningless. These words, *slavery* and *right,* are contradictory. They are mutually exclusive. Whether it is the statement of one man to another man, or one man to a people, the following sort of talk will always be equally nonsensical. *I make a convention with you which is wholly at your expense and wholly to my advantage; and, for as long as it pleases me, I will observe it and so will you.*

CHAPTER V / THAT IT IS ALWAYS NECESSARY TO RETURN TO A FIRST CONVENTION

Even if I were to grant all that I have thus far refuted, the supporters of despotism would not be any better off. There will always be a great difference between subduing a multitude and ruling a society. If scattered men, however many they may be, were successively enslaved by a single individual, I see nothing there but a master and slaves; I do not see a people and its leader. It is, if you will, an aggregation, but not an association. There is neither a public good nor a body politic there. Even if that man had enslaved half the world, he is always just a private individual. His interest, separated from that of others, is never anything but a private interest. If this same man is about to die, after his passing his empire remains scattered and disunited, just as an oak tree dissolves and falls into a pile of ashes after fire has consumed it.

A people, says Grotius, can give itself to a king. According to Grotius, therefore, a people is a people before it gives itself to a king. This gift itself is a civil act; it presupposes a public deliberation. Thus, before examining the act whereby a people chooses a king, it would be well to examine the act whereby a people is a people. For since this act is necessarily prior to the other, it is the true foundation of society.

In fact, if there were no prior convention, then, unless the vote were unanimous, what would become of the minority's obligation to submit to the majority's choice, and where do one hundred who want a master get the right to vote for ten who do not? The law of majority rule is itself an established convention, and presupposes unanimity on at least one occasion.

CHAPTER VI / ON THE SOCIAL COMPACT

I suppose that men have reached the point where obstacles that are harmful to their maintenance in the state of nature gain the upper hand by their resistance to the forces that each individual can bring to bear to maintain himself in that state. Such being the case, that original state cannot subsist any longer, and the human race would perish if it did not alter its mode of existence.

For since men cannot engender new forces, but merely unite and direct existing ones, they have no other means of maintaining themselves but to form by aggregation a sum of forces that could gain the upper hand over the resistance, so that their forces are directed by means of a single moving power and made to act in concert.

This sum of forces cannot come into being without the cooperation of many. But since each man's force and liberty are the primary instruments of his maintenance, how is he going to engage them without hurting himself and without neglecting the care that he owes himself? This difficulty, seen in terms of my subject, can be stated in the following terms:

"Find a form of association which defends and protects with all common forces the person and goods of each associate, and by means of which each one, while uniting with all, nevertheless obeys only himself and remains as free as before?" This is the fundamental problem for which the social contract provides the solution.

The clauses of this contract are so determined by the nature of the act that the least modification renders them vain and ineffectual, that, although perhaps they have never been formally promulgated, they are everywhere the same, everywhere tacitly accepted and acknowledged. Once the social compact is violated, each person then regains his first rights and resumes his natural liberty, while losing the conventional liberty for which he renounced it.

These clauses, properly understood, are all reducible to a single one, namely the total alienation of each associate, together with all of his rights, to the entire community. For first of all, since each person gives himself whole and entire, the condition is equal for everyone; and since the condition is equal for everyone, no one has an interest in making it burdensome for the others.

Moreover, since the alienation is made without reservation, the union is as perfect as possible, and no associate has anything further to demand. For if some rights remained with private individuals, in the absence of any common superior who could decide between them and the public, each person would eventually claim to be his own judge in all things, since he is on some point his own judge. The state of nature would subsist and the association would necessarily become tyrannical or hollow.

Finally, in giving himself to all, each person gives himself to no one. And since there is no associate over whom he does not acquire the same right that he would grant others over himself, he gains the equivalent of everything he loses, along with a greater amount of force to preserve what he has.

If, therefore, one eliminates from the social compact whatever is not essential to it, one will find that it is reducible to the following terms. *Each of us places his person and all his power in common under the supreme direction of the general will; and as one we receive each member as an indivisible part of the whole.*

At once, in place of the individual person of each contracting party, this act of association produces a moral and collective body composed of as many members as there are voices in the assembly, which receives from this same act its unity, its common *self*, its life and its will. This public person, formed thus by union of all the others formerly took the name *city*, and at present takes the name *republic* or *body politic*, which is called *state* by its members when it is passive, *sovereign* when it is active, *power* when compared to others like itself. As to the associates, they collectively take the name *people*; individually they are called *citizens*, insofar as participants in the sovereign authority, and *subjects,* insofar as they are subjected to the laws of the state. But these terms are often confused and mistaken for one another. It is enough to know how to distinguish them when they are used with absolute precision.

CHAPTER VII / ON THE SOVEREIGN

This formula shows that the act of association includes a reciprocal commitment between the public and private individuals, and that each individual, contracting, as it were, with himself, finds himself under a twofold commitment: namely as a member of the sovereign to private individuals, and as a member of the state toward the sovereign. But the maxim of civil law that no one is held to commitments made to himself cannot be applied here, for there is a considerable difference between being obligated to oneself, or to a whole of which one is a part.

It must be further noted that the public deliberation that can obligate all the subjects to the sovereign, owing to the two different relationships in which each of them is viewed, cannot, for the opposite reason, obligate the sovereign to itself, and that consequently it is contrary to the nature of the body politic that the sovereign impose upon itself a law it could not break. Since the sovereign can be considered under but one single relationship, it is then in the position of a private individual contracting with himself. Whence it is apparent that there neither is nor can be any type of fundamental law that is obligatory for the people as a body, not even the social contract. This does not mean that the whole body cannot perfectly well commit itself to another body with respect to things that do not infringe on this contract. For in regard to the foreigner, it becomes a simple being, as individual.

However, since the body politic or the sovereign derives its being exclusively from the sanctity of the contract, it can never obligate itself, not even to another power, to do anything that derogates from the original act, such as alienating some portion of itself or submitting to another sovereign. Violation of the act whereby it exists would be self-annihilation, and whatever is nothing produces nothing.

As soon as this multitude is thus united in a body, one cannot harm one of the members without attacking the whole body. It is even less likely that the body can be harmed without the members feeling it. Thus duty and interest equally obligate the two parties to come to one another's aid, and the same men should seek to combine in this two-fold relationship all the advantages that result from it.

For since the sovereign is formed entirely from the private individuals who make it up, it neither has nor could have an interest contrary to theirs. Hence, the sovereign power has no need to offer a guarantee to its subjects, since it is impossible for a body to want to harm all of its members, and, as we will see later, it cannot harm any one of them in particular. The sovereign, by the mere fact that it exists, is always all that it should be.

But the same thing cannot be said of the subjects in relation to the sovereign, for which, despite their common interest, their commitments would be without substance if it did not find ways of being assured of their fidelity.

In fact, each individual can, as a man, have a private will contrary to or different from the general will that he has as a citizen. His private interest can speak to him in an entirely different manner than the common interest. His absolute and naturally independent existence can cause him to envisage what he owes the common cause as a gratuitous contribution, the loss of which will be less harmful to others than its payment is burdensome to him. And in viewing the moral person which constitutes the state as a being of reason because it is not a man, he would enjoy the rights of a citizen without wanting to fulfill the duties of a subject, an injustice whose growth would bring about the ruin of the body politic.

Thus, in order for the social compact to avoid being an empty formula, it tacitly entails the commitment—which alone can give force to the others—that whoever refuses to obey the general will will be forced to do so by the entire body. This means merely that he will be forced to be free. For this is the sort of condition that, by giving each citizen to the homeland, guarantees him against all personal dependence—a condition that produces the skill and the performance of the political machine, and which alone bestows legitimacy upon civil commitments. Without it such commitments would be absurd, tyrannical and subject to the worst abuses.

CHAPTER VIII / ON THE CIVIL STATE

This passage from the state of nature to the civil state produces quite a remarkable change in man, for it substitutes justice for instinct in his behavior and gives his actions a moral quality they previously lacked. Only then, when the voice of duty replaces physical impulse and right replaces appetite, does man, who had hitherto taken only himself into account, find himself forced to act upon other principles and to consult his reason before listening to his inclinations. Although in this state he deprives himself of several of the advantages belonging to him in the state of nature, he regains such great ones. His faculties are exercised and developed, his ideas are broadened, his feelings are ennobled, his entire soul is elevated to such a height that, if the abuse of this new condition did not often lower his status to beneath the level he left, he ought constantly to bless the happy moment that pulled him away from it forever and which transformed him from a stupid, limited animal into an intelligent being and a man.

Let us summarize this entire balance sheet so that the credits and debits are easily compared. What man loses through the social contract is his natural liberty and an unlimited right to everything that tempts him and that he can acquire. What he gains is civil liberty and the proprietary ownership of all he possesses. So as not to be in error in these compensations, it is necessary to draw a careful distinction between natural liberty (which is limited solely by the force or the individual involved) and civil liberty (which is limited by the general will), and between possession (which is merely the effect of the force or the right of the first occupant) and proprietary ownership (which is based solely on a positive title).

To the preceding acquisitions could be added the acquisition in the civil state of moral liberty, which alone makes man truly the master of himself. For to be driven by appetite alone is slavery, and obedience to the law one has prescribed for oneself is liberty. But I have already said too much on this subject, and the philosophical meaning of the word *liberty* is not my subject here.

Book II

CHAPTER V / ON THE RIGHT OF LIFE OR DEATH

The question arises how private individuals who have no right to dispose of their own lives can transfer to the sovereign this very same right which they do not have. This question seems difficult to resolve only because it is poorly stated. Every man has the right to risk his own life in order to preserve it. Has it ever been said that a person who jumps out a window to escape a fire is guilty of committing suicide? Has this crime ever been imputed to someone who perishes in a storm, unaware of its danger when he embarked?

The social treaty has as its purpose the conservation of the contracting parties. Whoever wills the end also wills the means, and these means are inseparable from some risks, even from some losses. Whoever wishes to preserve his life at the expense of others should also give it up for them when necessary. For the citizen is no longer judge of the peril to which the law wishes he be exposed, and when the prince has said to him, "it is expedient for the state that you should die," he should die. Because it is under this condition alone that he has lived in security up to then, and because his life is not only a kindness of nature, but a conditional gift of the state.

The death penalty inflicted on criminals can be viewed from more or less the same point of view. It is in order to avoid being the victim of an assassin that a person consents to die, were he to become one. According to this treaty, far from disposing of his own life, one thinks only of guaranteeing it. And it cannot be presumed that any of the contracting parties is then planning to get himself hanged.

Moreover, every malefactor who attacks the social right becomes through his transgressions a rebel and a traitor to the homeland; in violating its laws, he ceases to be a member, and he even wages war with it. In that case the preservation of the state is incompatible with his own. Thus one of the two must perish; and when the guilty party is put to death, it is less as a citizen than as an enemy. The legal proceeding and the judgment are the proofs and the declaration that he has broken the social treaty, and consequently that he is no longer a member of the state. For since he has acknowledged himself to be such, at least by his living there, he ought to be removed from it by exile as a violator of the compact, or by death as a public enemy. For such an enemy is not a moral person, but a man, and in this situation the right of war is to kill the vanquished.

But it will be said that the condemnation of a criminal is a particular act. Fine. So this condemnation is not a function of the sovereign. It is a right the sovereign can confer without itself being able to exercise it. All of my opinions are consistent, but I cannot present them all at once.

In addition, frequency of physical punishment is always a sign of weakness or of torpor in the government. There is no wicked man who could not be made good for something. One has the right to put to death, even as an example, only someone who cannot be preserved without danger.

With regard to the right of pardon, or of exempting a guilty party from the penalty decreed by the law and pronounced by the judge, this belongs only to one who is above the judge and the law, that is, to the sovereign. Still its right in this regard is not clearly defined, and the cases in which it is used are quite rare. In a well governed state, there are few punishments, not because many pardons are granted, but because there are few criminals. When a state is in decline, the sheer number of crimes insures impunity. Under the Roman Republic, neither the senate nor the consuls ever tried to grant pardons. The people itself did not do so, even though it sometimes revoked its own judgment. Frequent pardons indicate that transgressions will eventually have no need of them, and everyone sees where that leads. But I feel that my heart murmurs and holds back my pen. Let us leave these questions to be discussed by a just man who has not done wrong and who himself never needed pardon.

CHAPTER VI / ON LAW

. . . Strictly speaking, laws are merely the conditions of civil association. The populace that is subjected to the laws ought to be their author. The regulating of the conditions of a society belongs to no one but those who are in association with one another. But how will they regulate these conditions? Will it be by a common accord, by a sudden inspiration? Does the body politic have an organ for making known its will? Who will give it the necessary foresight to formulate acts and to promulgate them in advance, or how will it announce them in time of need? How will a blind multitude, which often does not know what it wants (since it rarely knows what is good for it), carry out on its own an enterprise as great and as difficult as a system of legislation? By itself the populace always wants the good, but by itself it does not always see it. The general will is always right, but the judgment that guides it is not always enlightened. It must be made to see objects as they are, and sometimes as they ought to appear to it. The good path it seeks must be pointed out to it. It must be made safe from the seduction of private wills. It must be given a sense of time and place. It must weigh present, tangible advantages against the danger of distant, hidden evils. Private individuals see the good they reject. The public wills the good that it does not see. Everyone is equally in need of guides. The former must be obligated to conform their wills to their reason; the latter must learn to know what it wants. Then public enlightenment results in the union of the understanding and the will in the social body; hence the full cooperation of the parts, and finally the greatest force of the whole. Whence there arises the necessity of having a legislator.

CHAPTER VII / ON THE LEGISLATOR

Discovering the rules of society best suited to nations would require a superior intelligence that beheld all the passions of men without feeling any of them; who had no affinity with our nature, yet knew it through and through; whose happiness was independent of us, yet who nevertheless was willing to concern itself with ours; finally, who, in the passage of time, procures for himself a distant glory, being able to labor in one age and find enjoyment in another. Gods would be needed to give men laws.

The same reasoning used by Caligula regarding matters of fact was used by Plato regarding right in defining the civil or royal man he looks for in his dialogue *The Statesman.* But if it is true that a great prince is a rare man, what about a great legislator? The former merely has to follow the model the latter should propose to him. The latter is the engineer who invents the machine; the former is merely the workman who constructs it and makes it run. At the birth of societies, says Montesquieu, it is the leaders of republics who bring about the institution, and thereafter it is the institution that forms the leaders of the republic.

He who dares to undertake the establishment of a people should feel that he is, so to speak, in a position to change human nature, to transform each individual (who by himself is a perfect and solitary whole), into a part of a larger whole from which this individual receives, in a sense, his life and his being; to alter man's constitution in order to strengthen it; to substitute a partial and moral existence for the physical and independent existence we have all received from nature. In a word, he must deny man his own forces in order to give him forces that are alien to him and that he cannot make use of without the help of others. The more these natural forces are dead and obliterated, and the greater and more durable are the acquired forces, the more too is the institution solid and perfect. Thus if each citizen is nothing and can do nothing except in concert with all the others, and if the force acquired by the whole is equal or superior to the sum of the natural forces of all the individuals, one can say that the legislation has achieved the highest possible point of perfection.

The legislator is in every respect an extraordinary man in the state. If he ought to be so by his genius, he is no less so by his office, which is neither magistracy nor sovereignty. This office, which constitutes the republic, does not enter into its constitution. It is a particular and superior function having nothing in common with the dominion over men. For if he who has command over men must not have command over laws, he who has command over the laws must no longer have any authority over men. Otherwise, his laws, ministers of his passions, would often only serve to perpetuate his injustices, and he could never avoid private opinions altering the sanctity of his work.

When Lycurgus gave laws to his homeland, he began by abdicating the throne. It was the custom of most Greek cities to entrust the establishment of their laws to foreigners. The modern republics of Italy often imitated this custom. The republic of Geneva did the same and things worked out well. In its finest age Rome saw the revival within its midst of all the crimes of tyranny and saw itself on the verge of perishing as a result of having united the legislative authority and the sovereign power in the same hands.

Nevertheless, the decimvirs* themselves never claimed the right to have any law passed on their authority alone. *Nothing we propose,* they would tell the people, *can become law without your consent. Romans, be yourselves the authors of the laws that should bring about your happiness.*

He who frames the laws, therefore, does not or should not have any legislative right. And the populace itself cannot, even if it wanted to, deprive itself of this incommunicable right, because, according to the fundamental compact, only the general will obligates private individuals, and there can never be any assurance that a private will is in conformity with the general will until it has been submitted to the free vote of the people. I have already said this, but it is not a waste of time to repeat it.

Thus we find together in the work of legislation two things that seem incompatible: an undertaking that transcends human force, and, to execute it, an authority that is nil. . . .

---

*The decimvirs: Roman magistrates constituting a body of ten men acting as a commission; especially, members of two such bodies who drew up the laws of the Twelve Tables and ruled Rome absolutely in 451 and 450 B.C.E. —ED.

IMMANUEL KANT

from *Grounding of the Metaphysics of Morals* (1785)

Immanuel Kant (1724–1804) was born in Königsberg, in East Prussia (now Kaliningrad, part of the Russian republic). The son of a saddlemaker and grandson of a Scottish immigrant, Kant attended the University of Königsberg, from which he graduated at twenty-two. A year later he published his first philosophical work, a book on living forces. He was a private tutor for several years while continuing his studies. At twenty-nine he received a master's degree and began teaching at Königsberg as a Privatdozent*—roughly, an unpaid lecturer who collected fees from his students. He continued in that capacity for fifteen years. Finally, in 1770, he was appointed to a chair of logic and metaphysics at the University of Königsberg.*

At the age of fifty-seven, Kant published the Critique of Pure Reason, *a work that earned him fame and that contemporary philosophers regard as one of the greatest works of the Western philosophical tradition. The decade that followed was extremely productive for Kant.* Prolegomena to Any Future Metaphysics *appeared in 1783;* Grounding of the Metaphysics of Morals *in 1785; the second edition of the* Critique of Pure Reason *in 1787; the* Critique of Practical Reason *in 1788; and the* Critique of Judgment *in 1790. Kant continued writing well into his seventies.*

Though known for his wit and conversational skill as well as for his intellect, Kant never married and never traveled more than a few miles from the place of his birth. His habits were so regular that, according to legend, neighbors would set their clocks by his afternoon walks.

Kant's Grounding of the Metaphysics of Morals *argues that only one thing is good intrinsically, that is, in itself: a good will. He argues that rational beings will recognize that they are subject to the moral law, which he formulates in several versions of what he takes to be single moral principle: the categorical imperative. From it stem human rights, human dignity, and everything else essential to morality. (Source: Reprinted from* Grounding of the Metaphysics of Morals, *translated and edited by James A. Ellington. Copyright © 1987 by Hackett Publishing Company Inc., Indianapolis, IN, and Cambridge, MA.)*

QUESTIONS FOR REFLECTION

1. What is an imperative? What is the difference between hypothetical and categorical imperatives?

2. Why must a categorical imperative be established *a priori*, that is, independently of experience?

3. Kant gives several different formulations of the categorical imperative. What are they? Why does he take them to be equivalent?

4. Consider Kant's four examples. How does he apply the categorical imperative to each?

5. What is autonomy? How does it relate to dignity?

SECOND SECTION / TRANSITION FROM POPULAR MORALITY TO A METAPHYSICS OF MORALS

. . . Everything in nature works according to laws. Only a rational being has the power to act according to his conception of laws, i.e., according to principles, and thereby has he a will. Since the derivation of actions from laws requires reason, the will is nothing but practical reason. If reason infallibly determines the will, then in the case of such a being actions which are recognized to be objectively necessary are also subjectively necessary, i.e., the will is a faculty of choosing only that which reason, independently of inclination, recognizes as being practically necessary, i.e., as good. But if reason of itself does not sufficiently determine the will, and if the will submits also to subjective conditions (certain incentives) which do not always agree with objective conditions; in a word, if the will does not in itself completely accord with reason (as is actually the case with men), then actions which are recognized as objectively necessary are subjectively contingent, and the determination of such a will according to objective laws is necessitation. That is to say that the relation of objective laws to a will not thoroughly good is represented as the determination of the will of a rational being by principles of reason which the will does not necessarily follow because of its own nature.

The representation of an objective principle insofar as it necessitates the will is called a command (of reason), and the formula of the command is called an imperative.

All imperatives are expressed by an *ought* and thereby indicate the relation of an objective law of reason to a will that is not necessarily determined by this law because of its subjective constitution (the relation of necessitation). Imperatives say that something would be good to do or to refrain from doing, but they say it to a will that does not always therefore do something simply because it has been represented to the will as something good to do. That is practically good which determines the will by means of representations of reason and hence not by subjective causes, but objectively, i.e., on grounds valid for every rational being as such. It is

distinguished from the pleasant as that which influences the will only by means of sensation from merely subjective causes, which hold only for this or that person's senses but do not hold as a principle of reason valid for everyone.

A perfectly good will would thus be quite as much subject to objective laws (of the good), but could not be conceived as thereby necessitated to act in conformity with law, inasmuch as it can of itself, according to its subjective constitution, be determined only by the representation of the good. Therefore no imperatives hold for the divine will, and in general for a holy will; the *ought* is here out of place, because the *would* is already of itself necessarily in agreement with the law. Consequently, imperatives are only formulas for expressing the relation of objective laws of willing in general to the subjective imperfection of the will of this or that rational being, e.g., the human will.

Now all imperatives command either hypothetically or categorically. The former represent the practical necessity of a possible action as a means for attaining something else that one wants (or may possibly want). The categorical imperative would be one which represented an action as objectively necessary in itself, without reference to another end.

Every practical law represents a possible action as good and hence as necessary for a subject who is practically determinable by reason; therefore all imperatives are formulas for determining an action which is necessary according to the principle of a will that is good in some way. Now if the action would be good merely as a means to something else, so is the imperative hypothetical. But if the action is represented as good in itself, and hence as necessary in a will which of itself conforms to reason as the principle of the will, then the imperative is categorical.

An imperative thus says what action possible by me would be good, and it presents the practical rule in relation to a will which does not forthwith perform an action simply because it is good, partly because the subject does not always know that the action is good and partly because (even if he does know it is good) his maxims might yet be opposed to the objective principles of practical reason.

A hypothetical imperative thus says only that an action is good for some purpose, either possible or actual. In the first case it is a problematic practical principal; in the second case an assertoric one. A categorical imperative, which declares an action to be of itself objectively necessary without reference to any purpose, i.e., without any other end, holds as an apodeictic practical principle.

Whatever is possible only through the powers of some rational being can be thought of as a possible purpose of some will. Consequently, there are in fact infinitely many principles of action insofar as they are represented as necessary for attaining a possible purpose achievable by them. All sciences have a practical part consisting of problems saying that some end is possible for us and of imperatives telling us how it can be attained. These can, therefore, be called in general imperatives of skill. Here there is no question at all whether the end is reasonable and good, but there is only a question as to what must be done to attain it. The prescriptions needed by a doctor in order to make his patient thoroughly healthy and by a poisoner in order to make sure of killing his victim are of equal value so far as each serves to bring about its purpose perfectly. Since there cannot be known in early youth what ends may be presented to us in the course of life, parents especially seek to have their children learn many different kinds of things, and they provide for skill in the use of means to all sorts of arbitrary ends, among which they cannot determine whether any one of them could in the future become an actual purpose for their ward, though there is always the possibility that he might adopt it. Their concern is so great that they commonly neglect to form and correct their children's judgment regarding the worth of things which might be chosen as ends.

There is, however, one end that can be presupposed as actual for all rational beings (so far as they are dependent beings to whom imperatives apply); and thus there is one purpose which they not merely can have but which can certainly be assumed to be such that they all do have by a natural necessity, and this is happiness. A hypothetical imperative which represents the practical necessity of an action as means for the promotion of happiness is assertoric. It may be expounded not simply as necessary to an uncertain, merely possible purpose,

but as necessary to a purpose which can be presupposed a priori and with certainty as being present in everyone because it belongs to his essence. Now skill in the choice of means to one's own greatest well-being can be called prudence in the narrowest sense. And thus the imperative that refers to the choice of means to one's own happiness, i.e., the precept of prudence, still remains hypothetical; the action is commanded not absolutely but only as a means to a further purpose.

Finally, there is one imperative which immediately commands a certain conduct without having as its condition any other purpose to be attained by it. This imperative is categorical. It is not concerned with the matter of the action and its intended result, but rather with the form of the action and the principle from which it follows; what is essentially good in the action consists in the mental disposition, let the consequences be what they may. This imperative may be called that of morality. . . .

If I think of a hypothetical imperative in general, I do not know beforehand what it will contain until its condition is given. But if I think of a categorical imperative, I know immediately what it contains. For since, besides the law, the imperative contains only the necessity that the maxim should accord with this law, while the law contains no condition to restrict it, there remains nothing but the universality of a law as such with which the maxim of the action should conform. This conformity alone is properly what is represented as necessary by the imperative.

Hence there is only one categorical imperatve and it is this: Act only according to that maxim whereby you can at the same time will that it should become a universal law.

Now if all imperatives of duty can be derived from this one imperative as their principle, then there can at least be shown what is understood by the concept of duty and what it means, even though there is left undecided whether what is called duty may not be an empty concept.

The universality of law according to which effects are produced constitutes what is properly called nature in the most general sense (as to form), i.e., the existence of things as far as determined by universal laws. Accordingly, the universal imperative of duty may be expressed thus: Act as if the maxim of your action were to become through your will a universal law of nature.

We shall now enumerate some duties, following the usual division of them into duties to ourselves and to others and into perfect and imperfect duties.

1. A man reduced to despair by a series of misfortunes feels sick of life but is still so far in possession of his reason that he can ask himself whether taking his own life would not be contrary to his duty to himself. Now he asks whether the maxim of his action could become a universal law of nature. But his maxim is this: from self-love I make as my principle to shorten my life when its continued duration threatens more evil than it promises satisfaction. There only remains the question as to whether this principle of self-love can become a universal law of nature. One sees at once a contradiction in a system of nature whose law would destroy life by means of the very same feeling that acts so as to stimulate the furtherance of life, and hence there could be no existence as a system of nature. Therefore, such a maxim cannot possibly hold as a universal law of nature and is, consequently, wholly opposed to the supreme principle of all duty.

2. Another man in need finds himself forced to borrow money. He knows well that he won't be able to repay it, but he sees also that he will not get any loan unless he firmly promises to repay it within a fixed time. He wants to make such a promise, but he still has conscience enough to ask himself whether it is not permissible and is contrary to duty to get out of difficulty in this way. Suppose, however, that he decides to do so. The maxim of his action would then be expressed as follows: when I believe myself to be in need of money, I will borrow money and promise to pay it back, although I know that I can never do so. Now this principle of self-love or personal advantage may perhaps be quite compatible with one's entire future welfare, but the question is now whether it is right. I then transform the requirement of self-love into a universal law and put the question thus: how would things stand if my maxim were to become a universal law? He then sees at once that such a maxim could never hold as a universal law of nature and be consistent with itself, but must necessarily be self-contradictory. For the universality of a law which says that anyone believ-

ing himself to be in difficulty could promise whatever he pleases with the intention of not keeping it would make promising itself and the end to be attained thereby quite impossible, inasmuch as no one would believe what was promised him but would merely laugh at all such utterances as being vain pretenses.

3. A third finds in himself a talent whose cultivation could make him a man useful in many respects. But he finds himself in comfortable circumstances and prefers to indulge in pleasure rather than to bother himself about broadening and improving his fortunate natural aptitudes. But he asks himself further whether his maxim of neglecting his natural gifts, besides agreeing of itself with his propensity to indulgence, might agree also with what is called duty. He then sees that a system of nature could indeed always subsist according to such a universal law, even though every man (like South Sea Islanders) should let his talents rust and resolve to devote his life entirely to idleness, indulgence, propagation, and, in a word, to enjoyment. But he cannot possibly will that this should become a universal law of nature or be implanted in us as such a law by a natural instinct. For as a rational being he necessarily wills that all his faculties should be developed, inasmuch as they are given him for all sorts of possible purposes.

4. A fourth man finds things going well for himself but sees others (whom he could help) struggling with great hardships; and he thinks: what does it matter to me? Let everybody be as happy as Heaven wills or as he can make himself; I shall take nothing from him nor even envy him; but I have no desire to contribute anything to his well-being or to his assistance when in need. If such a way of thinking were to become a universal law of nature, the human race admittedly could very well subsist and doubtless could subsist even better than when everyone prates about sympathy and benevolence and even on occasion exerts himself to practice them but, on the other hand, also cheats when he can, betrays the rights of man, or otherwise violates them. But even though it is possible that a universal law of nature could subsist in accordance with that maxim, still it is impossible to will that such a principle should hold everywhere as a law of nature. For

a will which resolved in this way would contradict itself, inasmuch as cases might often arise in which one would have need of the love and sympathy of others and in which he would deprive himself, by such a law of nature springing from his own will, of all hope of the aid he wants for himself.

These are some of the many actual duties, or at least what are taken to be such, whose derivation from the single principle cited above is clear. We must be able to will that a maxim of our action become a universal law; this is the canon for morally estimating any of our actions. Some actions are so constituted that their maxims cannot without contradition even be thought as a universal law of nature, much less be willed as what should become one. In the case of others this internal impossibility is indeed not found, but there is still no possibility of willing that their maxim should be raised to the universality of a law of nature, because such a will would contradict itself. There is no difficulty in seeing that the former kind of action conflicts with strict or narrow [perfect] (irremissible) duty, while the second kind conflicts only with broad [imperfect] (meritorious) duty. By means of these examples there has thus been fully set forth how all duties depend as regards the kind of obligation (not the object of their action) upon the one principle.

If we now attend to ourselves in any transgression of a duty, we find that we actually do not will that our maxim should become a universal law—because this is impossible for us—but rather that the opposite of this maxim should remain a law universally. We only take the liberty of making an exception to the law for ourselves (or just for this one time) to the advantage of our inclination. Consequently, if we weighed up everything from one and the same standpoint, namely, that of reason, we would find a contradiction in our own will, viz., that a certain principle be objectively necessary as a universal law and yet subjectively not hold universally but should admit of exceptions. But since we at one moment regard our action from the standpoint of a will wholly in accord with reason and then at another moment regard the very same action from the standpoint of a will affected by inclination, there is really no contradiction here. Rather, there is an opposition (*antagonismus*) of inclination to the pre-

cept of reason, whereby the universality (*universalitas*) of the principle is changed into a mere generality (*generalitas*) so that the practical principle of reason may meet the maxim halfway. Although this procedure cannot be justified in our own impartial judgment, yet it does show that we actually acknowledge the validity of the categorical imperative and (with all respect for it) merely allow ourselves a few exceptions which, as they seem to us, are unimportant and forced upon us.

We have thus at least shown that if duty is a concept which is to have significance and real legislative authority for our actions, then such duty can be expressed only in categorical imperatives but not at all in hypothetical ones. We have also—and this is already a great deal—exhibited clearly and definitely for every application what is the content of the categorical imperative, which must contain the principle of all duty (if there is such a thing at all). But we have not yet advanced far enough to prove a priori that there actually is an imperative of this kind, that there is a practical law which of itself commands absolutely and without any incentives, and that following this law is duty. . . .

The will is thought of as a faculty of determining itself to action in accordance with the representation of certain laws, and such a faculty can be found only in rational beings. Now what serves the will as the objective ground of its self-determination is an end; and if this end is given by reason alone, then it must be equally valid for all rational beings. On the other hand, what contains merely the ground of the possibility of the action, whose effect is an end, is called the means. The subjective ground of desire is the incentive; the objective ground of volition is the motive. Hence there arises the distinction between subjective ends, which rest on incentives, and objective ends, which depend on motives valid for every rational being. Practical principles are formal when they abstract from all subjective ends; they are material, however, when they are founded upon subjective ends, and hence upon certain incentives. The ends which a rational being arbitrarily proposes to himself as effects of this action (material ends) are all merely relative, for only their relation to a specially constituted faculty of desire in the subject gives them their worth. Consequently, such worth cannot provide any universal principles, which are valid and necessary for all rational beings and, furthermore, are valid for every volition, i.e., cannot provide any practical laws. Therefore, all such relative ends can be grounds only for hypothetical imperatives.

But let us suppose that there were something whose existence has in itself an absolute worth, something which as an end in itself could be a ground of determinate laws. In it, and in it alone, would there be the ground of a possible categorical imperative, i.e., of a practical law.

Now I say that man, and in general every rational being, exists as an end in himself and not merely as a means to be arbitrarily used by this or that will. He must in all his actions, whether directed to himself or to other rational beings, always be regarded at the same time as an end. All the objects of inclinations have only a conditioned value; for if there were not these inclinations and the needs founded on them, then their object would be without value. But the inclinations themselves, being sources of needs, are so far from having an absolute value such as to render them desirable for their own sake that the universal wish of every rational being must be, rather, to be wholly free from them. Accordingly, the value of any object obtainable by our action is always conditioned. Beings whose existence depends not on our will but on nature have, nevertheless, if they are not rational beings, only a relative value as means and are therefore called things. On the other hand, rational beings are called persons inasmuch as their nature already marks them out as ends in themselves, i.e., as something which is not to be used merely as means and hence there is imposed thereby a limit on all arbitrary use of such beings, which are thus objects of respect. Persons are, therefore, not merely subjective ends, whose existence as an effect of our actions has a value for us; but such beings are objective ends, i.e., exist as ends in themselves. Such an end is one for which there can be substituted no other end to which such beings should serve merely as means, for otherwise nothing at all of absolute value would be found anywhere. But if all value were conditioned and hence contingent, then no supreme practical principle could be found for reason at all.

If then there is to be a supreme practical principle and, as far as the human will is concerned, a categorical imperative, then it must be such that from the conception of what is necessarily an end for everyone because this end is an end in itself it constitutes an objective principle of the will and can hence serve as a practical law. The ground of such a principle is this: rational nature exists as an end in itself. In this way man necessarily thinks of his own existence; thus far is it a subjective principle of human actions. But in this way also does every other rational being think of his existence on the same rational ground that holds also for me; hence it is at the same time an objective principle, from which, as a supreme practical ground, all laws of the will must be able to be derived. The practical imperative will therefore be the following: Act in such a way that you treat humanity, whether in your own person or in the person of another, always at the same time as an end and never simply as a means. We now want to see whether this can be carried out in practice.

Let us keep to our previous examples.

First, as regards the concept of necessary duty to oneself, the man who contemplates suicide will ask himself whether his action can be consistent with the idea of humanity as an end in itself. If he destroys himself in order to escape from a difficult situation, then he is making use of his person merely as a means so as to maintain a tolerable condition till the end of his life. Man, however, is not a thing and hence is not something to be used merely as a means; he must in all his actions always be regarded as an end in himself. Therefore, I cannot dispose of man in my own person by mutilating, damaging, or killing him. (A more exact determination of this principle so as to avoid all misunderstanding, e.g., regarding the amputation of limbs in order to save oneself, or the exposure of one's life to danger in order to save it, and so on, must here be omitted; such questions belong to morals proper.)

Second, as concerns necessary or strict duty to others, the man who intends to make a false promise will immediately see that he intends to make use of another man merely as a means to an end which the latter does not likewise hold. For the man whom I want to use for my own purposes by such a promise cannot possibly concur with my way of acting toward him and hence cannot himself hold the end of this action. This conflict with the principle of duty to others becomes even clearer when instances of attacks on the freedom and property of others are considered. For then it becomes clear that a transgressor of the rights of men intends to make use of the persons of others merely as a means, without taking into consideration that, as rational beings, they should always be esteemed at the same time as ends, i.e., be esteemed only as beings who must themselves be able to hold the very same action as an end.

Third, with regard to contingent (meritorious) duty to oneself, it is not enough that the action does not conflict with humanity in our own person as an end in itself; the action must also harmonize with this end. Now there are in humanity capacities for greater perfection which belong to the end that nature has in view as regards humanity in our own person. To neglect these capacities might perhaps be consistent with the maintenance of humanity as an end in itself, but would not be consistent with the advancement of this end.

Fourth, concerning meritorious duty to others, the natural end that all men have is their own happiness. Now humanity might indeed subsist if nobody contributed anything to the happiness of others, provided he did not intentionally impair their happiness. But this, after all, would harmonize only negatively and not positively with humanity as an end in itself, if everyone does not also strive, as much as he can, to further the ends of others. For the ends of any subject who is an end in himself must as far as possible be my ends also, if that conception of an end in itself is to have its full effect in me.

This principle of humanity and of every rational nature generally as an end in itself is the supreme limiting condition of every man's freedom of action. This principle is not borrowed from experience, first, because of its universality, inasmuch as it applies to all rational beings generally, and no experience is capable of determining anything about them; and, secondly, because in experience (subjectively) humanity is not thought of as an end of men, i.e., as an object that we of ourselves actually make our end which as a law ought to constitute the supreme limiting condition of all subjective ends (whatever they may be); and hence this principle must arise from pure reason [and not from experience]. That is to say that the ground of all practical legislation lies objectively in the rule and in the form of universality, which (according to the first principle) makes the rule capable of being a law (say, for example, a law of nature). Subjectively, however, the ground of all practical legislation lies in the end; but (according to the second principle) the subject of all ends is every rational being as an end in himself. From this there now follows the third practical principle of the will as the supreme condition of the will's conformity with universal practical reason, viz., the idea of the will of every rational being as a will that legislates universal law.

According to this principle all maxims are rejected which are not consistent with the will's own legislation of universal law. The will is thus not merely subject to the law but is subject to the law in such a way that it must be regarded also as legislating for itself and only on this account as being subject to the law (of which it can regard itself as the author). . . .

When we look back upon all previous attempts that have been made to discover the principle of morality, these is no reason now to wonder why they one and all had to fail. Man was viewed as bound to laws by his duty; but it was not seen that man is subject only to his own, yet universal, legislation and that he is bound only to act in accordance with his own will, which is, however, a will purposed by nature to legislate universal laws. For when man is thought as being merely subject to a law (whatever it might be), then the law had to carry with it some interest functioning as an attracting stimulus or as a constraining force for obedience, inasmuch as the law did not arise as a law from his own will. Rather, in order that his will conform with law, it had to be necessitated by something else to act in a certain way. By this absolutely necessary conclusion, however, all the labor spent in finding a supreme ground for duty was irretrievably lost; duty was never discovered, but only the necessity of acting from a certain interest. This might be either one's own interest or another's, but either way the imperative had to be always conditional and could never possibly serve as a moral command. I want, therefore, to call my principle the principle of the autonomy of the will, in contrast with every other principle, which I accordingly count under heteronomy.

The concept of every rational being as one who must regard himself as legislating universal law by all his will's maxims, so that he may judge himself and his actions from this point of view, leads to another very fruitful concept, which depends on the aforementioned one, viz., that of a kingdom of ends.

By "kingdom" I understand a systematic union of different rational beings through common laws. Now laws determine ends as regards their universal validity; therefore, if one abstracts from the personal differences of rational beings and also from all content of their private ends, then it will be possible to think of a whole of all ends in systematic connection (a whole both of rational being as ends in themselves and also of the particular ends which each may set for himself); that is, one can think of a kingdom of ends that is possible on the aforesaid principles.

For all rational beings stand under the law that each of them should treat himself and all others never merely as means but always at the same time as an end in himself. Hereby arises a systematic union of rational beings through common objective laws, i.e., a kingdom that may be called a kingdom of ends (certainly only an ideal), inasmuch as these laws have in view the very relation of such beings to one another as ends and means.

A rational being belongs to the kingdom of ends as a member when he legislates in it universal laws while also being himself subject to these laws. He belongs to it as sovereign, when as legislator he is himself subject to the will of no other.

A rational being must always regard himself as legislator in a kingdom of ends rendered possible by freedom of the will, whether as member or as sovereign. The position of the latter can be maintained not merely through the maxims of his will but only if he is a completely independent being without needs and with unlimited power adequate to his will.

Hence morality consists in the relation of all action to that legislation whereby alone a kingdom of ends is possible. This legislation must be found in every rational being and must be able to arise from his will, whose principle then is never to act on any maxim except such as can also be a universal law and hence such as the will can thereby regard itself as at the same time the legislator of universal law. If now the maxims do not by their very nature already necessarily conform with this objective principle of rational beings as legislating universal laws, then the necessity of acting on that principle is called practi-

cal necessitation, i.e., duty. Duty does not apply to the sovereign in the kingdom of ends, but it does apply to every member and to each in the same degree.

The practical necessity of acting according to this principle, i.e., duty, does not rest at all on feelings, impulses, and inclinations, but only on the relation of rational beings to one another, a relation in which the will of a rational being must always be regarded at the same time as legislative, because otherwise he could not be thought of as an end in himself. Reason, therefore, relates every maxim of the will as legislating universal laws to every other will and also to every action toward oneself; it does so not on account of any other practical motive or future advantage but rather from the idea of the dignity of a rational being who obeys no law except what he at the same time enacts himself.

In the kingdom of ends everything has either a price or a dignity. Whatever has a price can be replaced by something else as its equivalent; on the other hand, whatever is above all price, and therefore admits of no equivalent, has a dignity.

Whatever has reference to general human inclinations and needs has a market price; whatever, without presupposing any need, accords with a certain taste, i.e., a delight in the mere unpurposive play of our mental powers, has an affective price; but that which constitutes the condition under which alone something can be an end in itself has not merely a relative worth, i.e., a price, but has an intrinsic worth, i.e., dignity.

Now morality is the condition under which alone a rational being can be an end in himself, for only thereby can he be a legislating member in the kingdom of ends. Hence morality and humanity, insofar as it is capable of morality, alone have dignity. Skill and diligence in work have a market price; wit, lively imagination, and humor have an affective price; but fidelity to promises and benevolence based on principles (not on instinct) have intrinsic worth. Neither nature nor art contain anything which in default of these could be put in their place; for their worth consists, not in the effects which arise from them, nor in the advantage and profit which they provide, but in mental dispositions, i.e., in the maxims of the will which are ready in this way to manifest themselves in action, even if they are not favored with success. Such actions also need no recommendation from any subjective disposition or taste so as to meet with immediate favor and delight; there is no need of any immediate propensity or feeling toward them. They exhibit the will performing them as an object of immediate respect; and nothing but reason is required to impose them upon the will, which is not to be cajoled into them, since in the case of duties such cajoling would be a contradiction. This estimation, therefore, lets the worth of such a disposition be recognized as dignity and puts it infinitely beyond all price, with which it cannot in the least be brought into competition or comparison without, as it were, violating its sanctity.

What then is it that entitles the morally good disposition, or virtue, to make such lofty claims? It is nothing less than the share which such a disposition affords the rational being of legislating universal laws, so that he is fit to be a member in a possible kingdom of ends, for which his own nature has already determined him as an end in himself and therefore as a legislator in the kingdom of ends. Thereby is he free as regards all laws of nature, and he obeys only those laws which he gives to himself. Accordingly, his maxims can belong to a universal legislation to which he at the same time subjects himself. For nothing can have any worth other than what the law determines. But the legislation itself which determines all worth must for that very reason have dignity, i.e., unconditional and incomparable worth; and the word "respect" alone provides a suitable expression for the esteem which a rational being must have for it. Hence autonomy is the ground of the dignity of human nature and of every rational nature. . . .

We can now end where we started in the beginning, viz., the concept of an unconditionally good will. That will is absolutely good which cannot be evil, i.e., whose maxim, when made into a universal law, can never conflict with itself. This principle is therefore also its supreme law: Act always according to that maxim whose universality as a law you can at the same time will. This is the only condition under which a will can never be in conflict with itself, and such an imperative is categorical. Inasmuch as the validity of the will as a universal law for possible actions is analogous to the universal connection of the existence of things in accordance with universal laws, which is the formal aspect of nature in general, the categorical imperative can

also be expressed thus: Act according to maxims which can at the same time have for their object themselves as universal laws of nature. In this way there is provided the formula for an absolutely good will.

Rational nature is distinguished from the rest of nature by the fact that it sets itself an end. This end would be the matter of every good will. But in the idea of an absolutely good will—good without any qualifying condition (of attaining this or that end)—complete abstraction must be made from every end that has to come about as an effect (since such would make every will only relatively good). And so the end must here be conceived, not as an end to be effected, but as an independently existing end. Hence it must be conceived only negatively, i.e., as an end which should never be acted against and therefore as one which in all willing must never be regarded merely as means but must always be esteemed at the same time as an end. Now this end can be nothing but the subject of all possible ends themselves, because this subject is at the same time the subject of a possible absolutely good will; for such a will cannot without contradiction be subordinated to any other object. The principle: So act in regard to every rational being (yourself and others) that he may at the same time count in your maxim as an end in himself, is thus basically the same as the principle: Act on a maxim which at the same time contains in itself its own universal validity for every rational being. That in the use of means for every end my maxim should be restricted to the condition of its universal validity as a law for every subject says just the same as that a subject of ends, i.e., a rational being himself, must be made the ground for all maxims of actions and must thus be used never merely as means but as the supreme limiting condition in the use of all means, i.e., always at the same time as an end.

Now there follows incontestably from this that every rational being as an end in himself must be able to regard himself with reference to all laws to which he may be subject as being at the same time the legislator of universal law, for just this very fitness of his maxims for the legislation of universal law distinguishes him as an end in himself. There follows also that his dignity (prerogative) of being above all the mere things of nature implies that his maxims must be taken from the viewpoint that regards himself, as well as every other rational being, as being legislative beings (and hence are they called persons). In this way there is possible a world of rational beings (*mundus intelligibilis*) as a kingdom of ends, because of the legislation belonging to all persons as members. Therefore, every rational being must so act as if he were through his maxim always a legislating member in the universal kingdom of ends. The formal principle of these maxims is this: So act as if your maxims were to serve at the same time as a universal law (for all rational beings). Thus a kingdom of ends is possible only on the analogy of a kingdom of nature; yet the former is possible only through maxims, i.e., self-imposed rules, while the latter is possible only through laws of efficient causes necessitated from without. Regardless of this difference and even though nature as a whole is viewed as a machine, yet insofar as nature stands in a relation to rational beings as its ends, it is on this account given the name of a kingdom of nature. Such a kingdom of ends would actually be realized through maxims whose rule is prescribed to all rational beings by the categorical imperative, if these maxims were universally obeyed. But even if a rational being himself strictly obeys such a maxim, he cannot for that reason count on everyone else's being true to it, nor can he expect the kingdom of nature and its purposive order to be in harmony with him as a fitting member of a kingdom of ends made possible by himself, i.e., he cannot expect the kingdom of nature to favor his expectation of happiness. Nevertheless, the law: Act in accordance with the maxims of a member legislating universal laws for a merely possible kingdom of ends, remains in full force, since it commands categorically. And just in this lies the paradox that merely the dignity of humanity as rational nature without any further end or advantage to be thereby gained—and hence respect for a mere idea—should yet serve as an inflexible precept for the will; and that just this very independence of the maxims from all such incentives should constitute the sublimity of maxims and the worthiness of every rational subject to be a legislative member in the kingdom of ends, for otherwise he would have to be regarded as subject only to the natural law of his own needs. And even if the kingdom of nature as well as the kingdom of ends were thought of as both united under one sovereign so that the latter kingdom would thereby no longer remain a mere idea but would acquire true reality, then indeed the kingdom of ends would gain the addition of a strong incentive, but never any increase in its intrinsic worth. For this sole absolute legislator must, in spite of all this, always be thought of as judging the worth of rational beings solely by the disinterested conduct prescribed to themselves by means of this idea alone. The essence of things is not altered by their external relations; and whatever without reference to such relations alone constitutes the absolute worth of man is also what he must be judged by, whoever the judge may be, even the Supreme Being. Hence morality is the relation of actions to the autonomy of the will, i.e., to the possible legislation of universal law by means of the maxims of the will. That action which is compatible with the autonomy of the will is permitted; that which is not compatible is forbidden. That will whose maxims are necessarily in accord with the laws of autonomy is a holy, or absolutely good, will. The dependence of a will which is not absolutely good upon the principle of autonomy (i.e., moral necessitation) is obligation, which cannot therefore be applied to a holy will. The objective necessity of an action from obligation is called duty.

From what has just been said, there can now easily be explained how it happens that, although in the concept of duty we think of subjection to the law, yet at the same time we thereby ascribe a certain dignity and sublimity to the person who fulfills all his duties. For not insofar as he is subject to the moral law does he have sublimity, but rather has it only insofar as with regard to this very same law he is at the same time legislative, and only thereby is he subject to the law. We have also shown above how neither fear nor inclination, but solely respect for the law, is the incentive which can give an action moral worth. Our own will, insofar as it were to act only under the condition of its being able to legislate universal law by means of its maxims—this will, ideally possible for us, is the proper object of respect. And the dignity of humanity consists just in its capacity to legislate universal law, though with the condition of humanity's being at the same time itself subject to this very same legislation.

EDMUND BURKE

from *Reflections on the Revolution in France* (1790)

(*Source: Reprinted from Edmund Burke,* Reflections on the Revolution in France. *London: Printed for J. Dodsley, 1790.*)

QUESTIONS FOR REFLECTION

1. How does Burke distinguish "real rights" from pretenders?

2. What real rights, in Burke's opinion, do people have? On what are these rights based?

3. What, according to Burke, is the purpose of government? Why does this lead Burke to claim that "the restraints on men, as well as their liberties, are to be reckoned among their rights"?

4. Why does reform require "infinite caution," in Burke's view? Why does Burke stress the importance of tradition?

5. What is the role of "natural feeling" and prejudice in Burke's theory?

6. How do we resolve conflicts between rights, according to Burke?

I t is no wonder, therefore, that with these ideas of everything in their constitution and government at home, either in church or state, as illegitimate and usurped, or at best as a vain mockery, they look abroad with an eager and passionate enthusiasm. Whilst they are possessed by these notions, it is vain to talk to them of the practice of their ancestors, the fundamental laws of their country, the fixed form of a constitution whose merits are confirmed by the solid test of long experience and an increasing public strength and national prosperity. They despise experience as the wisdom of unlettered men; and as for the rest, they have wrought underground a mine that will blow up, at one grand explosion, all examples of antiquity, all precedents, charters, and acts of parliament. They have "the rights of men." Against these there can be no prescription, against these no agreement is binding; these admit no temperament and no compromise; anything withheld from their full demand is so much of fraud and injustice. Against these their rights of men let no government look for security in the length of its continuance, or in the justice and lenity of its administration. The objections of these speculatists, if its forms do not quadrate with their theories, are as valid against such an old and beneficent government as against the most violent tyranny or the greenest unsurpation. They are always at issue with governments, not on a question of abuse, but a question of competency and a question of title. I have nothing to say to the clumsy subtilty of their political metaphysics. Let them be their amusement in the schools.—*"Illa se jactet in aula Aeolus, et clauso ventorum carcere regnet".** —But let them not break prison to burst like a *Levanter,* to sweep the earth with their hurricane and to break up the fountains of the great deep to overwhelm us.

Far am I from denying in theory, full as far is my heart from withholding in practice (if I were of power to give or to withhold) the *real* rights of men.

* "Let Aeolus bluster [literally, "fling himself about"] in that hall, and reign in the closed prison of the winds" (Virgil, *Aeneid* I, 140–41). —ED.

In denying their false claims of right, I do not mean to injure those which are real, and are such as their pretended rights would totally destroy. If civil society be made for the advantage of man, all the advantages for which it is made become his right. It is an institution of beneficence; and law itself is only beneficence acting by a rule. Men have a right to live by that rule; they have a right to do justice, as between their fellows, whether their fellows are in public function or in ordinary occupation. They have a right to the fruits of their industry and to the means of making their industry fruitful. They have a right to the acquisitions of their parents, to the nourishment and improvement of their offspring, to instruction in life, and to consolation in death. Whatever each man can separately do, without trespassing upon others, he has a right to do for himself; and he has a right to a fair portion of all which society, with all its combinations of skill and force, can do in his favor. In this partnership all men have equal rights, but not to equal things. He that has but five shillings in the partnership has as good a right to it as he that has five hundred pounds has to his larger proportion. But he has not a right to an equal dividend in the product of the joint stock; and as to the share of power, authority, and direction which each individual ought to have in the management of the state, that I must deny to be amongst the direct original rights of man in civil society; for I have in my contemplation the civil social man, and no other. It is a thing to be settled by convention.

If civil society be the offspring of convention, that convention must be its law. That convention must limit and modify all the descriptions of constitution which are formed under it. Every sort of legislative, judicial, or executory power are its creatures. They can have no being in any other state of things; *and how can any man claim under the conventions of civil rights which do not so much as suppose its existence— rights which are absolutely repugnant to it?* One of the first motives to civil society, and which becomes one of its fundamental rules, is *that no man should be judge in his own cause.* By this each person has at once divested himself of the first fundamental right of uncovenanted man, that is, to judge for himself and to assert his own cause. He abdicates all right to be his own governor. He inclusively, in a great measure, abandons the right of self-defense, the first law

of nature. Men cannot enjoy the rights of an uncivil and of a civil state together. That he may obtain justice, he gives up his right of determining what it is in points the most essential to him. That he may secure some liberty, he makes a surrender in trust of the whole of it.

Government is not made in virtue of natural rights, which may and do exist in total independence of it, and exist in much greater clearness and in a much greater degree of abstract perfection; but their abstract perfection is their practical defect. By having a right to everything they want everything. Government is a contrivance of human wisdom to provide for human *wants.* Men have a right that these wants should be provided for by this wisdom. Among these wants is to be reckoned the want, out of civil society, of a sufficient restraint upon their passions. Society requires not only that the passions of individuals should be subjected, but that even in the mass and body, as well as in the individuals, the inclinations of men should frequently be thwarted, their will controlled, and their passions brought into subjection. This can only be done *by a power out of themselves,* and not, in the exercise of its function, subject to that will and to those passions which it is its office to bridle and subdue. In this sense the restraints on men, as well as their liberties, are to be reckoned among their rights. But as the liberties and the restrictions vary with times and circumstances and admit to infinite modifications, they cannot be settled upon any abstract rule; and nothing is so foolish as to discuss them upon that principle.

The moment you abate anything from the full rights of men, each to govern himself, and suffer any artificial, positive limitation upon those rights, from that moment the whole organization of government becomes a consideration of convenience. This it is which makes the constitution of a state and the due distribution of its powers a matter of the most delicate and complicated skill. It requires a deep knowledge of human nature and human necessities, and of the things which facilitate or obstruct the various ends which are to be pursued by the mechanism of civil institutions. The state is to have recruits to its strength, and remedies to its distempers. What is the use of discussing a man's abstract right to food or medicine? The question is upon the method of procuring and administering them. In that deliberation I shall always advise to call in the aid of the farmer and the physician rather than the professor of metaphysics.

The science of constructing a commonwealth, or renovating it, or reforming it, is, like every other experimental science, not to be taught *a priori*. Nor is it a short experience that can instruct us in that practical science, because the real effects of moral causes are not always immediate; but that which in the first instance is prejudicial may be excellent in its remoter operation, and its excellence may arise even from the ill effects it produces in the beginning. The reverse also happens: and very plausible schemes, with very pleasing commencements, have often shameful and lamentable conclusions. In states there are often some obscure and almost latent causes, things which appear at first view of little moment, on which a very great part of its prosperity or adversity may most essentially depend. The science of government being therefore so practical in itself and intended for such practical purposes—a matter which requires experience, and even more experience than any person can gain in his whole life, however sagacious and observing he may be—it is with infinite caution that any man ought to venture upon pulling down an edifice which has answered in any tolerable degree for ages the common purposes of society, or on building it up again without having models and patterns of approved utility before his eyes.

These metaphysic rights entering into common life, like rays of light which pierce into a dense medium, are by the laws of nature refracted from their straight line. Indeed, in the gross and complicated mass of human passions and concerns the primitive rights of men undergo such a variety of refractions and reflections that it becomes absurd to talk of them as if they continued in the simplicity of their original direction. The nature of man is intricate; the objects of society are of the greatest possible complexity; and, therefore, no simple disposition or direction of power can be suitable either to man's nature or to the quality of his affairs. When I hear the simplicity of contrivance aimed at and boasted of in any new political constitutions, I am at no loss to decide that the artificers are grossly ignorant of

their trade or totally negligent of their duty. The simple governments are fundamentally defective, to say no worse of them. If you were to contemplate society in but one point of view, all these simple modes of polity are infinitely captivating. In effect each would answer its single end much more perfectly than the more complex is able to attain all its complex purposes. But it is better that the whole should be imperfectly and anomalously answered than that, while some parts are provided for with great exactness, others might be totally neglected or perhaps materially injured by the over-care of a favorite member.

The pretended rights of these theorists are all extremes; and in proportion as they are metaphysically true, they are morally and politically false. The rights of men are in a sort of *middle,* incapable of definition, but not impossible to be discerned. The rights of men in governments are their advantages; and these are often in balances between differences of good, in compromises sometimes between good and evil, and sometimes between evil and evil. Political reason is a computing principle: adding, subtracting, multiplying, and dividing, morally and not metaphysically or mathematically, true moral denominations.

By these theorists the right of the people is almost sophistically confounded with their power. The body of the community, whenever it can come to act, can meet with no effectual resistance; but till power and right are the same, the whole body of them has no right inconsistent with virtue, and the first of all virtues, prudence. Men have no right to what is not reasonable and to what is not for their benefit; for though a pleasant writer said, *liceat perire poetis,** when one of them, in cold blood, is said to have leaped into the flames of a volcanic revolution, *ardentem frigidus Aetnam insiluit,†* I consider such a frolic rather as an unjustifiable poetic license than as one of the franchises of Parnassus‡; and whether he was a poet, or divine, or politician that chose to

---

* "Poets are permitted to perish." —Ed.

† "In cold blood he jumped into burning Etna" (Horace, *Ars Poetica* 465–66). "He" refers to Empedocles. —Ed.

‡ Parnassus: a mountain that in Greek mythology was sacred to Apollo and the Muses; later used as a symbol of poetry and literature in general. —Ed.

exercise this kind of right, I think that more wise, because more charitable, thoughts would urge me rather to save the man than to preserve his brazen slippers as the monuments of his folly. . . .

. . . But the age of chivalry is gone. That of sophisters, economists, and calculators has succeeded, and the glory of Europe is extinguished forever. Never, never more shall we behold that generous loyalty to rank and sex, that proud submission, that dignified obedience, that subordination of the heart which kept alive, even in servitude itself, the spirit of an exalted freedom. The unbought grace of life, the cheap defense of nations, the nurse of manly sentiment and heroic enterprise, is gone! It is gone, that sensibility of principle, that chastity of honor which felt a stain like a wound, which inspired courage whilst it mitigated ferocity, which ennobled whatever it touched, and under which vice itself lost half its evil by losing all its grossness.

This mixed system of opinion and sentiment had its origin in the ancient chivalry; and the principle, though varied in its appearance by the varying state of human affairs, subsisted and influenced through a long succession of generations even to the time we live in. If it should ever be totally extinguished, the loss I fear will be great. It is this which has given its character to modern Europe. It is this which has distinguished it under all its forms of government, and distinguished it to its advantage, from the states of Asia and possibly from those states which flourished in the most brilliant periods of the antique world. It was this which, without confounding ranks, had produced a noble equality and handed it down through all the gradations of social life. It was this opinion which mitigated kings into companions and raised private men to be fellows with kings. Without force or opposition, it subdued the fierceness of pride and power, it obliged sovereigns to submit to the soft collar of social esteem, compelled stern authority to submit to elegance, and gave a domination, vanquisher of laws, to be subdued by manners.

But now all is to be changed. All the pleasing illusions which made power gentle and obedience liberal, which harmonized the different shades of life, and which, by a bland assimilation, incorpo-

rated into politics the sentiments which beautify and soften private society, are to be dissolved by this new conquering empire of light and reason. All the decent drapery of life is to be rudely torn off. All the superadded ideas, furnished from the wardrobe of a moral imagination, which the heart owns and the understanding ratifies as necessary to cover the defects of our naked, shivering nature, and to raise it to dignity in our own estimation, are to be exploded as a ridiculous, absurd, and antiquated fashion. . . .

On the scheme of this barbarous philosophy, which is the offspring of cold hearts and muddy understandings, and which is as void of solid wisdom as it is destitute of all taste and elegance, laws are to be supported only by their own terrors and by the concern which each individual may find in them from his own private speculations or can spare to them from his own private interests. In the groves of *their* academy, at the end of every vista, you see nothing but the gallows. Nothing is left which engages the affections on the part of the commonwealth. On the principles of this mechanic philosophy, our institutions can never be embodied, if I may use the expression, in persons, so as to create in us love, veneration, admiration, or attachment. But that sort of reason which banishes the affections is incapable of filling their place. These public affections, combined with manners, are required sometimes as supplements, sometimes as correctives, always as aids to law. The precept given by a wise man, as well as a great critic, for the construction of poems is equally true as to states:—*Non satis est pulchra esse poemata, dulcia sunto.** There ought to be a system of manners in every nation which a well-informed mind would be disposed to relish. To make us love our country, our country ought to be lovely.

But power, of some kind or other, will survive the shock in which manners and opinions perish; and it will find other and worse means for its support. The usurpation which, in order to subvert ancient institutions, has destroyed ancient principles will hold power by arts similar to those by which it has

---

* "It is not enough for poems to be beautiful; they must be delightful" (Horace, *Ars Poetica* 99). —ED.

acquired it. When the old feudal and chivalrous spirit of *fealty,* which, by freeing kings from fear, freed both kings and subjects from the precautions of tyranny, shall be extinct in the minds of men, plots and assassinations will be anticipated by preventive murder and preventive confiscation, and that long roll of grim and bloody maxims which form the political code of all power not standing on its own honor and the honor of those who are to obey it. Kings will be tyrants from policy when subjects are rebels from principle.

When ancient opinions and rules of life are taken away, the loss cannot possibly be estimated. From that moment we have no compass to govern us; nor can we know distinctly to what port we steer. . . .

Why do I feel so differently from the Reverend Dr. Price* and those of his lay flock who will choose to adopt the sentiments of his discourse?—For this plain reason: because it is *natural* I should; because we are so made as to be affected at such spectacles with melancholy sentiments upon the unstable condition of mortal prosperity and the tremendous uncertainty of human greatness; because in those natural feelings we learn great lessons; because in events like these our passions instruct our reason; because when kings are hurled from their thrones by the Supreme Director of this great drama and become the objects of insult to the base and of pity to the good, we behold such disasters in the moral as we should behold a miracle in the physical order of things. We are alarmed into reflection; our minds (as it has long since been observed) are purified by terror and pity, our weak, unthinking pride is humbled under the dispensations of a mysterious wisdom. . . .

. . . Thanks to our sullen resistance to innovation, thank to the cold sluggishness of our national character, we still bear the stamp of our forefathers. We have not (as I conceive) lost the generosity and dignity of thinking of the fourteenth century, nor as yet have we subtilized ourselves into savages. We are not the converts of Rousseau; we are not the disciples of Voltaire; Helvetius has made no progress

* Richard Price (1723–1791) wrote *Observations on the Nature of Civil Liberty* in 1777 to defend the American Revolution and *A Discourse on the Love of Our Country,* a sermon to the Revolution Society, in 1789 to support the French Revolution. —ED.

amongst us. Atheists are not our preachers; madmen are not our lawgivers. We know that we have made no discoveries, and we think that no discoveries are to be made in morality, nor many in the great principles of government, nor in the ideas of liberty, which were understood long before we were born, altogether as well as they will be after the grace has heaped its mold upon our presumption and the silent tomb shall have imposed its law on our pert loquacity. In England we have not yet been completely embowelled of our natural entrails; we still feel within us, and we cherish and cultivate, those inbred sentiments which are the faithful guardians, the active monitors of our duty, the true supporters of all liberal and manly morals. We have not been drawn and trussed, in order that we may be filled, like stuffed birds in a museum, with chaff and rags and paltry blurred shreds of paper about the rights of men. We preserve the whole of our feelings still native and entire, unsophisticated by pedantry and infidelity. We have real hearts of flesh and blood beating in our bosoms. We fear God; we look up with awe to kings, with affection to parliaments, with duty to magistrates, with reverence to priests, and with respect to nobility. Why? Because when such ideas are brought before our minds, it is *natural* to be so affected; because all other feelings are false and spurious and tend to corrupt our minds, to vitiate our primary morals, to render us unfit for rational liberty, and, by teaching us a servile, licentious, and abandoned insolence, to be our low sport for a few holidays, to make us perfectly fit for, and justly deserving of, slavery through the whole course of our lives.

You see, Sir, that in this enlightened age I am bold enough to confess that we are generally men of untaught feelings, that, instead of casting away all our old prejudices, we cherish them to a very considerable degree, and, to take more shame to ourselves, we cherish them because they are prejudices; and the longer they have lasted and the more generally they have prevailed, the more we cherish them. We are afraid to put men to live and trade each on his own private stock of reason, because we suspect that this stock in each man is small, and that the individuals would do better to avail themselves of the general bank and capital of nations and of ages. Many of our men of speculation, instead of exploding general prejudices, employ their sagacity to discover the latent wisdom which prevails in them. If they find what they seek, and they seldom fail, they think it more wise to continue the prejudice, with the reason involved, than to cast away the coat of prejudice and to leave nothing but the naked reason; because prejudice, with its reason, has a motive to give action to that reason, and an affection which will give it permanence. Prejudice is of ready application in the emergency; it previously engages the mind in a steady course of wisdom and virtue and does not leave the man hesitating in the moment of decision skeptical, puzzled, and unresolved. Prejudice renders a man's virtue his habit, and not a series of unconnected acts. Through just prejudice, his duty becomes a part of his nature. . . .

. . . Rage and frenzy will pull down more in half an hour than prudence, deliberation, and foresight can build up in a hundred years. The errors and defects of old establishments are visible and palpable. It calls for little ability to point them out; and where absolute power is given, it requires but a word wholly to abolish the vice and the establishment together. The same lazy but restless disposition which loves sloth and hates quiet directs the politicians when they come to work for supplying the place of what they have destroyed. To make everything the reverse of what they have seen is quite as easy as to destroy. No difficulties occur in what has never been tried. Criticism is almost baffled in discovering the defects of what has not existed; and eager enthusiasm and cheating hope have all the wide field of imagination in which they may expatiate with little or no opposition.

At once to preserve and to reform is quite another thing. When the useful parts of an old establishment are kept, and what is superadded is to be fitted to what is retained, a vigorous mind, steady, persevering attention, various powers of comparison and combination, and the resources of an understanding fruitful in expedients are to be exercised; they are to be exercised in a continued conflict with the combined force of opposite vices, with the obstinacy that rejects all improvement and

the levity that is fatigued and disgusted with everything of which it is in possession. But you may object—"A process of this kind is slow. It is not fit for an assembly which glories in performing in a few months the work of ages. Such a mode of reforming, possibly, might take up many years". Without question it might; and it ought. It is one of the excellences of a method in which time is amongst the assistants, that its operation is slow and in some cases almost imperceptible. If circumspection and caution are a part of wisdom when we work only upon inanimate matter, surely they become a part of duty, too, when the subject of our demolition and construction is not brick and timber but sentient beings, by the sudden alteration of whose state, condition, and habits multitudes may be rendered miserable. But it seems as if it were the prevalent opinion in Paris that an unfeeling heart and an undoubting confidence are the sole qualifications for a perfect legislator. Far different are my ideas of that high office. The true lawgiver ought to have a heart full of sensibility. He ought to love and respect his kind, and to fear himself. It may be allowed to his temperament to catch his ultimate object with an intuitive glance, but his movements toward it ought to be deliberate. Political arrangement, as it is a work for social ends, is to be only wrought by social means. There mind must conspire with mind. Time is required to produce that union of minds which alone can produce all the good we aim at. Our patience will achieve more than our force. If I might venture to appeal to what is so much out of fashion in Paris, I mean to experience, I should tell you that in my course I have known and, according to my measure, have co-operated with great men; and I have never yet seen any plan which has not been mended by the observation of those who were much inferior in understanding to the person who took the lead in the business. By a slow but well-sustained progress the effect of each step is watched; the good or ill success of the first gives light to us in the second; and so, from light to light, we are conducted with safety through the whole series. We see that the parts of the system do not clash. The evils latent in the most promising contrivances are provided for as they arise. One advantage is as little as possible sacrificed to another. We compensate, we reconcile, we balance. We are enabled to unite into a consistent whole the various anomalies and contending principles that are found in the minds and affairs of men. From hence arises, not an excellence in simplicity, but one far superior, an excellence in composition. Where the great interests of mankind are concerned through a long succession of generations, that succession ought to be admitted into some share in the councils which are so deeply to affect them. If justice requires this, the work itself requires the aid of more minds than one age can furnish. It is from this view of things that the best legislators have been often satisfied with the establishment of some sure, solid, and ruling principle in government—a power like that which some of the philosophers have called a plastic nature; and having fixed the principle, they have left it afterwards to its own operation. . . .

Abortion

Abortion raises notoriously difficult ethical problems. At root, these problems seem to revolve around rights. Opponents of abortion speak of the right to life of the fetus; pro-choice advocates speak of a woman's right to choose. Obviously, these two putative rights come into conflict over abortion. One cannot respect both the right to life of the fetus and the woman's right to choose if the woman chooses to abort. Consequently, the abortion issue seems to call for some neutral or well-grounded way of deciding when some rights take precedence over others.

Of course, not everyone grants the rights in question. Some argue that the fetus is not a person and, indeed, is sufficiently unlike a person that it has no rights. Others argue that the woman may have obligations toward a fetus inside her even if it is there through no choice of her own. They deny that, at least in some cases, a woman has a right to choose abortion. The abortion problem thus raises two other very difficult issues: (1) What kinds of beings have rights? Fetuses, severely ill or injured people, and animals all share many basic human characteristics but lack others common to typical, healthy adults. Which characteristics, if any, are essential to having rights? In general, how do we decide the boundaries of our moral categories? (2) What kinds of obligations do we have toward others? Under what circumstances do other people have rights against us—rights to have us do certain things to help them and to refrain from doing things to harm them? To what extent do such obligations depend on our willingness to assume them? These questions are crucial to the abortion issue and, moreover, reach far beyond it.

Abortion had been illegal in most areas of the United States until 1973, when the Supreme Court decided, in *Roe v. Wade,* that the Constitution guarantees a right to privacy implying that the state may not restrict abortions in the first trimester (the first three months of pregnancy). The Court backed away from any decision about the ultimate moral status of the fetus; it treated fetuses as "potential people," having value if not rights. (Opponents of the decision contend that this failure to decide the status of the fetus is itself a decision, since the Court does not take the rights of fetuses into account.) Instead, the Court based its decision on the medical fact that first-trimester abortions are less risky than carrying a child to term, whereas later abortions are riskier. The government's interest in preserving the health and safety of the mother thus gives the government reason to restrict abortions, but only after the first trimester. The value of the fetus also gives the government reason to restrict abortions, but only after the fetus becomes "viable"—that is, able to survive outside the mother's body. Until then, the mother's right to privacy takes precedence. The Court's decision in *Roe v. Wade* raises profound Constitutional questions and analogous moral questions: Is there a right to privacy? If so, what is it? How far does it extend? How does it relate to other rights? What obligations does it place on others?

The last question is especially important in *Webster v. Reproductive Heath Services*. Missouri had passed a law limiting abortions, (*a*) specifying that abortions not needed to save the mother's life could not be performed in public hospitals and (*b*) requiring physicians to test for the viability of any fetus believed to be at least twenty weeks old. The Court, in 1989, upheld these restrictions, maintaining (1) that the right to privacy does not require public subsidies for abortion and (2) that if viability is indeed the "compelling point" that *Roe v. Wade* claimed, then testing for viability is justifiable. The Court additionally questioned the trimester framework of *Roe v. Wade*, suggesting that it had little Constitutional or moral foundation.

In her article reprinted on pp. 287–296, Judith Jarvis Thomson contends that the unacceptability of abortion does not follow automatically from the right to life of the fetus. She grants, for the sake of argument, that the fetus has such a right. She then maintains that under many circumstances, a woman nevertheless has no obligation to carry a child to term. She distinguishes some important conceptions of our obligations to others and argues that only on a very (and, she thinks, unacceptably) strong conception does the woman generally have an obligation not to abort.

Jane English argues that both conservative and liberal positions on abortions are mistaken. She contends moreover that questions of personhood and rights are not as important to the moral issues surrounding abortion as many believe. Even if fetuses are persons with rights to life, she maintains, abortion is sometimes justifiable. And even if fetuses are not persons and have no rights, abortion is sometimes wrong. She concludes that we cannot resolve the abortion issue by reflecting on rights alone; we must reflect generally on our obligations to others.

Don Marquis, in contrast, contends that abortion is immoral for the same reason that murdering an adult human is immoral—it deprives something that would have had a human life of its future. Marquis does not argue, as many anti-abortionists have, that the fetus has a right to life or that abortion is murder; he argues instead that it is *like* murder in that it deprives something that would have gone on to experience a human life of that very opportunity.

Roe v. Wade (1973)

(*Source:* Roe v. Wade *410 U.S. 113 [1973]. Most legal references have been omitted.*)

QUESTIONS FOR REFLECTION

1. What, according to the majority, are the chief interests of the state in making a decision about abortion?

2. The majority bases its decision on the right of privacy. What is this right? How does the majority argue for it? What are its limitations?

3. The majority contends that the "compelling point" for balancing the rights and interests involved is viability. What is viability? Why does the majority settle on it as the compelling point? Do you find the argument convincing?

4. What fundamental rights and liberties does Justice Douglas advocate? How does he argue for them?

5. Suppose that a fetus has rights. Does Justice Douglas's analysis settle the issue of how to balance its rights against the mother's?

6. Justice Rehnquist argues that the right to an abortion should not be taken as fundamental. Why?

Mr. Justice Blackmun delivered the opinion of the Court. . . .

I

The Texas statutes that concern us here are Arts. 1191–1194 and 1196 of the State's Penal Code. These make it a crime to "procure an abortion," as therein defined, or to attempt one, except with respect to "an abortion procured or attempted by medical advice for the purpose of saving the life of the mother." Similar statutes are in existence in a majority of the States. . . .

II

Jane Roe, a single woman who was residing in Dallas County, Texas, instituted this federal action in March 1970 against the District Attorney of the county. She sought a declaratory judgment that the Texas criminal abortion statutes were unconstitutional on their face, and an injunction restraining the defendant from enforcing the statutes.

Roe alleged that she was unmarried and pregnant; that she wished to terminate her pregnancy by an abortion "performed by a competent, licensed physician, under safe, clinical conditions"; that she was unable to get a "legal" abortion in Texas because her life did not appear to be threatened by the continuation of her pregnancy; and that she could not afford to travel to another jurisdiction in order to secure a legal abortion under safe conditions. She claimed that the Texas statutes were unconstitutionally vague and that they abridged her right of personal privacy, protected by the First, Fourth, Fifth, Ninth, and Fourteenth Amendments. By an amendment to her complaint Roe purported to sue "on behalf of herself and all other women" similarly situated. . . .

VII

Three reasons have been advanced to explain historically the enactment of criminal abortion laws in the 19th century and to justify their continued existence.

It has been argued occasionally that these laws were the product of a Victorian social concern to discourage illicit sexual conduct. Texas, however, does not advance this justification in the present case, and it appears that no court or commentator has taken the argument seriously. The appellants and *amici* contend, moreover, that this is not a proper state purpose at all and suggest that, if it were, the Texas statutes are overbroad in protecting it since the law fails to distinguish between married and unwed mothers.

A second reason is concerned with abortion as a medical procedure. When most criminal abortion laws were first enacted, the procedure was a hazardous one for the woman. This was particularly true prior to the development of antisepsis. Antiseptic techniques, of course, were based on discoveries by Lister, Pasteur, and others first announced in 1867, but were not generally accepted and employed until about the turn of the century. Abortion mortality was high. Even after 1900, and perhaps until as late as the development of antibiotics in the 1940's, standard modern techniques such as dilation and curettage were not nearly so safe as they are today. Thus, it has been argued that a State's real concern in enacting a criminal abortion law was to protect the pregnant woman, that is, to restrain her from submitting to a procedure that placed her life in serious jeopardy.

Modern medical techniques have altered this situation. Appellants and various *amici* refer to medical data indicating that abortion in early pregnancy, that is, prior to the end of the first trimester, although not without its risk, is now relatively safe. Mortality rates for women undergoing early abortions, where the procedure is legal, appear to be as low as or lower than the rates for normal childbirth. Consequently, any interest of the State in protecting the woman from an inherently hazardous procedure, except when it would be equally dangerous for her to forgo it, has largely disappeared. Of course, important state interests in the areas of health and medical standards do remain. The State has a legitimate interest in seeing to it that abortion, like any other medical procedure, is performed under circumstances that insure maximum safety for the patient. This interest obviously extends at least to the performing physician and his staff, to the facilities involved, to the availability of after-care, and to adequate provision for any complication or emergency that might arise. The prevalence of high mortality rates at illegal "abortion mills" strengthens, rather than weakens, the State's interest in regulating the conditions under which abortions are performed. Moreover, the risk to the woman increases as her pregnancy continues. Thus, the State retains a definite interest in protecting the woman's own health and safety when an abortion is proposed at a late stage of pregnancy.

The third reason is the State's interest—some phrase it in terms of duty—in protecting prenatal life. Some of the argument for this justification rests on the theory that a new human life is present from the moment of conception. The State's interest and general obligation to protect life then extends, it is argued, to prenatal life. Only when the life of the pregnant mother herself is at stake, balanced against the life she carries within her, should the interest of the embryo or fetus not prevail. Logically, of course, a legitimate state interest in this area need not stand or fall on acceptance of the belief that life begins at conception or at some other point prior to live birth. In assessing the State's interest, recognition may be given to the less rigid claim that as long as at least *potential* life is involved, the State may assert interests beyond the protection of the pregnant woman alone.

Parties challenging state abortion laws have sharply disputed in some courts the contention that a purpose of these laws, when enacted, was to protect prenatal life. Pointing to the absence of legislative history to support the contention, they claim that most state laws were designed solely to protect the woman. Because medical advances have lessened this concern, at least with respect to abortion in early pregnancy, they argue that with respect to such abortions the laws can no longer be justified by any state interest. There is some scholarly support for this view of original purpose. The few state courts called upon to interpret their laws in the late

19th and early 20th centuries did focus on the State's interest in protecting the woman's health rather than in preserving the embryo and fetus. Proponents of this view point out that in many States, including Texas, by statute or judicial interpretation, the pregnant woman herself could not be prosecuted for self-abortion or for cooperating in an abortion performed upon her by another. They claim that adoption of the "quickening" distinction through received common law and state statutes tacitly recognizes the greater health hazards inherent in late abortion and impliedly repudiates the theory that life begins at conception.

It is with these interests, and the weight to be attached to them, that this case is concerned.

VIII

The Constitution does not explicitly mention any right of privacy. In a line of decisions, however, going back perhaps as far as *Union Pacific R. Co.* v. *Botsford* (1891), the Court has recognized that a right of personal privacy, or a guarantee of certain areas or zones of privacy, does exist under the Constitution. . . . The decisions make it clear that only personal rights that can be deemed "fundamental" or "implicit in the concept of ordered liberty" are included in this guarantee of personal privacy. They also make it clear that the right has some extension to activities relating to marriage, procreation, contraception, family relationships, and child rearing and education.

This right of privacy, whether it be founded in the Fourteenth Amendment's concept of personal liberty and restrictions upon state action, as we feel it is, or, as the District Court determined, in the Ninth Amendment's reservation of rights to the people, is broad enough to encompass a woman's decision whether or not to terminate her pregnancy. The detriment that the State would impose upon the pregnant woman by denying this choice altogether is apparent. Specific and direct harm medically diagnosable even in early pregnancy may be involved. Maternity, or additional offspring, may force upon the woman a distressful life and future. Psychological harm may be imminent. Mental and physical health may be taxed by child care. There is also the

distress, for all concerned, associated with the unwanted child, and there is the problem of bringing a child into a family already unable, psychologically and otherwise, to care for it. In other cases, as in this one, the additional difficulties and continuing stigma of unwed motherhood may be involved. All these are factors the woman and her responsible physician necessarily will consider in consultation.

On the basis of elements such as these, appellant and some *amici* argue that the woman's right is absolute and that she is entitled to terminate her pregnancy at whatever time, in whatever way, and for whatever reason she alone chooses. With this we do not agree. Appellant's arguments that Texas either has no valid interest at all in regulating the abortion decision, or no interest strong enough to support any limitation upon the woman's sole determination, are unpersuasive. The Court's decisions recognizing a right of privacy also acknowledge that some state regulation in areas protected by that right is appropriate. As noted above, a State may properly assert important interests in safeguarding health, in maintaining medical standards, and in protecting potential life. At some point in pregnancy, these respective interests become sufficiently compelling to sustain regulation of the factors that govern the abortion decision. The privacy right involved, therefore, cannot be said to be absolute. In fact, it is not clear to us that the claim asserted by some *amici* that one has an unlimited right to do with one's body as one pleases bears a close relationship to the right of privacy previously articulated in the Court's decisions. The Court has refused to recognize an unlimited right of this kind in the past.

We, therefore, conclude that the right of personal privacy includes the abortion decision, but that this right is not unqualified and must be considered against important state interests in regulation.

We note that those federal and state courts that have recently considered abortion law challenges have reached the same conclusion. A majority, in addition to the District Court in the present case, have held state laws unconstitutional, at least in part, because of vagueness or because of overbreadth and abridgment of rights.

Others have sustained state statutes.

Although the results are divided, most of these courts have agreed that the right of privacy, however based, is broad enough to cover the abortion decision; that the right, nonetheless, is not absolute and is subject to some limitations; and that at some point the state interests as to protection of health, medical standards, and prenatal life, become dominant. We agree with this approach.

Where certain "fundamental rights" are involved, the Court has held that regulation limiting these rights may be justified only by a "compelling state interest" and that legislative enactments must be narrowly drawn to express only the legitimate state interests at stake.

In . . . recent abortion cases . . . courts have recognized these principles. Those striking down state laws have generally scrutinized the State's interests in protecting health and potential life, and have concluded that neither interest justified broad limitations on the reasons for which a physician and his pregnant patient might decide that she should have an abortion in the early stages of pregnancy. Courts sustaining the state laws have held that the State's determinations to protect health or prenatal life are dominant and constitutionally justifiable.

IX

The District Court held that the appellee failed to meet his burden of demonstrating that the Texas statute's infringement upon Roe's rights was necessary to support a compelling state interest, and that, although the appellee presented "several compelling justifications for state presence in the area of abortions," the statutes outstripped these justifications and swept "far beyond any areas of compelling state interest." Appellant and appellee both contest that holding. Appellant, as has been indicated, claims an absolute right that bars any state imposition of criminal penalties in the area. Appellee argues that the State's determination to recognize and protect prenatal life from and after conception constitutes a compelling state interest. As noted above, we do not agree fully with either formulation.

A. The appellee and certain *amici* argue that the fetus is a "person" within the language and meaning of the Fourteenth Amendment. In support of this, they outline at length and in detail the well-known facts of fetal development. If this suggestion of personhood is established, the appellant's case, of course, collapses, for the fetus' right to life would then be guaranteed specifically by the Amendment. The appellant conceded as much on reargument. On the other hand, the appellee conceded on reargument that no case could be cited that holds that a fetus is a person within the meaning of the Fourteenth Amendment.

The Constitution does not define "person" in so many words. Section 1 of the Fourteenth Amendment contains three references to "person." The first, in defining "citizens," speaks of "persons born or naturalized in the United States." The word also appears both in the Due Process Clause and in the Equal Protection Clause. "Person" is used in other places in the Constitution. . . . But in nearly all these instances, the use of the word is such that it has application only postnatally. None indicates, with any assurance, that it has any possible prenatal application.

All this, together with our observation that throughout the major portion of the 19th century prevailing legal abortion practices were far freer than they are today, persuades us that the word "person," as used in the Fourteenth Amendment, does not include the unborn. This is in accord with the results reached in those few cases where the issue has been squarely presented. Indeed, our decision in *United States* v. *Vuitch* (1971), inferentially is to the same effect, for we there would not have indulged in statutory interpretation favorable to abortion in specified circumstances if the necessary consequence was the termination of life entitled to Fourteenth Amendment protection.

This conclusion, however, does not of itself fully answer the contentions raised by Texas, and we pass on to other considerations.

B. The pregnant woman cannot be isolated in her privacy. She carries an embryo and, later, a fetus, if one accepts the medical definitions of the developing young in the human uterus. . . . The situation therefore is inherently different from marital intimacy, or bedroom possession of obscene material, or marriage, or procreation, or education, with which *Eisenstadt* and *Griswold, Stanley, Loving, Skinner,* and *Pierce* and *Meyer* were respectively concerned. As we have intimated above, it is reasonable and appropriate for a State to decide that at some point in time another interest, that of health of the mother or that of potential human life, becomes significantly involved. The woman's privacy is no longer sole and any right of privacy she possesses must be measured accordingly.

Texas urges that, apart from the Fourteenth Amendment, life begins at conception and is present throughout pregnancy, and that, therefore, the State has a compelling interest in protecting that life from and after conception. We need not resolve the difficult question of when life begins. When those trained in the respective disciplines of medicine, philosophy, and theology are unable to arrive at any consensus, the judiciary, at this point in the development of man's knowledge, is not in a position to speculate as to the answer.

It should be sufficient to note briefly the wide divergence of thinking on this most sensitive and difficult question. There has always been strong support for the view that life does not begin until live birth. This was the belief of the Stoics. It appears to be the predominant, though not the unanimous, attitude of the Jewish faith. It may be taken to represent also the position of a large segment of the Protestant community, insofar as that can be ascertained; organized groups that have taken a formal position on the abortion issue have generally regarded abortion as a matter for the conscience of the individual and her family. As we have noted, the common law found greater significance in quickening. Physicians and their scientific colleagues have regarded that event with less interest and have tended to focus either upon conception, upon live birth, or upon the interim point at which the fetus becomes "viable," that is, potentially able to live outside the mother's womb, albeit with artificial aid. Viability is usually placed at about seven months (28 weeks) but may occur earlier, even at 24 weeks. The Aristotelian theory of "mediate animation," that held sway throughout the Middle Ages and the Renaissance in Europe, continued to be official Roman Catholic dogma until the 19th century, despite opposition to this "ensoulment" theory from those in the Church who would recognize the existence of life from the moment of conception. The latter is now, of course, the official belief of the Catholic Church. As one brief *amicus* discloses, this is a

view strongly held by many non-Catholics as well, and by many physicians. Substantial problems for precise definition of this view are posed, however, by new embryological data that purport to indicate that conception is a "process" over time, rather than an event, and by new medical techniques such as menstrual extraction, the "morning-after" pill, implantation of embryos, artificial insemination, and even artificial wombs.

In areas other than criminal abortion, the law has been reluctant to endorse any theory that life, as we recognize it, begins before live birth or to accord legal rights to the unborn except in narrowly defined situations and except when the rights are contingent upon live birth. For example, the traditional rule of tort law denied recovery for prenatal injuries even though the child was born alive. That rule has been changed in almost every jurisdiction. In most States, recovery is said to be permitted only if the fetus was viable, or at least quick, when the injuries were sustained, though few courts have squarely so held. In a recent development, generally opposed by the commentators, some States permit the parents of a stillborn child to maintain an action for wrongful death because of prenatal injuries. Such an action, however, would appear to be one to vindicate the parents' interest and is thus consistent with the view that the fetus, at most, represents only the potentiality of life. Similarly, unborn children have been recognized as acquiring rights or interests by way of inheritance or other devolution of property, and have been represented by guardians *ad litem*. Perfection of the interests involved, again, has generally been contingent upon live birth. In short, the unborn have never been recognized in the law as persons in the whole sense.

X

In view of all this, we do not agree that, by adopting one theory of life, Texas may override the rights of the pregnant woman that are at stake. We repeat, however, that the State does have an important and legitimate interest in preserving and protecting the health of the pregnant woman, whether she be a resident of the State or a nonresident who seeks medical consultation and treatment there, and that it has still *another* important and legitimate interest in protecting the potentiality of human life. These interests are separate and distinct. Each grows in substantiality as the woman approaches term and, at a point during pregnancy, each becomes "compelling."

With respect to the State's important and legitimate interest in the health of the mother, the "compelling" point, in the light of present medical knowledge, is at approximately the end of the first trimester. This is so because of the now-established medical fact . . . that until the end of the first trimester mortality in abortion may be less than mortality in normal childbirth. It follows that, from and after this point, a State may regulate the abortion procedure to the extent that the regulation reasonably relates to the preservation and protection of maternal health. Examples of permissible state regulation in this area are requirements as to the qualifications of the person who is to perform the abortion; as to the licensure of that person; as to the facility in which the procedure is to be performed, that is, whether it must be a hospital or may be a clinic or some other place of less-than-hospital status; as to the licensing of the facility; and the like.

This means, on the other hand, that, for the period of pregnancy prior to this "compelling" point, the attending physician, in consultation with his patient, is free to determine, without regulation by the State, that, in his medical judgment, the patient's pregnancy should be terminated. If that decision is reached, the judgment may be effectuated by an abortion free of interference by the State.

With respect to the State's important and legitimate interest in potential life, the "compelling" point is at viability. This is so because the fetus then presumably has the capability of meaningful life outside the mother's womb. State regulation protective of fetal life after viability thus has both logical and biological justifications. If the State is interested in protecting fetal life after viability, it may go so far as to proscribe abortion during that period, except when it is necessary to preserve the life or health of the mother.

Measured against these standards, Art. 1196 of the Texas Penal Code, in restricting legal abortions to those "procured or attempted by medical advice for the purpose of saving the life of the mother," sweeps too broadly. The statute makes no distinc-

tion between abortions performed early in pregnancy and those performed later, and it limits to a single reason, "saving" the mother's life, the legal justification for the procedure. The statute, therefore, cannot survive the constitutional attack made upon it here. . . .

XI

To summarize and to repeat:

1. A state criminal abortion statute of the current Texas type, that excepts from criminality only a *life-saving* procedure on behalf of the mother, without regard to pregnancy stage and without recognition of the other interests involved, is violative of the Due Process Clause of the Fourteenth Amendment.

   (a) For the stage prior to approximately the end of the first trimester, the abortion decision and its effectuation must be left to the medical judgment of the pregnant woman's attending physician.

   (b) For the stage subsequent to approximately the end of the first trimester, the State, in promoting its interest in the health of the mother, may, if it chooses, regulate the abortion procedure in ways that are reasonably related to maternal health.

   (c) For the stage subsequent to viability, the State in promoting its interest in the potentiality of human life may, if it chooses, regulate, and even proscribe, abortion except where it is necessary, in appropriate medical judgment, for the preservation of the life or health of the mother.

2. The State may define the term "physician," as it has been employed in the preceding paragraphs of this Part XI of this opinion, to mean only a physician currently licensed by the State, and may proscribe any abortion by a person who is not a physician as so defined. . . .

Mr. Justice Douglas, concurring. . . .

The Ninth Amendment obviously does not create federally enforceable rights. It merely says, "The enumeration in the Constitution of certain rights, shall not be construed to deny or disparage others retained by the people." But a catalogue of these rights includes customary, traditional, and time-honored rights, amenities, privileges, and immunities that come within the sweep of "the Blessings of Liberty" mentioned in the preamble to the Constitution. Many of them in my view come within the meaning of the term "liberty" as used in the Fourteenth Amendment.

First is the autonomous control over the development and expression on one's intellect, interests, tastes, and personality.

These are rights protected by the First Amendment and in my view they are absolute, permitting of no exceptions. . . . The Free Exercise Clause of the First Amendment is one facet of this constitutional right. The right to remain silent as respects one's own beliefs, . . . is protected by the First and the Fifth. The First Amendment grants the privacy of first-class mail, . . . All of these aspects of the right of privacy are "rights retained by the people" in the meaning of the Ninth Amendment.

Second is freedom of choice in the basic decisions of one's life respecting marriage, divorce, procreation, contraception, and the education and upbringing of children.

These rights, unlike those protected by the First Amendment, are subject to some control by the police power. Thus the Fourth Amendment speaks only of "unreasonable searches and seizures" and of "probable cause." These rights are "fundamental" and we have held that in order to support legislative action the statute must be narrowly and precisely drawn and that a "compelling state interest" must be shown in support of the limitation. . . .

. . . the right of procreation, . . . and the privacy of the marital relation, . . . are in this category. . . .

This right of privacy was called by Mr. Justice Brandeis the right "to be let alone." That right includes the privilege of an individual to plan his own affairs, for "outside areas of plainly harmful conduct, every American is left to shape his own life as he thinks best, do what he pleases, go where he pleases."

Third is the freedom to care for one's health and person, freedom from bodily restraint or compulsion, freedom to walk, stroll, or loaf.

These rights, though fundamental, are likewise subject to regulation on a showing of "compelling state interest." . . .

The Georgia statute is at war with the clear message of these cases—that a woman is free to make the basic decision whether to bear an unwanted child. Elaborate argument is hardly necessary to demonstrate that childbirth may deprive a woman of her preferred life style and force upon her a radically different and undesired future. For example, rejected applicants under the Georgia statute are required to endure the discomforts of pregnancy; to incur the pain, higher mortality rate, and aftereffects of childbirth; to abandon educational plans; to sustain loss of income; to forgo the satisfactions of careers; to tax further mental and physical health in providing childcare; and, in some cases, to bear the lifelong stigma of unwed motherhood, a badge which may haunt, if not deter, later legitimate family relationships.

Such a holding is, however, only the beginning of the problem. The State has interests to protect. Vaccinations to prevent epidemics are one example, as *Jacobson* holds. The Court held that compulsory sterilization of imbeciles afflicted with hereditary forms of insanity or imbecility is another. . . . Abortion affects another. While childbirth endangers the lives of some women, voluntary abortion at any time and place regardless of medical standards would impinge on the rightful concern of society. The woman's health is part of that concern; as is the life of the fetus after quickening. These concerns justify the State in treating the procedure as a medical one.

One difficulty is that this statute as construed and applied apparently does not give full sweep to the "psychological as well as physical well-being" of women patients which saved the concept "health" from being void for vagueness in *United States* v. *Vuitch.* But apart from that, Georgia's enactment has a constitutional infirmity because, as stated by the District Court, it "limits the number of reasons for which an abortion may be sought." I agree with the holding of the District Court, "This the State may not do, because such action unduly restricts a decision sheltered by the Constitutional right of privacy." . . .

The vicissitudes of life produce pregnancies which may be unwanted, or which may impair "health" in the broad *Vuitch* sense of the term, or which may imperil the life of the mother, or which in the full setting of the case may create such suffering, dislocations, misery, or tragedy as to make an early abortion the only civilized step to take. These hardships may be properly embraced in the "health" factor of the mother as appraised by a person of insight. Or they may be part of a broader medical judgment based on what is "appropriate" in a given case, though perhaps not "necessary" in a strict sense.

The "liberty" of the mother, though rooted as it is in the Constitution, may be qualified by the State for the reasons we have stated. But where fundamental personal rights and liberties are involved, the corrective legislation must be "narrowly drawn to prevent the supposed evil". . . . Unless regulatory measures are so confined and are addressed to the specific areas of compelling legislative concern, the police power would become the great leveller of constitutional rights and liberties.

There is no doubt that the State may require abortions to be performed by qualified medical personnel. The legitimate objective of preserving the mother's health clearly supports such laws. Their impact upon the woman's privacy is minimal. But the Georgia statute outlaws virtually all such operations—even in the earliest stages of pregnancy. In light of modern medical evidence suggesting that an early abortion is safer healthwise than childbirth itself, it cannot be seriously urged that so comprehensive a ban is aimed at protecting the woman's health. Rather, this expansive proscription of all abortions along the temporal spectrum can rest only on a public goal of preserving both embryonic and fetal life.

The present statute has struck a balance between the woman and the State's interests wholly in favor of the latter. I am not prepared to hold that a State may equate, as Georgia has done, all phases of maturation preceding birth. We held in *Griswold* that the States may not preclude spouses from attempting to avoid the joinder of sperm and egg. If this is true, it is difficult to perceive any overriding public necessity which might attach precisely at the moment of conception. As Mr. Justice Clark has said:

To say that life is present at conception is to give recognition to the potential, rather than the actual. The unfertilized egg has life, and if fertilized, it takes on human proportions. But the law deals in reality, not obscurity—the known rather than the unknown. When sperm meets egg, life may eventually form, but quite often it does not. The law does not deal in speculation. The phenomenon of life takes time to develop, and until it is actually present, it cannot be destroyed. Its interruption prior to formation would hardly be homicide, and as we have seen, society does not regard it as such. The rites of Baptism are not performed and death certificates are not required when a miscarriage occurs. No prosecutor has ever returned a murder indictment charging the taking of the life of a fetus. This would not be the case if the fetus constituted human life.

In summary, the enactment is overbroad. It is not closely correlated to the aim of preserving pre-natal life. In fact, it permits its destruction in several cases, including pregnancies resulting from sex acts in which unmarried females are below the statutory age of consent. At the same time, however, the measure broadly proscribes aborting other pregnancies which may cause severe mental disorders. Additionally, the statute is overbroad because it equates the value of embryonic life immediately after conception with the worth of life immediately before birth. . . .

The right to seek advice on one's health and the right to place his reliance on the physician of his choice are basic to Fourteenth Amendment values. We deal with fundamental rights and liberties, which, as already noted, can be contained or controlled only by discretely drawn legislation that preserves the "liberty" and regulates only those phases of the problem of compelling legislative concern. The imposition by the State of group controls over the physician-patient relation is not made on any medical procedure apart from abortion, no matter how dangerous the medical step may be. The oversight imposed on the physician and patient in abortion cases denies them their "liberty," *viz.,* their right of privacy, without any compelling, discernible state interest.

Georgia has constitutional warrant in treating abortion as a medical problem. To protect the woman's right of privacy, however, the control must be through the physician of her choice and the standards set for his performance.

The protection of the fetus when it has acquired life is a legitimate concern of the State. Georgia's law makes no rational, discernible decision on that score. For under the Act the developmental stage of the fetus is irrelevant when pregnancy is the result of rape or when the fetus will very likely be born with a permanent defect or when a continuation of the pregnancy will endanger the life of the mother or permanently injure her health. When life is present is a question we do not try to resolve. While basically a question for medical experts, as stated by Mr. Justice Clark, it is, of course, caught up in matters of religion and morality.

In short, I agree with the Court that endangering the life of the woman or seriously and permanently injuring her health are standards too narrow for the right of privacy that are at stake. . . .

Mr. Justice Rehnquist, dissenting.

The Court's opinion brings to the decision of this troubling question both extensive historical fact and a wealth of legal scholarship. While the opinion thus commands my respect, I find myself nonetheless in fundamental disagreement with those parts of it that invalidate the Texas statute in question, and therefore dissent.

I

The Court's opinion decides that a State may impose virtually no restriction on the performance of abortions during the first trimester of pregnancy. Our previous decisions indicate that a necessary predicate for such an opinion is a plaintiff who was in her first trimester of pregnancy at some time during the pendency of her lawsuit. While a party may vindicate his own constitutional rights, he may not seek vindication for the rights of others. The Court's statement of facts in this case makes clear, however, that the record in no way indicates the presence of such a plaintiff. We know only that plaintiff Roe at the time of filing her complaint was a pregnant woman; for aught that appears in this record, she may have been in her *last* trimester of pregnancy as of the date the complaint was filed.

Nothing in the Court's opinion indicates that Texas might not constitutionally apply its proscrip-

tion of abortion as written to a woman in that stage of pregnancy. Nonetheless, the Court uses her complaint against the Texas statute as a fulcrum for deciding that States may impose virtually no restrictions on medical abortions performed during the *first* trimester of pregnancy. In deciding such a hypothetical lawsuit, the Court departs from the longstanding admonition that it should never "formulate a rule of constitutional law broader than is required by the precise facts to which it is to be applied."

II

Even if there were a plaintiff in this case capable of litigating the issue which the Court decides, I would reach a conclusion opposite to that reached by the Court. I have difficulty in concluding, as the Court does, that the right of "privacy" is involved in this case. Texas, by the statute here challenged, bars the performance of a medical abortion by a licensed physician on a plaintiff such as Roe. A transaction resulting in an operation such as this is not "private" in the ordinary usage of that word. Nor is the "privacy" that the Court finds here even a distant relative of the freedom from searches and seizures protected by the Fourth Amendment to the Constitution, which the Court has referred to as embodying a right to privacy.

If the Court means by the term "privacy" no more than that the claim of a person to be free from unwanted state regulation of consensual transactions may be a form of "liberty" protected by the Fourteenth Amendment, there is no doubt that similar claims have been upheld in our earlier decisions on the basis of that liberty. I agree with the statement of Mr. Justice Stewart in his concurring opinion that the "liberty," against deprivation of which without due process the Fourteenth Amendment protects, embraces more than the rights found in the Bill of Rights. But that liberty is not guaranteed absolutely against deprivation, only against deprivation without due process of law. The test traditionally applied in the area of social and economic legislation is whether or not a law such as that challenged has a rational relation to a valid state objective. The Due Process Clause of the Fourteenth

Amendment undoubtedly does place a limit, albeit a broad one, on legislative power to enact laws such as this. If the Texas statute were to prohibit an abortion even where the mother's life is in jeopardy, I have little doubt that such a statute would lack a rational relation to a valid state objective. . . . But the Court's sweeping invalidation of any restrictions on abortion during the first trimester is impossible to justify under that standard, and the conscious weighing of competing factors that the Court's opinion apparently substitutes for the established test is far more appropriate to a legislative judgment than to a judicial one.

The Court eschews the history of the Fourteenth Amendment in its reliance on the "compelling state interest" test. But the Court adds a new wrinkle to this test by transposing it from the legal considerations associated with the Equal Protection Clause of the Fourteenth Amendment to this case arising under the Due Process Clause of the Fourteenth Amendment. Unless I misapprehend the consequences of this transplanting of the "compelling state interest test," the Court's opinion will accomplish the seemingly impossible feat of leaving this area of the law more confused than it found it.

While the Court's opinion quotes from the dissent of Mr. Justice Holmes in *Lochner* v. *New York* (1905), the result it reaches is more closely attuned to the majority opinion of Mr. Justice Peckham in that case. As in *Lochner* and similar cases applying substantive due process standards to economic and social welfare legislation, the adoption of the compelling state interest standard will inevitably require this Court to examine the legislative policies and pass on the wisdom of these policies in the very process of deciding whether a particular state interest put forward may or may not be "compelling." The decision here to break pregnancy into three distinct terms and to outline the permissible restrictions the State may impose in each one, for example, partakes more of judicial legislation than it does of determination of the intent of the drafters of the Fourteenth Amendment.

The fact that a majority of the States reflecting, after all, the majority sentiment in those States, have had restrictions on abortions for at least a century is a strong indication, it seems to me, that the asserted right to an abortion is not "so rooted in the traditions and conscience of our people as to be ranked as fundamental." Even today, when society's views on abortion are changing, the very existence of the debate is evidence that the "right" to an abortion is not so universally accepted as the appellant would have us believe.

To reach its result, the Court necessarily has had to find within the scope of the Fourteenth Amendment a right that was apparently completely unknown to the drafters of the Amendment. As early as 1821, the first state law dealing directly with abortion was enacted by the Connecticut Legislature. By the time of the adoption of the Fourteenth Amendment in 1868, there were at least 36 laws enacted by state or territorial legislatures limiting abortion. While many States have amended or updated their laws, 21 of the laws on the books in 1868 remain in effect today. Indeed, the Texas statute struck down today was, as the majority notes, first enacted in 1857 and "has remained substantially unchanged to the present time."

There apparently was no question concerning the validity of this provision or of any of the other state statutes when the Fourteenth Amendment was adopted. The only conclusion possible from this history is that the drafters did not intend to have the Fourteenth Amendment withdraw from the States the power to legislate with respect to this matter.

III

Even if one were to agree that the case that the Court decides were here, and that the enunciation of the substantive constitutional law in the Court's opinion were proper, the actual disposition of the case by the Court is still difficult to justify. The Texas statute is struck down *in toto,* even though the Court apparently concedes that at later periods of pregnancy Texas might impose these selfsame statutory limitations on abortion. My understanding of past practice is that a statute found to be invalid as applied to a particular plaintiff, but not unconstitutional as a whole, is not simply "struck down" but is, instead, declared unconstitutional as applied to the fact situation before the Court.

For all of the foregoing reasons, I respectfully dissent.

Webster v. Reproductive Health Services (1989)

(*Source:* Webster v. Reproductive Health Services *[1989]. Most legal references have been omitted.*)

QUESTIONS FOR REFLECTION

1. The majority argues that even if women have a right to have an abortion, the government has no obligation to subsidize the cost of abortions. How does the majority distinguish these issues?

2. The majority upholds the viability-testing provision of the Missouri law. How does it justify this decision?

3. The majority concludes by criticizing the framework of *Roe v. Wade*. What criticisms does the majority offer? Do you agree?

4. How does the dissent defend the *Roe v. Wade* framework against the majority's criticisms?

... Chief Justice Rehnquist announced the judgment of the Court and delivered the opinion of the Court with respect to Parts I, II-A, II-B, and II-C, and an opinion with respect to Parts II-D and III, in which Justice White and Justice Kennedy join.

This appeal concerns the constitutionality of a Missouri statute regulating the performance of abortions. The United States Court of Appeals for the Eighth Circuit struck down several provisions of the statute on the ground that they violated this Court's decision in *Roe* v. *Wade* (1973), and cases following it. We noted probable jurisdiction and now reverse.

I

In June 1986, the Governor of Missouri signed into law Missouri Senate Committee Substitute for House Bill No. 1596 (hereinafter Act or statute) which amended existing state law concerning unborn children and abortions. The Act consisted of 20 provisions, 5 of which are now before the Court. The first provision, or preamble, contains "findings" by the state legislature that "[t]he life of each human being begins at conception," and that "unborn chil-

dren have protectable interests in life, health, and well-being." The Act further requires that all Missouri laws be interpreted to provide unborn children with the same rights enjoyed by other persons, subject to the Federal Constitution and this Court's precedents.

Among its other provisions, the Act requires that, prior to performing an abortion on any woman whom a physician has reason to believe is 20 or more weeks pregnant, the physician ascertain whether the fetus is viable by performing "such medical examinations and tests as are necessary to make a finding of the gestational age, weight, and lung maturity of the unborn child." The Act also prohibits the use of public employees and facilities to perform or assist abortions not necessary to save the mother's life, and it prohibits the use of public funds, employees, or facilities for the purpose of "encouraging or counseling" a woman to have an abortion not necessary to save her life.

In July 1986, five health professionals employed by the State and two nonprofit corporations brought this class action in the United States District Court for the Western District of Missouri to challenge the constitutionality of the Missouri statute. Plaintiffs, appellees in this Court, sought declaratory and injunctive relief on the ground that certain statutory provisions violated the First, Fourth, Ninth, and Fourteenth Amendments to the Federal Constitution. They asserted violations of various rights, including the "privacy rights of pregnant women seeking abortions"; the "woman's right to an abortion"; the "righ[t] to privacy in the physician-patient relationship"; the physician's "righ[t] to practice medicine"; the pregnant woman's "right to life due to inherent risks involved in childbirth"; and the woman's right to "receive . . . adequate medical advice and treatment" concerning abortions.

Plaintiffs filed this suit "on their own behalf and on behalf of the entire class consisting of facilities and Missouri licensed physicians or other health care professionals offering abortion services or pregnancy counseling and on behalf of the entire class of pregnant females seeking abortion services or pregnancy counseling within the State of Missouri." The two nonprofit corporations are Reproductive Health Services, which offers family planning and gynecological services to the public, including abortion services up to 22 weeks "gestational age," and Planned Parenthood of Kansas City, which provides abortion services up to 14 weeks gestational age. The individual plaintiffs are three physicians, one nurse, and a social worker. All are "public employees" at "public facilities" in Missouri, and they are paid for their services with "public funds," as those terms are defined by Mo. Rev. Stat. §188.200 (1986). The individual plaintiffs, within the scope of their public employment, encourage and counsel pregnant women to have nontherapeutic abortions. Two of the physicians perform abortions. . . .

II

[A . . .]

B

Section 188.210 provides that "[i]t shall be unlawful for any public employee within the scope of his employment to perform or assist an abortion, not necessary to save the life of the mother," while §188.215 makes it "unlawful for any public facility to be used for the purpose of performing or assisting an abortion not necessary to save the life of the mother." The Court of Appeals held that these provisions contravened this Court's abortion decisions. We take the contrary view.

As we said earlier this Term in *DeShaney* v. *Winnebago County Dept. of Social Services* (1989) "our cases have recognized that the Due Process Clauses generally confer no affirmative right to governmental aid, even where such aid may be necessary to secure life, liberty, or property interests of which the government itself may not deprive the individual." In *Maher* v. *Roe,* the Court upheld a Connecticut welfare regulation under which Medicaid recipients received payments for medical services related to childbirth, but not for nontherapeutic abortions. The Court rejected the claim that this unequal subsidization of childbirth and abortion was impermissible under *Roe v. Wade.* As the Court put it:

> "The Connecticut regulation before us is different in kind from the laws invalidated in our previous abortion decisions. The Connecticut regulation places no obstacles—absolute or otherwise—in the pregnant woman's path to an abortion. An indigent woman who desires an abortion suffers no disadvantage as a consequence of Connecticut's decision to fund childbirth; she continues as before to be dependent on private sources for the service she desires. The State may have made childbirth a more attractive alternative, thereby influencing the woman's decision, but it has imposed no restriction on access to abortions that was not already there. The indigency that may make it difficult—and in some cases, perhaps, impossible—for some women to have abortions is neither created nor in any way affected by the Connecticut regulation."

Relying on *Maher,* the Court in *Poelker* v. *Doe* (1977) held that the city of St. Louis committed "no constitutional violation . . . in electing, as a policy choice, to provide publicly financed hospital services for childbirth without providing corresponding services for nontherapeutic abortions."

More recently, in *Harris* v. *McRae* (1980), the Court upheld "the most restrictive version of the Hyde Amendment," which withheld from States federal funds under the Medicaid program to re-imburse the costs of abortions, "'except where the life of the mother would be endangered if the fetus were carried to term.'" As in *Maher* and *Poelker,* the Court required only a showing that Congress' authorization of "reimbursement for medically necessary services generally, but not for certain medically necessary abortions" was rationally related to the legitimate governmental goal of encouraging childbirth.

The Court of Appeals distinguished these cases on the ground that "[t]o prevent access to a public facility does more than demonstrate a political choice in favor of childbirth; it clearly narrows and in some cases forecloses the availability of abortion to women." The court reasoned that the ban on the use of public facilities "could prevent a woman's chosen doctor from performing an abortion because of his unprivileged status at other hospitals or because a private hospital adopted a similar anti-abortion stance." It also thought that "[s]uch a rule could increase the cost of obtaining an abortion and delay the timing of it as well."

We think that this analysis is much like that which we rejected in *Maher, Poelker,* and *McRae.* As in those cases, the State's decision here to use public facilities and staff to encourage childbirth over abortion "places no governmental obstacle in the path of a woman who chooses to terminate her pregnancy." Just as Congress' refusal to fund abortions in *McRae* left "an indigent woman with at least the same range of choice in deciding whether to obtain a medically necessary abortion as she would have had if Congress had chosen to subsidize no health care costs at all," Missouri's refusal to allow public employees to perform abortions in public hospitals leaves a pregnant woman with the same choices as if the State had chosen not to operate any public hospitals at all. The challenged provisions only restrict a woman's ability to obtain an abortion to the extent that she chooses to use a physician affiliated with a public hospital. This circumstance is more easily remedied, and thus considerably less burdensome, than indigency, which "may make it difficult—and in some cases, perhaps, impossible—for some women to have abortions" without public funding. Having held that the State's refusal to fund abortions does not violate *Roe* v. *Wade,* it strains logic to reach a

contrary result for the use of public facilities and employees. If the State may "make a value judgment favoring childbirth over abortion and ... implement that judgment by the allocation of public funds," surely it may do so through the allocation of other public resources, such as hospitals and medical staff.

The Court of Appeals sought to distinguish our cases on the additional ground that "[t]he evidence here showed that all of the public facility's costs in providing abortion services are recouped when the patient pays." Absent any expenditure of public funds, the court thought that Missouri was "expressing" more than "its preference for childbirth over abortions," but rather was creating an "obstacle to exercise of the right to choose an abortion [that could not] stand absent a compelling state interest." We disagree.

"Constitutional concerns are greatest," we said in *Maher,* "when the State attempts to impose its will by the force of law; the State's power to encourage actions deemed to be in the public interest is necessarily far broader." Nothing in the Constitution requires States to enter or remain in the business of performing abortions. Nor, as appellees suggest, do private physicians and their patients have some kind of constitutional right of access to public facilities for the performance of abortions. Indeed, if the State does recoup all of its costs in performing abortions, and no state subsidy, direct or indirect, is available, it is difficult to see how any procreational choice is burdened by the State's ban on the use of its facilities or employees for performing abortions.

Maher, Poelker, and *McRae* all support the view that the State need not commit any resources to facilitating abortions, even if it can turn a profit by doing so. In *Poelker,* the suit was filed by an indigent who could not afford to pay for an abortion, but the ban on the performance of nontherapeutic abortions in city-owned hospitals applied whether or not the pregnant woman could pay. The Court emphasized that the Mayor's decision to prohibit abortions in city hospitals was "subject to public debate and approval or disapproval at the polls," and that "the Constitution does not forbid a State or city, pursuant to democratic processes, from expressing a preference for normal childbirth as St. Louis has done." Thus we uphold the Act's restrictions on the use of public employees and facilities for the performance or assistance of nontherapeutic abortions.

[C . . .]

D

. . . The viability-testing provision of the Missouri Act is concerned with promoting the State's interest in potential human life rather than in maternal health. Section 188.029 creates what is essentially a presumption of viability at 20 weeks, which the physician must rebut with tests indicating that the fetus is not viable prior to performing an abortion. It also directs the physician's determination as to viability by specifying consideration, if feasible, of gestational age, fetal weight, and lung capacity. The District Court found that "the medical evidence is uncontradicted that a 20-week fetus is *not* viable," and that "23½ to 24 weeks gestation is the earliest point in pregnancy where a reasonable possibility of viability exists." But it also found that there may be a 4-week error in estimating gestational age, which supports testing at 20 weeks.

In *Roe* v. *Wade,* the Court recognized that the State has "important and legitimate" interests in protecting maternal health and in the potentiality of human life. During the second trimester, the State "may, if it chooses, regulate the abortion procedure in ways that are reasonably related to maternal health." After viability, when the State's interest in potential human life was held to become compelling, the State "may, if it chooses, regulate, and even proscribe, abortion except where it is necessary, in appropriate medical judgment, for the preservation of the life or health of the mother."

In *Colautti* v. *Franklin*, upon which appellees rely, the Court held that a Pennsylvania statute regulating the standard of care to be used by a physician performing an abortion of a possibly viable fetus was void for vagueness. But in the course of reaching that conclusion, the Court reaffirmed its earlier statement in *Planned Parenthood of Central Missouri* v. *Danforth* (1976) that "'the determination of whether a particular fetus is viable is, and must be, a matter for the judgment of the responsible attending physician.'" The dissent ignores the statement in

Colautti that "neither the legislature nor the courts may proclaim one of the elements entering into the ascertainment of viability—be it weeks of gestation or fetal weight or any other single factor—as the determinant of when the State has a compelling interest in the life or health of the fetus." To the extent that §188.029 regulates the method for determining viability, it undoubtedly does superimpose state regulation on the medical determination of whether a particular fetus is viable. The Court of Appeals and the District Court thought it unconstitutional for this reason. To the extent that the viability tests increase the cost of what are in fact second-trimester abortions, their validity may also be questioned under *Akron,* where the Court held that a requirement that second trimester abortions must be performed in hospitals was invalid because it substantially increased the expense of those procedures.

We think that the doubt cast upon the Missouri statute by these cases is not so much a flaw in the statute as it is a reflection of the fact that the rigid trimester analysis of the course of a pregnancy enunciated in *Roe* has resulted in subsequent cases like *Colautti* and *Akron* making constitutional law in this area a virtual Procrustean bed. Statutes specifying elements of informed consent to be provided abortion patients, for example, were invalidated if they were thought to "structur[e] . . . the dialogue between the woman and her physician." *Thornburgh* v. *American College of Obstetricians and Gynecologists* (1986). As the dissenters in *Thornburgh* pointed out, such a statute would have been sustained under any traditional standard of judicial review or for any other surgical procedure except abortion.

Stare decisis is a cornerstone of our legal system,* but it has less power in constitutional cases, where, save for constitutional amendments, this Court is the only body able to make needed changes. We have not refrained from reconsideration of a prior construction of the Constitution that has proved "unsound in principle and unworkable in practice." We think the *Roe* trimester framework falls into that category.

* Literally, "let the decision stand," *stare decisis* is the principle of respect for legal precedent, directing courts to follow decisions in previous cases. —Ed.

In the first place, the rigid *Roe* framework is hardly consistent with the notion of a Constitution cast in general terms, as ours is, and usually speaking in general principles, as ours does. The key elements of the *Roe* framework—trimesters and viability—are not found in the text of the Constitution or in any place else one would expect to find a constitutional principle. Since the bounds of the inquiry are essentially indeterminate, the result has been a web of legal rules that have become increasingly intricate, resembling a code of regulations rather than a body of constitutional doctrine. As Justice White has put it, the trimester framework has left this Court to serve as the country's *"ex officio medical board with powers to approve or disapprove medical and operative practices and standards throughout the United States."*

In the second place, we do not see why the State's interest in protecting potential human life should come into existence only at the point of viability, and that there should therefore be a rigid line allowing state regulation after viability but prohibiting it before viability. The dissenters in *Thornburgh,* writing in the context of the *Roe* trimester analysis, would have recognized this fact by positing against the "fundamental right" recognized in *Roe* the State's "compelling interest" in protecting potential human life throughout pregnancy. "[T]he State's interest, if compelling after viability, is equally compelling before viability." . . .

The tests that §188.029 requires the physician to perform are designed to determine viability. The State here has chosen viability as the point at which its interest in potential human life must be safeguarded. . . . It is true that the tests in question increase the expense of abortion, and regulate the discretion of the physician in determining the viability of the fetus. Since the tests will undoubtedly show in many cases that the fetus is not viable, the tests will have been performed for what were in fact second-trimester abortions. But we are satisfied that the requirement of these tests permissibly furthers the State's interest in protecting potential human life, and we therefore believe §188.029 to be constitutional.

The dissent takes us to task for our failure to join in a "great issues" debate as to whether the Constitution includes an "unenumerated" general right to privacy as recognized in cases such as *Griswold* v. *Connecticut* (1965) and *Roe.* But *Griswold* v. *Connecticut,* unlike *Roe,* did not purport to adopt a whole framework, complete with detailed rules and distinctions, to govern the cases in which the asserted liberty interest would apply. As such, it was far different from the opinion, if not the holding, of *Roe* v. *Wade,* which sought to establish a constitutional framework for judging state regulation of abortion during the entire term of pregnancy. That framework sought to deal with areas of medical practice traditionally subject to state regulation, and it sought to balance once and for all by reference only to the calendar the claims of the State to protect the fetus as a form of human life against the claims of a woman to decide for herself whether or not to abort a fetus she was carrying. The experience of the Court in applying *Roe* v. *Wade* in later cases suggests to us that there is wisdom in not unnecessarily attempting to elaborate the abstract differences between a "fundamental right" to abortion, as the Court described it in *Akron,* a "limited fundamental constitutional right," which Justice Blackmun's dissent today treats *Roe* as having established, or a liberty interest protected by the Due Process Clause, which we believe it to be. The Missouri testing requirement here is reasonably designed to ensure that abortions are not performed where the fetus is viable—an end which all concede is legitimate—and that is sufficient to sustain its constitutionality.

The dissent also accuses us, *inter alia,* of cowardice and illegitimacy in dealing with "the most politically divisive domestic legal issue of our time." There is no doubt that our holding today will allow some governmental regulation of abortion that would have been prohibited under the language of cases such as *Colautti* v. *Franklin* (1979) and *Akron* v. *Akron Center for Reproductive Health, Inc.* But the goal of constitutional adjudication is surely not to remove inexorably "politically divisive" issues from the ambit of the legislative process, whereby the people through their elected representatives deal with matters of concern to them. The goal of constitutional adjudication is to hold true the balance between that which the Constitution puts beyond the reach of the democratic process and that which it does not. We think we have done that today. The dissent's suggestion that legislative bodies, in a

Nation where more than half of our population is women, will treat our decision today as an invitation to enact abortion regulation reminiscent of the dark ages not only misreads our views but does scant justice to those who serve in such bodies and the people who elect them.

III

Both appellants and the United States as *Amicus Curiae* have urged that we overrule our decision in *Roe* v. *Wade.* The facts of the present case, however, differ from those at issue in *Roe.* Here, Missouri has determined that viability is the point at which its interest in potential human life must be safeguarded. In *Roe*, on the other hand, the Texas statue criminalized the performance of *all* abortions, except when the mother's life was at stake. This case therefore affords us no occasion to revisit the holding of *Roe,* which was that the Texas statute unconstitutionally infringed the right to an abortion derived from the Due Process Clause, and we leave it undisturbed. To the extent indicated in our opinion, we would modify and narrow *Roe* and succeeding cases.

Because none of the challenged provisions of the Missouri Act properly before us conflict with the Constitution, the judgment of the Court of Appeals is reversed.

Justice Blackmun, with whom Justice Brennan and Justice Marshall join, concurring in part and dissenting in part.

Today, *Roe* v. *Wade* and the fundamental constitutional right of women to decide whether to terminate a pregnancy, survive but are not secure. Although the Court extricates itself from this case without making a single, even incremental, change in the law of abortion, the plurality and Justice Scalia would overrule *Roe* (the first silently, the other explicitly) and would return to the States virtually unfettered authority to control the quintessentially intimate, personal, and life-directing decision whether to carry a fetus to term. Although today, no less than yesterday, the Constitution and the decisions of this Court prohibit a State from enacting

laws that inhibit women from the meaningful exercise of that right, a plurality of this Court implicitly invites every state legislature to enact more and more restrictive abortion regulations in order to provoke more and more test cases, in the hope that sometime down the line the Court will return the law of procreative freedom to the severe limitations that generally prevailed in this country before January 22, 1973. Never in my memory has a plurality announced a judgment of this Court that so foments disregard for the law and for our standing decisions.

Nor in my memory has a plurality gone about its business in such a deceptive fashion. At every level of its review, from its effort to read the real meaning out of the Missouri statute, to its intended evisceration of precedents and its deafening silence about the constitutional protections that it would jettison, the plurality obscures the portent of its analysis. With feigned restraint, the plurality announces that its analysis leaves *Roe* "undisturbed," albeit "modif[ied] and narrow[ed]." But this disclaimer is totally meaningless. The plurality opinion is filled with winks, and nods, and knowing glances to those who would do away with *Roe* explicitly, but turns a stone face to anyone in search of what the plurality conceives as the scope of a woman's right under the Due Process Clause to terminate a pregnancy free from the coercive and brooding influence of the State. The simple truth is that *Roe* would not survive the plurality's analysis, and that the plurality provides no substitute for *Roe's* protective umbrella.

I fear for the future. I fear for the liberty and equality of the millions of women who have lived and come of age in the 16 years since *Roe* was decided. I fear for the integrity of, and public esteem for, this Court.

I dissent.

I

. . . In the plurality's view, the viability-testing provision imposes a burden on second-trimester abortions as a way of furthering the State's interest in protecting the potential life of the fetus. Since under the *Roe* framework, the State may not fully regulate abortion in the interest of potential life (as opposed to maternal health) until the third trimester, the plurality finds it necessary, in order to save the Missouri testing provision, to throw out *Roe's* trimester framework. In flat contradiction to *Roe,* the plurality concludes that the State's interest in potential life is compelling before viability), and upholds the testing provision because it "permissibly furthers" that state interest.

A

. . . No one contests that under the *Roe* framework the State, in order to promote its interest in potential human life, may regulate and even proscribe non-therapeutic abortions once the fetus becomes viable. If, as the plurality appears to hold, the testing provision simply requires a physician to use appropriate and medically sound tests to determine whether the fetus is actually viable when the estimated gestational age is greater than 20 weeks (and therefore within what the District Court found to be the margin of error for viability), then I see little or no conflict with *Roe.* Nothing in *Roe,* or any of its progeny, holds that a State may not effectuate its compelling interest in the potential life of a viable fetus by seeking to ensure that no viable fetus is mistakenly aborted because of the inherent lack of precision in estimates of gestational age. A requirement that a physician make a finding of viability, one way or the other, for every fetus that falls within the range of possible viability does no more than preserve the State's recognized authority. Although, as the plurality correctly points out, such a testing requirement would have the effect of imposing additional costs on second-trimester abortions where the tests indicated that the fetus was not viable, these costs would be merely incidental to, and a necessary accommodation of, the State's unquestioned right to prohibit non-therapeutic abortions after the point of viability. In short, the testing provision, as construed by the plurality is consistent with the *Roe* framework and could be upheld effortlessly under current doctrine.

How ironic it is, then, and disingenuous, that the plurality scolds the Court of Appeals for adopting a construction of the statute that fails to avoid constitutional difficulties. By distorting the statute, the plurality manages to avoid invalidating the testing provision on what should have been noncontroversial constitutional grounds; having done so, however, the plurality rushes headlong into a much deeper constitutional thicket, brushing past an obvious basis for upholding §188.029 in search of a pretext for scuttling the trimester framework. Evidently, from the plurality's perspective, the real problem with the Court of Appeals' construction of §188.029 is not that it raised a constitutional difficulty, but that it raised the wrong constitutional difficulty—one not implicating *Roe.* The plurality has remedied that, traditional canons of construction and judicial forbearance notwithstanding.

B

Having set up the conflict between §188.029 and the *Roe* trimester framework, the plurality summarily discards *Roe's* analytic core as "'unsound in principle and unworkable in practice.'" This is so, the plurality claims, because the key elements of the framework do not appear in the text of the Constitution, because the framework more closely resembles a regulatory code than a body of constitutional doctrine, and because under the framework the State's interest in potential human life is considered compelling only after viability, when, in fact, that interest is equally compelling throughout pregnancy. The plurality does not bother to explain these alleged flaws in *Roe.* Bald assertion masquerades as reasoning. The object, quite clearly, is not to persuade, but to prevail.

1

The plurality opinion is far more remarkable for the arguments that it does not advance than for those that it does. The plurality does not even mention, much less join, the true jurisprudential debate underlying this case: whether the Constitution includes an "unenumerated" general right to privacy as recognized in many of our decisions, most notably *Griswold* v. *Connecticut* (1965) and *Roe,* and, more specifically, whether and to what extent such a right to privacy extends to matters of childbearing and family life, including abortion. These are questions of unsurpassed significance in this Court's interpretation of the Constitution, and mark the battleground upon which this case was fought, by the parties, by the Solicitor General as *amicus* on behalf of petitioners, and by an unprecedented number of *amici*. On these grounds, abandoned by the plurality, the Court should decide this case.

But rather than arguing that the text of the Constitution makes no mention of the right to privacy, the plurality complains that the critical elements of the *Roe* framework—trimesters and viability—do not appear in the Constitution and are, therefore, somehow inconsistent with a Constitution cast in general terms. Were this a true concern, we would have to abandon most of our constitutional jurisprudence. As the plurality well knows, or should know, the "critical elements" of countless constitutional doctrines nowhere appear in the Constitution's text. The Constitution makes no mention, for example, of the First Amendment's "actual malice" standard for proving certain libels or of the standard for determining when speech is obscene. Similarly, the Constitution makes no mention of the rational-basis test, or the specific verbal formulations of intermediate and strict scrutiny by which this Court evaluates claims under the Equal Protection Clause. The reason is simple. Like the *Roe* framework, these tests or standards are not, and do not purport to be, rights protected by the Constitution. Rather, they are judge-made methods for evaluating and measuring the strength and scope of constitutional rights or for balancing the constitutional rights of individuals against the competing interests of government.

With respect to the *Roe* framework, the general consitutional principle, indeed the fundamental constitutional right, for which it was developed is the right to privacy, a species of "liberty" protected by the Due Process Clause, which under our past decisions safeguards the right of women to exercise some control over their own role in procreation. As we recently reaffirmed in *Thornburgh* v. *American College of Obstetricians and Gynecologists* (1986), few decisions are "more basic to individual dignity and autonomy" or more appropriate to that "certain private sphere of individual liberty" that the Constitution reserves

from the intrusive reach of government than the right to make the uniquely personal, intimate, and self-defining decision whether to end a pregnancy. It is this general principle, the "'moral fact that a person belongs to himself and not others nor to society as a whole,'" that is found in the Constitution. The trimester framework simply defines and limits that right to privacy in the abortion context to accommodate, not destroy, a State's legitimate interest in protecting the health of pregnant women and in preserving potential human life. Fashioning such accommodations between individual rights and the legitimate interests of government, establishing benchmarks and standards with which to evaluate the competing claims of individuals and government, lies at the the very heart of consitutional adjudication. To the extent that the trimester framework is useful in this enterprise, it is not only consistent with constitutional interpretation, but necessary to the wise and just exercise of this Court's paramount authority to define the scope of constitutional rights.

2

The plurality next alleges that the result of the trimester framework has "been a web of legal rules that have become increasingly intricate, resembling a code of regulations rather than a body of constitutional doctrine." Again, if this were a true and genuine concern, we would have to abandon vast areas of our constitutional jurisprudence. The plurality complains that under the trimester framework the Court has distinguished between a city ordinance requiring that second-trimester abortions be performed in clinics and a state law requiring that these abortions be performed in hospitals, or between laws requiring that certain information be furnished to a woman by a physician or his assistant and those requiring that such information be furnished by the physician exclusively. Are these distinctions any finer, or more "regulatory," than the distinctions we have often drawn in our First Amendment jurisprudence, where, for example, we have held that a "release time" program permitting public-school students to leave school grounds during school hours to receive religious instruction does not violate the Establishment Clause, even though a release-time program permitting religious instruction on school grounds does violate the Clause? Our Fourth Amendment jurisprudence recognizes factual distinctions no less intricate. Just this Term, for example, we held that while an aerial observation from a helicopter hovering at 400 feet does not violate any reasonable expectation of privacy, such an expectation of privacy would be violated by a helicopter observation from an unusually low altitude. Similarly, in a Sixth Amendment case, the Court held that although an overnight ban on attorney-client communication violated the constitutionally guaranteed right to counsel, that right was not violated when a trial judge separated a defendant from his lawyer during a 15-minute recess after the defendant's direct testimony.

That numerous constitutional doctrines result in narrow differentiations between similar circumstances does not mean that this Court has abandoned adjudication in favor of regulation. Rather, these careful distinctions reflect the process of constitutional adjudication itself, which is often highly fact-specific, requiring such determinations as whether state laws are "unduly burdensome" or "reasonable" or bear a "rational" or "necessary" relation to asserted state interests. In a recent due process case, the Chief Justice wrote for the Court: "[M]any branches of the law abound in nice distinctions that may be troublesome but have been thought nonetheless necessary: 'I do not think we need trouble ourselves with the thought that my view depends upon differences of degree. The whole law does so as soon as it is civilized.'"

These "differences of degree" fully account for our holdings in Simopoulos and Akron. Those decisions rest on this Court's reasoned and accurate judgment that hospitalization and doctor-counselling requirements unduly burdened the right of women to terminate a pregnancy and were not rationally related to the State's asserted interest in the health of pregnant women, while Virginia's substantially less restrictive regulations were not unduly burdensome and did rationally serve the State's interest. That the Court exercised its best judgment in evaluating these markedly different statutory schemes no more established the Court as an "'ex officio medical board,'" than our decisions involving religion in the

public schools establish the Court as a national school board, or our decisions concerning prison regulations establish the Court as a bureau of prisons. If, in delicate and complicated areas of constitutional law, our legal judgments "have become increasingly intricate," it is not, as the plurality contends, because we have overstepped our judicial role. Quite the opposite: the rules are intricate because we have remained conscientious in our duty to do justice carefully, especially when fundamental rights rise or fall with our decisions.

3

Finally, the plurality asserts that the trimester framework cannot stand because the State's interest in potential life is compelling throughout pregnancy, not merely after viability. The opinion contains not one word of rationale for its view of the State's interest. This "it-is-so-because-we-say-so" jurisprudence constitutes nothing other than an attempted exercise of brute force; reason, much less persuasion, has no place.

In answering the plurality's claim that the State's interest in the fetus is uniform and compelling throughout pregnancy, I cannot improve upon what Justice Stevens has written:

"I should think it obvious that the State's interest in the protection of an embryo—even if that interest is defined as 'protecting those who will be citizens' . . . —increases progressively and dramatically as the organism's capacity to feel pain, to experience pleasure, to survive, and to react to its surroundings increases day by day. The development of a fetus—and pregnancy itself—are not static conditions, and the assertion that the government's interest is static simply ignores this reality. . . . [U]nless the religious view that a fetus is a 'person' is adopted . . . there is a fundamental and well-recognized difference between a fetus and a human being; indeed, if there is not such a difference, the permissibility of terminating the life of a fetus could scarcely be left to the will of the state legislatures. And if distinctions may be drawn between a fetus and a human being in terms of the state interest in their protection—even though the fetus represents one of 'those who will be citizens'—it seems to me quite odd to argue that distinctions may not also be drawn between the state interest in protecting the freshly fertilized egg and the state interest in protecting the 9-month-gestated, fully sentient fetus on the eve of birth. Recognition of this distinction is supported not only by logic, but also by history and by our shared experiences." *Thornburgh*.

For my own part, I remain convinced, as six other Members of this Court 16 years ago were convinced, that the *Roe* framework, and the viability standard in particular, fairly, sensibly, and effectively functions to safeguard the constitutional liberties of pregnant women while recognizing and accommodating the State's interest in potential human life. The viability line reflects the biological facts and truths of fetal development; it marks that threshold moment prior to which a fetus cannot survive separate from the woman and cannot reasonably and objectively be regarded as a subject of rights or interests distinct from, or paramount to, those of the pregnant woman. At the same time, the viability standard takes account of the undeniable fact that as the fetus evolves into its postnatal form, and as it loses its dependence on the uterine environment, the State's interest in the fetus' potential human life, and in fostering a regard for human life in general, becomes compelling. As a practical matter, because viability follows "quickening"—the point at which a woman feels movement in her womb—and because viability occurs no earlier than 23 weeks gestational age, it establishes an easily applicable standard for regulating abortion while providing a pregnant woman ample time to exercise her fundamental right with her responsible physician to terminate her pregnancy. Although I have stated previously for a majority of this Court that "[c]onstitutional rights do not always have easily ascertainable boundaries," to seek and establish those boundaries remains the special responsibility of this Court. In *Roe*, we discharged that responsibility as logic and science compelled. The plurality today advances not one reasonable argument as to why our judgment in that case was wrong and should be abandoned.

C

Having contrived an opportunity to reconsider the *Roe* framework, and then having discarded that framework, the plurality finds the testing provision unobjectionable because it "permissibly furthers the State's interest in protecting potential human life." This newly minted standard is circular and totally meaningless. Whether a challenged abortion regulation "permissibly furthers" a legitimate state interest is the *question* that courts must answer in abortion cases, not the standard for courts to apply. In keeping with the rest of its opinion, the plurality makes no attempt to explain or to justify its new standard, either in the abstract or as applied in this case. Nor could it. The "permissibly furthers" standard has no independent meaning, and consists of nothing other than what a majority of this Court may believe at any given moment in any given case. The plurality's novel test appears to be nothing more than a dressed-up version of rational-basis review, this Court's most lenient level of scrutiny. One thing is clear, however: were the plurality's "permissibly furthers" standard adopted by the Court, for all practical purposes, *Roe* would be overruled.

The "permissibly furthers" standard completely disregards the irreducible minimum of *Roe*: the Court's recognition that a woman has a limited fundamental constitutional right to decide whether to terminate a pregnancy. That right receives no meaningful recognition in the plurality's written opinion. Since, in the plurality's view, the State's interest in potential life is compelling as of the moment of conception, and is therefore served only if abortion is abolished, every hindrance to a woman's ability to obtain an abortion must be "permissible." Indeed, the more severe the hindrance, the more effectively (and permissibly) the State's interest would be furthered. A tax on abortions or a criminal prohibition would both satisfy the plurality's standard. So, for that matter, would a requirement that a pregnant woman memorize and recite today's plurality opinion before seeking an abortion.

The plurality pretends that *Roe* survives, explaining that the facts of this case differ from those in *Roe*: here, Missouri has chosen to assert its interest in potential life only at the point of viability, whereas, in *Roe*, Texas had asserted that interest from the point of conception, criminalizing all abortions, except where the life of the mother was at stake. This, of course, is a distinction without a difference. The plurality repudiates every principle for which *Roe* stands; in good conscience, it cannot possibly believe that *Roe* lies "undisturbed" merely because this case does not call upon the Court to reconsider the Texas statute, or one like it. If the Constitution permits a State to enact any statute that reasonably furthers its interest in potential life, and if that interest arises as of conception, why would the Texas statute fail to pass muster? One suspects that the plurality agrees. It is impossible to read the plurality opinion and especially its final paragraph, without recognizing its implicit invitation to every State to enact more and more restrictive abortion laws, and to assert their interest in potential life as of the moment of conception. All these laws will satisfy the plurality's non-scrutiny, until sometime, a new regime of old dissenters and new appointees will declare what the plurality intends: that *Roe* is no longer good law.

D

Thus, "not with a bang, but a whimper," the plurality discards a landmark case of the last generation, and casts into darkness the hopes and visions of every woman in this country who had come to believe that the Constitution guaranteed her the right to exercise some control over her unique ability to bear children. The plurality does so either oblivious or insensitive to the fact that millions of women, and their families, have ordered their lives around the right to reproductive choice, and that this right has become vital to the full participation of women in the economic and political walks of American life. The plurality would clear the way once again for government to force upon women the physical labor and specific and direct medical and psychological harms that may accompany carrying a fetus to term. The plurality would clear the way again for the State to conscript a woman's body and to force upon her a "distressful life and future."

The result, as we know from experience, would be that every year hundreds of thousands of women, in desperation, would defy the law, and place their health and safety in the unclean and unsympathetic hands of back-alley abortionists, or they would attempt to perform abortions upon themselves, with disastrous results. Every year, many women, especially poor and minority women, would die or suffer debilitating physical trauma, all in the name of enforced morality or religious dictates or lack of compassion, as it may be.

Of the aspirations and settled understandings of American women, of the inevitable and brutal consequences of what it is doing, the tough-approach plurality utters not a word. This silence is callous. It is also profoundly destructive of this Court as an institution. To overturn a constitutional decision is a rare and grave undertaking. To overturn a constitutional decision that secured a fundamental personal liberty to millions of persons would be unprecedented in our 200 years of constitutional history. Although the doctrine of *stare decisis* applies with somewhat diminished force in constitutional cases generally, even in ordinary constitutional cases "any departure from *stare decisis* demands special justification." . . . This requirement of justification applies with unique force where, as here, the Court's abrogation of precedent would destroy people's firm belief, based on past decisions of this Court, that they possess an unabridgeable right to undertake certain conduct.

As discussed at perhaps too great length above, the plurality makes no serious attempt to carry "the heavy burden of persuading . . . that changes in society or in the law dictate" the abandonment of *Roe* and its numerous progeny, much less the greater burden of explaining the abrogation of a fundamental personal freedom. Instead, the plurality pretends that it leaves *Roe* standing, and refuses even to discuss the real issue underlying this case: whether the Constitution includes an unenumerated right to privacy that encompasses a woman's right to decide whether to terminate a pregnancy. To the extent that the plurality does criticize the *Roe* framework, these criticisms are pure *ipse dixit*.

This comes at a cost. The doctrine of *stare decisis* "permits society to presume that bedrock principles are founded in the law rather than in the proclivities of individuals, and thereby contributes to the integrity of our constitutional system of government, both in appearance and in fact." Today's decision involves the most politically divisive domestic legal issue of our time. By refusing to explain or to justify its proposed revolutionary revision in the law of abortion, and by refusing to abide not only by our precedents, but also by our canons for reconsidering those precedents, the plurality invites charges of cowardice and illegitimacy to our door. I cannot say that these would be undeserved.

II

For today, at least, the law of abortion stands undisturbed. For today, the women of this Nation still retain the liberty to control their destinies. But the signs are evident and very ominous, and a chill wind blows.

I dissent.

JUDITH JARVIS THOMSON

A Defense of Abortion

Judith Jarvis Thomson is Professor of Philosophy at the Massachusetts Institute of Technology. (Source: From Philosophy and Public Affairs *Vol. I, No. 1 [Fall 1971], pp. 47–66. Copyright © 1971 by Princeton University Press. Reprinted by permission of Princeton University Press.)*

QUESTIONS FOR REFLECTION

1. What conclusions does Thomson draw from the violinist example? Do you agree with her interpretation of the example?

2. How does Thomson argue against what she calls "the extreme view"?

3. What is a right to life, for Thomson? Why does she reject other accounts of this right?

4. What is Good Samaritanism? Minimally Decent Samaritanism? Which, according to Thomson, is required of us? What does this imply for the morality of abortion?

Most opposition to abortion relies on the premise that the fetus is a human being, a person, from the moment of conception. The premise is argued for, but, as I think, not well. Take, for example, the most common argument. We are asked to notice that the development of a human being from conception through birth into childhood is continuous; then it is said that to draw a line, to choose a point in this development and say "before this point the thing is not a person, after this point it is a person" is to make an arbitrary choice, a choice for which in the nature of things no good reason can be given. It is concluded that the fetus is, or anyway that we had better say it is, a person from the moment of conception. But this conclusion does not follow. Similar things might be said about the development of an acorn into an oak tree, and it does not follow that acorns are oak trees, or that we had better say they are. Arguments of this form are sometimes called "slippery slope arguments"—the phrase is perhaps self-explanatory—and it is dismaying that opponents of abortion rely on them so heavily and uncritically.

I am inclined to agree, however, that the prospects for "drawing a line" in the development of the fetus look dim. I am inclined to think also that we shall probably have to agree that the fetus has already become a human person well before birth. Indeed, it comes as a surprise when one first learns how early in its life it begins to acquire human characteristics. By the tenth week, for example, it already has a face, arms and legs, fingers and toes; it has internal organs, and brain activity is detectable. On the other hand, I think that the premise is false, that the fetus is not a person from the moment of conception. A newly fertilized ovum, a newly implanted clump of cells, is no more a person than an acorn is an oak tree. But I shall not discuss any of this. For it seems to me to be of great interest to ask what happens if, for the sake of argument, we allow the premise. How, precisely, are we supposed to get from there to the conclusion that abortion is morally impermissible? Opponents of abortion commonly spend most of their time establishing that the fetus is a person, and hardly any time explaining the step from there to the impermissibility of abortion. Perhaps they think the step too simple and obvious to require much comment. Or perhaps instead they are simply being economical in argument. Many of those who defend abortion rely on the premise that the fetus is not a person, but only a bit of tissue that will become a person at birth; and why pay out more arguments than you have to? Whatever the explanation, I suggest that the step they take is neither easy nor obvious, that it calls for closer examination than it is commonly given, and that when we do give it this closer examination we shall feel inclined to reject it.

I propose, then, that we grant that the fetus is a person from the moment of conception. How does the argument go from here? Something like this, I take it. Every person has a right to life. So the fetus has a right to life. No doubt the mother has a right to decide what shall happen in and to her body; everyone would grant that. But surely a person's right to life is stronger and more stringent than the mother's right to decide what happens in and to her body, and so outweighs it. So the fetus may not be killed; an abortion may not be performed.

It sounds plausible. But now let me ask you to imagine this. You wake up in the morning and find yourself back to back in bed with an unconscious violinist. A famous unconscious violinist. He has been found to have a fatal kidney ailment, and the Society of Music Lovers has canvassed all the available medical records and found that you alone have the right blood type to help. They have therefore kidnapped you, and last night the violinist's circulatory system was plugged into yours, so that your kidneys can be used to extract poisons from his blood as well as your own. The director of the hospital now tells you, "Look, we're sorry the Society of Music Lovers did this to you—we would never have permitted it if we had known. But still, they did it, and the violinist now is plugged into you. To unplug you would be to kill him. But never mind, it's only for nine months. By then he will have recovered from his ailment, and can safely be unplugged from you." Is it morally incumbent on you to accede to this situation? No doubt it would be very nice of you if you

did, a great kindness. But do you *have* to accede to it? What if it were not nine months, but nine years? Or longer still? What if the director of the hospital says, "Tough luck, I agree, but you've now got to stay in bed, with the violinist plugged into you, for the rest of your life. Because remember this. All persons have a right to life, and violinists are persons. Granted you have a right to decide what happens in and to your body, but a person's right to life outweighs your right to decide what happens in and to your body. So you cannot ever be unplugged from him." I imagine you would regard this as outrageous, which suggests that something really is wrong with that plausible-sounding argument I mentioned a moment ago.

In this case, of course, you were kidnapped; you didn't volunteer for the operation that plugged the violinist into your kidneys. Can those who oppose abortion on the ground I mentioned make an exception for a pregnancy due to rape? Certainly. They can say that persons have a right to life only if they didn't come into existence because of rape; or they can say that all persons have a right to life, but that some have less of a right to life than others, in particular, that those who came into existence because of rape have less. But these statements have a rather unpleasant sound. Surely the question of whether you have a right to life at all, or how much of it you have, shouldn't turn on the question of whether or not you are the product of a rape. And in fact the people who oppose abortion on the ground I mentioned do not make this distinction, and hence do not make an exception in case of rape.

Nor do they make an exception for a case in which the mother has to spend the nine months of her pregnancy in bed. They would agree that would be a great pity, and hard on the mother; but all the same, all persons have a right to life, the fetus is a person, and so on. I suspect, in fact, that they would not make an exception for a case in which, miraculously enough, the pregnancy went on for nine years, or even the rest of the mother's life.

Some won't even make an exception for a case in which continuation of the pregnancy is likely to shorten the mother's life; they regard abortion as impermissible even to save the mother's life. Such cases are nowadays very rare, and many opponents of abortion do not accept this extreme view. All the

THOMSON • A DEFENSE OF ABORTION

same, it is a good place to begin: a number of points of interest come out in respect to it.

1. Let us call the view that abortion is impermissible even to save the mother's life "the extreme view." I want to suggest first that it does not issue from the argument I mentioned earlier without the addition of some fairly powerful premises. Suppose a woman has become pregnant, and now learns that she has a cardiac condition such that she will die if she carries the baby to term. What may be done for her? The fetus, being a person, has a right to life, but as the mother is a person too, so has she a right to life. Presumably they have an equal right to life. How is it supposed to come out that an abortion may not be performed? If mother and child have an equal right to life, shouldn't we perhaps flip a coin? Or should we add to the mother's right to life her right to decide what happens in and to her body, which everybody seems to be ready to grant—the sum of her rights now outweighing the fetus' right to life?

The most familiar argument here is the following. We are told that performing the abortion would be directly killing the child, whereas doing nothing would not be killing the mother, but only letting her die. Moreover, in killing the child, one would be killing an innocent person, for the child has committed no crime, and is not aiming at his mother's death. And then there are a variety of ways in which this might be continued. (1) But as directly killing an innocent person is always and absolutely impermissible, an abortion may not be performed. Or, (2) as directly killing an innocent person is murder, and murder is always and absolutely impermissible, an abortion may not be performed. Or, (3) as one's duty to refrain from directly killing an innocent person is more stringent than one' duty to keep a person from dying, an abortion may not be performed. Or, (4) if one's only options are directly killing an innocent person or letting a person die, one must prefer letting the person die, and thus an abortion may not be performed.

Some people seem to have thought that these are not further premises which must be added if the conclusion is to be reached, but that they follow from the very fact that an innocent person has a right to life. But this seems to me to be a mistake, and perhaps the simplest way to show this is to bring out that while we must certainly grant that

innocent persons have a right to life, the theses in (1) through (4) are all false. Take (2), for example. If directly killing an innocent person is murder, and thus is impermissible, then the mother's directly killing the innocent person inside her is murder, and thus is impermissible. But it cannot seriously be thought to be murder if the mother performs an abortion on herself to save her life. It cannot seriously be said that she *must* refrain, that she *must* sit passively by and wait for her death. Let us look again at the case of you and the violinist. There you are, in bed with the violinist, and the director of the hospital says to you, "It's all most distressing, and I deeply sympathize, but you see this is putting an additional strain on your kidneys, and you'll be dead within the month. But you *have* to stay where you are all the same. Because unplugging you would be directly killing an innocent violinist, and that's murder, and that's impermissible." If anything in the world is true, it is that you do not commit murder, you do not do what is impermissible, if you reach around to your back and unplug yourself from that violinist to save your life.

The main focus of attention in writings on abortion has been on what a third party may or may not do in answer to a request from a woman for an abortion. This is in a way understandable. Things being as they are, there isn't much a woman can safely do to abort herself. So the question asked is what a third party may do, and what the mother may do, if it is mentioned at all, is deduced, almost as an afterthought, from what it is concluded that third parties may do. But it seems to me that to treat the matter in this way is to refuse to grant to the mother that very status of person which is so firmly insisted on for the fetus. For we cannot simply read off what a person may do from what a third party may do. Suppose you find yourself trapped in a tiny house with a growing child. I mean a very tiny house, and a rapidly growing child—you are already up against the wall of the house and in a few minutes you'll be crushed to death. The child on the other hand won't be crushed to death; if nothing is done to stop him from growing he'll be hurt, but in the end he'll simply burst open the house and walk out a free man. Now I could well understand it if a bystander were to say, "There's nothing we can do for you. We cannot choose between your life and his, we cannot be the ones to decide who is to live, we cannot inter- vene." But it cannot be concluded that you too can do nothing, that you cannot attack it to save your life. However innocent the child may be, you do not have to wait passively while it crushes you to death. Perhaps a pregnant woman is vaguely felt to have the status of house, to which we don't allow the right of self-defense. But if the woman houses the child, it should be remembered that she is a person who houses it.

I should perhaps stop to say explicitly that I am not claiming that people have a right to do anything whatever to save their lives. I think, rather, that there are drastic limits to the right of self-defense. If some- one threatens you with death unless you torture someone else to death, I think you have not the right, even to save your life, to do so. But the case under consideration here is very different. In our case there are only two people involved, one whose life is threatened, and one who threatens it. Both are innocent: the one who is threatened is not threat- ened because of any fault, the one who threatens does not threaten because of any fault. For this rea- son we may feel that we bystanders cannot inter- vene. But the person threatened can.

In sum, a woman surely can defend her life against the threat to it posed by the unborn child, even if doing so involves its death. And this shows not merely that the theses in (1) through (4) are false; it shows also that the extreme view of abortion is false, and so we need not canvass any other possi- ble ways of arriving at it from the argument I men- tioned at the outset.

2. The extreme view could of course be weak- ened to say that while abortion is permissible to save the mother's life, it may not be performed by the third party, but only by the mother herself. But this cannot be right either. For what we have to keep in mind is that the mother and the unborn child are not like two tenants in a small house which has, by an unfortunate mistake, been rented to both: the mother *owns* the house. The fact that she does adds to the offensiveness of deducing that the mother can do nothing from the supposition that third parties can do nothing. But it does more than this: it casts a bright light on the supposition that third parties can do nothing. Certainly it lets us see that a third party who says "I cannot choose between you" is

fooling himself if he thinks this is impartiality. If Jones has found and fastened on a certain coat, which he needs to keep him from freezing, but which Smith also needs to keep him from freezing, then it is not impartiality that says "I cannot choose between you" when Smith owns the coat. Women have said again and again "This body is *my* body!" and they have reason to feel angry, reason to feel that it has been like shouting into the wind. Smith, after all, is hardly likely to bless us if we say to him, "Of course it's your coat, anybody would grant that it is. But no one may choose between you and Jones who is to have it."

We should really ask what it is that says "no one may choose" in the face of the fact that the body that houses the child is the mother's body. It may be sim- ply a failure to appreciate this fact. But it may be something more interesting, namely the sense that one has a right to refuse to lay hands on people, even where it would be just and fair to do so, even where justice seems to require that somebody do so. Thus justice might call for somebody to get Smith's coat back from Jones, and yet you have a right to refuse to be the one to lay hands on Jones, a right to refuse to do physical violence to him. This, I think, must be granted. But then what should be said is not "no one may choose," but only "I cannot choose," and indeed not even this, but "I will not *act*," leaving it open that somebody else can or should, and in particular that anyone in a position of authority, with the job of securing people's rights, both can and should. So this is no difficulty. I have not been arguing that any given third party must accede to the mother's request that he perform an abortion to save her life, but only that he may.

I suppose that in some views of human life the mother's body is only on loan to her, the loan not being one which gives her any prior claim to it. One who held this view might well think it impartiality to say "I cannot choose." But I shall simply ignore this possibility. My own view is that if a human being has any just, prior claim to anything at all, he has a just, prior claim to his own body. And perhaps this needn't be argued for here anyway, since, as I mentioned, the arguments against abortion we are looking at do grant that the woman has a right to decide what happens in and to her body.

But although they do grant it, I have tried to show

that they do not take seriously what is done in granting it. I suggest the same thing will reappear even more clearly when we turn away from cases in which the mother's life is at stake, and attend, as I propose we now do, to the vastly more common cases in which a woman wants an abortion for some less weighty reason than preserving her own life.

3. Where the mother's life is not at stake, the argument I mentioned at the outset seems to have a much stronger pull. "Everyone has a right to life, so the unborn person has a right to life." And isn't the child's right to life weightier than anything other than the mother's own right to life, which she might put forward as ground for an abortion?

This argument treats the right to life as if it were unproblematic. It is not, and this seems to me to be precisely the source of the mistake.

For we should now, at long last, ask what it comes to, to have a right to life. In some views having a right to life includes having a right to be given at least the bare minimum one needs for continued life. But suppose that what in fact *is* the bare minimum a man needs for continued life is something he has no right at all to be given? If I am sick unto death, and the only thing that will save my life is the touch of Henry Fonda's cool hand on my fevered brow, then all the same, I have no right to be given the touch of Henry Fonda's cool hand on my fevered brow. It would be frightfully nice of him to fly in from the West Coast to provide it. It would be less nice, though no doubt well meant, if my friends flew out to the West Coast and carried Henry Fonda back with them. But I have no right at all against anybody that he should do this for me. Or again, to return to the story I told earlier, the fact that for continued life that violinist needs the continued use of your kidneys does not establish that he has a right to be given the continued use of your kidneys. He certainly has no right against you that *you* should give him continued use of your kidneys. For nobody has any right to use your kidneys unless you give him such a right; and nobody has the right against you that you shall give him this right—if you do allow him to go on using your kidneys, this is kindness on your part, and not something he can claim from you as his due. Nor has he any right against anybody else that *they* should give him continued use of your kidneys. Certainly he had no right against the Society of

Music Lovers that they should plug him into you in the first place. And if you now start to unplug yourself, having learned that you will otherwise have to spend nine years in bed with him, there is nobody in the world who must try to prevent you, in order to see to it that he is given something he has a right to be given.

Some people are rather stricter about the right to life. In their view, it does not include the right to be given anything, but amounts to, and only to, the right not to be killed by anybody. But here a related difficulty arises. If everybody is to refrain from killing that violinist, then everybody must refrain from doing a great many different sorts of things. Everybody must refrain from slitting his throat, everybody must refrain from shooting him—and everybody must refrain from unplugging you from him. But does he have a right against everybody that they shall refrain from unplugging you from him? To refrain from doing this is to allow him to continue to use your kidneys. It could be argued that he has a right against us that *we* should allow him to continue to use your kidneys. That is, while he had no right against us that we should give him the use of your kidneys, it might be argued that he anyway has a right against us that we shall not now intervene and deprive him of the use of your kidneys. I shall come back to third-party interventions later. But certainly the violinist has no right against you that *you* shall allow him to continue to use your kidneys. As I said, if you do allow him to use them, it is a kindness on your part, and not something you owe him.

The difficulty I point to here is not peculiar to the right to life. It reappears in connection with all the other natural rights; and it is something which an adequate account of rights must deal with. For present purposes it is enough just to draw attention to it. But I would stress that I am not arguing that people do not have a right to life—quite to the contrary, it seems to me that the primary control we must place on the acceptability of an account of rights is that it should turn out in that account to be a truth that all persons have a right to life. I am arguing only that having a right to life does not guarantee having either a right to be given the use of or a right to be allowed continued use of another person's body—even if one needs it for life itself. So the right to life will not serve the opponents of abortion in the very simple and clear way in which they seem to have thought it would.

4. There is another way to bring out the difficulty. In the most ordinary sort of case, to deprive someone of what he has a right to is to treat him unjustly. Suppose a boy and his small brother are jointly given a box of chocolates for Christmas. If the older boy takes the box and refuses to give his brother any of the chocolates, he is unjust to him, for the brother has been given a right to half of them. But suppose that, having learned that otherwise it means nine years in bed with that violinist, you unplug yourself from him. You surely are not being unjust to him, for you gave him no right to use your kidneys, and no one else can have given him any such right. But we have to notice that in unplugging yourself, you are killing him; and violinists, like everybody else, have a right to life, and thus in the view we were considering just now, the right not to be killed. So here you do what he supposedly has a right you shall not do, but you do not act unjustly to him in doing it.

The emendation which may be made at this point is this: the right to life consists not in the right not to be killed, but rather in the right not to be killed unjustly. This runs a risk of circularity, but never mind: it would enable us to square the fact that the violinist has a right to life with the fact that you do not act unjustly toward him in unplugging yourself, thereby killing him. For if you do not kill him unjustly, you do not violate his right to life, and so it is no wonder you do him no injustice.

But if this emendation is accepted, the gap in the argument against abortion stares us plainly in the face: it is by no means enough to show that the fetus is a person, and to remind us that all persons have a right to life—we need to be shown also that killing the fetus violates its right to life, i.e., that abortion is unjust killing. And is it?

I suppose we may take it as a datum that in a case of pregnancy due to rape the mother has not given the unborn person a right to the use of her body for food and shelter. Indeed, in what pregnancy could it be supposed that the mother has given the unborn person such a right? It is not as if there were unborn persons drifting about the world, to whom a woman who wants a child says "I invite you in."

But it might be argued that there are other ways one can have acquired a right to the use of another person's body than by having been invited to use it by that person. Suppose a woman voluntarily indulges in intercourse, knowing of the chance it will issue in pregnancy, and then she does become pregnant; is she not in part responsible for the presence, in fact the very existence, of the unborn person inside her? No doubt she did not invite it in. But doesn't her partial responsibility for its being there itself give it a right to the use of her body? If so, then her aborting it would be more like the boy's taking away the chocolates, and less like your unplugging yourself from the violinist—doing so would be depriving it of what it does have a right to, and thus would be doing it an injustice.

And then, too, it might be asked whether or not she can kill it even to save her own life: If she voluntarily called it into existence, how can she now kill it, even in self-defense?

The first thing to be said about this is that it is something new. Opponents of abortion have been so concerned to make out the independence of the fetus, in order to establish that it has a right to life, just as its mother does, that they have tended to overlook the possible support they might gain from making out that the fetus is *dependent* on the mother, in order to establish that she has a special kind of responsibility for it, a responsibility that gives it rights against her which are not possessed by any independent person—such as an ailing violinist who is a stranger to her.

On the other hand, this argument would give the unborn person a right to its mother's body only if her pregnancy resulted from a voluntary act, undertaken in full knowledge of the chance a pregnancy might result from it. It would leave out entirely the unborn person whose existence is due to rape. Pending the availability of some further argument, then, we would be left with the conclusion that unborn persons whose existence is due to rape have no right to the use of their mothers' bodies, and thus that aborting them is not depriving them of anything they have a right to and hence is not unjust killing.

And we should also notice that it is not at all plain that this argument really does go even as far as it purports to. For there are cases and cases, and the details make a difference. If the room is stuffy, and I therefore open a window to air it, and a burglar climbs in, it would be absurd to say, "Ah, now he can stay, she's given him a right to the use of her house—for she is partially responsible for his presence there, having voluntarily done what enabled him to get in, in full knowledge that there are such things as burglars, and that burglars burgle." It would be still more absurd to say this if I had had bars installed outside my windows, precisely to prevent burglars from getting in, and a burglar got in only because of a defect in the bars. It remains equally absurd if we imagine it is not a burglar who climbs in, but an innocent person who blunders or falls in. Again, suppose it were like this: people-seeds drift about in the air like pollen, and if you open your windows, one may drift in and take root in your carpets or upholstery. You don't want children, so you fix up your windows with fine mesh screens, the very best you can buy. As can happen, however, and on very, very rare occasions does happen, one of the screens is defective; and a seed drifts in and takes root. Does the person-plant who now develops have a right to the use of your house? Surely not—despite the fact that you voluntarily opened your windows, you knowingly kept carpets and upholstered furniture, and you knew that screens were sometimes defective. Someone may argue that you are responsible for its rooting, that it does have a right to your house, because after all you *could* have lived out your life with bare floors and furniture, or with sealed windows and doors. But this won't do—for by the same token anyone can avoid a pregnancy due to rape by having a hysterectomy, or anyway by never leaving home without a (reliable!) army.

It seems to me that the argument we are looking at can establish at most that there are *some* cases in which the unborn person has a right to the use of its mother's body, and therefore *some* cases in which abortion is unjust killing. There is room for much discussion and argument as to precisely which, if any. But I think we should sidestep this issue and leave it open, for at any rate the argument certainly does not establish that all abortion is unjust killing.

5. There is room for yet another argument here, however. We surely must all grant that there may be cases in which it would be morally indecent to detach a person from your body at the cost of his life. Suppose you learn that what the violinist needs is not nine years of your life, but only one hour: all you need do to save his life is to spend one hour in that bed with him. Suppose also that letting him use your kidneys for that one hour would not affect your

health in the slightest. Admittedly you were kidnapped. Admittedly you did not give anyone permission to plug him into you. Nevertheless it seems to me plain you *ought* to allow him to use your kidneys for that hour—it would be indecent to refuse.

Again, suppose pregnancy lasted only an hour, and constituted no threat to life or health. And suppose that a woman becomes pregnant as a result of rape. Admittedly she did not voluntarily do anything to bring about the existence of a child. Admittedly she did nothing at all which would give the unborn person a right to the use of her body. All the same it might well be said, as in the newly emended violinist story, that she *ought* to allow it to remain for that hour—that it would be indecent in her to refuse.

Now some people are inclined to use the term "right" in such a way that it follows from the fact that you ought to allow a person to use your body for the hour he needs, that he has a right to use your body for the hour he needs, even though he has not been given that right by any person or act. They may say that it follows also that if you refuse, you act unjustly toward him. This use of the term is perhaps so common that it cannot be called wrong; nevertheless it seems to me to be an unfortunate loosening of what we would do better to keep a tight rein on. Suppose that box of chocolates I mentioned earlier had not been given to both boys jointly, but was given only to the older boy. There he sits, stolidly eating his way through the box, his small brother watching enviously. Here we are likely to say "You ought not to be so mean. You ought to give your brother some of those chocolates." My own view is that it just does not follow from the truth of this that the brother has any right to any of the chocolates. If the boy refuses to give his brother any, he is greedy, stingy, callous—but not unjust. I suppose that the people I have in mind will say it does follow that the brother has a right to some of the chocolates, and thus that the boy does act unjustly if he refuses to give his brother any. But the effect of saying this is to obscure what we should keep distinct, namely the difference between the boy's refusal in this case and the boy's refusal in the earlier case, in which the box was given to both boys jointly, and in which the small brother thus had what was from any point of view clear title to half.

A further objection to so using the term "right" that from the fact that A ought to do a thing for B, it follows that B has a right against A that A do it for him, is that it is going to make the question of whether or not a man has a right to a thing turn on how easy it is to provide him with it; and this seems not merely unfortunate, but morally unacceptable. Take the case of Henry Fonda again. I said earlier that I had no right to the touch of his cool hand on my fevered brow, even though I needed it to save my life. I said it would be frightfully nice of him to fly in from the West Coast to provide me with it, but that I had no right against him that he should do so. But suppose he isn't on the West Coast. Suppose he has only to walk across the room, place a hand briefly on my brow—and lo, my life is saved. Then surely he ought to do it, it would be indecent to refuse. Is it to be said "Ah, well, it follows that in this case she has a right to the touch of his hand on her brow, and so it would be an injustice in him to refuse"? So that I have a right to it when it is easy for him to provide it, though no right when it's hard? It's rather a shocking idea that anyone's rights should fade away and disappear as it gets harder and harder to accord them to him.

So my own view is that even though you ought to let the violinist use your kidneys for the one hour he needs, we should not conclude that he has a right to do so—we would say that if you refuse, you are, like the boy who owns all the chocolates and will give none away, self-centered and callous, indecent in fact, but not unjust. And similarly, that even supposing a case in which a woman pregnant due to rape ought to allow the unborn person to use her body for the hour he needs, we should not conclude that he has a right to do so; we should conclude that she is self-centered, callous, indecent, but not unjust, if she refuses. The complaints are no less grave; they are just different. However, there is no need to insist on this point. If anyone does wish to deduce "he has a right" from "you ought," then all the same he must surely grant that there are cases in which it is not morally required of you that you allow that violinist to use your kidneys, and in which he does not have a right to use them, and in which you do not do him an injustice if you refuse. And so also for mother and unborn child. Except in such cases as the unborn person has a right to demand it—and we were leaving open the possibility that there may be such cases—nobody is morally *required* to make large

sacrifices, of health, of all other interests and concerns, of all other duties and commitments, for nine years, or even for nine months, in order to keep another person alive.

6. We have in fact to distinguish between two kinds of Samaritan: the Good Samaritan and what we might call the Minimally Decent Samaritan. The story of the Good Samaritan, you will remember, goes like this:

> A certain man went down from Jerusalem to Jericho, and fell among thieves, which stripped him of his raiment, and wounded him, and departed, leaving him half dead.
>
> And by chance there came down a certain priest that way; and when he saw him, he passed by on the other side.
>
> And likewise a Levite, when he was at the place, came and looked on him, and passed by on the other side.
>
> But a certain Samaritan, as he journeyed, came where he was; and when he saw him he had compassion on him.
>
> And went to him, and bound up his wounds, pouring in oil and wine, and set him on his own beast, and brought him to an inn, and took care of him.
>
> And on the morrow, when he departed, he took out two pence, and gave them to the host, and said unto him, "Take care of him; and whatsoever thou spendest more, when I come again, I will repay thee."
>
> (Luke 10:30–35)

The Good Samaritan went out of his way, at some cost to himself, to help one in need of it. We are not told what the options were, that is, whether or not the priest and the Levite could have helped by doing less than the Good Samaritan did, but assuming they could have, then the fact they did nothing at all shows they were not even Minimally Decent Samaritans, not because they were not Samaritans, but because they were not even minimally decent.

These things are a matter of degree, of course, but there is a difference, and it comes out perhaps most clearly in the story of Kitty Genovese, who, as you will remember, was murdered while thirty-eight people watched or listened, and did nothing at all to help her. A Good Samaritan would have rushed out to give direct assistance against the murderer. Or perhaps we had better allow that it would have been a Splendid Samaritan who did this, on the ground that it would have involved a risk of death for himself. But the thirty-eight not only did not do this, they did not even trouble to pick up a phone to call the police. Minimally Decent Samaritanism would call for doing at least that, and their not having done it was monstrous.

After telling the story of the Good Samaritan, Jesus said "Go, and do thou likewise." Perhaps he meant that we are morally required to act as the Good Samaritan did. Perhaps he was urging people to do more than is morally required of them. At all events it seems plain that it was not morally required of any of the thirty-eight that he rush out to give direct assistance at the risk of his own life, and that it is not morally required of anyone that he give long stretches of his life—nine years or nine months—to sustaining the life of a person who has no special right (we were leaving open the possibility of this) to demand it.

Indeed, with one rather striking class of exceptions, no one in any country in the world is *legally* required to do anywhere near as much as this for anyone else. The class of exceptions is obvious. My main concern here is not the state of the law in respect to abortion, but it is worth drawing attention to the fact that in no state in this country is any man compelled by law to be even a Minimally Decent Samaritan to any person; there is no law under which charges could be brought against the thirty-eight who stood by while Kitty Genovese died. By contrast, in most states in this country women are compelled by law to be not merely Minimally Decent Samaritans, but Good Samaritans to unborn persons inside them. This doesn't by itself settle anything one way or the other, because it may well be argued that there should be laws in this country—as there are in many European countries—compelling at least Minimally Decent Samaritanism. But it does show that there is a gross injustice in the existing state of the law. And it shows also that the groups currently working against liberalization of abortion laws, in fact working toward having it declared unconstitutional for a state to permit abortion, had better start working for the adoption of Good Samaritan laws generally, or earn the charge that they are acting in bad faith.

I should think, myself, that Minimally Decent Samaritan laws would be one thing, Good Samaritan laws quite another, and in fact highly improper. But we are not here concerned with the law. What we should ask is not whether anybody should be compelled by law to be a Good Samaritan, but whether we must accede to a situation in which somebody is being compelled—by nature, perhaps—to be a Good Samaritan. We have, in other words, to look now at third-party interventions. I have been arguing that no person is morally required to make large sacrifices to sustain the life of another who has no right to demand them, and this even where the sacrifices do not include life itself; we are not morally required to be Good Samaritans or anyway Very Good Samaritans to one another. But what if a man cannot extricate himself from such a situation? What if he appeals to us to extricate him? It seems to me plain that there are cases in which we can, cases in which a Good Samaritan would extricate him. There you are, you were kidnapped, and nine years in bed with that violinist lie ahead of you. You have your own life to lead. You are sorry, but you simply cannot see giving up so much of your life to the sustaining of his. You cannot extricate yourself, and ask us to do so. I should have thought that—in light of his having no right to the use of your body—it was obvious that we do not have to accede to your being forced to give up so much. We can do what you ask. There is no injustice to the violinist in our doing so.

7. Following the lead of the opponents of abortion, I have throughout been speaking of the fetus merely as a person, and what I have been asking is whether or not the argument we began with, which proceeds only from the fetus' being a person, really does establish its conclusion. I have argued that it does not.

But of course there are arguments and arguments, and it may be said that I have simply fastened on the wrong one. It may be said that what is important is not merely the fact that the fetus is a person, but that it is a person for whom the woman has a special kind of responsibility issuing from the fact that she is its mother. And it might be argued that all my analogies are therefore irrelevant—for you do not have that special kind of responsibility for that violinist, Henry Fonda does not have that special kind of responsibility for me. And our attention might be drawn to the fact that men and women both *are* compelled by law to provide support for their children.

I have in effect dealt (briefly) with this argument in section 4 above; but a (still briefer) recapitulation now may be in order. Surely we do not have any such "special responsibility" for a person unless we have assumed it, explicitly or implicitly. If a set of parents do not try to prevent pregnancy, do not obtain an abortion, and then at the time of birth of the child do not put it out for adoption, but rather take it home with them, then they have assumed responsibility for it, they have given it rights, and they cannot *now* withdraw support from it at the cost of its life because they now find it difficult to go on providing for it. But if they have taken all reasonable precautions against having a child, they do not simply by virtue of their biological relationship to the child who comes into existence have a special responsibility for it. They may wish to assume responsibility for it, or they may not wish to. And I am suggesting that if assuming responsibility for it would require large sacrifices, then they may refuse. A Good Samaritan would not refuse—or anyway, a Splendid Samaritan, if the sacrifices that had to be made were enormous. But then so would a Good Samaritan assume responsibility for that violinist; so would Henry Fonda, if he is a Good Samaritan, fly in from the West Coast and assume responsibility for me.

8. My argument will be found unsatisfactory on two counts by many of those who want to regard abortion as morally permissible. First, while I do argue that abortion is not impermissible, I do not argue that it is always permissible. There may well be cases in which carrying the child to term requires only Minimally Decent Samaritanism of the mother, and this is a standard we must not fall below. I am inclined to think it a merit of my account precisely that it does *not* give a general yes or a general no. It allows for and supports our sense that, for example, a sick and desperately frightened fourteen-year-old schoolgirl, pregnant due to rape, may *of course* choose abortion, and that any law which rules this out is an insane law. And it also allows for and sup-

ports our sense that in other cases resort to abortion is even positively indecent. It would be indecent in the women to request an abortion, and indecent in a doctor to perform it, if she is in her seventh month, and wants the abortion just to avoid the nuisance of postponing a trip abroad. The very fact that the arguments I have been drawing attention to treat all cases of abortion, or even all cases of abortion in which the mother's life is not at stake, as morally on a par ought to have made them suspect at the outset.

Secondly, while I am arguing for the permissibility of abortion in some cases, I am not arguing for the right to secure the death of the unborn child. It is easy to confuse these two things in that up to a certain point in the life of the fetus it is not able to survive outside the mother's body; hence removing it from her body guarantees its death. But they are importantly different. I have argued that you are not morally required to spend nine months in bed, sustaining the life of that violinist; but to say this is by no means to say that if, when you unplug yourself, there is a miracle and he survives, you then have a right to turn round and slit his throat. You may detach yourself even if this costs him his life; you have no right to be guaranteed his death, by some other means, if unplugging yourself does not kill him. There are some people who will feel dissatisfied by this feature of my argument. A woman may be utterly devastated by the thought of a child, a bit of herself, put out for adoption and never seen or heard of again. She may therefore want not merely that the child be detached from her, but more, that it die. Some opponents of abortion are inclined to regard this as beneath contempt—thereby showing insensitivity to what is surely a powerful source of despair. All the same, I agree that the desire for the child's death is not one which anybody may gratify, should it turn out to be possible to detach the child alive.

At this place, however, it should be remembered that we have only been pretending throughout that the fetus is a human being from the moment of conception. A very early abortion is surely not the killing of a person, and so is not dealt with by anything I have said here.

JANE ENGLISH

Abortion and the Concept of a Person

Jane English was Associate Professor of Philosophy at the University of North Carolina when she died in 1978.
(Source: Reprinted from The Canadian Journal of Philosophy *5, 2 [October 1975], pp. 233–243. Copyright © 1975 by the Canadian Journal of Philosophy.)*

QUESTIONS FOR REFLECTION

1. English argues that "our concept of a person is not sharp or decisive enough" to resolve the abortion controversy. How does she reach this conclusion?

2. What is the point of English's arguments concerning self-defense? What do you think they show?

3. How does English distinguish abortion from infanticide?

4. Why, according to English, are some abortions impermissible?

The abortion debate rages on. Yet the two most popular positions seem to be clearly mistaken. Conservatives maintain that a human life begins at conception and that therefore abortion must be wrong because it is murder. But not all killings of humans are murders. Most notably, self defense may justify even the killing of an innocent person.

Liberals, on the other hand, are just as mistaken in their argument that since a fetus does not become a person until birth, a woman may do whatever she pleases in and to her own body. First, you cannot do as you please with your own body if it affects other people adversely. Second, if a fetus is not a person, that does not imply that you can do to it anything you wish. Animals, for example, are not persons, yet to kill or torture them for no reason at all is wrong.

At the center of the storm has been the issue of just when it is between ovulation and adulthood that a person appears on the scene. Conservatives draw the line at conception, liberals at birth. In this paper I first examine our concept of a person and conclude that no single criterion can capture the concept of a person and no sharp line can be drawn.

Next I argue that if a fetus is a person, abortion is still justifiable in many cases; and if a fetus is not a person, killing it is still wrong in many cases. To a large extent, these two solutions are in agreement. I conclude that our concept of a person cannot and need not bear the weight that the abortion controversy has thrust upon it.

I

The several factions in the abortion argument have drawn battle lines around various proposed criteria for determining what is and what is not a person. For example, Mary Anne Warren lists five features (capacities for reasoning, self-awareness, complex communication, etc.) as her criteria for personhood and argues for the permissibility of abortion because a fetus falls outside this concept. Baruch Brody uses brain waves. Michael Tooley picks having-a-concept-of-self as his criterion and concludes that infanticide and abortion are justifiable, while the killing of adult animals is not. On the other side, Paul Ramsey claims a certain gene structure is the defining characteristic. John Noonan prefers conceived-of-humans and presents counterexamples to various other candidate criteria. For instance, he argues against viability as the criterion because the newborn and infirm would then be non-persons, since they cannot live without the aid of others. He rejects any criterion that calls upon the sorts of sentiments a being can evoke in adults on the grounds that this would allow us to exclude other races as non-persons if we could just view them sufficiently unsentimentally.

These approaches are typical: foes of abortion propose sufficient conditions for personhood which fetuses satisfy, while friends of abortion counter with necessary conditions for personhood which fetuses lack. But these both presuppose that the concept of a person can be captured in a strait jacket of necessary and/or sufficient conditions. Rather, "person" is a cluster of features, of which rationality, having a self concept and being conceived of humans are only part.

What is typical of persons? Within our concept of a person we include, first, certain biological factors: descended from humans, having a certain genetic makeup, having a head, hands, arms, eyes, capable of locomotion, breathing, eating, sleeping. There are psychological factors: sentience, perception, having a concept of self and of one's own interests and desires, the ability to use tools, the ability to use language or symbol systems, the ability to joke, to be angry, to doubt. There are rationality factors: the ability to reason and draw conclusions, the ability to generalize and to learn from past experience, the ability to sacrifice present interests for greater gains in the future. There are social factors: the ability to work in groups and respond to peer pressures, the ability to recognize and consider as valuable the interests of others, seeing oneself as one among "other minds," the ability to sympathize, encourage, love, the ability to evoke from others the responses of sympathy, encouragement, love, the ability to work with others for mutual advantage. Then there are legal factors: being subject to the law and protected by it, having the ability to sue and enter contracts, being counted in the census, having a name and citizenship, the ability to own property, inherit, and so forth.

Now the point is not that this list is incomplete, or that you can find counterinstances to each of its points. People typically exhibit rationality, for instance, but someone who was irrational would not thereby fail to qualify as a person. On the other hand, something could exhibit the majority of these features and still fail to be a person, as an advanced robot might. There is no single core of necessary and sufficient features which we can draw upon with the assurance that they constitute what really makes a person; there are only features that are more or less typical.

This is not to say that no necessary or sufficient conditions can be given. Being alive is a necessary condition for being a person, and being a U.S. Senator is sufficient. But rather than falling inside a sufficient condition or outside a necessary one, a fetus lies in the penumbra region where our concept of a person is not so simple. For this reason I think a conclusive answer to the question whether a fetus is a person is unattainable.

Here we might note a family of simple fallacies that proceed by stating a necessary condition for personhood and showing that a fetus has that characteristic. This is a form of the fallacy of affirming the consequent. For example, some have mistakenly reasoned from the premise that a fetus is human (after all, it is a human fetus rather than, say, a canine fetus), to the conclusion that it is *a* human. Adding an equivocation on "being," we get the fallacious argument that since a fetus is something both living and human, it is a human being.

Nonetheless, it does seem clear that a fetus has very few of the above family of characteristics, whereas a newborn baby exhibits a much larger proportion of them—and a two-year-old has even more. Note that one traditional anti-abortion argument has centered on pointing out the many ways in which a fetus resembles a baby. They emphasize its development ("It already has ten fingers. . . . ") without mentioning its dissimilarities to adults (it still has gills and a tail). They also try to evoke the sort of sympathy on our part that we only feel toward other persons ("Never to laugh . . . or feel the sunshine?"). This all seems to be a relevant way to argue, since its purpose is to persuade us that a fetus satisfies so many of the important features on the list that it ought to be treated as a person. Also note that a fetus near the time of birth satisfies many more of these factors than a fetus in the early months of development. This could provide reason for making distinctions among the different stages of pregnancy, as the U.S. Supreme Court has done.

Historically, the time at which a person has been said to come into existence has varied widely. Muslims date personhood from fourteen days after conception. Some medievals followed Aristotle in placing ensoulment at forty days after conception for a male fetus and eighty days for a female fetus. In European common law since the Seventeenth Century, abortion was considered the killing of a person only after quickening, the time when a pregnant woman first feels the fetus move on its own. Nor is this variety of opinions surprising. Biologically, a human being develops gradually. We shouldn't expect there to be any specific time or sharp dividing point when a person appears on the scene.

For these reasons I believe our concept of a person is not sharp or decisive enough to bear the weight of a solution to the abortion controversy. To use it to solve that problem is to clarify *obscurum per obscurius*.

II

Next let us consider what follows if a fetus is a person after all. Judith Jarvis Thomson's landmark article, "A Defense of Abortion," correctly points out that some additional argumentation is needed at this point in the conservative argument to bridge the gap between the premise that a fetus is an innocent person and the conclusion that killing it is always wrong. To arrive at this conclusion, we would need the additional premise that killing an innocent person is always wrong. But killing an innocent person is sometimes permissible, most notably in self defense. Some examples may help draw out our intuitions or ordinary judgments about self defense.

Suppose a mad scientist, for instance, hypnotized innocent people to jump out of the bushes and attack innocent passers-by with knives. If you are so attacked, we agree you have a right to kill the attacker in self defense, if killing him is the only way to protect your life or to save yourself from serious injury. It does not seem to matter here that the attacker is not malicious but himself an innocent pawn, for your killing of him is not done in a spirit of retribution but only in self defense.

How severe an injury may you inflict in self defense? In part this depends upon the severity of the injury to be avoided: you may not shoot someone merely to avoid having your clothes torn. This might lead one to the mistaken conclusion that the defense may only equal the threatened injury in severity; that to avoid death you may kill, but to avoid a black eye you may only inflict a black eye or the equivalent. Rather, our laws and customs seem to say that you may create an injury somewhat, but not enormously, greater than the injury to be avoided. To fend off an attack whose outcome would be as serious as rape, a severe beating or the loss of a finger, you may shoot; to avoid having your clothes torn, you may blacken an eye.

Aside from this, the injury you may inflict should only be the minimum necessary to deter or incapacitate the attacker. Even if you know he intends to kill you, you are not justified in shooting him if you could equally well save yourself by the simple expedient of running away. Self defense is for the purpose of avoiding harms rather than equalizing harms.

Some cases of pregnancy present a parallel situation. Though the fetus is itself innocent, it may pose a threat to the pregnant woman's well-being, life prospects or health, mental or physical. If the pregnancy presents a slight threat to her interests, it seems self defense cannot justify abortion. But if the threat is on a par with a serious beating or the loss of a finger, she may kill the fetus that poses such a threat, even if it is an innocent person. If a lesser harm to the fetus could have the same defensive effect, killing it would not be justified. It is unfortunate that the only way to free the woman from the pregnancy entails the death of the fetus (except in very late stages of pregnancy). Thus a self defense model supports Thomson's point that the woman has a right only to be freed from the fetus, not a right to demand its death.

The self defense model is most helpful when we take the pregnant woman's point of view. In the pre-Thomson literature, abortion is often framed as a question for a third party: do you, a doctor, have a right to choose between the life of the woman and that of the fetus? Some have claimed that if you were a passer-by who witnessed a struggle between the innocent hypnotized attacker and his equally innocent victim, you would have no reason to kill either in defense of the other. They have concluded that the self defense model implies that a woman may attempt to abort herself, but that a doctor should not assist her. I think the position of the third party is somewhat more complex. We do feel some inclination to intervene on behalf of the victim rather than the attacker, other things equal. But if both parties are innocent, other factors come into consideration. You would rush to the aid of your husband whether he was attacker or attackee. If a hypnotized famous violinist were attacking a skid row bum, we would try to save the individual who is of more value to society. These considerations would tend to support abortion in some cases.

But suppose you are a frail senior citizen who wishes to avoid being knifed by one of these innocent hypnotics, so you have hired a bodyguard to accompany you. If you are attacked, it is clear we believe that the bodyguard, acting as your agent, has a right to kill the attacker to save you from a serious beating. Your rights of self defense are transferred to your agent. I suggest that we should similarly view the doctor as the pregnant woman's agent in carrying out a defense she is physically incapable of accomplishing herself.

Thanks to modern technology, the cases are rare in which pregnancy poses as clear a threat to a woman's bodily health as an attacker brandishing a switchblade. How does self defense fare when more subtle, complex and long-range harms are involved?

To consider a somewhat fanciful example, suppose you are a highly trained surgeon when you are kidnapped by the hypnotic attacker. He says he does not intend to harm you but to take you back to the mad scientist who, it turn out, plans to hypnotize you to have a permanent mental block against all your knowledge of medicine. This would automatically destroy your career which would in turn have a serious adverse impact on your family, your per-sonal relationships and your happiness. It seems to me that if the only way you can avoid this outcome is to shoot the innocent attacker, you are justified in so doing. You are defending yourself from a drastic injury to your life prospects. I think it is no exaggeration to claim that unwanted pregnancies (most obviously among teenagers) often have such adverse life-long consequences as the surgeon's loss of livelihood.

Several parallels arise between various views on abortion and the self defense model. Let's suppose further that these hypnotized attackers only operate at night, so that it is well known that they can be avoided completely by the considerable inconvenience of never leaving your house after dark. One view is that since you could stay home at night, therefore if you go out and are selected by one of these hypnotized people, you have no right to defend yourself. This parallels the view that abstinence is the only acceptable way to avoid pregnancy. Others might hold that you ought to take along some defense such as Mace which will deter the hypnotized person without killing him, but that if this defense fails, you are obliged to submit to the resulting injury, no matter how severe it is. This parallels the view that contraception is all right but abortion is always wrong, even in cases of contraceptive failure.

A third view is that you may kill the hypnotized person only if he will actually kill you, but not if he will only injure you. This is like the position that abortion is permissible only if it is required to save a woman's life. Finally we have the view that it is all right to kill the attacker, even if only to avoid a very slight inconvenience to yourself and even if you knowingly walked down the very street where all these incidents have been taking place without taking along any Mace or protective escort. If we assume that a fetus is a person, this is the analogue of the view that abortion is always justifiable, "on demand."

The self defense model allows us to see an important difference that exists between abortion and infanticide, even if a fetus is a person from conception. Many have argued that the only way to justify abortion without justifying infanticide would be to find some characteristic of personhood that is acquired at birth. Michael Tooley, for one, claims infanticide is justifiable because the really significant characteristics of person are acquired some time after birth. But all such approaches look to characteristics of the developing human and ignore the relation between the fetus and the woman. What if, after birth, the presence of an infant or the need to support it posed a grave threat to the woman's sanity or life prospects? She could escape this threat by the simple expedient of running away. So a solution that does not entail the death of the infant is available. Before birth, such solutions are not available because of the biological dependence of the fetus on the woman. Birth is the crucial point not because of any characteristics the fetus gains, but because after birth the woman can defend herself by a means less drastic than killing the infant. Hence self defense can be used to justify abortion without necessarily thereby justifying infanticide.

III

On the other hand, supposing a fetus is not after all a person, would abortion always be morally permissible? Some opponents of abortion seem worried that if a fetus is not a full-fledged person, then we are justified in treating it in any way at all. However, this does not follow. Non-persons do get some consideration in our moral code, though of course they do not have the same rights as persons have (and in general they do not have moral responsibilities), and though their interests may be overridden by the interests of persons. Still, we cannot just treat them in any way at all.

Treatment of animals is a case in point. It is wrong to torture dogs for fun or to kill wild birds for no reason at all. It is wrong Period, even though dogs and birds do not have the same rights persons do. However, few people think it is wrong to use dogs as experimental animals, causing them considerable suffering in some cases, provided that the resulting research will probably bring discoveries of great benefit to people. And most of us think it all right to kill birds for food or to protect our crops. People's rights are different from the consideration we give to animals, then, for it is wrong to experiment on people, even if others might later benefit a great deal as

a result of their suffering. You might volunteer to be a subject, but this would be supererogatory; you certainly have a right to refuse to be a medical guinea pig.

But how do we decide what you may or may not do to non-persons? This is a difficult problem, one for which I believe no adequate account exists. You do not want to say, for instance, that torturing dogs is all right whenever the sum of its effects on people is good—when it doesn't warp the sensibilities of the torturer so much that he mistreats people. If that were the case, it would be all right to torture dogs if you did it in private, or if the torturer lived on a desert island or died soon afterward, so that his actions had no effect on people. This is an inadequate account, because whatever moral consideration animals get, it has to be indefeasible, too. It will have to be a general proscription of certain actions, not merely a weighing of the impact on people on a case-by-case basis.

Rather, we need to distinguish two levels on which consequences of actions can be taken into account in moral reasoning. The traditional objections to Utilitarianism focus on the fact that it operates solely on the first level, taking all the consequences into account in particular cases only. Thus Utilitarianism is open to "desert island" and "lifeboat" counterexamples because these cases are rigged to make the consequences of actions severely limited.

Rawls' theory could be described as a teleological sort of theory, but with teleology operating on a higher level. In choosing the principles to regulate society from the original position, his hypothetical choosers make their decision on the basis of the total consequences of various systems. Furthermore, they are constrained to choose a general set of rules which people can readily learn and apply. An ethical theory must operate by generating a set of sympathies and attitudes toward others which reinforces the functioning of that set of moral principles. Our prohibition against killing people operates by means of certain moral sentiments including sympathy, compassion and guilt. But if these attitudes are to form a coherent set, they carry us further: we tend to perform supererogatory actions, and we tend to feel similar compassion toward person-like non-persons.

It is crucial that psychological facts play a role here. Our psychological constitution makes it the case that for our ethical theory to work, it must prohibit certain treatment of non-persons which are significantly person-like. If our moral rules allowed people to treat some person-like non-persons in ways we do not want people to be treated, this would undermine the system of sympathies and attitudes that makes the ethical system work. For this reason, we would choose in the original position to make mistreatment of some sorts of animals wrong in general (not just wrong in the cases with public impact), even though animals are not themselves parties in the original position. Thus it makes sense that it is those animals whose appearance and behavior are most like those of people that get the most consideration in our moral scheme.

It is because of "coherence of attitudes," I think, that the similarity of a fetus to a baby is very significant. A fetus one week before birth is so much like a newborn baby in our psychological space that we cannot allow any cavalier treatment of the former while expecting full sympathy and nurturative support for the latter. Thus, I think that anti-abortion forces are indeed giving their strongest arguments when they point to the similarities between a fetus and a baby, and when they try to evoke our emotional attachment to and sympathy for the fetus. An early horror story from New York about nurses who were expected to alternate between caring for six-week premature infants and disposing of viable 24-week aborted fetuses is just that—a horror story. These beings are so much alike that no one can be asked to draw a distinction and treat them so very differently.

Remember, however, that in the early weeks after conception, a fetus is very much unlike a person. It is hard to develop these feelings for a set of genes which doesn't yet have a head, hands, beating heart, response to touch or the ability to move by itself. Thus it seems to me that the alleged "slippery slope" between conception and birth is not so very slippery. In the early stages of pregnancy, abortion can hardly be compared to murder for psychological reasons, but in the latest stages it is psychologically akin to murder.

Another source of similarity is the bodily continuity between fetus and adult. Bodies play a surprisingly central role in our attitudes toward persons. One has only to think of the philosophical literature on how far physical identity suffices for personal identity or Wittgenstein's remark that the best picture of the human soul is the human body. Even after death, when all agree the body is no longer a person, we still observe elaborate customs of respect for the human body; like people who torture dogs, necrophiliacs are not to be trusted with people. So it is appropriate that we show respect to a fetus as the body continuous with the body of a person. This is a degree of resemblance to persons that animals cannot rival.

Michael Tooley also utilizes a parallel with animals. He claims that it is always permissible to drown newborn kittens and draws conclusions about infanticide. But it is only permissible to drown kittens when their survival would cause some hardship. Perhaps it would be a burden to feed and house six more cats or to find other homes for them. The alternative of letting them starve produces even more suffering than the drowning. Since the kittens get their rights second-hand, so to speak, *via* the need for coherence in our attitudes, their interests are often overridden by the interests of fullfledged persons. But if their survival would be no inconvenience to people at all, then it is wrong to drown them, *contra* Tooley.

Tooley's conclusions about abortion are wrong for the same reason. Even if a fetus is not a person, abortion is not always permissible, because of the resemblance of a fetus to a person. I agree with Thomson that it would be wrong for a woman who is seven months pregnant to have an abortion just to avoid having to postpone a trip to Europe. In the early months of pregnancy when the fetus hardly resembles a baby at all, then, abortion is permissible whenever it is in the interests of the pregnant woman or her family. The reasons would only need to outweigh the pain and inconvenience of the abortion itself. In the middle months, when the fetus comes to resemble a person, abortion would be justifiable only when the continuation of the pregnancy or the birth of the child would cause harms—physical, psychological, economic or social—to the woman. In the late months of pregnancy, even on our current assumption that a fetus is not a person, abortion seems to be wrong except to save a woman from significant injury or death.

The Supreme Court has recognized similar gradations in the alleged slippery slope stretching between conception and birth. To this point, the present paper has been a discussion of the moral status of abortion only, not its legal status. In view of the great physical, financial and sometimes psychological costs of abortion, perhaps the legal arrangement most compatible with the proposed moral solution would be the absence of restrictions, that is, so-called abortion "on demand."

So I conclude, first, that application of our concept of a person will not suffice to settle the abortion issue. After all, the biological development of a human being is gradual. Second, whether a fetus is a person or not, abortion is justifiable early in pregnancy to avoid modest harms and seldom justifiable late in pregnancy except to avoid significant injury or death.

DON MARQUIS

Why Abortion Is Immoral

Don Marquis is Associate Professor of Philosophy at the University of Kansas. (Source: Reprinted from The Journal of Philosophy *LXXXVI, 4 (April 1989): 183–202, with permission of the author and* The Journal of Philosophy. *Copyright © 1989 by the Journal of Philosophy, Inc.)*

QUESTIONS FOR REFLECTION

1. Marquis argues that usual anti-abortion and pro-choice arguments have symmetric problems and so are at a standoff. Review his reasoning. Do you agree?

2. Why, according to Marquis, is it wrong to kill an adult human being?

3. Marquis argues that it is wrong to kill a fetus for just the same reason that it is wrong to kill an adult. How does his argument go? Do you find it convincing?

4. Marquis compares his argument to one for the wrongness of the wanton infliction of pain on animals. Do you find the arguments analogous?

5. What are the discontinuation and desire accounts? Why does Marquis reject them?

The view that abortion is, with rare exceptions, seriously immoral has received little support in the recent philosophical literature. No doubt most philosophers affiliated with secular institutions of higher education believe that the anti-abortion position is either a symptom of irrational religious dogma or a conclusion generated by seriously confused philosophical argument. The purpose of this essay is to undermine this general belief. This essay sets out an argument that purports to show, as well as any argument in ethics can show, that abortion is, except possibly in rare cases, seriously immoral, that it is in the same moral category as killing an innocent adult human being.

The argument is based on a major assumption. Many of the most insightful and careful writers on the ethics of abortion—such as Joel Feinberg, Michael Tooley, Mary Anne Warren, H. Tristram Engelhardt, Jr., L. W. Sumner, John T. Noonan, Jr., and Philip Devine—believe that whether or not abortion is morally permissible stands or falls on whether or not a fetus is the sort of being whose life it is seriously wrong to end. The argument of this essay will assume, but not argue, that they are correct.

Also, this essay will neglect issues of great importance to a complete ethics of abortion. Some anti-abortionists will allow that certain abortions, such as abortion before implantation or abortion when the life of a woman is threatened by a pregnancy or abortion after rape, may be morally permissible. This essay will not explore the casuistry of these hard cases. The purpose of this essay is to develop a general argument for the claim that the overwhelming majority of deliberate abortions are seriously immoral.

I

A sketch of standard anti-abortion and pro-choice arguments exhibits how those arguments possess certain symmetries that explain why partisans of those positions are so convinced of the correctness of their own positions, why they are not successful in convincing their opponents, and why, to others, this issue seems to be unresolvable. An analysis of the nature of this standoff suggests a strategy for surmounting it.

Consider the way a typical anti-abortionist argues. She will argue or assert that life is present from the moment of conception or that fetuses look like babies or that fetuses possess a characteristic such as a genetic code that is both necessary and sufficient for being human. Anti-abortionists seem to believe that (1) the truth of all of these claims is quite obvious, and (2) establishing any of these claims is sufficient to show that abortion is morally akin to murder.

A standard pro-choice strategy exhibits similarities. The pro-choicer will argue or assert that fetuses are not persons or that fetuses are not rational agents or that fetuses are not social beings. Pro-choicers seem to believe that (1) the truth of any of these claims is quite obvious, and (2) establishing any of these claims is sufficient to show that an abortion is not a wrongful killing.

In fact, both the pro-choice and the anti-abortion claims do seem to be true, although the "it looks like a baby" claim is more difficult to establish the earlier the pregnancy. We seem to have a standoff. How can it be resolved?

As everyone who has taken a bit of logic knows, if any of these arguments concerning abortion is a good argument, it requires not only some claim characterizing fetuses, but also some general moral principle that ties a characteristic of fetuses to having or not having the right to life or to some other moral characteristic that will generate the obligation or the lack of obligation not to end the life of a fetus. Accordingly, the arguments of the anti-abortionist and the pro-choicer need a bit of filling in to be regarded as adequate.

Note what each partisan will say. The anti-abortionist will claim that her position is supported by such generally accepted moral principles as "It is always prima facie seriously wrong to take a human life" or "It is always prima facie seriously wrong to end the life of a baby." Since these are generally accepted moral principles, her position is certainly

not obviously wrong. The pro-choicer will claim that her position is supported by such plausible moral principles as "Being a person is what gives an individual intrinsic moral worth" or "It is only seriously prima facie wrong to take the life of a member of the human community." Since these are generally accepted moral principles, the pro-choice position is certainly not obviously wrong. Unfortunately, we have again arrived at a standoff.

Now, how might one deal with this standoff? The standard approach is to try to show how the moral principles of one's opponent lose their plausibility under analysis. It is easy to see how this is possible. On the one hand, the anti-abortionist will defend a moral principle concerning the wrongness of killing which tends to be broad in scope in order that even fetuses at an early stage of pregnancy will fall under it. The problem with broad principles is that they often embrace too much. In this particular instance, the principle "It is always prima facie wrong to take a human life" seems to entail that it is wrong to end the existence of a living human cancer-cell culture, on the grounds that the culture is both living and human. Therefore, it seems that the anti-abortionist's favored principle is too broad.

On the other hand, the pro-choicer wants to find a moral principle concerning the wrongness of killing which tends to be narrow in scope in order that fetuses will *not* fall under it. The problem with narrow principles is that they often do not embrace enough. Hence, the needed principles such as "It is prima facie seriously wrong to kill only persons" or "It is prima facie wrong to kill only rational agents" do not explain why it is wrong to kill infants or young children or the severely retarded or even perhaps the severely mentally ill. Therefore, we seem again to have a standoff. The anti-abortionist charges, not unreasonably, that pro-choice principles concerning killing are too narrow to be acceptable; the pro-choicer charges, not unreasonably, that anti-abortionist principles concerning killing are too broad to be acceptable.

Attempts by both sides to patch up the difficulties in their positions run into further difficulties. The anti-abortionist will try to remove the problem in her position by reformulating her principle concerning killing in terms of human beings. Now we end up with: "It is always prima facie seriously wrong to end the life of a human being." This principle has the advantage of avoiding the problem of the human cancer-cell culture counterexample. But this advantage is purchased at a high price. For although it is clear that a fetus is both human and alive, it is not at all clear that a fetus is a human *being*. There is at least something to be said for the view that something becomes a human being only after a process of development, and that therefore first trimester fetuses and perhaps all fetuses are not yet human beings. Hence, the anti-abortionist, by this move, has merely exchanged one problem for another.

The pro-choicer fares no better. She may attempt to find reasons why killing infants, young children, and the severely retarded is wrong which are independent of her major principle that is supposed to explain the wrongness of taking human life, but which will not also make abortion immoral. This is no easy task. Appeals to social utility will seem satisfactory only to those who resolve not to think of the enormous difficulties with a utilitarian account of the wrongness of killing and the significant social costs of preserving the lives of the unproductive. A pro-choice strategy that extends the definition of 'person' to infants or even to young children seems just as arbitrary as an anti-abortion strategy that extends the definition of 'human being' to fetuses. Again, we find symmetries in the two positions and we arrive at a standoff.

There are even further problems that reflect symmetries in the two positions. In addition to counterexample problems, or the arbitrary application problems that can be exchanged for them, the standard anti-abortionist principle "It is prima facie seriously wrong to kill a human being," or one of its variants, can be objected to on the grounds of ambiguity. If 'human being' is taken to be a *biological* category, then the anti-abortionist is left with the problem of explaining why a merely biological category should make a moral difference. Why, it is asked, is it any more reasonable to base a moral conclusion on the number of chromosomes in one's cells than on the color of one's skin? If 'human being', on the other hand, is taken to be a *moral* category, then the claim that a fetus is a human being cannot be taken to be a premise in the anti-abortion argument, for it is precisely what needs to be established. Hence, either the anti-abortionist's main cat-

egory is a morally irrelevant, merely biological category, or it is of no use to the anti-abortionist in establishing (noncircularly, of course) that abortion is wrong.

Although this problem with the anti-abortionist position is often noticed, it is less often noticed that the pro-choice position suffers from an analogous problem. The principle "Only persons have the right to life" also suffers from an ambiguity. The term 'person' is typically defined in terms of psychological characteristics, although there will certainly be disagreement concerning which characteristics are most important. Supposing that this matter can be settled, the pro-choicer is left with the problem of explaining why *psychological* characteristics should make a *moral* difference. If the pro-choicer should attempt to deal with this problem by claiming that an explanation is not necessary, that in fact we do treat such a cluster of psychological properties as having moral significance, the sharp-witted anti-abortionist should have a ready response. We do treat being both living and human as having moral significance. If it is legitimate for the pro-choicer to demand that the anti-abortionist provide an explanation of the connection between the biological character of being a human being and the wrongness of being killed (even though people accept this connection), then it is legitimate for the anti-abortionist to demand that the pro-choicer provide an explanation of the connection between psychological criteria for being a person and the wrongness of being killed (even though that connection is accepted).

Feinberg has attempted to meet this objection (he calls psychological personhood "commonsense personhood"):

The characteristics that confer commonsense personhood are not arbitrary bases for rights and duties, such as race, sex or species membership; rather they are traits that make sense out of rights and duties and without which those moral attributes would have no point or function. It is because people are conscious; have a sense of their personal identities; have plans, goals, and projects; experience emotions; are liable to pains, anxieties, and frustrations; can reason and bargain, and so on—it is because of these attributes that people have values and interests, desires and expectations of their own, including a stake in their own futures, and a personal well-being of a sort we cannot ascribe to unconscious or nonrational beings. Because of their developed capacities they can assume duties and responsibilities and can have and make claims on one another. Only because of their sense of self, their life plans, their value hierarchies, and their stakes in their own futures can they be ascribed fundamental rights. There is nothing arbitrary about these linkages.

The plausible aspects of this attempt should not be taken to obscure its implausible features. There is a great deal to be said for the view that being a psychological person under some description is a necessary condition for having duties. One cannot have a duty unless one is capable of behaving morally, and a being's capability of behaving morally will require having a certain psychology. It is far from obvious, however, that having rights entails consciousness or rationality, as Feinberg suggests. We speak of the rights of the severely retarded or the severely mentally ill, yet some of these persons are not rational. We speak of the rights of the temporarily unconscious. The New Jersey Supreme Court based their decision in the Quinlan case on Karen Ann Quinlan's right to privacy, and she was known to be permanently unconscious at that time. Hence, Feinberg's claim that having rights entails being conscious is, on its face, obviously false.

Of course, it might not make sense to attribute rights to a being that would never in its natural history have certain psychological traits. This modest connection between psychological personhood and moral personhood will create a place for Karen Ann Quinlan and the temporarily unconscious. But then it makes a place for fetuses also. Hence, it does not serve Feinberg's pro-choice purposes. Accordingly, it seems that the pro-choicer will have as much difficulty bridging the gap between psychological personhood and personhood in the moral sense as the anti-abortionist has bridging the gap between being a biological human being and being a human being in the moral sense.

Furthermore, the pro-choicer cannot any more escape her problem by making person a purely moral category than the anti-abortionist could escape by the analogous move. For if person is a moral category, then the pro-choicer is left without the resources for establishing (noncircularly, of course) the claim that a fetus is not a person, which is an essential premise in her argument. Again, we have both a symmetry and a standoff between pro-choice and anti-abortion views.

Passions in the abortion debate run high. There are both plausibilities and difficulties with the standard positions. Accordingly, it is hardly surprising that partisans of either side embrace with fervor the moral generalizations that support the conclusions they preanalytically favor, and reject with disdain the moral generalizations of their opponents as being subject to inescapable difficulties. It is easy to believe that the counterexamples to one's own moral principles are merely temporary difficulties that will dissolve in the wake of further philosophical research, and that the counterexamples to the principles of one's opponents are as straightforward as the contradiction between *A* and *O* propositions in traditional logic. This might suggest to an impartial observer (if there are any) that the abortion issue is unresolvable.

There is a way out of this apparent dialectical quandary. The moral generalizations of both sides are not quite correct. The generalizations hold for the most part, for the usual cases. This suggests that they are all *accidental* generalizations, that the moral claims made by those on both sides of the dispute do not touch on the *essence* of the matter.

This use of the distinction between essence and accident is not meant to invoke obscure metaphysical categories. Rather, it is intended to reflect the rather atheoretical nature of the abortion discussion. If the generalization a partisan in the abortion dispute adopts were derived from the reason why ending the life of a human being is wrong, then there could not be exceptions to that generalization unless some special case obtains in which there are even more powerful countervailing reasons. Such generalizations would not be merely accidental generalizations; they would point to, or be based upon, the essence of the wrongness of killing, what it is that makes killing wrong. All this suggests that a necessary condition of resolving the abortion controversy is a more theoretical account of the wrongness of killing. After all, if we merely believe, but do not understand, why killing adult human beings such as ourselves is wrong, how could we conceivably show that abortion is either immoral or permissible?

II

In order to develop such an account, we can start from the following unproblematic assumption concerning our own case: it is wrong to kill us. Why is it wrong? Some answers can be easily eliminated. It might be said that what makes killing us wrong is that a killing brutalizes the one who kills. But the brutalization consists of being inured to the performance of an act that is hideously immoral; hence, the brutalization does not explain the immorality. It might be said that what makes killing us wrong is the great loss others would experience due to our absence. Although such hubris is understandable, such an explanation does not account for the wrongness of killing hermits, or those whose lives are relatively independent and whose friends find it easy to make new friends.

A more obvious answer is better. What primarily makes killing wrong is neither its effect on the murderer nor its effect on the victim's friends and relatives, but its effect on the victim. The loss of one's life is one of the greatest losses one can suffer. The loss of one's life deprives one of all the experiences, activities, projects, and enjoyments that would otherwise have constituted one's future. Therefore, killing someone is wrong, primarily because the killing inflicts (one of) the greatest possible losses on the victim. To describe this as the loss of life can be misleading, however. The change in my biological state does not by itself make killing me wrong. The effect of the loss of my biological life is the loss to me of all those activities, projects, experiences, and enjoyments which would otherwise have constituted my future personal life. These activities, projects, experiences, and enjoyments are either valuable for their own sakes or are means to something else that is valuable for its own sake. Some parts of my future are not valued by me now, but will come to be valued by me as I grow older and as my values and capacities change. When I am killed, I am deprived both of what I now value which would have been part of my future personal life, but also what I would come to value. Therefore, when I

die, I am deprived of all of the value of my future. Inflicting this loss on me is ultimately what makes killing me wrong. This being the case, it would seem that what makes killing *any* adult human being prima facie seriously wrong is the loss of his or her future.

How should this rudimentary theory of the wrongness of killing be evaluated? It cannot be faulted for deriving an 'ought' from an 'is', for it does not. The analysis assumes that killing me (or you, reader) is prima facie seriously wrong. The point of the analysis is to establish which natural property ultimately explains the wrongness of the killing, given that it is wrong. A natural property will ultimately explain the wrongness of killing, only if (1) the explanation fits with our intuitions about the matter and (2) there is no other natural property that provides the basis for a better explanation of the wrongness of killing. This analysis rests on the intuition that what makes killing a particular human or animal wrong is what it does to that particular human or animal. What makes killing wrong is some natural effect or other of the killing. Some would deny this. For instance, a divine-command theorist in ethics would deny it. Surely this denial is, however, one of those features of divine-command theory which renders it so implausible.

The claim that what makes killing wrong is the loss of the victim's future is directly supported by two considerations. In the first place, this theory explains why we regard killing as one of the worst of crimes. Killing is especially wrong, because it deprives the victim of more than perhaps any other crime. In the second place, people with AIDS or cancer who know they are dying believe, of course, that dying is a very bad thing for them. They believe that the loss of a future to them that they would otherwise have experienced is what makes their premature death a very bad thing for them. A better theory of the wrongness of killing would require a different natural property associated with killing which better fits with the attitudes of the dying. What could it be?

The view that what makes killing wrong is the loss to the victim of the value of the victim's future gains additional support when some of its implications are examined. In the first place, it is incompatible with the view that it is wrong to kill only beings who are biologically human. It is possible that there exists a different species from another planet whose members have a future like ours. Since having a future like that is what makes killing someone wrong, this theory entails that it would be wrong to kill members of such a species. Hence, this theory is opposed to the claim that only life that is biologically human has great moral worth, a claim which many anti-abortionists have seemed to adopt. This opposition, which this theory has in common with personhood theories, seems to be a merit of the theory.

In the second place, the claim that the loss of one's future is the wrong-making feature of one's being killed entails the possibility that the futures of some actual nonhuman mammals on our own planet are sufficiently like ours that it is seriously wrong to kill them also. Whether some animals do have the same right to life as human beings depends on adding to the account of the wrongness of killing some additional account of just what it is about my future or the futures of other adult human beings which makes it wrong to kill us. No such additional account will be offered in this essay. Undoubtedly, the provision of such an account would be a very difficult matter. Undoubtedly, any such account would be quite controversial. Hence, it surely should not reflect badly on this sketch of an elementary theory of the wrongness of killing that it is indeterminate with respect to some very difficult issues regarding animal rights.

In the third place, the claim that the loss of one's future is the wrong-making feature of one's being killed does not entail, as sanctity of human life theories do, that active euthanasia is wrong. Persons who are severely and incurably ill, who face a future of pain and despair, and who wish to die will not have suffered a loss if they are killed. It is, strictly speaking, the value of a human's future which makes killing wrong in this theory. This being so, killing does not necessarily wrong some persons who are sick and dying. Of course, there may be other reasons for a prohibition of active euthanasia, but that is another matter. Sanctity-of-human-life theories seem to hold that active euthanasia is seriously wrong even in an individual case where there seems to be good reason for it independently of public policy considerations. This consequence is most implausible, and it is a plus for the claim that

the loss of a future of value is what makes killing wrong that it does not share this consequence.

In the fourth place, the account of the wrongness of killing defended in this essay does straightforwardly entail that it is prima facie seriously wrong to kill children and infants, for we do presume that they have futures of value. Since we do believe that it is wrong to kill defenseless little babies, it is important that a theory of the wrongness of killing easily account for this. Personhood theories of the wrongness of killing, on the other hand, cannot straightforwardly account for the wrongness of killing infants and young children. Hence, such theories must add special ad hoc accounts of the wrongness of killing the young. The plausibility of such ad hoc theories seems to be a function of how desperately one wants such theories to work. The claim that the primary wrong-making feature of a killing is the loss to the victim of the value of its future accounts for the wrongness of killing young children and infants directly; it makes the wrongness of such acts as obvious as we actually think it is. This is a further merit of this theory. Accordingly, it seems that this value of a future-like-ours theory of the wrongness of killing shares strengths of both sanctity-of-life and personhood accounts while avoiding weaknesses of both. In addition, it meshes with a central intuition concerning what makes killing wrong.

The claim that the primary wrong-making feature of a killing is the loss to the victim of the value of its future has obvious consequences for the ethics of abortion. The future of a standard fetus includes a set of experiences, projects, activities, and such which are identical with the futures of adult human beings and are identical with the futures of young children. Since the reason that is sufficient to explain why it is wrong to kill human beings after the time of birth is a reason that also applies to fetuses, it follows that abortion is prima facie seriously morally wrong.

This argument does not rely on the invalid inference that, since it is wrong to kill persons, it is wrong to kill potential persons also. The category that is morally central to this analysis is the category of having a valuable future like ours; it is not the category of personhood. The argument to the conclusion that abortion is prima facie seriously morally wrong proceeded independently of the notion of person or potential person or any equivalent. Someone may wish to start with this analysis in terms of the value of a human future, conclude that abortion is, except perhaps in rare circumstances, seriously morally wrong, infer that fetuses have the right to life, and then call fetuses "persons" as a result of their having the right to life. Clearly, in this case, the category of person is being used to state the *conclusion* of the analysis rather than to generate the *argument* of the analysis.

The structure of this anti-abortion argument can be both illuminated and defended by comparing it to what appears to be the best argument for the wrongness of the wanton infliction of pain on animals. This latter argument is based on the assumption that it is prima facie wrong to inflict pain on me (or you, reader). What is the natural property associated with the infliction of pain which makes such infliction wrong? The obvious answer seems to be that the infliction of pain causes suffering and that suffering is a misfortune. The suffering caused by the infliction of pain is what makes the wanton infliction of pain on me wrong. The wanton infliction of pain on other adult humans causes suffering. The wanton infliction of pain on animals causes suffering. Since causing suffering is what makes the wanton infliction of pain wrong and since the wanton infliction of pain on animals causes suffering, it follows that the wanton infliction of pain on animals is wrong.

This argument for the wrongness of the wanton infliction of pain on animals shares a number of structural features with the argument for the serious prima facie wrongness of abortion. Both arguments start with an obvious assumption concerning what it is wrong to do to me (or you, reader). Both then look for the characteristic or the consequence of the wrong action which makes the action wrong. Both recognize that the wrong-making feature of these immoral actions is a property of actions sometimes directed at individuals other than postnatal human beings. If the structure of the argument for the wrongness of the wanton infliction of pain on animals is sound, then the structure of the argument for the prima facie serious wrongness of abortion is also sound, for the structure of the two arguments is the same. The structure common to both is the key

to the explanation of how the wrongness of abortion can be demonstrated without recourse to the category of person. In neither argument is that category crucial.

This defense of an argument for the wrongness of abortion in terms of a structurally similar argument for the wrongness of the wanton infliction of pain on animals succeeds only if the account regarding animals is the correct account. Is it? In the first place, it seems plausible. In the second place, its major competition is Kant's account. Kant believed that we do not have direct duties to animals at all, because they are not persons. Hence, Kant had to explain and justify the wrongness of inflicting pain on animals on the grounds that "he who is hard in his dealings with animals becomes hard also in his dealing with men." The problem with Kant's account is that there seems to be no reason for accepting this latter claim unless Kant's account is rejected. If the alternative to Kant's account is accepted, then it is easy to understand why someone who is indifferent to inflicting pain on animals is also indifferent to inflicting pain on humans, for one is indifferent to what makes inflicting pain wrong in both cases. But, if Kant's account is accepted, there is no intelligible reason why one who is hard in his dealings with animals (or crabgrass or stones) should also be hard in his dealings with men. After all, men are persons: animals are no more persons than crabgrass or stones. Persons are Kant's crucial moral category. Why, in short, should a Kantian accept the basic claim in Kant's argument?

Hence, Kant's argument for the wrongness of inflicting pain on animals rests on a claim that, in a world of Kantian moral agents, is demonstrably false. Therefore, the alternative analysis, being more plausible anyway, should be accepted. Since this alternative analysis has the same structure as the anti-abortion argument being defended here, we have further support for the argument for the immorality of abortion being defended in this essay.

Of course, this value of a future-like-ours argument, if sound, shows only that abortion is prima facie wrong, not that it is wrong in any and all circumstances. Since the loss of the future to a standard fetus, if killed, is, however, at least as great a loss as the loss of the future to a standard adult human being who is killed, abortion, like ordinary killing, could be justified only by the most compelling reasons. The loss of one's life is almost the greatest misfortune that can happen to one. Presumably abortion could be justified in some circumstances, only if the loss consequent on failing to abort would be at least as great. Accordingly, morally permissible abortions will be rare indeed unless, perhaps, they occur so early in pregnancy that a fetus is not yet definitely an individual. Hence, this argument should be taken as showing that abortion is presumptively very seriously wrong, where the presumption is very strong—as strong as the presumption that killing another adult human being is wrong.

III

How complete an account of the wrongness of killing does the value of a future-like-ours account have to be in order that the wrongness of abortion is a consequence? This account does not have to be an account of the necessary conditions for the wrongness of killing. Some persons in nursing homes may lack valuable human futures, yet it may be wrong to kill them for other reasons. Furthermore, this account does not obviously have to be the sole reason killing is wrong where the victim did have a valuable future. This analysis claims only that, for any killing where the victim did have a valuable future like ours, having that future by itself is sufficient to create the strong presumption that the killing is seriously wrong.

One way to overturn the value of a future-like-ours argument would be to find some account of the wrongness of killing which is at least as intelligible and which has different implications for the ethics of abortion. Two rival accounts possess at least some degree of plausibility. One account is based on the obvious fact that people value the experience of living and wish for that valuable experience to continue. Therefore, it might be said, what makes killing wrong is the discontinuation of that experience for the victim. Let us call this the *discontinuation account*. Another rival account is based upon the obvious fact that people strongly desire to continue to live. This suggests that what makes killing us so wrong is that it interferes with the fulfillment of a strong and fundamental desire, the fulfillment of which is necessary for the fulfillment of any other desires we might have. Let us call this the *desire account*.

Consider first the desire account as a rival account of the ethics of killing which would provide the basis for rejecting the anti-abortion position. Such an account will have to be stronger than the value of a future-like-ours account of the wrongness of abortion if it is to do the job expected of it. To entail the wrongness of abortion, the value of a future-like-ours account has only to provide a sufficient, but not a necessary, condition for the wrongness of killing. The desire account, on the other hand, must provide us also with a necessary condition for the wrongness of killing in order to generate a pro-choice conclusion on abortion. The reason for this is that presumably the argument from the desire account moves from the claim that what makes killing wrong is interference with a very strong desire to the claim that abortion is not wrong because the fetus lacks a strong desire to live. Obviously, this inference fails if someone's having the desire to live is not a necessary condition of its being wrong to kill that individual.

One problem with the desire account is that we do regard it as seriously wrong to kill persons who have little desire to live or who have no desire to live or, indeed, have a desire not to live. We believe it is seriously wrong to kill the unconscious, the sleeping, those who are tired of life, and those who are suicidal. The value-of-a-human-future account renders standard morality intelligible in these cases; these cases appear to be incompatible with the desire account.

The desire account is subject to a deeper difficulty. We desire life, because we value the goods of this life. The goodness of life is not secondary to our desire for it. If this were not so, the pain of one's own premature death could be done away with merely by an appropriate alteration in the configuration of one's desires. This is absurd. Hence, it would seem that it is the loss of the goods of one's future, not the interference with the fulfillment of a strong desire to live, which accounts ultimately for the wrongness of killing.

It is worth noting that, if the desire account is modified so that it does not provide a necessary, but only a sufficient, condition for the wrongness of killing, the desire account is compatible with the value of a future-like-ours account. The combined accounts will yield an anti-abortion ethic. This suggests that one can retain what is intuitively plausible about the desire account without a challenge to the basic argument of this paper.

It is also worth noting that, if future desires have moral force in a modified desire account of the wrongness of killing, one can find support for an anti-abortion ethic even in the absence of a value of a future-like-ours account. If one decides that a morally relevant property, the possession of which is sufficient to make it wrong to kill some individual, is the desire at some future time to live—one might decide to justify one's refusal to kill suicidal teenagers on these grounds, for example—then, since typical fetuses will have the desire in the future to live, it is wrong to kill typical fetuses. Accordingly, it does not seem that a desire account of the wrongness of killing can provide a justification of a pro-choice ethic of abortion which is nearly as adequate as the value of a human-future justification on an anti-abortion ethic.

The discontinuation account looks more promising as an account of the wrongness of killing. It seems just as intelligible as the value of a future-like-ours account, but it does not justify an anti-abortion position. Obviously, if it is the continuation of one's activities, experiences, and projects, the loss of which makes killing wrong, then it is not wrong to kill fetuses for that reason, for fetuses do not have experiences, activities, and projects to be continued or discontinued. Accordingly, the discontinuation account does not have the anti-abortion consequences that the value of a future-like-ours account has. Yet, it seems as intelligible as the value of a future-like-ours account, for when we think of what would be wrong with our being killed, it does seem as if it is the discontinuation of what makes our lives worthwhile which makes killing us wrong.

Is the discontinuation account just as good an account as the value of a future-like-ours account? The discontinuation account will not be adequate at all, if it does not refer to the *value* of the experience that may be discontinued. One does not want the discontinuation account to make it wrong to kill a patient who begs for death and who is in severe pain that cannot be relieved short of killing. (I leave open the question of whether it is wrong for other reasons.) Accordingly, the discontinuation account must be more than a bare discontinuation account. It must make some reference to the positive value of the patient's experiences. But, by the same token, the value of a future-like-ours account cannot be a bare future account either. Just having a future surely does not itself rule out killing the above patient. This account must make some reference to the value of the patient's future experiences and projects also. Hence, both accounts involve the value of experiences, projects, and activities. So far we still have symmetry between the accounts.

The symmetry fades, however, when we focus on the time period of the value of the experiences, etc., which has moral consequences. Although both accounts leave open the possibility that the patient in our example may be killed, this possibility is left open only in virtue of the utterly bleak future for the patient. It makes no difference whether the patient's immediate past contains intolerable pain, or consists in being in a coma (which we can imagine is a situation of indifference), or consists in a life of value. If the patient's future is a future of value, we want our account to make it wrong to kill the patient. If the patient's future is intolerable, whatever his or her immediate past, we want our account to allow killing the patient. Obviously, then, it is the value of that patient's future which is doing the work in rendering the morality of killing the patient intelligible.

This being the case, it seems clear that whether one has immediate past experiences or not does no work in the explanation of what makes killing wrong. The addition the discontinuation account makes to the value of a human future account is otiose. Its addition to the value-of-a-future account plays no role at all in rendering intelligible the wrongness of killing. Therefore, it can be discarded with the discontinuation account of which it is a part.

IV

The analysis of the previous section suggests that alternative general accounts of the wrongness of killing are either inadequate or unsuccessful in getting around the anti-abortion consequences of the value of a future-like-ours argument. A different strategy for avoiding these anti-abortion consequences involves limiting the scope of the value of a future argument. More precisely, the strategy involves arguing that fetuses lack a property that is essential for the value-of-a-future argument (or for any anti-abortion argument) to apply to them.

One move of this sort is based upon the claim that a necessary condition of one's future being valuable is that one values it. Value implies a valuer. Given this one might argue that, since fetuses cannot value their futures, their futures are not valuable to them. Hence, it does not seriously wrong them deliberately to end their lives.

This move fails, however, because of some ambiguities. Let us assume that something cannot be of value unless it is valued by someone. This does not entail that my life is of no value unless it is valued by me. I may think, in a period of despair, that my future is of no worth whatsoever, but I may be wrong because others rightly see value—even great value—in it. Furthermore, my future can be valuable to me even if I do not value it. This is the case when a young person attempts suicide, but is rescued and goes on to significant human achievements. Such young people's futures are ultimately valuable to them, even though such futures do not seem to be valuable to them at the moment of attempted suicide. A fetus's future can be valuable to it in the same way. Accordingly, this attempt to limit the anti-abortion argument fails.

Another similar attempt to reject the anti-abortion position is based on Tooley's claim that an entity cannot possess the right to life unless it has the capacity to desire its continued existence. It follows that, since fetuses lack the conceptual capacity to desire to continue to live, they lack the right to life. Accordingly, Tooley concludes that abortion cannot be seriously prima facie wrong. . . .

What could be the evidence for Tooley's basic claim? Tooley once argued that individuals have a prima facie right to what they desire and that the lack of the capacity to desire something undercuts the basis of one's right to it. . . . This argument plainly will not succeed in the context of the analysis of this essay, however, since the point here is to establish the fetus's right to life on other grounds. Tooley's argument assumes that the right to life cannot be established in general on some basis other than the desire for life. This position was considered and rejected in the preceding section of this paper.

One might attempt to defend Tooley's basic claim on the grounds that, because a fetus cannot apprehend continued life as a benefit, its continued life cannot be a benefit or cannot be something it has a right to or cannot be something that is in its interest. This might be defended in terms of the general proposition that, if an individual is literally incapable of caring about or taking an interest in some X, then one does not have a right to X or X is not a benefit or X is not something that is in one's interest.

Each member of this family of claims seems to be open to objections. As John C. Stevens has pointed out, one may have a right to be treated with a certain medical procedure (because of a health insurance policy one has purchased), even though one cannot conceive of the nature of the procedure. And, as Tooley himself has pointed out, persons who have been indoctrinated, or drugged, or rendered temporarily unconscious may be literally incapable of caring about or taking an interest in something that is in their interest or is something to which they have a right, or is something that benefits them. Hence, the Tooley claim that would restrict the scope of the value of a future-like-ours argument is undermined by counterexamples.

Finally, Paul Bassen has argued that, even though the prospects of an embryo might seem to be a basis for the wrongness of abortion, an embryo cannot be a victim and therefore cannot be wronged. An embryo cannot be a victim, he says, because it lacks sentience. His central argument for this seems to be that, even though plants and the permanently unconscious are alive, they clearly cannot be victims. What is the explanation of this? Bassen claims that the explanation is that their lives consist of mere metabolism and mere metabolism is not enough to ground victimizability. Mentation is required.

The problem with this attempt to establish the absence of victimizability is that both plants and the permanently unconscious clearly lack what Bassen calls "prospects" or what I have called "a future life like ours." Hence, it is surely open to one to argue that the real reason we believe plants and the permanently unconscious cannot be victims is that killing them cannot deprive them of a future life like ours; the real reason is not their absence of present mentation.

Bassen recognizes that his view is subject to this difficulty, and he recognizes that the case of children seems to support this difficulty, for "much of what we do for children is based on prospects." He argues, however, that, in the case of children and in other such cases, "potentiality comes into play only where victimizability has been secured on other grounds". . . .

Bassen's defense of his view is patently question-begging, since what is adequate to secure victimizability is exactly what is at issue. His examples do not support his own view against the thesis of this essay. Of course, embryos can be victims: when their lives are deliberately terminated, they are deprived of their futures of value, their prospects. This makes them victims, for it directly wrongs them.

The seeming plausibility of Bassen's view stems from the fact that paradigmatic cases of imagining someone as a victim involve empathy, and empathy requires mentation of the victim. The victims of flood, famine, rape, or child abuse are all persons with whom we can empathize. That empathy seems to be part of seeing them as victims.

In spite of the strength of these examples, the attractive intuition that a situation in which there is victimization requires the possibility of empathy is subject to counterexamples. Consider a case that Bassen himself offers: "Posthumous obliteration of an author's work constitutes a misfortune for him only if he had wished his work to endure". . . . The conditions Bassen wishes to impose upon the possibility of being victimized here seem far too strong. Perhaps this author, due to his unrealistic standards of excellence and his low self-esteem, regarded his work as unworthy of survival, even though it possessed genuine literary merit. Destruction of such work would surely victimize its author. In such a case, empathy with the victim concerning the loss is clearly impossible.

Of course, Bassen does not make the possibility of empathy a necessary condition of victimizability; he requires only mentation. Hence, on Bassen's actual view, this author, as I have described him, can be a victim. The problem is that the basic intuition

that renders Bassen's view plausible is missing in the author's case. In order to attempt to avoid counterexamples, Bassen has made his thesis too weak to be supported by the intuitions that suggested it.

Even so, the mentation requirement on victimizability is still subject to counterexamples. Suppose a severe accident renders me totally unconscious for a month, after which I recover. Surely killing me while I am unconscious victimizes me, even though I am incapable of mentation during that time. It follows that Bassen's thesis fails. Apparently, attempts to restrict the value of a future-like-ours argument so that fetuses do not fall within its scope do not succeed.

V

In this essay, it has been argued that the correct ethic of the wrongness of killing can be extended to fetal life and used to show that there is a strong presumption that any abortion is morally impermissible. If the ethic of killing adopted here entails, however, that contraception is also seriously immoral, then there would appear to be a difficulty with the analysis of this essay.

But this analysis does not entail that contraception is wrong. Of course, contraception prevents the actualization of a possible future of value. Hence, it follows from the claim that futures of value should be maximized that contraception is prima facie immoral. This obligation to maximize does not exist, however; furthermore, nothing in the ethics of killing in this paper entails that it does. The ethics of killing in this essay would entail that contraception is wrong only if something were denied a human future of value by contraception. Nothing at all is denied such a future by contraception, however.

Candidates for a subject of harm by contraception fall into four categories: (1) some sperm or other, (2) some ovum or other, (3) a sperm and an ovum separately, and (4) a sperm and an ovum together. Assigning the harm to some sperm is utterly arbitrary, for no reason can be given for making a sperm the subject of harm rather than an ovum. Assigning the harm to some ovum is utterly arbitrary, for no reason can be given for making an ovum the subject of harm rather than a sperm. One might attempt to avoid these problems by insisting that contraception deprives both the sperm and the ovum separately of a valuable future like ours. On this alternative, too many futures are lost. Contraception was supposed to be wrong, because it deprived us of one future of value, not two. One might attempt to avoid this problem by holding that contraception deprives the combination of sperm and ovum of a valuable future like ours. But here the definite article misleads. At the time of contraception, there are hundreds of millions of sperm, one (released) ovum and millions of possible combinations of all of these. There is no actual combination at all. Is the subject of the loss to be a merely possible combination? Which one? This alternative does not yield an actual subject of harm either. Accordingly, the immorality of contraception is not entailed by the loss of a future-like-ours argument simply because there is no nonarbitrarily identifiable subject of the loss in the case of contraception.

VI

The purpose of this essay has been to set out an argument for the serious presumptive wrongness of abortion subject to the assumption that the moral permissibility of abortion stands or falls on the moral status of the fetus. Since a fetus possesses a property, the possession of which in adult human beings is sufficient to make killing an adult human being wrong, abortion is wrong. This way of dealing with the problem of abortion seems superior to other approaches to the ethics of abortion, because it rests on an ethics of killing which is close to self-evident, because the crucial morally relevent property clearly applies to fetuses, and because the argument avoids the usual equivocations on 'human life', 'human being', or 'person'. The argument rests neither on religious claims nor on Papal dogma. It is not subject to the objection of "speciesism." Its soundness is compatible with the moral permissibility of euthanasia and contraception. It deals with our intuitions concerning young children.

Finally, this analysis can be viewed as resolving a standard problem—indeed, *the* standard problem—concerning the ethics of abortion. Clearly, it is wrong to kill adult human beings. Clearly, it is not wrong to end the life of some arbitrarily chosen single human cell. Fetuses seem to be like arbitrarily chosen human cells in some respects and like adult humans in other respects. The problem of the ethics of abortion is the problem of determining the fetal property that settles this moral controversy. The thesis of this essay is that the problem of the ethics of abortion, so understood, is solvable.

Euthanasia

Euthanasia, or mercy killing, presents some very difficult and painful dilemmas for doctors, patients, family members, and moral philosophers. Sometimes a patient's condition is so poor and holds so little hope of future recovery that death seems better than life. Is it ever morally justifiable to allow such patients to die by withholding treatment that would otherwise be given? Is it ever justifiable to kill them?

Clearly, this topic concerns both rights and liberty. The patient has a right to life and perhaps a right to die. The patient may also have the liberty to make certain fundamental decisions about whether to continue treatment. Frequently, however, euthanasia becomes a serious issue only after the patient is comatose or otherwise incapable of making a competent decision. Moreover, many factors seem to be morally relevant to the decision between life and death. Is the patient conscious? Suffering? If so, how much? What are the prospects for improvement? Is the patient terminally ill? What kind of life can the patient hope to lead, and for how long? The course of action being contemplated may also matter: Cessation of "heroic" lifesaving efforts? Withdrawal of food and water? A lethal injection?

The Supreme Court of New Jersey, in a much-publicized case, decided in 1976 to allow the parents of Karen Ann Quinlan to remove her from a respirator. She was comatose and diagnosed as having no chance of regaining consciousness. The court decided that Quinlan's right of privacy gave her or her guardian the right to decide the course of her treatment, since a respirator, which might be deemed ordinary for a curable patient, should count as extraordinary for someone with her poor prognosis.

Eight years later, the Supreme Court of Missouri reached the opposite verdict in a related case. Nancy Cruzan, after an automobile accident, was "in a persistent vegetative state." She was nevertheless not terminally ill and not reliant on a respirator or other extraordinary machinery for support. However, she did require a feeding tube. Her guardians requested that fluids and nutrition be withdrawn. The court found no justification for granting that request, arguing that Cruzan's condition was significantly different from Quinlan's and that the relevant state interest is life, not the quality of life, as the *Quinlan* court seemed to suggest.

J. Gay-Williams argues that euthanasia is invariably wrong. It is, he contends, contrary to everyone's natural inclination to continue living. Moreover, it is extremely dangerous for several reasons. First, we can never know that death is really preferable to continued life. Second, people may choose death out of ignorance, a temporary feeling of hopelessness, or consideration for their families. Finally, euthanasia would lead to a lowered respect for life that could have serious consequences for medical care and society's treatment of the infirm.

James Rachels cites the policy of the American Medical Association on euthanasia, maintaining that it rests on a distinction between active and passive euthanasia that makes no moral sense. Rachels argues that there is no moral difference between killing someone and letting them die. Yet active killing is illegal and denounced by the AMA, whereas letting a patient die is accepted in some cases, even though patients might suffer great and unnecessary pain by being allowed to die slowly. Rachels urges the AMA to alter its stand and recommend active euthanasia in certain carefully restricted cases.

Bonnie Steinbock criticizes Rachels's position. She holds that the AMA's policy rests not on the distinction between active and passive euthanasia but on the concept of the intentional termination of life. She maintains that there is a significant moral difference between ordinary and extraordinary care. Although it is justifiable at times to refrain from extraordinary measures, she argues, it is never permissible to end life intentionally by withholding ordinary care or active killing.

Matter of Quinlan (1976)

(*Source:* Matter of Quinlan *70 N.J. 10, 355 A. 2d. 647 [1976]. Most legal references have been omitted.*)

QUESTIONS FOR REFLECTION

1. Which features of Karen Ann Quinlan's condition did the court find relevant to reaching a decision? Do you agree that these are all the relevant factors?

2. How did the court justify its decision? Do you find the justification persuasive?

3. In fact, when Karen Ann Quinlan was disconnected from life-support machinery after this decision, she did not die. If the court had known she would survive without the equipment, would the justification the court offered be weakened?

The Litigation

The central figure in this tragic case is Karen Ann Quinlan, a New Jersey resident. At the age of 22, she lies in a debilitated and allegedly moribund state at Saint Clare's Hospital in Denville, New Jersey. The litigation has to do, in final analysis, with her life—its continuance or cessation—and the responsibilities, rights and duties, with regard to any fateful decision concerning it, of her family, her guardian, her doctors, the hospital, the State through its law enforcement authorities, and finally the courts of justice.

Due to extensive physical damage fully described in the able opinion of the trial judge, Judge Muir, supporting that judgment, Karen allegedly was incompetent. Joseph Quinlan sought the adjudication of that incompetency. He wished to be appointed guardian of the person and property of his daughter. It was proposed by him that such letters of guardianship, if granted, should contain an express power to him as guardian to authorize the discontinuance of all extraordinary medical procedures now allegedly sustaining Karen's vital processes and hence her life, since these measures, he asserted, present no hope of her eventual recovery. A guardian *ad litem* was appointed by Judge Muir to represent the interest of the alleged incompetent.

The Factual Base

On the night of April 15, 1975, for reasons still unclear, Karen Quinlan ceased breathing for at least two 15 minute periods. She received some ineffectual mouth-to-mouth resuscitation from friends. She was taken by ambulance to Newton Memorial Hospital. There she had a temperature of 100 degrees, her pupils were unreactive and she was unresponsive even to deep pain. The history at the time of her admission to that hospital was essentially incomplete and uninformative.

Three days later, Dr. Morse examined Karen at the request of the Newton admitting physician, Dr. McGee. He found her comatose with evidence of decortication, a condition relating to derangement of the cortex of the brain causing a physical posture in which the upper extremities are flexed and the lower extremities are extended. She required a respirator to assist her breathing. Dr. Morse was unable to obtain an adequate account of the circumstances and events leading up to Karen's admission to the Newton Hospital. Such initial history or etiology is crucial in neurological diagnosis. Relying as he did upon the Newton Memorial records and his own examination, he concluded that prolonged lack of oxygen in the bloodstream, anoxia, was identified with her condition as he saw it upon first observation. When she was later transferred to Saint Clare's Hospital she was still unconscious, still on a respirator and a tracheotomy had been performed. On her arrival Dr. Morse conducted extensive and detailed examinations. An electroencephalogram (EEG) measuring electrical rhythm of the brain was performed and Dr. Morse characterized the result as "abnormal but it showed some activity and was consistent with her clinical state." Other significant neurological tests, including a brain scan, an angiogram, and a lumbar puncture were normal in result. Dr. Morse testified that Karen has been in a state of coma, lack of consciousness, since he began treating her. He explained that there are basically two types of coma, sleep-like unresponsiveness and awake unresponsiveness. Karen was originally in a sleep-like unresponsive condition but soon developed "sleep-wake" cycles, apparently a normal improvement for comatose patients occurring within three to four weeks. In the awake cycle she blinks, cries out and does things of that sort but is still totally unaware of anyone or anything around her.

Dr. Morse and other expert physicians who examined her characterized Karen as being in a "chronic persistent vegetative state." Dr. Fred Plum, one of such expert witnesses, defined this as a "subject who remains with the capacity to maintain the vegetative parts of neurological function but who . . . no longer has any cognitive function." . . .

It seemed to be the consensus not only of the treating physicians but also of the several qualified experts who testified in the case, that removal from the respirator would not conform to medical practices, standards and traditions.

The further medical consensus was that Karen in addition to being comatose is in a chronic and persistent "vegetative" state, having no awareness of anything or anyone around her and existing at a primitive reflex level. Although she does have some brain stem function (ineffective for respiration) and has other reactions one normally associates with being alive, such as moving, reacting to light, sound and noxious stimuli, blinking her eyes, and the like, the quality of her feeling impulses is unknown. She grimaces, makes stereotyped cries and sounds and has chewing motions. Her blood pressure is normal.

Karen is described as emaciated, having suffered a weight loss of at least 40 pounds, and undergoing a continuing deteriorative process. Her posture is described as fetal-like and grotesque; there is extreme flexion-rigidity of the arms, legs and related muscles and her joints are severely rigid and deformed.

From all of this evidence, and including the whole testimonial record, several basic findings in the physical area are mandated. Severe brain and associated damage, albeit of uncertain etiology, has left Karen in a chronic and persistent vegetative state. No form of treatment which can cure or improve that condition is known or available. As nearly as may be determined, considering the guarded area of remote uncertainties characteristic of most medical science predictions, she can *never* be restored to cognitive or sapient life. Even with regard to the vegetative level and improvement therein (if such it may be called) the prognosis is extremely poor and the extent unknown if it should in fact occur.

She is debilitated and moribund and although fairly stable at the time of argument before us (no new information having been filed in the meanwhile in expansion of the record), no physician risked the opinion that she could live more than a year and indeed she may die much earlier. Excellent medical and nursing care so far has been able to ward off the constant threat of infection, to which she is peculiarly susceptible because of the respirator, the tracheal tube and other incidents of care in her vulnerable condition. Her life accordingly is sustained by the respirator and tubal feeding, and removal from the respirator would cause her death soon, although the time cannot be stated with more precision.

It is from this factual base that the Court confronts and responds to three basic issues:

1. Was the trial court correct in denying the specific relief requested by plaintiff, i.e., authorization for termination of the life-supporting apparatus, on the case presented to him? Our determination on that question is in the affirmative.

2. Was the court correct in withholding letters of guardianship from the plaintiff and appointing in his stead a stranger? On that issue our determination is in the negative.

3. Should this Court, in the light of the foregoing conclusions, grant declaratory relief to the plaintiff? On that question our Court's determination is in the affirmative.

This brings us to a consideration of the constitutional and legal issues underlying the foregoing determinations.

Constitutional and Legal Issues

The Right of Privacy

It is the issue of the constitutional right of privacy that has given us most concern, in the exceptional circumstances of this case. Here a loving parent, *qua* parent and raising the rights of his incompetent and profoundly damaged daughter, probably irreversibly doomed to no more than a biologically vegetative remnant of life, is before the court. He seeks authorization to abandon specialized technological procedures which can only maintain for a time a body having no potential for resumption or continuance of other than a "vegetative" existence.

We have no doubt, in these unhappy circumstances, that if Karen were herself miraculously lucid for an interval (not altering the existing prognosis of the condition to which she would soon return) and perceptive of her irreversible condition, she could effectively decide upon discontinuance of the life-support apparatus, even if it meant the prospect of natural death. . . .

We have no hesitancy in deciding . . . that no external compelling interest of the State could compel Karen to endure the unendurable, only to vegetate a few measurable months with no realistic possibility of returning to any semblance of cognitive or sapient life. We perceive no thread of logic distinguishing between such a choice on Karen's part and a similar choice which, under the evidence in this case, could be made by a competent patient terminally ill, riddled by cancer and suffering great pain; such a patient would not be resuscitated or put on a respirator . . . and *a fortiori* would not be kept *against his will* on a respirator.

Although the Constitution does not explicitly mention a right of privacy, Supreme Court decisions have recognized that a right of personal privacy exists and that certain areas of privacy are guaranteed under the Constitution. . . .

The court in *Griswold* found the unwritten constitutional right of privacy to exist in the penumbra of specific guarantees of the Bill of Rights "formed by emanations from those guarantees that help give them life and substance." Presumably this right is broad enough to encompass a patient's decision to decline medical treatment under certain circumstances, in much the same way as it is broad enough to encompass a woman's decision to terminate pregnancy under certain conditions. . . .

The claimed interests of the State in this case are essentially the preservation and sanctity of human life and defense of the right of the physician to administer medical treatment according to his best judgment. In this case the doctors say that removing Karen from the respirator will conflict with their professional judgment. The plaintiff answers that Karen's present treatment serves only a maintenance function; that the respirator cannot cure or improve her condition but at best can only prolong her inevitable slow deterioration and death; and that the interests of the patient, as seen by her surrogate, the guardian, must be evaluated by the court as predominant, even in the face of an opinion *contra* by the present attending physicians. Plaintiff's distinction is significant. The nature of Karen's care and the realistic chances of her recovery are quite unlike those of the patients discussed in many of the cases where treatments were ordered. In many of those cases the medical procedure required (usually a transfusion) constituted a minimal bodily invasion and the chances of recovery and return to functioning life were very good. We think that the State's interest *contra* weakens and the individual's right to privacy grows as the degree of bodily invasion increases and the prognosis dims. Ultimately there comes a point at which the individual's rights overcome the State interest. It is for that reason that we believe Karen's choice, if she were competent to make it, would be vindicated by the law. Her prognosis is extremely poor—she will never resume cognitive life. And the bodily invasion is very great—she requires 24 hour intensive nursing care, antibiotics, the assistance of a respirator, a catheter and feeding tube.

Our affirmation of Karen's independent right of choice, however, would ordinarily be based upon her competency to assert it. The sad truth, however, is that she is grossly incompetent and we cannot discern her supposed choice based on the testimony of her previous conversations with friends, where such testimony is without sufficient probative weight. . . . Nevertheless we have concluded that Karen's right of privacy may be asserted on her behalf by her guardian under the peculiar circumstances here present.

If a putative decision by Karen to permit this non-cognitive, vegetative existence to terminate by natural forces is regarded as a valuable incident of her right of privacy, as we believe it to be, then it should not be discarded solely on the basis that her condition prevents her conscious exercise of the choice. The only practical way to prevent destruction of the right is to permit the guardian and family of Karen to render their best judgment, subject to the qualifications hereinafter stated, as to whether she would exercise it in these circumstances. If their conclusion is in the affirmative this decision should be accepted by a society the overwhelming majority of whose members would, we think, in similar circumstances, exercise such a choice in the same way for themselves or for those closest to them. It is for this reason that we determine that Karen's right of privacy may be asserted in her behalf, in this respect, by her guardian and family under the particular circumstances presented by this record.

Regarding Mr. Quinlan's right of privacy, we agree with Judge Muir's conclusion that there is no parental constitutional right that would entitle him to a grant of relief *in propria persona.* . . . Insofar as a parental right of privacy has been recognized, it has been in the context of determining the rearing of infants and, as Judge Muir put it, involved "continuing life styles." . . . Karen Quinlan is a 22-year-old adult. Her right of privacy in respect of the matter before the court is to be vindicated by Mr. Quinlan as guardian, as hereinabove determined.

The Medical Factor

. . . We glean from the record here that physicians distinguish between curing the ill and comforting and easing the dying; that they refuse to treat the curable as if they were dying or ought to die, and that they have sometimes refused to treat the hopeless and dying as if they were curable. In this sense, as we were reminded by the testimony of Drs. Korein and Diamond, many of them have refused to inflict an undesired prolongation of the process of dying on a patient in irreversible condition when it is clear that such "therapy" offers neither human nor humane benefit. We think these attitudes represent a balanced implementation of a profoundly realistic perspective on the meaning of life and death and that they respect the whole Judeo-Christian tradition of regard for human life. No less would they seem consistent with the moral matrix of medicine, "to heal," very much in the sense of the endless mission of the law, "to do justice."

Yet this balance, we feel, is particularly difficult to perceive and apply in the context of the development by advanced technology of sophisticated and artificial life-sustaining devices. For those possibly curable, such devices are of great value, and, as ordinary medical procedures, are essential. Consequently, as pointed out by Dr. Diamond, they are necessary because of the ethic of medical practice. But in light of the situation in the present case (while the record here is somewhat hazy in distinguishing between "ordinary" and "extraordinary" measures), one would have to think that the use of the same respirator or life support could be considered "ordinary" in the context of the possibly curable patient but "extraordinary" in the context of the forced sustaining by cardiorespiratory processes of an irreversibly doomed patient. . . .

The evidence in this case convinces us that the focal point of decision should be the prognosis as to the reasonable possibility of return to cognitive and sapient life, as distinguished from the forced continuance of that biological vegetative existence to which Karen seems to be doomed.

In summary of the present Point of this opinion, we conclude that the state of the pertinent medical standards and practices which guided the attending physicians in this matter is not such as would justify this Court in deeming itself bound or controlled thereby in responding to the case for declaratory relief established by the parties on the record before us. . . .

Declaratory Relief

. . . [W]e herewith declare the following affirmative relief on behalf of the plaintiff. Upon the concurrence of the guardian and family of Karen, should the responsible attending physicians conclude that there is no reasonable possibility of Karen's ever emerging from her present comatose condition to a cognitive, sapient state and that the life-support apparatus now being administered to Karen should be discontinued, they shall consult with the hospital "Ethics Committee" or like body of the institution in which Karen is then hospitalized. If that consultative body agrees that there is no reasonable possibility of Karen's ever emerging from her present comatose condition to a cognitive, sapient state, the present life-support system may be withdrawn and said action shall be without any civil or criminal liability therefor on the part of any participant, whether guardian, physician, hospital or others. We herewith specifically so hold.

Cruzan v. Harmon (1984)

(*Source*: Cruzan v. Harmon *760 SW 2nd 408 [1978].
Most legal references have been omitted.*)

QUESTIONS FOR REFLECTION

1. Which features of Nancy Cruzan's condition did
the court find relevant to reaching a decision? Do
you agree that these are all the relevant factors?

2. How did the court justify its decision? Do you
find the justification persuasive?

3. How does this case differ from that of Karen Ann
Quinlan? Why does the court reject *Quinlan* as a
guide?

...At 12:54 A.M., January 11, 1983, the Missouri
Highway Patrol dispatched Trooper Dale Penn to the
scene of a single car accident in Jasper County, Missouri. Penn arrived six minutes later to find Nancy
Beth Cruzan lying face down in a ditch, approximately thirty-five feet from her overturned vehicle.
The trooper examined Nancy and found her without
detectable respiratory or cardiac function.

At 1:09 A.M., Paramedics Robert Williams and
Rick Maynard arrived at the accident scene; they
immediately initiated efforts to revive Nancy. By
1:12 A.M., cardiac function and spontaneous respiration had recommenced. The ambulance crew transported Nancy to the Freeman Hospital where exploratory surgery revealed a laceration of the liver. A
CAT scan showed no significant abnormalities of
her brain. The attending physician diagnosed a
probable cerebral contusion compounded by significant anoxia (deprivation of oxygen) of unknown
duration. The trial judge found that a deprivation of
oxygen to the brain approaching six minutes would
result in permanent brain damage; the best estimate
of the period of Nancy's anoxia was twelve to fourteen minutes.

Nancy remained in a coma for approximately
three weeks following the accident. Thereafter, she
seemed to improve somewhat and was able to take

nutrition orally. Rehabilitative efforts began. In
order to assist her recovery and to ease the feeding
process, a gastrostomy feeding tube was surgically
implanted on February 7, 1983, with the consent of
her (then) husband.

Over a substantial period of time, valiant efforts
to rehabilitate Nancy took place, without success.
She now lies in the Mount Vernon State Hospital.
She receives the totality of her nutrition and hydration through the gastrostomy tube.

The trial court found that (1) her respiration and
circulation are not artificially maintained and are
within the normal limits of a thirty-year-old female;
(2) she is "oblivious to her environment except for
reflexive responses to sound and perhaps painful
stimuli"; (3) she suffered anoxia of the brain resulting in a "massive enlargement of the ventricles
filling with cerebrospinal fluid in the area where the
brain has degenerated" and that "cerebral cortical
atrophy is irreversible, permanent, progressive and
ongoing"; (4) "her highest cognitive brain function
is exhibited by her grimacing perhaps in recognition
of ordinarily painful stimuli, indicating the experience of pain and apparent response to sound";
(5) she is a spastic quadriplegic; (6) her four extremities are contracted with irreversible muscular
and tendon damage to all extremities; (7) "she has

no cognitive or reflexive ability to swallow food or water to maintain her daily essential needs" and that "she will never recover her ability to swallow sufficient [sic] to satisfy her needs." In sum, Nancy is diagnosed as in a persistent vegetative state. She is not dead. She is not terminally ill. Medical experts testified that she could live another thirty years.

The trial court found that Nancy expressed, in "somewhat serious conversation" that if sick or injured she would not want to continue her life unless she could live "halfway normally." Based on this conversation, the trial court concluded that "she would not wish to continue with nutrition and hydration."

The court concluded that no state interest outweighed Nancy's "right to liberty" and that to deny Nancy's co-guardians authority to act under these circumstances would deprive Nancy of equal protection of the law. The court ordered state employees to "cause the request of the co-guardians to withdraw nutrition or hydration to be carried out."

As we said, this case presents a single issue for resolution: May a guardian order that food and water be withheld from an incompetent ward who is in a persistent vegetative state but who is otherwise alive . . . and not terminally ill? As the parties carefully pointed out in their thoughtful briefs, this issue is a broad one, invoking consideration of the authority of guardians of incompetent wards, the public policy of Missouri with regard to the termination of life-sustaining treatment and the amorphous mass of constitutional rights generally described as the "right to liberty", "the right to privacy", equal protection and due process.

This is also a case in which euphemisms readily find their way to the fore, perhaps to soften the reality of what is really at stake. But this is not a case in which we are asked to let someone die. Nancy is not dead. Nor is she terminally ill. This is a case in which we are asked to allow the medical profession to make Nancy die by starvation and dehydration. The debate here is thus not between life and death; it is between quality of life and death. We are asked to hold that the cost of maintaining Nancy's present life is too great when weighed against the benefit that life conveys both to Nancy and her loved ones and that she must die. . . .

The Right to Refuse Treatment

The common law recognizes the right of individual autonomy over decisions relating to one's health and welfare. From this root of autonomy, the common law developed the principle that a battery occurs when a physician performs a medical procedure without valid consent. . . . The doctrine of informed consent arose in recognition of the value society places on a person's autonomy and as the primary vehicle by which a person can protect the integrity of his body. If one can consent to treatment, one can also refuse it. Thus, as a necessary corollary to informed consent, the right to refuse treatment arose. "The patient's ability to control his bodily integrity . . . is significant only when one recognizes that this right also encompasses a right to informed refusal." . . .

A decision as to medical treatment must be informed.

> There are three basic prerequisites for informed consent: the patient must have the capacity to reason and make judgments, the decision must be made voluntarily and without coercion, and the patient must have a clear understanding of the risks and benefits of the proposed treatment alternatives or nontreatment, along with a full understanding of the nature of the disease and the prognosis.

. . . In the absence of these three elements, neither consent nor refusal can be informed. Thus, it is definitionally impossible for a person to make an informed decision—either to consent or to refuse—under hypothetical circumstances; under such circumstances, neither the benefits nor the risks of treatment can be properly weighed or fully appreciated.

The Right to Privacy

Quinlan, and cases which follow it, announce that a patient's right to refuse medical treatment also arises from a constitutional right of privacy. Although some courts find that right embedded in their state constitutions, the privacy argument is most often founded on decisions of the United States Supreme Court, primarily *Roe v. Wade,* . . . (1973). Unfortunately, the bare statement that the right of privacy extends to treatment decisions is seldom accompanied by any reasoned analysis as to the scope of that right or its application to the refusal of life-sustaining treatment.

. . . We . . . find no unfettered right of privacy under our constitution that would support the right of a person to refuse medical treatment in every circumstance.

If Nancy possesses such a right, it must be found to derive from the federal constitutional right to privacy announced by the United States Supreme Court. That Court "has recognized that a right of personal privacy, or a guarantee of certain areas or zones of privacy, does exist under the [United States] Constitution." . . . The Supreme Court has not, however, extended the right of privacy to permit a patient or her guardian to direct the withdrawal of food and water. We are left to determine for ourselves whether the penumbral right of privacy encompasses a right to refuse life-sustaining medical treatment.

Quinlan is the first case to apply a right of privacy to decisions regarding the termination of life-sustaining treatment. In deciding the applicability of the right to such determinations, *Quinlan* first cites *Griswold v. Connecticut,* . . . (1965), for the proposition that the right of privacy exists and, without further analysis states: "Presumably this right is broad enough to encompass a patient's decision to decline medical treatment under certain circumstances, in much the same way as it is broad enough to encompass a woman's decision to terminate a pregnancy under certain conditions." . . . The presumption invoked by the New Jersey Supreme Court provides the precedent for the extension of this right of privacy by other courts whose decisions permitting the termination of life-sustaining treatment is founded on privacy.

Yet *Roe* itself counsels against such a broad reading.

> The privacy right involved, therefore, cannot be said to be absolute. In fact, it is not clear to us that the claim asserted by some amici that one has an unlimited right to do with one's body as one pleases bears a close relationship to the right of privacy previously articulated in the Court's decisions. The Court has refused to recognize an unlimited right of this kind in the past. . . .

The language in *Roe* is not an aberration. The Supreme Court's most recent privacy decision resisted expansion of the privacy right. In *Bowers v. Hardwick,* . . . (1986), the Supreme Court considered whether the right to privacy extended to the conduct of homosexuals. Noting that the prior right to privacy cases focused on a common theme of procreation and relationships within the bonds of marriage, the court refused to extend the right of privacy beyond those bounds, arguing that such an extension amounted to the discovery of a new right. . . .

Based on our analysis of the right to privacy decisions of the Supreme Court, we carry grave doubts as to the applicability of privacy rights to decisions to terminate the provision of food and water to an incompetent patient. As will be seen, however, even if we recognize such a broadly sweeping right of privacy, a decision by Nancy's co-guardians to withdraw food and water under these circumstances cannot be sustained. . . .

It is tempting to equate the state's interest in the preservation of life with some measure of quality of life. As the discussion which follows shows, some courts find quality of life a convenient focus when justifying the termination of treatment. But the state's interest is not in quality of life. The broad policy statements of the legislature make no such distinction; nor shall we. Were quality of life at issue, persons with all manner of handicaps might find the state seeking to terminate their lives. Instead, the state's interest is in life; that interest is unqualified.

Balancing the Patient's Rights and the State's Interest

1

In casting the balance between the patient's common law right to refuse treatment/constitutional right to privacy and the state's interest in life, we acknowledge that the great majority of courts allow the termination of life-sustaining treatment. In doing so, these courts invariably find that the patient's right to refuse treatment outweighs the state's interest in preserving life. In some cases, that result is the product of a hopeless medical prognosis; in others, the court allows concerns with quality of life to discount the state's interest in life. *Quinlan,* of course, is the source in each instance. . . .

Prior to *Quinlan,* the common law preferred to err on the side of life. Choices for incompetents were made to preserve life, not hasten death. *Quinlan* changed the calculus. Moving from the common law's prejudice in favor of life, *Quinlan* subtly recast the state's interest in life as an interest in the quality of life (cognitive and sapient), struck a balance between quality of life and Karen Quinlan's right to privacy and permitted the termination of a life-sustaining procedure. . . .

As we previously stated, however, the state's interest is not in quality of life. The state's interest is an unqualified interest in life. . . .

. . . Nancy's counsel argues that her treatment is invasive. The invasion took place when the gastrostomy tube was inserted with consent at a time when hope remained for recovery. Presently, the tube merely provides a conduit for the introduction of food and water. The *continuation* of feeding through the tube is not heroically invasive. . . .

The state's relevant interest is in life, both its preservation and its sanctity. Nancy is not dead. Her life expectancy is thirty years.

Nancy's care requirements, while total, are not burdensome to Nancy. The evidence at trial showed that the care provided did not cause Nancy pain. Nor is that care particularly burdensome for her, given that she does not respond to it.

Finally, there is no evidence that Nancy is terminally ill. The quality of her life is severely diminished to be sure. Yet if food and water are supplied, she will not die.

Given the fact that Nancy is alive and that the burdens of her treatment are not excessive for her, we do not believe her right to refuse treatment, whether that right proceeds from a constitutional right of privacy or a common law right to refuse treatment, outweighs the immense, clear fact of life in which the state maintains a vital interest. . . .

J. GAY-WILLIAMS

The Wrongfulness of Euthanasia

(*Source: Reprinted from Ronald Munson [ed.],* Intervention and Reflection: Basic Issues in Medical Ethics. *Copyright © 1979 by Wadsworth Publishing Company, Inc.*)

QUESTIONS FOR REFLECTION

1. Why does Gay-Williams object to the phrase "passive euthanasia"?

2. Gay-Williams argues that euthanasia is unnatural. In what way? How does this argument lead to the moral conclusion that euthanasia is wrong?

3. Can euthanasia ever be in a patient's self-interest, according to Gay-Williams? Do you agree?

4. What is Gay-Williams's "slippery slope" argument? How persuasive is it?

My impression is that euthanasia—the idea, if not the practice—is slowly gaining acceptance within our society. Cynics might attribute this to an increasing tendency to devalue human life, but I do not believe this is the major factor. The acceptance is much more likely to be the result of unthinking sympathy and benevolence. Well-publicized, tragic stories like that of Karen Quinlan elicit from us deep feelings of compassion. We think to ourselves, "She and her family would be better off if she were dead." It is an easy step from this very human response to the view that if someone (and others) would be better off dead, then it must be all right to kill that person. Although I respect the compassion that leads to this conclusion, I believe the conclusion is wrong. I want to show that euthanasia is wrong. It is inherently wrong, but it also wrong judged from the standpoints of self-interest and of practical effects.

Before presenting my arguments to support this claim, it would be well to define "euthanasia." An essential aspect of euthanasia is that it involves taking a human life, either one's own or that of another. Also, the person whose life is taken must be someone who is believed to be suffering from some disease or injury from which recovery cannot reasonably be expected. Finally, the action must be deliberate and intentional. Thus, euthanasia is intentionally taking the life of a presumably hopeless person. Whether the life is one's own or that of another, the taking of it is still euthanasia.

It is important to be clear about the deliberate and intentional aspect of the killing. If a hopeless person is given an injection of the wrong drug by mistake and this causes his death, this is wrongful killing but not euthanasia. The killing cannot be the result of accident. Furthermore, if the person is given an injection of a drug that is believed to be necessary to treat his disease or better his condition and the person dies as a result, then this is neither wrongful killing nor euthanasia. The intention was to make the patient well, not kill him. Similarly, when a patient's condition is such that it is not reasonable to hope that any medical procedures or treatments will save his life, a failure to implement the procedures or treatments is not euthanasia. If the person dies, this will be as a result of his injuries or disease and not because of his failure to receive treatment.

The failure to continue treatment after it has been realized that the patient has little chance of benefitting from it has been characterized by some as "passive euthanasia." This phrase is misleading and mistaken. In such cases, the person involved is not killed (the first essential aspect of euthanasia), nor is the death of the person intended by the withholding of additional treatment (the third essential aspect of euthanasia). The aim may be to spare the person additional and unjustifiable pain, to save him from the indignities of hopeless manipulations, and to avoid increasing the financial and emotional burden on his family. When I buy a pencil it is so that I can use it to write, not to contribute to an increase in the gross national product. This may be the unintended consequence of my action, but it is not the aim of my action. So it is with failing to continue the treatment of a dying person. I intend his death no more than I intend to reduce the GNP by not using medical supplies. His is an unintended dying, and so-called "passive euthanasia" is not euthanasia at all.

1 The Argument from Nature

Every human being has a natural inclination to continue living. Our reflexes and responses fit us to fight attackers, flee wild animals, and dodge out of the way of trucks. In our daily lives we exercise the caution and care necessary to protect ourselves. Our bodies are similarly structured for survival right down to the molecular level. When we are cut, our capillaries seal shut, our blood clots, and fibrogen is produced to start the process of healing the wound. When we are invaded by bacteria, antibodies are produced to fight against the alien organisms, and their remains are swept out of the body by special cells designed for clean-up work.

Euthanasia does violence to this natural goal of survival. It is literally acting against nature because all the processes of nature are bent towards the end of bodily survival. Euthanasia defeats these subtle mechanisms in a way that, in a particular case, disease and injury might not.

It is possible, but not necessary, to make an appeal to revealed religion in this connection. Man as trustee of his body acts against God, its rightful possessor, when he takes his own life. He also violates the commandment to hold life sacred and never to take it without just and compelling cause. But since this appeal will persuade only those who are prepared to accept that religion has access to revealed truths, I shall not employ this line of argument.

It is enough, I believe, to recognize that the organization of the human body and our patterns of behavioral responses make the continuation of life a natural goal. By reason alone, then, we can recognize that euthanasia sets us against our own nature. Furthermore, in doing so, euthanasia does violence to our dignity. Our dignity comes from seeking our ends. When one of our goals is survival, and actions are taken that eliminate that goal, then our natural dignity suffers. Unlike animals, we are conscious through reason of our nature and our ends. Euthanasia involves acting as if this dual nature—inclination towards survival and awareness of this as an end—did not exist. Thus, euthanasia denies our basic human character and requires that we regard ourselves or others as something less than fully human.

2 The Argument from Self-Interest

The above arguments are, I believe, sufficient to show that euthanasia is inherently wrong. But there are reasons for considering it wrong when judged by standards other than reason. Because death is final and irreversible, euthanasia contains within it the possibility that we will work against our own interest if we practice it or allow it to be practiced on us.

Contemporary medicine has high standards of excellence and a proven record of accomplishment, but it does not possess perfect and complete knowledge. A mistaken diagnosis is possible, and so is a mistaken prognosis. Consequently, we may believe that we are dying of a disease when, as a matter of fact, we may not be. We may think that we have no hope of recovery when, as a matter of fact, our chances are quite good. In such circumstances, if euthanasia were permitted, we would die needlessly. Death is final and the chance of error too great to approve the practice of euthanasia.

Also, there is always the possibility that an

experimental procedure or a hitherto untried technique will pull us through. We should at least keep this option open, but euthanasia closes it off. Furthermore, spontaneous remission does occur in many cases. For no apparent reason, a patient simply recovers when those all around him, including his physicians, expected him to die. Euthanasia would just guarantee their expectations and leave no room for the "miraculous" recoveries that frequently occur.

Finally, knowing that we can take our life at any time (or ask another to take it) might well incline us to give up too easily. The will to live is strong in all of us, but it can be weakened by pain and suffering and feelings of hopelessness. If during a bad time we allow ourselves to be killed, we never have a chance to reconsider. Recovery from a serious illness requires that we fight for it, and anything that weakens our determination by suggesting that there is an easy way out is ultimately against our own interest. Also, we may be inclined towards euthanasia because of our concern for others. If we see our sickness and suffering as an emotional and financial burden on our family, we may feel that to leave our life is to make their lives easier. The very presence of the possibility of euthanasia may keep us from surviving when we might.

3 The Argument from Practical Effects

Doctors and nurses are, for the most part, totally committed to saving lives. A life lost is, for them, almost a personal failure, an insult to their skills and knowledge. Euthanasia as a practice might well alter this. It could have a corrupting influence so that in any case that is severe doctors and nurses might not try hard enough to save the patient. They might decide that the patient would simply be "better off dead" and take the steps necessary to make that come about. This attitude could then carry over to their dealings with patients less seriously ill. The result would be an overall decline in the quality of medical care.

Finally, euthanasia as a policy is a slippery slope. A person apparently hopelessly ill may be allowed to take his own life. Then he may be permitted to deputize others to do it for him should he no longer be able to act. The judgment of others then becomes the ruling factor. Already at this point euthanasia is not personal and voluntary, for others are acting "on behalf of" the patient as they see fit. This may well incline them to act on behalf of other patients who have not authorized them to exercise their judgment. It is only a short step, then, from voluntary euthanasia (self-inflicted or authorized), to directed euthanasia administered to a patient who has given no authorization, to involuntary euthanasia conducted as part of a social policy. Recently many psychiatrists and sociologists have argued that we define as "mental illness" those forms of behavior that we disapprove of. This gives us license then to lock up those who display the behavior. The category of the "hopelessly ill" provides the possibility of even worse abuse. Embedded in a social policy, it would give society or its representatives the authority to eliminate all those who might be considered too "ill" to function normally any longer. The dangers of euthanasia are too great to all to run the risk of approving it in any form. The first slippery step may well lead to a serious and harmful fall.

I hope that I have succeeded in showing why the benevolence that inclines us to give approval of euthanasia is misplaced. Euthanasia is inherently wrong because it violates the nature and dignity of human beings. But even those who are not convinced by this must be persuaded that the potential personal and social dangers inherent in euthanasia are sufficient to forbid our approving it either as a personal practice or as a public policy.

Suffering is surely a terrible thing, and we have a clear duty to comfort those in need and to ease their suffering when we can. But suffering is also a natural part of life with values for the individual and for others that we should not overlook. We may legitimately seek for others and for ourselves an easeful death. Euthanasia, however, is not just an easeful death. It is a wrongful death. Euthanasia is not just dying. It is killing.

JAMES RACHELS

Active and Passive Euthanasia

James Rachels is Professor of Philosophy at the University of Alabama at Birmingham. (Source: James Rachels, "Active and Passive Euthanasia." Reprinted from The New England Journal of Medicine 292, Number 2 [January 9, 1975], pp. 78–80. Copyright © 1975 by the Massachusetts Medical Society.)

QUESTIONS FOR REFLECTION

1. What is the difference between active and passive euthanasia?

2. Why, according to Rachels, is active euthanasia sometimes preferable?

3. Rachels's conclusion that killing and letting die are morally equivalent rests, in part, on his bathtub example. Do you agree with his analysis of that example? Can you think of cases just alike, except for the difference between killing and letting die, where there is a significant moral difference?

4. Are there cases in which active euthanasia is justifiable?

The distinction between active and passive euthanasia is thought to be crucial for medical ethics. The idea is that it is permissible, at least in some cases, to withhold treatment and allow a patient to die, but it is never permissible to take any direct action designed to kill the patient. This doctrine seems to be accepted by most doctors, and it is endorsed in a statement adopted by the House of Delegates of the American Medical Association on December 4, 1973:

> The intentional termination of the life of one human being by another—mercy killing—is contrary to that for which the medical profession stands and is contrary to the policy of the American Medical Association.
>
> The cessation of the employment of extraordinary means to prolong the life of the body when there is irrefutable evidence that biological death is imminent is the decision of the patient and/or his immediate family. The advice and judgment of the physician should be freely available to the patient and/or his immediate family.

However, a strong case can be made against this doctrine. In what follows, I will set out some of the relevant arguments, and urge doctors to reconsider their views on this matter.

To begin with a familiar type of situation, a patient who is dying of incurable cancer of the throat is in terrible pain, which can no longer be satisfactorily alleviated. He is certain to die within a few days, even if present treatment is continued, but he does not want to go on living for those days since the pain is unbearable. So he asks the doctor for an end to it, and his family joins in the request.

Suppose the doctor agrees to withhold treatment, as the conventional doctrine says he may. The justification for his doing so is that the patient is in terrible agony, and since he is going to die anyway, it would be wrong to prolong his suffering needlessly. But now notice this. If one simply withholds treatment, it may take the patient longer to die, and so he may suffer more than he would if more direct action were taken and a lethal injection given. This fact provides strong reason for thinking that, once the initial decision not to prolong his agony has been made, active euthanasia is actually preferable to passive euthanasia, rather than the reverse. To say otherwise is to endorse the option that leads to more suffering rather than less, and is contrary to the humanitarian impulse that prompts the decision not to prolong his life in the first place.

Part of my point is that the process of being "allowed to die" can be relatively slow and painful, whereas being given a lethal injection is relatively quick and painless. Let me give a different sort of example. In the United States about one in 600 babies is born with Down's syndrome. Most of these babies are otherwise healthy—that is, with only the usual pediatric care, they will proceed to an otherwise normal infancy. Some, however, are born with congenital defects such as intestinal obstructions that require operations if they are to live. Sometimes, the parents and the doctor will decide not to operate, and let the infant die. Anthony Shaw describes what happens then:

> . . . When surgery is denied [the doctor] must try to keep the infant from suffering while natural forces sap the baby's life away. As a surgeon whose natural inclination is to use the scalpel to fight off death, standing by and watching a salvageable baby die is the most emotionally exhausting experience I know. It is easy at a conference, in a theoretical discussion, to decide that such infants should be allowed to die. It is altogether different to stand by in the nursery and watch as dehydration and infection wither a tiny being over hours and days. This is a terrible ordeal for me and the hospital staff—much more so than for the parents who never set foot in the nursery.

I can understand why some people are opposed to all euthanasia, and insist that such infants must be allowed to live. I think I can also understand why other people favor destroying these babies quickly and painlessly. But why should anyone favor letting "dehydration and infection wither a tiny being over hours and days?" The doctrine that says that a baby may be allowed to dehydrate and wither, but may not be given an injection that would end its life without suffering, seems so patently cruel as to require no further refutation. The strong language is not intended to offend, but only to put the point in the clearest possible way.

My second argument is that the conventional doctrine leads to decisions concerning life and death made on irrelevant grounds.

Consider again the case of the infants with Down's syndrome who need operations for congenital defects unrelated to the syndrome to live. Sometimes, there is no operation, and the baby dies, but when there is no such defect, the baby lives on. Now, an operation such as that to remove an intestinal obstruction is not prohibitively difficult. The reason why such operations are not performed in these cases is, clearly, that the child has Down's syndrome and the parents and doctor judge that because of that fact it is better for the child to die.

But notice that this situation is absurd, no matter what view one takes of the lives and potentials of such babies. If the life of such an infant is worth preserving, what does it matter if it needs a simple operation? Or, if one thinks it better that such a baby should not live on, what difference does it make that it happens to have an unobstructed intestinal tract? In either case, the matter of life and death is being decided on irrelevant grounds. It is the Down's syndrome, and not the intestines, that is the issue. The matter should be decided, if at all, on that basis, and not be allowed to depend on the essentially irrelevant question of whether the intestinal tract is blocked.

What makes this situation possible, of course, is the idea that when there is an intestinal blockage, one can "let the baby die," but when there is no such defect there is nothing that can be done, for one must not "kill" it. The fact that this idea leads to such results as deciding life or death on irrelevant grounds is another good reason why the doctrine should be rejected.

One reason why so many people think that there is an important moral difference between active and passive euthanasia is that they think killing someone is morally worse than letting someone die. But is it? Is killing, in itself, worse than letting die? To investigate this issue, two cases may be considered that are exactly alike except that one involves killing whereas the other involves letting someone die. Then, it can be asked whether this difference makes any difference to the moral assessments. It is important that the cases be exactly alike, except for this one difference, since otherwise one cannot be confident that it is this difference and not some other that accounts for any variation in the assessments of the two cases. So, let us consider this pair of cases:

In the first, Smith stands to gain a large inheritance if anything should happen to his six-year-old cousin. One evening while the child is taking his bath, Smith sneaks into the bathroom and drowns the child, and then arranges things so that it will look like an accident.

In the second, Jones also stands to gain if anything should happen to his six-year-old cousin. Like Smith, Jones sneaks in planning to drown the child in his bath. However, just as he enters the bathroom Jones sees the child slip and hit his head, and fall face down in the water. Jones is delighted; he stands by, ready to push the child's head back under if it is necessary, but it is not necessary. With only a little thrashing about the child drowns all by himself, "accidentally," as Jones watches and does nothing.

Now Smith killed the child, whereas Jones "merely" let the child die. That is the only difference between them. Did either man behave better, from a moral point of view? If the difference between killing and letting die were in itself a morally important matter, one should say that Jones's behavior was less reprehensible than Smith's. But does one really want to say that? I think not. In the first place, both men acted from the same motive, personal gain, and both had exactly the same end in view when they acted. It may be inferred from Smith's conduct that he is a bad man, although that judgment may be withdrawn or modified if certain further facts are learned about him—for example, that he is mentally deranged. But would not the very same thing be inferred about Jones from his conduct? And would not the same further considerations also be relevant to any modification of this judgment? Moreover, suppose Jones pleaded, in his own defense, "After all, I didn't do anything except just stand there and watch the child drown. I didn't kill him; I only let him die." Again, if letting die were in itself less bad than killing, this defense should have at least some weight. But it does not. Such a "defense" can only be regarded as a grotesque perversion of moral reasoning. Morally speaking, it is no defense at all.

Now, it may be pointed out, quite properly, that the cases of euthanasia with which doctors are concerned are not like this at all. They do not involve personal gain or the destruction of normally healthy children. Doctors are concerned only with cases in which the patient's life is of no further use to him, or in which the patient's life has become or will soon become a terrible burden. However, the point is the same in these cases: the bare difference between killing and letting die does not, in itself, make a moral difference. If a doctor lets a patient die, for humane reasons, he is in the same moral position as if he had given the patient a lethal injection for humane reasons. If his decision was wrong —if, for example, the patient's illness was in fact curable—the decision would be equally regrettable no matter which method was used to carry it out. And if the doctor's decision was the right one, the method used is not in itself important.

The AMA policy statement isolates the crucial issue very well; the crucial issue is "the intentional termination of the life of one human being by another." But after identifying this issue, and forbidding "mercy killing," the statement goes on to deny that the cessation of treatment is the intentional termination of a life. This is where the mistake comes in, for what is the cessation of treatment, in these circumstances, if it is not "the intentional termination of the life of one human being by another?" Of course, it is exactly that, and if it were not, there would be no point to it.

Many people will find this judgment hard to accept. One reason, I think, is that it is very easy to conflate the question of whether killing is, in itself, worse than letting die, with the very different question of whether most actual cases of killing are more reprehensible than most actual cases of letting die. Most actual cases of killing are clearly terrible (think, for example, of all the murders reported in the newspapers), and one hears of such cases every day. On the other hand, one hardly ever hears of a case of letting die, except for the actions of doctors who are motivated by humanitarian reasons. So one learns to think of killing in a much worse light than of letting die. But this does not mean that there is something about killing that makes it in itself worse than letting die, for it is not the bare difference between killing and letting die that makes the difference in these cases. Rather, the other factors—the murderer's motive of personal gain, for example, contrasted with the doctor's humanitarian motivation —account for different reactions to the different cases.

I have argued that killing is not in itself any worse than letting die; if my contention is right, it follows that active euthanasia is not any worse than passive euthanasia. What arguments can be given on the other side? The most common, I believe, is the following:

"The important difference between active and passive euthanasia is that, in passive euthanasia, the doctor does not do anything to bring about the patient's death. The doctor does nothing, and the patient dies of whatever ills already afflict him. In active euthanasia, however, the doctor does something to bring about the patient's death: he kills him. The doctor who gives the patient with cancer a lethal injection has himself caused his patient's death; whereas if he merely ceases treatment, the cancer is the cause of the death."

A number of points need to be made here. The first is that it is not exactly correct to say that in passive euthanasia the doctor does nothing, for he does do one thing that is very important: he lets the patient die. "Letting someone die" is certainly different, in some respects, from other types of action— mainly in that it is a kind of action that one may perform by way of not performing certain other actions. For example, one may let a patient die by way of not giving medication, just as one may insult someone by way of not shaking his hand. But for any purpose of moral assessment, it is a type of action nonetheless. The decision to let a patient die is subject to moral appraisal in the same way that a decision to kill him would be subject to moral appraisal: it may be assessed as wise or unwise, compassionate or sadistic, right or wrong. If a doctor deliberately let a patient die who was suffering from a routinely curable illness, the doctor would certainly be to blame for what he had done, just as he would be to blame if he had needlessly killed the patient. Charges against him would then be appropriate. If so, it would be no defense at all for him to insist that he didn't "do anything." He would have done something very serious indeed, for he let his patient die.

Fixing the cause of death may be very important from a legal point of view, for it may determine whether criminal charges are brought against the doctor. But I do not think that this notion can be used to show a moral difference between active and passive euthanasia. The reason why it is considered bad to be the cause of someone's death is that death is regarded as a great evil—and so it is. However, if it has been decided that euthanasia—even passive euthanasia—is desirable in a given case, it has also been decided that in this instance death is no greater an evil than the patient's continued existence. And if this is true, the usual reason for not wanting to be the cause of someone's death simply does not apply.

Finally, doctors may think that all of this is only of academic interest—the sort of thing that philosophers may worry about but that has no practical bearing on their own work. After all, doctors must be concerned about the legal consequences of what they do, and active euthanasia is clearly forbidden by the law. But even so, doctors should also be concerned with the fact that the law is forcing upon them a moral doctrine that may well be indefensible, and has a considerable effect on their practices. Of course, most doctors are not now in the position of being coerced in this matter, for they do not regard themselves as merely going along with what the law requires. Rather, in statements such as the AMA policy statement that I have quoted, they are endorsing this doctrine as a central point of medical ethics. In that statement, active euthanasia is condemned not merely as illegal but as "contrary to that for which the medical profession stands," whereas passive euthanasia is approved. However, the preceding considerations suggest that there is really no moral difference between the two, considered in themselves (there may be important moral differences in some cases in their *consequences,* but, as I pointed out, these differences may make active euthanasia, and not passive euthanasia, the morally preferable option). So, whereas doctors may have to discriminate between active and passive euthanasia to satisfy the law, they should not do any more than that. In particular, they should not give the distinction any added authority and weight by writing it into official statements of medical ethics.

BONNIE STEINBOCK

The Intentional Termination of Life

Bonnie Steinbock is Professor of Philosophy at the State University of New York at Albany. (Source: Reprinted from Ethics in Science and Medicine *6, Number 1 [1979], pp. 59–64. Copyright © 1979 by Pergamon Press, Ltd.)*

QUESTIONS FOR REFLECTION

1. Steinbock maintains that, in some cases, ceasing life-prolonging treatment does not amount to intentional termination of life. In what cases? Do you agree?

2. What is extraordinary treatment? Why is it important to Steinbock's argument?

3. How does Steinbock criticize Rachels's analysis of decisions concerning infants with Down's syndrome? Does she disagree with Rachels's views concerning which babies should be saved or how babies should be treated?

4. What, for Steinbock, is the significance of the patient's right to refuse treatment?

According to James Rachels and Michael Tooley . . . a common mistake in medical ethics is the belief that there is a moral difference between active and passive euthanasia. This is a mistake, they argue, because the rationale underlying the distinction between active and passive euthanasia is the idea that there is a significant moral difference between intentionally killing and intentionally letting die. "The idea," Tooley says, "is admittedly very common. But I believe that it can be shown to reflect either confused thinking or a moral point of view unrelated to the interests of individuals." Whether or not the belief that there is a significant moral difference is mistaken is not my concern here. For it is far from clear that this distinction *is* the basis of the doctrine of the American Medical Association which Rachels attacks. And if the killing/letting die distinction is not the basis of the AMA doctrine, then arguments showing that the distinction has no moral force do not, in themselves, reveal in the doctrine's adherents either "confused thinking" or "a moral point of view unrelated to the interests of individuals." Indeed, as we examine the AMA doctrine, I think it will become clear that it appeals to and makes use of a number of overlapping distinctions, which may have moral significance in particular cases, such as the distinction between intending and foreseeing, or between ordinary and extraordinary care. Let us then turn to the 1973 statement, from the House of Delegates of the American Medical Association, which Rachels cites:

> The intentional termination of the life of one human being by another—mercy killing—is contrary to that for which the medical profession stands and is contrary to the policy of the American Medical Association.
>
> The cessation of the employment of extraordinary means to prolong the life of the body when there is irrefutable evidence that biological death is imminent is the decision of the patient and/or his immediate family. The advice and judgment of the physician should be freely available to the patient and/or his immediate family.

Rachels attacks this statement because he believes

that it contains a moral distinction between active and passive euthanasia. Tooley also believes this to be the position of the AMA, saying:

> Many people hold that there is an important moral distinction between passive euthanasia and active euthanasia. Thus, while the AMA maintains that people have a right "to die with dignity," so that it is morally permissible for a doctor to allow someone to die if that person wants to and is suffering from an incurable illness causing pain that cannot be sufficiently alleviated, the AMA is unwilling to countenance active euthanasia for a person who is in similar straits, but who has the misfortune not to be suffering from an illness that will result in a speedy death.

Both men, then, take the AMA position to prohibit active euthanasia, while allowing, under certain conditions, passive euthanasia.

I intend to show that the AMA statement does not imply support of the active/passive euthanasia distinction. In forbidding the intentional termination of life, the statement rejects both active and passive euthanasia. It does allow for "the cessation of the employment of extraordinary means" to prolong life. The mistake Rachels and Tooley make is in identifying the cessation of life-prolonging treatment with passive euthanasia, or intentionally letting die. If it were right to equate the two, then the AMA statement would be self-contradictory, for it would begin by condemning, and end by allowing, the intentional termination of life. But if the cessation of life-prolonging treatment is not always or necessarily passive euthanasia, then there is no confusion and no contradiction.

Why does Rachels think that the cessation of life-prolonging treatment is the intentional termination of life? He says:

> The AMA policy statement isolates the crucial issue very well: the crucial issue is "the intentional termination of the life of one human being by another." But after identifying this issue, and forbidding "mercy killing," the statement goes on to deny that the cessation of treatment is the intentional termination of a life. This is where the mistake comes in, for what is the cessation of treatment, in these circumstances, if it is not "the intentional termination of the life of one human being by another"? Of course it is exactly that, and if it were not, there would be no point to it.

However, there *can* be a point (to the cessation of life-prolonging treatment) other than an endeavor to bring about the patient's death, and so the blanket identification of cessation of treatment with the intentional termination of a life is inaccurate. There are at least two situations in which the termination of life-prolonging treatment cannot be identified with the intentional termination of the life of one human being by another.

The first situation concerns the patient's right to refuse treatment. Both Tooley and Rachels give the example of a patient dying of an incurable disease, accompanied by unrelievable pain, who wants to end the treatment which cannot cure him but can only prolong his miserable existence. Why, they ask, may a doctor accede to the patient's request to stop treatment, but not provide a patient in a similar situation with a lethal dose? The answer lies in the patient's right to refuse treatment. In general, a competent adult has the right to refuse treatment, even where such treatment is necessary to prolong life. Indeed, the right to refuse treatment has been upheld even when the patient's reason for refusing treatment is generally agreed to be inadequate. This right can be overridden (if, for example, the patient has dependent children) but, in general, no one may legally compel you to undergo treatment to which you have not consented. "Historically, surgical intrusion has always been considered a technical battery upon the person and one to be excused or justified by consent of the patient or justified by necessity created by the circumstances of the moment. . . ."

At this point, an objection might be raised that if one has the right to refuse life-prolonging treatment, then consistency demands that one have the right to decide to end his or her life, and to obtain help in doing so. The idea is that the right to refuse treatment somehow implies a right to voluntary euthanasia, and we need to see why someone might think this. The right to refuse treatment has been considered by legal writers as an example of the right to privacy or, better, the right to bodily self-determination. You have the right to decide what happens to your own body, and the right to refuse treatment is an instance of that right. But if you have the right to determine what happens to your own body, then should you not have the right to choose to end your life, and even a right to get help in doing so?

However, it is important to see that the right to refuse treatment is not the same as, nor does it entail, a right to voluntary euthanasia, even if both can be derived from the right to bodily self-determination. The right to refuse treatment is not itself a "right to die"; that one may choose to exercise this right even at the risk of death, or even *in order to die,* is irrelevant. The purpose of the right to refuse medical treatment is not to give persons a right to decide whether to live or die, but to protect them from the unwanted interferences of others. Perhaps we ought to interpret the right to bodily self-determination more broadly, so as to include a right to die; but this would be a substantial extension of our present understanding of the right to bodily self-determination, and not a consequence of it. If we were to recognize a right to voluntary euthanasia, we would have to agree that people have the right not merely to be left alone but also the right to be killed. I leave to one side that substantive moral issue. My claim is simply that there can be a reason for terminating life-prolonging treatment other than "to bring about the patient's death."

The second case in which termination of treatment cannot be identified with intentional termination of life is where continued treatment has little chance of improving the patient's condition and brings greater discomfort than relief.

The question here is what treatment is appropriate to the particular case. A cancer specialist describes it in this way:

My general rule is to administer therapy as long as a patient responds well and has the potential for a reasonably good quality of life. But when all feasible therapies have been administered and a patient shows signs of rapid deterioration, the continuation of therapy can cause more discomfort than the cancer. From that time I recommended surgery, radiotherapy, or chemotherapy only as a means of relieving pain. But if a patient's condition should once again stabilize after the withdrawal of active therapy and if it should appear that he could still gain some good time, I would immediately reinstitute active therapy. The decision to cease anticancer treatment is never irrevocable, and

often the desire to live will push a patient to try for another remission, or even a few more days of life.

The decision here to cease anticancer treatment cannot be construed as a decision that the patient die, or as the intentional termination of life. It is a decision to provide the most appropriate treatment for that patient at that time. Rachels suggests that the point of the cessation of treatment is the intentional termination of life. But here the point of discontinuing treatment is not to bring about the patient's death but to avoid treatment that will cause more discomfort than the cancer and has little hope of benefiting the patient. Treatment that meets this description is often called "extraordinary." The concept is flexible, and what might be considered "extraordinary" in one situation might be ordinary in another. The use of a respirator to sustain a patient through a severe bout with a respiratory disease would be considered ordinary; its use to sustain the life of a severely brain-damaged person in an irreversible coma would be considered extraordinary.

Contrasted with extraordinary treatment is ordinary treatment, the care a doctor would normally be expected to provide. Failure to provide ordinary care constitutes neglect, and can even be construed as the intentional infliction of harm, where there is a legal obligation to provide care. The importance of the ordinary/extraordinary care distinction lies partly in its connection to the doctor's intention. The withholding of extraordinary care should be seen as a decision not to inflict painful treatment on a patient without reasonable hope of success. The withholding of ordinary care, by contrast, must be seen as neglect. Thus, one doctor says, "We have to draw a distinction between ordinary and extraordinary means. We never withdraw what's needed to make a baby comfortable, we would never withdraw the care a parent would provide. We never kill a baby. . . . But we may decide certain heroic interventions are not worthwhile."

We should keep in mind the ordinary/extraordinary care distinction when considering an example given by both Tooley and Rachels to show the irrationality of the active/passive distinction with regard to infanticide. The example is this: a child is born with Down's syndrome and also has an intestinal obstruction that requires corrective surgery. If the surgery is not performed, the infant will starve to death, since it cannot take food orally. This may take days or even weeks, as dehydration and infection set in. Commenting on this situation in his article in this book Rachels says:

> I can understand why some people are opposed to all euthanasia, and insist that such infants must be allowed to live. I think I can also understand why other people favor destroying these babies quickly and painlessly. But why should anyone favor letting "dehydration and infection wither a tiny being over hours and days"? The doctrine that says that a baby may be allowed to dehydrate and wither, but may not be given an injection that would end its life without suffering, seems so patently cruel as to require no further refutation.

Such a doctrine perhaps does not need further refutation; but this is not the AMA doctrine. The AMA statement criticized by Rachels allows only for the cessation of extraordinary means to prolong life when death is imminent. Neither of these conditions is satisfied in this example. Death is not imminent in this situation, any more than it would be if a normal child had an attack of appendicitis. Neither the corrective surgery to remove the intestinal obstruction nor the intravenous feeding required to keep the infant alive until such surgery is performed can be regarded as extraordinary means, for neither is particularly expensive, nor does either place an overwhelming burden on the patient or others. (The continued existence of the child might be thought to place an overwhelming burden on its parents, but that has nothing to do with the characterization of the means to prolong its life as extraordinary. If it had, then *feeding* a severely defective child who required a great deal of care could be regarded as extraordinary.) The chances of success if the operation is undertaken are quite good, though there is always a risk in operating on infants. Though the Down's syndrome will not be alleviated, the child will proceed to an otherwise normal infancy.

It cannot be argued that the treatment is withheld for the infant's sake, unless one is prepared to argue that all mentally retarded babies are better off dead. This is particularly implausible in the case of Down's syndrome babies, who generally do not suffer and are capable of giving and receiving love, of learning and playing, to varying degrees.

In a film on this subject entitled, "Who Should Survive?", a doctor defended a decision not to operate, saying that since the parents did not consent to the operation, the doctors' hands were tied. As we have seen, surgical intrusion requires consent, and in the case of infants, consent would normally come from the parents. But, as legal guardians, parents are required to provide medical care for their children, and failure to do so can constitute criminal neglect or even homicide. In general, courts have been understandably reluctant to recognize a parental right to terminate life-prolonging treatment. Although prosecution is unlikely, physicians who comply with invalid instructions from the parents and permit the infant's death could be liable for aiding and abetting, failure to report child neglect, or even homicide. So it is not true that, in this situation, doctors are legally bound to do as the parents wish.

To sum up, I think that Rachels is right to regard the decision not to operate in the Down's syndrome example as the intentional termination of life. But there is no reason to believe that either the law or the AMA would regard it otherwise. Certainly the decision to withhold treatment is not justified by the AMA statement. That such infants have been allowed to die cannot be denied; but this, I think, is the result of doctors misunderstanding the law and the AMA position.

Withholding treatment in this case is the intentional termination of life because the infant is deliberately allowed to die; that is the point of not operating. But there are other cases in which that is not the point. If the point is to avoid inflicting painful treatment on a patient with little or no reasonable hope of success, this is not the intentional termination of life. The permissibility of such withholding of treatment, then, would have no implications for the permissibility of euthanasia, active or passive.

The decision whether or not to operate, or to institute vigorous treatment, is particularly agonizing in the case of children born with spina bifida, an opening in the base of the spine usually accompanied by hydrocephalus and mental retardation. If left unoperated, these children usually die of meningitis or kidney failure within the first few years of life. Even if they survive, all affected children face a lifetime of illness, operations, and varying degrees of disability. The policy used to be to save as many as possible, but the trend now is toward selective treatment, based on the physician's estimate of the chances of success. If operating is not likely to improve significantly the child's condition, parents and doctors may agree not to operate. This is not the intentional termination of life, for again the purpose is not the termination of the child's life but the avoidance of painful and pointless treatment. Thus, the fact that withholding treatment is justified does not imply that killing the child would be equally justified.

Throughout the discussion, I have claimed that intentionally ceasing life-prolonging treatment is not the intentional termination of life unless the doctor has, as his or her purpose in stopping treatment, the patient's death.

It may be objected that I have incorrectly characterized the conditions for the intentional termination of life. Perhaps it is enough that the doctor intentionally ceases treatment, foreseeing that the patient will die.

In many cases, if one acts intentionally, foreseeing that a particular result will occur, one can be said to have brought about that result intentionally. Indeed, this is the general legal rule. Why, then, am I not willing to call the cessation of life-prolonging treatment, in compliance with the patient's right to refuse treatment, the intentional termination of life? It is not because such an *identification* is necessarily opprobrious; for we could go on to *discuss* whether such cessation of treatment is a *justifiable* intentional termination of life. Even in the law, some cases of homicide are justifiable; e.g., homicide in self-defense.

However, the cessation of life-prolonging treatment, in the cases which I have discussed, is not regarded in law as being justifiable homicide, because it is not homicide at all. Why is this? Is it because the doctor "doesn't do anything," and so cannot be guilty of homicide? Surely not, since, as I have indicated, the law sometimes treats an omission as the cause of death. A better explanation, I think, has to do with the fact that in the context of

the patient's right to refuse treatment, a doctor is not at liberty to continue treatment. It seems a necessary ingredient of intentionally letting die that one could have done something to prevent the death. In this situation, of course, the doctor can physically prevent the patient's death, but since we do not regard the doctor as *free* to continue treatment, we say that there is "nothing he can do." Therefore he does not intentionally let the patient die.

To discuss this suggestion fully, I would need to present a full-scale theory of intentional action. However, at least I have shown, through the discussion of the above examples, that such a theory will be very complex, and that one of the complexities concerns the agent's reason for acting. The reason why an agent acted (or failed to act) may affect the characterization of what he did intentionally. The mere fact that he did *something* intentionally, foreseeing a certain result, does not necessarily mean that he brought about that *result* intentionally.

In order to show that the cessation of life-prolonging treatment, in the cases I've discusssed, is the intentional termination of life, one would either have to show that treatment was stopped in order to bring about the patient's death, or provide a theory of intentional action according to which the reason for ceasing treatment is irrelevant to its characterization as the intentional termination of life. I find this suggestion implausible, but am willing to consider arguments for it. Rachels has provided no such arguments: indeed, he apparently shares my view about the intentional termination of life. For when he claims that the cessation of life-prolonging treatment *is* the intentional termination of life, his reason for making the claim is that "if it were not, there would be no point to it." Rachels believes that the point of ceasing treatment, "in these cases," is to bring about the patient's death. If that were not the point, he suggests, why would the doctor cease treatment? I have shown, however, that there can be a point to ceasing treatment which is not the death of the patient. In showing this, I have refuted Rachels' reason for identifying the cessation of life-prolonging treatment with the intentional termination of life, and thus his argument against the AMA doctrine.

Here someone might say: Even if the withholding of treatment is not the intentional termination of life, does that make a difference, morally speaking?

If life-prolonging treatment may be withheld, for the sake of the child, may not an easy death be provided, for the sake of the child, as well? The unoperated child with spina bifida may take months or even years to die. Distressed by the spectacle of children "lying around, waiting to die," one doctor has written, "It is time that society and medicine stopped perpetuating the fiction that withholding treatment is ethically different from terminating a life. It is time that society began to discuss mechanisms by which we can alleviate the pain and suffering for those individuals whom we cannot help."

I do not deny that there may be cases in which death is in the best interests of the patient. In such cases, a quick and painless death may be the best thing. However, I do not think that, once active or vigorous treatment is stopped, a quick death is always preferable to a lingering one. We must be cautious about attributing to defective children *our* distress at seeing them linger. Waiting for them to die may be tough on parents, doctors, and nurses—it isn't necessarily tough on the child. The decision not to operate need not mean a decision to neglect, and it may be possible to make the remaining months of the child's life comfortable, pleasant, and filled with love. If this alternative is possible, surely it is more decent and humane than killing the child. In such a situation, withholding treatment, foreseeing the child's death, is not ethically equivalent to killing the child, and we cannot move from the permissibility of the former to that of the latter. I am worried that there will be a tendency to do precisely that if active euthanasia is regarded as morally equivalent to the withholding of life-prolonging treatment.

Conclusion

The AMA statement does not make the distinction Rachels and Tooley wish to attack, that between active and passive euthanasia. Instead, the statement draws a distinction between the intentional termination of life, on the one hand, and the cessation of the employment of extraordinary means to prolong life, on the other. Nothing said by Rachels and Tooley shows that this distinction is confused. It may be that doctors have misinterpreted the AMA statement, and that this has led, for example, to decisions to allow defective infants to starve slowly to death. I quite agree with Rachels and Tooley that the decisions to which they allude were cruel and made on irrelevant grounds. Certainly it is worth pointing out that allowing someone to die *can* be the intentional termination of life, and that it can be just as bad as, or worse than, killing someone. However, the withholding of life-prolonging treatment is not necessarily the intentional termination of life, so that if it is permissible to withhold life-prolonging treatment it does not follow that, other things being equal, it is permissible to kill. Furthermore, most of the time, other things are not equal. In many of the cases in which it would be right to cease treatment, I do not think that it would also be right to kill.

Capital Punishment

Ordinarily, we think that people have a right to life and that governments, if they have any obligations at all, are obliged to protect that right. But many people believe that the government is nevertheless justified in putting certain kinds of criminals to death. Generally, they believe that the government needs to deprive some people of the right to life in order to protect that right for others—indeed, for the vast majority of its citizens. From this belief arises the issue of capital punishment: Can the government be justified in putting someone to death?

The death penalty raises important questions about the origin, status, and extent of the right to life. Most people believe that they have the right to defend themselves against an assailant. They believe, in particular, that they have the right to kill an attacker if their own lives are in danger. Some philosophers have extended this reasoning to the state as a whole. The murderer, for example, can be seen as attacking society; society is justified in using lethal force to defend itself. Of course, once apprehended, the murderer no longer threatens society in quite the same way. But if murderers are likely to murder again, the self-protection argument may apply. This strategy argues that the right to life is limited so that those who threaten death to others lose their own right to life or, at least, deserve to have it overridden by the rights of others.

Other philosophers have argued in favor of a right to revenge. Society, having suffered a serious harm, has the right to take retribution by punishing the offender. Moreover, the punishment that seems appropriate for causing death is suffering death. They have thus maintained that justice sometimes requires the death penalty.

Still others have stressed deterrence as a justification for capital punishment. Putting a criminal to death, on this view, deters others from committing similar crimes. Enforcing the death penalty thus promotes the good of society; it may save more lives than it costs. Statistical studies of the effects of capital punishment tend to be inconclusive; it is not clear whether the death penalty actually has this effect. But some studies report that each execution saves several lives by deterring prospective murderers.

These arguments raise large issues beyond those involving the right to life itself. What rights does society have to defend itself against criminal activity? What is the moral justification for punishment? When can the interests of a larger group justify violating the rights of an individual? Under what circumstances does a person lose or surrender rights? In each case, arguments for and against capital punishment take or presuppose controversial stands.

In *Furman v. Georgia,* in 1972, the Supreme Court held that a Georgia capital punishment law was unconstitutional. The Court found that the death penalty, under the circumstances of its application there, was incompatible with human dignity and violated the Eighth Amendment prohibiting "cruel and unusual" punishment. Some members of the Court argued that the death penalty was in itself objectionable. The majority, however, concluded simply that its application was too haphazard, unprincipled, and unjust to count as constitutional.

In *Gregg v. Georgia,* four years later, the Court upheld Georgia's revision of its capital punishment law. Under that revision, the jury receives detailed instructions about the appropriateness of the death penalty. Certain kinds of circumstances are aggravating, tending to justify the death penalty; others are mitigating, tending to justify an alternative sentence. The Court decided that the death penalty, administered in this way, is constitutionally acceptable.

Strictly speaking, these decisions rest on legal rather than moral grounds. They are not, however, morally irrelevant. Cruel and unusual punishments are ethically as well as legally objectionable. Consequently, the legal arguments of the justices in these cases parallel moral arguments about the permissibility of capital punishment.

Ernest van den Haag goes beyond typical defenses of capital punishment in at least two ways. First, he argues that deterrence provides an argument for the death penalty, even if we cannot determine whether it succeeds in deterring or not. If there is a chance that it does, he contends, then we place innocent lives at risk by failing to carry it out. Second, he argues that certain special cases justify capital punishment, even if it is unacceptable in most cases. Thus, we may be justified in executing war criminals and criminals who murder in prison while already serving life terms, even if we are not justified in executing most murderers.

Hugo Bedau argues that the death penalty is unacceptable in all circumstances. He reviews the main arguments for capital punishment and rejects them. He then argues that even if its social goals are acceptable, the death penalty is a poor way of meeting them. Finally, he formulates several moral principles, arguing that they rule out capital punishment completely.

Furman v. Georgia [1972]

(*Source:* Furman v. Georgia *408 U.S. 238 [1972]. Most legal references have been omitted.*)

QUESTIONS FOR REFLECTION

1. Justice Brennan offers four principles for deter-mining whether a punishment "comports with human dignity." Explain them.

2. Justice Brennan argues that all four principles rule out the death penalty. Review his arguments. Do you find them persuasive?

3. What are Justice Marshall's chief arguments against capital punishment?

... **M**r. Justice Brennan, concurring.

The question presented in these cases is whether death is today a punishment for crime that is "cruel and unusual" and consequently, by virtue of the Eighth and Fourteenth Amendments, beyond the power of the State to inflict. . . .

[I . . .]

II

Ours would indeed be a simple task were we required merely to measure a challenged punishment against those that history has long condemned. That narrow and unwarranted view of the Clause, how-ever, was left behind with the 19th century. Our task today is more complex. We know "that the words of the [Clause] are not precise, and that their scope is not static." We know, therefore, that the Clause "must draw its meaning from the evolving standards of decency that mark the progress of a maturing society." That knowledge, of course, is but the begin-ning of the inquiry.

In *Trop* v. *Dulles*, it was said that "[t]he question is whether [a] penalty subjects the individual to a fate forbidden by the principle of civilized treatment guaranteed by the [Clause]." It was also said that a challenged punishment must be examined "in light of the basic prohibition against inhuman treatment" embodied in the Clause. It was said, finally, that:

> "The basic concept underlying the [Clause] is nothing less than the dignity of man. While the State has the power to punish, the [Clause] stands to assure that this power be exercised within the limits of civilized standards."

At bottom, then, the Cruel and Unusual Punish-ments Clause prohibits the infliction of uncivilized and inhuman punishments. The State, even as it punishes, must treat its members with respect for their intrinsic worth as human beings. A punish-ment is "cruel and unusual," therefore, if it does not comport with human dignity.

This formulation, of course, does not of itself yield principles for assessing the constitutional validity of particular punishments. Nevertheless, even though "[t]his Court has had little occasion to give precise content to the [Clause]," there are prin-ciples recognized in our cases and inherent in the

Clause sufficient to permit a judicial determination whether a challenged punishment comports with human dignity.

The primary principle is that a punishment must not be so severe as to be degrading to the dignity of human beings. Pain, certainly, may be a factor in the judgment. The infliction of an extremely severe punishment will often entail physical suffering. Yet the Framers also knew "that there could be exercises of cruelty by laws other than those which inflicted bodily pain or mutilation." Even though "[t]here may be involved no physical mistreatment, no primitive torture," *Trop* v. *Dulles,* severe mental pain may be inherent in the infliction of a particular punishment. That, indeed, was one of the conclusions underlying the holding of the plurality in *Trop* v. *Dulles* that the punishment of expatriation violates the Clause. And the physical and mental suffering inherent in the punishment of *cadena temporal** was an obvious basis for the Court's decision in *Weems* v. *United States* that the punishment was "cruel and unusual."

More than the presence of pain, however, is comprehended in the judgment that the extreme severity of a punishment makes it degrading to the dignity of human beings. The barbaric punishments condemned by history, "punishments which inflict torture, such as the rack, the thumbscrew, the iron boot, the stretching of limbs and the like," are, of course, "attended with acute pain and suffering." When we consider why they have been condemned, however, we realize that the pain involved is not the only reason. The true significance of these punishments is that they treat members of the human race as nonhumans, as objects to be toyed with and discarded. They are thus inconsistent with the fundamental premise of the Clause that even the vilest criminal remains a human being possessed of common human dignity.

The infliction of an extremely severe punishment, then, like the one before the Court in *Weems* v. *United States,* from which "[n]o circumstance of

degradation [was] omitted," may reflect the attitude that the person punished is not entitled to recognition as a fellow human being. That attitude may be apparent apart from the severity of the punishment itself. In *Louisiana ex rel. Francis v. Resweber* (1947), for example, the unsuccessful electrocution, although it caused "mental anguish and physical pain," was the result of "an unforeseeable accident." Had the failure been intentional, however, the punishment would have been, like torture, so degrading and indecent as to amount to a refusal to accord the criminal human status. Indeed, a punishment may be degrading to human dignity solely because it is a punishment. A State may not punish a person for begin "mentally ill, or a leper, or . . . afflicted with a venereal disease," or for being addicted to narcotics. To inflict punishment for having a disease is to treat the individual as a diseased thing rather than as a sick human being. That the punishment is not severe, "in the abstract," is irrelevant; "[e]ven one day in prison would be a cruel and unusual punishment for the 'crime' of having a common cold." Finally, of course, a punishment may be degrading simply by reason of its enormity. A prime example is expatriation, a "punishment more primitive than torture," for it necessarily involves a denial by society of the individual's existence as a member of the human community.

In determining whether a punishment comports with human dignity, we are aided also by a second principle inherent in the Clause—that the State must not arbitrarily inflict a severe punishment. This principle derives from the notion that the State does not respect human dignity when, without reason, it inflicts upon some people a severe punishment that it does not inflict upon others. Indeed, the very words "cruel and unusual punishments" imply condemnation of the arbitrary infliction of severe punishments. And, as we now know, the English history of the Clause reveals a particular concern with the establishment of a safeguard against arbitrary punishments. . . .

A third principle inherent in the Clause is that a severe punishment must not be unacceptable to contemporary society. Rejection by society, of course, is a strong indication that a severe punishment does not comport with human dignity. In applying this principle, however, we must make certain that the

---

* *Cadena temporal:* a punishment requiring a period of hard and painful labor in chains, followed by perpetual probation. In *Weems v. United States,* the period of hard and painful labor was twelve years. —Ed.

judicial determination is as objective as possible. Thus, for example, *Weems* v. *United States* and *Trop* v. *Dulles* suggest that one factor that may be considered is the existence of the punishment in jurisdictions other than those before the Court. *Wilkerson* v. *Utah* suggests that another factor to be considered is the historic usage of the punishment. *Trop* v. *Dulles* combined present acceptance with past usage by observing that "the death penalty has been employed throughout our history, and, in a day when it is still widely accepted, it cannot be said to violate the constitutional concept of cruelty." In *Robinson* v. *California*, which involved the infliction of punishment for narcotics addiction, the Court went a step further, concluding simply that "in the light of contemporary human knowledge, a law which made a criminal offense of such a disease would doubtless be universally thought to be an infliction of cruel and unusual punishment."

The question under this principle, then, is whether there are objective indicators from which a court can conclude that contemporary society considers a severe punishment unacceptable. Accordingly, the judicial task is to review the history of a challenged punishment and to examine society's present practices with respect to its use. Legislative authorization, of ocurse, does not establish acceptance. The acceptability of a severe punishment is measured, not by its availability, for it might become so offensive to society as never to be inflicted, but by its use.

The final principle inherent in the Clause is that a severe punishment must not be excessive. A punishment is excessive under this principle if it is unnecessary: The infliction of a severe punishment by the State cannot comport with human dignity when it is nothing more than the pointless infliction of suffering. If there is a significantly less severe punishment adequate to achieve the purposes for which the punishment is inflicted, the punishment inflicted is unnecessary and therefore excessive. . . .

There are, then, four principles by which we may determine whether a particular punishment is "cruel and unusual." The primary principle, which I believe supplies the essential predicate for the application of the others, is that a punishment must not by its severity be degrading to human dignity. The paradigm violation of this principle would be the infliction of a torturous punishment of the type that the Clause has always prohibited. Yet "[i]t is unlikely that any State at this moment in history" would pass a law providing for the infliction of such a punishment. Indeed, no such punishment has ever been before this Court. The same may be said of the other principles. It is unlikely that this Court will confront a severe punishment that is obviously inflicted in wholly arbitrary fashion; no State would engage in a reign of blind terror. Nor is it likely that this Court will be called upon to review a severe punishment that is clearly and totally rejected throughout society; no legislature would be able even to authorize the infliction of such a punishment. Nor, finally, is it likely that this Court will have to consider a severe punishment that is patently unnecessary; no State today would inflict a severe punishment knowing that there was no reason whatever for doing so. In short, we are unlikely to have occasion to determine that a punishment is fatally offensive under any one principle.

Since the Bill of Rights was adopted, this Court has adjudged only three punishments to be within the prohibition of the Clause. See *Weems* v. *United States* (1910) (12 years in chains at hard and painful labor); *Trop* v. *Dulles* (1958) (expatriation); *Robinson* v. *California* (1962) (imprisonment for narcotics addiction). Each punishment, of course, was degrading to human dignity, but of none could it be said conclusively that it was fatally offensive under one or the other of the principles. Rather, these "cruel and unusual punishments" seriously implicated several of the priniciples, and it was the application of the principles in combination that supported the judgment. That, indeed, is not surprising. The function of these principles, after all, is simply to provide means by which a court can determine whether a challenged punishment comports with human dignity. They are, therefore, interrelated, and in most cases it will be their convergence that will justify the conclusion that a punishment is "cruel and unusual." The test, then, will ordinarily be a cumulative one: If a punishment is unusually severe, if there is a strong probability that it is inflicted arbitrarily, if it is substantially rejected by contemporary society, and if there is no reason to believe that it serves any penal purpose more effectively than some less severe punishment, then the continued infliction of that punishment violates the command of the Clause that the State may not inflict inhuman and uncivilized punishments upon those convicted of crimes.

III

... The question, then, is whether the deliberate infliction of death is today consistent with the command of the Clause that the State may not inflict punishments that do not comport with human dignity. I will analyze the punishment of death in terms of the principles set out above and the cumulative test to which they lead: It is a denial of human dignity for the State arbitrarily to subject a person to an unusually severe punishment that society has indicated it does not regard as acceptable, and that cannot be shown to serve any penal purpose more effectively than a significantly less drastic punishment. Under these principles and this test, death is today a "cruel and unusual" punishment.

Death is a unique punishment in the United States. In a society that so strongly affirms the sanctity of life, not surprisingly the common view is that death is the ultimate sanction. This natural human feeling appears all about us. There has been no national debate about punishment, in general or by imprisonment, comparable to the debate about the punishment of death. No other punishment has been so continuously restricted, nor has any State yet abolished prisons, as some have abolished this punishment. And those States that still inflict death reserve it for the most heinous crimes. Juries, of course, have always treated death cases differently, as have governors exercising their commutation powers. Criminal defendants are of the same view. "As all practicing lawyers know, who have defended persons charged with capital offenses, often the only goal possible is to avoid the death penalty." Some legislatures have required particular procedures, such as two-stage trials and automatic appeals, applicable only in death cases. "It is the universal experience in the administration of criminal justice that those charged with capital offenses are granted special considerations." This Court, too, almost always treats death cases as a class apart. And the unfortunate effect of this punishment upon the functioning of the judicial process is well known; no other punishment has a similar effect.

The only explanation for the uniqueness of death is its extreme severity. Death is today an unusually severe punishment, unusual in its pain, in its finality, and in its enormity. No other existing punishment is comparable to death in terms of physical and mental suffering. Although our information is not conclusive, it appears that there is no method available that guarantees an immediate and painless death. Since the discontinuance of flogging as a constitutionally permissible punishment, death remains as the only punishment that may involve the conscious infliction of physical pain. In addition, we know that mental pain is an inseparable part of our practice of punishing criminals by death, for the prospect of pending execution exacts a frightful toll during the inevitable long wait between the imposition of sentence and the actual infliction of death. As the California Supreme Court pointed out, "the process of carrying out a verdict of death is often so degrading and brutalizing to the human spirit as to constitute psychological torture." Indeed, as Mr. Justice Frankfurter noted, "the onset of insanity while awaiting execution of a death sentence is not a rare phenomenon." The "fate of ever-increasing fear and distress" to which the expatriate is subjected can only exist to a greater degree for a person confined in prison awaiting death.

The unusual severity of death is manifested most clearly in its finality and enormity. Death, in these respects, is in a class by itself. Expatriation, for example, is a punishment that "destroys for the individual the political existence that was centuries in the development," that "strips the citizen of his status in the national and international political community," and that puts "[h]is very existence" in jeopardy. Expatriation thus inherently entails "the total destruction of the individual's status in organized society." "In short, the expatriate has lost the right to have rights." Yet, demonstrably, expatriation is not "a fate worse than death." Although death, like expatriation, destroys the individual's "political existence" and his "status in organized society," it does more, for, unlike expatriation, death also destroys "[h]is very existence." There is, too, at least the possibility that the expatriate will in the future regain "the right to have rights." Death forecloses even that possibility.

Death is truly an awesome punishment. The calculated killing of a human being by the State involves, by its very nature, a denial of the executed person's humanity. The contrast with the plight of a person punished by imprisonment is evident. An individual in prison does not lose "the right to have rights." A prisoner retains, for example, the constitutional rights to the free exercise of religion, to be free of cruel and unusual punishments, and to treatment as a "person" for purposes of due process of law and the equal protection of the laws. A prisoner remains a member of the human family. Moreover, he retains the right of access to the courts. His punishment is not irrevocable. Apart from the common charge, grounded upon the recognition of human fallibility, that the punishment of death must inevitably be inflicted upon innocent men, we know that death has been the lot of men whose convictions were unconstitutionally secured in view of later, retroactively applied, holdings of this Court. The punishment itself may have been unconstitutionally inflicted, yet the finality of death precludes relief. An executed person has indeed "lost the right to have rights." As one 19th century proponent of punishing criminals by death declared, "When a man is hung, there is an end of our relations with him. His execution is a way of saying, 'You are not fit for this world, take your chance elsewhere.'"

In comparison to all other punishments today, then, the deliberate extinguishment of human life by the State is uniquely degrading to human dignity. I would not hesitate to hold, on that ground alone, that death is today a "cruel and unusual" punishment, were it not that death is a punishment of long-standing usage and acceptance in this country. I therefore turn to the second principle—that the State may not arbitrarily inflict an unusually severe punishment.

The outstanding characteristic of our present practice of punishing criminals by death is the infrequency with which we resort to it. The evidence is conclusive that death is not the ordinary punishment for any crime.

There has been a steady decline in the infliction of this punishment in every decade since the 1930's, the earliest period for which accurate statistics are available. In the 1930's, executions averaged 167 per year; in the 1940's, the average was 128; in the 1950's, it was 72; and in the years 1960–1962, it was 48. There have been a total of 46 executions since then, 36 of them in 1963–1964. Yet our population and the number of capital crimes committed have increased greatly over the past four decades. The contemporary rarity of the infliction of this punishment is thus the end result of a long-continued decline. That rarity is plainly revealed by an examination of the years 1961–1970, the last 10-year period for which statistics are available. During that time, an average of 106 death sentences was imposed each year. Not nearly that number, however, could be carried out, for many were precluded by commutations to life or a term of years, transfers to mental institutions because of insanity, resentences to life or a term of years, grants of new trials and orders for resentencing, dismissals of indictments and reversals of convictions, and deaths by suicide and natural causes. On January 1, 1961, the death row population was 219; on December 31, 1970, it was 608; during that span, there were 135 executions. Consequently, had the 389 additions to death row also been executed, the annual average would have been 52. In short, the country might, at most, have executed one criminal each week. In fact, of course, far fewer were executed. Even before the moratorium on executions began in 1967, executions totaled only 42 in 1961 and 47 in 1962, an average of less than one per week; the number dwindled to 21 in 1963, to 15 in 1964, and to seven in 1965; in 1966, there was one execution, and in 1967, there were two.

When a country of over 200 million people inflicts an unusually severe punishment no more than 50 times a year, the inference is strong that the punishment is not being regularly and fairly applied. To dispel it would indeed require a clear showing of nonarbitrary infliction.

Although there are not exact figures available, we know that thousands of murders and rapes are committed annually in States where death is an authorized punishment for those crimes. However the rate of infliction is characterized—as "freakishly" or "spectacularly" rare, or simply as rare—it would take the purest sophistry to deny that death is inflicted in only a minute fraction of these cases. How much rarer, after all, could the infliction of death be?

When the punishment of death is inflicted in a trivial number of the cases in which it is legally available, the conclusion is virtually inescapable that it is being inflicted arbitrarily. Indeed, it smacks of little more than a lottery system. The States claim, however, that this rarity is evidence not of arbitrariness, but of informed selectivity: Death is inflicted, they say, only in "extreme" cases.

Informed selectivity, of course, is a value not to be denigrated. Yet presumably the States could make precisely the same claim if there were 10 executions per year, or five, or even if there were but one. That there may be as many as 50 per year does not strengthen the claim. When the rate of infliction is at this low level, it is highly implausible that only the worst criminals or the criminals who commit the worst crimes are selected for this punishment. No one has yet suggested a rational basis that could differentiate in those terms the few who die from the many who go to prison. Crimes and criminals simply do not admit of a distinction that can be drawn so finely as to explain, on that ground, the execution of such a tiny sample of those eligible. Certainly the laws that provide for this punishment do not attempt to draw that distinction; all cases to which the laws apply are necessarily "extreme." Nor is the distinction credible in fact. If, for example, petitioner Furman or his crime illustrates the "extreme," then nearly all murderers and their murders are also "extreme."* Furthermore, our procedures in death cases, rather than resulting in the selection of "extreme" cases for this punishment, actually sanction an arbitrary selection. For this Court has held that juries may, as they do, make the decision whether to impose a death sentence wholly unguided by standards governing that decision. In other words, our procedures are not constructed to guard against the totally capricious selection of criminals for the punishment of death.

Although it is difficult to imagine what further facts would be necessary in order to prove that death is, as my Brother Stewart puts it, "wantonly and . . . freakishly" inflicted, I need not conclude that arbitrary infliction is patently obvious. I am not considering this punishment by the isolated light of one principle. The probability of arbitrariness is sufficiently substantial that it can be relied upon, in combination with the other principles, in reaching a judgment on the constitutionality of this punishment.

When there is a strong probability that an unusually severe and degrading punishment is being inflicted arbitrarily, we may well expect that society will disapprove of its infliction. I turn, therefore, to the third principle. An examination of the history and present operation of the American practice of punishing criminals by death reveals that this punishment has been almost totally rejected by contemporary society.

I cannot add to my Brother Marshall's comprehensive treatment of the English and American history of this punishment. I emphasize, however, one significant conclusion that emerges from that history. From the beginning of our Nation, the punishment of death has stirred acute public controversy. Although pragmatic arguments for and against the punishment have been frequently advanced, this longstanding and heated controversy cannot be

---

* The victim surprised Furman in the act of burglarizing the victim's home in the middle of the night. While escaping, Furman killed the victim with one pistol shot fired through the closed kitchen door from the outside. At the trial, Furman gave his version of the killing:

"They got me charged with murder and I admit, I admit going to these folks' home and they did caught me in there and I was coming back out, backing up and there was a wire down there on the floor. I was coming out backwards and fell back and I didn't intend to kill nobody. I didn't know they was behind the door. The gun went off and I didn't know nothing about no murder until they arrested me, and when the gun went off I was down on the floor and I got up and ran. That's all to it."

The Georgia Supreme Court accepted that version:

"The admission in open court by the accused . . . that during the period in which he was involved in the commission of a criminal act at the home of the deceased, he accidentally tripped over a wire in leaving the premises causing the gun to go off, together with other facts and circumstances surrounding the death of the deceased by violent means, was sufficient to support the verdict of guilty of murder. . . . "

About Furman himself, the jury knew only that he was black and that, according to his statement at trial, he was 26 years old and worked at "Superior Upholstery." It took the jury one hour and 35 minutes to return a verdict of guilt and a sentence of death.

explained solely as the result of differences over the practical wisdom of a particular government policy. At bottom, the battle has been waged on moral grounds. The country has debated whether a society for which the dignity of the individual is the supreme value can, without a fundamental inconsistency, follow the practice of deliberately putting some of its members to death. In the United States, as in other nations of the western world, "the struggle about this punishment has been one between ancient and deeply rooted beliefs in retribution, atonement or vengeance on the one hand, and, on the other, beliefs in the personal value and dignity of the common man that were born of the democratic movement of the eighteenth century, as well as beliefs in the scientific approach to an understanding of the motive forces of human conduct, which are the result of the growth of the sciences of behavior during the nineteenth and twentieth centuries." It is this essentially moral conflict that forms the backdrop for the past changes in and the present operation of our system of imposing death as a punishment for crime.

Our practice of punishing criminals by death has changed greatly over the years. One significant change has been in our methods of inflicting death. Although this country never embraced the more violent and repulsive methods employed in England, we did for a long time rely almost exclusively upon the gallows and the firing squad. Since the development of the supposedly more humane methods of electrocution late in the 19th century and lethal gas in the 20th, however, hanging and shooting have virtually ceased. Our concern for decency and human dignity, moreover, has compelled changes in the circumstances surrounding the execution itself. No longer does our society countenance the spectacle of public executions, once thought desirable as a deterrent to criminal behavior by others. Today we reject public executions as debasing and brutalizing to us all.

Also significant is the drastic decrease in the crimes for which the punishment of death is actually inflicted. While esoteric capital crimes remain on the books, since 1930 murder and rape have accounted for nearly 99% of the total executions, and murder alone for about 87%. In addition, the crime of capital murder has itself been limited. As the Court noted in *McGautha* v. *California,* there was in this country a "rebellion against the common-law rule imposing a mandatory death sentence on all convicted murderers." Initially, that rebellion resulted in legislative definitions that distinguished between degrees of murder, retaining the mandatory death sentence only for murder in the first degree. Yet "[t]his new legislative criterion for isolating crimes appropriately by death soon proved as unsuccessful as the concept of 'malice aforethought,'" the common-law means of separating murder from manslaughter. Not only was the distinction between degrees of murder confusing and uncertain in practice, but even in clear cases of first-degree murder juries continued to take the law into their own hands: if they felt that death was an inappropriate punishment, "they simply refused to convict of the capital offense." The phenomenon of jury nullification thus remained to counteract the rigors of mandatory death sentences. Bowing to reality, "legislatures did not try, as before, to refine further the definition of capital homicides. Instead they adopted the method of forthrightly granting juries the discretion which they had been exercising in fact." In consequence, virtually all death sentences today are discretionarily imposed. Finally, it is significant that nine States no longer inflict the punishment of death under any circumstances, and five others have restricted it to extremely rare crimes.

Thus, although "the death penalty has been employed throughout our history," in fact the history of this punishment is one of successive restriction. What was once a common punishment has become, in the context of a continuing moral debate, increasingly rare. The evolution of this punishment evidences, not that it is an inevitable part of the American scene, but that it has proved progressively more troublesome to the national conscience. The result of this movement is our current system of administering the punishment, under which death sentences are rarely imposed and death is even more rarely inflicted. It is, of course, "We, the People" who are responsible for the rarity both of the imposition and the carrying out of this punishment. Juries, "express[ing] the conscience of the community on the ultimate question of life or death," *Witherspoon* v. *Illinois,* have been able to bring themselves to vote for death in a mere 100 or so cases among the thousands tried each year where the punishment is available. Governors, elected by and acting for us, have regularly commuted a substantial number of those sentences. And it is our society that insists upon due process of law to the end that no person will be unjustly put to death, thus ensuring that many more of those sentences will not be carried out. In sum, we have made death a rare punishment today.

The progressive decline in, and the current rarity of, the infliction of death demonstrate that our society seriously questions the appropriateness of this punishment today. The States point out that many legislatures authorize death as the punishment for certain crimes and that substantial segments of the public, as reflected in opinion polls and referendum votes, continue to support it. Yet the availability of this punishment through statutory authorization, as well as the polls and referenda, which amount simply to approval of that authorization, simply underscores the extent to which our society has in fact rejected this punishment. When an unusually severe punishment is authorized for wide-scale application but not, because of society's refusal, inflicted save in a few instances, the inference is compelling that there is a deep-seated reluctance to inflict it. Indeed, the likelihood is great that the punishment is tolerated only because of its disuse. The objective indicator of society's view of an unusually severe punishment is what society does with it, and today society will inflict death upon only a small sample of the eligible criminals. Rejection could hardly be more complete without becoming absolute. At the very least, I must conclude that contemporary society views this punishment with substantial doubt.

The final principle to be considered is that an unusually severe and degrading punishment may not be excessive in view of the purposes for which it is inflicted. This principle, too, is related to the others. When there is a strong probability that the State is arbitrarily inflicting an unusually severe punishment that is subject to grave societal doubts, it is likely also that the punishment cannot be shown to be serving any penal purpose that could not be served equally well by some less severe punishment.

The States' primary claim is that death is a necessary punishment because it prevents the commission of capital crimes more effectively than any less severe punishment. The first part of this claim is that the infliction of death is necessary to stop the individuals executed from committing further crimes. The sufficient answer to this is that if a criminal convicted of a capital crime poses a danger to society, effective administration of the State's pardon and parole laws can delay or deny his release from prison, and techniques of isolation can eliminate or minimize the danger while he remains confined.

The more significant argument is that the threat of death prevents the commission of capital crimes because it deters potential criminals who would not be deterred by the threat of imprisonment. The argument is not based upon evidence that the threat of death is a superior deterrent. Indeed, as my Brother Marshall establishes, the available evidence uniformly indicates, although it does not conclusively prove, that the threat of death has no greater deterrent effect than the threat of imprisonment. The States argue, however, that they are entitled to rely upon common human experience, and that experience, they say, supports the conclusion that death must be a more effective deterrent than any less severe punishment. Because people fear death the most, the argument runs, the threat of death must be the greatest deterrent.

It is important to focus upon the precise import of this argument. It is not denied that many, and probably most, capital crimes cannot be deterred by the threat of punishment. Thus the argument can apply only to those who think rationally about the commission of capital crimes. Particularly is that true when the potential criminal, under this argument, must not only consider the risk of punishment, but also distinguish between two possible punishments. The concern, then, is with a particular type of potential criminal, the rational person who will commit a capital crime knowing that the punishment is long-term imprisonment, which may well be for the rest of his life, but will not commit the crime knowing that the punishment is death. On the face of it, the assumption that such persons exist is implausible.

In any event, this argument cannot be appraised in the abstract. We are not presented with the theoretical question whether under any imaginable circumstances the threat of death might be a greater deterrent to the commission of capital crimes than the threat of imprisonment. We are concerned with the practice of punishing criminals by death as it exists in the United States today. Proponents of this argument necessarily admit that its validity depends upon the existence of a system in which the punishment of death is invariably and swiftly imposed. Our system, of course, satisfies neither condition. A rational person contemplating a murder or rape is confronted, not with the certainty of a speedy death, but with the slightest possibility that he will be executed in the distant future. The risk of death is remote and improbable; in contrast, the risk of long-term imprisonment is near and great. In short, whatever the speculative validity of the assumption that the threat of death is a superior deterrent, there is no reason to believe that as currently administered the punishment of death is necessary to deter the commission of capital crimes. Whatever might be the case were all or substantially all eligible criminals quickly put to death, unverifiable possibilities are an insufficient basis upon which to conclude that the threat of death today has any greater deterrent efficacy than the threat of imprisonment.*

There is, however, another aspect to the argument that the punishment of death is necessary for the protection of society. The infliction of death, the States urge, serves to manifest the community's outrage at the commission of the crime. It is, they say, a concrete public expression of moral indignation that inculcates respect for the law and helps assure a more peaceful community. Moreover, we are told, not only does the punishment of death exert this widespread moralizing influence upon community

values, it also satisfies the popular demand for grievous condemnation of abhorrent crimes and thus prevents disorder, lynching, and attempts by private citizens to take the law into their own hands.

The question, however, is not whether death serves these supposed purposes of punishment, but whether death serves them more effectively than imprisonment. There is no evidence whatever that utilization of imprisonment rather than death encourages private blood feuds and other disorders. Surely if there were such a danger, the execution of a handful of criminals each year would not prevent it. The assertion that death alone is a sufficiently emphatic denunciation for capital crimes suffers from the same defect. If capital crimes require the punishment of death in order to provide moral reinforcement for the basic values of the community, those values can only be undermined when death is so rarely inflicted upon the criminals who commit the crimes. Furthermore, it is certainly doubtful that the infliction of death by the State does in fact strengthen the community's moral code; if the deliberate extinguishment of human life has any effect at all, it more likely tends to lower our respect for life and brutalize our values. That, after all, is why we no longer carry out public executions. In any event, this claim simply means that one purpose of punishment is to indicate social disapproval of crime. To serve that purpose our laws distribute punishments according to the gravity of crimes and punish more severely the crimes society regards as more serious. That purpose cannot justify any particular punishment as the upper limit of severity.

There is, then, no substantial reason to believe that the punishment of death, as currently administered, is necessary for the protection of society. The only other purpose suggested, one that is independent of protection for society, is retribution. Shortly stated, retribution in this context means that criminals are put to death because they deserve it.

Although it is difficult to believe that any State today wishes to proclaim adherence to "naked vengeance," the States claim, in reliance upon its statutory authorization, that death is the only fit punishment for capital crimes and that this retributive purpose justifies its infliction. In the past, judged by its statutory authorization, death was con-

* There is also the more limited argument that death is a necessary punishment when criminals are already serving or subject to a sentence of life imprisonment. If the only punishment available is further imprisonment, it is said, those criminals will have nothing to lose by committing further crimes, and accordingly the threat of death is the sole deterrent. But "life" imprisonment is a misnomer today. Rarely, if ever, do crimes carry a mandatory life sentence without possibility of parole. That possibility ensures that criminals do not reach the point where further crimes are free of consequences. Moreover, if this argument is simply an assertion that the threat of death is a more effective deterrent than the threat of increased imprisonment by denial of release on parole, then, as noted above, there is simply no evidence to support it.

sidered the only fit punishment for the crime of forgery, for the first federal criminal statute provided a mandatory death penalty for that crime. Obviously, concepts of justice change; no immutable moral order requires death for murderers and rapists. The claim that death is a just punishment necessarily refers to the existence of certain public beliefs. The claim must be that for capital crimes death alone comports with society's notion of proper punishment. As administered today, however, the punishment of death cannot be justified as a necessary means of exacting retribution from criminals. When the overwhelming number of criminals who commit capital crimes go to prison, it cannot be concluded that death serves the purpose of retribution more effectively than imprisonment. The asserted public belief that murderers and rapists deserve to die is flatly inconsistent with the execution of a random few. As the history of the punishment of death in this country shows, our society wishes to prevent crime; we have no desire to kill criminals simply to get even with them.

In sum, the punishment of death is inconsistent with all four principles: Death is an unusually severe and degrading punishment; there is a strong probability that it is inflicted arbitrarily; its rejection by contemporary society is virtually total; and there is no reason to believe that it serves any penal purpose more effectively than the less severe punishment of imprisonment. The function of these principles is to enable a court to determine whether a punishment comports with human dignity. Death, quite simply, does not. . . .

Mr. Justice Marshall, concurring. . . .

V

In order to assess whether or not death is an excessive or unnecessary penalty, it is necessary to consider the reasons why a legislature might select it as punishment for one or more offenses, and examine whether less severe penalties would satisfy the legitimate legislative wants as well as capital punishment. If they would, then the death penalty is unnecessary cruelty, and, therefore, unconstitutional.

There are six purposes conceivably served by capital punishment: retribution, deterrence, prevention of repetitive criminal acts, encouragement of guilty pleas and confessions, eugenics, and economy. These are considered *seriatim* below.

A. The concept of retribution is one of the most misunderstood in all of our criminal jurisprudence. The principal source of confusion derives from the fact that, in dealing with the concept, most people confuse the question "why do men in fact punish?" with the question "what justifies men in punishing?" Men may punish for any number of reasons, but the one reason that punishment is morally good or morally justifiable is that someone has broken the law. Thus, it can correctly be said that breaking the law is the *sine qua non* of punishment, or, in other words, that we only tolerate punishment as it is imposed on one who deviates from the norm established by the criminal law.

The fact that the State may seek retribution against those who have broken its laws does not mean that retribution may then become the State's sole end in punishing. Our jurisprudence has always accepted deterrence in general, deterrence of individual recidivism, isolation of dangerous persons, and rehabilitation as proper goals of punishment. Retaliation, vengeance, and retribution have been roundly condemned as intolerable aspirations for a government in a free society.

Punishment as retribution has been condemned by scholars for centuries, and the Eighth Amendment itself was adopted to prevent punishment from becoming synonymous with vengeance. . . .

B. The most hotly contested issue regarding capital punishment is whether it is better than life imprisonment as a deterrent to crime.

While the contrary position has been argued, it is my firm opinion that the death penalty is a more severe sanction than life imprisonment. Admittedly, there are some persons who would rather die than languish in prison for a lifetime. But, whether or not they should be able to choose death as an alternative is a far different question from that presented here —*i. e.,* whether the State can impose death as a punishment. Death is irrevocable; life imprisonment is not. Death, of course, makes rehabilitation impossible; life imprisonment does not. In short, death has always been viewed as the ultimate sanction, and it seems perfectly reasonable to continue to view it as such.

It must be kept in mind, then, that the question to be considered is not simply whether capital punishment is a deterrent, but whether it is a better deterrent than life imprisonment.

There is no more complex problem than determining the deterrent efficacy of the death penalty. "Capital punishment has obviously failed as a deterrent when a murder is committed. We can number its failures. But we cannot number its successes. No one can ever know how many people have refrained from murder because of the fear of being hanged." This is the nub of the problem and it is exacerbated by the paucity of useful data. The United States is more fortunate than most countries, however, in that it has what are generally considered to be the world's most reliable statistics.

The two strongest arguments in favor of capital punishment as a deterrent are both logical hypotheses devoid of evidentiary support, but persuasive nonetheless. The first proposition was best stated by Sir James Stephen in 1864:

> "No other punishment deters men so effectually from committing crimes as the punishment of death. This is one of those propositions which it is difficult to prove, simply because they are in themselves more obvious than any proof can make them. It is possible to display ingenuity in arguing against it, but that is all. The whole experience of mankind is in the other direction. The threat of instant death is the one to which resort has always been made when there was an absolute necessity for producing some result. . . . No one goes to certain inevitable death except by compulsion. Put the matter the other way. Was there ever yet a criminal who, when sentenced to death and brought out to die, would refuse the offer of a commutation of his sentence for the severest secondary punishment? Surely not. Why is this? It can only be because 'All that a man has will he give for his life.' In any secondary punishment, however terrible, there is hope; but death is death; its terrors cannot be described more forcibly."

This hypothesis relates to the use of capital punishment as a deterrent for any crime. The second proposition is that "if life imprisonment is the maximum penalty for a crime such as murder, an offender who is serving a life sentence cannot then be deterred from murdering a fellow inmate or a prison officer." This hypothesis advocates a limited deterrent effect under particular circumstances.

Abolitionists attempt to disprove these hypotheses by amassing statistical evidence to demonstrate that there is no correlation between criminal activity and the existence or nonexistence of a capital sanction. Almost all of the evidence involves the crime of murder, since murder is punishable by death in more jurisdictions than are other offenses, and almost 90% of all executions since 1930 have been pursuant to murder convictions.

Thorsten Sellin, one of the leading authorities on capital punishment, has urged that if the death penalty deters prospective murderers, the following hypotheses should be true:

"(a) Murders should be less frequent in states that have the death penalty than in those that have abolished it, other factors being equal. Comparisons of this nature must be made among states that are as alike as possible in all other respects—character of population, social and economic condition, etc.—in order not to introduce factors known to influence murder rates in a serious manner but present in only one of these states.

"(b) Murders should increase when the death penalty is abolished and should decline when it is restored.

"(c) The deterrent effect should be greatest and should therefore affect murder rates most powerfully in those communities where the crime occurred and its consequences are most strongly brought home to the population.

"(d) Law enforcement officers would be safer from murderous attacks in states that have the death penalty than in those without it."

Sellin's evidence indicates that not one of these propositions is true. This evidence has its problems, however. One is that there are no accurate figures for capital murders; there are only figures on homicides and they, of course, include noncapital killings. A second problem is that certain murders undoubtedly are misinterpreted as accidental deaths or suicides, and there is no way of estimating the number of such undetected crimes. A third problem is that not all homicides are reported. Despite these difficulties, most authorities have assumed that the proportion of capital murders in a State's or nation's homicide statistics remains reasonably constant, and that the homicide statistics are therefore useful.

Sellin's statistics demonstrate that there is no correlation between the murder rate and the presence or absence of the capital sanction. He compares States that have similar characteristics and finds that irrespective of their position on capital punishment, they have similar murder rates. In the New England States, for example, there is no correlation between executions and homicide rates. The same is true for Midwestern States, and for all others studied. Both the United Nations and Great Britain have acknowledged the validity of Sellin's statistics.

Sellin also concludes that abolition and/or reintroduction of the death penalty had no effect on the homicide rates of the various States involved. This conclusion is borne out by others who have made similar inquiries and by the experience of other countries. Despite problems with the statistics, Sellin's evidence has been relied upon in international studies of capital punishment.

Statistics also show that the deterrant effect of capital punishment is no greater in those communities where executions take place than in other communities. In fact, there is some evidence that imposition of capital punishment may actually encourage crime, rather than deter it. And, while police and law enforcement officers are the strongest advocates of capital punishment, the evidence is overwhelming that police are no safer in communities that retain the sanction than in those that have abolished it.

There is also a substantial body of data showing that the existence of the death penalty has virtually no effect on the homicide rate in prisons. Most of the persons sentenced to death are murderers, and murderers tend to be model prisoners. . . .

C. Much of what must be said about the death penalty as a device to prevent recidivism is obvious —if a murderer is executed, he cannot possibly commit another offense. The fact is, however, that murderers are extremely unlikely to commit other crimes either in prison or upon their release. For the most part, they are first offenders, and when released from prison they are known to become model citizens. Furthermore, most persons who

commit capital crimes are not executed. With respect to those who are sentenced to die, it is critical to note that the jury is never asked to determine whether they are likely to be recidivists. In light of these facts, if capital punishment were justified purely on the basis of preventing recidivism, it would have to be considered to be excessive; no general need to obliterate all capital offenders could have been demonstrated, nor any specific need in individual cases.

D. The three final purposes which may underlie utilization of a capital sanction—encouraging guilty pleas and confessions, eugenics, and reducing state expenditures—may be dealt with quickly. If the death penalty is used to encourage guilty pleas and thus to deter suspects from exercising their rights under the Sixth Amendment to jury trials, it is unconstitutional. Its elimination would do little to impair the State's bargaining position in criminal cases, since life imprisonment remains a severe sanction which can be used as leverage for bargaining for pleas or confessions in exchange either for charges of lesser offenses or recommendations of leniency.

Moreover, to the extent that capital punishment is used to encourage confessions and guilty pleas, it is not being used for punishment purposes. A State that justifies capital punishment on its utility as part of the conviction process could not profess to rely on capital punishment as a deterrent. Such a State's system would be structured with twin goals only: obtaining guilty pleas and confessions and imposing *imprisonment* as the maximum sanction. Since life imprisonment is sufficient for bargaining purposes, the death penalty is excessive if used for the same purposes.

In light of the previous discussion on deterrence, any suggestions concerning the eugenic benefits of capital punishment are obviously meritless. As I pointed out above, there is not even any attempt made to discover which capital offenders are likely to be recidivists, let alone which are positively incurable. No test or procedure presently exists by which incurables can be screened from those who would benefit from treatment. On the one hand, due process would seem to require that we have some procedure to demonstrate incurability before execution; and, on the other hand, equal protection would then seemingly require that all incurables be executed. In addition, the "cruel and unusual" language would require that life imprisonment, treatment, and sterilization be inadequate for eugenic purposes. More importantly, this Nation has never formally professed eugenic goals, and the history of the world does not look kindly on them. If eugenics is one of our purposes, then the legislatures should say so forthrightly and design procedures to serve this goal. Until such time, I can only conclude, as has virtually everyone else who has looked at the problem, that capital punishment cannot be defended on the basis of any eugenic purposes.

As for the argument that it is cheaper to execute a capital offender than to imprison him for life, even assuming that such an argument, if true, would support a capital sanction, it is simply incorrect. A disproportionate amount of money spent on prisons is attributable to death row. Condemned men are not productive members of the prison community, although they could be, and executions are expensive. Appeals are often automatic, and courts admittedly spend more time with death cases.

At trial, the selection of jurors is likely to become a costly, time-consuming problem in a capital case, and defense counsel will reasonably exhaust every possible means to save his client from execution, no matter how long the trial takes.

During the period between conviction and execution, there are an inordinate number of collateral attacks on the conviction and attempts to obtain executive clemency, all of which exhaust the time, money, and effort of the State. There are also continual assertions that the condemned prisoner has gone insane. Because there is a formally established policy of not executing insane persons, great sums of money may be spent on detecting and curing mental illness in order to perform the execution. Since no one wants the responsibility for the execution, the condemned man is likely to be passed back and forth from doctors to custodial officials to courts like a ping-pong ball. The entire process is very costly.

When all is said and done, there can be no doubt that it costs more to execute a man than to keep him in prison for life.

E.   There is but one conclusion that can be drawn from all of this—i. e., the death penalty is an excessive and unnecessary punishment that violates the Eighth Amendment. The statistical evidence is not convincing beyond all doubt, but it is persuasive. It is not improper at this point to take judicial notice of the fact that for more than 200 years men have labored to demonstrate that capital punishment serves no purpose that life imprisonment could not serve equally well. And they have done so with great success. Little, if any, evidence has been adduced to prove the contrary. The point has now been reached at which deference to the legislatures is tantamount to abdication of our judicial roles as factfinders, judges, and ultimate arbiters of the Constitution. We know that at some point the presumption of constitutionality accorded legislative acts gives way to a realistic assessment of those acts. This point comes when there is sufficient evidence available so that judges can determine, not whether the legislature acted wisely, but whether it had any rational basis whatsoever for acting. We have this evidence before us now. There is no rational basis for concluding that capital punishment is not excessive. It therefore violates the Eighth Amendment. . . .

Gregg v. Georgia (1976)

(*Source:* Gregg v. Georgia *428 U.S. 153 [1976]. Most legal references have been omitted.*)

QUESTIONS FOR REFLECTION

1. The majority argues that the death penalty is sometimes justified. What are the majority's chief arguments?

2. In *Furman v. Georgia*, Justice Brennan outlined four principles for determining the acceptability of a punishment. Does the majority in *Gregg v. Georgia* accept those principles? Does it present arguments that the death penalty can satisfy them?

Judgment of the Court, and opinion of Mr. Justice Stewart, Mr. Justice Powell, and Mr. Justice Stevens, announced by Mr. Justice Stewart. . . .

III

. . . The Court on a number of occasions has both assumed and asserted the constitutionality of capital punishment. In several cases that assumption provided a necessary foundation for the decision, as the Court was asked to decide whether a particular method of carrying out a capital sentence would be allowed to stand under the Eighth Amendment. But until *Furman v. Georgia,* the Court never confronted squarely the fundamental claim that the punishment of death always, regardless of the enormity of the offense or the procedure followed in imposing the sentence, is cruel and unusual punishment in violation of the Constitution. Although this issue was presented and addressed in *Furman,* it was not resolved by the Court. Four Justices would have held that capital punishment is not unconstitutional *per se;* two Justices would have reached the opposite conclusion; and three Justices, while agreeing that the statutes then before the Court were invalid as

applied, left open the question whether such punishment may ever be imposed. We now hold that the punishment of death does not invariably violate the Constitution.

A

The history of the prohibition of "cruel and unusual" punishment already has been reviewed at length. The phrase first appeared in the English Bill of Rights of 1689, which was drafted by Parliament at the accession of William and Mary. The English version appears to have been directed against punishments unauthorized by statute and beyond the jurisdiction of the sentencing court, as well as those disproportionate to the offense involved. The American draftsmen, who adopted the English phrasing in drafting the Eighth Amendment, were primarily concerned, however, with proscribing "tortures" and other "barbarous" methods of punishment. . . .

. . . A penalty also must accord with "the dignity of man," which is the "basic concept underlying the Eighth Amendment." This means, at least, that the punishment not be "excessive." When a form of punishment in the abstract (in this case, whether capital punishment may ever be imposed as a sanction for murder) rather than in the particular (the propriety of death as a penalty to be applied to a specific defendant for a specific crime) is under consideration, the inquiry into "excessiveness" has two aspects. First, the punishment must not involve the unnecessary and wanton infliction of pain. Second, the punishment must not be grossly out of proportion to the severity of the crime.

B

Of course, the requirement of the Eighth Amendment must be applied with an awareness of the limited role to be played by the courts. This does not mean that judges have no role to play, for the Eighth Amendment is a restraint upon the exercise of legislative power. . . .

But, while we have an obligation to insure that constitutional bounds are not overreached, we may not act as judges as we might as legislators.

> "Courts are not representative bodies. They are not designed to be a good reflex of a democratic society. Their judgment is best informed, and therefore most dependable, within narrow limits. Their essential quality is detachment, founded on independence. History teaches that the independence of the judiciary is jeopardized when courts become embroiled in the passions of the day and assume primary responsibility in choosing between competing political, economic and social pressures."

Therefore, in assessing a punishment selected by a democratically elected legislature against the constitutional measure, we presume its validity. We may not require the legislature to select the least severe penalty possible so long as the penalty selected is not cruelly inhumane or disproportionate to the crime involved. And a heavy burden rests on those who would attack the judgment of the representatives of the people.

This is true in part because the constitutional test is intertwined with an assessment of contemporary standards and the legislative judgment weighs heavily in ascertaining such standards. "[I]n a democratic society legislatures, not courts, are constituted to respond to the will and consequently the moral values of the people." The deference we owe to the decisions of the state legislatures under our federal system is enhanced where the specification of punishments is concerned, for "these are peculiarly questions of legislative policy." Caution is necessary lest this Court become, "under the aegis of the Cruel and Unusual Punishment Clause, the ultimate arbiter of the standards of criminal responsibility . . . throughout the country." A decision that a given punishment is impermissible under the Eighth Amendment cannot be reversed short of a constitutional amendment. The ability of the people to express their preference through the normal democratic processes, as well as through ballot referenda, is shut off. Revisions cannot be made in the light of further experience.

C

In the discussion to this point we have sought to identify the principles and considerations that guide a court in addressing an Eighth Amendment claim. We now consider specifically whether the sentence of death for the crime of murder is a *per se* violation of the Eighth and Fourteenth Amendments to the Constitution. We note first that history and precedent strongly support a negative answer to this question.

The imposition of the death penalty for the crime of murder has a long history of acceptance both in the United States and in England. The common-law rule imposed a mandatory death sentence on all convicted murderers. And the penalty continued to be used into the 20th century by most American States, although the breadth of the common-law rule was diminished, initially by narrowing the class of murders to be punished by death and subsequently by widespread adoption of laws expressly granting juries the discretion to recommend mercy.

It is apparent from the text of the Constitution itself that the existence of capital punishment was accepted by the Framers. At the time the Eighth Amendment was ratified, capital punishment was a common sanction in every State. Indeed, the First Congress of the United States enacted legislation providing death as the penalty for specified crimes. The Fifth Amendment, adopted at the same time as the Eighth, contemplated the continued existence of the capital sanction by imposing certain limits on the prosecution of capital cases:

> "No person shall be held to answer for a capital, or otherwise infamous crime, unless on a presentment or indictment of a Grand Jury . . . ; nor shall any person be subject for the same offense to be twice put in jeopardy of life or limb; . . . nor be deprived of life, liberty, or property, without due process of law. . . . "

And the Fourteenth Amendment, adopted over three-quarters of a century later, similarly contemplates the existence of the capital sanction in providing that no State shall deprive any person of "life, liberty, or property" without due process of law.

For nearly two centuries, this Court, repeatedly and often expressly, has recognized that capital punishment is not invalid *per se*. . . .

Four years ago, the petitioners in *Furman* and its companion cases predicated their argument primarily upon the asserted proposition that standards of decency had evolved to the point where capital punishment no longer could be tolerated. The petitioners in those cases said, in effect, that the evolutionary process had come to an end, and that standards of decency required that the Eighth Amendment be construed finally as prohibiting capital punishment for any crime regardless of its depravity and impact on society. This view was accepted by two Justices. Three other Justices were unwilling to go so far; focusing on the procedures by which convicted defendants were selected for the death penalty rather than on the actual punishment inflicted, they joined in the conclusion that the statutes before the Court were constitutionally invalid.

The petitioners in the capital cases before the Court today renew the "standards of decency" argument, but developments during the four years since *Furman* have undercut substantially the assumptions upon which their argument rested. Despite the continuing debate, dating back to the 19th century, over the morality and utility of capital punishment, it is now evident that a large proportion of American society continues to regard it as an appropriate and necessary criminal sanction.

The most marked indication of society's endorsement of the death penalty for murder is the legislative response to *Furman*. The legislatures of at least 35 States have enacted new statutes that provide for the death penalty for at least some crimes that result in the death of another person. And the Congress of the United States, in 1974, enacted a statute providing the death penalty for aircraft piracy that results in death. These recently adopted statutes have attempted to address the concerns expressed by the Court in *Furman* primarily (i) by specifying the factors to be weighed and the procedures to be followed in deciding when to impose a capital sentence, or (ii) by making the death penalty mandatory for specified crimes. But all of the post-*Furman* statutes make clear that capital punishment itself has not been rejected by the elected representatives of the people.

In the only statewide referendum occurring since *Furman* and brought to our attention, the people of California adopted a constitutional amendment that authorized capital punishment, in effect negating a prior ruling by the Supreme Court of California in *People* v. *Anderson* (1972) that the death penalty violated the California Constitution.

The jury also is a significant and reliable objective index of contemporary values because it is so directly involved. The Court has said that "one of the most important functions any jury can perform in making . . . a selection [between life imprisonment and death for a defendant convicted in a capital case] is to maintain a link between contemporary community values and the penal system." It may be true that evolving standards have influenced juries in recent decades to be more discriminating in imposing the sentence of death. But the relative infrequency of jury verdicts imposing the death sentence does not indicate rejection of capital punishment *per se*. Rather, the reluctance of juries in many cases to impose the sentence may well reflect the humane feeling that this most irrevocable of sanctions should be reserved for a small number of extreme cases. Indeed, the actions of juries in many States since *Furman* are fully compatible with the legislative judgments, reflected in the new statutes, as to the continued utility and necessity of capital punishment in approriate cases. At the close of 1974 at least 254 persons had been sentenced to death since *Furman,* and by the end of March 1976, more than 460 persons were subject to death sentences.

As we have seen, however, the Eighth Amendment demands more than that a challenged punishment be acceptable to contemporary society. The Court also must ask whether it comports with the basic concept of human dignity at the core of the Amendment. Although we cannot "invalidate a category of penalties because we deem less severe penalties adequate to serve the ends of penology," the sanction imposed cannot be so totally without penological justification that it results in the gratuitous infliction of suffering.

The death penalty is said to serve two principal social purposes: retribution and deterrence of capital crimes by prospective offenders.

In part, capital punishment is an expression of society's moral outrage at particularly offensive conduct. This function may be unappealing to many, but it is essential in an ordered society that asks its citizens to rely on legal processes rather than self-help to vindicate their wrongs.

> "The instinct for retribution is part of the nature of man, and channeling that instinct in the administration of criminal justice serves an important purpose in promoting the stability of a society governed by law. When people begin to believe that organized society is unwilling or unable to impose upon criminal offenders the punishment they 'deserve,' then there are sown the seeds of anarchy—of self-help, vigilante justice, and lynch law." *Furman v. Georgia* (Stewart, J., concurring).

"Retribution is no longer the dominant objective of the criminal law," but neither is it a forbidden objective nor one inconsistent with our respect for the dignity of men. Indeed, the decision that capital punishment may be the appropriate sanction in extreme cases is an expression of the community's belief that certain crimes are themselves so grievous an affront to humanity that the only adequate response may be the penalty of death.

Statistical attempts to evaluate the worth of the death penalty as a deterrent to crimes by potential offenders have occasioned a great deal of debate. The results simply have been inconclusive. As one opponent of capital punishment has said:

> "[A]fter all possible inquiry, including the probing of all possible methods of inquiry, we do not know, and for systematic and easily visible reasons cannot know, what the truth about this 'deterrent' effect may be. . . .
>
> "The inescapable flaw is . . . that social conditions

in any state are not constant through time, and that social conditions are not the same in any two states. If an effect were observed (and the observed effects, one way or another, are not large) then one could not at all tell whether any of this effect is attributable to the presence or absence of capital punishment. A 'scientific'— that is to say, a soundly based—conclusion is simply impossible, and no methodological path out of this tangle suggests itself."

Although some of the studies suggest that the death penalty may not function as a significantly greater deterrent than lesser penalties, there is no convincing empirical evidence either supporting or refuting this view. We may nevertheless assume safely that there are murderers, such as those who act in passion, for whom the threat of death has little or no deterrent effect. But for many others, the death penalty undoubtedly is a significant deterrent. There are carefully contemplated murders, such as murder for hire, where the possible penalty of death may well enter into the cold calculus that precedes the decision to act. And there are some categories of murder, such as murder by a life prisoner, where other sanctions may not be adequate.

The value of capital punishment as a deterrent of crime is a complex factual issue the resolution of which properly rests with the legislatures, which can evaluate the results of statistical studies in terms of their own local conditions and with a flexibility of approach that is not available to the courts. Indeed, many of the post-*Furman* statutes reflect just such a responsible effort to define those crimes and those criminals for which capital punishment is most probably an effective deterrent.

In sum, we cannot say that the judgment of the Georgia Legislature that capital punishment may be necessary in some cases is clearly wrong. Considerations of federalism, as well as respect for the ability of a legislature to evaluate, in terms of its particular State, the moral consensus concerning the death penalty and its social utility as a sanction, require us to conclude, in the absence of more convincing evidence, that the infliction of death as a punishment for murder is not without justification and thus is not unconstitutionally severe.

Finally, we must consider whether the punishment of death is disproportionate in relation to the crime for which it is imposed. There is no question that death as a punishment is unique in its severity and irrevocability. When a defendant's life is at stake, the Court has been particularly sensitive to insure that every safeguard is observed. But we are concerned here only with the imposition of capital punishment for the crime of murder, and when a life has been taken deliberately by the offender, we cannot say that the punishment is invariably disproportionate to the crime. It is an extreme sanction, suitable to the most extreme of crimes.

We hold that the death penalty is not a form of punishment that may never be imposed, regardless of the circumstances of the offense, regardless of the character of the offender, and regardless of the procedure followed in reaching the decision to impose it.

IV

[A . . .]

B

We now turn to consideration of the constitutionality of Georgia's capital-sentencing procedures. In the wake of *Furman,* Georgia amended its capital punishment statute, but chose not to narrow the scope of its murder provisions. Thus, now as before *Furman,* in Georgia "[a] person commits murder when he unlawfully and with malice aforethought, either express or implied, causes the death of another human being." All persons convicted of murder "shall be punished by death or by imprisonment for life."

Georgia did act, however, to narrow the class of murderers subject to capital punishment by specifying 10 statutory aggravating circumstances, one of which must be found by the jury to exist beyond a reasonable doubt before a death sentence can ever be imposed. In addition, the jury is authorized to consider any other appropriate aggravating or mitigating circumstances. The jury is not required to find any mitigating circumstances in order to make a recommendation of mercy that is binding on the trial court, but it must find a *statutory* aggravating circumstance before recommending a sentence of death.

These procedures require the jury to consider the circumstances of the crime and the criminal before it recommends sentence. No longer can a Georgia jury do as Furman's jury did: reach a finding of the defendant's guilt and then, without guidance or direction, decide whether he should live or die. Instead, the jury's attention is directed to the specific circumstances of the crime: Was it committed in the course of another capital felony? Was it committed for money? Was it committed upon a peace officer or judicial officer? Was it committed in a particularly heinous way or in a manner that endangered the lives of many persons? In addition, the jury's attention is focused on the characteristics of the person who committed the crime: Does he have a record of prior convictions for capital offenses? Are there any special facts about this defendant that mitigate against imposing capital punishment (*e. g.,* his youth, the extent of his cooperation with the police, his emotional state at the time of the crime). As a result, while some jury discretion still exists, "the discretion to be exercised is controlled by clear and objective standards so as to produce non-discriminatory application."

As an important additional safeguard against arbitrariness and caprice, the Georgia statutory scheme provides for automatic appeal of all death sentences to the State's Supreme Court. That court is required by statute to review each sentence of death and determine whether it was imposed under the influence of passion or prejudice, whether the evidence supports the jury's finding of a statutory aggravating circumstance, and whether the sentence is disproportionate compared to those sentences imposed in similar cases.

In short, Georgia's new sentencing procedures require as a prerequisite to the imposition of the death penalty, specific jury findings as to the circumstances of the crime or the character of the defendant. Moreover, to guard further against a situation comparable to that presented in *Furman,* the Supreme Court of Georgia compares each death sentence with the sentences imposed on similarly situated defendants to ensure that the sentence of death in a particular case is not disproportionate.

On their face these procedures seem to satisfy the concerns of *Furman*. No longer should there be "no meaningful basis for distinguishing the few cases in which [the death penalty] is imposed from the many cases in which it is not." . . .

V

The basic concern of *Furman* centered on those defendants who were being condemned to death capriciously and arbitrarily. Under the procedures before the Court in that case, sentencing authorities were not directed to give attention to the nature or circumstances of the crime committed or to the character or record of the defendant. Left unguided, juries imposed the death sentence in a way that could only be called freakish. The new Georgia sentencing procedures, by contrast, focus the jury's attention on the particularized nature of the crime and the particularized characteristics of the individual defendant. While the jury is permitted to consider any aggravating or mitigating circumstances, it must find and identify at least one statutory aggravating factor before it may impose a penalty of death. In this way the jury's discretion is channeled. No longer can a jury wantonly and freakishly impose the death sentence; it is always circumscribed by the legislative guidelines. In addition, the review function of the Supreme Court of Georgia affords additional assurance that the concerns that prompted our decision in *Furman* are not present to any significant degree in the Georgia procedure applied here.

For the reasons expressed in this opinion, we hold that the statutory system under which Gregg was sentenced to death does not violate the Constitution. Accordingly, the judgment of the Georgia Supreme Court is affirmed. . . .

ERNEST VAN DEN HAAG

from *The Death Penalty Debate*

Ernest van den Haag is Professor of Jurisprudence and Public Policy at Fordham University. (Source: Excerpts from Ernest van den Haag and Joseph P. Conrad, The Death Penalty: A Debate, *Plenum Press, 1983. Copyright © 1983 by Plenum Publishing Corporation.)*

QUESTIONS FOR REFLECTION

1. Van den Haag argues that we should accept the deterrent value of the death penalty, despite the inconclusive results of most statistical studies. What are his arguments?

2. In what special circumstances, according to van den Haag, is capital punishment justified, even if it is unacceptable in most cases? Do you agree?

3. Why, in van den Haag's view, is the death penalty compatible with human dignity?

CHAPTER 4 / MORE ON THE DETERRENT EFFECT OF THE DEATH PENALTY

If it is difficult, perhaps impossible, to prove statistically—and just as hard to disprove—that the death penalty deters more from capital crimes than available alternative punishments do (such as life imprisonment), why do so many people believe so firmly that the death penalty is a more effective deterrent?

Some are persuaded by irrelevant arguments. They insist that the death penalty at least makes sure that the person who suffered it will not commit other crimes. True. Yet this confuses incapacitation with a specific way to bring it about: death. Death is the surest way to bring about the most total incapacitation, and it is irrevocable. But does incapacitation need to be that total? And is irrevocability necessarily an advantage? Obviously it makes correcting mistakes and rehabilitation impossible. What is the advantage of execution, then, over alternative ways of achieving the desired incapacitation?

More important, the argument for incapacitation confuses the elimination of one murderer (or of any number of murderers) with a reduction in the homicide rate. But the elimination of any specific number of actual or even of potential murderers—and there is some doubt that the actual murderers of the past are the most likely future (potential) murderers—will not affect the homicide rate, except through deterrence. There are enough potential murderers around to replace all those incapacitated. Deterrence may prevent the potential from becoming actual murderers. But incapacitation of some or all actual murderers is not likely to have much effect by itself. Let us then return to the question: Does capital punishment deter more than life imprisonment?

Science, logic, or statistics often have been unable to prove what common sense tells us to be true. Thus, the Greek philosopher Zeno some 2000 years ago found that he could not show that motion is possible; indeed, his famous paradoxes appear to show that motion is impossible. Though nobody believed them to be true, nobody succeeded in showing the fallacy of these paradoxes until the rise of mathematical logic less than a hundred years ago. But meanwhile, the world did not stand still. Indeed, nobody argued that motion should stop because it had not been shown to be logically possible. There is no more reason to abolish the death penalty than there was to abolish motion simply because the death penalty has not been, and perhaps cannot be, shown statistically to be a deterrent over and above other penalties. Indeed, there are two quite satisfactory, if nonstatistical, indications of the marginal deterrent effect of the death penalty.

In the first place, our experience shows that the greater the threatened penalty, the more it deters. *Ceteris paribus,* the threat of 50 lashes, deters more than the threat of 5; a $1000 fine deters more than a $10 fine; 10 years in prison deter more than 1 year in prison—just as, conversely, the promise of a $1000 reward is a greater incentive than the promise of a $10 reward, etc. There may be diminishing returns. Once a reward exceeds, say, $1 million, the additional attraction may diminish. Once a punishment exceeds, say, 10 years in prison (net of parole), there may be little additional deterrence in threatening additional years. We know hardly anything about diminishing returns of penalties. It would still seem likely, however, that the threat of life in prison deters more than any other term of imprisonment.

The threat of death may deter still more. For it is a mistake to regard the death penalty as though it were of the same kind as other penalties. If it is not, then diminishing returns are unlikely to apply. And death differs significantly, in kind, from any other penalty. Life in prison is still life, however unpleasant. In contrast, the death penalty does not just threaten to make life unpleasant—it threatens to take life altogether. This difference is perceived by those affected. We find that when they have the choice between life in prison and execution, 99% of all prisoners under sentence of death prefer life in prison. By means of appeals, pleas for commutation, indeed by all means at their disposal, they indicate that they prefer life in prison to execution.

From this unquestioned fact a reasonable conclusion can be drawn in favor of the superior deterrent effect of the death penalty. Those who have the choice in practice, those whose choice has actual and immediate effects on their life and death, fear death more than they fear life in prison or any other available penalty. If they do, it follows that the threat of the death penalty, all other things equal, is likely to deter more than the threat of life in prison. One is most deterred by what one fears most. From which it follows that whatever statistics fail, or do not fail, to show, the death penalty is likely to be more deterrent than any other.

Suppose now one is not fully convinced of the superior deterrent effect of the death penalty. I believe I can show that even if one is genuinely uncertain as to whether the death penalty adds to deterrence, one should still favor it, from a purely deterrent viewpoint. For if we are not sure, we must choose either to (1) trade the certain death, by execution, of a convicted murderer for the probable survival of an indefinite number of murder victims whose future murder is less likely (whose survival is more likely)—if the convicted murderer's execution deters prospective murderers, as it might, or to (2) trade the certain survival of the convicted murderer for the probable loss of the lives of future murder victims more likely to be murdered because the convicted murderer's nonexecution might not deter prospective murderers, who could have been deterred by executing the convicted murderer.

To restate the matter: If we were quite ignorant about the marginal deterrent effects of execution, we would have to choose—like it or not—between the certainty of the convicted murderer's death by execution and the likelihood of the survival of future victims of other murderers on the one hand, and on the other his certain survival and the likelihood of the death of new victims. I'd rather execute a man convicted of having murdered others than to put the lives of innocents at risk. I find it hard to understand the opposite choice.

However, I doubt that those who insist that the death penalty has not been demonstrated to be more deterrent than other penalties really believe that it is not. Or that it matters. I am fairly certain that the deterrent effect of the death penalty, or its absence, is not actually important to them. Rather, I think, they use the lack of statistical demonstration of a marginal deterrent effect to rationalize an opposition to the death penalty that has nonrational sources yet to be examined. In fact, although they use the alleged inconclusiveness of statistical demonstrations of deterrence as an argument to dissuade others from the death penalty, it can be shown that most abolitionists are not quite serious about the relevance of their own argument from insufficient deterrence.

In numerous discussions I have asked those who oppose capital punishment because, in their opinion, it will not deter capital crimes enough, whether they would favor the death penalty if it could be shown to deter more than life imprisonment does. My question usually led to some embarrassment and to attempts to dodge it by saying that additional deterrence has not been shown. However, when I persisted, conceding as much but asking abolitionists to give a hypothetical answer to a hypothetical question, they would admit that they would continue to oppose the death penalty—even if it were shown to deter more than life imprisonment. Which is to say that the argument based on the alleged lack of superior deterrence is factitious.

At times I have pursued the question. I would ask: "Suppose it were shown that every time we execute a person convicted of murder, ten fewer homicides are committed annually than were otherwise expected —would you still favor abolition?" The answer has been "yes" in all cases I can recall. I would persist: "Suppose every time we execute a convicted murderer, 500 fewer persons are murdered than otherwise would be expected to be murdered; suppose that, by executing the convicted murderer, we so much more deter others, who are not deterred by the threat of life imprisonment, that 500 victims will be spared?" After some hesitation, such staunch abolitionists as Professor Hugo Adam Bedau (Tufts University); Ramsey Clark, attorney general of the United States under President Johnson; Professor Charles Black (Yale); and Mr. Henry Schwarzchild, capital punishment project director of the American Civil Liberties Union, admitted that if they had the choice, they would rather see 500 innocents murdered than execute one convict found guilty of murder. This leads me to doubt the sincerity of abolitionist arguments based on the alleged lack of significant additional deterrent effect of capital punishment.

I also wonder why anyone would hold more precious the life of a convicted murderer than that of 500 innocents, if by executing him he could save them. . . .

CHAPTER 10 / SPECIAL CASES

There are some special cases—special because the threat of the death penalty is the only threat that may deter the crime. We do not know that it will. We do know that in these cases no other threat can.

Unless threatened with the death penalty, prisoners serving life sentences without parole can murder fellow prisoners or guards with impunity. Without the death penalty we give effective immunity, we promise impunity, to just those persons who are most likely to need deterrent threats if they are to be restrained. From a moral viewpoint one may add that if a prisoner already convicted of a crime sufficient to send him to prison for life commits a murder, the death penalty seems likely to be well deserved. At any rate, without the death penalty his fellow prisoners and the correctional officers can and will be victimized with impunity should he decide to murder them. To avoid threatening the convict with the only punishment available to restrain him, their lives are put at risk. This seems hard to justify.

The matter is all too well illustrated by the following:

> Two hard-case inmates apparently wangled their way into the warden's offices and stabbed the warden and his deputy to death with sharpened mess-hall knives.
>
> . . . investigators said that the death mission had been specifically ordered the night before at a meeting of Muslim inmates because Fromhold had resisted their demands "once too often." Fromhold was stabbed thirteen times in the back and chest; Warden Patrick Curran, 47, who dashed into his deputy's first-floor office, was stabbed three times in the back.
>
> Neither inmate had much to lose. Burton was doing life in the cold-blooded execution of a Philadelphia police sergeant, and Bowen was awaiting trial in another cop-killing and the shooting of an elderly couple.*

I can think of no reason for giving permanent immunity to homicidal life prisoners, thereby victimizing guards and other prisoners.

Outside prison, too, the threat of the death penalty is the only threat that is likely to restrain some

* *Newsweek*, 11 June 1973.

criminals. Without the death penalty an offender having committed a crime that leads to imprisonment for life has nothing to lose if he murders the arresting officer. By murdering the officer or, for that matter, witnesses to their crimes, such criminals increase their chances of escape, without increasing the severity of the punishment they will suffer if caught. This is the case for all criminals likely to be given life imprisonment if caught who commit an additional crime such as murdering the arresting officer. Only the death penalty could rationally restrain them.

In some states the death penalty is threatened to those who murder a police officer in the performance of his duties. Thus, special protection is extended to police officers, who, after all, are specially exposed. They deserve that extra protection. But it seems to me that everyone deserves the protection against murder that the death penalty can provide.

There are still other cases in which the death penalty alone is likely to be perceived as the threat that may deter from the crime. Thus, there is little point in imprisoning a spy in wartime: He expects his side to win, to be liberated by it, and to become a hero. On the other hand, if he had to fear immediate execution, the victory of his side would help the spy little. This may deter some people from becoming spies. It may not deter the man who does not mind becoming a patriotic martyr, but it may deter a man who does his spying for money.

A deserter, too, afraid of the risk of death on the battlefield, afraid enough to desert, is not going to be restrained by the threat of a prison sentence. But he may be afraid of certain death by firing squad. So may be anyone who deserts for any reason whatsoever.

Even the death penalty cannot restrain certain crimes. Once a man has committed a first murder for which, if convicted, he would be punished by execution, he can commit additional murders without fear of additional punishment. The range of punishments is limited. The range of crimes is not. The death penalty is the most severe punishment we can impose. It is reserved for the most serious crimes. But we can add nothing for still more serious crimes such as multiple murders or torture murders.

Unlike death, which we will all experience, torture is repulsive to us. Thus, we will not apply it

even to those who richly deserve it. It is, moreover, most unlikely that anyone not deterred by death would be deterred by torture or that death with torture would be more deterrent than death without. Thus, there is little point in trying to extend the range of punishment upward, beyond death.

Unfortunately, criminals can and sometimes do torture victims. They also can and sometimes do murder more than one person. The law cannot threaten more than death. But at least it should not threaten less. Although the threat of the death penalty may not restrain the second murder, it may restrain the first. . . .

CHAPTER 16 / THE ADVOCATE ADVOCATES

There are two basic arguments for the death penalty; they are independent of, yet consistent with, one another.

The first argument is moral: The death penalty is just; it is deserved for certain crimes. One can explain why one feels that certain crimes deserve the death penalty. But as usual with moral arguments, one cannot show this conviction to be *factually* correct (or, for that matter, incorrect) since moral arguments rest not on facts but on our evaluation of them. My evaluation leads me to believe that, e.g., premeditated murder or treason (a fact) is so grave and horrible a crime (an evaluation) as to deserve nothing less than the death penalty, that only the death penalty (a fact) is proportionate to the gravity of the crime (an evaluation).

My widely shared view is opposed by abolitionists, who claim that the death penalty is unjust for any crime, and inconsistent with human dignity. . . . Since most abolitionists believe, as I do, that punishments should be proportionate to the perceived gravity of crimes, the abolitionist claim seems to me logically precarious. It implies either that murder is not so horrible after all—not horrible enough, at any rate, to deserve death—or that the death penalty is too harsh a punishment for it, and indeed for any conceivable crime. I find it hard to believe that one can hold either view seriously, let alone both. . . .

I must confess that I have never understood the assorted arguments claiming that the death penalty is inconsistent with human dignity or that, somehow, society has no right to impose it. One might as well claim that death generally, or at least death from illness, is inconsistent with human dignity, or that birth is, or any suffering or any undesirable social condition. Most of these are unavoidable. At least death by execution can be avoided by not killing someone else, by not committing murder. One can preserve one's dignity in this respect if one values it. Incidentally, execution may be physically less humiliating and painful than death in a hospital. It is, however, morally more humiliating and meant to be: It indicates the extreme blame we attach to the crime of murder by deliberately expelling the murderer from among the living.

As for the dignity of society, it seems to me that by executing murderers it tries to keep its promise to secure the lives of innocents, to vindicate the law, and to impose retribution on those who so horribly violate it. To do anything less would be inconsistent with the dignity of society.

I see no evidence for society somehow not having "the right" to execute murderers. It has always done so. Traditional laws and Scriptures have always supported the death penalty. I know of no reasoning, even in a religious (theocratic) state, that denies the right of secular courts to impose it. We in America have a secular republic, of course, and therefore, the suggestion that the right to punish belongs only to God, or that the right to impose capital punishment does, is clearly out of place. It is not a religious but a secular task to put murderers to death. Our Constitution does provide for it (Amendments V and XIV). However much we believe in divine justice, it is to occur after, not in, this life. As for justice here and now, it is done by the courts, which are authorized in certain cases to impose the death penalty. A secular state cannot leave it to God. And incidentally, no theocratic state ever has. If they make mistakes, one can hope that God will correct the courts hereafter—but this is no ground for depriving courts of their duty to impose the penalties provided by law where required, nor is it a ground for depriving the law of the ability to prescribe the punishments felt to be just, including the death penalty.

The second argument in favor of capital punish-

ment is material, grounded on empirical facts. They are contested, as readers of this book know, but no one would deny that what is contested are facts. The factual question is: Does the death penalty deter murder more than life imprisonment, or does it make no difference? . . .

Statistics have their place. But here I think they scarcely are needed. Harsher penalties are more deterrent than milder ones. Not only does our whole criminal justice system accept this view; we all do to the extent to which deterrence is aimed at in our everyday life. All other things equal, we penalize our children, our friends, or our business partners the more harshly the more we feel we must deter them and others in the future from a wrong they have done. Social life would not be possible if we did not believe that we can attract people to actions we desire by giving them incentives, and deter them from actions we do not desire by disincentives. The incentives and disincentives are usually proportionate to the felt desirability or undesirability of what we want to attract to or deter from. Why should murder be an exception? Why should we not believe that the greatest disincentive—the threat of death—is most likely to be the greatest deterrent?

Where there is life there is hope. This certainly is one major argument in favor of the death penalty. The murderer who premeditates his crime—and crimes of passion are not subject to capital punishment—if he contemplates the risk of life imprisonment is not likely to believe that, if convicted, he will remain in prison for life. He knows, however inchoately, about parole, pardons, commutations—he believes above all that he, a smart and superior fellow, will find a way to escape. Few prisoners actually do escape. But practically all "lifers" believe that they will, at least when they start their sentence. So believing, they do not greatly fear a sentence of life imprisonment and are not deterred by it. This is why the rate of stranger-murders—murders in which victim and murderer do not know one another and to which the threat of the death penalty should apply—as a proportion of all murders has steadily climbed in the last twenty years. The murderers knew that in practice they would get away with life imprisonment, from which they would be paroled after a few years. Or they hoped they would escape. After all, we executed all of five prisoners in 1981, only one of whom was executed against his wishes. (All of them were white, to the great disappointment of the civil liberties lobby.) At this rate no murderer can foresee execution or be deterred by it.

I find it hard to believe . . . that most men are incapable of murder. . . . I am optimistic, however, in my own way, which seems more realistic to me: I believe that most men can be deterred from murder by the threat of the death penalty.

Even if . . . only a few men would ever become murderers in the absence of the threat of punishment were correct, I should continue to advocate the death penalty to deter these few men. And even if only some of these men need the threat of capital punishment to be deterred, while others would be deterred by the threat of life imprisonment, I should advocate the death penalty to deter the very few who . . . do, or even just may, require it to be deterred. The lives of the innocents that will or may be spared because of the death penalty are more valuable to me, and to any civilized society, than the lives of murderers. I do not want to risk their lives for the sake of the lives of murderers.

The reader will have to decide for himself on which side he wants to be.

HUGO BEDAU

How to Argue About the Death Penalty

Hugo Adam Bedau is Justin B. Fletcher Professor of Philosophy at Tufts University. (Source: Reprinted from Hugo Adam Bedau [ed.], The Death Penalty in America. *Copyright © 1982 by Oxford University Press, Inc.)*

QUESTIONS FOR REFLECTION

1. What, in Bedau's view, are the legitimate social goals of capital punishment? Why does Bedau hold that it is an inefficient way of achieving these goals?

2. What are the moral principles on which Bedau bases his opposition to the death penalty? Do you accept these principles? How does he argue from them to the unacceptability of the death penalty?

I

Argument over the death penalty—especially in the United States during the past generation—has been concentrated in large part on trying to answer various disputed *questions of fact*. Among them two have been salient: Is the death penalty a better deterrent to crime (especially murder) than the alternative of imprisonment? Is the death penalty administered in a discriminatory way, and, in particular, are black or other nonwhite offenders (or offenders whose victims are white) more likely to be tried, convicted, sentenced to death, and executed than whites (or offenders whose victims are nonwhite)? Other questions of fact have also been explored, including these two: What is the risk that an innocent person could actually be executed for a crime he did not commit? What is the risk that a person convicted of a capital felony but not executed will commit another capital felony?

Varying degrees of effort have been expended in trying to answer these questions. Although I think the current answers are capable of further refinement, I also think anyone who studies the evidence today must conclude that the best current answers to these four questions are as follows. (1) There is little or no evidence that the death penalty is a better deterrent to murder than is imprisonment; on the contrary, most evidence shows that these two punishments are about equally (in)effective as deterrents to murder. Furthermore, as long as the death penalty continues to be used relatively rarely, there is no prospect of gaining more decisive evidence on the question. (2) There is evidence that the death penalty has been and continues to be administered, whether intentionally or not, in a manner that produces arbitrary and racially discriminatory results in death sentencing. At the very least, this is true in those jurisdictions where the question has been investigated in recent years. (3) It is impossible to calculate the risk that an innocent person will be executed, but the risk is not zero, as the record of convicted, sentenced, and executed innocents shows. (4) Recidivism data show that some murderers have killed after a conviction and prison sentence for murder; so there is a risk that others will do so as well.

Let us assume that my summary of the results of research on these four questions is correct, and that further research will not significantly change these answers. The first thing to notice is that even if everyone agreed on these answers, this would not by itself settle the dispute over whether to keep, expand, reduce, or abolish the death penalty. Knowing these empirical truths about the administration and effects of the death penalty in our society does not entail knowing whether one should support its retention or abolition. This would still be true even if we knew with finality the answers to *all* the factual questions that can be asked about it.

There are two reasons for this. The facts as they currently stand and as seen from the abolitionist perspective do not point strongly and overwhelmingly to the futility of the death penalty or to the harm it does, at least as long as it continues to be used only in the limited and restricted form of the past decade: confined to the crime of murder, with trial courts empowered to exercise "guided discretion" in sentencing, with defense counsel able to introduce anything as mitigating evidence, and with automatic review of both conviction and sentence by some appellate court. Nor do the facts show that the alternative of life imprisonment is on balance a noticeably superior punishment. For example, the evidence of racial discrimination in the administration of the death penalty, while incontestable, may be no worse than the racial discrimination that occurs where lesser crimes and punishments are concerned. No one who has studied the data thinks that the administration of justice for murder approaches the level of racial discrimination reached a generation ago in the South by the administration of justice for rape. Besides, it is always possible to argue that such discrimination is diminishing, or will diminish over time, and that, in any case, since the fault does not lie in the capital statutes themselves—they are color-blind on their face—the remedy does not lie in repealing them.

But the marginal impact of the empirical evidence is not the major factor in explaining why settling disputes over matters of fact does not and cannot settle the larger controversy over the death penalty itself. As a matter of sheer logic, it is not possible to deduce a policy conclusion (such as the desirability of abolishing the death penalty) from any set of factual premises, however general and well supported. Any argument intended to recommend continuing or reforming current policy on the death penalty must include among its premises one or more normative propositions. Unless disputants over the death penalty can agree about these normative propositions, their agreement on the general facts will never suffice to resolve their dispute.

II

Accordingly, the course of wisdom for those interested in arguing about the death penalty is to focus attention on the normative propositions crucial to the dispute, in the hope that some headway may be made in narrowing disagreement over their number, content, and weight.

If this is to be done effectively, the context of these norms in general political ideology needs to be fixed. Suffice it to say here that I proceed from within the context of liberal pluralistic constitutional democracy and the conception of punishment appropriate therein.

Logically prior to the idea of punishment is the idea of a crime. What counts as a criminal harm depends in part on our conception of persons as bearers of rights deserving respect and protection. In this setting, liability to punishment and its actual infliction serve the complex function of reinforcing compliance with a set of laws deemed necessary to protect the fundamental equal rights of all members of society. The normative propositions relevant to the death penalty controversy are interwoven with the basic purposes and principles of liberal society, including the recognition and protection of individual rights to life and liberty, and to security of person and property.

These norms can be divided into two groups: those that express relevant and desirable *social goals* or *purposes,* and those that express relevant and respectable *moral principles.* Punishment is thus a practice or institution defined through various policies—such as the death penalty for murder—and intended to be the means or instrument whereby certain social goals are achieved within the constraints imposed by acknowledged moral principles.

Reduction of crime, or at least prevention of an increase in crime, is an example of such a goal. This goal influences the choice of punishments because of their impact (hypothesized or verified) on the crime rate. No one, except for purists of a retributive stripe, would dissent from the view that this goal is relevant to the death penalty controversy. Because of its relevance, there is continuing interest in the outcome of research on the differential deterrent efficacy of death versus imprisonment. The only questions normally in dispute are what that research shows (I have summarized it above) and how important this goal is (some regard it as decisive).

Similarly, that no one should be convicted and sentenced to death without a fair trial (i.e., in violation of "due process of law") is a principle of law and morality generally respected. Its general acceptance explains the considerable reformation in the laws governing the death penalty in the United States that have been introduced since 1972 by the Supreme Court. The Court argued that capital trials and death sentencing were in practice unfair (in constitutional jargon, they were in violation of the Eighth and Fourteenth Amendments, which bar "cruel and un-usual punishments" and require "equal protection of the laws," respectively). State legislatures and thoughtful observers agreed. Here again the only questions concern how important it is to comply with this principle (some regard it as decisive) and the extent to which the death penalty currently violates it (I have remarked on this point above, too).

The chief use of a moral principle in the present setting is to constrain the methods used in pursuit of policy (as when respect for "due process" rules out curbstone justice as a tactic in crime fighting). However, identifying the relevant goals, acknowl-edging the force of the relevant principles, and agreeing on the relevant general facts will still not suffice to resolve the dispute. The relative impor-tance of achieving a given goal and the relative weight of a given principle remain to be settled, and disagreement over these matters is likely to show up in disagreement over the justification of the death penalty itself.

If this is a correct sketch of the structural char-acter of debate and disagreement over the death penalty, then (as I noted earlier) the best hope for progress may lie in looking more carefully at the nonfactual normative ingredients so far isolated in the dispute. Ideally, we would identify and evaluate the policy goals relevant to punishment generally, as

well as the moral principles that constrain the struc-ture and content of the penalty schedule. We would also settle the proper relative weights to attach to these goals and constraints, if not in general, then at least for their application in the present context. Then, with whatever relevant general facts are at our disposal, we would be in a position to draw the appropriate inferences and resolve the entire dis-pute, confident that we have examined and duly weighed everything that reason and morality can bring to bear on the problem.

As an abstract matter, therefore, the question is whether the set of relevant policies and principles, taken in conjunction with the relevant facts, favors reduction (even complete abolition) of the death penalty, or whether it favors retention (or even extension) of the death penalty. Lurking in the back-ground, of course, is the troubling possibility that the relevant norms and facts underdetermine the resolution of the dispute. But let us not worry about sharks on dry land, not yet.

III

Where choice of punishments is concerned, the relevant social goals, I suggest, are few. Two in partic-ular generally commend themselves:

(G 1) Punishment should contribute to the reduc-tion of crime; accordingly, the punishment for a crime should not be so idle a threat or so slight a deprivation that it has no deterrent or incapacitative effects; and it certainly should not contribute to an increase in crime.

(G 2) Punishments should be "economical"—they should not waste valuable social resources in futile or unnecessarily costly endeavors.

The instrumental character of these purposes and goals is evident. They reflect the fact that society does not institute and maintain the practice of punishment for its own sake, as though it were a good in itself. Rather, punishment is and is seen to be a means to an end or ends. The justification of a society's punitive policies and practices must there-fore involve two steps: first, it must be shown that these ends are desirable; second, it must be shown that the practice of punishment is the best means to these ends. What is true of the justification of punishment generally is true a fortiori of justifying the death penalty.

Endorsement of these two policy goals tends to encourage support for the death penalty. Opponents of capital punishment need not reject these goals, however, and its defenders cannot argue that accepting these goals vindicates their preferred policy. Traditionally, it is true, the death penalty has often been supported on the ground that it provides the best social defense and is extremely cheap to administer. But since the time of Beccaria and Bentham, these empirical claims have been challenged, and rightly so. If support for the death penalty today in a country such as the United States rests on the high priority placed on these goals, then there is much (some would say compelling) evidence to undermine this support. The most that can be said solely by reference to these goals is that recognition of their importance can always be counted on to kindle interest in capital punishment, and to that extent put its opponents on the defensive.

Whether punishment is intended to serve only the two goals so far identified is disputable. An argument can be made that there are two or three further goals:

(G 3) Punishment should rectify the harm and injustice caused by crime.

(G 4) Punishment should serve as a recognized channel for the release of public indignation and anger at the offender.

(G 5) Punishment should make convicted offenders into better persons rather than leave them as they are or make them worse.

Obviously, anyone who accepts the fifth goal must reject the death penalty. I shall not try here to argue the merits of this goal, either in itself or relative to the other goals of punishment. Whatever its merits, this goal is less widely sought than the others, and for that reason alone is less useful in trying to develop rational agreement over the death penalty. Its persuasive power for those not already persuaded against the death penalty on other grounds is likely to be slight to zero. Although I am unwilling

to strike it from the list of goals that punishment in general is and should be practiced to achieve, it would be unreasonable to stress its pre-eminence in the present context.

The proposed third goal is open to the objection that rectification of injustice is not really a goal of punishment, even if it is a desirable goal in other settings. (Indeed, it is widely believed that rectification is not a goal of punishment but of noncriminal tort judgments.) But even if it is a goal of punishment generally, it seems irrelevant to the death penalty controversy, because neither death nor imprisonment (as practiced in the United States) rectifies anything. Nonetheless, this goal may be indirectly important for the death penalty controversy. To the extent that one believes punishments ought to serve this goal, and that there is no possible way to rectify the crime of murder, one may come to believe that the fourth goal is of even greater importance than would otherwise be the case. Indeed, striving to achieve this fourth goal and embracing the death penalty as a consequence is quite parallel to striving to achieve the fifth goal and consequently embracing its abolition.

Does this fourth goal have a greater claim on our support than I have allowed is true of the fifth goal, so obviously incompatible with it? Many would say that it does. Some would even argue that it is this goal, not any of the others, that is the paramount purpose of punishment under law. Whatever else punishment does, its threat and infliction are to be seen as the expression of social indignation at deliberate harm to the innocent. Preserving a socially acceptable vehicle for the expression of anger at offenders is absolutely crucial to the health of a just society.

There are in principle three ways to respond to this claim insofar as it is part of an argument for capital punishment. One is to reject it out of hand as a false proposition from start to finish. A second is to concede that the goal of providing a visible and acceptable channel for the emotion of anger is legitimate, but to argue that this goal could at best justify the death penalty only in a very small number of cases (the occasional Adolf Eichmann, for example), since otherwise its importance would be vastly exaggerated. A third response is to concede both the legitimacy and the relative importance of this goal, but to point out that its pursuit, like that of all other goals, is nonetheless constrained by moral principles (yet to be examined), and that once these principles are properly employed, the death penalty ceases to be a permissible method of achieving this goal. I think both the second and third objections are sound, and a few further words here about each are appropriate.

First of all, anger is not the same as resentment or indignation, since the latter feeling or emotion can be aroused only through the perceived violation of some moral principle, whereas the former does not have this constraint. But whether the feeling aroused by a horrible murder is really only anger rather than indignation is just the question whether the principles of morality have been violated or not. Knowing that the accused offender has no legal excuse or justification for his criminal conduct is not enough to warrant the inference that he and his conduct are appropriate objects of our unqualified moral hostility. More about the context of the offense and its causation must be supplied; it may well be that in ordinary criminal cases one rarely or never knows enough to reach such a condemnatory judgment with confidence. Even were this not so, one has no reason to suppose that justified anger at offenders is of overriding importance, and that all countervailing considerations must yield to its pre-eminence. For one thing, the righteous anger needed for that role is simply not available in a pluralistic secular society. Even if it were, we have been assured from biblical times that it passes all too easily into self-righteous and hypocritical repression by some sinners or others.

Quite apart from such objections, there is a certain anomaly, even irony, in the defense of the death penalty by appeal to this goal. On the one hand, we are told of the importance of a publicly recognized ritual for extermination of convicted murderers as a necessary vent for otherwise unchanneled disruptive public emotions. On the other hand, our society scrupulously rejects time-honored methods of execution that truly do express hatred and anger at offenders: beheading, crucifixion, dismemberment, and even hanging and the electric chair are disappearing. Execution by lethal injection, increasingly the popular option, hardly seems appropriate as the outlet of

choice for such allegedly volatile energies! And is it not ironic that this technique, invented to facilitate life-saving surgery, now turns out to be the preferred channel for the expression of moral indignation?

IV

If the purposes or goals of punishment lend a utilitarian quality to the practice of punishment, the moral principles relevant to the death penalty operate as deontological constraints on their pursuit. Stating all and only the principles relevant to the death penalty controversy is not easy, and the list that follows is no more than the latest approximation to the task. . . . With some overlap here and there, these principles are six:

(P 1) No one should deliberately and intentionally take another's life where there is a feasible alternative.

(P 2) The more severe a penalty is, the more important it is that it be imposed only on those who truly deserve it.

(P 3) The more severe a penalty is, the weightier the justification required to warrant its imposition on anyone.

(P 4) Whatever the criminal offense, the accused and convicted offender does not forfeit all his rights and dignity as a person. Accordingly, there is an upper limit to the severity—cruelty, destructiveness, finality—of permissible punishments, regardless of the offense.

(P 5) Fairness requires that punishments should be graded in their severity according to the gravity of the offense.

(P 6) If human lives are to be risked, the risk should fall more heavily on wrong-doers (the guilty) than on others (the innocent).

I cannot argue here for all these principles, but they really need no argument from me. Each is recognized implicitly or explicitly in our practice; each can be seen to constrain our conduct as individuals and as officers in democratic institutions. Outright repudiation or cynical disregard of any of these principles would disqualify one from engaging in serious discourse and debate over punishment in a liberal society. All can be seen as corollaries or theorems of the general proposition that life, limb, and security of person—of *all* persons—are of paramount value. Thus, only minimal interference (in the jargon of the law, "the least restrictive means") is warranted with anyone's life, limb, and security in order to protect the rights of others.

How do these principles direct or advise us in regard to the permissibility or desirability of the death penalty? The first thing to note is that evidently none directly rules it out. I know of no moral principle that is both sufficiently rigid and sufficiently well established for us to point to it and say: "The practice of capital punishment is flatly contradictory to the requirements of this moral principle." (Of course, we could invent a principle that would have this consequence, but that is hardly to the point.) This should not be surprising; few if any of the critics or the defenders of the death penalty have supposed otherwise. Second, several of these principles do reflect the heavy burden that properly falls on anyone who advocates that certain human beings be deliberately killed by others, when those to be killed are not at the time a danger to anyone. For example, whereas the first principle may permit lethal force in self-defense, it directly counsels against the death penalty in *all* cases without exception. The second and third principles emphasize the importance of "due process" and "equal protection" as the finality and incompensability of punishments increase. The fourth principle draws attention to the nature and value of persons, even those convicted of terrible crimes. It reminds us that even if crimes know no upper limit in their wantonness, cruelty, destructiveness, and horror, punishments under law in a civilized society cannot imitate crimes in this regard. Punishment does operate under limits, and these limits are not arbitrary.

The final two principles, however, seem to be exceptions to the generalization that the principles as a group tend to favor punishments other than death. The fifth principle seems to entail that if murder is the gravest crime, then it should receive the severest punishment. This does not, of course, *require* a society to invoke the death penalty for murder—unless one accepts *lex talionis* ("a life for a life, an eye for an eye") in a singularly literal-minded manner. Since *lex talionis* is not a sound principle on which to construct the penalty schedule generally, appealing to this interpretation of the fifth principle here simply begs the question. Nevertheless, the principle that punishments should be graded to fit the crime does encourage consideration of the death penalty, especially if it seems that there is no other way to punish murder with the utmost permissible severity.

Of rather more interest is the sixth principle. Some make it the cornerstone of their defense of the death penalty. They argue that it is better to execute all convicted murderers, lest on a future occasion any of them murder again, than it is to execute none of them, thereby averting the risk of executing any who may be innocent. A policy of complete abolition—at least in the United States today—would result in thousands of convicted killers (only a few of whom are innocent) being held behind bars for life. This cohort would constitute a permanent risk to the safety of many millions of innocent citizens. The sole gain to counterbalance this risk is the guarantee that no lives (innocent or guilty) will be lost through legal executions. The practice of executions thus protects far more innocent citizens than the same practice puts in jeopardy.

This argument is far less conclusive than it may at first seem. Even if we grant it full weight, it is simply unreasonable to use it (or any other argument) as a way of dismissing the relevance of principles that counsel a different result, or as a tactic to imply the subordinate importance of those other principles. If used in this manner, the sixth principle would be thoroughly transformed. It has become a disguised version of the first policy goal (viz., Reduce crime!) and in effect would elevate that goal to pre-eminence over every competing and constraining consideration. The argument also fosters the illusion that we can in fact reasonably estimate, if not actually calculate, the number of lives risked by a policy of abolition as opposed to a policy of capital punishment. This is false; we do not and cannot reasonably hope to know what the risk is of convicting the innocent, even if we could estimate the risk of recidivist murder. We therefore cannot really compare the two risks with any precision. Finally, the argument gains whatever strength it appears to have by tacitly ignoring the following dilemma. If the policy of killing the convicted in order to reduce risk to the innocent is to achieve maximum effect, then death must be the *mandatory* penalty for everyone convicted of murder (never mind other crimes). But such a policy cannot really be carried out. It flies in the face of two centuries of political reality, which demonstrates the impossibility of enforcing truly mandatory death penalties for murder and other crimes against the person. The only realistic policy alternative is some version of a *discretionary* death penalty. However, every version of this policy actually tried has proved vulnerable to criticism on grounds of inequity in its administration, as critic after critic has shown. Meanwhile, history tells us that our society is unable to avoid all risk of recidivist murder.

The upshot is that we today run both the risk of executing the innocent and the risk of recidivist murder, even though it is necessary to run only one of these risks.

V

What has our examination of the relevant goals and principles shown about the possibility of resolving the death penalty controversy on rational grounds? First, the death penalty is primarily a means to one or more ends or goals, but it is not the only (and arguably not the best) means to them. Second, several principles of relevance to sound punitive policy in general favor (although they do not demand) abolition of the death penalty. Third, there is no goal or principle that constitutes a conclusive reason favoring either side in the dispute. Unless, of course, some one goal or principle is interpreted or weighted in such a manner (cf. the fifth goal, or the fifth principle). But in that case, one side or the other will refuse to accept it. Finally, the several goals and principles of punishment that have been identified have no obvious rank order or relative weighting. As they stand, these goals and principles do indeed underdetermine the policy dispute over capital punishment. Perhaps such a ranking could be pro-

vided by some comprehensive socioethical theory. But the failure of every known such theory to secure general acceptance so far does not bode well for prompt and rational resolution of the controversy along these lines.

Despite the absence of any conclusive reasons or decisive ranking of principles, we may take refuge in the thought . . . that a preponderance of reasons does favor one side rather than the other. Such a preponderance emerges, however, only when the relevant goals and principles of punishment are seen in a certain light, or from a particular angle of vision. Perhaps this amounts to one rather than another weighting of goals and principles but without conscious reliance upon any manifest theory. In any case, I shall mention three such considerations that are important in my assessment of the moral objections to the death penalty.

The first and by far the most important concerns the role and function of power in the hands of government. It is in general preferable, *ceteris paribus,* that such power over individuals should shrink rather than expand. Where such power must be used, then let it be devoted to constructive rather than destructive purposes, thus enhancing the autonomy and liberty of those directly affected. But the death penalty contradicts this concern; it is government power used in a dramatically destructive manner upon individuals in the absence of any compelling social necessity. No wonder it is the ultimate symbol of such power.

Another consideration that shapes my interpretation of the goals and principles of evaluation is an orientation to the *future* rather than to the past. We cannot do anything for the dead victims of crime. (How many of those who oppose the death penalty would continue to do so if, *mirabile dictu,* executing the murderer brought the victim back to life?) But we can—or at least we can try to—do something for the living: we can protect the innocent, prevent illegitimate violence, and help those in despair over their own victimization. None of these constructive tasks involves punishing anyone for expressive, vindictive, or retributive reasons. The more we stress these factors in our choice of punishments, the more we orient our punitive policies toward the past—toward trying to use government power over the lives of a few as a socially approved instrument of moral bookkeeping.

Finally, the death penalty projects a false and misleading picture of man and society. Its professed message for those who support it is this: justice requires killing the convicted murderer. So we focus on the death that all murderers supposedly deserve and overlook our inability to give a rational account of why so few actually get it. Hence, the lesson taught by the practice of capital punishment is really quite different. Far from being a symbol of justice, it is a symbol of brutality and stupidity. Perhaps if we lived in a world of autonomous Kantian moral agents, where all the criminals freely expressed their rational will in the intention to kill others without their consent or desert, then death for the convicted murderer might be just (as even Karl Marx was inclined to think). But a closer look at the convicts who actually are on our death rows shows that these killers are a far cry from the rational agents of Kant's metaphysical imagination. We fool ourselves if we think a system of ideal retributive justice designed for such persons is the appropriate model for the penal system in our society.

Have I implicitly conceded that argument over the death penalty is irrational? If I am right that the death penalty controversy does not really turn on controversial social goals or controversial moral principles, any more than it does on disputed general facts, but instead turns on how all three are to be balanced or weighed, does it follow that reason alone cannot resolve the controversy, because reason alone cannot determine which weighting or balancing is the correct one? Or can reason resolve this problem, perhaps by appeal to further theory, theory that would deepen our appreciation of what truly underlies a commitment to liberal institutions and a belief in the possibilities for autonomy of all persons? I think it can—but this is the right place to end the present investigation because we have reached the launching platform for another one.

PART IV　**Justice**

Aristotle distinguishes several different senses of justice. He identifies one sense of justice with virtue as a whole, but specifically in relation to other people. Another sense of justice pertains to rectification—setting right previous wrongs. This section concerns distributive justice: the problem of distributing goods and obligations among the members of a society.

Aristotle holds a simple but extremely powerful theory of distributive justice. He believes that both goods and obligations ought to be distributed according to merit. He considers a group of people who have somehow obtained a flute. Who in the group should get the flute? The best flute player, Aristotle answers. Similarly, goods ought to go to those who deserve them—that is, those who can make the best use of them. This answer has very strong intuitive appeal. How should a professor assign grades? The top grades should go to those with the most merit, those who have performed best. Who should receive a Grammy award? Those who have produced the best music. Who should receive political power? Those who have the most political virtue, Aristotle answers—the people with the greatest ability to bring about good government.

Aristotle's theory is a *structural* theory of justice. It says that people should receive goods of a certain kind to the extent that they have merit of that kind. Thus, it answers the question of distributive justice in terms of who has what other characteristics now or at some other definite time. Jean-Jacques Rousseau, Karl Marx, Friedrich Engels, and John Rawls all propose very different theories of justice, but all are similarly structural; all specify who should get what in terms of who has what now or at some other time.

Rousseau's analysis of distributive justice is somewhat vague. He makes clear that no one should have too much and no one too little. Within the bounds this principle establishes, however, the general will rules. Recall that according to Rousseau's conception of the social contract, we would agree to form a government because we hope to gain from the cooperation it makes possible. We are willing to commit everything we have in the interests of cooperation and expect to receive in return our share of everything that anyone else has. Distribution, then, is in the hands of the community as a whole. Rousseau treats the community as a body with its own interests. He characterizes limits on the community's behavior in terms of the general will. Roughly, the community can legitimately do only what accords with the general will—that is, with the community's own self-interest. This seems to imply that a just distribution is one that accords with the interests of the community as a whole. What this distribution is, of course, is an empirical matter. But Rousseau feels confident enough to say that the multitude should not lack necessities and that the fortunate should not be able to pursue luxuries.

Marx and Engels take Rousseau's position to a more definite conclusion. They analyze social structures in terms of class struggle. They see moral language as little more than a tool in class struggle; consequently, they are reluctant to offer a general theory of justice. But Marx does provide a slogan that embodies such a theory: "From each according to his abilities, to each according to his needs!" This, too, is a structural theory. It determines who should receive what by considering who has what abilities and needs. Note that Marx's theory has something in common with Aristotle's; both agree that responsibilities are functions of ability. Aristotle, however, believes that rewards should also be proportionate to ability; Marx believes that they should go to those in need, regardless of merit or contribution.

John Rawls offers another development of Rousseau's approach. Imagine being in the state of nature, choosing whether or not to submit to a government. To determine principles of justice, Rawls says, we must imagine that we make the choice based not on any contingent features of our own characters, but on the basis of what we share with all other human beings. Rawls thus imagines us making the choice from behind the veil of ignorance, in which we know everything we need to know about economics, political science, sociology, and so on, but know nothing about our own position in the social structure. What principles, Rawls asks, would we choose from behind the veil of ignorance? What institutions would be rational choices? He concludes that we would choose to minimize risk and so opt for a system that would make the least well-off in society as well-off as possible; that is, we would choose to maximize the welfare of the least advantaged. We would not choose to maximize good overall, as a utilitarian would, for we would fear coming out a loser in the social order. We would not choose absolute equality, for we have no reason to object to inequality as long as it does not disadvantage us, no matter where we might end up in the resulting society. Rawls thus advocates two principles of justice. The first is a principle of liberty, that each person should have the most liberty compatible with an equal liberty for all. The second has two parts: (a) inequalities should be to everyone's advantage (that is, those who receive less would be even worse off if others weren't receiving more) and (b) the positions to which benefits attach should be open to everyone. Part (a) is often called the *difference principle;* part (b) is a principle of equal opportunity. The difference principle, by far, has stirred the most controversy concerning Rawls's theory.

Rawls's approach to distributive justice is also a structural theory. We determine whether a set of institutions is just by looking at the distribution they produce—not now, perhaps, but at some point in the future when the distribution stabilizes. John Locke and Robert Nozick offer a very different theory of justice. How do we determine whether people hold their possessions justly? Locke and Nozick deny that any sort of structural account can provide an answer. Do you, for example, possess this book justly? To answer that question, in their view, we need to ask, not about your abilities or your needs or your total wealth or whether your possession of the book benefits everyone, but about how you obtained it. Did you steal it? Did you buy it from someone who had the right to sell it? Locke takes property as a fundamental natural and civil right. The purpose of government, Locke insists, is to preserve property. Consequently, government cannot consider every good in society its own and reflect abstractly on how to distribute it. People acquire goods justly from nature. They buy and sell them justly. When an injustice occurs, they try to compensate for it. To determine whether a distribution is just, according to Locke and Nozick, we must see how it came about. Were the initial acquisitions just? Were subsequent transfers just? Were any injustices sufficiently rectified? If we can answer yes to these questions, then, Locke and Nozick believe, the distribution is just. Their theories are thus *historical* theories: whether a distribution is just depends on how it came about.

ARISTOTLE

from *Nicomachean Ethics*

(*Source: Reprinted from* Aristotle's Nichomachean Ethics, *translated by W. D. Ross [1925], by permission of Oxford University Press.*)

QUESTIONS FOR REFLECTION

1. What does Aristotle mean by his assertion that the unjust are "grasping"?

2. How does justice in the broadest sense relate to virtue?

3. What particular kinds of justice does Aristotle discuss? Explain each.

4. According to Aristotle's theory of distributive justice, the just is the proportional. What does this mean? What should be proportional to what?

Book V

1

. . . Now 'justice' and 'injustice' seem to be ambiguous, but because their different meanings approach near to one another the ambiguity escapes notice and is not obvious as it is, comparatively, when the meanings are far apart, e. g. (for here the difference in outward form is great) as the ambiguity in the use of *kleis* for the collar-bone of an animal and for that with which we lock a door. Let us take as a starting-point, then, the various meanings of 'an unjust man'. Both the lawless man and the grasping and unfair man are thought to be unjust, so that evidently both the law-abiding and the fair man will be just. The just, then, is the lawful and the fair, the unjust the unlawful and the unfair.

Since the unjust man is grasping, he must be concerned with goods—not all goods, but those with which prosperity and adversity have to do, which taken absolutely are always good, but for a particular person are not always good. Now men pray for and pursue these things; but they should not, but should pray that the things that are good absolutely may also be good for them, and should choose the things that *are* good for them. The unjust man does not always choose the greater, but also the less—in the case of things bad absolutely; but because the lesser evil is itself thought to be in a sense good, and graspingness is directed at the good, therefore he is thought to be grasping. And he is unfair; for this contains and is common to both.

Since the lawless man was seen to be unjust and the law-abiding man just, evidently all lawful acts are in a sense just acts; for the acts laid down by the legislative art are lawful, and each of these, we say, is just. Now the laws in their enactments on all subjects aim at the common advantage either of all or of the best or of those who hold power, or something of the sort; so that in one sense we call those acts just that tend to produce and preserve happiness and its components for the political society. And the law bids us do both the acts of a brave man (e. g. not to desert our post nor take to flight nor throw away our arms), and those of a temperate man (e. g. not to commit adultery nor to gratify one's lust), and those of a good-tempered man (e. g. not to strike another nor to speak evil), and similarly with regard to the other virtues and forms of wickedness, commanding some acts and forbidding others; and the rightly-framed law does this rightly, and the hastily conceived one less well.

This form of justice, then, is complete virtue, but not absolutely, but in relation to our neighbour. And therefore justice is often thought to be the greatest of virtues, and "neither evening nor morning star" is so wonderful; and proverbially "in justice is every virtue comprehended." And it is complete virtue in its fullest sense, because it is the actual exercise of complete virtue. It is complete because he who possesses it can exercise his virtue not only in himself but towards his neighbour also; for many men can exercise virtue in their own affairs, but not in their relations to their neighbour. This is why the saying of Bias is thought to be true, that "rule will show the man"; for a ruler is necessarily in relation to other men and a member of a society. For this same reason justice, alone of the virtues, is thought to be "another's good," because it is related to our neighbour; for it does what is advantageous to another, either a ruler or a copartner. Now the worst man is he who exercises his wickedness both towards himself and towards his friends, and the best man is not he who exercises his virtue towards himself but he who exercises it towards another; for this is a difficult task. Justice in this sense, then, is not part of virtue but virtue entire, nor is the contrary injustice a part of vice but vice entire. What the difference is between virtue and justice in this sense is plain from what we have said; they are the same but their essence is not the same; what, as a relation to one's neighbour, is justice is, as a certain kind of state without qualification, virtue.

2

But at all events what we are investigating is the justice which is a *part* of virtue; for there is a justice of this kind, as we maintain. Similarly it is with injustice in the particular sense that we are concerned.

That there is such a thing is indicated by the fact that while the man who exhibits in action the other forms of wickedness acts wrongly indeed, but not graspingly (e. g. the man who throws away his shield through cowardice or speaks harshly through bad temper or fails to help a friend with money through

meanness), when a man acts graspingly he often exhibits none of these vices—no, nor all together, but certainly wickedness of some kind (for we blame him) and injustice. There is, then, another kind of injustice which is a part of injustice in the wide sense, and a use of the word 'unjust' which answers to a part of what is unjust in the wide sense of "contrary to the law." Again, if one man commits adultery for the sake of gain and makes money by it, while another does so at the bidding of appetite though he loses money and is penalized for it, the latter would be held to be self-indulgent rather than grasping, but the former is unjust, but not self-indulgent; evidently, therefore, he is unjust by reason of his making gain by his act. Again, all other unjust acts are ascribed invariably to some particular kind of wickedness, e. g. adultery to self-indulgence, the desertion of a comrade in battle to cowardice, physical violence to anger; but if a man makes gain, his action is ascribed to no form of wickedness but injustice. Evidently, therefore, there is apart from injustice in the wide sense another, "particular," injustice which shares the name and nature of the first, because its definition falls within the same genus; for the significance of both consists in a relation to one's neighbour, but the one is concerned with honour or money or safety—or that which includes all these, if we had a single name for it—and its motive is the pleasure that arises from gain; while the other is concerned with all the objects with which the good man is concerned.

It is clear, then, that there is more than one kind of justice, and that there is one which is distinct from virtue entire; we must try to grasp its genus and differentia.

The unjust has been divided into the unlawful and the unfair, and the just into the lawful and the fair. To the unlawful answers the afore-mentioned sense of injustice. But since the unfair and the unlawful are not the same, but are different as a part is from its whole (for all that is unfair is unlawful, but not all that is unlawful is unfair), the unjust and injustice in the sense of the unfair are not the same as but different from the former kind, as part from whole; for injustice in this sense is a part of injustice in the wide sense, and similarly justice in the one sense of justice in the other. Therefore we must speak also about particular justice and particular injustice, and similarly about the just and the unjust. The justice, then, which answers to the whole of virtue, and the corresponding injustice, one being the exercise of virtue as a whole, and the other that of vice as a whole, towards one's neighbour, we may leave on one side. And how the meanings of 'just' and 'unjust' which answer to these are to be distinguished is evident; for practically the majority of the acts commanded by the law are those which are prescribed from the point of view of virtue taken as a whole; for the law bids us practise every virtue and forbids us to practise any vice. And the things that tend to produce virtue taken as a whole are those of the acts prescribed by the law which have been prescribed with a view to education for the common good. But with regard to the education of the individual as such, which makes him without qualification a good *man,* we must determine later whether this is the function of the political art or of another; for perhaps it is not the same to be a good man and a good citizen of any state taken at random.

Of particular justice and that which is just in the corresponding sense, (A) one kind is that which is manifested in distributions of honour or money or the other things that fall to be divided among those who have a share in the constitution (for in these it is possible for one man to have a share either unequal or equal to that of another), and (B) one is that which plays a rectifying part in transactions between man and man. Of this there are two divisions; of transactions (1) some are voluntary and (2) others involuntary—voluntary such transactions as sale, purchase, loan for consumption, pledging, loan for use, depositing, letting (they are called voluntary because the origin of these transactions is voluntary), while of the involuntary (a) some are clandestine, such as theft, adultery, poisoning, procuring, enticement of slaves, assassination, false witness, and (b) others are violent, such as assault, imprisonment, murder, robbery with violence, mutilation, abuse, insult.

3

(A) We have shown that both the unjust man and the unjust act are unfair or unequal; now it is clear that there is also an intermediate between the two unequals involved in either case. And this is the equal;

for in any kind of action in which there is a more and a less there is also what is equal. If, then, the unjust is unequal, the just is equal, as all men suppose it to be, even apart from argument. And since the equal is intermediate, the just will be an intermediate. Now equality implies at least two things. The just, then, must be both intermediate and equal and relative (i. e. for certain persons). And *qua* intermediate it must be between certain things (which are respectively greater and less); *qua* equal, it involves *two* things; *qua* just, it is for certain people. The just, therefore, involves at least four terms; for the persons for whom it is in fact just are two, and the things in which it is manifested, the objects distributed, are two. And the same equality will exist between the persons and between the things concerned; for as the latter—the things concerned—are related, so are the former; if they are not equal, they will not have what is equal, but this is the origin of quarrels and complaints—when either equals have and are awarded unequal shares, or unequals equal shares. Further, this is plain from the fact that awards should be 'according to merit'; for all men agree that what is just in distribution must be according to merit in some sense, though they do not all specify the same sort of merit, but democrats identify it with the status of freeman, supporters of oligarchy with wealth (or with noble birth), and supporters of aristocracy with excellence.

The just, then, is a species of the proportionate (proportion being not a property only of the kind of number which consists of abstract units, but of number in general). For proportion is equality of ratios, and involves four terms at least (that discrete proportion involves four terms is plain, but so does continuous proportion, for it uses one term as two and mentions it twice; e. g. "as the line A is to the line B, so is the line B to the line C"; the line B, then, has been mentioned twice, so that if the line B be assumed twice, the proportional terms will be four); and the just, too, involves at least four terms, and the ratio between one pair is the same as that between the other pair; for there is a similar distinction between the persons and between the things. As the term A, then, is to B, so will C be to D, and therefore, *alternando,* as A is to C, B will be to D. Therefore also the whole is in the same ratio to the whole; and this coupling the distribution effects, and, if the terms are so combined, effects justly. The conjuction, then, of the term A with C and of B with D is what is just in distribution, and this species of the just is intermediate, and the unjust is what violates the proportion; for the proportional is intermediate, and the just is proportional. (Mathematicians call this kind of proportion geometrical; for it is in geometrical proportion that it follows that the whole is to the whole as either part is to the corresponding part.) This proportion is not continuous; for we cannot get a single term standing for a person and a thing.

This, then, is what the just is—the proportional; the unjust is what violates the proportion. Hence one term becomes too great, the other too small, as indeed happens in practice; for the man who acts unjustly has too much, and the man who is unjustly treated too little, of what is good. In the case of evil the reverse is true; for the lesser evil is reckoned a good in comparison with the greater evil, since the lesser evil is rather to be chosen than the greater, and what is worthy of choice is good, and what is worthier of choice a greater good. . . .

JOHN LOCKE

from *Second Treatise of Government* (1690)

(*Source: Reprinted from John Locke,* Two Treatises of Government. *London: Printed for Awnsham Churchill, 1690.*)

QUESTIONS FOR REFLECTION

1. Locke takes the right to property as natural. Why? What allows me to appropriate things I find in nature? Are there limits to my right of appropriation?

2. What, for Locke, justifies allowing a person to appropriate more than he or she needs?

3. How does money affect principles of property, in Locke's view?

4. What, for Locke, is the chief end of government? How does it limit government action?

5. Why, according to Locke, is the minority bound to follow the majority's decision?

CHAPTER V / OF PROPERTY

§. 25. Whether we consider natural reason, which tells us that men, being once born, have a right to their preservation and consequently to meat and drink and such other things as nature affords for their subsistence, or revelation, which gives us an account of those grants God made of the world to Adam and to Noah and his sons, it is very clear that God, as king David says, Psal. cxv. 16. has given the earth to the children of men: given it to mankind in common. But this being supposed, it seems to some a very great difficulty how anyone should ever come to have a property in any thing: I will not content myself to answer that if it be difficult to make out property upon a supposition that God gave the world to Adam and his posterity in common, it is impossible that any man, but one universal monarch, should have any property upon a supposition that God gave the world to Adam and his heirs in succession, exclusive of all the rest of his posterity.

EDITOR'S NOTE: Spelling and punctuation have been modernized for clarity.

But I shall endeavour to show how men might come to have a property in several parts of that which God gave to mankind in common, and that without any express compact of all the commoners.

§. 26. God, who has given the world to men in common, has also given them reason to make use of it to the best advantage of life and convenience. The earth and all that is therein is given to men for the support and comfort of their being. And though all the fruits it naturally produces and beasts it feeds belong to mankind in common, as they are produced by the spontaneous hand of nature, and nobody has originally a private dominion exclusive of the rest of mankind, in any of them, as they are thus in their natural state; yet being given for the use of men, there must of necessity be a means to appropriate them some way or other before they can be of any use or at all beneficial to any particular man. The fruit or venison which nourishes the wild Indian, who knows no inclosure and is still a tenant in common, must be his, and so his, i.e. a part of him, that another can no longer have any right to it before it can do him any good for the support of his life.

§. 27. Though the earth and all inferior creatures be common to all men, yet every man has a property in his own person: this no body has any right to but himself. The labour of his body and the work of his hands, we may say, are properly his. Whatsoever then he removes out of the state that nature has provided, and left in it, he has mixed his labour with and joined to it something that is his own and thereby makes it his property. It being by him removed from the common state nature has placed it in, it has by this labour something annexed to it that excludes the common right of other men: for this labour being the unquestionable property of the labourer, no man but he can have a right to what that is once joined to, at least where there is enough, and as good, left in common for others.

§. 28. He that is nourished by the acorns he picked up under an oak or the apples he gathered from the trees in the wood has certainly appropriated them to himself. Nobody can deny but the nourishment is his. I ask then, when did they begin to be his? when he digested? or when he ate? or when he boiled? or when he brought them home? or when he picked them up? and it is plain, if the first gathering made them not his, nothing else could. That labour put a distinction between them and common: that added something to them more than nature, the common mother of all, had done; and so they became his private right. And will anyone say he had no right to those acorns or apples he thus appropriated, because he had not the consent of all mankind to make them his? Was it a robbery thus to assume to himself what belonged to all in common? If such a consent as that was necessary, man had starved, notwithstanding the plenty God had given him. We see in commons, which remain so by compact, that it is the taking any part of what is common and removing it out of the state nature leaves it in, which begins the property, without which the common is of no use. And the taking of this or that part does not depend on the express consent of all the commoners. Thus the grass my horse has bit, the turfs my servant has cut, and the ore I have digged in any place where I have a right to them in common with others became my property, without the assignation or consent of any body. The labour that was mine, removing them out of that common state they were in, has fixed my property to them.

§. 29. By making an explicit consent of every commoner necessary to anyone's appropriating to himself any part of what is given in common, children or servants could not cut the meat which their father or master had provided for them in common without assigning to every one his peculiar part. Though the water running in the fountain be everyone's, yet who can doubt but that in the pitcher is his only who drew it out? His labour has taken it out of the hands of nature, where it was common and belonged equally to all her children, and has thereby appropriated it to himself.

§. 30. Thus this law of reason makes the deer that Indian's who has killed it; it is allowed to be his goods, who has bestowed his labour upon it, though before it was the common right of everyone. And amongst those who are counted the civilized part of mankind, who have made and multiplied positive laws to determine property, this original law of nature, for the beginning of property, in what was before common, still takes place; and by virtue thereof, what fish anyone catches in the ocean, that great and still remaining common of mankind, or what ambergris anyone takes up here, is by the labour that removes it out of that common state nature left it in made his property, who takes that pains about it. And even amongst us, the hare that anyone is hunting is thought his who pursues her during the chase: for being a beast that is still looked upon as common and no man's private possession, whoever has employed so much labour about any of that kind as to find and pursue her has thereby removed her from the state of nature, wherein she was common, and has begun a property.

§. 31. It will perhaps be objected to this, that if gathering the acorns, or other fruits of the earth, &c. makes a right to them, then any one may ingross as much as he will. To which I answer, Not so. The same law of nature that does by this means give us property does also bound that property too. *God has given us all things richly,* 1 Tim. vi. 12. is the voice of reason confirmed by inspiration. But how far has he given it us? To enjoy. As much as anyone can make use of to any advantage of life before it spoils, so much he may by his labour fix a property in: whatever is beyond this is more than his share and belongs to others. Nothing was made by God for man to spoil or destroy. And thus, considering the plenty of natural provisions there was a long time in the world and the few spenders and to how small a part of that provision the industry of one man could extend itself and ingross it to the prejudice of others, especially keeping within the bounds, set by reason, of what might serve for his use, there could be then little room for quarrels or contentions about property so established.

§. 32. But the chief matter of property being now not the fruits of the earth and the beasts that subsist on it, but the earth itself, as that which takes in and carries with it all the rest; I think it is plain that property in that too is acquired as the former. As much land as a man tills, plants, improves, cultivates, and can use the product of, so much is his property. He by his labour does, as it were, enclose it from the common. Nor will it invalidate his right to say everybody else has an equal title to it and therefore he cannot appropriate, he cannot enclose, without the consent of all his fellow-commoners, all mankind. God, when he gave the world in common to all mankind, commanded man also to labour, and the penury of his condition required it of him. God and his reason commanded him to subdue the earth, i. e. improve it for the benefit of life, and therein lay out something upon it that was his own, his labour. He that in obedience to this command of God, subdued, tilled and sowed any part of it thereby annexed to it something that was his property, which another had no title to nor could without injury take from him.

§. 33. Nor was this appropriation of any parcel of land, by improving it, any prejudice to any other man, since there was still enough and as good left; and more than the yet unprovided could use. So that, in effect, there was never the less left for others because of his enclosure for himself: for he that leaves as much as another can make use of does as good as take nothing at all. Nobody could think himself injured by the drinking of another man, though he took a good draught, who had a whole river of the same water left him to quench his thirst; and the case of land and water, where there is enough of both, is perfectly the same.

§. 34. God gave the world to men in common, but since he gave it them for their benefit and the greatest conveniencies of life they were capable to draw from it, it cannot be supposed he meant it should always remain common and uncultivated. He gave it to the use of the industrious and rational (and labour was to be his title to it), not to the fancy or covetousness of the quarrelsome and contentious. He that had as good left for his improvement as was already taken up needed not complain, ought not meddle with what was already improved by another's labour; if he did, it is plain he desired the benefit of another's pains, which he had no right to, and not the ground which God had given him in common with others to labour on and whereof there was as good left as that already possessed, and more than he knew what to do with or his industry could reach to. . . .

§. 37. This is certain, that in the beginning, before the desire of having more than man needed had altered the intrinsic value of things, which depends only on their usefulness to the life of man or had agreed that a little piece of yellow metal which would keep without wasting or decay should be worth a great piece of flesh or a whole heap of corn; though men had a right to appropriate by their labour each one of himself as much of the things of nature as he could use, yet this could not be much, nor to the prejudice of others, where the same plenty was still left to those who would use the same industry. To which let me add, that he who appropriates land to himself by his labour does not lessen, but increases the common stock of mankind; for the provisions serving to the support of human life produced by one acre of enclosed and cultivated land are (to speak much within compass) ten times more than those which are yielded by an acre of land of an equal richness lying waste in common. And therefore he that encloses land and has a greater plenty of the conveniencies of life from ten acres than he could have from an hundred left to nature may truly be said to give ninety acres to mankind: for his labour now supplies him with provisions out of ten acres which were but the product of an hundred lying in common. I have here rated the improved land very low in making its product but as ten to one, when it is much nearer a hundred to one; for I ask whether in the wild woods and uncultivated waste of America, left to nature, without any improvement, tillage or husbandry, a thousand acres yield the needy and wretched inhabitants as many conveniencies of life as ten acres of equally fertile land do in Devonshire, where they are well cultivated?

Before the appropriation of land, he who gathered as much of the wild fruit, killed, caught, or tamed as many of the beasts as he could; he that so employed his pains about any of the spontaneous products of nature as any way to alter them from the state which nature put them in, by placing any of his labour on them, did thereby acquire a propriety in them: but if they perished in his possession, without their due use; if the fruits rotted or the venison putrified before he could spend it, he offended against the common law of nature and was liable to be punished; he invaded his neighbour's share, for he had no right farther than his use called for any of them, and they might serve to afford him conveniencies of life. . . .

§. 44. From all which it is evident that though the things of nature are given in common, yet man, by being master of himself, and proprietor of his own person and the actions or labour of it had still in himself the great foundation of property; and that which made up the great part of what he applied to the support or comfort of his being, when invention and arts had improved the conveniencies of life, was perfectly his own and did not belong in common to others.

§. 45. Thus labour, in the beginning, gave a right of property wherever anyone was pleased to employ it upon what was common, which remained a long while the far greater part and is yet more than mankind makes use of. Men, at first, for the most part, contented themselves with what unassisted nature offered to their necessities; and though afterwards, in some parts of the world (where the increase of people and stock, with the use of money, had made land scarce and so of some value), the several communities settled the bounds of their distinct territories, and by laws within themselves regulated the properties of the private men of their society, and so, by compact and agreement, settled the property which labour and industry began; and the leagues that have been made between several states and kingdoms, either expressly or tacitly disowning all claim and right to the land in the others' possession, have, by common consent, given up their pretences

to their natural common right, which originally they had to those countries, and so have, by positive agreement, settled a property amongst themselves in distinct parts and parcels of the earth; yet there are still great tracts of ground to be found, which (the inhabitants thereof not having joined with the rest of mankind in the consent of the use of their common money) lie waste and are more than the people who dwell on it do or can make use of and so still lie in common; though this can scarce happen amongst that part of mankind that have consented to the use of money.

§. 46. The greatest part of things really useful to the life of man, and such as the necessity of subsisting made the first commoners of the world look after, as it does the Americans now, are generally things of short duration such as, if they are not consumed by use, will decay and perish of themselves; gold, silver and diamonds are things that fancy or agreement has put the value on, more than real use and the necessary support of life. Now of those good things which nature has provided in common, everyone had a right (as has been said) to as much as he could use, and property in all that he could effect with his labour; all that his industry could extend to, to alter from the state nature had put in it, was his. He that gathered a hundred bushels of acorns or apples had thereby a property in them; they were his goods as soon as gathered. He was only to look that he used them before they spoiled, else he took more than his share and robbed others. And indeed it was a foolish thing, as well as dishonest, to hoard up more than he could make use of. If he gave away a part to any body else, so that it perished not uselessly in his possession, these he also made use of. And if he also bartered away plums that would have rotted in a week for nuts that would last good for his eating a whole year, he did no injury; he wasted not the common stock, destroyed no part of the portion of goods that belonged to others, so long as nothing perished uselessly in his hands. Again, if he would give his nuts for a piece of metal, pleased with its colour; or exchange his sheep for shells, or wool for a sparkling pebble or a diamond, and keep those by him all his life, he invaded not the right of others; he might heap up as much of these durable things as he pleased, the exceeding of the bounds of his just property not lying in the largeness of his possession, but the perishing of any thing uselessly in it.

§. 47. And thus came in the use of money, some lasting thing that men might keep without spoiling and that by mutual consent men would take in exchange for the truly useful but perishable supports of life.

§. 48. And as different degrees of industry were apt to give men possessions in different proportions, so this invention of money gave them the opportunity to continue and enlarge them: for supposing an island, separate from all possible commerce with the rest of the world, wherein there were but a hundred families, but there were sheep, horses and cows, with other useful animals, wholesome fruits, and land enough for corn for a hundred thousand times as many, but nothing in the island, either because of its commonness or perishableness fit to supply the place of money; what reason could any one have there to enlarge his possessions beyond the use of his family and a plentiful supply to its consumption, either in what their own industry produced or they could barter for like perishable, useful commodities with others? Where there is not something both lasting and scarce and so valuable to be hoarded up, there men will not be apt to enlarge their possessions of land, were it never so rich, never so free for them to take: for I ask, what would a man value ten thousand or a hundred thousand acres of excellent land, ready cultivated and well stocked too with cattle, in the middle of the inland parts of America, where he had no hopes of commerce with other parts of the world, to draw money to him by the sale of the product? It would not be worth the enclosing, and we should see him give up again to the wild common of nature whatever was more than would supply the conveniencies of life to be had there for him and his family.

§. 49. Thus in the beginning all the world was America, and more so than that is now; for no such thing as money was any where known. Find out something that has the use and value of money amongst his neighbours; you shall see the same man will begin presently to enlarge his possessions.

§. 50. But since gold and silver, being little useful to the life of man in proportion to food, raiment, and carriage, has its value only from the consent of men, whereof labour yet makes in great part the measure, it is plain that men have agreed to a disproportionate and unequal possession of the earth, they having by a tacit and voluntary consent found out a way how a man may fairly possess more land than he himself can use the product of, by receiving in exchange for the overplus gold and silver which may be hoarded up without injury to anyone, these metals not spoiling or decaying in the hands of the possessor. This partage of things in an inequality of private possessions, men have made practicable out of the bounds of society, and without compact, only by putting a value on gold and silver and tacitly agreeing in the use of money; for in governments, the laws regulate the right of property, and the possession of land is determined by positive constitutions.

§. 51. And thus, I think, it is very easy to conceive, without any difficulty, how labour could at first begin a title of property in the common things of nature and how the spending it upon our uses bounded it. So that there could then be no reason of quarrelling about title nor any doubt about the largeness of possession it gave. Right and convenience went together; for as a man had a right to all he could employ his labour upon, so he had no temptation to labour for more than he could make use of. This left no room for controversy about the title, nor for encroachment on the right of others; what portion a man carved to himself was easily seen; and it was useless, as well as dishonest, to carve himself too much or take more than he needed.

CHAPTER VIII / OF THE BEGINNING OF POLITICAL SOCIETIES

§. 95. Men being, as has been said, by nature all free, equal, and independent, no one can be put out of this estate and subjected to the political power of another without his own consent. The only way whereby any one divests himself of his natural liberty and puts on the bonds of civil society is by agreeing with other men to join and unite into a community for their comfortable, safe, and peaceable living one amongst another, in a secure enjoyment of their properties and a greater security against any that are not of it. This any number of men may do, because it injures not the freedom of the rest; they are left as they were in the liberty of the state of nature. When any number of men have so consented to make one community or government, they are thereby presently encorporated and make one body politic, wherein the majority have a right to act and conclude the rest.

§. 96. For when any number of men have, by the consent of every individual, made a community, they have thereby made that community one body, with a power to act as one body, which is only by the will and determination of the majority: for that which acts any community, being only the consent of the individuals of it, and it being necessary to that which is one body to move one way, it is necessary the body should move that way whither the greater force carries it, which is the consent of the majority; or else it is impossible it should act or continue one body, one community, which the consent of every individual that united into it agreed that it should; and so everyone is bound by that consent to be concluded by the majority. And therefore we see that in assemblies empowered to act by positive laws, where no number is set by that positive law which impowers them, the act of the majority passes for the act of the whole and of course determines as having, by the law of nature and reason, the power of the whole.

§. 97. And thus every man, by consenting with others to make one body politic under one government, puts himself under an obligation to everyone of that society to submit to the determination of the majority and to be concluded by it; or else this original compact, whereby he with others incorporated into one society, would signify nothing and be no compact if he be left free and under no other ties than he was in before in the state of nature. For what appearance would there be of any compact? what new engagement if he were no farther tied by any decrees of the society than he himself thought fit and did actually consent to? This would be still as great a liberty as he himself had before his compact, or anyone else in the state of nature has, who may submit himself and consent to any acts of it if he thinks fit.

§. 98. For if the consent of the majority shall not, in reason, be received as the act of the whole and conclude every individual, nothing but the consent of every individual can make anything to be the act of the whole: but such a consent is next to impossible ever to be had, if we consider the infirmities of health and avocations of business, which in a number, though much less than that of a commonwealth, will necessarily keep many away from the public assembly. To which if we add the variety of opinions and contrariety of interest which unavoidably happen in all collections of men, the coming into society upon such terms would be only like Cato's coming into the theatre only to go out again. Such a constitution as this would make the mighty Leviathan of a shorter duration than the feeblest creatures and not let it outlast the day it was born in, which cannot be supposed until we can think that rational creatures should desire and constitute societies only to be dissolved, for where the majority cannot conclude the rest, there they cannot act as one body and consequently will be immediately dissolved again.

§. 99. Whosoever therefore out of a state of nature unite into a community must be understood to give up all the power necessary to the ends for which they unite into society to the majority of the community, unless they expressly agreed in any number greater than the majority. And this is done by barely agreeing to unite into one political society, which is all the compact that is, or needs be, between the individuals that enter into or make up a commonwealth. And thus that which begins and actually constitutes any political society is nothing but the consent of any number of freemen capable of a majority to unite and incorporate into such a society. And this is that, and that only, which did or could give beginning to any lawful government in the world. . . .

CHAPTER IX / OF THE ENDS OF POLITICAL SOCIETY AND GOVERNMENT

§. 123. If man in the state of nature be so free, as has been said; if he be absolute lord of his own person and possessions, equal to the greatest and subject to nobody, why will he part with his freedom? why will he give up this empire and subject himself to the dominion and control of any other power? To which it is obvious to answer that though in the state of nature he hath such a right, yet the enjoyment of it is very uncertain and constantly exposed to the invasion of others; for all being kings as much as he, every man his equal, and the greater part no strict observers of equity and justice, the enjoyment of the property he has in this state is very unsafe, very unsecure. This makes him willing to quit a condition which, however free, is full of fears and continual dangers; and it is not without reason that he seeks out and is willing to join in society with others who are already united, or have a mind to unite, for the mutual preservation of their lives, liberties and estates, which I call by the general name *property*.

§. 124. The great and chief end, therefore, of men's uniting into commonwealths, and putting themselves under government is the preservation of their property. To which in the state of nature there are many things wanting.

First, there wants an established, settled, known law, received and allowed by common consent to be the standard of right and wrong, and the common measure to decide all controversies between them; for though the law of nature be plain and intelligible to all rational creatures, yet men being biased by their interest, as well as ignorant for want of study of it, are not apt to allow of it as a law binding to them in the application of it to their particular cases.

§. 125. *Secondly,* in the state of nature there wants a known and indifferent judge with authority to determine all differences according to the established law; for everyone in that state being both judge and executioner of the law of nature, men being partial to themselves, passion and revenge is very apt to carry them too far and with too much heat in their own cases, as well as negligence and unconcernedness to make them too remiss in other men's.

§. 126. *Thirdly,* in the state of nature there often wants power to back and support the sentence when right and to give it due execution. They who by any injustice offended will seldom fail where they are able by force to make good their injustice; such resistance many times makes the punishment dangerous and frequently destructive to those who attempt it.

§. 127. Thus mankind, notwithstanding all the privileges of the state of nature, being but in an ill condition while they remain in it, are quickly driven into society. Hence it comes to pass that we seldom find any number of men live any time together in this state. The inconveniences that they are therein exposed to by the irregular and uncertain exercise of the power every man has of punishing the transgressions of others make them take sanctuary under the established laws of government and therein seek the preservation of their property. It is this makes them so willingly give up every one his single power of punishing, to be exercised by such alone as shall be appointed to it amongst them and by such rules as the community, or those authorized by them to that purpose, shall agree on. And in this we have the original right and rise of both the legislative and executive power, as well as of the governments and societies themselves.

§. 128. For in the state of nature, to omit the liberty he has of innocent delights, a man has two powers.

The first is to do whatsoever he thinks fit for the preservation of himself and others within the permission of the law of nature, by which law, common to them all, he and all the rest of mankind are one community, make up one society, distinct from all other creatures. And were it not for the corruption and vitiousness of degenerate men, there would be no need of any other, no necessity that men should separate from this great and natural community and by positive agreements combine into smaller and divided associations.

The other power a man has in the state of nature is the power to punish the crimes committed against that law. Both these he gives up when he joins in a private, if I may so call it, or particular politic society and encorporates into any commonwealth separate from the rest of mankind.

§. 129. The first power, viz. of doing whatsoever he thought for the preservation of himself and the rest of mankind, he gives up to be regulated by laws made by the society, so far forth as the preservation of himself and the rest of that society shall require; which laws of the society in many things confine the liberty he had by the law of nature.

§. 130. Secondly, the power of punishing he wholly gives up and engages his natural force (which he might before employ in the execution of the law of nature, by his own single authority, as he thought fit) to assist the executive power of the society, as the law thereof shall require; for being now in a new state, wherein he is to enjoy many conveniencies from the labour, assistance, and society of others in the same community, as well as protection from its whole strength, he is to part also with as much of his natural liberty in providing for himself as the good, prosperity, and safety of the society shall require; which is not only necessary, but just, since the other members of the society do the like.

§. 131. But though men, when they enter into society, give up the equality, liberty, and executive power they had in the state of nature, into the hands of the society to be so far disposed of by the legislative as the good of the society shall require, yet, it being only with an intention in everyone the better to preserve himself, his liberty and property (for no rational creature can be supposed to change his condition with an intention to be worse), the power of the society, or legislative constituted by them, can never be supposed to extend farther than the common good but is obliged to secure everyone's property by providing against those three defects above mentioned that made the state of nature so unsafe and uneasy. And so whoever has the legislative or supreme power of any commonwealth is bound to govern by established standing laws promulgated and known to the people, and not by extemporary decrees; by indifferent and upright judges, who are to decide controversies by those laws and to employ the force of the community at home only in the execution of such laws or abroad to prevent or redress foreign injuries and secure the community from inroads and invasion. And all this to be directed to no other end but the peace, safety, and public good of the people.

CHAPTER XI / OF THE EXTENT OF THE LEGISLATIVE POWER

§. 134. The great end of men's entering into society, being the enjoyment of their properties in peace and safety, and the great instrument and means of that being the laws established in that society, the first and fundamental positive law of all commonwealths is the establishing of the legislative power; as the first and fundamental natural law, which is to govern even the legislative itself, is the preservation of the society and (as far as will consist with the public good) of every person in it. This legislative is not only the supreme power of the commonwealth, but sacred and unalterable in the hands where the community have once placed it; nor can any edict of anybody else, in what form soever conceived or by what power soever backed, have the force and obligation of a law which has not its sanction from that legislative which the public has chosen and appointed; for without this the law could not have that which is absolutely necessary to its being a law, the consent of the society, over whom no body can have a power to make laws but by their own consent and by authority received from them; and therefore all the obedience, which by the most solemn ties any one can be obliged to pay, ultimately terminates in this supreme power and is directed by those laws which it enacts; nor can any oaths to any foreign power whatsoever or any domestic subordinate power discharge any member of the society from his obedience to the legislative acting pursuant to their trust, nor oblige him to any obedience contrary to the laws so enacted or farther than they do allow, it being ridiculous to imagine one can be tied ultimately to obey any power in the society which is not the supreme.

§. 135. Though the legislative, whether placed in one or more, whether it be always in being or only by intervals, though it be the supreme power in every commonwealth; yet,

First, it is not nor can possibly be absolutely arbitrary over the lives and fortunes of the people; for it being but the joint power of every member of the society given up to that person, or assembly which is legislator, it can be no more than those persons had in a state of nature before they entered into society and gave up to the community; for nobody can transfer to another more power than he has in himself, and nobody has an absolute arbitrary power over himself or over any other to destroy his own life or take away the life or property of another. A man, as has been proved, cannot subject himself to the arbitrary power of another; and having in the state of nature no arbitrary power over the life, liberty, or possession of another, but only so much as the law of nature gave him for the preservation of himself and the rest of mankind, this is all he does, or can give up to the commonwealth, and by it to the legislative power, so that the legislative can have no more than this. Their power, in the utmost bounds of it, is limited to the public good of the society. It is a power that has no other end but preservation and therefore can never have a right to destroy, enslave, or designedly to impoverish the subjects. The obligations of the law of nature cease not in society, but only in many cases are drawn closer and have by human laws known penalties annexed to them to enforce their observation. Thus the law of nature stands as an eternal rule to all men, legislators as well as others. The rules that they make for other men's actions, must, as well as their own and other men's actions, be conformable to the law of nature, i. e. to the will of God, of which that is a declaration, and the fundamental law of nature being the preservation of mankind, no human sanction can be good or valid against it.

§. 136. *Secondly,* the legislative, or supreme authority, cannot assume to itself a power to rule by extemporary arbitrary decrees, but is bound to dispense justice and decide the rights of the subject by promulgated standing laws and known authorized judges; for the law of nature being unwritten and so nowhere to be found but in the minds of men, they who through passion or interest shall miscite or misapply it cannot so easily be convinced of their mistake where there is no established judge; and so it serves not, as it ought, to determine the rights and fence the properties of those that live under it, especially where everyone is judge, interpreter, and executioner of it too, and that in his own case; and he that has right on his side, having ordinarily but his own single strength, has not force enough to defend himself from injuries or to punish delinquents. To avoid these inconveniences, which disorder men's properties in the state of nature, men unite into societies that they may have the united strength of the whole society to secure and defend their properties and may have standing rules to bound it, by which everyone may know what is his. To this end it is that men give up all their natural power to the society which they enter into, and the community put the legislative power into such hands as they think fit, with this trust, that they shall be governed by declared laws, or else their peace, quiet, and prop-

erty will still be at the same uncertainty as it was in the state of nature.

§. 137. Absolute arbitrary power, or governing without settled standing laws, can neither of them consist with the ends of society and government, which men would not quit the freedom of the state of nature for, and tie themselves up under, were it not to preserve their lives, liberties and fortunes, and by stated rules of right and property to secure their peace and quiet. It cannot be supposed that they should intend, had they a power so to do, to give to anyone, or more, an absolute arbitrary power over their persons and estates and put a force into the magistrate's hand to execute his unlimited will arbitrarily upon them. This were to put themselves into a worse condition than the state of nature, wherein they had a liberty to defend their right against the injuries of others and were upon equal terms of force to maintain it, whether invaded by a single man or many in combination. Whereas by supposing they have given up themselves to the absolute arbitrary power and will of a legislator, they have disarmed themselves and armed him to make a prey of them when he pleases; he being in a much worse condition, who is exposed to the arbitrary power of one man who has the command of 100,000, then he that is exposed to the arbitrary power of 100,000 single men; nobody being secure, that his will, who has such a command, is better than that of other men, though his force be 100,000 times stronger. And therefore, whatever form the commonwealth is under, the ruling power ought to govern by declared and received laws, and not by extemporary dictates and undetermined resolutions: for then mankind will be in a far worse condition than in the state of nature, if they shall have armed one, or a few men with the joint power of a multitude, to force them to obey at pleasure the exorbitant and unlimited decrees of their sudden thoughts or unrestrained, and until that moment unkown wills, without having any measures set down which may guide and justify their actions; for all the power the government has, being only for the good of the society, as it ought not to be arbitrary and at pleasure, so it ought to be exercised by established and promulgated laws that both the people may know their duty and be safe and secure within the limits of the law and the rulers too kept within their bounds and not be tempted by the power they have in their hands to employ it to such purposes and by such measures as they would not have known and own not willingly.

§. 138. *Thirdly,* the supreme power cannot take from any man any part of his property without his own consent; for the preservation of property being the end of government and that for which men enter into society, it necessarily supposes and requires that the people should have property, without which they must be supposed to lose that, by entering into society, which was the end for which they entered into it; too gross an absurdity for any man to own. Men therefore in society having property, they have such a right to the goods which by the law of the community are theirs, that nobody has a right to take their substance or any part of it from them without their own consent: without this they have no property at all; for I have truly no property in that which another can by right take from me when he pleases against my consent. Hence it is a mistake to think that the supreme or legislative power of any commonwealth can do what it will and dispose of the estates of the subject arbitrarily or take any part of them at pleasure. This is not much to be feared in governments where the legislative consists, wholly or in part, in assemblies which are variable, whose members upon the dissolution of the assembly are subjects under the common laws of their country equally with the rest. But in governments, where the legislative is in one lasting assembly always in being, or in one man, as in absolute monarchies, there is danger still that they will think themselves to have a distinct interest from the rest of the community and so will be apt to increase their own riches and power by taking what they think fit from the people; for a man's property is not at all secure, though there be good and equitable laws to set the bounds of it between him and his fellow subjects, if he who commands those subjects have power to take from any private man what part he pleases of his property and use and dispose of it as he thinks good.

§. 139. But government, into whatsoever hands it is put, being, as I have before shown, entrusted with this condition and for this end, that men might have and secure their properties, the prince or senate, however it may have power to make laws for the regulating of property between the subjects one amongst another, yet can never have a power to take to themselves the whole or any part of the subjects property without their own consent: for this would be in effect to leave them no property at all. And to let us see that even absolute power, where it is necessary, is not arbitrary by being absolute but is still limited by that reason and confined to those ends which required it in some cases to be absolute, we need look no farther than the common practice of martial discipline: for the preservation of the army, and in it of the whole commonwealth, requires an absolute obedience to the command of every superior officer, and it is justly death to disobey or dispute the most dangerous or unreasonable of them; but yet we see that neither the sergeant that could command a soldier to march up to the mouth of a cannon or stand in a breach where he is almost sure to perish can command that soldier to give him one penny of his money; nor the general that can condemn him to death for deserting his post or for not obeying the most desperate orders can yet, with all his absolute power of life and death, dispose of one farthing of that soldier's estate or seize one jot of his goods, whom yet he can command anything, and hang for the least disobedience; because such a blind obedience is necessary to that end for which the commander has his power, *viz.* the preservation of the rest, but the disposing of his goods has nothing to do with it.

§. 140. It is true, governments cannot be supported without great charge, and it is fit everyone who enjoys his share of the protection should pay out of his estate his proportion for the maintenance of it. But still it must be with his own consent, i. e. the consent of the majority, giving it either by themselves or their representatives chosen by them; for if any one shall claim a power to lay and levy taxes on the people by his own authority and without such consent of the people, he thereby invades the fundamental law of property and subverts the end of government: for what property have I in that which another may be right take when he pleases to himself?

§. 141. *Fourthly,* the legislative cannot transfer the power of making laws to any other hands, for it being but a delegated power from the people, they who have it cannot pass it over to others. The people alone can appoint the form of the commonwealth, which is by constituting the legislative and appointing in whose hands that shall be. And when the people have said, We will submit to rules and be governed by laws made by such men and in such forms, nobody else can say other men shall make laws for them; nor can the people be bound by any laws but such as are enacted by those whom they have chosen and authorized to make laws for them. The power of the legislative, being derived from the people by a positive voluntary grant and institution, can be no other than what that positive grant conveyed, which being only to make laws and not to make legislators, the legislative can have no power to transfer their authority to making laws and place it in other hands.

§. 142. These are the bounds which the trust that is put in them by the society and the law of God and nature have set to the legislative power of every commonwealth, in all forms of government.

First, they are to govern by promulgated established laws, not to be varied in particular cases, but to have one rule for rich and poor, for the favourite at court, and the country man at plough.

Secondly, these laws also ought to be designed for no other end ultimately but the good of the people.

Thirdly, they must not raise taxes on the property of the people without the consent of the people, given by themselves or their deputies. And this properly concerns only such governments where the legislative is always in being, or at least where the people have not reserved any part of the legislative to deputies, to be from time to time chosen by themselves.

Fourthly, the legislative neither must nor can transfer the power of making laws to any body else or place it anywhere but where the people have.

JEAN-JACQUES ROUSSEAU

from *Discourse on the Origin of Inequality* (1755) and *On the Social Contract* (1762)

(*Source: Reprinted from* The Basic Political Writings of Jean-Jacques Rousseau, *translated and edited by Donald A. Cress. Copyright © 1987 by Hackett Publishing Company.*)

QUESTIONS FOR REFLECTION

1. What is Rousseau's conception of the state of nature in the *Discourse on the Origin of Inequality*? Does it differ from that of *On the Social Contract*?

2. Why, in Rousseau's view, does property give rise to deception?

3. How does Rousseau criticize the right to property?

4. What stages of inequality does Rousseau discuss? What is the final stage?

5. What principles of distributive justice does Rousseau advocate? Are they compatible with one another?

6. According to Rousseau, are there any limits on government power? If so, what are they?

from *Discourse on the Origin of Inequality*

Part Two

The first person who, having enclosed a plot of land, took it into his head to say *this is mine* and found people simple enough to believe him, was the true founder of civil society. What crimes, wars, murders, what miseries and horrors would the human race have been spared, had someone pulled up the stakes or filled in the ditch and cried out to his fellow men: "Do not listen to this imposter. You are lost if you forget that the fruits of the earth belong to all and the earth to no one!" But it is quite likely that by then things had already reached the point where they could no longer continue as they were. For this idea of property, depending on many prior ideas which could only have arisen successively, was not formed all at once in the human mind. It was necessary to make great progress, to acquire much industry and enlightenment, and to transmit and augment them from one age to another, before arriving at this final stage in the state of nature. Let us therefore take things farther back and try to piece together under a single viewpoint that slow succession of events and advances in knowledge in their most natural order.

Man's first sentiment was that of his own existence; his first concern was that of his preservation. The products of the earth provided him with all the help he needed; instinct led him to make use of them. With hunger and other appetites making him experience by turns various ways of existing, there was one appetite that invited him to perpetuate his species; and this blind inclination, devoid of any sentiment of the heart, produced a purely animal act. Once this need had been satisfied, the two sexes no longer took cognizance of one another, and even the child no longer meant anything to the mother once it could do without her. . . .

Although his fellowmen were not for him what they are for us, and although he had hardly anything more to do with them than with other animals, they were not forgotten in his observations. The conformities that time could make him perceive among them, his female, and himself, made him judge those he did not perceive. And seeing that they all acted as he would have done under similar circumstances, he concluded that their way of thinking and feeling was in complete conformity with his own. And this important truth, well established in his mind, made him follow, by a presentiment as sure as dialectic and more prompt, the best rules of conduct that it was appropriate to observe toward them for his advantage and safety. . . .

In proportion as ideas and sentiments succeed one another and as the mind and heart are trained, the human race continues to be tamed, relationships spread and bonds are tightened. People grew accustomed to gather in front of their huts or around a large tree; song and dance, true children of love and leisure, became the amusement or rather the occupation of idle men and women who flocked together. Each one began to look at the others and to want to be looked at himself, and public esteem had a value. The one who sang or danced the best, the handsomest, the strongest, the most adroit or the most eloquent became the most highly regarded. And this was the first step toward inequality and, at the same time, toward vice. From these first preferences were born vanity and contempt on the one hand, and shame and envy on the other. And the fermentation caused by these new leavens eventually produced compounds fatal to happiness and innocence.

As soon as men had begun mutually to value one another, and the idea of esteem was formed in their minds, each one claimed to have a right to it, and it was no longer possible for anyone to be lacking it with impunity. From this came the first duties of civility, even among savages; and from this every voluntary wrong became an outrage, because along with the harm that resulted from the injury, the offended party saw in it contempt for his person, which often was more insufferable than the harm itself. Hence each man punished the contempt shown him in a manner proportionate to the esteem in which he held himself; acts of revenge became terrible, and men became bloodthirsty and cruel. This is precisely the stage reached by most of the savage people known to us; and it is for want of having made adequate distinctions among their ideas or of having noticed how far these peoples already were from the original state of nature that many have hastened to conclude that man is naturally cruel, and that he needs civilization in order to soften him. On the contrary, nothing is so gentle as man in his primitive state, when, placed by nature at an equal distance from the stupidity of brutes and the fatal enlightenment of civil man, and limited equally by instinct and reason to protecting himself from the harm that threatens himself, he is restrained by natural pity from needlessly harming anyone himself, even if he has been harmed. For according to the axiom of the wise Locke, *where there is no property, there is no injury.*

But is must be noted that society in its beginning stages and the relations already established among men required in them qualities different from those they derived from their primitive constitution; that, with morality beginning to be introduced into human actions, and everyone, prior to the existence of laws, being sole judge and avenger of the offenses he had received, the goodness appropriate to the pure state of nature was no longer what was appropriate to an emerging society; that it was necessary for punishments to become more severe in proportion as the occasions for giving offense became more frequent; and that it was for the fear of vengeance to take the place of the deterrent character of laws. Hence although men had become less forebearing, and although natural pity had already undergone

some alteration, this period of the development of human faculties, maintaining a middle position between the indolence of our primitive state and the petulant activity of our egocentrism, must have been the happiest and most durable epoch. The more one reflects on it, the more one finds that this state was the least subject to upheavals and the best for man, and that he must have left it only by virtue of some fatal chance happening that, for the common good, ought never have happened. The example of savages, almost all of whom have been found in this state, seems to confirm that the human race had been made to remain in it always; that this state is the veritable youth of the world; and that all the subsequent progress has been in appearance so many steps toward the perfection of the individual, and in fact toward the decay of the species.

As long as men were content with the rustic huts, as long as they were limited to making their clothing out of skins sewn together with thorns or fish bones, adorning themselves with feathers and shells, painting their bodies with various colors, perfecting or embellishing their bows and arrows, using sharp-edged stones to make some fishing canoes or some crude musical instuments; in a word, as long as they applied themselves exclusively to tasks that a single individual could do and to the arts that did not require the cooperation of several hands, they lived as free, healthy, good and happy as they could in accordance with their nature; and they continued to enjoy among themselves the sweet rewards of independent intercourse. But as soon as one man needed the help of another, as soon as one man realized that it was useful for a single individual to have provisions for two, equality disappeared, property came into existence, labor became necessary. Vast forests were transformed into smiling fields which had to be watered with men's sweat, and in which slavery and misery were soon seen to germinate and grow with the crops.

Metallurgy and agriculture were the two arts whose invention produced this great revolution. For the poet, it is gold and silver; but for the philosopher, it is iron and wheat that have civilized men and ruined the human. Thus they were both unknown to the savages of America, who for that reason have always remained savages. Other peoples even appear to have remained barbarous, as long as they practiced one of those arts without the other. And perhaps one of the best reasons why Europe has been, if not sooner, at least more constantly and better governed than the other parts of the world, is that it is at the same time the most abundant in iron and the most fertile in wheat. . . .

From the cultivation of land, there necessarily followed the division of land; and from property once recognized, the first rules of justice. For in order to render everyone what is his, it is necessary that everyone can have something. Moreover, as men began to look toward the future and as they saw that they all had goods to lose, there was not one of them who did not have to fear reprisals against himself for wrongs he might do to another. This origin is all the more natural as it is impossible to conceive of the idea of property arising from anything but manual labor, for it is not clear what man can add, beyond his own labor, in order to appropriate things he has not made. It is labor alone that, in giving the cultivator a right to the product of the soil he has tilled, consequently gives him a right, at least until the harvest, and thus from year to year. With this possession continuing uninterrupted, it is easily transformed into property. When the ancients, say Grotius, gave Ceres* the epithet of legislatrix, gave the name Thesmophories to a festival celebrated in her honor, they thereby made it apparent that the division of lands has produced a new kind of right: namely, the right of property, different from that which results from the natural law.

Things in this state could have remained equal, if talents had been equal, and if the use of iron and the consumption of foodstuffs had always been in precise balance. But this proportion, which was not maintained by anything, was soon broken. The strongest did the most work; the most adroit turned theirs to better advantage: the most ingenious found ways to shorten their labor. The farmer had a greater need for iron, or the blacksmith had a greater need for wheat; and in laboring equally, the one earned a great deal while the other barely had enough to live. Thus it is that natural inequality imperceptibly manifests itself together with inequality occasioned

by the socialization process. Thus it is that the differences among men, developed by those of circumstances, make themselves more noticeable, more permanent in their effects, and begin to influence the fate of private individuals in the same proportion.

With things having reached this point, it is easy to imagine the rest. I will not stop to describe the successive invention of the arts, the progress of languages, the testing and use of talents, the inequality of fortunes, the use or abuse of wealth, nor all the details that follow these and that everyone can easily supply. I will limit myself exclusively to taking a look at the human race placed in this new order of things.

Thus we find here all our faculties developed, memory and imagination in play, egocentrism looking out for its interests, reason rendered active, and the mind having nearly reached the limit of the perfection of which it is capable. We find here all the natural qualities put into action, the rank and fate of each man established not only on the basis of the quantity of goods and the power to serve or harm, but also on the basis of mind, beauty, strength or skill, on the basis of merit or talents. And since these qualities were the only ones that could attract consideration, he was soon forced to have them or affect them. It was necessary, for his advantage, to show himself to be something other than what he in fact was. Being something and appearing to be something became two completely different things; and from this distinction there arose grand ostentation, deceptive cunning, and all the vices that follow in their wake. On the other hand, although man had previously been free and independent, we find him, so to speak, subject, by virtue of a multitude of fresh needs, to all of nature and particularly to his fellowmen, whose slave in a sense he becomes even in becoming their master; rich, he needs their services; poor, he needs their help; and being midway between wealth and poverty does not put him in a position to get along without them. It is therefore necessary for him to seek incessantly to interest them in his fate and to make them find their own profit, in fact or in appearance, in working for his. This makes him two-faced and crooked with some, imperious and harsh with others, and puts him in the position of having to abuse everyone he needs

* Ceres was the goddess of agriculture. —Ed.

when he cannot make them fear him and does not find it in his interests to be of useful service to them. Finally, consuming ambition, the zeal for raising the relative level of his fortune, less out of real need than in order to put himself above others, inspires in all men a wicked tendency to harm one another, a secret jealousy all the more dangerous because, in order to strike its blow in greater safety, it often wears the mask of benevolence; in short, competition and rivalry on the one hand, opposition of interest[s] on the other, and always the hidden desire to profit at the expense of someone else. All these ills are the first effect of property and the inseparable offshoot of incipient inequality.

Before representative signs of wealth had been invented, it could hardly have consisted of anything but lands and livestock, the only real goods men can possess. Now when inheritances had grown in number and size to the point of covering the entire landscape and of all bordering on one another, some could no longer be enlarged except at the expense of others; and the supernumeraries, whom weakness or indolence had prevented from acquiring an inheritance in their turn, became poor without having lost anything, because while everything changed around them, they alone had not changed at all. Thus they were forced to receive or steal their subsistence from the hands of the rich. And from that there began to arise, according to the diverse characters of the rich and the poor, domination and servitude, or violence and thefts. For their part, the wealthy had no sooner known the pleasure of domination, than before long they disdained all others, and using their old slaves to subdue new ones, they thought of nothing but the subjugation and enslavement of their neighbors, like those ravenous wolves which, on having once tasted human flesh, reject all other food and desire to devour only men.

Thus, when both the most powerful or the most miserable made of their strength or their needs a sort of right to another's goods, equivalent, according to them, to the right of property, the destruction of equality was followed by the most frightful disorder. Thus the usurpations of the rich, the acts of brigandage by the poor, the unbridled passions of all, stifling natural pity and the still weak voice of justice, made men greedy, ambitious and wicked. There arose between the right of the strongest and the right of the first occupant a perpetual conflict that ended only in fights and murders. Emerging society gave way to the most horrible state of war; since the human race, vilified and desolated, was no longer able to retrace its steps or give up the unfortunate acquisitions it had made, and since it labored only toward its shame by abusing the faculties that honor it, it brought itself to the brink of ruin. *Horrified by the newness of the ill, both the poor man and the rich man hope to flee from wealth, hating what they once had prayed for.*

It is not possible that men should not have eventually reflected upon so miserable a situation and upon the calamities that overwhelm them. The rich in particular must have soon felt how disadvantageous to them it was to have a perpetual war in which they alone paid all the costs, and in which the risk of losing one's life was common to all and the risk of losing one's goods was personal. Moreover, regardless of the light in which they tried to place their usurpations, they knew full well that they were established on nothing but a precarious and abusive right, and that having been acquired merely by force, force might take them away from them without their having any reason to complain. Even those enriched exclusively by industry could hardly base their property on better claims. They could very well say: "I am the one who built that wall; I have earned this land with my labor." In response to them it could be said: "Who gave you the boundary lines? By what right do you claim to exact payment at our expense for labor we did not impose upon you? Are you unaware that a multitude of your brothers perish or suffer from need of what you have in excess, and that you needed explicit and unanimous consent from the human race for you to help yourself to anything from the common subsistence that went beyond your own?" Bereft of valid reasons to justify himself and sufficient forces to defend himself; easily crushing a private individual, but himself crushed by troops of bandits; alone against all and unable on account of mutual jealousies to unite with his equals against enemies united by the common hope of plunder, the rich, pressed by necessity, finally conceived the most thought-out project that ever entered the human mind. It was to use in his favor the very strength of those who attacked him, to turn his adversaries into his defenders, to instill in them other maxims, and to give them other institutions which were as favorable to him as natural right was unfavorable to him.

With this end in mind, after having shown his neighbors the horror of a situation which armed them all against each other and made their possessions as burdensome as their needs, and in which no one could find safety in either poverty or wealth, he easily invented specious reasons to lead them to his goal. "Let us unite," he says to them, "in order to protect the weak from oppression, restrain the ambitious, and assure everyone of possessing what belongs to him. Let us institute rules of justice and peace to which all will be obliged to conform, which will make special exceptions for no one, and which will in some way compensate for the caprices of fortune by subjecting the strong and weak to mutual obligations. In short, instead of turning our forces against ourselves, let us gather them into one supreme power that governs us according to wise laws, that protects and defends all the members of the association, repulses common enemies, and maintains us in an eternal concord."

Considerably less than the equivalent of this discourse was needed to convince crude, easily seduced men who also had too many disputes to settle among themselves to be able to get along without arbiters, and too much greed and ambition to be able to get along without masters for long. They all ran to chain themselves, in the belief that they secured their liberty, for although they had enough sense to realize the advantages of a political establishment, they did not have enough experience to foresee its dangers. Those most capable of anticipating the abuses were precisely those who counted on profiting from them; and even the wise saw the need to be resolved to sacrifice one part of their liberty to preserve the other, just as a wounded man has his arm amputated to save the rest of his body.

Such was, or should have been, the origin of society and laws, which gave new fetters to the weak and new forces to the rich, irretrievably destroyed natural liberty, established forever the law of property and of inequality, changed adroit usurpation into an irrevocable right, and for the profit of a few ambitious men henceforth subjected the entire human race to labor, servitude and misery. It is readily apparent how the establishment of a single society rendered indispensable that of all the others, and how, to stand head to head against the united forces, it was necessary to unite in turn. Societies, multiplying or spreading rapidly, soon covered the entire surface of the earth; and it was no longer possible to find a single corner in the universe where someone could free himself from the yoke and withdraw his head from the often ill-guided sword which everyone saw perpetually hanging over his own head. With civil right thus having become the common rule of citizens, the law of nature no longer was operative except between the various societies, when, under the name of the law of nations, it was tempered by some tacit conventions in order to make intercourse possible and to serve as a substitute for natural compassion which, losing between one society and another nearly all the force it had between one man and another, no longer resides anywhere but in a few great cosmopolitan souls, who overcome the imaginary barriers that separate peoples, and who, following the example of the sovereign being who has created them, embrace the entire human race in their benevolence.

Remaining thus among themselves in the state of nature, the bodies politic soon experienced the inconveniences that had forced private individuals to leave it; and that state became even more deadly among these great bodies than that state had among the private individuals of whom they were composed. Whence came the national wars, battles, murders, and reprisals that make nature tremble and offend reason, and all those horrible prejudices that rank the honor of shedding human blood among the virtues. The most decent people learned to consider it one of their duties to kill their fellow men. Finally, men were seen massacring one another by the thousands without knowing why. More murders were committed in a single day of combat and more horrors in the capture of a single city than were committed in the state of nature during entire centuries over the entire face of the earth. Such are the first effects one glimpses of the division of mankind into different societies. . . .

If we follow the progress of inequality in these various revolutions, we will find that the first stage was the establishment of the law and of the right of property, the second stage was the institution of the magistracy, and the third and final stage was the transformation of legitimate power into arbitrary power. Thus the class of rich and poor was authorized by the first epoch, that of the strong and the weak by the second, and that of master and slave by the third: the ultimate degree of inequality and the limit to which all the others finally lead, until new revolutions completely dissolve the government or bring it nearer to its legitimate institution.

To grasp the necessity of this progress, we must consider less the motives for the establishment of the body politic than the form it takes in its execution and the disadvantages that follow in its wake. For the vices that make social institutions necessary are the same ones that make their abuses inevitable. . . .

Here is the final stage of inequality, and the extreme point that closes the circle and touches the point from which we started. Here all private individuals become equals again, because they are nothing. And since subjects no longer have any law other than the master's will, nor the master any rule other than his passions, the notions of good and the principles of justice again vanish. Here everything is returned solely to the law of the strongest, and consequently to a new state of nature different from the one with which we began, in that the one was the state of nature in its purity, and this last one is the fruit of an excess of corruption. Moreover, there is so little difference between these two states, and the governmental contract is so utterly dissolved by despotism, that the despot is master only as long as he is the strongest; and as soon as he can be ousted, he has no cause to protest against violence. The uprising that ends in the strangulation or the dethronement of a sultan is as lawful an act as those by which he disposed of the lives and goods of his subjects the day before. Force alone maintained him; force alone brings him down. Thus everything happens in accordance with the natural order, and whatever the outcome of these brief and frequent upheavals may be, no one can complain about someone else's injustice, but only of his own imprudence or his misfortune.

In discovering and following thus the forgotten and lost routes that must have led man from the natural state to the civil state; in reestablishing, with

the intermediate positions I have just taken note of, those that time constraints on me have made me suppress or that the imagination has not suggested to me, no attentive reader can fail to be struck by the immense space that separates these two states. It is in this slow succession of things that he will see the solution to an infinity of moral and political problems which the philosophers are unable to resolve. He will realize that, since the human race of one age is not the human race of another age, the reason why Diogenes did not find his man is because he searched among his contemporaries for a man who no longer existed. Cato, he will say, perished with Rome and liberty because he was out of place in his age; and this greatest of men merely astonished the world, which five hundred years earlier he would have governed. In short, he will explain how the soul and human passions are imperceptibly altered and, as it were, change their nature; why, in the long run, our needs and our pleasures change their objects; why, with original man gradually disappearing, society no longer offers to the eyes of the wise man anything but an assemblage of artificial men and factitious passions which are the work of all these new relations and have no true foundation in nature. What reflection teaches us on this subject is perfectly confirmed by observation: savage man and civilized man differ so greatly in the depths of their hearts and in their inclinations, that what constitutes the supreme happiness of the one would reduce the other to despair. Savage man breathes only tranquillity and liberty; he wants simply to live and rest easy; and not even the unperturbed tranquillity of the Stoic approaches his profound indifference for any other objects. On the other hand, the citizen is always active and in a sweat, always agitated, and unceasingly tormenting himself in order to seek still more laborious occupations. He works until he dies; he even runs to his death in order to be in a position to live, or renounces life in order to acquire immortality. He pays court to the great whom he hates and to the rich whom he scorns. He stops at nothing to obtain the honor of serving them. He proudly crows about his own baseness and their protection; and proud of his slavery, he speaks with disdain about those who do not have the honor of taking part in it. What a spectacle for the Carib are the difficult and envied labors of the

European minister! How many cruel deaths would that indolent savage not prefer to the horror of such a life, which often is not mollified even by the pleasure of doing good. But in order to see the purpose of so many cares, the words *power* and *reputation* would have to have a meaning in his mind; he would have to learn that there is a type of men who place some value on the regard the rest of the world has for them, and who know how to be happy and content with themselves on the testimony of others rather than on their own. Such, in fact, is the true cause of all these differences; the savage lives in himself; the man accustomed to the ways of society is always outside himself and knows how to live only in the opinion of others. And it is, as it were, from their judgment alone that he draws the sentiment of his own existence. It is not pertinent to my subject to show how, from such a disposition, so much indifference for good and evil arises, along with such fine discourse on morality; how, with everything reduced to appearances, everything becomes factitious and bogus: honor, friendship, virtue, and often even our vices, about which we eventually find the secret of boasting; how, in a word, always asking others what we are and never daring to question ourselves on this matter, in the midst of so much philosophy, humanity, politeness, and sublime maxims, we have merely a deceitful and frivolous exterior: honor without virtue, reason without wisdom, and pleasure without happiness. It is enough for me to have proved that this is not the original state of man, and that this is only the spirit of society, and the inequality that society engenders, which thus change and alter all our natural inclinations.

I have tried to set forth the origin and progress of inequality, the establishment and abuse of political societies, to the extent that these things can be deduced from the nature of man by the light of reason alone, and independently of the sacred dogmas that give to sovereign authority the sanction of divine right. It follows from this presentation that, since inequality is practically non-existent in the state of nature, it derives its force and growth from the development of our faculties and the progress of the human mind, and eventually becomes stable and legitimate through the establishment of property and laws. Moreover, it follows that moral inequality, authorized by positive right alone, is contrary to natural right whenever it is not combined in the same proportion with physical inequality: a distinction that is sufficient to determine what one should think in this regard about the sort of inequality that reigns among all civilized people, for it is obviously contrary to the law of nature, however it may be defined, for a child to command an old man, for an imbecile to lead a wise man, and for a handful of people to gorge themselves on superfluities while the starving multitude lacks necessities.

from *On the Social Contract*

Book 1

CHAPTER IX / ON THE REAL [I.E., PROPRIETARY] DOMAIN

Each member of the community gives himself to it at the instant of its constitution, just as he actually is, himself and all his forces, including all the goods in his possession. This is not to say that by this act possession changes its nature as it changes hands and becomes property in the hands of the sovereign. Rather, since the forces of the city are incomparably greater than those of a private individual, public possession is by that very fact stronger and more irrevocable, without being more legitimate, at least to strangers. For with regard to its members, the state is master of all their goods in virtue of the social contract, which serves in the state as the basis of all rights. But with regard to other powers, the state is master only in virtue of the right of the first occupant, which it derives from private individuals.

The right of first occupant, though more real than the right of the strongest, does not become a true right until after the establishment of the right of property. Every man by nature has a right to everything he needs; however, the positive act whereby he becomes a proprietor of some goods excludes him from all the rest. Once his lot has been determined, he should limit himself thereto, no longer having any right against the community. This is the reason why the right of the first occupant, so weak in the state of nature, is able to command the respect of every man living in the civil state. In this right, one respects not so much what belongs to others as what does not belong to oneself.

In general, the following rules must obtain in order to authorize the right of the first occupant on any land. First, this land may not already be occupied by anyone. Second, no one may occupy more than the amount needed to subsist. Third, one is to take possession of it not by an empty ceremony, but by working and cultivating it—the only sign of property that ought, in the absence of legal titles, to be respected by others. . . .

It can also happen, as men begin to unite before possessing anything and later appropriate a piece of land sufficient for everyone, that they enjoy it in common or divide it among themselves either in equal shares or according to proportions laid down by the sovereign. In whatever way this acquisition is accomplished, each private individual's right to his very own store is always subordinate to the community's right to all, without which there could be neither solidity in the social fabric nor real force in the exercise of sovereignty.

I will end this chapter and this book with a remark that should serve as a basis for every social system. It is that instead of destroying natural equality, the fundamental compact, on the contrary, substitutes a moral and legitimate equality to whatever physical inequality nature may have been able to impose upon men, and that, however, unequal in force or intelligence they may be, men all become equal by convention and by right.*

---

* Under bad governments this equality is only apparent and illusory. It serves merely to maintain the poor man in his misery and the rich man in his usurpation. In actuality, laws are always useful to those who have possessions and harmful to those who have nothing. Whence it follows that the social state is advantageous to men only insofar as they all have something and none of them has too much.

Book II

CHAPTER III / WHETHER THE GENERAL WILL CAN ERR

It follows from what has preceded that the general will is always right and always tends toward the public utility. However, it does not follow that the deliberations of the people always have the same rectitude. We always want what is good for us, but we do not always see what it is. The populace is never corrupted, but it is often tricked, and only then does it appear to want what is bad.

There is often a great deal of difference between the will of all and the general will. The latter considers only the general interest, whereas the former considers private interest and is merely the sum of private wills. But remove from these same wills the pluses and minuses that cancel each other out, and what remains as the sum of the differences is the general will.

If, when a sufficiently informed populace deliberates, the citizens were to have no communication among themselves, the general will would always result from the large number of small differences, and the deliberation would always be good. But when intrigues and partial associations come into being at the expense of the large association, the will of each of these associations becomes general in relation to its members and particular in relation to the state. It can be said, then, that there are no longer as many voters as there are men, but merely as many as there are associations. The differences become less numerous and yield a result that is less general. Finally, when one of these associations is so large that it dominates all the others, the result is no longer a sum of minor differences, but a single difference. Then there is no longer a general will, and the opinion that dominates is merely a private opinion.

For the general will to be well articulated, it is therefore important that there should be no partial society in the state and that each citizen make up his own mind. Such was the unique and sublime institution of the great Lycurgus. If there are partial societies, their number must be multiplied and in-

equality among them prevented, as was done by Solon, Numa* and Servius. These precautions are the only effective way of bringing it about that the general will is always enlightened and that the populace is not tricked.

CHAPTER IV / ON THE LIMITS OF SOVEREIGN POWER

If the state or the city is merely a moral person whose life consists in the union of its members, and if the most important of its concerns is that of its own conservation, it ought to have a universal compulsory force to move and arrange each part in the manner best suited to the whole. Just as nature gives each man an absolute power over all his members, the social compact gives the body politic an absolute power over all its members, and it is the same power which, as I have said, is directed by the general will and bears the name sovereignty.

But over and above the public person, we need to consider the private persons who make it up and whose life and liberty are naturally independent of it. It is, therefore, a question of making a rigorous distinction between the respective rights of the citizens and the sovereign, and between the duties the former have to fulfill as subjects and the natural right they should enjoy as men.

We grant that each person alienates, by the social compact, only that portion of his power, his goods, and liberty whose use is of consequence to the community; but we must also grant that only the sovereign is the judge of what is of consequence.

A citizen should render to the state all the service he can as soon as the sovereign demands them. However, for its part, the sovereign cannot impose on the subjects any fetters that are of no use to the community. It cannot even will to do so, for under the law of reason nothing takes place without a cause, any more than under the law of nature.

The commitments that bind us to the body poli-

---

* Lycurgus was a legendary Spartan lawgiver of about the ninth century B.C.E. Solon was an Athenian lawgiver, and Numa was Rome's second king. —ED.

tic are obligatory only because they are mutual, and their nature is such that in fulfilling them one cannot work for someone else without also working for oneself. Why is the general will always right, and why do all constantly want the happiness of each of them, if not because everyone applies the word *each* to himself and thinks of himself as he votes for all? This proves that the quality of right and the notion of justice it produces are derived from the preference each person gives himself, and thus from the nature of man; that the general will, to be really such, must be general in its object as well as in its essence; that it must derive from all in order to be applied to all; and that it loses its natural rectitude when it tends toward any individual, determinate object. For then, judging what is foreign to us, we have no true principle of equity to guide us. . . .

. . . the social compact establishes among the citizens an equality of such a kind that they all commit themselves under the same conditions and should all enjoy the same rights. Thus by the very nature of the compact, every act of sovereignty (that is, every authentic act of the general will) obligates or favors all citizens equally, so that the sovereign knows only the nation as a body and does not draw distinctions between any of those members that make it up. Strictly speaking, then, what is an act of sovereignty? It is not a convention between a superior and an inferior, but a convention of the body with each of its members. This convention is legitimate, because it has the social contract as a basis; equitable, because it is common to all; useful, because it can have only the general good for its object; and solid, because it has the public force and the supreme power as a guarantee. So long as the subjects are subordinated only to such convention, they obey no one but their own will alone. And asking how far the respective rights of the sovereign and the citizens extend is asking how far the latter can commit themselves to one another, each to all and all to each.

We can see from this that the sovereign power, absolute, wholly sacred and inviolable as it is, does not and cannot exceed the limits of general conventions, and that every man can completely dispose of such goods and freedom as has been left to him by these conventions. This results in the fact that the sovereign never has the right to lay more charges on one subject than on another, because in that case the matter becomes particular, no longer within the range of the sovereign's competence.

Once these distinctions are granted, it is so false that there is, in the social contract, any genuine renunciation on the part of private individuals that their situation, as a result of this contract, is really preferable to what it was beforehand; and, instead of an alienation, they have merely made an advantageous exchange of an uncertain and precarious mode of existence for another that is better and surer. Natural independence is exchanged for liberty; the power to harm others is exchanged for their own security; and their force, which others could overcome, for a right which the social union renders invincible. Their life itself, which they have devoted to the state, is continually protected by it; and when they risk their lives for its defense, what are they then doing but returning to the state what they have received from it? What are they doing, that they did not do more frequently and with greater danger in the state of nature, when they would inevitably have to fight battles, defending at the peril of their lives the means of their preservation? It is true that everyone has to fight, if necessary, for the homeland; but it also is the case that no one ever has to fight on his own behalf. Do we not still gain by running, for something that brings about our security, a portion of the risks we would have to run for ourselves once our security is taken away?

CHAPTER XI / ON THE VARIOUS SYSTEMS OF LEGISLATION

If one enquires into precisely wherein the greatest good of all consists, which should be the purpose of every system of legislation, one will find that it boils down to the two principal objects, *liberty* and *equality*. Liberty, because all particular dependence is that much force taken from the body of the state; equality, because liberty cannot subsist without it.

I have already said what civil liberty is. Regarding equality, we need not mean by this word that degrees of power and wealth are to be absolutely the same, but rather that, with regard to power, it should transcend all violence and never be exercised except by virtue of rank and laws; and, with regard to wealth, no citizen should be so rich as to be capable of buying another citizen, and none so poor that he is forced to sell himself. This presupposes moderation in goods and credit on the part of the great, and moderation in avarice and covetousness* on the part of the lowly.

This equality is said to be a speculative fiction that cannot exist in practice. But if abuse is inevitable, does it follow that it should not at least be regulated? It is precisely because the force of things tends always to destroy equality that the force of legislation should always tend to maintain it.

---

* Do you therefore want to give constancy to the State? Bring the extremes as close together as possible. Tolerate neither rich men nor beggars. These two estates, which are naturally inseparable, are equally fatal to the common good. From the one come the fomenters of tyranny, and from the other the tyrants. It is always between them that public liberty becomes a matter of commerce. The one buys it and the other sells it.

KARL MARX AND FRIEDRICH ENGELS

from *Manifesto of the Communist Party* (1848)

and

KARL MARX

from *Critique of the Gotha Program* (1872)

Karl Marx (1818–1883) was born in Treves, in the German Rhineland, to a Jewish family that had converted to Lutheranism. After studying law in Bonn and philosophy and history in Berlin, he earned his doctorate at Jena in 1841 with a dissertation on the ancient Greek philosophers Epicurus and Democritus. He became editor of a liberal Cologne newspaper, which was suppressed in 1843. He fled to Paris; two years later he was expelled from France and fled to Brussels.

Friedrich Engels (1820–1895), born in Barmen, also in the Rhineland, was the son of a textile manufacturer. He worked for his father in a cotton mill in Manchester, England, as a clerk, manager, and part owner. He met Marx in Cologne in 1842 and again in Paris in 1844. In 1848, they collaborated to write The Communist Manifesto. *Engels returned to England. Marx also ended up there a year later, after being expelled from Belgium, France, and Germany. He lived for the rest of his life in London, supported by Engels.*

Though a vision of justice lies behind much of their work, Marx and Engels wrote little about it. The Communist Manifesto and the Critique of the Gotha Program contain some of their most explicit comments about distributive justice. The former work details the theory of class struggle; the latter presents Marx's famous slogan, "From each according to his abilities, to each according to his needs!" which summarizes his conception of just distribution. (Source: Reprinted from Karl Marx and Friedrich Engels, Manifesto of the Communist Party, New York: International Publishers, 1932, and Karl Marx, Critique of the Gotha Program: New York, International Publishers, 1933.)

QUESTIONS FOR REFLECTION

1. What is the bourgeoisie? What is the proletariat?

2. Why, according to Marx and Engels, are the bourgeoisie and the proletariat in conflict?

3. What is communism?

4. What arguments do Marx and Engels advance for the abolition of private property? What objections might be raised against that program?

5. What practical measures do Marx and Engels advocate? How do they relate to the primary aim of communism?

6. What is Marx's conception of distributive justice?

from *Manifesto of the Communist Party*

I. Bourgeois and Proletarians*

The history of all hitherto existing society is the history of class struggles.

Freeman and slave, patrician and plebeian, lord and serf, guild-master and journeyman, in a word, oppressor and oppressed, stood in constant opposition to one another, carried on an uninterrupted, now hidden, now open fight, a fight that each time ended, either in a revolutionary re-constitution of society at large, or in the common ruin of the contending classes.

In the earlier epochs of history, we find almost everywhere a complicated arrangement of society into various orders, a manifold gradation of social rank. In ancient Rome we have patricians, knights, plebeians, slaves; in the Middle Ages, feudal lords, vassals, guild-masters, journeymen, apprentices, serfs; in almost all of these classes, again, subordinate gradations.

The modern bourgeois society that has sprouted from the ruins of feudal society has not done away with class antagonisms. It has but establishsed new classes, new conditions of oppression, new forms of struggle in place of the old ones.

Our epoch, the epoch of the bourgeoisie, possesses, however, this distinctive feature: it has simplified the class antagonisms: Society as a whole is more and more splitting up into two great hostile camps, into two great classes directly facing each other: Bourgeoisie and Proletariat. . . .

The bourgeoisie, historically, has played a most revolutionary part.

The bourgeoisie, wherever it has got the upper hand, has put an end to all feudal, patriarchal, idyllic relations. It has pitilessly torn asunder the motley feudal ties that bound man to his "natural superiors," and has left remaining no other nexus between man and man than naked self-interest, than callous "cash payment." It has drowned the most heavenly ecstasies of religious fervour, of chivalrous enthusiasm, of philistine sentimentalism, in the icy water of egotistical calculation. It has resolved personal worth into exchange value, and in place of the numberless indefeasible chartered freedoms, has set up that single, unconscionable freedom—Free Trade. In one word, for exploitation, veiled by religious and political illusions, it has substituted naked, shameless, direct, brutal exploitation.

The bourgeoisie has stripped of its halo every occupation hitherto honoured and looked up to with reverent awe. It has converted the physician, the lawyer, the priest, the poet, the man of science, into its paid wage-labourers.

The bourgeoisie has torn away from the family its sentimental veil, and has reduced the family relation to a mere money relation.

The bourgeoisie has disclosed how it came to pass that the brutal display of vigour in the Middle Ages, which Reactionists so much admire, found its fitting complement in the most slothful indolence. It has been the first to show what man's activity can bring about. It has accomplished wonders far surpassing Egyptian pyramids, Roman aqueducts, and Gothic cathedrals; it has conducted expeditions that put in the shade all former Exoduses of nations and crusades.

The bourgeoisie cannot exist without constantly revolutionising the instruments of production, and thereby the relations of production, and with them the whole relations of society. Conservation of the old modes of production in unaltered form, was, on

* By bourgeoisie is meant the class of modern Capitalists, owners of the means of social production and employers of wage-labour. By proletariat, the class of modern wage-labourers who, having no means of production of their own, are reduced to selling their labour-power in order to live.

the contrary, the first condition of existence for all earlier industrial classes. Constant revolutionising of production, uninterrupted disturbance of all social conditions, everlasting uncertainty and agitation distinguish the bourgeois epoch from all earlier ones. All fixed, fast-frozen relations, with their train of ancient and venerable prejudices and opinions, are swept away, all new-formed ones become antiquated before they can ossify. All that is solid melts into air, all that is holy is profaned, and man is at last compelled to face with sober senses, his real conditions of life, and his relations with his kind.

The need of a constantly expanding market for its products chases the bourgeoisie over the whole surface of the globe. It must nestle everywhere, settle everywhere, establish connexions everywhere.

The bourgeoisie has through its exploitation of the world-market given a cosmopolitan character to production and consumption in every country. To the great chagrin of Reactionists, it has drawn from under the feet of industry the national ground on which it stood. All old-established national industries have been destroyed or are daily being destroyed. They are dislodged by new industries, whose introduction becomes a life and death question for all civilised nations, by industries that no longer work up indigenous raw material, but raw material drawn from the remotest zones; industries whose products are consumed, not only at home, but in every quarter of the globe. In place of the old wants, satisfied by the productions of the country, we find new wants, requiring for their satisfaction the products of distant lands and climes. In place of the old local and national seclusion and self-sufficiency, we have intercourse in every direction, universal interdependence of nations. And as in material, so also in intellectual production. The intellectual creations of individual nations become common property. National one-sidedness and narrow-mindedness become more and more impossible, and from the numerous national and local literatures, there arises a world literature.

The bourgeoisie, by the rapid improvement of all instruments of production, by the immensely facilitated means of communication, draws all, even the most barbarian, nations into civilisation. The cheap prices of its commodities are the heavy artillery with which it batters down all Chinese walls, with which

it forces the barbarians' intensely obstinate hatred of foreigners to capitulate. It compels all nations, on pain of extinction, to adopt the bourgeois mode of production; it compels them to introduce what it calls civilisation into their midst, i.e., to become bourgeois themselves. In one word, it creates a world after its own image.

The bourgeoisie has subjected the country to the rule of the towns. It has created enormous cities, has greatly increased the urban population as compared with the rural, and has thus rescued a considerable part of the population from the idiocy of rural life. Just as it has made the country dependent on the towns, so it has made barbarian and semi-barbarian countries dependent on the civilised ones, nations of peasants on nations of bourgeois, the East on the West.

The bourgeoisie keeps more and more doing away with the scattered state of the population, of the means of production, and of property. It has agglomerated population, centralised means of production, and has concentrated property in a few hands. The necessary consequence of this was political centralisation. Independent, or but loosely connected provinces, with separate interests, laws, government and systems of taxation, became lumped together into one nation, with one government, one code of laws, one national class-interest, one frontier and one customs-tariff. . . .

. . . Modern bourgeois society with its relations of production, of exchange and of property, a society that has conjured up such gigantic means of production and of exchange, is like the sorcerer, who is no longer able to control the powers of the nether world whom he has called up by his spells. For many a decade past the history of industry and commerce is but the history of the revolt of modern productive forces against modern conditions of production, against the property relations that are the conditions for the existence of the bourgeoisie and of its rule. It is enough to mention the commercial crises that by their periodical return put on its trial, each time more threateningly, the existence of the entire bourgeois society. In these crises a great part not only of the existing products, but also of the previously created productive forces, are periodically destroyed. In these crises there breaks out an epidemic that, in all earlier epochs, would have seemed an absurdity—the epidemic of over-production. Society suddenly finds itself put back into a state of momentary barbarism; it appears as if a famine, a universal war of devastation had cut off the supply of every means of subsistence; industry and commerce seem to be destroyed; and why? Because there is too much civilisation, too much means of subsistence, too much industry, too much commerce. The productive forces at the disposal of society no longer tend to further the development of the conditions of bourgeois property; on the contrary, they have become too powerful for these conditions, by which they are fettered, and so soon as they overcome these fetters, they bring disorder into the whole of bourgeois society, endanger the existence of bourgeois property. The conditions of bourgeois society are too narrow to comprise the wealth created by them. And how does the bourgeoisie get over these crises? On the one hand by enforced destruction of a mass of productive forces; on the other, by the conquest of new markets, and by the more thorough exploitation of the old ones. That is to say, by paving the way for more extensive and more destructive crises, and by diminishing the means whereby crises are prevented.

The weapons with which the bourgeoisie felled fuedalism to the ground are now turned against the bourgeoisie itself.

But not only has the bourgeoisie forged the weapons that bring death to itself; it has also called into existence the men who are to wield those weapons—the modern working class—the proletarians.

In proportion as the bourgeoisie, *i.e.*, capital, is developed, in the same proportion is the proletariat, the modern working class, developed—a class of labourers, who live only so long as they find work, and who find work only so long as their labour increases capital. These labourers, who must sell themselves piece-meal, are a commodity, like every other article of commerce, and are consequently exposed to all the vicissitudes of competition, to all the fluctuations of the market.

Owing to the extensive use of machinery and to division of labour, the work of the proletarians has lost all individual character, and consequently, all charm for the workman. He becomes an appendage of the machine, and it is only the most simple, most monotonous, and most easily acquired knack, that

is required of him. Hence, the cost of production of a workman is restricted, almost entirely, to the means of subsistence that he requires for his maintenance, and for the propagation of his race. But the price of a commodity, and therefore also of labour, is equal to its cost of production. In proportion, therefore, as the repulsiveness of the work increases, the wage decreases. Nay more, in proportion as the use of machinery and division of labour increases, in the same proportion the burden of toil also increases, whether by prolongation of the working hours, by increase of the work exacted in a given time or by increased speed of the machinery, etc.

Modern industry has converted the little workshop of the patriarchal master into the great factory of the industrial capitalist. Masses of labourers, crowded into the factory, are organised like soldiers. As privates of the industrial army they are placed under the command of a perfect hierarchy of officers and sergeants. Not only are they slaves of the bourgeois class, and of the bourgeois State; they are daily and hourly enslaved by the machine, by the over-looker, and, above all, by the individual bourgeois manufacturer himself. The more openly this despotism proclaims gain to be its end and aim, the more petty, the more hateful and the more embittering it is.

The less the skill and exertion of strength implied in manual labour, in other words, the more modern industry becomes developed, the more is the labour of men superseded by that of women. Differences of age and sex have no longer any distinctive social validity for the working class. All are instruments of labour, more or less expensive to use, according to their age and sex. . . .

Now and then the workers are victorious, but only for a time. The real fruit of their battles lies, not in the immediate result, but in the ever-expanding union of the workers. This union is helped on by the improved means of communication that are created by modern industry and that place the workers of different localities in contact with one another. It was just this contact that was needed to centralise the numerous local struggles, all of the same character, into one national struggle between classes. But every class struggle is a political struggle. And that union, to attain which the burghers of the Middle Ages, with their miserable highways, required centuries, the modern proletarians, thanks to railways, achieve in a few years.

This organisation of the proletrians into a class, and consequently into a political party, is continually being upset again by the competition between the workers themselves. But it ever rises up again, stronger, firmer, mightier. It compels legislative recognition of particular interests of the workers, by taking advantage of the divisions among the bourgeoisie itself. Thus the ten-hours' bill in England was carried.

Altogether collisions between the classes of the old society further, in many ways, the course of development of the proletariat. The bourgeoisie finds itself involved in a constant battle. At first with the aristocracy; later on, with those portions of the bourgeoisie itself, whose interests have become antagonistic to the progress of industry; at all times, with the bourgeoisie of foreign countries. In all these battles it sees itself compelled to appeal to the proletariat, to ask for its help, and thus, to drag it into the political arena. The bourgeoisie itself, therefore, supplies the proletariat with its own elements of political and general education, in other words, it furnishes the proletariat with weapons for fighting the bourgeoisie.

Further, as we have already seen, entire sections of the ruling classes are, by the advance of industry, precipitated into the proletariat, or are at least threatened in their conditions of existence. These also supply the proletariat with fresh elements of enlightenment and progress.

Finally, in times when the class struggle nears the decisive hour, the process of dissolution going on within the ruling class, in fact within the whole range of society, assumes such a violent, glaring character, that a small section of the ruling class cuts itself adrift, and joins the revolutionary class, the class that holds the future in its hands. Just as, therefore, at an earlier period, a section of the nobility went over to the bourgeoisie, so now a portion of the bourgeoisie goes over to the proletariat, and in particular, a portion of the bourgeois ideologists, who have raised themselves to the level of comprehending theoretically the historical movement as a whole.

Of all the classes that stand face to face with the bourgeoisie today, the proletariat alone is a really revolutionary class. The other classes decay and finally disappear in the face of Modern Industry; the proletariat is its special and essential product. . . .

Hitherto, every form of society has been based, as we have already seen, on the antagonism of oppressing and oppressed classes. But in order to oppress a class, certain conditions must be assured to it under which it can, at least, continue its slavish existence. The serf, in the period of serfdom, raised himself to membership in the commune, just as the petty bourgeois, under the yoke of feudal absolutism, managed to develop into a bourgeois. The modern labourer, on the contrary, instead of rising with the progress of industry, sinks deeper and deeper below the conditions of existence of his own class. He becomes a pauper, and pauperism develops more rapidly than population and wealth. And here it becomes evident, that the bourgeoisie is unfit any longer to be the ruling class in society, and to impose its conditions of existence upon society as an over-riding law. It is unfit to rule because it is incompetent to assure an existence to its slave within his slavery, because it cannot help letting him sink into such a state, that it has to feed him, instead of being fed by him. Society can no longer live under this bourgeoisie, in other words, its existence is no longer compatible with society.

The essential condition for the existence, and for the sway of the bourgeois class, is the formation and augmentation of capital; the condition for capital is wage-labour. Wage-labour rests exclusively on competition between the labourers. The advance of industry, whose involuntary promoter is the bourgeoisie, replaces the isolation of the labourers, due to competition, by their revolutionary combination, due to association. The development of Modern Industry, therefore, cuts from under its feet the very foundation on which the bourgeoisie produces and appropriates products. What the bougeoisie, therefore, produces, above all, is its own grave-diggers. Its fall and the victory of the proletariat are equally inevitable.

II. Proletarians and Communists

In what relation do the Communists stand to the proletarians as a whole?

The Communists do not form a separate party opposed to other working-class parties.

They have no interests separate and apart from those of the proletariat as a whole.

They do not set up any sectarian principles of their own, by which to shape and mould the proletarian movement.

The Communists are distinguished from the other working-class parties by this only: (1) In the national stuggles of the proletarians of the different countries, they point out and bring to the front the common interests of the entire proletariat, independently of all nationality. (2) In the various stages of development which the struggle of the working class against the bourgeoisie has to pass through, they always and everywhere represent the interests of the movement as a whole.

The Communists, therefore, are on the one hand, practically, the most advanced and resolute section of the working-class parties of every country, that section which pushes forward all others; on the other hand, theoretically, they have over the great mass of the proletariat the advantage of clearly understanding the line of march, the conditions, and the ultimate general results of the proletarian movement.

The immediate aim of the Communists is the same as that of all the other proletarian parties: formation of the proletariat into a class, overthrow of the bourgeois supremacy, conquest of political power by the proletariat.

The thoretical conclusions of the Communists are in no way based on ideas or principles that have been invented, or discovered, by this or that would-be universal reformer.

They merely express, in general terms, actual relations springing from an existing class struggle, from a historical movement going on under our very eyes. The abolition of existing property relations is not at all a distinctive feature of Communism.

All property relations in the past have continually been subject to historical change consequent upon the change in historical conditions.

The French Revolution, for example, abolished feudal property in favour of bourgeois property.

The distinguishing feature of Communism is not the abolition of property generally, but the abolition of bourgeois property. But modern bourgeois private property is the final and most complete expression of the system of producing and appropriating products, that is based on class antagonisms, on the exploitation of the many by the few.

In this sense, the theory of the Communists may be summed up in the single sentence: Abolition of private property. . . .

You are horrified at our intending to do away with private property. But in your existing society, private property is already done away with for nine-tenths of the population; its existence for the few is solely due to its non-existence in the hands of those nine-tenths. You reproach us, therefore, with intending to do away with a form of property, the necessary condition for whose existence is the non-existence of any property for the immense majority of society.

In one word, you reproach us with intending to do away with your property. Precisely so; that is just what we intend.

From the moment when labour can no longer be converted into capital, money, or rent, into a social power capable of being monopolised, *i.e.*, from the moment when individual property can no longer be transformed into bourgeois property, into capital, from that moment, you say, individuality vanishes.

You must, therefore, confess that by "individual" you mean no other person than the bourgeois, than the middle-class owner of property. This person must, indeed, be swept out of the way, and made impossible.

Communism deprives no man of the power to appropriate the products of society; all that it does is to deprive him of the power to subjugate the labour of others by means of such appropriation.

It has been objected that upon the abolition of private property all work will cease, and universal laziness will overtake us.

According to this, bourgeois society ought long ago to have gone to the dogs through sheer idleness; for those of its members who work, acquire nothing, and those who acquire anything, do not work. The whole of this objection is but another expression of the tautology: that there can no longer be any wage-labour when there is no longer any capital.

All objections urged against the Communistic

mode of producing and appropriating material products, have, in the same way, been urged against the Communistic modes of producing and appropriating intellectual products. Just as, to the bourgeois, the disappearance of class property is the disappearance of production itself, so the disappearance of class culture is to him identical with the dissappearance of all culture.

That culture, the loss of which he laments, is, for the enormous majority, a mere training to act as a machine.

But don't wrangle with us so long as you apply, to our intended abolition of bourgeois property, the standard of your bourgeois notions of freedom, culture, law, &c. Your very ideas are but the outgrowth of the conditions of your bourgeois production and bourgeois property, just as your jurisprudence is but the will of your class made into a law for all, a will, whose essential character and direction are determined by the economical conditions of existence of your class. . . .

Does it require deep intuition to comprehend that man's ideas, views and conceptions, in one word, man's consciousness, changes with every change in the conditions of his material existence, in his social relations and in his social life?

What else does the history of ideas prove, than that intellectual production changes its character in proportion as material production is changed? The ruling ideas of each age have ever been the ideas of its ruling class. . . .

We have seen above, that the first step in the revolution by the working class, is to raise the proletariat to the position of ruling class, to win the battle of democracy.

The proletariat will use its political supremacy to wrest, by degrees, all capital from the bourgeoisie, to centralise all instruments of production in the hands of the State, i. e., of the proletariat organised as the ruling class; and to increase the total of productive forces as rapidly as possible.

Of course, in the beginning, this cannot be effected except by means of despotic inroads on the rights of property, and on the conditions of bourgeois production; by means of measures, therefore, which appear economically insufficient and untenable, but which, in the course of the movement,

outstrip themselves, necessitate further inroads upon the old social order, and are unavoidable as a means of entirely revolutionising the mode of production.

These measures will of course be different in different countries.

Nevertheless in the most advanced countries, the following will be pretty generally applicable.

1. Abolition of property in land and application of all rents of land to public purposes.

2. A heavy progressive or graduated income tax.

3. Abolition of all right of inheritance.

4. Confiscation of the property of all emigrants and rebels.

5. Centralisation of credit in the hands of the State, by means of a national bank with State capital and an exclusive monopoly.

6. Centralisation of the means of communication and transport in the hands of the State.

7. Extention of factories and instruments of production owned by the State; the bringing into cultivation of waste-lands, and the improvement of the soil generally in accordance with a common plan.

8. Equal liability of all to labour. Establishment of industrial armies, especially for agriculture.

9. Combination of agriculture with manufacturing industries; gradual abolition of the distinction between town and country, by a more equable distribution of the population over the country.

10. Free education for all children in public schools. Abolition of children's factory labour in its present form. Combination of education with industrial production, &c., &c.

When, in the course of development, class distinctions have disappeared, and all production has been concentrated in the hands of a vast association of the whole nation, the public power will lose its political character. Political power, properly so called, is merely the organised power of one class for oppressing another. If the proletariat during its contest with the bourgeoisie is compelled, by the force of circumstances, to organise itself as a class, if, by means of a revolution, it makes itself the ruling class, and, as such, sweeps away by force the old conditions of production, then it will, along with these conditions, have swept away the conditions for the existence of class antagonisms and of classes generally, and will thereby have abolished its own supremacy as a class.

In place of the old bourgeois society, with its classes and class antagonisms, we shall have an association, in which the free development of each is the condition for the free development of all.

IV. Position of the Communists in Relation to the Various Existing Opposition Parties

. . . In short, the Communists everywhere support every revolutionary movement against the existing social and political order of things.

In all these movements they bring to the front, as the leading question in each, the property question, no matter what its degree of development at the time.

Finally, they labour everywhere for the union and agreement of the democratic parties of all countries.

The Communists disdain to conceal their views and aims. They openly declare that their ends can be attained only by the forcible overthrow of all existing social conditions. Let the ruling classes tremble at a Communistic revolution. The proletarians have nothing to lose but their chains. They have a world to win.

WORKING MEN OF ALL COUNTRIES, UNITE!

from *Critique of the Gotha Program*

... What is "a fair distribution"?

Do not the bourgeois assert that the present-day distribution is "fair"? And is it not, in fact, the only "fair" distribution on the basis of the present-day mode of production? Are economic relations regulated by legal conceptions or do not, on the contrary, legal relations arise from economic ones? Have not also the socialist sectarians the most varied notions about "fair" distribution?

To understand what is implied in this connection by the phrase "fair distribution," we must take the first paragraph and this one together. The latter presupposes a society wherein "the instruments of labour are common property and the total labour is cooperatively regulated," and from the first paragraph we learn that "the proceeds of labour belong undiminished with equal right to all members of society."

"To all members of society"? To those who do not work as well? What remains then of the "undiminished proceeds of labour"? Only to those members of society who work? What remains then of the "equal right" of all members of society?

But "all members of society" and "equal right" are obviously mere phrases. The kernel consists in this, that in this communist society every worker must receive the "undiminished" Lassallean* "proceeds of labour."

Let us take first of all the words "proceeds of labour" in the sense of the product of labour; then the co-operative proceeds of labour are the *total social product.*

From this must now be deducted:

First, cover for replacement of the means of production used up.

Secondly, additional portion for expansion of production.

Thirdly, reserve or insurance funds to provide against accidents, dislocations caused by natural calamities, etc.

These deductions from the "undiminished proceeds of labour" are an economic necessity and their magnitude is to be determined according to available means and forces, and partly by computation of probabilities, but they are in no way calculable by equity.

There remains the other part of the total product, intended to serve as means of consumption.

Before this is divided among the individuals, there has to be deducted again, from it:

First, the general costs of administration not belonging to production.

This part will, from the outset, be very considerably restricted in comparison with present-day society and it diminishes in proportion as the new society develops.

Secondly, that which is intended for the common satisfaction of needs, such as schools, health services, etc.

From the outset this part grows considerably in comparison with present-day society and it grows in proportion as the new society develops.

Thirdly, funds for those unable to work, etc., in short, for what is included under so-called official poor relief today.

Only now do we come to the "distribution" which the programme, under Lassallean influence, alone has in view in its narrow fashion, namely, to that part of the means of consumption which is divided among the individual producers of the co-operative society.

The "undiminished proceeds of labour" have already unnoticeably become converted into the "diminished" proceeds, although what the producer is deprived of in his capacity as a private individual

*Ferdinand Lassalle (1825–1864), German socialist and correspondent of Marx, founded the first political party for German workers in 1863. It is the ancestor of today's German Social Democratic Party. —Ed.

benefits him directly or indirectly in his capacity as a member of society.

Just as the phrase of the "undiminished proceeds of labour" has disappeared, so now does the phrase of the "proceeds of labour" disappear altogether.

Within the co-operative society based on common ownership of the means of production, the producers do not exchange their products; just as little does the labour employed on the products appear here *as the value* of these products, as a material quality possessed by them, since now, in contrast to capitalist society, individual labour no longer exists in an indirect fashion but directly as a component part of the total labour. The phrase "proceeds of labour," objectionable also today on account of its ambiguity, thus loses all meaning.

What we have to deal with here is a communist society, not as it has *developed* on its own foundations, but, on the contrary, just as it *emerges* from capitalist society; which is thus in every respect, economically, morally and intellectually, still stamped with the birth marks of the old society from whose womb it emerges. Accordingly, the individual producer receives back from society—after the deductions have been made—exactly what he gives to it. What he has given to it is his individual quantum of labour. For example, the social working day consists of the sum of the individual hours of work; the individual labour time of the individual producer is the part of the social working day contributed by him, his share in it. He receives a certificate from society that he has furnished such and such an amount of labour (after deducting his labour for the common funds), and with this certificate he draws from the social stock of means of consumption as much as costs the same amount of labour. The same amount of labour which he has given to society in one form he receives back in another.

Here obviously the same principle prevails as that which regulates the exchange of commodities, as far as this is exchange of equal values. Content and form are changed, because under the altered circumstances no one can give anything except his labour, and because, on the other hand, nothing can pass to the ownership of individuals except individual means of consumption. But, as far as the distribution of the latter among the individual producers

is concerned, the same principle prevails as in the exchange of commodity equivalents: a given amount of labour in one form is exchanged for an equal amount of labour in another form.

Hence, *equal right* here is still in principle—*bourgeois right,* although principle and practice are no longer at loggerheads, while the exchange of equivalents in commodity exchange only exists *on the average* and not in the individual case.

In spite of this advance, this *equal right* is still constantly stigmatised by a bourgeois limitation. The right of the producers is *proportional* to the labour they supply; the equality consists in the fact that measurement is made with an *equal standard,* labour.

But one man is superior to another physically or mentally and so supplies more labour in the same time, or can labour for a longer time; and labour, to serve as a measure, must be defined by its duration or intensity, otherwise it ceases to be a standard of measurement. This *equal* right is an unequal right for unequal labour. It recognises no class differences, because everyone is only a worker like everyone else; but it tacitly recognises unequal individual endowment and thus productive capacity as natural privileges. *It is, therefore, a right of inequality, in its content, like every right.* Right by its very nature can consist only in the application of an equal standard; but unequal individuals (and they would not be different individuals if they were not unequal) are measurable only by an equal standard in so far as they are brought under an equal point of view, are taken from one *definite* side only, for instance, in the present case, are regarded *only as workers* and nothing more is seen in them, everything else being ignored. Further, one worker is married, another not; one has more children than another, and so on and so forth. Thus, with an equal performance of labour, and hence an equal share in the social consumption fund, one will in fact receive more than another, one will be richer than another, and so on. To avoid all these defects, right instead of being equal would have to be unequal.

But these defects are inevitable in the first phase of communist society as it is when it has just emerged after prolonged birth pangs from capitalist society. Right can never be higher that the economic structure of society and its cultural development conditioned thereby.

In a higher phase of communist society, after the enslaving subordination of the individual to the division of labour, and therewith also the antithesis between mental and physical labour, has vanished; after labour has become not only a means of life but life's prime want; after the productive forces have also increased with the all-round development of the individual, and all the springs of co-operative wealth flow more abundantly—only then can the narrow horizon of bourgeois right be crossed in its entirety and society inscribe on its banner: From each according to his ability, to each according to his needs!

I have dealt more at length with the "undiminished proceeds of labour," on the one hand, and with "equal right" and "fair distribution," on the other, in order to show what a crime it is to attempt, on the one hand, to force on our Party again, as dogmas, ideas which in a certain period had some meaning but have now become obsolete verbal rubbish, while again perverting, on the other, the realistic outlook, which it cost so much effort to instil into the Party but which has now taken root in it, by means of ideological nonsense about right and other trash so common among the democrats and French Socialists.

Quite apart from the analysis so far given, it was in general a mistake to make a fuss about so-called *distribution* and put the principal stress on it.

Any distribution whatever of the means of consumption is only a consequence of the distribution of the conditions of production themselves. The latter distribution, however, is a feature of the mode of production itself. The capitalist mode of production, for example, rests on the fact that the material conditions of production are in the hands of non-workers in the form of property in capital and land, while the masses are only owners of the personal condition of production, of labour power. If the elements of production are so distributed, then the present-day distribution of the means of consumption results automatically. If the material conditions of production are the co-operative property of the workers themselves, then there likewise results a distribution of the means of consumption different from the present one. Vulgar socialism (and from it in turn a section of the democracy) has taken over from the bourgeois economists the consideration and treatment of distribution as independent of the mode of production and hence the presentation of socialism as turning principally on distribution. After the real relation has long been made clear, why retrogress again? . . .

JOHN RAWLS

from *A Theory of Justice* (1970)

John Rawls is Professor of Philosophy at Harvard University. (Source: Reprinted by permission of the publishers from A Theory of Justice *by John Rawls, Cambridge, Mass.: Harvard University Press. Copyright © 1971 by the President and Fellows of Harvard College.)*

QUESTIONS FOR REFLECTION

1. What is a well-ordered society?

2. What is the original position? What is the role of the veil of ignorance?

3. What is reflective equilibrium? What is its significance for moral theory?

4. What are Rawls's two principles of justice? Can they come into conflict? If so, how can the conflict be resolved?

CHAPTER I / JUSTICE AS FAIRNESS

1. The Role of Justice

Justice is the first virtue of social institutions, as truth is of systems of thought. A theory however elegant and economical must be rejected or revised if it is untrue; likewise laws and institutions no matter how efficient and well-arranged must be reformed or abolished if they are unjust. Each person possesses an inviolability founded on justice that even the welfare of society as a whole cannot override. For this reason justice denies that the loss of freedom for some is made right by a greater good shared by others. It does not allow that the sacrifices imposed on a few are outweighed by the larger sum of advantages enjoyed by many. Therefore in a just society the liberties of equal citizenship are taken as settled; the rights secured by justice are not subject to political bargaining or to the calculus of social interests. The only thing that permits us to acquiesce in an erroneous theory is the lack of a better one; analogously, an injustice is tolerable only when it is necessary to avoid an even greater injustice. Being first virtues of human activities, truth and justice are uncompromising.

These propositions seem to express our intuitive conviction of the primacy of justice. No doubt they are expressed too strongly. In any event I wish to inquire whether these contentions or others similar to them are sound, and if so how they can be accounted for. To this end it is necessary to work out a theory of justice in the light of which these assertions can be interpreted and assessed. I shall begin by considering the role of the principles of justice. Let us assume, to fix ideas, that a society is a more or less self-sufficient association of persons who in their relations to one another recognize certain rules of conduct as binding and who for the most part act in accordance with them. Suppose further that these rules specify a system of cooperation designed to advance the good of those taking part in it. Then, although a society is a cooperative venture for mutual advantage, it is typically marked by a conflict as well as by an identity of interests. There is an identity of interests since social cooperation makes possible a better life for all than any would have if each were to live solely by his own efforts. There is a conflict of interests since persons are not indifferent as to how the greater benefits produced by their collaboration are distributed, for in order to pursue their ends they each prefer a larger to a lesser share. A set of principles is required for choosing among the various social arrangements which determine this division of advantages and for underwriting an agreement on the proper distributive shares. These principles are the principles of social justice: they provide a way of assigning rights and duties in the basic institutions of society and they define the appropriate distribution of the benefits and burdens of social cooperation.

Now let us say that a society is well-ordered when it is not only designed to advance the good of its members but when it is also effectively regulated by a public conception of justice. That is, it is a society in which (1) everyone accepts and knows that the others accept the same principles of justice, and (2) the basic social institutions generally satisfy and are generally known to satisfy these principles. In this case while men may put forth excessive demands on one another, they nevertheless acknowledge a common point of view from which their claims may be adjudicated. If men's inclination to self-interest makes their vigilance against one another necessary, their public sense of justice makes their secure association together possible. Among individuals with disparate aims and purposes a shared conception of justice establishes the bonds of civic friendship; the general desire for justice limits the pursuit of other ends. One may think of a public conception of justice as constituting the fundamental charter of a well-ordered human association.

Existing societies are of course seldom well-ordered in this sense, for what is just and unjust is usually in dispute. Men disagree about which principles should define the basic terms of their association. Yet we may still say, despite this disagreement, that they each have a conception of justice. That is, they understand the need for, and they are prepared to affirm, a characteristic set of principles for assigning basic rights and duties and for determining what they take to be the proper distribution of the benefits and burdens of social cooperation. Thus it seems natural to think of the concept of justice as distinct from the various conceptions of justice and as being specified by the role which these different sets of principles, these different conceptions, have in common. Those who hold different conceptions of justice can, then, still agree that institutions are just when no arbitrary distinctions are made between persons in the assigning of basic rights and duties and when the rules determine a proper balance between competing claims to the advantages of social life. Men can agree to this description of just institutions since the notions of an arbitrary distinction and of a proper balance, which are included in the concept of justice, are left open for each to interpret according to the principles of justice that he accepts. These principles single out which similarities and differences among persons are relevant in determining rights and duties and they specify which division of advantages is appropriate. Clearly this distinction between the concept and the various conceptions of justice settles no important questions. It simply helps to identify the role of the principles of social justice.

Some measure of agreement in conceptions of justice is, however, not the only prerequisite for a viable human community. There are other fundamental social problems, in particular those of coordination, efficiency, and stability. Thus the plans of individuals need to be fitted together so that their activities are compatible with one another and they can all be carried through without anyone's legitimate expectations being severely disappointed. Moreover, the execution of these plans should lead to the achievement of social ends in ways that are efficient and consistent with justice. And finally, the scheme of social cooperation must be stable: it must be more or less regularly complied with and its basic rules willingly acted upon; and when infractions occur, stabilizing forces should exist that prevent further violations and tend to restore the arrangement. Now it is evident that these three problems are connected with that of justice. In the absence of a certain measure of agreement on what is just and unjust, it is clearly more difficult for individuals to coordinate their plans efficiently in order to insure that mutually beneficial arrangements are maintained. Distrust and resentment corrode the ties of civility, and suspicion and hostility tempt men to act in ways they would otherwise avoid. So while the distinctive role of conceptions of justice is to specify basic rights and duties and to determine the appropriate distributive shares, the way in which a conception does this is bound to affect the problems of efficiency, coordination, and stability. We cannot, in general, assess a conception of justice by its distributive role alone, however useful this role may be in identifying the concept of justice. We must take into account its wider connections; for even though justice has a certain priority, being the most important virtue of institutions, it is still true that, other things equal, one conception of justice is preferable to another when its broader consequences are more desirable. . . .

3. The Main Idea of the Theory of Justice

My aim is to present a conception of justice which generalizes and carries to a higher level of abstraction the familiar theory of the social contract as found, say, in Locke, Rousseau, and Kant. In order to do this we are not to think of the original contract as one to enter a particular society or to set up a particular form of government. Rather, the guiding idea is that the principles of justice for the basic structure of society are the object of the original agreement. They are the principles that free and rational persons concerned to further their own interests would accept in an initial position of equality as defining the fundamental terms of their association. These principles are to regulate all further agreements; they specify the kinds of social cooperation that can be entered into and the forms of government that can be established. This way of regarding the principles of justice I shall call justice as fairness.

Thus we are to imagine that those who engage in social cooperation choose together, in one joint act, the principles which are to assign basic rights and duties and to determine the division of social benefits. Men are to decide in advance how they are to regulate their claims against one another and what is to be the foundation charter of their society. Just as each person must decide by rational reflection what constitutes his good, that is, the system of ends which it is rational for him to pursue, so a group of persons must decide once and for all what is to count among them as just and unjust. The

choice which rational men would make in this hypothetical situation of equal liberty, assuming for the present that this choice problem has a solution, determines the principles of justice.

In justice as fairness the original position of equality corresponds to the state of nature in the traditional theory of the social contract. This original position is not, of course, thought of as an actual historical state of affairs, much less as a primitive condition of culture. It is understood as a purely hypothetical situation characterized so as to lead to a certain conception of justice. Among the essential features of this situation is that no one knows his place in society, his class position or social status, nor does any one know his fortune in the distribution of natural assets and abilities, his intelligence, strength, and the like. I shall even assume that the parties do not know their conceptions of the good or their special psychological propensities. The principles of justice are chosen behind a veil of ignorance. This ensures that no one is advantaged or disadvantaged in the choice of principles by the outcome of natural chance or the contingency of social circumstances. Since all are similarly situated and no one is able to design principles to favor his particular condition, the principles of justice are the result of a fair agreement or bargain. For given the circumstances of the original position, the symmetry of everyone's relations to each other, this initial situation is fair between individuals as moral persons, that is, as rational beings with their own ends and capable, I shall assume, of a sense of justice. The original position is, one might say, the appropriate initial status quo, and thus the fundamental agreements reached in it are fair. This explains the propriety of the name "justice as fairness": it conveys the idea that the principles of justice are agreed to in an initial situation that is fair. The name does not mean that the concepts of justice and fairness are the same, any more than the phrase "poetry as metaphor" means that the concepts of poetry and metaphor are the same.

Justice as fairness begins, as I have said, with one of the most general of all choices which persons might make together, namely, with the choice of the first principles of a conception of justice which is to regulate all subsequent criticism and reform of institutions. Then, having chosen a conception of justice, we can suppose that they are to choose a constitution and a legislature to enact laws, and so on, all in accordance with the principles of justice initially agreed upon. Our social situation is just if it is such that by this sequence of hypothetical agreements we would have contracted into the general system of rules which defines it. Moreover, assuming that the original position does determine a set of principles (that is, that a particular conception of justice would be chosen), it will then be true that whenever social institutions satisfy these principles those engaged in them can say to one another that they are cooperating on terms to which they would agree if they were free and equal persons whose relations with respect to one another were fair. They could all view their arrangements as meeting the stipulations which they would acknowledge in an initial situation that embodies widely accepted and reasonable constraints on the choice of principles. The general recognition of this fact would provide the basis for a public acceptance of the corresponding principles of justice. No society can, of course, be a scheme of cooperation which men enter voluntarily in a literal sense; each person finds himself placed at birth in some particular position in some particular society, and the nature of this position materially affects his life prospects. Yet a society satisfying the principles of justice as fairness comes as close as a society can to being a voluntary scheme, for it meets the principles which free and equal persons would assent to under circumstances that are fair. In this sense its members are autonomous and the obligations they recognize self-imposed.

One feature of justice as fairness is to think of the parties in the initial situation as rational and mutually disinterested. This does not mean that the parties are egoists, that is, individuals with only certain kinds of interests, say in wealth, prestige, and domination. But they are conceived as not taking an interest in one another's interests. They are to presume that even their spiritual aims may be opposed, in the way that the aims of those of different religions may be opposed. Moreover, the concept of rationality must be interpreted as far as possible in the narrow sense, standard in economic theory, of taking the most effective means to given ends. I shall modify this concept to some extent, . . . but one must try to avoid introducing into it any controversial ethical elements. The initial situation must be characterized by stipulations that are widely accepted.

In working out the conception of justice as fairness one main task clearly is to determine which principles of justice would be chosen in the original position. To do this we must describe this situation in some detail and formulate with care the problem of choice which it presents. . . . It may be observed, however, that once the principles of justice are thought of as arising from an original agreement in a situation of equality, it is an open question whether the principle of utility would be acknowledged. Offhand it hardly seems likely that persons who view themselves as equals, entitled to press their claims upon one another, would agree to a principle which may require lesser life prospects for some simply for the sake of a greater sum of advantages enjoyed by others. Since each desires to protect his interests, his capacity to advance his conception of the good, no one has a reason to acquiesce in an enduring loss for himself in order to bring about a greater net balance of satisfaction. In the absence of strong and lasting benevolent impulses, a rational man would not accept a basic structure merely because it maximized the algebraic sum of advantages irrespective of its permanent effects on his own basic rights and interests. Thus it seems that the principle of utility is incompatible with the conception of social cooperation among equals for mutual advantage. It appears to be inconsistent with the idea of reciprocity implicit in the notion of a well-ordered society. Or, at any rate, so I shall argue.

I shall maintain instead that the persons in the initial situation would choose two rather different principles: the first requires equality in the assignment of basic rights and duties, while the second holds that social and economic inequalities, for example inequalities of wealth and authority, are just only if they result in compensating benefits for everyone, and in particular for the least advantaged members of society. These principles rule out justifying institutions on the grounds that the hardships of some are offset by a greater good in the aggregate. It may be expedient but it is not just that some should have less in order that others may prosper. But there is no injustice in the greater benefits earned by a few provided that the situation of persons not so fortunate is thereby improved. The intuitive idea is that since everyone's well-being depends upon a scheme of cooperation without which no one could have a satisfactory life, the division of advantages should be such as to draw forth the willing cooperation of everyone taking part in it, including those less well situated. Yet this can be expected only if reasonable terms are proposed. The two principles mentioned seem to be a fair agreement on the basis of which those better endowed, or more fortunate in their social position, neither of which we can be said to deserve, could expect the willing cooperation of others when some workable scheme is a necessary condition of the welfare of all. Once we decide to look for a conception of justice that nullifies the accidents of natural endowment and the contingencies of social circumstance as counters in quest for political and economic advantage, we are led to these principles. They express the result of leaving aside those aspects of the social world that seem arbitrary from a moral point of view.

The problem of the choice of principles, however, is extremely difficult. I do not expect the answer I shall suggest to be convincing to everyone. It is, therefore, worth noting from the outset that justice as fairness, like other contract views, consists of two parts: (1) an interpretation of the initial situation and of the problem of choice posed there, and (2) a set of principles which, it is argued, would be agreed to. One may accept the first part of the theory (or some variant thereof), but not the other, and conversely. The concept of the initial contractual situation may seem reasonable although the particular principles proposed are rejected. . . .

4. The Original Position and Justification

I have said that the original position is the appropriate initial status quo which insures that the fundamental agreements reached in it are fair. This fact yields the name "justice as fairness." It is clear, then, that I want to say that one conception of justice is more reasonable than another, or justifiable with respect to it, if rational persons in the initial situation would choose its principles over those of the other for the role of justice. Conceptions of justice are to be ranked by their acceptability to persons so circumstanced. Understood in this way the question of justification is settled by working out a problem of deliberation: we have to ascertain which principles it would be rational to adopt given the contractual situation. This connects the theory of justice with the theory of rational choice.

If this view of the problem of justification is to succeed, we must, of course, describe in some detail the nature of this choice problem. A problem of rational decision has a definite answer only if we know the beliefs and interests of the parties, their relations with respect to one another, the alternatives between which they are to choose, the procedure whereby they make up their minds, and so on. As the circumstances are presented in different ways, correspondingly different principles are accepted. The concept of the original position, as I shall refer to it, is that the most philosophically favored interpretation of this initial choice situation for the purposes of a theory of justice.

But how are we to decide what is the most favored interpretation? I assume, for one thing, that there is a broad measure of agreement that principles of justice should be chosen under certain conditions. To justify a particular description of the initial situation one shows that it incorporates these commonly shared presumptions. One argues from widely accepted but weak premises to more specific conclusions. Each of the presumptions should by itself be natural and plausible; some of them may seem innocuous or even trivial. The aim of the contract approach is to establish that taken together they impose significant bounds on acceptable principles of justice. The ideal outcome would be that these conditions determine a unique set of principles; but I shall be satisfied if they suffice to rank the main traditional conceptions of social justice.

One should not be misled, then, by the somewhat unusual conditions which characterize the original position. The idea here is simply to make vivid to ourselves the restrictions that it seems reasonable to impose on arguments for principles of justice, and therefore on these principles themselves. Thus it seems reasonable and generally acceptable that no one should be advantaged or disadvantaged by natural fortune or social circumstances in the choice of principles. It also seems widely agreed that it should be impossible to tailor principles to the circumstances of one's own case. We should insure further that particular inclinations and aspirations, and persons' conceptions of their good do not affect the principles adopted. The aim is to rule out those principles that it would be rational to propose for acceptance, however little the chance of success, only if one knew certain things that are irrelevant from the standpoint of justice. For example, if a man knew that he was wealthy, he might find it rational to advance the principle that various taxes for welfare measures be counted unjust; if he knew that he was poor, he would most likely propose the contrary principle. To represent the desired restrictions one imagines a situation in which everyone is deprived of this sort of information. One excludes the knowledge of those contingencies which sets men at odds and allows them to be guided by their prejudices. In this manner the veil of ignorance is arrived at in a natural way. This concept should cause no difficulty if we keep in mind the constraints on arguments that it is meant to express. At any time we can enter the original position, so to speak, simply by following a certain procedure, namely, by arguing for principles of justice in accordance with these restrictions.

It seems reasonable to suppose that the parties in the original position are equal. That is, all have the same rights in the procedure for choosing principles; each can make proposals, submit reasons for their acceptance, and so on. Obviously the purpose of these conditions is to represent equality between human beings as moral persons, as creatures having a conception of their good and capable of a sense of justice. The basis of equality is taken to be similarity in these two respects. Systems of ends are not ranked in value; and each man is presumed to have the requisite ability to understand and to act upon whatever principles are adopted. Together with the veil of ignorance, these conditions define the principles of justice as those which rational persons concerned to advance their interests would consent to as equals when none are known to be advantaged or disadvantaged by social and natural contingencies.

There is, however, another side to justifying a particular description of the original position. This is to see if the principles which would be chosen match our considered convictions of justice or extend them in an acceptable way. We can note whether applying these principles would lead us to make the same judgments about the basic structure of society which we now make intuitively and in which we have the greatest confidence; or whether, in cases where our present judgments are in doubt and given with hesitation, these principles offer a resolution which we can affirm on reflection. There are questions which we feel sure must be answered in a certain way. For example, we are confident that religious intolerance and racial discrimination are unjust. We think that we have examined these things with care and have reached what we believe is an impartial judgment not likely to be distorted by an excessive attention to our own interests. These convictions are provisional fixed points which we presume any conception of justice must fit. But we have much less assurance as to what is the correct distribution of wealth and authority. Here we may be looking for a way to remove our doubts. We can check an interpretation of the initial situation, then, by the capacity of its principles to accommodate our firmest convictions and to provide guidance where guidance is needed.

In searching for the most favored description of this situation we work from both ends. We begin by describing it so that it represents generally shared and preferably weak conditions. We then see if these conditions are strong enough to yield a significant set of principles. If not, we look for further premises equally reasonable. But if so, and these principles match our considered convictions of justice, then so far well and good. But presumably there will be discrepancies. In this case we have a choice. We can either modify the account of the initial situation or we can revise our existing judgments, for even the judgments we take provisionally as fixed points are liable to revision. By going back and forth, sometimes altering the conditions of the contractual circumstances, at others withdrawing our judgments and conforming them to principle, I assume that eventually we shall find a description of the initial situation that both expresses reasonable conditions and yields principles which match our considered judgments duly pruned and adjusted. This state of affairs I refer to as reflective equilibrium. It is an equilibrium because at last our principles and judgments coincide; and it is reflective since we know to what principles our judgments conform and the premises of their derivation. At the moment everything is in order. But this equilibrium is not necessarily stable. It is liable to be upset by further examination of the conditions which should be imposed on the contractual situation and by particular cases which may lead us to revise our judgments. Yet for the time being we have done what we can to render coherent and to justify our convictions of social justice. We have reached a conception of the original position.

I shall not, of course, actually work through this process. Still, we may think of the interpretation of the original position that I shall present as the result of such a hypothetical course of reflection. It represents the attempt to accommodate within one scheme both reasonable philosophical conditions on principles as well as our considered judgments of justice. In arriving at the favored interpretation of the initial situation there is no point at which an appeal is made to self-evidence in the traditional sense either of general conceptions or particular convictions. I do not claim for the principles of justice proposed that they are necessary truths or derivable from such truths. A conception of justice cannot be deduced from self-evident premises or conditions on principles; instead, its justification is a matter of the mutual support of many considerations, of everything fitting together into one coherent view.

A final comment. We shall want to say that certain principles of justice are justified because they would be agreed to in an initial situation of equality. I have emphasized that this original position is purely hypothetical. It is natural to ask why, if this agreement is never actually entered into, we should take any interest in these principles, moral or otherwise. The answer is that the conditions embodied in the description of the original position are ones that we do in fact accept. Or if we do not, then perhaps we can be persuaded to do so by philosophical reflection. Each aspect of the contractual situation can be given supporting grounds. Thus what we shall do is to collect together into one conception a number of conditions on principles that we are ready upon due consideration to recognize as reasonable. These constraints express what we are prepared to regard as limits on fair terms of social cooperation. One way to look at the idea of the original position, therefore, is to see it as an expository device which sums up the meaning of these conditions and helps us to extract their consequences. On the other hand, this conception is also an intuitive notion that suggests its own elaboration, so that led on by it we are drawn to define more clearly the standpoint from which we can best interpret moral relationships. We need a conception that enables us to envision our objective from afar: the intuitive notion of the original position is to do this for us.

11. Two Principles of Justice

I shall now state in a provisional form the two principles of justice that I believe would be chosen in the original position. In this section I wish to make only the most general comments, and therefore the first formulation of these principles is tentative. . . .

The first statement of the two principles reads as follows.

First: each person is to have an equal right to the most extensive basic liberty compatible with a similar liberty for others.

Second: social and economic inequalities are to be arranged so that they are both (a) reasonably expected to be to everyone's advantage, and (b) attached to positions and offices open to all. . . .

By way of general comment, these principles primarily apply, as I have said, to the basic structure of society. They are to govern the assignment of rights and duties and to regulate the distribution of social and economic advantages. As their formulation suggests, these principles presuppose that the social structure can be divided into two more or less distinct parts, the first principle applying to the one, the second to the other. They distinguish between those aspects of the social system that define and secure the equal liberties of citizenship and those that specify and establish social and economic inequalities. The basic liberties of citizens are, roughly speaking, political liberty (the right to vote and to be eligible for public office) together with freedom of speech and assembly; liberty of conscience and freedom of thought; freedom of the person along with the right to hold (personal) property; and freedom from arbitrary arrest and seizure as defined by the concept of the rule of law. These liberties are all required to be equal by the first principle, since citizens of a just society are to have the same basic rights.

The second principle applies, in the first approximation, to the distribution of income and wealth and to the design of organizations that make use of differences in authority and responsibility, or chains of command. While the distribution of wealth and income need not be equal, it must be to everyone's advantage, and at the same time, positions of authority and offices of command must be accessible to all. One applies the second principle by holding positions open, and then, subject to this constraint, arranges social and economic inequalities so that everyone benefits.

These principles are to be arranged in a serial order with the first principle prior to the second. This ordering means that a departure from the institutions of equal liberty required by the first principle cannot be justified by, or compensated for, by greater social and economic advantages. The distribution of wealth and income, and the hierarchies of authority, must be consistent with both the liberties of equal citizenship and equality of opportunity.

It is clear that these principles are rather specific in their content, and their acceptance rests on certain assumptions that I must eventually try to explain and justify. A theory of justice depends upon a theory of society in ways that will become evident as we proceed. For the present, it should be observed that the two principles (and this holds for all formulations) are a special case of a more general conception of justice that can be expressed as follows.

All social values—liberty and opportunity, income and wealth, and the bases of self-respect—are to be distributed equally unless an unequal distribution of any, or all, of these values is to everyone's advantage.

Injustice, then, is simply inequalities that are not to the benefit of all. Of course, this conception is extremely vague and requires interpretation.

As a first step, suppose that the basic structure of society distributes certain primary goods, that is,

things that every rational man is presumed to want. These goods normally have a use whatever a person's rational plan of life. For simplicity, assume that the chief primary goods at the disposition of society are rights and liberties, powers and opportunities, income and wealth. . . . These are the social primary goods. Other primary goods such as health and vigor, intelligence and imagination, are natural goods; although their possession is influenced by the basic structure, they are not so directly under its control. Imagine, then, a hypothetical initial arrangement in which all the social primary goods are equally distributed: everyone has similar rights and duties, and income and wealth are evenly shared. This state of affairs provides a benchmark for judging improvements. If certain inequalities of wealth and organizational powers would make everyone better off than in this hypothetical starting situation, then they accord with the general conception.

Now it is possible, at least theoretically, that by giving up some of their fundamental liberties men are sufficiently compensated by the resulting social and economic gains. The general conception of justice imposes no restrictions on what sort of inequalities are permissible; it only requires that everyone's position be improved. We need not suppose anything so drastic as consenting to a condition of slavery. Imagine instead that men forego certain political rights when the economic returns are significant and their capacity to influence the course of policy by the exercise of these rights would be marginal in any case. It is this kind of exchange which the two principles as stated rule out; being arranged in serial order they do not permit exchanges between basic liberties and economic social gains. The serial ordering of principles expresses an underlying preference among primary social goods. When this preference is rational so likewise is the choice of these principles in this order.

In developing justice as fairness I shall, for the most part, leave aside the general conception of justice and examine instead the special case of the two principles in serial order. The advantage of this procedure is that from the first the matter of priorities is recognized and an effort made to find principles to deal with it. One is lead to attend throughout to the conditions under which the acknowledgment of the absolute weight of liberty with respect to social and economic advantages, as defined by the lexical order of the two principles, would be reasonable. Offhand, this ranking appears extreme and too special a case to be of much interest; but there is more justification for it than would appear at first sight. Or at any rate, so I shall maintain. . . . Furthermore, the distinction between fundamental rights and liberties and economic and social benefits marks a difference among primary social goods that one should try to exploit. It suggests an important division in the social system. Of course, the distinctions drawn and the ordering proposed are bound to be at best only approximations. There are surely circumstances in which they fail. But it is essential to depict clearly the main lines of a reasonable conception of justice; and under many conditions anyway, the two principles in serial order may serve well enough. When necessary we can fall back on the more general conception.

The fact that the two principles apply to institutions has certain consequences. Several points illustrate this. First of all, the rights and liberties referred to by these principles are those which are defined by the public rules of the basic structure. Whether men are free is determined by the rights and duties established by the major institutions of society. Liberty is a certain pattern of social forms. The first principle simply requires that certain sorts of rules, those defining basic liberties, apply to everyone equally and that they allow the most extensive liberty compatible with a like liberty for all. The only reason for circumscribing the rights defining liberty and making men's freedom less extensive than it might otherwise be is that these equal rights as institutionally defined would interfere with one another.

Another thing to bear in mind is that when principles mention persons, or require that everyone gain from an inequality, the reference is to representative persons holding the various social positions, or offices, or whatever, established by the basic structure. Thus in applying the second principle I assume that it is possible to assign an expectation of well-being to representative individuals holding these positions. This expectation indicates their life prospects as viewed from their social station. In general, the expectations of representative persons depend upon the distribution of rights and duties throughout the basic structure. When this changes, expectations change. I assume, then, that expectations are connected: by raising the prospects of the representative man in one position we presumably increase or decrease the prospects of representative men in other positions. Since it applies to institutional forms, the second principle (or rather the first part of it) refers to the expectations of representative individuals. . . . neither principle applies to distributions of particular goods to particular individuals who may be identified by their proper names. The situation where someone is considering how to allocate certain commodities to needy persons who are known to him is not within the scope of the principles. They are meant to regulate basic institutional arrangements. We must not assume that there is much similarity from the standpoint of justice between an administrative allotment of goods to specific persons and the appropriate design of society. Our common sense intuitions for the former may be a poor guide to the latter.

Now the second principle insists that each person benefit from permissible inequalities in the basic structure. This means that it must be reasonable for each relevant representative man defined by this structure, when he views it as a going concern, to prefer his prospects with the inequality to his prospects without it. One is not allowed to justify differences in income or organizational powers on the ground that the disadvantages of those in one position are outweighed by the greater advantages of those in another. Much less can infringements of liberty be counterbalanced in this way. Applied to the basic structure, the principle of utility would have us maximize the sum of expectations of representative men (weighted by the number of persons they represent, on the classical view); and this would permit us to compensate for the losses of some by the gains of others. Instead, the two principles require that everyone benefit from economic and social inequalities. . . .

ROBERT NOZICK

from *Anarchy, State, and Utopia* (1974)

QUESTIONS FOR REFLECTION

1. Outline Nozick's entitlement theory. What principles would be required, if the world were perfect? What principle is needed because it is not?

2. How do historical principles differ from end-result principles?

3. What is a patterned theory of justice? Is Nozick's theory patterned? Can a theory be both patterned and historical?

4. Why, according to Nozick, are patterned theories of justice incompatible with liberty?

CHAPTER 7 / DISTRIBUTIVE JUSTICE

The minimal state is the most extensive state that can be justified. Any state more extensive violates people's rights. Yet many persons have put forth reasons purporting to justify a more extensive state. . . . In this chapter we consider the claim that a more extensive state is justified, because necessary (or the best instrument) to achieve distributive justice.

The term "distributive justice" is not a neutral one. Hearing the term "distribution," most people presume that some thing or mechanism uses some principle or criterion to give out a supply of things. Into this process of distributing shares some error may have crept. So it is an open question, at least, whether *re*distribution should take place; whether we should do again what has already been done once, though poorly. However, we are not in the position of children who have been given portions of pie by someone who now makes last minute adjustments to rectify careless cutting. There is no *central* distribution, no person or group entitled to control all the resources, jointly deciding how they are to be doled out. What each person gets, he gets from others who give to him in exchange for something, or as a gift. In a free society, diverse persons control different resources, and new holdings arise out of the voluntary exchanges and actions of persons. There is no more a distributing or distribution of shares than there is a distributing of mates in a society in which persons choose whom they shall marry. The total result is the product of many individual decisions which the different individuals involved are entitled to make. Some uses of the term "distribution," it is true, do not imply a previous distributing appropriately judged by some criterion (for example, "probability distribution"); nevertheless, despite the title of this chapter, it would be best to use a terminology that clearly is neutral. We shall speak of people's holdings; a principle of justice in holdings describes (part of) what justice tells us (requires) about holdings. I shall state first what I take to be the correct view about justice in holdings, and then turn to the discussion of alternate views.

Section I

The Entitlement Theory

The subject of justice in holdings consists of three major topics. The first is the *original acquisition of holdings,* the appropriation of unheld things. This includes the issues of how unheld things may come to be held, the process, or processes, by which unheld things may come to be held, the things that may come to be held by these processes, the extent of what comes to be held by a particular process, and so on. We shall refer to the complicated truth about this topic, which we shall not formulate here, as the principle of justice in acquisition. The second topic concerns the *transfer of holdings* from one person to another. By what processes may a person transfer holdings to another? How may a person acquire a holding from another who holds it? Under this topic come general descriptions of voluntary exchange, and gift and (on the other hand) fraud, as well as reference to particular conventional details fixed upon in a given society. The complicated truth about this subject (with placeholders for conventional details) we shall call the principle of justice in transfer. (And we shall suppose it also includes principles governing how a person may divest himself of a holding, passing it into an unheld state.)

If the world were wholly just, the following inductive definition would exhaustively cover the subject of justice in holdings.

1. A person who acquires a holding in accordance with the principle of justice in acquisition is entitled to that holding.

2. A person who acquires a holding in accordance with the principle of justice in transfer, from someone else entitled to the holding, is entitled to the holding.

3. No one is entitled to a holding except by (repeated) applications of 1 and 2.

The complete principle of distributive justice would say simply that a distribution is just if everyone is entitled to the holdings they possess under the distribution.

A distribution is just if it arises from another just distribution by legitimate means. The legitimate means of moving from one distribution to another are specified by the principle of justice in transfer. The legitimate first "moves" are specified by the principle of justice in acquisition. Whatever arises from a just situation by just steps is itself just. The means of change specified by the principle of justice in transfer preserve justice. As correct rules of inference are truth-preserving, and any conclusion deduced via repeated application of such rules from only true premises is itself true, so the means of transition from one situation to another specified by the principle of justice in transfer are justice-preserving, and any situation actually arising from repeated transitions in accordance with the principle from a just situation is itself just. The parallel between justice-preserving transformations and truth-preserving transformations illuminates where it fails as well as where it holds. That a conclusion could have been deduced by truth-preserving means from premises that are true suffices to show its truth. That from a just situation a situation *could* have arisen via justice-preserving means does not suffice to show its justice. The fact that a thief's victims voluntarily *could* have presented him with gifts does not entitle the thief to his ill-gotten gains. Justice in holdings is historical; it depends upon what actually has happened. We shall return to this point later.

Not all actual situations are generated in accordance with the two principles of justice in holdings: the principle of justice in acquisition and the principle of justice in transfer. Some people steal from others, or defraud them, or enslave them, seizing their product and preventing them from living as they choose, or forcibly exclude others from competing in exchanges. None of these are permissible modes of transition from one situation to another. And some persons acquire holdings by means not sanctioned by the principle of justice in acquisition. The existence of past injustice (previous violations of the first two principles of justice in holdings) raises the third major topic under justice in holdings: the rectification of injustice in holdings. If past injustice has shaped present holdings in various ways, some identifiable and some not, what now, if anything, ought to be done to rectify these injustices? What obligations do the performers of injustice have toward those whose position is worse than it would have been had the injustice not been done? Or, than it would have been had compensation been paid promptly? How, if at all, do things change if the beneficiaries and those made worse off are not the direct parties in the act of injustice, but, for example, their descendants? Is an injustice done to someone whose holding was itself based upon an unrectified injustice? How far back must one go in wiping clean the historical slate of injustices? What may victims of injustice permissibly do in order to rectify the injustices being done to them, including the many injustices done by persons acting through their government? I do not know of a thorough or theoretically sophisticated treatment of such issues. Idealizing greatly, let us suppose theoretical investigation will produce a principle of rectification. This principle uses historical information about previous situations and injustices done in them (as defined by the first two principles of justice and rights against interference), and information about the actual course of events that flowed from these injustices, until the present, and it yields a description (or descriptions) of holdings in the society. The principle of rectification presumably will make use of its best estimate of subjunctive information about what would have occurred (or a probability distribution over what might have occurred, using the expected value) if the injustice had not taken place. If the actual description of holdings turns out not to be one of the descriptions yielded by the principle, then one of the descriptions yielded must be realized.

The general outlines of the theory of justice in holdings are that the holdings of a person are just if he is entitled to them by the principles of justice in acquisition and transfer, or by the principle of rectification of injustice (as specified by the first two principles). If each person's holdings are just, then the total set (distribution) of holdings is just. To turn these general outlines into a specific theory we would have to specify the details of each of the three principles of justice in holdings: the principle of acquisition of holdings, the principle of transfer of holdings, and the principle of rectification of violations of the first two principles. I shall not attempt that task here. (Locke's principle of justice in acquisition is discussed below.)

Historical Principles and End-Result Principles

The general outlines of the entitlement theory illuminate the nature and defects of other conceptions of distributive justice. The entitlement theory of justice in distribution is *historical;* whether a distribution is just depends upon how it came about. In contrast, *current time-slice principles* of justice hold that the justice of a distribution is determined by how things are distributed (who has what) as judged by some *structural* principle(s) of just distribution. A utilitarian who judges between any two distributions by seeing which has the greater sum of utility and, if the sums tie, applies some fixed equality criterion to choose the more equal distribution, would hold a current time-slice principle of justice. As would someone who had a fixed schedule of trade-offs between the sum of happiness and equality. According to a current time-slice principle, all that needs to be looked at, in judging the justice of a distribution, is who ends up with what; in comparing any two distributions one need look only at the matrix presenting the distributions. No further information need be fed into a principle of justice. It is a consequence of such principles of justice that any two structurally identical distributions are equally just. (Two distributions are structurally identical if they present the same profile, but perhaps have different persons occupying the particular slots. My having ten and your having five, and my having five and your having ten are structurally identical distributions.) Welfare economics is the theory of current time-slice principles of justice. The subject is conceived as operating on matrices representing only current information about distribution. This, as well as some of the usual conditions (for example, the choice of distribution is invariant under relabeling of columns), guarantees that welfare economics will be a current time-slice theory, with all of its inadequacies.

Most persons do not accept current time-slice principles as constituting the whole story about distributive shares. They think it relevant in assessing the justice of a situation to consider not only the distribution it embodies, but also how that distribution came about. If some persons are in prisons for murder or war crimes, we do not say that to assess the justice of the distribution in the society we must look only at what this person has, and that person has, and that person has, . . . at the current time. We think it relevant to ask whether someone did something so that he *deserved* to be punished, deserved to have a lower share. Most will agree to the relevance of further information with regard to punishments and penalties. Consider also desired things. One traditional socialist view is that workers are entitled to the produce and full fruits of their labor; they have earned it; a distribution is unjust if it does not give the workers what they are entitled to. Such entitlements are based upon some past history. No socialist holding this view would find it comforting to be told that because the actual distribution *A* happens to coincide structurally with the one he desires *D*, *A* therefore is no less just than *D*; it differs only in that the "parasitic" owners of capital receive under *A* what the workers are entitled to under *D*, and the workers receive under *A* what the owners are entitled to under *D*, namely very little. This socialist rightly, in my view, holds onto the notions of earning, producing, entitlement, desert, and so forth, and he rejects current time-slice principles that look only to the structure of the resulting set of holdings. (The set of holdings resulting from what? Isn't it implausible that how holdings are produced and come to exist has no effect at all on who should hold what?) His mistake lies in his view of what entitlements arise out of what sorts of productive processes.

We construe the position we discuss too narrowly by speaking of *current* time-slice principles. Nothing is changed if structural principles operate upon a time sequence of current time-slice profiles and, for example, give someone more now to counterbalance the less he has had earlier. A utilitarian or an egalitarian or any mixture of the two over time will inherit the difficulties of his more myopic comrades. He is not helped by the fact that *some* of the information others consider relevant in assessing a distribution is reflected, unrecoverably, in past matrices. Henceforth, we shall refer to such unhistorical principles of distributive justice, including the current time-slice principles, as *end-result principles* or *end-state principles*.

In contrast to end-result principles of justice, *historical principles* of justice hold that past circumstances or actions of people can create differential entitlements or differential deserts to things. An injustice can be worked by moving from one distribution to another structurally identical one, for the second, in profile the same, may violate people's entitlements or deserts; it may not fit the actual history.

Patterning

The entitlement principles of justice in holdings that we have sketched are historical principles of justice. To better understand their precise character, we shall distinguish them from another subclass of the historical principles. Consider, as an example, the principle of distribution according to moral merit. This principle requires that total distributive shares vary directly with moral merit; no person should have a greater share than anyone whose moral merit is greater. (If moral merit could be not merely ordered but measured on an interval or ratio scale, stronger principles could be formulated.) Or consider the principle that results by substituting "usefulness to society" for "moral merit" in the previous principle. Or instead of "distribute according to moral merit," or "distribute according to usefulness to society," we might consider "distribute according to the weighted sum of moral merit, usefulness to society, and need," with the weights of the different dimensions equal. Let us call a principle of distribution *patterned* if it specifies that a distribution is to vary along with some natural dimension, weighted sum of natural dimensions, or lexicographic ordering of natural dimensions. And let us say a distribution is patterned if it accords with some patterned principle. (I speak of natural dimensions, admittedly without a general criterion for them, because for any set of holdings some artificial dimensions can be gimmicked up to vary along with the distribution of the set.) The principle of distribution in accordance with moral merit is a patterned historical principle, which specifies a patterned distribution. "Distribute according to I.Q." is a patterned principle that looks to information not contained in distributional matrices. It is not historical, however, in that it does not look to any past actions creating differential entitlements to evaluate a distribution; it requires only distributional matrices whose columns are labeled by I.Q. scores. The distribution in a society, however, may be composed of such simple patterned distributions, without itself being simply patterned. Different sectors may operate different patterns, or some combination of patterns may operate in different proportions across a society. A distribution composed in this manner, from a small number of patterned distributions, we also shall term "patterned." And we extend the use of "pattern" to include the overall designs put forth by combinations of end-state principles.

Almost every suggested principle of distributive justice is patterned: to each according to his moral merit, or needs, or marginal product, or how hard he tries, or the weighted sum of the foregoing, and so on. The principle of entitlement we have sketched is *not* patterned. There is no one natural dimension or weighted sum or combination of a small number of natural dimensions that yields the distributions generated in accordance with the principle of entitlement. The set of holdings that results when some persons receive their marginal products, others win at gambling, others receive a share of their mate's income, others receive gifts from foundations, others receive interest on loans, others receive gifts from admirers, others receive returns on investment, others make for themselves much of what they have, others find things, and so on, will not be patterned. Heavy strands of patterns will run through it; significant portions of the variance in holdings will be accounted for by pattern-variables. If most people most of the time choose to transfer some of their entitlements to others only in exchange for something from them, then a large part of what many people hold will vary with what they held that others wanted. More details are provided by the theory of marginal productivity. But gifts to relatives, charitable donations, bequests to children, and the like, are not best conceived, in the first instance, in this manner. Ignoring the strands of pattern, let us suppose for the moment that a distribution actually arrived at by the operation of the principle of entitlement is random with respect to any pattern. Though the resulting set of holdings

will be unpatterned, it will not be incomprehensible, for it can be seen as arising from the operation of a small number of principles. These principles specify how an initial distribution may arise (the principle of acquisition of holdings) and how distributions may be transformed into others (the principle of transfer of holdings). The process whereby the set of holdings is generated will be intelligible, though the set of holdings itself that results from this process will be unpatterned.

The writings of F. A. Hayek focus less than is usually done upon what patterning distributive justice requires. Hayek argues that we cannot know enough about each person's situation to distribute to each according to his moral merit (but would justice demand we do so if we did have this knowledge?); and he goes on to say, "our objection is against all attempts to impress upon society a deliberately chosen pattern of distribution, whether it be an order of equality or of inequality." However, Hayek concludes that in a free society there will be distribution in accordance with value rather than moral merit; that is, in accordance with the perceived value of a person's actions and services to others. Despite his rejection of a patterned conception of distributive justice, Hayek himself suggests a pattern he thinks justifiable: distribution in accordance with the perceived benefits given to others, leaving room for the complaint that a free society does not realize exactly this pattern. Stating this patterned strand of a free capitalist society more precisely, we get "To each according to how much he benefits others who have the resources for benefiting those who benefit them." This will seem arbitrary unless some acceptable initial set of holdings is specified, or unless it is held that the operation of the system over time washes out any significant effects from the initial set of holdings. As an example of the latter, if almost anyone would have bought a car from Henry Ford, the supposition that it was an arbitrary matter who held the money then (and so bought) would not place Henry Ford's earnings under a cloud. In any event, *his* coming to hold it is not arbitrary. Distribution according to benefits to others *is* a major patterned strand in a free capitalist society, as Hayek correctly points out, but it is only a strand and does not constitute the whole pattern of a system of entitlements (namely, inheritance, gifts for arbitrary reasons, charity, and so on) or a standard that one should insist a society fit. Will people tolerate for long a system yielding distributions that they believe are unpatterned? No doubt people will not long accept a distribution they believe is *unjust*. People want their society to be and to look just. But must the look of justice reside in a resulting pattern rather than in the underlying generating principles? We are in no position to conclude that the inhabitants of a society embodying an entitlement conception of justice in holdings will find it unacceptable. Still, it must be granted that were people's reasons for transferring some of their holdings to others always irrational or arbitrary, we would find this disturbing. (Suppose people always determined what holdings they would transfer, and to whom, by using a random device.) We feel more comfortable upholding the justice of an entitlement system if most of the transfers under it are done for reasons. This does not mean necessarily that all deserve what holdings they receive. It means only that there is a purpose or point to someone's transferring a holding to one person rather than to another; that usually we can see what the transferrer thinks he's gaining, what cause he thinks he's serving, what goals he thinks he's helping to achieve, and so forth. Since in a capitalist society people often transfer holdings to others in accordance with how much they perceive these others benefiting them, the fabric constituted by the individual transactions and transfers is largely reasonable and intelligible. (Gifts to loved ones, bequests to children, charity to the needy also are nonarbitrary components of the fabric.) In stressing the large strand of distribution in accordance with benefit to others, Hayek shows the point of many transfers, and so shows that the system of transfer of entitlements is not just spinning its gears aimlessly. The system of entitlements is defensible when constituted by the individual aims of individual transactions. No overarching aim is needed, no distributional pattern is required.

To think that the task of a theory of distributive justice is to fill in the blank in "to each according to his _____" is to be predisposed to search for a pattern; and the separate treatment of "from each according to his _____" treats production and distribution as two separate and indepen-

dent issues. On an entitlement view these are *not* two separate questions. Whoever makes something, having bought or contracted for all other held resources used in the process (transferring some of his holdings for these cooperating factors), is entitled to it. The situation is *not* one of something's getting made, and there being an open question of who is to get it. Things come into the world already attached to people having entitlements over them. From the point of view of the historical entitlement conception of justice in holdings, those who start afresh to complete "to each according to his _____" treat objects as if they appeared from nowhere, out of nothing. A complete theory of justice might cover this limit case as well; perhaps here is a use for the usual conceptions of distributive justice.

So entrenched are maxims of the usual form that perhaps we should present the entitlement conception as a competitor. Ignoring acquisition and rectification, we might say:

> From each according to what he chooses to do, to each according to what he makes for himself (perhaps with the contracted aid of others) and what others choose to do for him and choose to give him of what they've been given previously (under this maxim) and haven't yet expended or transferred.

This, the discerning reader will have noticed, has its defects as a slogan. So as a summary and great simplification (and not as a maxim with any independent meaning) we have:

> *From each as they choose, to each as they are chosen.*

How Liberty Upsets Patterns

It is not clear how those holding alternative conceptions of distributive justice can reject the entitlement conception of justice in holdings. For suppose a distribution favored by one of these nonentitlement conceptions is realized. Let us suppose it is your favorite one and let us call this distribution D_1; perhaps everyone has an equal share, perhaps shares vary in accordance with some dimension you treasure. Now suppose that Wilt Chamberlain is greatly in demand by basketball teams, being a great gate attraction. (Also suppose contracts run only for a year, with players being free agents.) He signs the following sort of contract with a team: In each home game, twenty-five cents from the price of each ticket of admission goes to him. (We ignore the question of whether he is "gouging" the owners, letting them look out for themselves.) The season starts, and people cheerfully attend his team's games; they buy their tickets, each time dropping a separate twenty-five cents of their admission price into a special box with Chamberlain's name on it. They are excited about seeing him play; it is worth the total admission price to them. Let us suppose that in one season one million persons attend his home games, and Wilt Chamberlain winds up with $250,000, a much larger sum than the average income and larger even than anyone else has. Is he entitled to this income? Is this new distribution D_2, unjust? If so, why? There is *no* question about whether each of the people was entitled to the control over the resources they held in D_1; because that was the distribution (your favorite) that (for the purposes of argument) we assumed was acceptable. Each of these persons *chose* to give twenty-five cents of their money to Chamberlain. They could have spent it on going to the movies, or on candy bars, or on copies of *Dissent* magazine, or of *Monthly Review.* But they all, at least one million of them, converged on giving it to Wilt Chamberlain in exchange for watching him play basketball. If D_1 was a just distribution, and people voluntarily moved from it to D_2, transferring parts of their shares they were given under D_1 (what was it for if not to do something with?), isn't D_2 also just? If the people were entitled to dispose of the resources to which they were entitled (under D_1), didn't this include their being entitled to give it to, or exchange it with, Wilt Chamberlain? Can anyone else complain on grounds of justice? Each other person already has his legitimate share under D_1, Under D_1, there is nothing that anyone has that anyone else has a claim of justice against. After someone transfers something to Wilt Chamberlain, third parties *still* have their legitimate shares; *their* shares are not changed. By what process could such a transfer among two persons give rise to a legitimate claim of distributive justice on a portion of what was transferred, by a third party who had no claim of justice on any holding of the others *before* the transfer? To cut off objections irrelevant here, we might imagine the exchanges occurring in a socialist society, after hours. After playing whatever basketball he does in his daily work, or doing whatever other daily work he does, Wilt Chamberlain decides to put in *overtime* to earn additional money. (First his work quota is set; he works time over that.) Or imagine it is a skilled juggler people like to see, who puts on shows after hours.

Why might someone work overtime in a society in which it is assumed their needs are satisfied? Perhaps because they care about things other than needs. I like to write in books that I read, and to have easy access to books for browsing at odd hours. It would be very pleasant and convenient to have the resources of Widener Library in my back yard. No society, I assume, will provide such resources close to each person who would like them as part of his regular allotment (under D_1). Thus, persons either must do without some extra things that they want, or be allowed to do something extra to get some of these things. On what basis could the inequalities that would eventuate be forbidden? Notice also that small factories would spring up in a socialist society, unless forbidden. I melt down some of my personal possessions (under D_1) and build a machine out of the material. I offer you, and others, a philosophy lecture once a week in exchange for your cranking the handle on my machine, whose products I exchange for yet other things, and so on. (The raw materials used by the machine are given to me by others who possess them under D_1, in exchange for hearing lectures.) Each person might participate to gain things over and above their allotment under D_1. Some persons even might want to leave their job in socialist industry and work full time in this private sector. I shall say something more about these issues in the next chapter. Here I wish merely to note how private property even in means of production would occur in a socialist society that did not forbid people to use as they wished some of the resources they are given under the socialist distribution D_1. The socialist society would have to forbid capitalist acts between consenting adults.

The general point illustrated by the Wilt Chamberlain example and the example of the entrepreneur in a socialist society is that no end-state principle or distributional patterned principle of justice can be continuously realized without continuous interference with people's lives. Any favored pattern would be transformed into one unfavored by the principle, by people choosing to act in various ways; for example, by people exchanging goods and services with other people, or giving things to other people, things the transferrers are entitled to under the favored distributional pattern. To maintain a pattern one must either continually interfere to stop people from transferring resources as they wish to, or continually (or periodically) interfere to take from some persons resources that others for some reason chose to transfer to them. (But if some time limit is to be set on how long people may keep resources others voluntarily transfer to them, why let them keep these resources for *any* period of time? Why not have immediate confiscation?) It might be objected that all persons voluntarily will choose to refrain from actions which would upset the pattern. This presupposes unrealistically (1) that all will most want to maintain the pattern (are those who don't, to be "reeducated" or forced to undergo "self-criticism"?), (2) that each can gather enough information about his own actions and the ongoing activities of others to discover which of his actions will upset the pattern, and (3) that diverse and far-flung persons can coordinate their actions to dovetail into the pattern. Compare the manner in which the market is neutral among persons' desires, as it reflects and transmits widely scattered information via prices, and coordinates persons' activities.

It puts things perhaps a bit too strongly to say that every patterned (or end-state) principle is liable to be thwarted by the voluntary actions of the individual parties transferring some of their shares they receive under the principle. For perhaps some *very* weak patterns are not so thwarted. Any distributional pattern with any egalitarian component is overturnable by the voluntary actions of individual persons over time; as is every patterned condition with sufficient content so as actually to have been proposed as presenting the central core of distributive justice. Still, given the possibility that some weak conditions or patterns may not be unstable in this way, it would be better to formulate an explicit description of the kind of interesting and contentful patterns under discussion, and to prove a theorem about their instability. Since the weaker the patterning, the more likely it is that the entitlement system itself satisfies it, a plausible conjecture is that any patterning either is unstable or is satisfied by the entitlement system. . . .

Welfare and World Hunger

The central problem of distributive justice is how goods should be allotted to members of a society. In many societies, the prevailing methods of allotment leave some with very little. Some may not have enough to eat; some may have inadequate housing or no housing at all. Some may lack basic medical care. Some may receive no, or very poor, education. How should society respond to these problems?

Clearly, this question raises two major issues. One is philosophical: What are the proper principles of distribution? What, in other words, is the correct theory of distributive justice? The other is practical: Given a set of principles of distribution, how can we devise policies to bring about distributions in accord with them? Answering the first question defines our obligations to help others; answering the second defines a way of fulfilling them in practice. The first question is prior. Only if we know what we are trying to accomplish can we judge how well various policies accomplish it.

These questions go to the root of our conception of political and economic organization. A society that alters its laws about capital punishment, abortion, or pornography, for example, may bring about significant changes by doing so, but it does not fundamentally change the way it is organized. Changing one's conception of distribution, however, can change social organization. Socialism, capitalism, communism, and other forms of economic organization aim at satisfying different principles of distribution. Within each system arise important questions about policies for satisfying them.

Carl Cohen, a philosopher, presents the case for socialism. He defines its conception of distributive justice and its basic strategies for bringing about a society in accord with that conception. Cohen argues that private ownership is unfair. Free enterprise, he contends, brings about a system in which the rich get richer, the poor get poorer, and the society gets more unjust. He maintains that public ownership of the means of production is compatible with liberty. Indeed, he proposes, it is required for fulfilling human liberty in its broadest and most important sense.

Garrett Hardin takes a global and pessimistic view of problems of poverty. He compares the world to a sea, with about one-third of the population in a lifeboat and the other two-thirds trying to avoid drowning and hoping to climb aboard. The lifeboat, he argues, has a limited capacity and cannot admit many more members. We have no obligation to admit anyone—and certainly no obligation to surrender our place. Hardin asserts further that aid to the poor does not help them; on the contrary, it damages the environment, leading to a "tragedy of the commons," and harms future generations.

Peter Singer, too, treats the problem on a global scale. People in wealthy countries enjoy a comfortable life, whereas many in poor countries suffer and starve. This, he contends, is not just unfair; it is tantamount to homicide. Inhabitants of wealthy countries could prevent the hungry from dying without large sacrifices. He rejects the theory of distributive justice proposed by Locke and Nozick, arguing that we have very serious moral obligations to help those in danger of starvation. He also contends that Hardin's lifeboat analogy is inappropriate.

Philosopher John Hospers argues in favor of libertarianism, the view that the government may act only to prevent harm to others. Taking Mill's harm principle and applying it broadly, Hospers finds little justification for any government action concerning distribution. The government may of course enforce laws against stealing, for example, because that involves direct harm to others. But nothing justifies government action to take from A and give to B simply because B has less than A. Hospers argues that all other conceptions of government and of distributive justice give people rights over the lives of others—rights that, in his view, they do not have.

Social worker and theorist Charles Murray addresses the practical problem of welfare. He assumes that government is justified in attempting to eliminate poverty, homelessness, and other social problems, but asks how it can do so. Murray draws several laws about social programs, which imply that such programs inevitably do more harm than good. Murray concludes that a society without any welfare programs at all would be better off than one in which government expends a great deal of energy and money trying to redistribute income and other goods. If Murray is right, there is a sense in which the practical problem of welfare policy may be prior to the question of distributive justice: perhaps no policies can achieve anything worth achieving—on any plausible conception of justice—without doing even greater harm. If so, then what conception of justice is correct makes no difference for social policy, for no combination of welfare programs could bring about a just distribution.

Finally, Nobel prizewinner James Buchanan, an economist, argues that socialism is dead; recent world events have shown that removing ownership from private hands removes incentives for success, leading to economic stagnation. By making ownership public, moreover, socialism invariably places decision-making power in the hands of bureaucrats. They act for the public good only in name; in fact, they act to promote the good of the bureaucracy, i.e., their own good. Buchanan sees the failure of socialist economies in practice as an indication that socialism is inadequate as a theory. In short, socialism makes most people worse off, rewarding only those with political power. It not only lowers people's welfare across the board but also leads to unjust distributions. Buchanan, however, sees a live threat in the "Leviathan" state, in which interest groups compete to manipulate public policy for their own private ends. As in socialist economies, those with political power can enforce distributions that benefit them while harming the society as a whole. Buchanan thus stresses the link between economic and political systems, arguing for restraints on political interference in the marketplace.

from *Four Systems*

Carl Cohen is Professor of Philosophy at the University of Michigan. (Source: Reprinted from Four Systems *by Carl Cohen. Copyright © 1982 by Random House, Inc.)*

QUESTIONS FOR REFLECTION

1. How does Cohen define socialism? What does it mean in practice?

2. What are Cohen's criticisms of free enterprise? Do you agree?

3. Why, according to Cohen, is private ownership unfair? What conception of justice does Cohen use?

4. How does Cohen try to reconcile socialism with individual liberty? Does he succeed?

Democracy Fulfilled

We socialists agree that democracy is necessary and absolutely right. But it is not enough. Democracy is completed, fulfilled, by socialism—which is simply the democratic control of *all* resources in the community by society *as a whole.*

Socialism makes democratic ideals concrete. In it the collective will of the people is put to the service of the people in their daily lives. Through socialism the common interests of all the citizens are protected, their common needs met.

The name "socialism" has—at least to many American ears—a negative, even a threatening, connotation. Yet most ordinary people warmly support—under a different name—many activities that are truly socialist in nature. We all know that some things must be done for the community as a whole. And some things can be undertaken *for* the community only *by* the community, acting *as* a community. Constructive collective action in this spirit is socialism.

How, for example, do we "provide for the common defense"? Why, through social action, of course. Armies and warships cannot be maintained by private groups or individuals. National defense, undertaken jointly with democratic consent, is only one of many socialist enterprises that no one seriously questions.

How do we make and enforce the criminal law? Collectively, of course. Citizens can neither establish criminal codes and courts as individuals, nor punish as individuals. That would be the war of each against all, in which the lives of people would indeed prove nasty, poor, brutish, and short. The adoption of laws, and their enforcement, is an essentially *social* activity. Nothing else would be feasible or sane. Everyone grants that; to this extent we are all socialists.

Is not the same true of national foreign policy? We may differ as individuals, but do we not agree upon the need for one community position? And of health regulations? Do we allow the meat packers or the drug manufacturers to decide for themselves what is fit to eat or prescribe? And everyone now agrees on the need for community policies, collective undertakings to protect the environment, our forests and fish, animals and birds. Shall we not have public parks or seashores? Shall we not join to protect our historical treasures and the beauties of our land? Absurd even to ask. To do these things we must, of course, act as a society, because as individuals we are relatively helpless and ineffective. We will succeed, if we succeed at all, cooperatively, because there is absolutely no other way to have successful armies, just courts, or beautiful parks. All democratic experience teaches the need for collective action. Real democracy *is* social democracy, democratic socialism.

While we all practice socialism in many spheres, its applicability to other spheres in which it is equally necessary is widely denied. Sometimes manipulated by the rich and powerful, sometimes blinded by our own slogans, sometimes dreading unreal philosophical ghosts, we fear to take social action where we ought. We fail to complete our democracy.

How can we complete it? Where would collective action have greatest impact on daily life? In the economy, of course. Action as a society is needed most of all in producing and distributing the necessities and comforts of ordinary human life. Socialism is democracy extended to the world of work and money.

Socialism and Popular Will

All the wealth of the world—the houses and food, the land and lumber and luxuries—is somehow divided and distributed. How is that done? And how should it be done? We socialists try to rethink such fundamental questions: Who gets what? And why?

Satisfactory answers to these questions must, of course, prove acceptable to the masses. Being democrats above all, we trust the judgment of the people. Their choices, when fully informed, will be rational and fair. We lay it down as a restriction upon ourselves, therefore, that the great changes socialism requires must come only as the honest expression of the will of the citizens, through action by their freely elected representatives. An organic transformation of society can succeed only when genuinely willed by its members. True socialists—unlike some who falsely parade under that banner—never have and never will force their solutions on an unwilling community. Democracies around the world, from India to Sweden, have enthusiastically applied socialist theory to their problems, devising socialist solutions specially suitable to their circumstances. The same basic theory can be applied successfully, with American ingenuity, to American circumstances. Confident that we can prove this to the satisfaction of the citizens concerned, we commit ourselves without reservations to abide by the judgment of the people after the case has been put fairly before them. We compel no one; our socialism is democratic, through and through.

Rich and Poor

How the wealth of most is now divided is very plain to see. A few people get a great deal, and most people get just barely enough, or a little less than enough, to live decently. Rich and poor are the great classes of society, and everyone knows it well. Early democracies accepted these stark inequities as natural and inevitable. We do not. Some democrats still accept them. Material success (they say) is open to everyone in a system of private enterprise, and rewards properly go to the industrious and the able, those ambitious enough to pull themselves out of poverty by effort and wit. Some succeed, some do not, and most (they conclude) receive their just deserts.

It isn't so. That picture of "free enterprise" is a myth and always has been. In fact, by putting control of industry and finance into private hands, free enterprise results in the ownership of more and more by fewer and fewer, making economic justice unattainable for most. For centuries, wherever capitalism has prevailed, the great body of wealth has rested in the pockets of a tiny fraction of the citizens, while the masses are divided between those who just get by on their wages, and those who are unemployed and poor, inadequately housed, and often hungry. That great division, between those who have and those who have not, is the leading feature of a private enterprise economy, even when democratic. Those who have get more, because money and property are instruments for the accumulation of more money and more property. Economic freedom in such a system, for the vast majority, is only the freedom to work for another.

Working men and women are free to sweat for pay-checks, free to look for another job, and maybe—if their needs are desperate—free to go on welfare. These are false freedoms, not deserving the name.

Why does it work out that way? Will the poor always be with us? Ought each person to look out only for himself or herself and devil take the hindmost? We deny that this is the spirit of a decent society. We do not accept the inevitability of poverty; we do not think a democracy need be a cutthroat enterprise, and we know that cooperative action by the members of a society in their joint interests can protect both the essential freedoms of each individual and the economic well-being of all. That rational cooperation is called socialism.

Parks and Industries

Consider this vivid contrast. No one questions the appropriateness of public parks—places for play and the enjoyment of nature, owned by the people, and operated by their elected representatives (and those they hire) in everyone's interest. Our parks (national, state, and municipal) are among our proudest possessions. Yes, possessions; we own them, each of us, and though some abuse them thoughtlessly, most of us love them and take satisfaction in their beauty. We do not begrudge the need to tax ourselves to maintain them. We could sell the forests and the land, reduce our tax burden thereby, and leave all citizens to take care of their own recreational needs as well as they can. If unable to pay for access to private parks or clubs, or to afford a private lake or a canyon—well, that would be their lookout. Simply to formulate this attitude is to exhibit its absurdity. Natural beauty and opportunity for relaxation and play for ourselves and our children are deep human needs; we fully understand how vital it is that the limited resources of nature, the lakes and forests, streams and wildlife, be preserved, in part at least, for our common and perpetual enjoyment.

Compare with this the condition of the steel industry. Virtually all of the steel in the United States is produced by three companies: U.S. Steel, Republic Steel, Inland Steel. The private owners of these three companies—a tiny fraction of our citi-zens—literally possess, own as their private property, the foundries, mills, and other facilities that constitute the literal foundation of almost all other industry. Virtually nothing works without steel. Steel mills are not as pretty as parks, true, but are they any less necessary to the well-being of a people? Can any of us do without steel? Not for a day. Cars, trucks, ships, and trains are made of it. Housing and communication depend utterly upon it. Kitchens and radios, elevators and pens—practically all tools and all conveniences require it. Hardly any activity, public or private, goes on without some use of iron or steel. Then why not exhibit the same community concern for steel that we exhibit for our parks? Why let a few capitalists charge us as they please (since we cannot control them) for what we must have? Why suppose that a fair price for steel includes an enormous profit—over and above all the costs of making and shipping the steel—for the private owners of the mills?

What explains so blind an infatuation with "private enterprise"? Under its spell we allow ourselves to be manipulated by the private owners of the steel foundries, gouged (even in our own homes!) by the private owners of the telephone wires. Oil wells and forests, precious resources from our common earth, are exploited by giant corporations whose ultimate object is profit alone. We must wake to see that productive industry, vital to the life of a society, is properly the possession of that society as a whole, not of private individuals or companies. The principles we apply unhesitatingly to parks apply with equal force to factories. Production as well as recreation can be a source of public pride and satisfaction—when socialized. Socialism is nothing more than the *general* application of collective intelligence.

Every democracy, socialist or not, will seek to protect citizens' political rights—but only socialist democracies protect citizens' *economic* rights. Freedom of speech and assembly are priceless; are not freedom from unemployment and hunger equally so? We think so. The same collective action needed to defend the citizens against aggression from without is needed to organize production rationally and to distribute wealth justly, within our own borders. In the economic sphere as much as any other, cooperation and foresight are central. The public ownership of industry is the only way to achieve them.

The Unfairness of Private Ownership

History confirms this. The private ownership of productive industry has always resulted in deprivation for most, luxury for a few. The owners of factories and mines are forced, by competition, to exploit both workers and resources. Where private interests have been the foundation of the system, they have always been advanced at the expense of public interests. Why not build a power project in the heart of the Hudson River valley or on the seashores of Maine? It is not a concern for beauty but for bookkeeping that pays off. Drill for oil wherever it can be found—in the last of the forests, on the beaches, on the lawn of the state capitol. Business is business. The great redwoods of California, each hundreds of years old and a monument to nature's grandeur, fall by the thousands; the forests are clear-cut, left as ugly, muddy hillsides. The drive for profit is the sharpest of all saws.

The system of private ownership encourages, even demands, selfishness at every turn. Let buyers, employees, the general public beware! Cornering the market in computing equipment, controlling access to the telephone system, delaying the marketing of steers in order to raise the price of beef, steadily increasing the price of gasoline when petroleum is in short supply—all such maneuvers are within the rules of the capitalist game. Sharp play and toughness yield riches; generosity yields bankruptcy; and no one may refuse to play.

To limit the injustices done in the name of private enterprise, some have tried to adjust the rules of the game. It does not work. Fair business practice codes, antitrust legislation, minimum-wage laws, and the like, do restrain some of the excesses of the capitalists. But such changes are no more than cosmetics, mitigating but not eliminating the real evil. Injustice flows not merely from the excesses of capitalism but from the essence of the system of private ownership itself.

Changing the rules cannot eliminate exploitation and gross inequality; only changing the entire game can. If everyone is to be free from economic need, everyone must have the right to participate in planning production and controlling distribution. That can be only when industrial production and distribution is entirely in public hands. Just as those who are not represented in parliament will suffer politically, those not represented in economic decision making will surely suffer in the market. The very argument that justifies democracy in the political sphere justifies democracy in the economic sphere as well. Economic injustice in a private enterprise system is not an accident but a necessary outcome. To eliminate that injustice we must end the disproportion in the powers of its elements, just as the disproportionate powers of political elements were finally ended by giving the vote to all citizens. The case for socialism is the case for economic democracy.

The Inhumanity of the Market

Socialism is simply economic good sense. The long-term fruits of capitalism have become too bitter: cycles of boom and bust, unemployment and welfare, personal dissatisfaction and business failure. Inflation steals from everyone (except those who can raise prices and rents quickly); depression demoralizes everyone. Disorder and distress are widespread. Our land itself is abused, our water poisoned, and our air fouled. When everything is left "up for grabs," the grabbing will be vicious and the outcome chaotic. There can be no intelligent planning for future needs, no rational distribution of products or materials in short supply, no reasonable deployment of human energies, in an economy in which the fundamental rule is dog-eat-dog. Legislation designed to blunt the fangs can do no more than reduce the depth of a serious wound.

Capitalism relies upon the so-called "market economy." The prices asked or offered for raw materials and finished products it leaves entirely to private parties, individuals or business firms, who enter a supposedly open market. This free market, it is argued, will be self-regulating; supply and demand will rationalize prices, fairness and productivity will be ensured by competition, enterprise encouraged by the hope of profit.

None of this actually works in the way capitalist mythology depicts it. The system relies upon the wisdom and power of economic fairies that never did exist. Nothing in the market is dependable, since everything within it fluctuates in response to unpredictable and uncontrollable factors: the tastes of buyers, the moods of sellers, the special circumstances of either, accidents causing short supply, or fashions transforming reasonable supply into glut.

Rationality and fairness through competition? No claim could be more fraudulent. In a capitalist market prices depend largely upon the relative strengths (or weaknesses) of the traders. If I own all the orchards, and am therefore the seller of all the cherries in the market, you, dear buyer, will pay my price or eat no cherries. Steel, timber, farm machinery are for sale in the market. Go, dear friend, and bargain with the sellers. Anyone tempted to believe capitalist propaganda about the give and take in the market should put it to the test. Reflect upon your own recent experiences as a shopper: You were told the price of the item you looked at—a TV set or a can of beans—and you paid that price or left without. That is how the market works for ordinary folks. Giant firms, manufacturers or chain retailers, may bargain with suppliers on occasion—but even then the stronger get the better deals. Those who control resources and money control the market, manipulating it in their own interests. Those who enter the market (either as buyer or seller) with great needs but little power are squeezed and exploited. The weak get twisted, the strong do the twisting. That's free enterprise.

Fairness? Markets do not know the meaning of the word. All's fair in war—and market competition is perpetual war, through guile and threat, on a thousand fronts. Rewards go to the aggressive; the keys to victory are accumulation, possession, control. And rules for fair dealing? They will be evaded, broken surreptitiously, even ignored—just like the rules of war—when it profits the combatants.

Private enterprise is worse than unfair. It is nofair; it does not recognize justice as any concern for *homo economicus*. The only things that count, for it, are the things that can be counted. Such a system is by its nature, explicitly *inhumane*. To render it humane it is necessary to transform it into an instrument for humans. Socialism makes human concerns the fundamental concerns in the design, manufacture, and distribution of material goods. Only thus can an economic system achieve justice. What should appear in that holiest of capitalist places, "the bottom line"? A record of increased human satisfactions? Or a record of profit?

The Cruelty of Capitalism

"Ah, but that callous system you attack," replies the capitalist, "is the most wonderfully productive in all the world. We do not, it is true, share everything and share alike—but by rewarding personal ambition and intellect, we encourage and tap the productivity of all. Capitalist societies may not be perfectly equitable, but they are rich—and that, in the end, is what we all want."

The true colors of the beast begin to show. Riches, material acquisition, is for it—but not for us —the paramount objective. Socialists think of human life in broader and deeper terms. For us money and goods are servants, not masters. General human well-being, we say, is the mark of a good society. Material wealth is only our tool.

Even on their own ground, however—measuring everything by prosperity—the case for capitalism fails. That private ownership leads to greater productivity is also myth. Enormous growth there has been, of course, in all modern economies; but that growth came with invention and discovery, with technological advance, with mass production and automation. It comes in capitalist countries *and* socialist countries, when relatively primitive methods of production are replaced by more efficient systems. Human intelligence, not capitalism, should get credit for that. There is no reason to believe that human intelligence must be less energetic, or less inventive, when put to common service than when serving private ends.

The ironic consequence of that private service is *deprivation*, the hidden *lack* of that very prosperity capitalism claims. In a system of private ownership the factories and mines must produce at a profit or not at all. Most steel foundries—under capitalism— operate well below capacity most of the time. Produce too much steel and the price will drop; what profit, after all, is there in that? Houses and apartments are needed by tens of millions of Americans; we have the capacity to build that housing, but it goes largely unused. Carpenters and masons wait impatiently in union halls for work; lumber yards and designers lay off workers; contractors and salesmen search desperately for buyers who can afford loans at high interest rates; banks wait cautiously for safe borrowers. The entire system permits even needed construction only when a profit is to be made. If there is no money in it, those in need of housing will simply wait. You cannot make a buck by being a nice guy. What does get built is outrageously expensive, affordable only by the rich. Building slows to a crawl while housing needs soar. The human need for housing plays second fiddle to the demand for profit, and the building industry floats like a chip on the waves of a capricious economic ocean.

So it is with every industry. Production within the plant may be organized and efficient in the highest degree—but the "free market" to which skills and products are brought is madness itself. Again and again capitalism carries itself, now with unbridled enthusiasm, now with unrelieved desperation, to the brink of dissolution. "Business cycles"—the euphemistic name for the manic booms and depressing busts of the capitalist market—are the inevitable consequence of stupid inaction, leaving to pure chance and private avarice the control of our essential common business. The resulting human misery has been incalculable. After a chain of depressions through the nineteenth and early twentieth centuries, capitalism produced the super depression of the 1930s—a slough of despair, fathomless in depth and a decade in length. It was cut short, at last, only by the productive impetus of a terrible war.

In that great depression the true face of capitalism showed itself. Hunger was rampant in the midst of plenty. While humiliated citizens waited in soup lines for a dole, food in warehouses could find no profitable market! Food there was, in great quantities, but because it could not be sold profitably it had to be destroyed. Destroyed! To hold up prices for the rest! We Americans actually burnt huge stores of wheat; we killed and buried great numbers of pigs; we milked the cows and literally poured out the milk onto the ground—because, in the free market, it yielded no profit.

Madness, you say? Yes, the madness of the market economy. A sane economy is a human economy, directed by human intelligence, to serve humans. It will not leave the fate of citizens to chance, or the supply of industrial goods to unpredictable market forces, or the control of essential foodstuffs to private greed. The market cannot be sane, because sanity is a human quality and the market has no humanity whatever. . . .

Public Ownership

Reasonable human beings can end all this. Production and distribution can be designed for human service. Cooperation is the key. Society must be organized with mutual service and mutual benefit as its fundamental theme. That theme is not alien to us; it lies at the core of our highest moral and religious ideals. We must realize these ideals in practice.

Economic cooperation entails two practical principles: (1) productive property must be publicly owned; and (2) production and distribution must be planned for the common good. *Public ownership* and *planning*—acting upon both we can readily achieve the substance of democratic socialism.

Public ownership is the base. Public ownership of what? Of the means by which goods are produced and work is carried on. Private persons are not entitled to own the instruments of our common good. A system enabling some to exact profit from the work of others, to wax rich while the glaring needs of others go unmet, is fundamentally corrupt. We would end that corruption by bringing all the elements of the productive economy—the electric utilities and the mines, agriculture and transport, the production of metals and paper and drugs, the airlines and the food chains and the telephone system—under public ownership.

We do not propose to confiscate anything. The capital now held by private owners we would have the community pay for, at a fair price. But we would end the surreptitious confiscation by a few of the common wealth. The people have a right to advance their own general welfare through state action. They have that right in the economic sphere as in every other. Individuals will not be deprived of their personal effects, their houses or cars, their books or boots. Indeed, we seek the enlargement of such private goods for individual satisfaction. Individual human beings, after all, are what government is created to serve. But productive property is our common good, our collective concern. We will move it—justly—from private to public hands.

The Elimination of Private Profit

The nationalization of all industry will have two consequences. First, *profit* for some from the work of others will be no more. If there is surplus produced by the operation of the utility companies, or the design of computers, or the distribution of any manufactured goods, let that surplus return to the treasury of the entire community. Let all productive systems be used, we say, not for private enrichment but for public benefit, and for continuing investment in the components of public production themselves. Workers should know that they labor each for all, and that any value they produce beyond what they receive in wages will not be taken from them but returned to them in some form of general benefit. One of those benefits will be the reduction of prices; when profits do not need to be squeezed from an enterprise, the consumer need only be charged the actual cost of that product or service. Goods and services will at last be fairly priced. . . .

Planning and Democracy

[One] major objection to economic planning is the claim that it will cost us our freedom. This is as false as the claim that it does not work, and more pernicious.

Here lies the nub of the conflict between democratic socialists and our private enterprise critics. Freedom, says the critic, is the paramount social value. The freedom of each individual as an economic agent must be curtailed, they argue, by any large-scale economic plan. Once the goals are set, and the role of each economic element fixed, every private person must be sharply restricted in the use of his own resources. What can be bought and what can be sold or invested will be determined by the plan. The individual will be forced to work where,

and when, and as the socialist bureaucrats have decided. Economic planning, they conclude, is but a pretty name for economic slavery.

The complaint is entirely unfounded. It is plausible only because it supposes, falsely, that economic planning under socialism will be imposed from above, by arbitrary authorities over whom we will have no control. Not so. Democratic socialism brings *democratic* planning. In an economy that is publicly owned and managed, *we* are the planners. Long-range designs for the allocation of resources, decisions about what is to be produced and how it is to be distributed, will come not from a secret, all-powerful elite but from *public* bodies, publicly selected, acting publicly, and answerable to the general public.

This genuine public accountability is absent, we agree, in some countries calling themselves "socialist." We despise that economic czarism as bitterly as do our capitalist friends. That is a false socialism which betrays the democratic spirit to which we are committed. Free citizens, accustomed to governing their own affairs, jealous of their own ultimate authority, will not be fooled by deceitful talk. They—we!—will know when our most important business is truly under our own control, and we will not stand for any other state of affairs. We will give up none of our freedom to do our own planning for our own needs. To the contrary, real freedom of action will be magnified in a truly *democratic* socialism by its increase of economic security for individuals and economic rationality in the whole society.

The critics' picture of socialist planning is a caricature of the real thing. They picture each citizen as a mindless cog in a great machine that grinds on unfeelingly, insensitive to mistakes or changing conditions. But the truly insensitive economy is the *un*-planned one, the economy that cannot respond to human needs because it responds to nothing human at all. In that disordered economy the individual is indeed helpless, a bobbing cork on uncontrolled currents. Those currents are brought under control only by giving each citizen a voice in the control of economic as well as political affairs. Democratic planning ensures that voice. The plans will be ours. We can adjust them as we make errors and learn from them; we can refine them as circumstances change. We can scrap bad plans and devise new ones as we develop new needs or new capacities. A planned economy, *honestly* socialized, will not be our master but our servant. Let our critics not forget that our first principle throughout is *self-government, democracy.*

Planning and Liberty

For self-governed citizens liberty is, indeed, a paramount concern. And what is liberty, after all? It consists of the ability and the right of individuals to make choices in determining their own conduct. The greater the range of their choices, the greater their freedom. No one supposes that liberty is absolute, that individuals can be free to do entirely as they please without restriction. Even the best of our laws limit each person's freedom to do some sorts of things in order that all of us may be genuinely free to do many other, more valuable sorts of things. The more complex a society, the more essential are some kinds of self-restriction for the extension of real freedom within it.

We witness this rational trade-off everywhere. Primary education is made compulsory in order that all may enjoy the freedom possible only for those who can read and write. Social security taxation ensures freedom from want in old age. We may resort to a military draft, reluctantly, to keep the country free. And so on. Having to send our children to school, being deprived of some of our income by taxation—these and other sound policies clearly limit us. We accept such limitations in the interest of the greater liberties they promote.

In the economic sphere such trade-offs are essential. Even advocates of "free enterprise" readily admit the necessity of legislation that hinders private monopolies, obliges honest business reports, forbids the sale of untested drugs or spoiled foods, and so on. Such restrictions are justified by their benefits in safeguarding other more essential economic goods.

Limits on the absolute freedom of private economic agents will be entailed by socialized planning; we make no bones about that. Some of these limits—on the freedom to own, buy, and sell productive resources like factories and farms—will be painful to some, just as universal taxation or compulsory schooling are burdensome now to many. The freedoms gained, from economic insecurity and injustice, will be vastly greater than those given up, and vastly more important. . . .

GARRETT HARDIN

The Case against Helping the Poor

Garrett Hardin is Professor of Biology at the University of California at Santa Barbara. (Source: Reprinted with permission from Psychology Today Magazine, *Copyright © 1974, Sussex Publishers, Inc.).*

QUESTIONS FOR REFLECTION

1. Explain Hardin's lifeboat analogy.

2. What role does population play in Hardin's argument? What are his factual premises about population? Do you find them plausible?

3. What is "the tragedy of the commons"?

4. What, in Hardin's view, would be the consequences of establishing a world food bank?

Environmentalists use the metaphor of the earth as a "spaceship" in trying to persuade countries, industries and people to stop wasting and polluting our natural resources. Since we all share life on this planet, they argue, no single person or institution has the right to destroy, waste, or use more than a fair share of its resources.

But does everyone on earth have an equal right to an equal share of its resources? The spaceship metaphor can be dangerous when used by misguided idealists to justify suicidal policies for sharing our resources through uncontrolled immigration and foreign aid. In their enthusiastic but unrealistic generosity, they confuse the ethics of a spaceship with those of a lifeboat.

A true spaceship would have to be under the control of a captain, since no ship could possibly survive if its course were determined by committee. Spaceship Earth certainly has no captain; the United Nations is merely a toothless tiger, with little power to enforce any policy upon its bickering members.

If we divide the world crudely into rich nations and poor nations, two thirds of them are desperately poor, and only one third comparatively rich, with the United States the wealthiest of all. Metaphorically each rich nation can be seen as a lifeboat full of comparatively rich people. In the ocean outside each lifeboat swim the poor of the world, who would like to get in, or at least to share some of the wealth. What should the lifeboat passengers do?

First, we must recognize the limited capacity of any lifeboat. For example, a nation's land has a limited capacity to support a population and as the current energy crisis has shown us, in some ways we have already exceeded the carrying capacity of our land.

Adrift in a Moral Sea

So here we sit, say fifty people in our lifeboat. To be generous, let us assume it has room for ten more, making a total capacity of sixty. Suppose the fifty of us in the lifeboat see 100 others swimming in the water outside, begging for admission to our boat or for handouts. We have several options: we may be tempted to try to live by the Christian ideal of being "our brother's keeper," or by the Marxist ideal of "to each according to his needs." Since the needs of all in the water are the same, and since they can all be seen as "our brothers," we could take them all into our boat, making a total of 150 in a boat designed for sixty. The boat swamps, everyone drowns. Complete justice, complete catastrophe.

Since the boat has an unused excess capacity of ten more passengers, we could admit just ten more to it. But which ten do we let in? How do we choose? Do we pick the best ten, the neediest ten, "first come, first served"? And what do we say to the ninety we exclude? If we do let an extra ten into our lifeboat, we will have lost our "safety factor," an engineering principle of critical importance. For example, if we don't leave room for excess capacity as a safety factor in our country's agriculture, a new plant disease or a bad change in the weather could have disastrous consequences.

Suppose we decide to preserve our small safety factor and admit no more to the lifeboat. Our survival is then possible, although we shall have to be constantly on guard against boarding parties.

While this last solution clearly offers the only means of our survival, it is morally abhorrent to many people. Some say they feel guilty about their good luck. My reply is simple: "Get out and yield your place to others." This may solve the problem of the guilt-ridden person's conscience, but it does not change the ethics of the lifeboat. The needy person to whom the guilt-ridden person yields his place will not himself feel guilty about his good luck. If he did, he would not climb aboard. The net result of conscience-striken people giving up their unjustly held seats is the elimination of that sort of conscience from the lifeboat.

This is the basic metaphor within which we must work out our solutions. Let us now enrich the image, step by step, with substantive additions from the real world, a world that must solve real and pressing problems of overpopulation and hunger.

The harsh ethics of the lifeboat become even harsher when we consider the reproductive differences between the rich nations and the poor nations. The people inside the lifeboats are doubling in numbers every eighty-seven years; those swimming around outside are doubling, on the average, every thirty-five years, more than twice as fast as the rich. And since the world's resources are dwindling, the difference in prosperity between the rich and the poor can only increase.

As of 1973, the U.S. had a population of 210 million people, who were increasing by 0.8 percent per year. Outside our lifeboat, let us imagine another 210 million people, (say the combined populations of Colombia, Ecuador, Venezuela, Morocco, Pakistan, Thailand, and the Philippines) who are increasing at a rate of 3.3 percent per year. Put differently, the doubling time for this aggregate population is twenty-one years, compared to eighty-seven years for the U.S.

Multiplying the Rich and the Poor

Now suppose the U.S. agreed to pool its resources with those seven countries, with everyone receiving an equal share. Initially the ratio of Americans to non-Americans in this model would be one-to-one. But consider what the ratio would be after eighty-seven years, by which time the Americans would have doubled to a population of 420 million. By then, doubling every twenty-one years, the other group would have swollen to 354 billion. Each American would have to share the available resources with more than eight people.

But, one could argue, this discussion assumes that current population trends will continue, and they may not. Quite so. Most likely the rate of population increase will decline much faster in the U.S. than it will in the other countries, and there does not seem to be much we can do about it. In sharing with "each according to his needs," we must recognize that needs are determined by population size, which is determined by the rate of reproduction, which at present is regarded as a sovereign right of every nation, poor or not. This being so, the philanthropic load created by the sharing ethic of the spaceship can only increase.

The Tragedy of the Commons

The fundamental error of spaceship ethics, and the sharing it requires, is that it leads to what I call "the tragedy of the commons." Under a system of private property, the men who own property recognize their responsibility to care for it, for if they don't they will eventually suffer. A farmer, for instance, will allow no more cattle in a pasture than its carrying capacity justifies. If he overloads it, erosion sets in, weeds take over, and he loses the use of the pasture.

If a pasture becomes a commons open to all, the right of each to use it may not be matched by a corresponding responsibility to protect it. Asking everyone to use it with discretion will hardly do, for the considerate herdsman who refrains from overloading the commons suffers more than a selfish one who says his needs are greater. If everyone would restrain himself, all would be well; but it takes only one less than everyone to ruin a system of voluntary restraint. In a crowded world of less than perfect human beings, mutual ruin is inevitable if there are no controls. This is the tragedy of the commons.

One of the major tasks of education today should be the creation of such an acute awareness of the dangers of the commons that people will recognize its many varieties. For example, the air and water have become polluted because they are treated as commons. Further growth in the population or per-capita conversion of natural resources into pollutants will only make the problem worse. The same holds true for the fish of the oceans. Fishing fleets have nearly disappeared in many parts of the world, technological improvements in the art of fishing are hastening the day of complete ruin. Only the replacement of the system of the commons with a responsible system of control will save the land, air, water and oceanic fisheries.

The World Food Bank

In recent years there has been a push to create a new commons called a World Food Bank, an international depository of food reserves to which nations would contribute according to their abilities and from which they would draw according to their needs. This humanitarian proposal has received support from many liberal international groups, and from such prominent citizens as Margaret Mead, U.N. Secretary General Kurt Waldheim, and Senators Edward Kennedy and George McGovern.

A world food bank appeals powerfully to our humanitarian impulses. But before we rush ahead with such a plan, let us recognize where the greatest political push comes from, lest we be disillusioned later. Our experience with the "Food for Peace program," or Public Law 480, gives us the answer. This program moved billions of dollars worth of U.S. surplus grain to food-short, population-long countries during the past two decades. But when P.L. 480 first became law, a headline in the business magazine *Forbes* revealed the real power behind it: "Feeding the World's Hungry Millions: How It Will Mean Billions for U.S. Business."

And indeed it did. In the years 1960 to 1970, U.S. taxpayers spent a total of $7.9 billion on the Food for Peace program. Between 1948 and 1970, they also paid an additional $50 billion for other economic-aid programs, some of which went for food and food-producing machinery and technology. Though all U.S. taxpayers were forced to contribute to the cost of P.L. 480, certain special interest groups gained handsomely under the program. Farmers did not have to contribute the grain; the Government, or rather the taxpayers, bought it from them at full market prices. The increased demand raised prices of farm products generally. The manufacturers of farm machinery, fertilizers and pesticides benefited by the farmers' extra efforts to grow more food. Grain elevators profited from storing the surplus until it could be shipped. Railroads made money hauling it to ports, and shipping lines profited from carrying it overseas. The implementation of P.L. 480 required the creation of a vast Government bureaucracy, which then acquired its own vested interest in continuing the program regardless of its merits.

Extracting Dollars

Those who proposed and defended the Food for Peace program in public rarely mentioned its importance to any of these special interests. The public emphasis was always on its humanitarian effects. The combination of silent selfish interests and highly vocal humanitarian apologists made a powerful and successful lobby for extracting money from taxpayers. We can expect the same lobby to push now for the creation of a World Food Bank.

However great the potential benefit to selfish interests, it should not be a decisive argument against a truly humanitarian program. We must ask if such a program would actually do more good than harm, not only momentarily but also in the long run. Those who propose the food bank usually refer to a current "emergency" or "crisis" in terms of world food supply. But what is an emergency? Although they may be infrequent and sudden, everyone knows that emergencies will occur from time to time. A well-run family, company, organization or country prepares for the likelihood of accidents and emergencies. It expects them, it budgets for them, it saves for them.

Learning the Hard Way

What happens if some organizations or countries budget for accidents and others do not? If each country is solely responsible for its own well-being, poorly managed ones will suffer. But they can learn from experience. They may mend their ways, and learn to budget for infrequent but certain emergencies. For example, the weather varies from year to year, and periodic crop failures are certain. A wise and competent government saves out of the production of the good years in anticipation of bad years to come. Joseph taught this policy to Pharaoh in Egypt more than 2,000 years ago. Yet the great majority of the governments in the world today do not follow such a policy. They lack either the wisdom or the competence, or both. Should those nations that do manage to put something aside be forced to come to the rescue each time an emergency occurs among the poor nations?

"But it isn't their fault!" some kindhearted liberals argue. "How can we blame the poor people who are caught in an emergency? Why must they suffer for the sins of their governments?" The concept of blame is simply not relevant here. The real question is, what are the operational consequences of establishing a world food bank? If it is open to every country every time a need develops, slovenly rulers will not be motivated to take Joseph's advice. Someone will always come to their aid. Some countries will deposit food in the world food bank, and others will withdraw it. There will be almost no overlap. As

a result of such solutions to food shortage emergencies, the poor countries will not learn to mend their ways, and will suffer progressively greater emergencies as their populations grow.

Population Control the Crude Way

On the average, poor countries undergo a 2.5 percent increase in population each year; rich countries, about 0.8 percent. Only rich countries have anything in the way of food reserves set aside, and even they do not have as much as they should. Poor countries have none. If poor countries received no food from the outside, the rate of their population growth would be periodically checked by crop failures and famines. But if they can always draw on a world food bank in time of need, their population can continue to grow unchecked, and so will their "need" for aid. In the short run, a world food bank may diminish that need, but in the long run it actually increases the need without limit.

Without some system of worldwide food sharing, the proportion of people in the rich and poor nations might eventually stabilize. The overpopulated poor countries would decrease in numbers, while the rich countries that had room for more people would increase. But with a well-meaning system of sharing, such as a world food bank, the growth differential between the rich and the poor countries will not only persist, it will increase. Because of the higher rate of population growth in the poor countries of the world, 88 percent of today's children are born poor, and only 12 percent rich. Year by year the ratio becomes worse, as the fast-reproducing poor outnumber the slow-reproducing rich.

A world food bank is thus a commons in disguise. People will have more motivation to draw from it than to add to any common store. The less provident and less able will multiply at the expense of the abler and more provident, bringing eventual ruin upon all who share in the commons. Besides, any system of "sharing" that amounts to foreign aid from the rich nations to the poor nations will carry the taint of charity, which will contribute little to the world peace so devoutly desired by those who support the idea of a world food bank.

As past U.S. foreign-aid programs have amply and depressingly demonstrated, international charity frequently inspires mistrust and antagonism rather than gratitude on the part of the recipient nation.

Chinese Fish and Miracle Rice

The modern approach to foreign aid stresses the export of technology and advice, rather than money and food. As an ancient Chinese proverb goes: "Give a man a fish and he will eat for a day; teach him how to fish and he will eat for the rest of his days." Acting on this advice, the Rockefeller and Ford Foundations have financed a number of programs for improving agriculture in the hungry nations. Known as the "Green Revolution," these programs have led to the development of "miracle rice" and "miracle wheat," new strains that offer bigger harvests and greater resistance to crop damage. Norman Borlaug, the Nobel Prize winning agronomist who, supported by the Rockefeller Foundation, developed "miracle wheat," is one of the most prominent advocates of a world food bank.

Whether or not the Green Revolution can increase food production as much as its champions claim is a debatable but possibly irrelevant point. Those who support this well-intended humanitarian effort should first consider some of the fundamentals of human ecology. Ironically, one man who did was the late Alan Gregg, a vice president of the Rockefeller Foundation. Two decades ago he expressed strong doubts about the wisdom of such attempts to increase food production. He likened the growth and spread of humanity over the surface of the earth to the spread of cancer in the human body, remarking that "cancerous growths demand food; but, as far as I know, they have never been cured by getting it."

Overloading the Environment

Every human born constitutes a draft on all aspects of the environment: food, air, water, forests, beaches, wildlife, scenery and solitude. Food can, perhaps, be significantly increased to meet a growing demand. But what about clean beaches, unspoiled forests, and solitude? If we satisfy a growing population's need for food, we necessarily decrease its per capita supply of the other resources needed by men.

India, for example, now has a population of 600 million, which increases by 15 million each year. This population already puts a huge load on a relatively impoverished environment. The country's forests are now only a small fraction of what they were three centuries ago, and floods and erosion continually destroy the insufficient farmland that remains. Every one of the 15 million new lives added to India's population puts an additional burden on the environment, and increases the economic and social costs of crowding. However humanitarian our intent, every Indian life saved through medical or nutritional assistance from abroad diminishes the quality of life for those who remain, and for subsequent generations. If rich countries make it possible, through foreign aid, for 600 million Indians to swell to 1.2 billion in a mere twenty-eight years, as their current growth rate threatens, will future generations of Indians thank us for hastening the destruction of their environment? Will our good intentions be sufficient excuse for the consequences of our actions?

My final example of a commons in action is one for which the public has the least desire for rational discussion—immigration. Anyone who publicly questions the wisdom of current U.S. immigration policy is promptly charged with bigotry, prejudice, ethnocentrism, chauvinism, isolationism or selfishness. Rather than encounter such accusations, one would rather talk about other matters, leaving immigration policy to wallow in the crosscurrents of special interests that take no account of the good of the whole, or the interests of posterity.

Perhaps we still feel guilty about things we said in the past. Two generations ago the popular press frequently referred to Dagos, Wops, Polacks, Chinks and Krauts, in articles about how America was being "overrun" by foreigners of supposedly inferior genetic stock. But because the implied inferiority of foreigners was used then as justification for keeping them out, people now assume that restrictive policies could only be based on such misguided notions. There are other grounds.

A Nation of Immigrants

Just consider the numbers involved. Our Government acknowledges a net inflow of 400,000 immigrants a year. While we have no hard data on the extent of illegal entries, educated guesses put the figure at about 600,000 a year. Since the natural increase (excess of births over deaths) of the resident population now runs about 1.7 million per year, the yearly gain from immigration amounts to at least 19 percent of the total annual increase, and may be as much as 37 percent if we include the estimate for illegal immigrants. Considering the growing use of birth-control devices, the potential effect of educational campaigns by such organizations as Planned Parenthood Federation of America and Zero Population Growth, and the influence of inflation and the housing shortage, the fertility rate of American women may decline so much that immigration could account for all the yearly increase in population. Should we not at least ask if that is what we want?

For the sake of those who worry about whether the "quality" of the average immigrant compares favorably with the quality of the average resident, let us assume that immigrants and nativeborn citizens are of exactly equal quality, however one defines that term. We will focus here only on quantity; and since our conclusions will depend on nothing else, all charges of bigotry and chauvinism become irrelevant.

Immigration vs. Food Supply

World food banks *move food to the people,* hastening the exhaustion of the environment of the poor countries. Unrestricted immigration, on the other hand, *moves people to the food,* thus speeding up the destruction of the environment of the rich countries. We can easily understand why poor people should want to make this latter transfer, but why should rich hosts encourage it?

As in the case of foreign-aid programs, immigration receives support from selfish interests and humanitarian impulses. The primary selfish interest in unimpeded immigration is the desire of employers for cheap labor, particularly in industries and trades that offer degrading work. In the past, one wave of foreigners after another was brought into the U.S. to work at wretched jobs for wretched wages. In recent years the Cubans, Puerto Ricans and Mexicans have had this dubious honor. The interests of the employers of cheap labor mesh well with the guilty silence of the country's liberal intelligentsia. White Anglo-Saxon Protestants are particularly reluctant to call for a closing of the doors to immigration for fear of being called bigots.

But not all countries have such reluctant leadership. Most educated Hawaiians, for example, are keenly aware of the limits of their environment, particularly in terms of population growth. There is only so much room on the islands, and the islanders know it. To Hawaiians, immigrants from the other forty-nine states present as great a threat as those from other nations. At a recent meeting of Hawaiian government officials in Honolulu, I had the ironic delight of hearing a speaker, who like most of his audience was of Japanese ancestry, ask how the country might practically and constitutionally close its doors to further immigration. One member of the audience countered: "How can we shut the doors now? We have many friends and relatives in Japan that we'd like to bring here some day so that they can enjoy Hawaii too." The Japanese-American speaker smiled sympathetically and answered: "Yes, but we have children now, and someday we'll have grandchildren too. We can bring more people here from Japan only by giving away some of the land that we hope to pass on to our grandchildren some day. What right do we have to do that?"

At this point, I can hear U.S. liberals asking: "How can you justify slamming the door once you're inside? You say that immigrants should be kept out. But aren't we all immigrants, or the descendants of immigrants? If we insist on staying, must we not admit all others?" Our craving for intellectual order leads us to seek and prefer symmetrical rules and morals: a single rule for me and everybody else; the same rule yesterday, today, and tomorrow. Justice, we feel, should not change with time and place.

We Americans of non-Indian ancestry can look upon ourselves as the descendants of thieves who are guilty morally, if not legally, of stealing this land from its Indian owners. Should we then give back the land to the now living American descendants of those Indians? However morally or logically sound this proposal may be, I, for one, am unwilling to live by it and I know no one else who is. Besides, the logical consequence would be absurd. Suppose that intoxicated with a sense of pure justice, we should decide to turn our land over to the Indians. Since all our wealth has also been derived from the land, wouldn't we be morally obliged to give that back to the Indians too?

Pure Justice vs. Reality

Clearly, the concept of pure justice produces an infinite regression to absurdity. Centuries ago, wise men invented statutes of limitations to justify the rejection of such pure justice, in the interest of preventing continual disorder. The law zealously defends property rights, but only relatively recent property rights. Drawing a line after an arbitrary time has elapsed may be unjust, but the alternatives are worse.

We are all the descendants of thieves, and the world's resources are inequitably distributed. But we must begin the journey to tomorrow from the point where we are today. We cannot remake the past. We cannot safely divide the wealth equitably among all peoples so long as people reproduce at different rates. To do so would guarantee that our grandchildren, and everyone else's grandchildren, would have only a ruined world to inhabit.

To be generous with one's own possessions is quite different from being generous with those of posterity. We should call this point to the attention of those who, from a commendable love of justice and equality, would institute a system of the commons, either in the form of a world food bank, or of unrestricted immigration. We must convince them if we wish to save at least some parts of the world from environmental ruin.

Without a true world government to control reproduction and the use of available resources, the sharing ethic of the spaceship is impossible. For the foreseeable future, our survival demands that we govern our actions by the ethics of a lifeboat, harsh though they may be. Posterity will be satisfied with nothing less.

Addendum 1989

Can anyone watch children starve on television without wanting to help? Naturally sympathetic, a normal human being thinks that he can imagine what it is like to be starving. We all want to do unto others as we would have them do unto us.

But wanting is not doing. Forty years of activity by the U.S. Agency for International Development, as well as episodic nongovernmental attempts to feed the world's starving, have produced mixed results. Before we respond to the next appeal we should ask, "Does what we call 'aid' really help?"

Some of the shortcomings of food aid can be dealt with briefly. Waste is unavoidable: Because most poor countries have wretched transportation systems, food may sit on a dock until it rots. Then there are the corrupt politicians who take donated food away from the poor and give it to their political supporters. In Somalia in the 1980s, fully 70 percent of the donated food went to the army.

We can school ourselves to accept such losses. Panicky projects are always inefficient: Waste and corruption are par for the course. But there is another kind of loss that we cannot—in fact, we should not—accept, and that is the loss caused by the boomerang effects of philanthropy. Before we jump onto the next "feed-the-starving" bandwagon we need to understand how well-intentioned efforts can be counterproductive.

Briefly put, it is a mistake to focus only on starving people while ignoring their surroundings. Where there is great starvation there is usually an impoverished environment: poor soil, scarce water and wildly fluctuating weather. As a result, the "carrying capacity" of the environment is low. The territory simply cannot support the population that is trying to live on it. Yet if the population were much smaller, and if it would stay smaller, the people would not need to starve.

Let us look at a particular example. Nigeria, like all the central African countries, has increased greatly in population in the last quarter-century. Over many generations, Nigerians learned that their farmlands would be most productive if crop-growing alternated with "fallow years"—years in which the land was left untilled to recover its fertility.

When modern medicine reduced the death rate,

the population began to grow. More food was demanded from the same land. Responding to that need, Nigerians shortened the fallow periods. The result was counterproductive. In one carefully studied village, the average fallow period was shortened from 5.3 to 1.4 years. As a result, the yearly production (averaged over both fallow and crop years) fell by 30 percent.

Are Nigerian farmers stupid? Not at all! They know perfectly well what they are doing. But a farmer whose family has grown too large for his farm has to take care of next year's need before he can provide for the future. To fallow or not to fallow translates into this choice: zero production in a fallow year or a 30 percent shortfall over the long run. Starvation cannot wait. Long-term policies have to give way to short-term ones. So the farmer plows up his overstressed fields, thus diminishing long-term productivity.

PETER SINGER

from *Practical Ethics*

Peter Singer is Professor of Philosophy and Director of the Center for Human Bioethics at Monash University, Australia. (Source: Reprinted from Peter Singer, Practical Ethics. *Copyright © 1979 by Cambridge University Press. Reprinted with the permission of Cambridge University Press.)*

QUESTIONS FOR REFLECTION

1. What is absolute poverty?
2. Can the world support its people, according to Singer? Why or why not?
3. Why, according to Singer, do some people go hungry?
4. Singer questions our intuitive moral sense that living affluently is different from murdering people. What are his arguments? Do you find them persuasive?
5. How does Singer criticize Locke's and Nozick's theories of rights?
6. Evaluate Singer's argument for our obligation to assist the absolutely poor.
7. How does Singer respond to Hardin's lifeboat argument?

Some Facts

Consider these facts: by the most cautious estimates, 400 million people lack the calories, protein, vitamins and minerals needed for a normally healthy life. Millions are constantly hungry; others suffer from deficiency diseases and from infections they would be able to resist on a better diet. Children are worst affected. According to one estimate, 15 million children under five die every year from the combined effects of malnutrition and infection. In some areas, half the children born can be expected to die before their fifth birthday.

Nor is lack of food the only hardship of the poor. To give a broader picture, Robert McNamara, President of the World Bank, has suggested the term "absolute poverty." The poverty we are familiar with in industrialized nations is relative poverty—meaning that some citizens are poor, relative to the wealth enjoyed by their neighbours. People living in relative poverty in Australia might be quite comfortably off by comparison with old-age pensioners in Britain, and British old-age pensioners are not poor in comparison with the poverty that exists in Mali or Ethiopia. Absolute poverty, on the other hand, is poverty by any standard. In McNamara's words:

> Poverty at the absolute level . . . is life at the very margin of existence.
>
> The absolute poor are severely deprived human beings struggling to survive in a set of squalid and degraded circumstances almost beyond the power of our sophisticated imaginations and privileged circumstances to conceive.
>
> Compared to those fortunate enough to live in developed countries individuals in the poorest nations have
>
> An infant mortality rate eight times higher
> A life expectancy one-third lower
> An adult literacy rate 60% less
> A nutritional level, for one out of every two in the population, below acceptable standards; and for millions of infants, less protein than is sufficient to permit optimum development of the brain.

And McNamara has summed up absolute poverty as:

> a condition of life so characterized by malnutrition, illiteracy, disease, squalid surroundings, high infant mortality and low life expectancy as to be beneath any reasonable definition of human decency.

Absolute poverty is, as McNamara has said, responsible for the loss of countless lives, especially among infants and young children. When absolute poverty does not cause death it still causes misery of a kind not often seen in the affluent nations. Malnutrition in young children stunts both physical and mental development. It has been estimated that the health, growth and learning capacity of nearly half the young children in developing countries are affected by malnutrition. Millions of people on poor diets suffer from deficiency diseases, like goitre, or blindness caused by a lack of vitamin A. The food value of what the poor eat is further reduced by parasites such as hookworm and ringworm, which are endemic in conditions of poor sanitation and health education.

Death and disease apart, absolute poverty remains a miserable condition of life, with inadequate food, shelter, clothing, sanitation, health services and education. According to World Bank estimates which define absolute poverty in terms of income levels insufficient to provide adequate nutrition, something like 800 million people—almost 40% of the people of developing countries—live in absolute poverty. Absolute poverty is probably the principal cause of human misery today.

This is the background situation, the situation that prevails on our planet all the time. It does not make headlines. People died from malnutrition and related diseases yesterday, and more will die tomorrow. The occasional droughts, cyclones, earthquakes and floods that take the lives of tens of thousands in one place and at one time are more newsworthy. They add greatly to the total amount of human suffering; but it is wrong to assume that when there are no major calamities reported, all is well.

The problem is not that the world cannot produce enough to feed and shelter its people. People in the poor countries consume, on average, 400 lbs. of grain a year, while North Americans average more than 2000 lbs. The difference is caused by the fact that in the rich countries we feed most of our grain to animals, converting it into meat, milk and eggs. Because this is an inefficient process, wasting up to 95% of the food value of the animal feed, people in rich countries are responsible for the consumption of far more food than those in poor countries who eat few animal products. If we stopped feeding animals on grains, soybeans and fishmeal the amount of food saved would—if distributed to those who need it—be more than enough to end hunger throughout the world.

These facts about animal food do not mean that we can easily solve the world food problem by cutting down on animal products, but they show that the problem is essentially one of distribution rather than production. The world does produce enough food. Moreover the poorer nations themselves could produce far more if they made more use of improved agricultural techniques.

So why are people hungry? Poor people cannot afford to buy grain grown by American farmers. Poor farmers cannot afford to buy improved seeds, or fertilizers, or the machinery needed for drilling wells and pumping water. Only by transferring some of the wealth of the developed nations to the poor of the underdeveloped nations can the situation be changed.

That this wealth exists is clear. Against the picture of absolute poverty that McNamara has painted, one might pose a picture of "absolute affluence." Those who are absolutely affluent are not necessarily affluent by comparison with their neighbours, but they are affluent by any reasonable definition of human needs. This means that they have more income than they need to provide themselves adequately with all the basic necessities of life. After buying food, shelter, clothing, necessary health services and education, the absolutely affluent are still able to spend money on luxuries. The absolutely affluent choose their food for the pleasures of the palate, not to stop hunger; they buy new clothes to look fashionable, not to keep warm; they move house to be in a better neighbourhood or have a play room for the children, not to keep out the rain; and after all this there is still money to spend on books and records, colour television, and overseas holidays.

At this stage I am making no ethical judgments about absolute affluence, merely pointing out that it exists. Its defining characteristic is a significant amount of income above the level necessary to provide for the basic human needs of oneself and one's dependents. By this standard Western Europe, North America, Japan, Australia, New Zealand and the oil-rich Middle Eastern states are all absolutely affluent, and so are many, if not all, of their citizens. The USSR and Eastern Europe might also be included on this list. To quote McNamara once more:

> The average citizen of a developed country enjoys wealth beyond the wildest dreams of the one billion people in countries with per capita incomes under $200. . . .

These, therefore, are the countries—and individuals—who have wealth which they could, without threatening their own basic welfare, transfer to the absolutely poor.

At present, very little is being transferred. Members of the Organization of Petroleum Exporting Countries lead the way, giving an average of 2.1% of their Gross National Product. Apart from them, only Sweden, The Netherlands and Norway have reached the modest UN target of 0.7% of GNP. Britain gives 0.38% of its GNP in official development assistance and a small additional amount in unofficial aid from voluntary organizations. The total comes to less than £1 per month per person, and compares with 5.5% of GNP spent on alcohol, and 3% on tobacco. Other, even wealthier nations, give still less: Germany gives 0.27%, the United States 0.22% and Japan 0.21%.

The Moral Equivalent of Murder?

If these are the facts, we cannot avoid concluding that by not giving more than we do, people in rich countries are allowing those in poor countries to suffer from absolute poverty, with consequent malnutrition, ill health and death. This is not a conclusion which applies only to governments. It applies to each absolutely affluent individual, for each of us has the opportunity to do something about the situation; for instance, to give our time or money to voluntary organizations like Oxfam, War on Want, Freedom From Hunger, and so on. If, then, allowing

someone to die is not intrinisically different from killing someone, it would seem that we are all murderers.

Is this verdict too harsh? Many will reject it as self-evidently absurd. They would sooner take it as showing that allowing to die cannot be equivalent to killing than as showing that living in an affluent style without contributing to Oxfam is ethically equivalent to going over to India and shooting a few peasants. And no doubt, put as bluntly as that, the verdict *is* too harsh.

There are several significant differences between spending money on luxuries instead of using it to save lives, and deliberately shooting people.

First, the motivation will normally be different. Those who deliberately shoot others go out of their way to kill; they presumably want their victims dead, from malice, sadism, or some equally unpleasant motive. A person who buys a colour television set presumably wants to watch television in colour—not in itself a terrible thing. At worst, spending money on luxuries instead of giving it away indicates selfishness and indifference to the sufferings of others, characteristics which may be understandable but are not comparable with actual malice or similar motives.

Second, it is not difficult for most of us to act in accordance with a rule against killing people: it is, on the other hand, very difficult to obey a rule which commands us to save all the lives we can. To live a comfortable, or even luxurious life it is not necessary to kill anyone; but it is necessary to allow some to die whom we might have saved, for the money that we need to live comfortably could have been given away. Thus the duty to avoid killing is much easier to discharge completely than the duty to save. Saving every life we could would mean cutting our standard of living down to the bare essentials needed to keep us alive.* To discharge this duty

---

* Strictly, we would need to cut down to the minimum level compatible with earning the income which, after providing for our needs, left us most to give away. Thus if my present position earns me, say, £10,000 a year, but requires me to spend £1,000 a year on dressing respectably and maintaining a car, I cannot save more people by giving away the car and clothes if that will mean taking a job which, although it does not involve me in these expenses, earns me only £5,000.

completely would require a degree of moral heroism utterly different from what is required by mere avoidance of killing.

A third difference is the greater certainty of the outcome of shooting when compared with not giving aid. If I point a loaded gun at someone and pull the trigger, it is virtually certain that the person will be injured, if not killed; whereas the money that I could give might be spent on a project than turns out to be unsuccessful and helps no one.

Fourth, when people are shot there are identifiable individuals who have been harmed. We can point to them and to their grieving families. When I buy my colour television, I cannot know who my money would have saved if I had given it away. In a time of famine I may see dead bodies and grieving families on my new television, and I might not doubt that my money would have saved some of them; even then it is impossible to point to a body and say that had I not bought the set, that person would have survived.

Fifth, it might be said that the plight of the hungry is not my doing, and so I cannot be held responsible for it. The starving would have been starving if I had never existed. If I kill, however, I am responsible for my victims' deaths, for those people would not have died if I had not killed them. . . .

Do the five differences not only explain, but also justify, our attitudes? Let us consider them one by one:

1. Take the lack of an identifiable victim first. Suppose that I am a travelling salesman, selling tinned food, and I learn that a batch of tins contains a contaminant, the known effect of which when consumed is to double the risk that the consumer will died from stomach cancer. Suppose I continue to sell the tins. My decision may have no identifiable victims. Some of those who eat the food will die from cancer. The proportion of consumers dying in this way will be twice that of the community at large, but which among the consumers died because they ate what I sold, and which would have contracted the disease anyway? It is impossible to tell; but surely this impossibility makes my decision no less reprehensible than it would have been had the contaminant had more readily detectable, though equally fatal, effects.

2. The lack of certainty that by giving money I could save a life does reduce the wrongness of not giving, by comparison with deliberate killing; but it is insufficient to show that not giving is acceptable conduct. The motorist who speeds through pedestrian crossings, heedless of anyone who might be on them, is not a murderer. She may never actually hit a pedestrian; yet what she does is very wrong indeed.

3. The notion of responsibility for acts rather than omissions is more puzzling. On the one hand we feel ourselves to be under a greater obligation to help those whose misfortunes we have caused. (It is for this reason that advocates of overseas aid often argue that Western nations have created the poverty of Third World nations, through forms of economic exploitation which go back to the colonial system.) On the other hand any consequentialist would insist that we are responsible for all the consequences of our actions, and if a consequence of my spending money on a luxury item is that someone dies, I am responsible for that death. It is true that the person would have died even if I had never existed, but what is the relevance of that? The fact is that I do exist, and the consequentialist will say that our responsibilities derive from the world as it is, not as it might have been.

One way of making sense of the nonconsequentialist view of responsibility is by basing it on a theory of rights of the kind proposed by John Locke or, more recently, Robert Nozick. If everyone has a right to life, and this right is a right *against* others who might threaten my life, but not a right *to* assistance from others when my life is in danger, then we can understand the feeling that we are responsible for acting to kill but not for omitting to save. The former violates the rights of others, the latter does not.

Should we accept such a theory of rights? If we build up our theory of rights by imagining, as Locke and Nozick do, individuals living independently from each other in a "state of nature," it may seem natural to adopt a conception of rights in which as long as each leaves the other alone, no rights are violated. I might, on this view, quite properly have maintained my independent existence if I had wished to do so. So if I do not make you any worse off than you would have been if I had had nothing at all to do with you, how can I have violated your rights? But why start from such an unhistorical, abstract and ultimately inexplicable idea as an independent individual? We now know that our ancestors were social beings long before they were human beings, and could not have developed the abilities and capacities of human beings if they had not been social beings first. In any case we are not, now, isolated individuals. If we consider people living together in a community, it is less easy to assume that rights must be restricted to rights against interference. We might, instead, adopt the view that taking rights to life seriously is incompatible with standing by and watching people die when one could easily save them.

4. What of the difference in motivation? That a person does not positively wish for the death of another lessens the severity of the blame she deserves; but not by as much as our present attitudes to giving aid suggest. The behaviour of the speeding motorist is again comparable, for such motorists usually have no desire at all to kill anyone. They merely enjoy speeding and are indifferent to the consequences. Despite their lack of malice, those who kill with cars deserve not only blame but also severe punishment.

5. Finally, the fact that to avoid killing people is normally not difficult, whereas to save all one possibly could save is heroic, must make an important difference to our attitude to failure to do what the respective principles demand. Not to kill is a minimum standard of acceptable conduct we can require of everyone; to save all one possibly could is not something that can realistically be required, especially not in societies accustomed to giving as little as ours do. Given the generally accepted standards, people who give, say, £100 a year to Oxfam are more aptly praised for above average generosity than blamed for giving less than they might. The appropriateness of praise and blame is, however, a separate issue from the rightness or wrongness of actions. The former evaluates the agent: the latter evaluates the action. Perhaps people who give £100 really ought to give at least £1,000, but to blame them for not giving more could be counterproductive. It might make them feel that what is required is too demanding, and if one is going to be blamed anyway, one might as well not give anything at all.

(That an ethic which put saving all one possibly can on the same footing as not killing would be an ethic for saints or heroes should not lead us to assume that the alternative must be an ethic which makes it obligatory not to kill, but puts us under no obligation to save anyone. There are positions in between these extremes, as we shall soon see.)

To summarize our discussion of the five differences which normally exist between killing and allowing to die, in the context of absolute poverty and overseas aid. The lack of an identifiable victim is of no moral significance, though it may play an important role in explaining our attitudes. The idea that we are directly responsible for those we kill, but not for those we do not help, depends on a questionable notion of responsibility, and may need to be based on a controversial theory of rights. Differences in certainty and motivation are ethically significant, and show that not aiding the poor is not to be condemned as murdering them; it could, however, be on a par with killing someone as a result of reckless driving, which is serious enough. Finally the difficulty of completely discharging the duty of saving all one possibly can makes it inappropriate to blame those who fall short of this target as we blame those who kill; but this does not show that the act itself is less serious. Nor does it indicate anything about those who, far from saving all they possibly can, make no effort to save anyone.

These conclusions suggest a new approach. Instead of attempting to deal with the contrast between affluence and poverty by comparing not saving with deliberate killing, let us consider afresh whether we have an obligation to assist those whose lives are in danger, and if so, how this obligation applies to the present world situation.

The Obligation to Assist

The Argument for an Obligation to Assist

The path from the library at my university to the Humanities lecture theatre passes a shallow ornamental pond. Suppose that on my way to give a lecture I notice that a small child has fallen in and is in danger of drowning. Would anyone deny that

I ought to wade in and pull the child out? This will mean getting my clothes muddy, and either cancelling my lecture or delaying it until I can find something dry to change into; but compared with the avoidable death of a child this is insignificant.

A plausible principle that would support the judgment that I ought to pull the child out is this: if it is in our power to prevent something very bad happening, without thereby sacrificing anything of comparable moral significance, we ought to do it. This principle seems uncontroversial. It will obviously win the assent of consequentialists; but non-consequentialists should accept it too, because the injunction to prevent what is bad applies only when nothing comparably significant is at stake. Thus the principle cannot lead to the kinds of actions of which non-consequentialists strongly disapprove—serious violations of individual rights, injustice, broken promises, and so on. If a non-consequentialist regards any of these as comparable in moral significance to the bad thing that is to be prevented, he will automatically regard the principle as not applying in those cases in which the bad thing can only be prevented by violating rights, doing injustice, breaking promises, or whatever else is at stake. Most non-consequentialists hold that we ought to prevent what is bad and promote what is good. Their dispute with consequentialists lies in their insistence that this is not the sole ultimate ethical principle; that it is *an* ethical principle is not denied by any plausible ethical theory.

Nevertheless the uncontroversial appearance of the principle that we ought to prevent what is bad when we can do so without sacrificing anything of comparable moral significance is deceptive. If it were taken seriously and acted upon, our lives and our world would be fundamentally changed. For the principle applies, not just to rare situations in which one can save a child from a pond, but to the everyday situation in which we can assist those living in absolute poverty. In saying this I assume that absolute poverty, with its hunger and malnutrition, lack of shelter, illiteracy, disease, high infant mortality and low life expectancy, is a bad thing. And I assume that it is within the power of the affluent to reduce absolute poverty, without sacrificing anything of comparable moral significance. If these two assumptions and the principle we have been discuss-

ing are correct, we have an obligation to help those in absolute poverty which is no less strong than our obligation to rescue a drowning child from a pond. Not to help would be wrong, whether or not it is intrinsically equivalent to killing. Helping is not, as conventionally thought, a charitable act which it is praiseworthy to do, but not wrong to omit; it is something that everyone ought to do.

This is the argument for an obligation to assist. Set out more formally, it would look like this.

First premise: If we can prevent something bad without sacrificing anything of comparable significance, we ought to do it.

Second premise: Absolute poverty is bad.

Third premise: There is some absolute poverty we can prevent without sacrificing anything of comparable moral significance.

Conclusion: We ought to prevent some absolute poverty.

The first premise is the substantive moral premise on which the argument rests, and I have tried to show that it can be accepted by people who hold a variety of ethical positions.

The second premise is unlikely to be challenged. Absolute poverty is, as McNamara put it, "beneath any reasonable definition of human decency" and it would be hard to find a plausible ethical view which did not regard it as a bad thing.

The third premise is more controversial, even though it is cautiously framed. It claims only that some absolute poverty can be prevented without the sacrifice of anything of comparable moral significance. It thus avoids the objection that any aid I can give is just "drops in the ocean" for the point is not whether my personal contribution will make any noticeable impression on world poverty as a whole (of course it won't) but whether it will prevent some poverty. This is all the argument needs to sustain its conclusion, since the second premise says that any absolute poverty is bad, and not merely the total amount of absolute poverty. If without sacrificing anything of comparable moral significance we can provide just one family with the means to raise itself out of absolute poverty, the third premise is vindicated.

I have left the notion of moral significance unexamined in order to show that the argument does not depend on any specific values or ethical principles. I think the third premise is true for most people living in industrialized nations, on any defensible view of what is morally significant. Our affluence means that we have income we can dispose of without giving up the basic necessities of life, and we can use this income to reduce absolute poverty. Just how much we will think ourselves obliged to give up will depend on what we consider to be of comparable moral significance to the poverty we could prevent: colour television, stylish clothes, expensive dinners, a sophisticated stereo system, overseas holidays, a (second?) car, a larger house, private schools for our children. . . . For a utilitarian, none of these is likely to be of comparable significance to the reduction of absolute poverty; and those who are not utilitarians surely must, if they subscribe to the principle of universalizability, accept that at least *some* of these things are of far less moral significance than the absolute poverty that could be prevented by the money they cost. . . .

Objections to the Argument

Property Rights

Do people have a right to private property, a right which contradicts the view that they are under an obligation to give some of their wealth away to those in absolute poverty? According to some theories of rights (for instance, Robert Nozick's) provided one has acquired one's property without the use of unjust means like force and fraud, one may be entitled to enormous wealth while others starve. This individualistic conception of rights is in contrast to other views, like the early Christian doctrine to be found in the works of Thomas Aquinas, which holds that since property exists for the satisfaction of human needs, "whatever a man has in superabundance is owed, of natural right, to the poor for their sustenance." A socialist would also, of course, see wealth as belonging to the community rather than the individual, while utilitarians, whether socialist or not, would be prepared to override property rights to prevent great evils.

Does the argument for an obligation to assist others therefore presuppose one of these other theories of property rights, and not an individualistic theory like Nozick's? Not necessarily. A theory of property rights can insist on our *right* to retain wealth without pronouncing on whether the rich *ought* to give to the poor. Nozick, for example, rejects the use of compulsory means like taxation to redistribute income, but suggests that we can achieve the ends we deem morally desirable by voluntary means. So Nozick would reject the claim that rich people have an "obligation" to give to the poor, in so far as this implies that the poor have a right to our aid, but might accept that giving is something we ought to do and failing to give, though within one's rights, is wrong—for rights is not all there is to ethics.

The argument for an obligation to assist can survive, with only minor modifications, even if we accept an individualistic theory of property rights. In any case, however, I do not think we should accept such a theory. It leaves too much to chance to be an acceptable ethical view. For instance, those whose forefathers happened to inhabit some sandy wastes around the Persian Gulf are now fabulously wealthy, because oil lay under those sands; while those whose forefathers settled on better land south of the Sahara live in absolute poverty, because of drought and bad harvests. Can this distribution be acceptable from an impartial point of view? If we imagine ourselves about to begin life as a citizen of either Kuwait or Chad—but we do not know which —would we accept the principle that citizens of Kuwait are under no obligation to assist people living in Chad?

Population and the Ethics of Triage

Perhaps the most serious objection to the argument that we have an obligation to assist is that since the major cause of absolute poverty is overpopulation, helping those now in poverty will only ensure that yet more people are born to live in poverty in the future.

In its most extreme form, this objection is taken to show that we should adopt a policy of "triage." The term comes from medical policies adopted in wartime. With too few doctors to cope with all the casualties, the wounded were divided into three categories: those who would probably survive without medical assistance, those who might survive if they received assistance, but otherwise probably would not, and those who even with medical assistance probably would not survive. Only those in the middle category were given medical assistance. The idea, of course, was to use limited medical resources as effectively as possible. For those in the first category, medical treatment was not strictly necessary; for those in the third category, it was likely to be useless. It has been suggested that we should apply the same policies to countries, according to their prospects of becoming self-sustaining. We would not aid countries which even without our help will soon be able to feed their populations. We would not aid countries which, even with our help, will not be able to limit their population to a level they can feed. We would aid those countries where our help might make the difference between success and failure in bringing food and population into balance.

Advocates of this theory are understandably reluctant to give a complete list of the countries they would place into the "hopeless" category; but Bangladesh is often cited as an example. Adopting the policy of triage would, then, mean cutting off assistance to Bangladesh and allowing famine, disease and natural disasters to reduce the population of that country (now around 80 million) to the level at which it can provide adequately for all.

In support of this view Garrett Hardin has offered a metaphor: we in the rich nations are like the occupants of a crowded lifeboat adrift in a sea full of drowning people. If we try to save the drowning by bringing them aboard our boat will be overloaded and we shall all drown. Since it is better that some survive than none, we should leave the others to drown. In the world today, according to Hardin, "lifeboat ethics" apply. The rich should leave the poor to starve, for otherwise the poor will drag the rich down with them.

Against this view, some writers have argued that over-population is a myth. The world produces ample food to feed its population, and could, according to some estimates, feed ten times as many. People are hungry not because there are too many but because of inequitable land distribution, the manipulation of Third World economies by the developed nations, wastage of food in the West, and so on.

Putting aside the controversial issue of the extent to which food production might one day be increased, it is true, as we have already seen, that the world now produces enough to feed its inhabitants —the amount lost by being fed to animals itself being enough to meet existing grain shortages. Nevertheless population growth cannot be ignored. Bangladesh could, with land reform and using better techniques, feed its present population of 80 million; but by the year 2000, according to World Bank estimates, its population will be 146 million. The enormous effort that will have to go into feeding an extra 66 million people, all added to the population within a quarter of a century, means that Bangladesh must develop at full speed to stay where she is. Other low income countries are in similar situations. By the end of the century, Ethiopia's population is expected to rise from 29 to 54 million; Somalia's from 3 to 7 million, India's from 620 to 958 million, Zaire's from 25 to 47 million. What will happen then? Population cannot grow indefinitely. It will be checked by a decline in birth rates or a rise in death rates. Those who advocate triage are proposing that we allow the population growth of some countries to be checked by a rise in death rates—that is, by increased malnutrition, and related diseases; by widespread famines; by increased infant mortality; and by epidemics of infectious diseases.

The consequences of triage on this scale are so horrible that we are inclined to reject it without further argument. How could we sit by our television sets, watching millions starve while we do nothing? Would not that be the end of all notions of human equality and respect for human life? Don't people have a right to our assistance, irrespective of the consequences?

Anyone whose initial reaction to triage was not one of repugnance would be an unpleasant sort of person. Yet initial reactions based on strong feelings are not always reliable guides. Advocates of triage are rightly concerned with the long-term consequences of our actions. They say that helping the poor and starving now merely ensures more poor and starving in the future. When our capacity to help is finally unable to cope—as one day it must be—the suffering will be greater than it would be if we stopped helping now. If this is correct, there is nothing we can do to prevent absolute starvation and poverty, in the long run, and so we have no obligation to assist. Nor does it seem reasonable to hold that under these circumstances people have a right to our assistance. If we do accept such a right, irrespective of the consequences, we are saying that, in Hardin's metaphor, we would continue to haul the drowning into our lifeboat until the boat sank and we all drowned.

If triage is to be rejected it must be tackled on its own ground, within the framework of consequentialist ethics. Here it is vulnerable. Any consequentialist ethics must take probability of outcome into account. A course of action that will certainly produce some benefit is to be preferred to an alternative course that may lead to a slightly larger benefit, but is equally likely to result in no benefit at all. Only if the greater magnitude of the uncertain benefit outweighs its uncertainty should we choose it. Better one certain unit of benefit than a 10% chance of 5 units; but better a 50% chance of 3 units than a single certain unit. The same principle applies when we are trying to avoid evils.

The policy of triage involves a certain, very great evil: population control by famine and disease. Tens of millions would die slowly. Hundreds of millions would continue to live in absolute poverty, at the very margin of existence. Against this prospect, advocates of the policy place a possible evil which is greater still: the same process of famine and disease, taking place in, say, fifty years time, when the world's population may be three times its present level, and the number who will die from famine, or struggle on in absolute poverty, will be that much greater. The question is: how probable is this forecast that continued assistance now will lead to greater disasters in the future?

Forecasts of population growth are notoriously fallible, and theories about the factors which affect it remain speculative. One theory, at least as plausible as any other, is that countries pass through a "demographic transition" as their standard of living rises. When people are very poor and have no access to modern medicine their fertility is high, but population is kept in check by high death rates. The introduction of sanitation, modern medical techniques and other improvements reduces the death rate, but initially has little effect on the birth rate. Then population grows rapidly. Most poor countries

are now in this phase. If standards of living continue to rise, however, couples begin to realize that to have the same number of children surviving to maturity as in the past, they do not need to give birth to as many children as their parents did. The need for children to provide economic support in old age diminishes. Improved education and the emancipation and employment of women also reduce the birthrate, and so population growth begins to level off. Most rich nations have reached this stage, and their populations are growing only very slowly.

If this theory is right, there is an alternative to the disasters accepted as inevitable by supporters of triage. We can assist poor countries to raise the living standards of the poorest members of their population. We can encourage the governments of these countries to enact land reform measures, improve education, and liberate women from a purely childbearing role. We can also help other countries to make contraception and sterilization widely available. There is a fair chance that these measures will hasten the onset of the demographic transition and bring population growth down to a manageable level. Success cannot be guaranteed; but the evidence that improved economic security and education reduce population growth is strong enough to make triage ethically unacceptable. We cannot allow millions to die from starvation and disease when there is a reasonable probability that population can be brought under control without such horrors.

Population growth is therefore not a reason against giving overseas aid, although it should make us think about the kind of aid to give. Instead of food handouts, it may be better to give aid that hastens the demographic transition. This may mean agricultural assistance for the rural poor, or assistance with education, or the provision of contraceptive services. Whatever kind of aid proves most effective in specific circumstances, the obligation to assist is not reduced.

One awkward question remains. What should we do about a poor and already overpopulated country which, for religious or nationalistic reasons, restricts the use of contraceptives and refuses to slow its population growth? Should we nevertheless offer development assistance? Or should we make our offer conditional on effective steps being taken to reduce the birthrate? To the latter course, some would object that putting conditions on aid is an attempt to impose our own ideas on independent sovereign nations. So it is—but is this imposition unjustifiable? If the argument for an obligation to assist is sound, we have an obligation to reduce absolute poverty: but we have no obligation to make sacrifices that, to the best of our knowledge, have no prospect of reducing poverty in the long run. Hence we have no obligation to assist countries whose governments have policies which will make our aid ineffective. This could be very harsh on poor citizens of these countries—for they may have no say in the government's policies—but we will help more people in the long run by using our resources where they are most effective. (The same principles may apply, incidentally, to countries that refuse to take other steps that could make assistance effective—like refusing to reform systems of land holding that impose intolerable burdens on poor tenant farmers.) . . .

Too High a Standard?

The final objection to the argument for an obligation to assist is that it sets a standard so high that none but a saint could attain it. How many people can we really expect to give away everything not comparable in moral significance to the poverty their donation could relieve? For most of us, with commonsense views about what is of moral significance, this would mean a life of real austerity. Might it not be counterproductive to demand so much? Might not people say: "As I can't do what is morally required anyway, I won't bother to give at all." If, however, we were to set a more realistic standard, people might make a genuine effort to reach it. Thus setting a lower standard might actually result in more aid being given.

It is important to get the status of this objection clear. Its accuracy as a prediction of human behaviour is quite compatible with the argument that we are obliged to give to the point at which by giving more we sacrifice something of comparable moral significance. What would follow from the objection is that public advocacy of this standard of giving is undesirable. It would mean that in order to do the maximum to reduce absolute poverty, we should advocate a standard lower than the amount we think people really ought to give. Of course we ourselves —those of us who accept the original argument, with its higher standard—would know that we ought to do more than we publicly propose people ought to do, and we might actually give more than we urge others to give. There is no inconsistency here, since in both our private and our public behaviour we are trying to do what will most reduce absolute poverty.

For a consequentialist, this apparent conflict between public and private morality is always a possibility, and not in itself an indication that the underlying principle is wrong. The consequences of a principle are one thing, the consequences of publicly advocating it another.

Is it true that the standard set by our argument is so high as to be counterproductive? There is not much evidence to go by, but discussions of the argument, with students and others have led me to think it might be. On the other hand the conventionally accepted standard—a few coins in a collection tin when one is waved under your nose—is obviously far too low. What level should we advocate? Any figure will be arbitrary, but there may be something to be said for a round percentage of one's income like, say, 10%—more than a token donation, yet not so high as to be beyond all but saints. (This figure has the additional advantage of being reminiscent of the ancient tithe, or tenth, which was traditionally given to the church, whose responsibilities included care of the poor in one's local community. Perhaps the idea can be revived and applied to the global community.) Some families, of course, will find 10% a considerable strain on their finances. Others may be able to give more without difficulty. No figure should be advocated as a rigid minimum or maximum; but it seems safe to advocate that those earning average or above average incomes in affluent societies, unless they have an unusually large number of dependents or other special needs, ought to give a tenth of their income to reducing absolute poverty. By any reasonable ethical standards this is the minimum we ought to do, and we do wrong if we do less.

JOHN HOSPERS

What Libertarianism Is

John Hospers is Professor Emeritus of Philosophy at the University of Southern California. He ran for president on the Libertarian Party ticket in 1972. (Source: Reprinted from Tibor R. Machan [ed.], The Libertarian Alternative: Essays in Social and Political Philosophy, *Nelson-Hall, 1974. Copyright © 1974 by Nelson-Hall, Inc.)*

QUESTIONS FOR REFECTION

1. How does Hospers define libertarianism?

2. What conception of rights emerges from Hospers's analysis?

3. What, according to Hospers, is the proper function of government? How does his view compare to Mill's? To Locke's?

4. How does Hospers respond to the charge that libertarianism fails to respond to real human needs? Do you find his answer convincing?

The political philosophy that is called libertarianism (from the Latin *libertas,* liberty) is the doctrine that every person is the owner of his own life, and that no one is the owner of anyone else's life; and that consequently every human being has the right to act in accordance with his own choices, unless those actions infringe on the equal liberty of other human beings to act in accordance with *their* choices.

There are several other ways of stating the same libertarian thesis:

1. *No one is anyone else's master, and no one is anyone else's slave.* Since I am the one to decide how my life is to be conducted, just as you decide about yours, I have no right (even if I had the power) to make you my slave and be your master, nor have you the right to become the master by enslaving me. Slavery is *forced* servitude, and since no one owns the life of anyone else, no one has the right to enslave another. Political theories past and present have traditionally been concerned with who should be the master (usually the king, the dictator, or government bureaucracy) and who should be the slaves, and what the extent of the slavery should be. Libertarianism holds that no one has the right to use force to enslave the life of another, or any portion or aspect of that life.

2. *Other men's lives are not yours to dispose of.* I enjoy seeing operas; but operas are expensive to produce. Opera-lovers often say, "The state (or the city, etc.) should subsidize opera, so that we can all see it. Also it would be for people's betterment, cultural benefit, etc." But what they are advocating is nothing more or less than legalized plunder. They can't pay for the productions themselves, and yet they want to see opera, which involves a large number of people and their labor; so what they are saying in effect is, "Get the money through legalized force. Take a little bit more out of every worker's paycheck every week to pay for the operas we want to see." But I have no right to take by force from the workers' pockets to pay for what I want.

Perhaps it would be better if he *did* go to see opera—then I should try to convince him to go voluntarily. But to take the money from him forcibly, because in my opinion it would be good for *him,* is still seizure of his earnings, which is plunder.

Besides, if I have the right to force him to help pay for my pet projects, hasn't he equally the right to force me to help pay for his? Perhaps he in turn wants the government to subsidize rock-and-roll, or his new car, or a house in the country? If I have the right to milk him, why hasn't he the right to milk me? If I can be a moral cannibal, why can't he too?

We should beware of the inventors of utopias. They would remake the world according to their vision—with the lives and fruits of the labor of *other* human beings. Is it someone's utopian vision that others should build pyramids to beautify the landscape? Very well, then other men should provide the labor; and if he is in a position of political power, and he can't get men to do it voluntarily, then he must *compel* them to "cooperate"—i.e. he must enslave them.

A hundred men might gain great pleasure from beating up or killing just one insignificant human being; but other men's lives are not theirs to dispose of. "In order to achieve the worthy goals of the next five-year-plan, we must forcibly collectivize the peasants . . ."; but other men's lives are not theirs to dispose of. Do you want to occupy, rent-free, the mansion that another man has worked for twenty years to buy? But other men's lives are not yours to dispose of. Do you want operas so badly that everyone is forced to work harder to pay for their subsidization through taxes? But other men's lives are not yours to dispose of. Do you want to have free medical care at the expense of other people, whether they wish to provide it or not? But this would require them to work longer for you whether they want to or not, and other men's lives are not yours to dispose of.

> The freedom to engage in any type of enterprise, to produce, to own and control property, to buy and sell on the free market, is derived from the rights to life, liberty, and property . . . which are stated in the Declaration of Independence . . . [but] when a government guarantees a "right" to an education or parity on farm products or a guaranteed annual income, it is staking a claim on the property of one group of citizens for the sake of another group. In short, it is violating one of the fundamental rights it was instituted to protect.*

3. *No human being should be a nonvoluntary mortgage on the life of another.* I cannot claim your life, your work, or the products of your efforts as mine. The fruit of one man's labor should not be fair game for every freeloader who comes along and demands it as his own. The orchard that has been carefully grown, nurtured, and harvested by its owner should not be ripe for the plucking for any bypasser who has a yen for the ripe fruit. The wealth that some men have produced should not be fair game for looting by government, to be used for whatever purposes its representatives determine, no matter what their motives in so doing may be. The theft of your money by a robber is not justified by the fact that he used it to help his injured mother.

It will already be evident that libertarian doctrine is embedded in a view of the rights of man. Each human being has the right to live his life as he chooses, compatibly with the equal right of all other human beings to live their lives as they choose.

All man's rights are implicit in the above statement. Each man has the right to life: any attempt by others to take it away from him, or even to injure him, violates this right, through the use of coercion against him. Each man has the right to liberty: to conduct his life in accordance with the alternatives open to him without coercive action by others. And every man has the right to property: to work to sustain his life (and the lives of whichever others he chooses to sustain, such as his family) and to retain the fruits of his labor.

People often defend the rights of life and liberty but denigrate property rights, and yet the right to property is as basic as the other two; indeed, without property rights no other rights are possible. Depriving you of property is depriving you of the means by which you live.

> . . . All that which an individual possesses by right (including his life and property) are morally his to use,

* William W. Bayes, "What Is Property?" *The Freeman,* July 1970, p. 348.

dispose of and even destroy, as he sees fit. If I own my life, then it follows that I am free to associate with whom I please and not to associate with whom I please. If I own my knowledge and services, it follows that I may ask any compensation I wish for providing them for another, or I may abstain from providing them at all, if I so choose. If I own my house, it follows that I may decorate it as I please and live in it with whom I please. If I control my own business, it follows that I may charge what I please for my products or services, hire whom I please and not hire whom I please. All that which I own in fact, I may dispose of as I choose to in reality. For anyone to attempt to limit my freedom to do so is to violate my rights.

Where do my rights end? Where yours begin. I may do anything I wish with my own life, liberty and property without your consent; but I may do nothing with your life, liberty and property without your consent. If we recognize the principle of man's rights, it follows that the individual is sovereign of the domain of his own life and property, and is sovereign of no other domain. To attempt to interfere forcibly with another's use, disposal or destruction of his own property is to initiate force against him and to violate his rights.

I have no right to decide how *you* should spend your time or your money. I can make that decision for myself, but not for you, my neighbor. I may deplore your choice of life-style, and I may talk with you about it provided you are willing to listen to me. But I have no right to use force to change it. Nor have I the right to decide how you should spend the money you have earned. I may appeal to you to give it to the Red Cross, and you may prefer to go to prizefights. But that is your decision, and however much I may chafe about it I do not have the right to interfere forcibly with it, for example by robbing you in order to use the money in accordance with *my* choices. (If I have the right to rob you, have you also the right to rob me?)

When I claim a right, I carve out a niche, as it were, in my life, saying in effect, "This activity I must be able to perform without interference from others. For you and everyone else, this is off limits." And so I put up a "no trespassing" sign, which marks off the area of my right. Each individual's right is his "no trespassing" sign in relation to me and others. I may not encroach upon his domain any more than he

upon mine, without my consent. Every right entails a duty, true—but the duty is only that of *forbearance* —that is, of *refraining* from violating the other person's right. If you have a right to life, I have no right to take your life; if you have a right to the products of your labor (property), I have no right to take it from you without your consent. The non-violation of these rights will not guarantee you protection against natural catastrophes such as floods and earthquakes, but it will protect you against the aggressive activities *of other men*. And rights, after all, have to do with one's relations to other human beings, not with one's relations to physical nature.

Nor were these rights created by government; governments—some governments, obviously not all —*recognize* and *protect* the rights that individuals already have. Governments regularly forbid homicide and theft; and, at a more advanced stage, protect individuals against such things as libel and breach of contract. . . .

Government is the most dangerous institution known to man. Throughout history it has violated the rights of men more than any individual or group of individuals could do: it has killed people, enslaved them, sent them to forced labor and concentration camps, and regularly robbed and pillaged them of the fruits of their expended labor. Unlike individual criminals, government has the power to arrest and try; unlike individual criminals, it can surround and encompass a person totally, dominating every aspect of one's life, so that one has no recourse from it but to leave the country (and in totalitarian nations even that is prohibited). Government throughout history has a much sorrier record than any individual, even that of a ruthless mass murderer. The signs we see on bumper stickers are chillingly accurate: "Beware: the Government is Armed and Dangerous."

The only proper role of government, according to libertarians, is that of the protector of the citizen against aggression by other individuals. The government, of course, should never initiate aggression; its proper role is as the embodiment of the *retaliatory* use of force against anyone who initiates its use.

If each individual had constantly to defend himself against possible aggressors, he would have to spend a considerable portion of his life in target practice, karate exercises, and other means of self-defenses, and even so he would probably be helpless against groups of individuals who might try to kill, maim, or rob him. He would have little time for cultivating those qualities which are essential to civilized life, nor would improvements in science, medicine, and the arts be likely to occur. The function of government is to take this responsibility off his shoulders: the government undertakes to defend him against aggressors and to punish them if they attack him. When the government is effective in doing this, it enables the citizen to go about his business unmolested and without constant fear for his life. To do this, of course, government must have physical power—the police, to protect the citizen from aggression within its borders, and the armed forces, to protect him from aggressors outside. Beyond that, the government should not intrude upon his life, either to run his business, or adjust his daily activities, or prescribe his personal moral code.

Government, then, undertakes to be the individual's protector; but historically governments have gone far beyond this function. Since they already have the physical power, they have not hesitated to use it for purposes far beyond that which was entrusted to them in the first place. Undertaking initially to protect its citizens against aggression, it has often itself become an aggressor—a far greater aggressor, indeed, than the criminals against whom it was supposed to protect its citizens. Governments have done what no private citizens can do: arrest and imprison individuals without a trial and send them to slave labor camps. Government must have power in order to be effective—and yet the very means by which alone it can be effective make it vulnerable to the abuse of power, leading to managing the lives of individuals and even inflicting terror upon them.

What then should be the function of government? In a word, the *protection of human rights*.

1. *The right to life*: libertarians support all such legislation as will protect human beings against the use of force by others, for example, laws against killing, attempted killing, maiming, beating, and all kinds of physical violence.

2. *The right to liberty*: there should be no laws compromising in any way freedom of speech, of the press, and of peaceable assembly. There should be no censorship of ideas, books, films, or of anything else by government.

3. *The right to property*: libertarians support legislation that protects the property rights of individuals against confiscation, nationalization, eminent domain, robbery, trespass, fraud and misrepresentation, patent and copyright, libel and slander.

Someone has violently assaulted you. Should he be legally liable? Of course. He has violated one of your rights. He has knowingly injured you, and since he has initiated aggression against you he should be made to expiate.

Someone has negligently left his bicycle on the sidewalk where you trip over it in the dark and injure yourself. He didn't do it intentionally; he didn't mean you any harm. Should he be legally liable? Of course; he has, however unwittingly, injured you, and since the injury is caused by him and you are the victim, he should pay.

Someone across the street is unemployed. Should you be taxed extra to pay for his expenses? Not at all. You have not injured him, you are not responsible for the fact that he is unemployed (unless you are a senator or bureaucrat who agitated for further curtailing of business, which legislation passed, with the result that your neighbor was laid off by the curtailed business). You may voluntarily wish to help him out, or better still, try to get him a job to put him on his feet again; but since you have initiated no aggressive act against him, and neither purposely nor accidentally injured him in any way, you should not be legally penalized for the fact of his unemployment. (Actually, it is just such penalties that increase unemployment.)

One man, A, works hard for years and finally earns a high salary as a professional man. A second man, B, prefers not to work at all, and to spend wastefully what money he has (through inheritance), so that after a year or two he has nothing left. At the end of this time he has a long siege of illness and lots of medical bills to pay. He demands that the bills be paid by the government—that is, by the taxpayers of the land, including Mr. A.

But of course B has no such right. He chose to lead his life in a certain way—that was his voluntary decision. One consequence of that choice is that he must depend on charity in case of later need. Mr. A chose not to live that way. (And if everyone lived like Mr. B, on whom would he depend in case of later need?) Each has a right to live in the way he pleases, but each must live with the consequences of his own decision (which, as always, fall primarily on himself). He cannot, in time of need, claim A's beneficence as his right . . .

Laws may be classified into three types: (1) laws protecting individuals against themselves, such as laws against fornication and other sexual behavior, alcohol, and drugs; (2) laws protecting individuals against aggressions by other individuals, such as laws against murder, robbery, and fraud; (3) laws requiring people to help one another; for example, all laws which rob Peter to pay Paul, such as welfare.

Libertarians reject the first class of laws totally. Behavior which harms no one else is strictly the individual's own affair. Thus, there should be no laws against becoming intoxicated, since whether or not to become intoxicated is the individual's own decision; but there should be laws against driving while intoxicated, since the drunken driver is a threat to every other motorist on the highway (drunken driving falls into type 2). Similarly, there should be no laws against drugs (except the prohibition of sale of drugs to minors) as long as the taking of these drugs poses no threat to anyone else. Drug addiction is a psychological problem to which no present solution exists. Most of the social harm caused by addicts, other than to themselves, is the result of thefts which they perform in order to continue their habit—and then the *legal* crime is the theft, not the addiction. The actual cost of heroin is about ten cents a shot; if it were legalized, the enormous traffic in illegal sale and purchase of it would stop, as well as the accompanying proselytization to get new addicts (to make more money for the pusher) and the thefts performed by addicts who often require eighty dollars a day just to keep up the habit. Addiction would not stop, but the crimes would: it is estimated that 75 percent of the burglaries in New York City today are performed by addicts, and all these crimes could be wiped out at one stroke through the legalization of drugs. (Only when the taking of drugs could be shown to constitute a threat to *others,* should it be prohibited by law.

It is only laws protecting people against *themselves* that libertarians oppose.)

Laws should be limited to the second class only: aggression by individuals against other individuals. These are laws whose function is to protect human beings against encroachment by others; and this, as we have seen, is (according to libertarianism) the sole function of government.

Libertarians also reject the third class of laws totally: no one should be forced by law to help others, not even to tell them the time of day if requested, and certainly not to give them a portion of one's weekly paycheck. Governments, in the guise of humanitarianism, have given to some by taking from others (charging a "handling fee" in the process, which, because of the government's waste and inefficiency, sometimes is several hundred percent). And in so doing they have decreased incentive, violated the rights of individuals, and lowered the standard of living of almost everyone.

All such laws constitute what libertarians call *moral cannibalism.* A cannibal in the physical sense is a person who lives off the flesh of other human beings. A *moral* cannibal is one who believes he has a right to live off the "spirit" of other human beings—who believes that he has a moral claim on the productive capacity, time, and effort expended by others.

It has become fashionable to claim virtually everything that one needs or desires as one's *right.* Thus, many people claim that they have a right to a job, the right to free medical care, to free food and clothing, to a decent home, and so on. Now if one asks, apart from any specific context, whether it would be desirable if everyone had these things, one might well say yes. But there is a gimmick attached to each of them: *At whose expense?* Jobs, medical care, education, and so on, don't grow on trees. These are goods and services *produced only by men.* Who, then, is to provide them, and under what conditions?

If you have a right to a job, who is to supply it? Must an employer supply it even if he doesn't want to hire you? What if you are unemployable, or incurably lazy? (If you say "the government must supply it," does that mean that a job must be created for you which no employer needs done, and that you must be kept in it regardless of how much or little you work?) If the employer is forced to supply it at his expense even if he doesn't need you, then isn't *he* being enslaved to that extent? What ever happened to *his* right to conduct his life and his affairs in accordance with his choices?

If you have a right to free medical care, then, since medical care doesn't exist in nature as wild apples do, some people will have to supply it to you for free: that is, they will have to spend their time and money and energy taking care of you whether they want to or not. What ever happened to *their* right to conduct their lives as they see fit? Or do you have a right to violate theirs? Can there be a right to violate rights?

All those who demand this or that as a "free service" are consciously or unconsciously evading the fact that there is in reality no such thing as free services. All man-made goods and services are the result of human expenditure of time and effort. There is no such thing as "something for nothing" in this world. If you demand something free, you are demanding that other men give their time and effort to you without compensation. If they voluntarily choose to do this, there is no problem; but if you demand that they be *forced* to do it, you are interfering with their right not to do it if they so choose. "Swimming in this pool ought to be free!" says the indignant passerby. What he means is that others should build a pool, others should provide the

materials, and still others should run it and keep it in functioning order, so that *he* can use it without fee. But what right has he to the expenditure of *their* time and effort? To expect something "for free" is to expect it *to be paid for by others* whether they choose to or not.

Many questions, particularly about economic matters, will be generated by the libertarian account of human rights and the role of government. Should government have no role in assisting the needy, in providing social security, in legislating minimum wages, in fixing prices and putting a ceiling on rents, in curbing monopolies, in erecting tariffs, in guaranteeing jobs, in managing the money supply? To these and all similar questions the libertarian answers with an unequivocal no.

"But then you'd let people go hungry!" comes the rejoinder. This, the libertarian insists, is precisely what would not happen; with the restrictions removed, the economy would flourish as never before. With the controls taken off business, existing enterprises would expand and new ones would spring into existence satisfying more and more consumer needs; millions more people would be gainfully employed instead of subsisting on welfare, and all kinds of research and production, released from the stranglehold of government, would proliferate, fulfilling man's needs and desires as never before. It has always been so whenever government has permitted men to be free traders on a free market. . . .

CHARLES MURRAY

from *Losing Ground: American Social Policy, 1950–1980*

Charles Murray is Bradley Fellow at the Manhattan Institute for Policy Research. (Source: From Losing Ground: American Social Policy, 1950–1980 *by Charles Murray. Copyright © 1984 by Charles Murray. Reprinted by permission of Basic Books, a division of HarperCollins Publishers Inc.)*

QUESTIONS FOR REFLECTION

1. Explain Murray's three laws.

2. Are you convinced that Murray's laws are true? Why or why not?

3. What benefits would accrue, according to Murray, if welfare programs were eliminated altogether?

4. Who might be harmed by eliminating welfare programs, in Murray's view? In your view?

[CHAPTER 16 / THE CONSTRAINTS ON HELPING]

Laws of Social Programs

. . . Let me suggest some characteristics . . . that occur so widely and for such embedded reasons that they suggest laws. That is, no matter how ingenious the design of a social transfer program may be, we cannot—in a free society—design programs that escape their influence. . . .

#1. The Law of Imperfect Selection. Any objective rule that defines eligibility for a social transfer program will irrationally exclude some persons.

It can always be demonstrated that some persons who are excluded from the Food Stamps program are in greater need than some persons who receive Food Stamps. It can always be demonstrated that someone who is technically ineligible for Medicaid really "ought" to be receiving it, given the intent of the legislation.

These inequities, which are observed everywhere, are not the fault of inept writers of eligibility rules, but an inescapable outcome of the task of rule-writing. Eligibility rules must convert the concept of "true need" into objectified elements. The rules constructed from these bits and pieces are necessarily subject to what Herbert Costner has called "epistemic error"—the inevitable gap between quantified measures and the concept they are intended to capture. We have no way of defining "truly needy" precisely—not those who truly need to stop smoking, nor those truly in need of college scholarships or subsidized loans or disability insurance. Any criterion we specify will inevitably include a range of people, some of whom are unequivocally the people we intended to help, others of whom are less so, and still others of whom meet the letter of the eligibility requirement but are much less needy than some persons who do not.

Social welfare policy in earlier times tended to deal with this problem by erring in the direction of exclusion—better to deny help to some truly needy persons than to let a few slackers slip through. Such

468

attitudes depended, however, on the assumption that the greater good was being served. Moral precepts had to be upheld. Whenever a person was inappropriately given help, it was bad for the recipient (undermining his character) and a bad example to the community at large.

When that assumption is weakened or dispensed with altogether, it follows naturally that the Law of Imperfect Selection leads to programs with constantly broadening target populations. If persons are not to blame for their plight, no real harm is done by giving them help they do not fully "need." No moral cost is incurred by permitting some undeserving into the program. A moral cost *is* incurred by excluding a deserving person. No one has a scalpel sharp enough to excise only the undeserving. Therefore it is not just a matter of political expedience to add a new layer to the eligible population rather than to subtract one (though that is often a factor in the actual decision-making process). It is also the morally correct thing to do, given the premises of the argument.

#2. The Law of Unintended Rewards. Any social transfer increases the net value of being in the condition that prompted the transfer.

A deficiency is observed—too little money, too little food, too little academic achievement—and a social transfer program tries to fill the gap—with a welfare payment, Food Stamps, a compensatory education program. An unwanted behavior is observed —drug addiction, crime, unemployability—and the program tries to change that behavior to some other, better behavior—through a drug rehabilitation program, psychotherapy, vocational training. In each case, the program, however unintentionally, *must* be constructed in such a way that it increases the net value of being in the condition that it seeks to change—either by increasing the rewards or by reducing the penalties.

For some people in some circumstances, it is absurd to think in terms of "net value," because they so clearly have no choice at all about the fix they are in or because the net value is still less desirable than virtually any alternative. Paraplegics receiving Medicaid cannot easily be seen as "rewarded" for becoming paraplegics by the existence of free medical care. Poor children in Head Start cannot be seen as re-warded for being poor. Persons who are in the unwanted condition *completely involuntarily* are not affected by the existence of the reward.

But the number of such pure examples is very small. Let us return to the case of the middle-aged worker who loses his job, wants desperately to work, but can find nothing. He receives Unemployment Insurance, hating every penny of it. He would seem to be "completely involuntarily" in his situation and his search for a job unaffected by the existence of Unemployment Insurance. In fact, however, his behavior (unless he is peculiarly irrational) *is* affected by the existence of the Unemployment Insurance. For example, the cushion provided by Unemployment Insurance may lead him to refuse to take a job that requires him to move to another town, whereas he would take the job and uproot his home if he were more desperate. Most people (including me) are glad that his behavior is so affected, that he does not have to leave the home and friends of a lifetime, that he can wait for a job opening nearby. But he is not "completely involuntarily" unemployed in such a case, and the reason he is not is that the Unemployment Insurance has made the condition of unemployment more tolerable.

Our paraplegic anchors one end of the continuum labeled "Degree of Voluntarism in the Conditions that Social Policy Seeks to Change or Make Less Painful," and our unemployed worker is only slightly to one side of him—but he is to one side, not in the same place. The apparent unattractiveness of most of the conditions that social policy seeks to change must not obscure the continuum involved. No one chooses to be a paraplegic, and perhaps no one chooses to be a heroin addict. But the distinction remains: very few heroin addicts developed their addiction by being tied down and forcibly injected with heroin. They may not have chosen to become addicts, but they *did* choose initially to take heroin.

Let us consider the implications in terms of the archetypical social program for helping the chronic unemployed escape their condition, the job-training program.

Imagine that a program is begun that has the most basic and benign inducement of all, the chance to learn a marketable skill. It is open to everybody. By opening it to all, we have circumvented (for the time being) the Law of Unintended Rewards. All may obtain the training, no matter what their job history, so no unintended reward is being given for the condition of chronic unemployment.

On assessing the results, we observe that the ones who enter the program, stick with it, and learn a skill include very few of the hardcore unemployed whom we most wanted to help. The typical "success" stories from our training program are persons with a history of steady employment who wanted to upgrade their earning power. This is admirable. But what about the hardcore unemployed? A considerable number entered the program, but almost all of them dropped out or failed to get jobs once they left. Only a small proportion used the training opportunity as we had hoped. The problem of the hardcore unemployed remains essentially unchanged.

We may continue to circumvent the Law of Unintended Rewards. All we need do is continue the job-training program unchanged. It will still be there, still available to all who want to enroll, but we will do nothing to entice participation. Our theory (should we adopt this stance) is that, as time goes on, we will continue to help at least a few of the hardcore unemployed who are in effect skimmed from the top of the pool. We may even hope that the number skimmed from the top will be larger than the number who enter the pool, so that, given enough time, the population of hardcore unemployed will diminish. But this strategy is a gradualist one and relies on the assumption that other conditions in society are not creating more hardcore unemployed than the program is skimming off.

The alternative is to do something to get more of the hardcore unemployed into the program, and to improve the content so that more of them profit from the training. And once this alternative is taken, the program planner is caught in the trap of unintended rewards. Because we cannot "draft" people into the program or otherwise coerce their participation, our only alternative is to make it more attractive by changing the rules a bit.

Suppose, for example, we find that the reason many did not profit from the earlier program was that they got fired from (or quit) their new jobs within a few days of getting them, and that the reason they did so had to do with the job-readiness problem. The ex-trainee was late getting to work, the

boss complained, the ex-trainee reacted angrily and was fired. We observe this to be a common pattern. We know the problem is not that the ex-trainee is lazy or unmotivated, but that he has never been socialized into the discipline of the workplace. He needs more time, more help, more patience than other workers until he develops the needed work habits. Suppose that we try to compensate—for example, by placing our trainees with employers who are being subsidized to hire such persons. The employer accepts lower productivity and other problems in return for a payment to do so (such plans have been tried frequently, with mixed results). Given identical work at identical pay, the ex-trainee is being rewarded for his "credential" of hardcore unemployment. He can get away with behavior that an ordinary worker cannot get away with.

May we still assume that the program is making progress in preparing its trainees for the real-world marketplace? Will the hardcore unemployed modify their unreliable behavior? What will be the effect on morale and self-esteem among those trainees who were succeeding in the program before the change of rules? It is tempting to conclude that the program has already ceased to function effectively for anyone anymore, that the change in rules has done more harm than good. But my proposition is for the moment a more restricted one: The reward for unproductive behavior (both past and present) now exists.

What of the case of a drug addict who is chronically unemployed because (let us assume) of the addiction? It might seem that the unintended reward in such a case is innocuous; it consists of measures to relieve the addict of his addiction, measures for which the nonaddict will have no need or use. If we were dealing with an involuntary disability—our paraplegic again—the argument would be valid. But in the case of drug addiction (or any other behavior that has its rewards), a painless cure generally increases the attractiveness of the behavior. Imagine, for example, a pill that instantly and painlessly relieved dependence on heroin, and the subsequent effects on heroin use.

Thus we are faced with the problem we observed in the thought experiment. The program that seeks to change behavior must offer an inducement that unavoidably either adds to the attraction of, or reduces the penalties of engaging in, the behavior in question. The best-known example in real life is the thirty-and-a-third rule for AFDC recipients. It becomes more advantageous financially to hold a job than not to hold a job (the intended inducement for AFDC recipients to work), but it also becomes more advantageous to be on AFDC (the unintended reward to nonrecipients).

We are now ready to tackle the question of when a social program can reasonably be expected to accomplish net good and when it can reasonably be expected to produce net harm. Again let us think in terms of a continuum. All social programs, I have argued, provide an unintended reward for being in the condition that the program is trying to change or make more tolerable. But some of these unintended rewards are so small that they are of little practical importance. Why then can we not simply bring a bit of care to the design of such programs, making sure that the unintended reward is *always* small? The reason we are not free to do so lies in the third law of social programs:

> #3. The Law of Net Harm. The less likely it is that the unwanted behavior will change voluntarily, the more likely it is that a program to induce change will cause net harm.

A social program that seeks to change behavior must do two things. It must induce participation by the persons who are to benefit, as described under the Law of Unintended Rewards. Then it must actually produce the desired change in behavior. It must succeed, and success depends crucially on one factor above all others: The price that the participant is willing to pay.

The more that the individual is willing to accept whatever needs to be done in order to achieve the desired state of affairs, the broader the discretion of the program designers. Thus, expensive health resorts can withhold food from their guests, hospitals can demand that their interns work inhuman schedules, and elite volunteer units in the armed forces can ask their trainees to take risks in training exercises that seem (to the rest of us) suicidal. Such programs need offer no inducement at all except the "thing in itself" that is the *raison d'être* of the program—a shapelier body, a career as a physician,

membership in the elite military unit. Similarly, the drug addict who is prepared to sign over to a program a great of deal of control over his own behavior may very well be successful—witness the sometimes impressive success rates of private treatment clinics.

The smaller the price that the participant is willing to pay, the greater the constraints on program design. It makes no difference to an official running a training program for the hardcore unemployed that (for example) the Marine Corps can install exemplary work habits in recruits who come to the Corps no more "job-ready" than the recruits to the job-training program. If the training program tried for one day to use the techniques that the Marine Corps uses, it would lose its participants. Boot camp was not part of the bargain the job trainees struck with the government when they signed on. Instead, the training program must not only induce persons to join the program (which may be fairly easy). It must also induce them to stay in the program, induce them to cooperate with its curriculum, and induce them, finally, to adopt major changes in outlook, habits, and assumptions. The program content must be almost entirely carrot.

There is nothing morally reprehensible in approaches that are constrained to use only positive inducements. The objections are practical.

First, it is guaranteed that success rates will be very low. The technology of changing human behavior depends heavily on the use of negative reinforcement in conjunction with positive reinforcement. The more deeply engrained the behavior to be changed and the more attractions it holds for the person whose behavior is involved, the more important it is that the program have both a full tool kit available to it *and* the participant's willingness to go along with whatever is required. The Marine Corps has both these assets. Social programs to deal with the hardcore unemployed, teenaged mothers, delinquents, and addicts seldom do.

Second, as inducements become large—as they must, if the program is dealing with the most intractable problems—the more attractive they become to people who were not in need of help in the first place. We do not yet know how large they must finally become. We do know from experience, however, that quite generous experimental programs have provided extensive counseling, training guaranteed jobs, and other supports—and failed. We can only guess at what would be enough—perhaps a matter of years of full-time residential training, followed by guaranteed jobs at double or triple the minimum wage; we do not know. Whatever they are, however, consider their effects on the people not in the program. At this point, it appears that any program that would succeed in helping large numbers of the hardcore unemployed will make hardcore unemployment a highly desirable state to be in.

The conditions that combine to produce net harm are somewhat different in the theoretical and the practical cases, but they come to the same thing. Theoretically, any program that mounts an intervention with sufficient rewards to sustain participation and an effective result will generate so much of the unwanted behavior (in order to become eligible for the program's rewards) that the net effect will be to increase the incidence of the unwanted behavior. In practice, the programs that deal with the most intractable behavior problems have included a package of rewards large enough to induce participation, but not large enough to produce the desired result.

My conclusion is that social programs in a democratic society tend to produce net harm in dealing with the most difficult problems. They will inherently tend to have enough of an inducement to produce bad behavior and not enough of a solution to stimulate good behavior; and the more difficult the problem, the more likely it is that this relationship will prevail. The lesson is not that we can do no good at all, but that we must pick our shots.

[CHAPTER 17 / CHOOSING A FUTURE]

A Proposal for Public Welfare

I begin with the proposition that it is within our resources to do enormous good for some people quickly. We have available to us a program that would convert a large proportion of the younger generation of hardcore unemployed into steady workers making a living wage. The same program would drastically reduce births to single teenage girls. It would reverse the trendline in the breakup of poor families. It would measurably increase the upward socioeconomic mobility of poor families. These improvements would affect some millions of persons.

All these are results that have eluded the efforts of the social programs installed since 1965, yet, from everything we know, there is no real question about whether they would occur under the program I propose. A wide variety of persuasive evidence from our own culture and around the world, from experimental data and longitudinal studies, from theory and practice, suggests that the program would achieve such results.

The proposed program, our final and most ambitious thought experiment, consists of scrapping the entire federal welfare and income-support structure for working-aged persons, including AFDC, Medicaid, Food Stamps, Unemployment Insurance, Worker's Compensation, subsidized housing, disability insurance, and the rest. It would leave the working-aged person with no recourse whatsoever except the job market, family members, friends, and public or private locally funded services. It is the Alexandrian solution: cut the knot, for there is no way to untie it.

It is difficult to examine such a proposal dispassionately. Those who dislike paying for welfare are for it without thinking. Others reflexively imagine bread lines and people starving in the streets. But as a means of gaining fresh perspective on the problem of effective reform, let us consider what this hypothetical society might look like.

A large majority of the population is unaffected. A surprising number of the huge American middle and working classes go from birth to grave without using any social welfare benefits until they receive their first Social Security check. Another portion of the population is technically affected, but the change in income is so small or so sporadic that it makes no difference in quality of life. A third group comprises persons who have to make new arrangements and behave in different ways. Sons and daughters who fail to find work continue to live with their parents or relatives or friends. Teenaged mothers have to rely on support from their parents or the father of the child and perhaps work as well. People laid off from work have to use their own savings or borrow from others to make do until the next job is found. All these changes involve great disruption in expectations and accustomed roles.

Along with the disruptions go other changes in behavior. Some parents do not want their young adult children continuing to live off their income, and become quite insistent about their children learning skills and getting jobs. This attitude is most prevalent among single mothers who have to depend most critically on the earning power of their offspring.

Parents tend to become upset at the prospect of a daughter's bringing home a baby that must be entirely supported on an already inadequate income. Some become so upset that they spend considerable parental energy avoiding such an eventuality. Potential fathers of such babies find themselves under more pressure not to cause such a problem, or to help with its solution if it occurs.

Adolescents who were not job-ready find they are job-ready after all. It turns out that they can work for low wages and accept the discipline of the workplace if the alternative is grim enough. After a few years, many—not all, but many—find that they have acquired salable skills, or that they are at the right place at the right time, or otherwise find that the original entry-level job has gradually been transformed into a secure job paying a decent wage. A few—not a lot, but a few—find that the process leads to affluence.

Perhaps the most rightful, deserved benefit goes to the much larger population of low-income families who have been doing things right all along and have been punished for it: the young man who has taken responsibility for his wife and child even though his friends with the same choice have called him a fool; the single mother who has worked full time and forfeited her right to welfare for very little extra money; the parents who have set an example for their children even as the rules of the game have taught their children that the example is outmoded. For these millions of people, the instantaneous result is that no one makes fun of them any longer. The longer-term result will be that they regain the status that is properly theirs. They will not only be the bedrock upon which the community is founded (which they always have been), they will be recognized as such. The process whereby they regain their position is not magical, but a matter of logic.

When it becomes highly dysfunctional for a person to be dependent, status will accrue to being independent, and in fairly short order. Noneconomic rewards will once again reinforce the economic rewards of being a good parent and provider.

The prospective advantages are real and extremely plausible. In fact, if a government program of the traditional sort (one that would "do" something rather than simply get out of the way) could *as plausibly* promise these advantages, its passage would be a foregone conclusion. Congress, yearning for programs that are not retreads of failures, would be prepared to spend billions. Negative side-effects (as long as they were the traditionally acceptable negative side-effects) would be brushed aside as trivial in return for the benefits. For let me be quite clear: I am not suggesting that we dismantle income support for the working-aged to balance the budget or punish welfare cheats. I am hypothesizing, with the advantage of powerful collateral evidence, that the lives of large numbers of poor people would be radically changed for the better.

There is, however, a fourth segment of the population yet to be considered, those who are pauperized by the withdrawal of government supports and unable to make alternate arrangements: the teenaged mother who has no one to turn to; the incapacitated or the inept who are thrown out of the house; those to whom economic conditions have brought long periods in which there is no work to be had; those with illnesses not covered by insurance. What of these situations?

The first resort is the network of local services. Poor communities in our hypothetical society are still dotted with storefront health clinics, emergency relief agencies, employment services, legal services. They depend for support on local taxes or local philanthropy, and the local taxpayers and philanthropists tend to scrutinize them rather closely. But, by the same token, they also receive considerably more resources than they formerly did. The dismantling of the federal services has poured tens of billions of dollars back into the private economy. Some of that money no doubt has been spent on Mercedes and summer homes on the Cape. But some has been spent on capital investments that generate new jobs. And some has been spent on increased local services to the poor, voluntarily or as decreed by the municipality. In many cities, the coverage provided by this network of agencies is more generous, more humane, more wisely distributed, and more effective in its results than the services formerly subsidized by the federal government.

But we must expect that a large number of people will fall between the cracks. How might we go about trying to retain the advantages of a zero-level welfare system and still address the residual needs?

As we think about the nature of the population still in need, it becomes apparent that their basic problem in the vast majority of the cases is the lack of a job, and this problem is temporary. What they need is something to tide them over while finding a new place in the economy. So our first step is to re-install the Unemployment Insurance program in more or less its previous form. Properly administered, unemployment insurance makes sense. Even if it is restored with all the defects of current practice, the negative effects of Unemployment Insurance *alone* are relatively minor. Our objective is not to wipe out chicanery or to construct a theoretically unblemished system, but to meet legitimate human needs without doing more harm than good. Unemployment Insurance is one of the least harmful ways of contributing to such ends. Thus the system has been amended to take care of the victims of short-term swings in the economy.

Who is left? We are now down to the hardest of the hard core of the welfare-dependent. They have no jobs. They have been unable to find jobs (or have not tried to find jobs) for a longer period of time than the unemployment benefits cover. They have no families who will help. They have no friends who will help. For some reason, they cannot get help from local services or private charities except for the soup kitchen and a bed in the Salvation Army hall.

What will be the size of this population? We have never tried a zero-level federal welfare system under conditions of late-twentieth-century national wealth, so we cannot do more than speculate. But we may speculate. Let us ask of whom the population might consist and how they might fare.

For any category of "needy" we may name, we find ourselves driven to one of two lines of thought. Either the person is in a category that is going to be at the top of the list of services that localities vote for themselves, and at the top of the list of private ser-

vices, or the person is in a category where help really is not all that essential or desirable. The burden of the conclusion is not that every single person will be taken care of, but that the extent of resources to deal with needs is likely to be very great—not based on wishful thinking, but on extrapolations from reality.

To illustrate, let us consider the plight of the stereotypical welfare mother—never married, no skills, small children, no steady help from a man. It is safe to say that, now as in the 1950s, there is no one who has less sympathy from the white middle class, which is to be the source of most of the money for the private and local services we envision. Yet this same white middle class is a soft touch for people trying to make it on their own, and a soft touch for "deserving" needy mothers—AFDC was one of the most widely popular of the New Deal welfare measures, intended as it was for widows with small children. Thus we may envision two quite different scenarios.

In one scenario, the woman is presenting the local or private service with this proposition: "Help me find a job and day-care for my children, and I will take care of the rest." In effect, she puts herself into the same category as the widow and the deserted wife—identifies herself as one of the most obviously deserving of the deserving poor. Welfare mothers who want to get into the labor force are likely to find a wide range of help. In the other scenario, she asks for an outright and indefinite cash grant—in effect, a private or local version of AFDC —so that she can stay with the children and not hold a job. In the latter case, it is very easy to imagine situations in which she will not be able to find a local service or a private philanthropy to provide the help she seeks. The question we must now ask is: What's so bad about that? If children were always better off being with their mother all day and if, by the act of giving birth, a mother acquired the inalienable right to be with the child, then her situation would be unjust to her and injurious to her children. Neither assertion can be defended, however—especially not in the 1980s, when more mothers of all classes work away from the home than ever before, and even more especially not in view of the empirical record for the children growing up under the current welfare system. Why should the mother be exempted by the system from the pressures that must affect every-one else's decision to work?

As we survey these prospects, important questions remain unresolved. The first of these is why, if federal social transfers are treacherous, should locally mandated transfers be less so? Why should a municipality be permitted to legislate its own AFDC or Food Stamp program if their results are so inherently bad?

Part of the answer lies in conceptions of freedom. I have deliberately avoided raising them—the discussion is about how to help the disadvantaged, not about how to help the advantaged cut their taxes, to which arguments for personal freedom somehow always get diverted. Nonetheless, the point is valid: Local or even state systems leave much more room than a federal system for everyone, donors and recipients alike, to exercise freedom of choice about the kind of system they live under. Laws are more easily made and changed, and people who find them unacceptable have much more latitude in going somewhere more to their liking.

But the freedom of choice argument, while legitimate, is not necessary. We may put the advantages of local systems in terms of the Law of Imperfect Selection. A federal system must inherently employ very crude, inaccurate rules for deciding who gets what kind of help, and the results are as I outlined them in chapter 16. At the opposite extreme—a neighbor helping a neighbor, a family member helping another family member—the law loses its validity nearly altogether. Very fine-grained judgments based on personal knowledge are being made about specific people and changing situations. In neighborhoods and small cities, the procedures can still bring much individualized information to bear on decisions. Even systems in large cities and states can do much better than a national system; a decaying industrial city in the Northeast and a booming sunbelt city of the same size can and probably should adopt much different rules about who gets what and how much.

A final and equally powerful argument for not impeding local systems is diversity. We know much more in the 1980s than we knew in the 1960s about what does not work. We have a lot to learn about what *does* work. Localities have been a rich source of experiments. Marva Collins in Chicago gives us an example of how a school can bring inner-city students up to national norms. Sister Falaka Fattah in Philadelphia shows us how homeless youths can be rescued from the streets. There are numberless such lessons waiting to be learned from the diversity of local efforts. By all means, let a hundred flowers bloom, and if the federal government can play a useful role in lending a hand and spreading the word of successes, so much the better.

The ultimate unresolved question about our proposal to abolish income maintenance for the working-aged is how many people will fall through the cracks. In whatever detail we try to foresee the consequences, the objection may always be raised: We cannot be *sure* that everyone will be taken care of in the degree to which we would wish. But this observation by no means settles the question. If one may point in objection to the child now fed by Food Stamps who would go hungry, one may also point with satisfaction to the child who would have an entirely different and better future. Hungry children should be fed; there is no argument about that. It is no less urgent that children be allowed to grow up in a system free of the forces that encourage them to remain poor and dependent. If a strategy reasonably promises to remove those forces, after so many attempts to "help the poor" have failed, it is worth thinking about.

But that rationale is too vague. Let me step outside the persona I have employed and put the issue in terms of one last intensely personal hypothetical example. Let us suppose that you, a parent, could know that tomorrow your own child would be made an orphan. You have a choice. You may put your child with an extremely poor family, so poor that your child will be badly clothed and will indeed sometimes be hungry. But you also know that the parents have worked hard all their lives, will make sure your child goes to school and studies, and will teach your child that independence is a primary value. Or you may put your child with a family with parents who have never worked, who will be incapable of overseeing your child's education—but who have plenty of food and good clothes, provided by others. If the choice about where one would put one's own child is as clear to you as it is to me, on what grounds does one justify support of a system that, indirectly but without doubt, makes the other choice for other children? The answer that "What we really want is a world where that choice is not forced upon us" is no answer. We have tried to have it that way. We failed. Everything we know about why we failed tells us that more of the same will not make the dilemma go away.

The Ideal of Opportunity

Billions for equal opportunity, not one cent for equal outcome—such is the slogan to inscribe on the banner of whatever cause my proposals constitute. Their common theme is to make it possible to get as far as one can go on one's merit, hardly a new ideal in American thought.

The ideal itself has never lapsed. What did lapse was the recognition that practical merit exists. Some people are better than others. They deserve more of society's rewards, of which money is only one small part. A principal function of social policy is to make sure they have the opportunity to reap those rewards. Government cannot identify the worthy, but it can protect a society in which the worthy can identify themselves.

I am proposing triage of a sort, triage by self-selection. In triage on the battlefield, the doctor makes the decision—this one gets treatment, that one waits, the other one is made comfortable while waiting to die. In our social triage, the decision is left up to the patient. The patient always has the right to say "I can do X" and get a chance to prove it. Society always has the right to hold him to that pledge. The patient always has the right to fail. Society always has the right to let him.

There is in this stance no lack of compassion but a presumption of respect. People—all people, black or white, rich or poor—may be unequally responsible for what has happened to them in the past, but all are equally responsible for what they do next. Just as in our idealized educational system a student can come back a third, fourth, or fifth time to a course, in our idealized society a person can fail repeatedly and always be qualified for another chance—to try again, to try something easier, to try something different. The options are always open. Opportunity is endless. There is no punishment for failure, only a total absence of rewards. Society—or our idealized society—should be preoccupied with making sure that achievement is rewarded.

There is no shortage of people to be rewarded. Go into any inner-city school and you will find students of extraordinary talent, kept from knowing how good they are by rules we imposed in the name of fairness. Go into any poor community, and you will find people of extraordinary imagination and perseverance, energy and pride, making tortured accommodations to the strange world we created in the name of generosity. The success stories of past generations of poor in this country are waiting to be repeated.

There is no shortage of institutions to provide the rewards. Our schools know how to educate students who want to be educated. Our industries know how to find productive people and reward them. Our police know how to protect people who are ready to cooperate in their own protection. Our system of justice knows how to protect the rights of individuals who know what their rights are. Our philanthropic institutions know how to multiply the effectiveness of people who are already trying to help themselves. In short, American society is very good at reinforcing the investment of an individual in himself. For the affluent and for the middle-class, these mechanisms continue to work about as well as they ever have, and we enjoy their benefits. Not so for the poor. American government, in its recent social policy, has been ineffectual in trying to stage-manage the decision to invest, and it has been unintentionally punitive toward those who would make the decision on their own. It is time to get out of the way. . . .

JAMES BUCHANAN

Socialism Is Dead; Leviathan Lives

James Buchanan is Distinguished Professor of Economics at George Mason University. He was awarded the Nobel Prize in economics in 1986. (Source: Reprinted from The Wall Street Journal, *July 18, 1990, p. A8. Copyright © 1990 by Dow Jones and Company, Inc.)*

QUESTIONS FOR REFLECTION

1. Buchanan argues that socialism is dead. Why, in his view, did it deserve to die?

2. Buchanan sees a new threat to human welfare that he describes as Leviathan. What is this threat? How does it relate to Hobbes's *Leviathan*?

More than a century ago, the German philosopher Friedrich Nietzsche announced the death of God. This dramatic statement was intended to suggest that religion had ceased to serve as an organizing principle for the lives of individuals or for the rules of their association. Since Nietzsche, the God pronounced dead was replaced in man's consciousness by "socialism." And I want to match Nietzsche's announcement with the comparable one that "socialism is dead"—a statement that seems much less shocking than Nietzsche's because it is being heard throughout the world in 1990.

In a very real sense, the loss of faith in socialism is more dramatic than the loss of faith in God, because the god that was socialism took on forms that were directly observable. There were no continuing unknowns waiting to be revealed only in another life, and the promised realization of the socialist ideal could not be infinitely postponed. Socialism promised quite specific results; it did not deliver.

One can only look back in amazement at the monumental folly that caused the intellectual leaders of the world, for more than a century, to buy into what F.A. Hayek called the "fatal conceit" that socialism embodied. How did we come to be trapped in the romantic myth that politically organized authority could satisfy our needs more adequately than we might satisfy them ourselves through voluntary agreement, association and exchange?

Socialists Everywhere

This fatal conceit was almost universal. Let us now beware of current attempts to limit acceptance of the socialist myth to those who were the explicit promulgators and defenders of the centrally planned authoritarian regimes of the Soviet Union and its satellites. There were socialists everywhere, in all societies and, even in the face of the evidence that continues to accumulate, there are many who still cannot escape from the socialist mind-set. And even for those of us who have, however begrudgingly, acknowledged that the socialist god is dead, there may not have emerged any faith or belief in any non-socialist alternative. We may accept socialism's failure; we may not accept the alternative represented by the free market or enterprise system, even as tempered by elements of the welfare state.

Socialists everywhere, confronted with the evidence that economies organized, wholly or partially, on socialist principles cannot deliver the goods, are now making desperate efforts to redefine the term "socialism," which British socialist and scholar Alex Nove defined in 1987 as a society in which "the means of production of goods and services are not in private hands."

It is now almost universally acknowledged that a private-ownership, free-enterprise economy "works better" than Mr. Nove's socialized economy, in which decisions are made by state or cooperative agencies. The individualized market economy "works better" than the socialized economy in the sense that it produces more goods. But it also works better in the sense that it allows individuals more liberty to choose where, when and to what purpose they will put their capacities to produce values that they expect others to demand.

A threshold was crossed in the 18th century when we learned how the rule of law, stability of private property and the withdrawal of political interference with private choices could unleash the entrepreneurial energies that are latent within each of us. Humankind seemed near to the ultimate realization of its social potential. How did the socialist vision emerge to threaten, and in part forestall, this future? And why did the principles of classical political economy, which seemed so strongly to suggest the relative superiority of a market economy, lose their persuasive powers so quickly?

We must, I think, appreciate the rhetorical genius of Marx and his ability to convert arguments advanced in support of market organization into what could be made to appear to be support for a particular distributional class, the capitalists. By clever substitution of emotion-laden terminology, the market system became "capitalism," and the search of every person for his own advantage became the profit-seeking of the greedy capitalists. This rhetorical genius, coupled with totally erroneous economic analysis embedded into pseudo-scientific jargon about the laws of history, was highly successful in elevating the distributional issue to center stage, to the relative neglect of the allocational and growth elements that were central in the classical teachings.

(I speak as one who shared fully in the socialist mind-set, from which, thanks to Frank Knight, I escaped relatively early in my career. But I appreciate the appeal of the Marxist-socialist ideas even if, now, I cannot explain it.)

Recall that during its early decades, the Soviet Union was held out as paradise by socialists in the West. After World War II, Eastern Europe was absorbed into the Soviet political orbit and the countries of Western Europe socialized their economies to greater or lesser degrees. Even where economies were largely allowed to remain free, Keynesian-inspired macromanagement was supported by arguments about the tendency of capitalism to generate massive unemployment.

Between the early 1960s and today, socialism became ill and died. What happened? There were two sides to the coin: "market success" and "political failure." The accumulation of empirical evidence must ultimately dispel romance. And the evidence did indeed accumulate to demonstrate that free-market economies performed much better than politically directed or planned economies. Contrast, for example the West German *Wirtschaftwunder* with the demonstrable failures of the socialist experiments in Britain in the late 1940s and early 1950s. Honest evaluation suggested that the centralized economies of the Soviet Union, China and East European countries were not successful in producing goods and services.

Ideas also matter. And here the record of the academic economists remains, at best, a very mixed bag. The welfare economists of the early and middle decades of this century were almost exclusively concerned with demonstrating the failures of markets, in order to provide a rationale for political interferences. But the public-choice revolution in ideas about politics, and political failures, was also sparked primarily by academic economists.

When the behavioral model of economics are applied to "public choosers"—to those who participate variously in political roles, as voters, politicians, bureaucrats, planners, party leaders, etc.—the romantic vision that was essential to the whole socialist myth vanishes. If those who make decisions for others are finally seen as just like everyone else, how can the awesome delegation of authority that must characterize the centralized economy be justified?

This loss of faith in politics, in socialism broadly defined, has not, however, been accompanied by any demonstrable renewal or reconversion to a faith in markets, the *laissez-faire* vision that was central to the teachings of the classical political economists. There remains a residual unwillingness to leave things alone, to allow the free market, governed by the rule of law, to organize itself. We are left, therefore, with what is essentially an attitude of nihilism toward economic organization. There seems to be no widely shared organizing principle upon which persons can begin to think about the operations of a political economy.

It is in this setting, which does seem to be descriptive of the era into which we are so rapidly moving, that the natural forces that generate the Leviathan state emerge and assume dominance. With no overriding principle that dictates how an economy is to be organized, the political structure is open to exploitation by the pressures of well-organized interests. The special-interest, rent-seeking, churning state finds fertile ground for growth in this environment. And, depending on the relative strength of organized interests, we observe quite arbitrary, politicized interferences with markets.

This setting, which I have referred to as Leviathan, has much in common with the mercantilist-protectionist politics that Adam Smith attacked so vehemently in "The Wealth of Nations" in 1776. The same barriers that Adam Smith sought to abolish are everywhere resurging; and the same arguments are heard, both in support and in opposition. The arguments for Leviathan's extensions are not versions of the socialist's dream; they are, instead, simple efforts to claim a public interest in a single sector's private profit.

Constitutional Constraints

There will be no escape from the protectionist-mercantilist regime that now threatens to be characteristic of the post-socialist politics in both Western and Eastern countries so long as we allow the ordinary or natural outcomes of majoritarian democratic processes to operate without adequate constitutional constraints. If we know that politics fails and that its natural proclivity is to extend its reach beyond tolerable bounds, we must incorporate constraints into a constitutional structure. A depoliticized economic order is within the realm of the possible, even if the accompanying faith in market organizations is not fully regained. We can protect ourselves against the appetites of the monster that the Leviathan state threatens to become.

The organized polities of the nation-states, and the associations among those states, must be kept within constitutional boundaries. The death throes of socialism should not be allowed to distract attention from the continuing necessity to prevent the overreaching of the state-as-Leviathan, which becomes all the more dangerous because it does not depend on an ideology to give it focus. Ideas, and the institutions that emerge as these ideas are put into practice, can be killed off and replaced by other ideas and other institutions. The machinations of interest-driven politics are much more difficult to dislodge. Let us get on with the task.

Affirmative Action

The United States, like many other countries, has a history of racial and sexual discrimination. Unlike many other countries, it also has a history of slavery. Discrimination and slavery have long been recognized as evils. Discrimination, for example, might be defined as making a judgment or decision on the basis of irrelevant factors. Race and sex are almost always irrelevant to decisions about whom to hire, whom to fire, whom to admit to a college or university, and other similar decisions. Kant's categorical imperative requires that we judge similar cases similarly—that we judge a case as if our judgment were universal law. To discriminate is to judge similar cases differently, depending on some irrelevant factor such as race or sex. Discrimination thus directly violates Kant's imperative.

The obligation to eliminate discrimination, therefore, is not controversial. What its elimination requires is. Racial or sexual discrimination, as a violation of Kant's principle, is by its very nature unfair. So, we might think that justice requires making decisions about hiring, firing, admissions, and other matters of economic and political significance in a "color-blind" way, without regard for race, sex, or other irrelevant factors. From another perspective, however, this apparent even-handedness is only apparent, for some of the players in the economic and political game have been harmed by prior discrimination. Setting things right requires, from this point of view, giving those players an advantage to balance the disadvantages they suffer as a result of past injustices. On this conception, then, race, sex, and perhaps other characteristics are no longer irrelevant. The history of discrimination has turned them into relevant factors.

From this perspective have sprung "affirmative-action" programs: programs that give preferences to some people because of their race, sex, ethnic background, or other characteristic. Generally, these programs try to "level the playing field" by granting preference to those who suffer from prior discrimination or are otherwise disadvantaged. Sometimes, the preference is general, of the form "all other things being equal, we prefer people with the following characteristics"; in other cases, there are explicit quotas for people of different groups. Affirmative-action programs have been a source of controversy. In the United States, they have provoked arguments and lawsuits. In other countries, they have provoked riots and bloodshed.

The University of California operated a quota system at its medical school at Davis. It reserved sixteen of the one hundred places in each class at the medical school for members of minority groups. Alan Bakke, a white male, applied and was rejected. He learned, however, that his grades and test scores were higher than those of many students admitted under the minority quota. Bakke sued, claiming that he had been discriminated against on account of his race. In 1978, the Supreme Court decided in Bakke's favor. The Court stopped short of declaring that taking race and similar qualities into account is unacceptable. The Court did, however, decide that quota systems like that operating at the University of California were unconstitutional, amounting themselves to a form of discrimination. Dissenters on the Court decried the decision, maintaining that there is a great moral difference between using a racial classification against a disadvantaged group and using it to benefit that group. In short, the dissenters insisted that race, sex, and other factors are not irrelevant in themselves, though there is a strong presumption of their irrelevance. Prior discrimination and economic disadvantage may, they claimed, make these factors relevant and even require that they be taken into account in decision-making.

Following Bakke was a series of decisions on affirmative action in various contexts: education, industry, unions, state government, and others. These decisions are extremely complex. They agree, however, that affirmative-action programs, to be constitutional, must pass strict scrutiny; that is, they must be necessary to achieve a compelling state interest. Racial equality is a compelling state interest, so the crucial question has been, Is this program necessary to achieve it? In the Court's jargon, Is it *narrowly tailored?* The Court has upheld several voluntary race-conscious affirmative-action plans, and even some court-imposed quota systems in cases where there appeared to be ongoing discrimination.

In 1989, the Court decided, in *City of Richmond v. Croson,* that set-asides—quotas, in effect, for minority contractors—are unconstitutional. The majority held that quotas, while not unacceptable in all cases, are very hard to justify. In particular, there must be some specific prior or continuing discrimination that the program will counteract. Moreover, the program must be the least intrusive way to counteract it. The Court found Richmond's provision that 30 percent of all construction contracts should go to minority firms unacceptable by both criteria. There was no specific discrimination being counteracted, and there was no evidence that a set-aside was the least intrusive way of counteracting discrimination. Once again, a minority on the Court argued that racial quotas do not constitute discrimination if they work to benefit the disadvantaged.

Myrl Duncan, a law professor, argues that affirmative action is justifiable. She reviews the chief arguments for such programs and considers criticisms of them. In each case, she argues that the criticisms are unjustified. She goes on to review arguments against affirmative action, contending that none succeeds. Finally, Thomas Sowell, an economist, argues that affirmative action brings about far more harm than good. He traces the history of affirmative action in many societies around the world, contending that it uniformly increases racial tensions. Advocates argue that affirmative-action plans are temporary repairs of harm brought about by prior discrimination. Sowell argues that there is no way to determine how much of the economic position of an individual or a group is due to prior discrimination. Consequently, there is no way to tell when the effects of prior discrimination have been eliminated. Once instituted, therefore, preferences never go away; indeed, they expand to more groups, few of whose claims can be founded on prior discrimination.

Regents of the University of California v. Bakke (1978)

(*Source:* Regents of the University of California v. Bakke *438 U.S. 265 [1978]. Most legal references have been omitted.*)

QUESTIONS FOR REFLECTION

1. Justice Powell argues that the University of California's racial classification should not simply be viewed as "benign." Why?

2. How did the University of California try to justify its affirmative-action program? Why does Justice Powell reject those arguments?

3. What sort of affirmative-action program does Justice Powell find acceptable? How does it differ from the University of California program?

4. Justices Brennan, White, Marshall, and Blackmun contend that human equality requires taking race into account. What arguments do they advance? On what issues do they most clearly disagree with Justice Powell?

5. What arguments does Justice Marshall's dissent add to those he advanced jointly with Brennan, White, and Blackmun?

...Mr. Justice Powell announced the judgment of the Court. . . .

I

The Medical School of the University of California at Davis opened in 1968 with an entering class of 50 students. In 1971, the size of the entering class was increased to 100 students, a level at which it remains. No admissions program for disadvantaged or minority students existed when the school opened, and the first class contained three Asians but no blacks, no Mexican-Americans, and no American Indians. Over the next two years, the faculty devised a special admissions program to increase the representation of "disadvantaged" students in each Medical School class. The special program consisted of a separate admissions system operating in coordination with the regular admissions process. . . .

The special admissions program operated with a separate committee, a majority of whom were members of minority groups. On the 1973 application form, candidates were asked to indicate whether they wished to be considered as "economically and/or educationally disadvantaged" applicants; on the 1974 form the question was whether they wished to be considered as members of a "minority group," which the Medical School apparently viewed as "Blacks," "Chicanos," "Asians," and "American Indians." If these questions were answered affirmatively, the application was forwarded to the special admissions committee. No formal definition of "disadvantaged" was ever produced, but the chairman of the special committee screened each application to see whether it reflected economic or educational deprivation. Having passed this initial hurdle, the applications then were rated by the special committee in a fashion similar to that used by the general admissions committee, except that special candidates did not have to meet the 2.5 grade point average cutoff applied to regular applicants. About one-fifth of the total number of special applicants were invited for interviews in 1973 and 1974. Following each interview, the special committee assigned each special applicant a benchmark score. The special committee then presented its top choices to the general admissions committee. The latter did not rate or compare the special candidates against the general applicants, but could reject recommended special candidates for failure to meet course requirements or other specific deficiencies. The special committee continued to recommend special applicants until a number prescribed by faculty vote were admitted. While the overall class size was still 50, the prescribed number was 8; in 1973 and 1974, when the class size had doubled to 100, the prescribed number of special admissions also doubled, to 16.

From the year of the increase in class size—1971 —through 1974, the special program resulted in the admission of 21 black students, 30 Mexican-Americans, and 12 Asians, for a total of 63 minority students. Over the same period, the regular admissions program produced 1 black, 6 Mexican-Americans, and 37 Asians, for a total of 44 minority students. Although disadvantaged whites applied to the special program in large numbers, none received an offer of admission through that process. Indeed, in 1974, at least, the special committee explicitly considered only "disadvantaged" special applicants who were members of one of the designated minority groups.

Allan Bakke is a white male who applied to the Davis Medical School in both 1973 and 1974. In both years Bakke's application was considered under the general admissions program, and he received an interview. His 1973 interview was with Dr. Theodore C. West, who considered Bakke "a very desirable applicant to [the] medical school." Despite a strong benchmark score of 468 out of 500, Bakke was rejected. His application had come late in the year, and no applicants in the general admissions process with scores below 470 were accepted after Bakke's application was completed. There were four special admissions slots unfilled at that time however, for which Bakke was not considered. After his 1973 rejection, Bakke wrote to Dr. George H. Lowrey, Associate Dean and Chairman of the Admissions Committee, protesting that the special admissions program operated as a racial and ethnic quota.

Bakke's 1974 application was completed early in the year. His student interviewer gave him an overall rating of 94, finding him "friendly, well tempered,

conscientious and delightful to speak with." His faculty interviewer was, by coincidence, the same Dr. Lowrey to whom he had written in protest of the special admissions program. Dr. Lowrey found Bakke "rather limited in his approach" to the problems of the medical profession and found disturbing Bakke's "very definite opinions which were based more on his personal viewpoints than upon a study of the total problem." Dr. Lowrey gave Bakke the lowest of his six ratings, an 86; his total was 549 out of 600. Again, Bakke's application was rejected. In neither year did the chairman of the admissions committee, Dr. Lowrey, exercise his discretion to place Bakke on the waiting list. In both years, applicants were admitted under the special program with grade point averages, MCAT scores, and benchmark scores significantly lower than Bakke's. The table on page 485 compares Bakke's science grade point average, overall grade point average, and MCAT scores with the average scores of regular admittees and of special admittees in both 1973 and 1974.

After the second rejection, Bakke filed the instant suit in the Superior Court of California. He sought mandatory, injunctive, and declaratory relief compelling his admission to the Medical School. He alleged that the Medical School's special admissions program operated to exclude him from the school on the basis of his race, in violation of his rights under the Equal Protection Clause of the Fourteenth Amendment, Art. I, § 21, of the California Constitution, and § 601 of Title VI of the Civil Rights Act of 1964. The University cross-complained for a declaration that its special admissions program was lawful. . . .

[II . . .]

III

A

. . . The guarantees of the Fourteenth Amendment extend to all persons. Its language is explicit: "No State shall . . . deny to any person within its jurisdiction the equal protection of the laws." It is settled

CLASS ENTERING IN 1973

| | SGPA | OGPA | MCAT (Percentiles) | | | |
			Verbal	Quanti-tative	Science	Gen. Infor.
Bakke	3.44	3.46	96	94	97	72
Average of regular admittees	3.51	3.49	81	76	83	69
Average of special admittees	2.62	2.88	46	24	35	33

CLASS ENTERING IN 1974

| | SGPA | OGPA | MCAT (Percentiles) | | | |
			Verbal	Quanti-tative	Science	Gen. Infor.
Bakke	3.44	3.46	96	94	97	72
Average of regular admittees	3.36	3.29	69	67	82	72
Average of special admittees	2.42	2.62	34	30	37	18

Applicants admitted under the special program also had benchmark scores significantly lower than many students, including Bakke, rejected under the general admissions program, even though the special rating system apparently gave credit for overcoming "disadvantage."

beyond question that the "rights created by the first section of the Fourteenth Amendment are, by its terms, guaranteed to the individual. The rights established are personal rights." The guarantee of equal protection cannot mean one thing when applied to one individual and something else when applied to a person of another color. If both are not accorded the same protection, then it is not equal.

Nevertheless, petitioner argues that the court below erred in applying strict scrutiny to the special admissions program because white males, such as respondent, are not a "discrete and insular minority" requiring extraordinary protection from the majoritarian political process. This rationale, however, has never been invoked in our decisions as a prerequisite to subjecting racial or ethnic distinctions to strict scrutiny. Nor has this Court held that

discreteness and insularity constitute necessary preconditions to a holding that a particular classification is invidious. These characteristics may be relevant in deciding whether or not to add new types of classifications to the list of "suspect" categories or whether a particular classification survives close examination. Racial and ethnic classifications, however, are subject to stringent examination without regard to these additional characteristics. We declared as much in the first cases explicitly to recognize racial distinctions as suspect:

"Distinctions between citizens solely because of their ancestry are by their very nature odious to a free people whose institutions are founded upon the doctrine of equality."

"[A]ll legal restrictions which curtail the civil rights

of a single racial group are immediately suspect. That is not to say that all such restrictions are unconstitutional. It is to say that courts must subject them to the most rigid scrutiny."

The Court has never questioned the validity of those pronouncements. Racial and ethnic distinctions of any sort are inherently suspect and thus call for the most exacting judicial examination.

B

This perception of racial and ethnic distinctions is rooted in our Nation's constitutional and demographic history. The Court's initial view of the Fourteenth Amendment was that its "one pervading purpose" was "the freedom of the slave race, the security and firm establishment of that freedom, and the protection of the newly-made freeman and citizen from the oppressions of those who had formerly exercised dominion over him." *Slaughter-House Cases* (1873). The Equal Protection Clause, however, was "[v]irtually strangled in infancy by post-civil-war judicial reactionism." It was relegated to decades of relative desuetude while the Due Process Clause of the Fourteenth Amendment, after a short germinal period, flourished as a cornerstone in the Court's defense of property and liberty of contract. In that cause, the Fourteenth Amendment's "one pervading purpose" was displaced. It was only as the era of substantive due process came to a close that the Equal Protection Clause began to attain a genuine measure of vitality.

By that time it was no longer possible to peg the guarantees of the Fourteenth Amendment to the struggle for equality of one racial minority. During the dormancy of the Equal Protection Clause, the United States had become a Nation of minorities. Each had to struggle—and to some extent struggles still—to overcome the prejudices not of a monolithic majority, but of a "majority" composed of various minority groups of whom it was said—perhaps unfairly in many cases—that a shared characteristic was a willingness to disadvantage other groups. As the Nation filled with the stock of many lands, the reach of the Clause was gradually extended to all ethnic groups seeking protection from official discrimination. The guarantees of equal protection,

said the Court in *Yick Wo,* "are universal in their application, to all persons within the territorial jurisdiction, without regard to any differences of race, of color, or of nationality; and the equal protection of the laws is a pledge of the protection of equal laws."

Although many of the Framers of the Fourteenth Amendment conceived of its primary function as bridging the vast distance between members of the Negro race and the white "majority," the Amendment itself was framed in universal terms, without reference to color, ethnic origin, or condition of prior servitude. As this Court recently remarked in interpreting the 1866 Civil Rights Act to extend to claims of racial discrimination against white persons, "the 39th Congress was intent upon establishing in the federal law a broader principle than would have been necessary simply to meet the particular and immediate plight of the newly freed Negro slaves." And that legislation was specifically broadened in 1870 to ensure that "all persons," not merely "citizens," would enjoy equal rights under the law. Indeed, it is not unlikely that among the Framers were many who would have applauded a reading of the Equal Protection Clause that states a principle of universal application and is responsive to the racial, ethnic, and cultural diversity of the Nation.

Over the past 30 years, this Court has embarked upon the crucial mission of interpreting the Equal Protection Clause with the view of assuring to all persons "the protection of equal laws," in a Nation confronting a legacy of slavery and racial discrimination. Because the landmark decisions in this area arose in response to the continued exclusion of Negroes from the mainstream of American society, they could be characterized as involving discrimination by the "majority" white race against the Negro minority. But they need not be read as depending upon that characterization for their results. It suffices to say that "[o]ver the years, this Court has consistently repudiated '[d]istinctions between citizens solely because of their ancestry' as being 'odious to a free people whose institutions are founded upon the doctrine of equality.'"

Petitioner urges us to adopt for the first time a more restrictive view of the Equal Protection Clause and hold that discrimination against members of the white "majority" cannot be suspect if its purpose can be characterized as "benign."* The clock of our liberties, however, cannot be turned back to 1868. It is far too late to argue that the guarantee of equal protection to *all* persons permits the recognition of special wards entitled to a degree of protection greater than that accorded others.† "The Fourteenth Amendment is not directed solely against discrimination due to a 'two-class theory'—that is, based upon differences between 'white' and Negro."

Once the artificial line of a "two-class theory" of the Fourteenth Amendment is put aside, the difficulties entailed in varying the level of judicial review according to a perceived "preferred" status of a particular racial or ethnic minority are intractable. The

* In the view of Mr. Justice Brennan, Mr. Justice White, Mr. Justice Marshall, and Mr. Justice Blackmun, the pliable notion of "stigma" is the crucial element in analyzing racial classifications. The Equal Protection Clause is not framed in terms of "stigma." Certainly the word has no clearly defined constitutional meaning. It reflects a subjective judgment that is standardless. *All* state-imposed classifications that rearrange burdens and benefits on the basis of race are likely to be viewed with deep resentment by the individuals burdened. The denial to innocent persons of equal rights and opportunities may outrage those so deprived and therefore may be perceived as invidious. These individuals are likely to find little comfort in the notion that the deprivation they are asked to endure is merely the price of membership in the dominant majority and that its imposition is inspired by the supposedly benign purpose of aiding others. One should not lightly dismiss the inherent unfairness of, and the perception of mistreatment that accompanies, a system of allocating benefits and privileges on the basis of skin color and ethnic origin. Moreover, Mr. Justice Brennan, Mr. Justice White, Mr. Justice Marshall, and Mr. Justice Blackmun offer no principle for deciding whether preferential classifications reflect a benign remedial purpose or a malevolent stigmatic classification, since they are willing in this case to accept mere *post hoc* declarations by an isolated state entity—a medical school faculty—unadorned by particularized findings of past discrimination, to establish such a remedial purpose.

† Professor Bickel noted the self-contradiction of that view:
    "The lesson of the great decisions of the Supreme Court and the lesson of contemporary history have been the same for at least a generation: discrimination on the basis of race is illegal, immoral, unconstitutional, inherently wrong, and destructive of democratic society. Now this is to be unlearned and we are told that this is not a matter of fundamental principle but only a matter of whose ox is gored. Those for whom racial equality was demanded are to be more equal than others. Having found support in the Constitution for equality, they now claim support for inequality under the same Constitution." A. Bickel, The Morality of Consent 133 (1975).

concepts of "majority" and "minority" necessarily reflect temporary arrangements and political judgments. As observed above, the white "majority" itself is composed of various minority groups, most of which can lay claim to a history of prior discrimination at the hands of the State and private individuals. Not all of these groups can receive preferential treatment and corresponding judicial tolerance of distinctions drawn in terms of race and nationality, for then the only "majority" left would be a new minority of white Anglo-Saxon Protestants. There is no principled basis for deciding which groups would merit "heightened judicial solicitude" and which would not. Courts would be asked to evaluate the extent of the prejudice and consequent harm suffered by various minority groups. Those whose societal injury is thought to exceed some arbitrary level of tolerability then would be entitled to preferential classifications at the expense of individuals belonging to other groups. Those classifications would be free from exacting judicial scrutiny. As these preferences began to have their desired effect, and the consequences of past discrimination were undone, new judicial rankings would be necessary. The kind of variable sociological and political analysis necessary to produce such rankings simply does not lie within the judicial competence—even if they otherwise were politically feasible and socially desirable.

Moreover, there are serious problems of justice connected with the idea of preference itself. First, it may not always be clear that a so-called preference is in fact benign. Courts may be asked to validate burdens imposed upon individual members of a particular group in order to advance the group's general interest. Nothing in the Constitution supports the notion that individuals may be asked to suffer otherwise impermissible burdens in order to enhance the societal standing of their ethnic groups. Second, preferential programs may only reinforce common stereotypes holding that certain groups are unable to achieve success without special protection based on a factor having no relationship to individual worth. Third, there is a measure of inequity in forcing innocent persons in respondent's position to bear the burdens of redressing grievances not of their making.

By hitching the meaning of the Equal Protection Clause to these transitory considerations, we would be holding, as a constitutional principle, that judicial scrutiny of classifications touching on racial and ethnic background may vary with the ebb and flow of political forces. Disparate constitutional tolerance of such classifications well may serve to exacerbate racial and ethnic antagonisms rather than alleviate them. Also, the mutability of a constitutional principle, based upon shifting political and social judgments, undermines the chances for consistent application of the Constitution from one generation to the next, a critical feature of its coherent interpretation. In expounding the Constitution, the Court's role is to discern "principles sufficiently absolute to give them roots throughout the community and continuity over significant periods of time, and to lift them above the level of the pragmatic political judgments of a particular time and place."

If it is the individual who is entitled to judicial protection against classifications based upon his racial or ethnic background because such distinctions impinge upon personal rights, rather than the individual only because of his membership in a particular group, then constitutional standards may be applied consistently. Political judgments regarding the necessity for the particular classification may be weighed in the constitutional balance, but the standard of justification will remain constant. This is as it should be, since those political judgments are the product of rough compromise struck by contending groups within the democratic process. When they touch upon an individual's race or ethnic background, he is entitled to a judicial determination that the burden he is asked to bear on that basis is precisely tailored to serve a compelling governmental interest. The Constitution guarantees that right to every person regardless of his background. . . .

IV

We have held that in "order to justify the use of a suspect classification, a State must show that its purpose or interest is both constitutionally permissible and substantial, and that its use of the classification is 'necessary . . . to the accomplishment' of its purpose or the safeguarding of its interest." The special admissions program purports to serve the purposes of: (i) "reducing the historic deficit of traditionally

disfavored minorities in medical schools and in the medical profession," (ii) countering the effects of societal discrimination; (iii) increasing the number of physicians who will practice in communities currently underserved; and (iv) obtaining the educational benefits that flow from an ethnically diverse student body. It is necessary to decide which, if any, of these purposes is substantial enough to support the use of a suspect classification.

A

If petitioner's purpose is to assure within its student body some specified percentage of a particular group merely because of its race or ethnic origin, such a preferential purpose must be rejected not as insubstantial but as facially invalid. Preferring members of any one group for no reason other than race or ethnic origin is discrimination for its own sake. This the Constitution forbids.

B

The State certainly has a legitimate and substantial interest in ameliorating, or eliminating where feasible, the disabling effects of identified discrimination. The line of school desegregation cases, commencing with *Brown*, attests to the importance of this state goal and the commitment of the judiciary to affirm all lawful means toward its attainment. In the school cases, the States were required by court order to redress the wrongs worked by specific instances of racial discrimination. That goal was far more focused than the remedying of the effects of "societal discrimination," an amorphous concept of injury that may be ageless in its reach into the past.

We have never approved a classification that aids persons perceived as members of relatively victimized groups at the expense of other innocent individuals in the absence of judicial, legislative, or administrative findings of constitutional or statutory violations. After such findings have been made, the governmental interest, in preferring members of the injured groups at the expense of others is substantial, since the legal rights of the victims must be vindicated. In such a case, the extent of the injury and the consequent remedy will have been judicially, legislatively, or administratively defined. Also, the remedial action usually remains subject to continuing oversight to assure that it will work the least harm possible to other innocent persons competing for the benefit. Without such findings of constitutional or statutory violations, it cannot be said that the government has any greater interest in helping one individual than in refraining from harming another. Thus, the government has no compelling justification for inflicting such harm. . . .

Hence, the purpose of helping certain groups whom the faculty of the Davis Medical School perceived as victims of "societal discrimination" does not justify a classification that imposes disadvantages upon persons like respondent, who bear no responsibility for whatever harm the beneficiaries of the special admissions program are thought to have suffered. To hold otherwise would be to convert a remedy heretofore reserved for violations of legal rights into a privilege that all institutions throughout the Nation could grant at their pleasure to whatever groups are perceived as victims of societal discrimination. That is a step we have never approved.

C

Petitioner identifies, as another purpose of its program, improving the delivery of health-care services to communities currently underserved. It may be assumed that in some situations a State's interest in facilitating the health care of its citizens is sufficiently compelling to support the use of a suspect classification. But there is virtually no evidence in the record indicating that petitioner's special admissions program is either needed or geared to promote that goal. The court below addressed this failure of proof:

> "The University concedes it cannot assure that minority doctors who entered under the program, all of whom expressed an 'interest' in practicing in a disadvantaged community, will actually do so. It may be correct to assume that some of them will carry out this intention, and that it is more likely they will practice in minority communities than the average white doctor. Nevertheless, there are more precise and reliable ways to identify applicants who are genuinely interested in the medical problems of minorities than by

race. An applicant of whatever race who has demonstrated his concern for disadvantaged minorities in the past and who declares that practice in such a community is his primary professional goal would be more likely to contribute to alleviation of the medical shortage than one who is chosen entirely on the basis of race and disadvantage. In short, there is no empirical data to demonstrate that any one race is more selflessly socially oriented or by contrast that another is more selfishly acquisitive."

Petitioner simply has not carried its burden of demonstrating that it must prefer members of particular ethnic groups over all other individuals in order to promote better health-care delivery to deprived citizens. Indeed, petitioner has not shown that its preferential classification is likely to have any significant effect on the problem.

D

The fourth goal asserted by petitioner is the attainment of a diverse student body. This clearly is a constitutionally permissible goal for an institution of higher education. Academic freedom, though not a specifically enumerated constitutional right, long has been viewed as a special concern of the First Amendment. The freedom of a university to make its own judgments as to education includes the selection of its student body. Mr. Justice Frankfurter summarized the "four essential freedoms" that constitute academic freedom:

> "'It is the business of a university to provide that atmosphere which is most conducive to speculation, experiment and creation. It is an atmosphere in which there prevail "the four essential freedoms" of a university—to determine for itself on academic grounds who may teach, what may be taught, how it shall be taught, and who may be admitted to study.'"

Our national commitment to the safeguarding of these freedoms within university communities was emphasized in *Keyishian v. Board of Regents* (1967):

> "Our Nation is deeply committed to safeguarding academic freedom which is of transcendent value to all of us and not merely to the teachers concerned. That freedom is therefore a special concern of the First

Amendment. . . . The Nation's future depends upon leaders trained through wide exposure to that robust exchange of ideas which discovers truth 'out of a multitude of tongues, [rather] than through any kind of authoritative selection.'"

The atmosphere of "speculation, experiment and creation"—so essential to the quality of higher education—is widely believed to be promoted by a diverse student body. As the Court noted in *Keyishian,* it is not too much to say that the "nation's future depends upon leaders trained through wide exposure" to the ideas and mores of students as diverse as this Nation of many peoples.

Thus, in arguing that its universities must be accorded the right to select those students who will contribute the most to the "robust exchange of ideas," petitioner invokes a countervailing constitutional interest, that of the First Amendment. In this light, petitioner must be viewed as seeking to achieve a goal that is of paramount importance in the fulfillment of its mission.

It may be argued that there is greater force to these views at the undergraduate level than in a medical school where the training is centered primarily on professional competency. But even at the graduate level, our tradition and experience lend support to the view that the contribution of diversity is substantial. In *Sweatt v. Painter,* the Court made a similar point with specific reference to legal education:

> "The law school, the proving ground for legal learning and practice, cannot be effective in isolation from the individuals and institutions with which the law interacts. Few students and no one who has practiced law would choose to study in an academic vacuum, removed from the interplay of ideas and the exchange of views with which the law is concerned."

Physicians serve a heterogeneous population. An otherwise qualified medical student with a particular background—whether it be ethnic, geographic, culturally advantaged or disadvantaged—may bring to a professional school of medicine experiences, outlooks, and ideas that enrich the training of its student body and better equip its graduates to render with understanding their vital service to humanity.

Ethnic diversity, however, is only one element in a range of factors a university properly may consider in attaining the goal of a heterogeneous student body. Although a university must have wide discretion in making the sensitive judgments as to who should be admitted, constitutional limitations protecting individual rights may not be disregarded. Respondent urges—and the courts below have held —that petitioner's dual admissions program is a racial classification that impermissibly infringes his rights under the Fourteenth Amendment. As the interest of diversity is compelling in the context of a university's admissions program, the question remains whether the program's racial classification is necessary to promote this interest.

V

A

It may be assumed that the reservation of a specified number of seats in each class for individuals from the preferred ethnic groups would contribute to the attainment of considerable ethnic diversity in the student body. But petitioner's argument that this is the only effective means of serving the interest of diversity is seriously flawed. In a most fundamental sense the argument misconceives the nature of the state interest that would justify consideration of race or ethnic background. It is not an interest in simple ethnic diversity, in which a specified percentage of the student body is in effect guaranteed to be members of selected ethnic groups, with the remaining percentage an undifferentiated aggregation of students. The diversity that furthers a compelling state interest encompasses a far broader array of qualifications and characteristics of which racial or ethnic origin is but a single though important element. Petitioner's special admissions program, focused *solely* on ethnic diversity, would hinder rather than further attainment of genuine diversity.

Nor would the state interest in genuine diversity be served by expanding petitioner's two-track system into a multitrack program with a prescribed number of seats set aside for each identifiable category of applicants. Indeed, it is inconceivable that a university would thus pursue the logic of petitioner's two-track program to the illogical end of insulating each category of applicants with certain desired qualifications from competition with all other applicants. . . .

B

In summary, it is evident that the Davis special admissions program involves the use of an explicit racial classification never before countenanced by this Court. It tells applicants who are not Negro, Asian, or Chicano that they are totally excluded from a specific percentage of the seats in an entering class. No matter how strong their qualifications, quantitative and extracurricular, including their own potential for contribution to educational diversity, they are never afforded the chance to compete with applicants from the preferred groups for the special admissions seats. At the same time, the preferred applicants have the opportunity to compete for every seat in the class.

The fatal flaw in petitioner's preferential program is its disregard of individual rights as guaranteed by the Fourteenth Amendment. Such rights are not absolute. But when a State's distribution of benefits or imposition of burdens hinges on ancestry or the color of a person's skin, that individual is entitled to a demonstration that the challenged classification is necessary to promote a substantial state interest. Petitioner has failed to carry this burden. For this reason, that portion of the California court's judgment holding petitioner's special admissions program invalid under the Fourteenth Amendment must be affirmed. . . .

Opinion of Mr. Justice Brennan, Mr. Justice White, Mr. Justice Marshall, and Mr. Justice Blackmun, concurring in the judgment in part and dissenting in part. . . .

I

Our Nation was founded on the principle that "all Men are created equal." Yet candor requires acknowledgment that the Framers of our Constitution, to forge the 13 Colonies into one Nation, openly compromised this principle of equality with its antithesis: slavery. The consequences of this compromise are well known and have aptly been called our "American Dilemma." Still, it is well to recount how recent the time has been, if it has yet come, when the promise of our principles has flowered into the actuality of equal opportunity for all regardless of race or color.

The Fourteenth Amendment, the embodiment in the Constitution of our abiding belief in human equality, has been the law of our land for only slightly more than half its 200 years. And for half of that half, the Equal Protection Clause of the Amendment was largely moribund so that, as late as 1927, Mr. Justice Holmes could sum up the importance of that Clause by remarking that it was the "last resort of constitutional arguments." Worse than desuetude, the Clause was early turned against those whom it was intended to set free, condemning them to a "separate but equal" status before the law, a status always separate but seldom equal. Not until 1954— only 24 years ago—was this odious doctrine interred by our decision in *Brown v. Board of Education* and its progeny, which proclaimed that separate schools and public facilities of all sorts were inherently unequal and forbidden under our Constitution. Even then inequality was not eliminated with "all deliberate speed." In 1968 and again in 1971, for example, we were forced to remind school boards of their obligation to eliminate racial discrimination root and branch. And a glance at our docket and at dockets of lower courts will show that even today officially sanctioned discrimination is not a thing of the past.

Against this background, claims that law must be "color-blind" or that the datum of race is no longer relevant to public policy must be seen as aspiration rather than as description of reality. This is not to denigrate aspiration; for reality rebukes us that race has too often been used by those who would stigmatize and oppress minorities. Yet we cannot—and, as we shall demonstrate, need not under our Constitution or Title VI, which merely extends the constraints of the Fourteenth Amendment to private parties who receive federal funds—let color blindness become myopia which masks the reality that many "created equal" have been treated within our lifetimes as inferior both by the law and by their fellow citizens.

II

The threshold question we must decide is whether Title VI of the Civil Rights Act of 1964 bars recipients of federal funds from giving preferential consideration to disadvantaged members of racial minorities as part of a program designed to enable such individuals to surmount the obstacles imposed by racial discrimination. . . .

In our view, Title VI prohibits only those uses of racial criteria that would violate the Fourteenth Amendment if employed by a State or its agencies; it does not bar the preferential treatment of racial minorities as a means of remedying past societal discrimination to the extent that such action is consistent with the Fourteenth Amendment. The legislative history of Title VI, administrative regulations interpreting the statute, subsequent congressional and executive action, and the prior decisions of this Court compel this conclusion. None of these sources lends support to the proposition that Congress intended to bar all race-conscious efforts to extend the benefits of federally financed programs to minorities who have been historically excluded from the full benefits of American life. . . .

III

A

The assertion of human equality is closely associated with the proposition that differences in color or creed, birth or status, are neither significant nor relevant to the way in which persons should be treated. Nonetheless, the position that such factors must be "constitutionally an irrelevance," summed up by the shorthand phrase "[o]ur Constitution is colorblind," has never been adopted by this Court as the proper meaning of the Equal Protection Clause.

Indeed, we have expressly rejected this proposition on a number of occasions.

Our cases have always implied that an "overriding statutory purpose" could be found that would justify racial classifications. More recently, in *McDaniel v. Barresi* (1971), this Court unanimously reversed the Georgia Supreme Court which had held that a desegregation plan voluntarily adopted by a local school board, which assigned students on the basis of race, was *per se* invalid because it was not colorblind. And in *North Carolina Board of Education v. Swann* we held, again unanimously, that a statute mandating color-blind school-assignment plans could not stand "against the background of segregation," since such a limit on remedies would "render illusory the promise of *Brown [I]*."

We conclude, therefore, that racial classifications are not *per se* invalid under the Fourteenth Amendment. Accordingly, we turn to the problem of articulating what our role should be in reviewing state action that expressly classifies by race.

B

Respondent argues that racial classifications are always suspect and, consequently, that this Court should weigh the importance of the objectives served by Davis' special admissions program to see if they are compelling. In addition, he asserts that this Court must inquire whether, in its judgment, there are alternatives to racial classifications which would suit Davis' purposes. Petitioner, on the other hand, states that our proper role is simply to accept petitioner's determination that the racial classifications used by its program are reasonably related to what it tells us are its benign purposes. We reject petitioner's view, but, because our prior cases are in many respects inapposite to that before us now, we find it necessary to define with precision the meaning of that inexact term, "strict scrutiny."

Unquestionably we have held that a government practice or statute which restricts "fundamental rights" or which contains "suspect classifications" is to be subjected to "strict scrutiny" and can be justified only if it furthers a compelling government purpose and, even then, only if no less restrictive alternative is available. But no fundamental right is involved here. Nor do whites as a class have any of the "traditional indicia of suspectness: the class is not saddled with such disabilities, or subjected to such a history of purposeful unequal treatment, or relegated to such a position of political powerlessness as to command extraordinary protection from the majoritarian political process."

Moreover, if the University's representations are credited, this is not a case where racial classifications are "irrelevant and therefore prohibited." Nor has anyone suggested that the University's purposes contravene the cardinal principle that racial classifications that stigmatize—because they are drawn on the presumption that one race is inferior to another or because they put the weight of government behind racial hatred and separatism—are invalid without more.

On the other hand, the fact that this case does not fit neatly into our prior analytic framework for race cases does not mean that it should be analyzed by applying the very loose rational-basis standard of review that is the very least that is always applied in equal protection cases. "'[T]he mere recitation of a benign, compensatory purpose is not an automatic shield which protects against any inquiry into the actual purposes underlying a statutory scheme.'" Instead, a number of considerations—developed in gender-discrimination cases but which carry even more force when applied to racial classifications—lead us to conclude that racial classifications designed to further remedial purposes "'must serve important governmental objectives and must be substantially related to achievement of those objectives.'"

First, race, like, "gender-based classifications too often [has] been inexcusably utilized to stereotype and stigmatize politically powerless segments of society." While a carefully tailored statute designed to remedy past discrimination could avoid these vices, we nonetheless have recognized that the line between honest and thoughtful appraisal of the effects of past discrimination and paternalistic stereotyping is not so clear and that a statute based on the latter is patently capable of stigmatizing all women with a badge of inferiority. State programs designed ostensibly to ameliorate the effects of past racial discrimination obviously create the same hazard of stigma, since they may promote racial separatism and reinforce the views of those who believe that members of racial minorities are inherently incapable of succeeding on their own.

Second, race, like gender and illegitimacy, is an immutable characteristic which its possessors are powerless to escape or set aside. While a classification is not *per se* invalid because it divides classes on the basis of an immutable characteristic, it is nevertheless true that such divisions are contrary to our deep belief that "legal burdens should bear some relationship to individual responsibility or wrongdoing" and that advancement sanctioned, sponsored, or approved by the State should ideally be based on individual merit or achievement, or at the least on factors within the control of an individual.

Because this principle is so deeply rooted it might be supposed that it would be considered in the legislative process and weighed against the benefits of programs preferring individuals because of their race. But this is not necessarily so: The "natural consequence of our governing process [may well be] that the most 'discrete and insular' of whites . . . will be called upon to bear the immediate, direct costs of benign discrimination." Moreover, it is clear from our cases that there are limits beyond which majorities may not go when they classify on the basis of immutable characteristics. Thus, even if the concern for individualism is weighed by the political process, that weighing cannot waive the personal rights of individuals under the Fourteenth Amendment.

In sum, because of the significant risk that racial classifications established for ostensibly benign purposes can be misused, causing effects not unlike those created by invidious classifications, it is inappropriate to inquire only whether there is any conceivable basis that might sustain such a classification. Instead, to justify such a classification an important and articulated purpose for its use must be shown. In addition, any statute must be stricken that stigmatizes any group or that singles out those least well represented in the political process to bear the brunt of a benign program. Thus, our review under the Fourteenth Amendment should be strict—not "'strict' in theory and fatal in fact," because it is stigma that causes fatality—but strict and searching nonetheless.

IV

Davis' articulated purpose of remedying the effects of past societal discrimination is, under our cases, sufficiently important to justify the use of race-conscious admissions programs where there is a sound basis for concluding that minority under-representation is substantial and chronic, and that the handicap of past discrimination is impeding access of minorities to the Medical School. . . .

[A . . .]

B

. . . Certainly, on the basis of the undisputed factual submissions before this Court, Davis had a sound basis for believing that the problem of under-representation of minorities was substantial and chronic and that the problem was attributable to handicaps imposed on minority applicants by past and present racial discrimination. Until at least 1973, the practice of medicine in this country was, in fact, if not in law, largely the prerogative of whites. In 1950, for example, while Negroes constituted 10% of the total population, Negro physicians consti-tuted only 2.2% of the total number of physicians. The overwhelming majority of these, moreover, were educated in two predominantly Negro medical schools, Howard and Meharry. By 1970, the gap between the proportion of Negroes in medicine and their proportion in the population had widened: The number of Negroes employed in medicine remained frozen at 2.2% while the Negro popula-tion had increased to 11.1%. The number of Negro admittees to predominantly white medical schools, moreover, had declined in absolute numbers during the years 1955 to 1964.

Moreover, Davis had very good reason to believe that the national pattern of underrepresentation of minorities in medicine would be perpetuated if it retained a single admissions standard. For example, the entering classes in 1968 and 1969, the years in which such a standard was used, included only 1 Chicano and 2 Negroes out of the 50 admittees for each year. Nor is there any relief from this pattern of underrepresentation in the statistics for the regular admissions program in later years.

Davis clearly could conclude that the serious and persistent underrepresentation of minorities in medicine depicted by these statistics is the result of handicaps under which minority applicants labor as a consequence of a background of deliberate, purposeful discrimination against minorities in ed-ucation and in society generally, as well as in the medical profession. From the inception of our na-tional life, Negroes have been subjected to unique legal disabilities impairing access to equal educa-tional opportunity. Under slavery, penal sanctions were imposed upon anyone attempting to educate Negroes. After enactment of the Fourteenth Amend-ment the States continued to deny Negroes equal educational opportunity, enforcing a strict policy of segregation that itself stamped Negroes as inferior, that relegated minorities to inferior educational institutions, and that denied them intercourse in the mainstream of professional life necessary to ad-vancement. Segregation was not limited to public facilities, moreover, but was enforced by criminal penalties against private action as well. Thus, as late as 1908, this Court enforced a state criminal convic-tion against a private college for teaching Negroes together with whites.

Green v. County School Board gave explicit recog-nition to the fact that the habit of discrimination and the cultural tradition of race prejudice culti-vated by centuries of legal slavery and segregation were not immediately dissipated when *Brown I,* announced the constitutional principle that equal educational opportunity and participation in all aspects of American life could not be denied on the basis of race. Rather, massive official and private resistance prevented, and to a lesser extent still pre-vents, attainment of equal opportunity in education at all levels and in the professions. The generation of minority students applying to Davis Medical School since it opened in 1968—most of whom were born before or about the time *Brown I* was decided—clearly have been victims of this discrimination. . . .

C

The second prong of our test—whether the Davis program stigmatizes any discrete group or individ-ual and whether race is reasonably used in light of the program's objectives—is clearly satisfied by the Davis program.

It is not even claimed that Davis' program in any way operates to stigmatize or single out any discrete and insular, or even any identifiable, nonminority group. Nor will harm comparable to that imposed upon racial minorities by exclusion or separation on grounds of race be the likely result of the program. It does not, for example, establish an exclusive preserve for minority students apart from and exclusive of whites. Rather, its purpose is to overcome the effects of segregation by bringing the races together. True, whites are excluded from participation in the special admissions program, but this fact only operates to reduce the number of whites to be admitted in the regular admissions program in order to permit admission of a reasonable percentage—less than their proportion of the California population—of otherwise underrepresented qualified minority applicants.

Nor was Bakke in any sense stamped as inferior by the Medical School's rejection of him. Indeed, it is conceded by all that he satisfied those criteria regarded by the school as generally relevant to academic performance better than most of the minority members who were admitted. Moreover, there is absolutely no basis for concluding that Bakke's rejection as a result of Davis' use of racial preference will affect him throughout his life in the same way as the segregation of the Negro schoolchildren in *Brown I* would have affected them. Unlike discrimination against racial minorities, the use of racial preferences for remedial purposes does not inflict a pervasive injury upon individual whites in the sense that wherever they go or whatever they do there is a significant likelihood that they will be treated as second-class citizens because of their color. This distinction does not mean that the exclusion of a white resulting from the preferential use of race is not sufficiently serious to require justification; but it does mean that the injury inflicted by such a policy is not distinguishable from disadvantages caused by a wide range of government actions, none of which has ever been thought impermissible for that reason alone.

In addition, there is simply no evidence that the Davis program discriminates intentionally or unintentionally against any minority group which it purports to benefit. The program does not establish a quota in the invidious sense of a ceiling on the number of minority applicants to be admitted. Nor can the program reasonably be regarded as stigmatizing the program's beneficiaries or their race as inferior. The Davis program does not simply advance less qualified applicants; rather, it compensates applicants, who it is uncontested are fully qualified to study medicine, for educational disadvantages which it was reasonable to conclude were a product of state-fostered discrimination. Once admitted, these students must satisfy the same degree requirements as regularly admitted students; they are taught by the same faculty in the same classes; and their performance is evaluated by the same standards by which regularly admitted students are judged. Under these circumstances, their performance and degrees must be regarded equally with the regularly admitted students with whom they compete for standing. Since minority graduates cannot justifiably be regarded as less well qualified than nonminority graduates by virtue of the special admissions program, there is no reasonable basis to conclude that minority graduates at schools using such programs would be stigmatized as inferior by the existence of such programs.

D

We disagree with the lower courts' conclusion that the Davis program's use of race was unreasonable in light of its objectives. First, as petitioner argues, there are no practical means by which it could achieve its end in the foreseeable future without the use of race-conscious measures. With respect to any factor (such as poverty or family educational background) that may be used as a substitute for race as an indicator of past discrimination, whites greatly outnumber racial minorities simply because whites make up a far larger percentage of the total population and therefore far outnumber minorities in absolute terms at every socioeconomic level. For example, of a class of recent medical school applicants from families with less than $10,000 income, at least 71% were white. Of all 1970 families headed by a person *not* a high school graduate which included related children under 18, 80% were white and 20% were racial minorities. Moreover, while race is positively correlated with differences in GPA and MCAT scores, economic disadvantage is not. Thus, it appears that economically disadvantaged whites do not score less well than economically advantaged whites, while economically advantaged blacks score less well than do disadvantaged whites. These statistics graphically illustrate that the University's purpose to integrate its classes by compensating for past discrimination could not be achieved by a general preference for the economically disadvantaged or the children of parents of limited education unless such groups were to make up the entire class.

Second, the Davis admissions program does not simply equate minority status with disadvantage. Rather, Davis considers on an individual basis each applicant's personal history to determine whether he or she has likely been disadvantaged by racial discrimination. The record makes clear that only minority applicants likely to have been isolated from the mainstream of American life are considered in the special program; other minority applicants are eligible only through the regular admissions program. True, the procedure by which disadvantage is detected is informal, but we have never insisted that educators conduct their affairs through adjudicatory proceedings, and such insistence here is misplaced. A case-by-case inquiry into the extent to which each individual applicant has been affected, either directly or indirectly, by racial discrimination, would seem to be, as a practical matter, virtually impossible, despite the fact that there are excellent reasons for concluding that such effects generally exist. When individual measurement is impossible or extremely impractical, there is nothing to prevent a State from using categorical means to achieve its ends, at least where the category is closely related to the goal. And it is clear from our cases that specific proof that a person has been victimized by discrimination is not a necessary predicate to offering him relief where the probability of victimization is great. . . .

Mr. Justice Marshall.

I agree with the judgment of the Court only insofar as it permits a university to consider the race of an applicant in making admissions decisions. I do not agree that petitioner's admissions program violates the Constitution. For it must be remembered that, during most of the past 200 years, the Constitution as interpreted by this Court did not prohibit the most ingenious and pervasive forms of discrimination against the Negro. Now, when a State acts to remedy the effects of that legacy of discrimination, I cannot believe that this same Constitution stands as a barrier.

I

A

Three hundred and fifty years ago, the Negro was dragged to this country in chains to be sold into slavery. Uprooted from his homeland and thrust into bondage for forced labor, the slave was deprived of all legal rights. It was unlawful to teach him to read; he could be sold away from his family and friends at the whim of his master; and killing or maiming him was not a crime. The system of slavery brutalized and dehumanized both master and slave. . . .

B

The status of the Negro as property was officially erased by his emancipation at the end of the Civil War. But the long-awaited emancipation, while freeing the Negro from slavery, did not bring him citizenship or equality in any meaningful way. Slavery was replaced by a system of "laws which imposed upon the colored race onerous disabilities and burdens, and curtailed their rights in the pursuit of life, liberty, and property to such an extent that their freedom was of little value." Despite the passage of the Thirteenth, Fourteenth, and Fifteenth Amendments, the Negro was systematically denied the rights those Amendments were supposed to secure. The combined actions and inactions of the State and Federal Governments maintained Negroes in a position of legal inferiority for another century after the Civil War. . . .

II

The position of the Negro today in America is the tragic but inevitable consequence of centuries of unequal treatment. Measured by any benchmark of comfort or achievement, meaningful equality remains a distant dream for the Negro.

A Negro child today has a life expectancy which is shorter by more than five years than that of a white child. The Negro child's mother is over three times more likely to die of complications in childbirth, and the infant mortality rate for Negroes is nearly twice that for whites. The median income of the Negro family is only 60% that of the median of a white family, and the percentage of Negroes who live in families with incomes below the poverty line is nearly four times greater than that of whites.

When the Negro child reaches working age, he finds that America offers him significantly less than it offers his white counterpart. For Negro adults, the unemployment rate is twice that of whites, and the unemployment rate for Negro teenagers is nearly three times that of white teenagers. A Negro male who completes four years of college can expect a median annual income of merely $110 more than a white male who has only a high school diploma. Although Negroes represent 11.5% of the population, they are only 1.2% of the lawyers, and judges, 2% of the physicians, 2.3% of the dentists, 1.1% of the engineers and 2.6% of the college and university professors.

The relationship between those figures and the history of unequal treatment afforded to the Negro cannot be denied. At every point from birth to death the impact of the past is reflected in the still disfavored position of the Negro.

In light of the sorry history of discrimination and its devastating impact on the lives of Negroes, bringing the Negro into the mainstream of American life should be a state interest of the highest order. To fail to do so is to ensure that America will forever remain a divided society.

III

I do not believe that the Fourteenth Amendment requires us to accept that fate. Neither its history nor our past cases lend any support to the conclusion that a university may not remedy the cumulative effects of society's discrimination by giving consideration to race in an effort to increase the number and percentage of Negro doctors. . . .

IV

While I applaud the judgment of the Court that a university may consider race in its admissions process, it is more than a little ironic that, after several hundred years of class-based discrimination against Negroes, the Court is unwilling to hold that a class-based remedy for that discrimination is permissible. In declining to so hold, today's judgment ignores the fact that for several hundred years Negroes have been discriminated against, not as individuals, but rather solely because of the color of their skins. It is unnecessary in 20th-century America to have individual Negroes demonstrate that they have been victims of racial discrimination; the racism of our society has been so pervasive that none, regardless of wealth or position, has managed to escape its impact. The experience of Negroes in America has been different in kind, not just in degree, from that of other ethnic groups. It is not merely the history of slavery alone but also that a whole people were marked as inferior by the law. And that mark has endured. The dream of America as the great melting pot has not been realized for the Negro; because of his skin color he never even made it into the pot.

These differences in the experience of the Negro make it difficult for me to accept that Negroes cannot be afforded greater protection under the Fourteenth Amendment where it is necessary to remedy the effects of past discrimination. In the *Civil Rights Cases,* the Court wrote that the Negro emerging from slavery must cease "to be the special favorite of the laws." We cannot in light of the history of the last century yield to that view. Had the Court in that decision and others been willing to "do for human liberty and the fundamental rights of American citizenship, what it did . . . for the protection of slavery and the rights of the masters of fugitive slaves," we would not need now to permit the recognition of any "special wards."

Most importantly, had the Court been willing in 1896, in *Plessy v. Ferguson,* to hold that the Equal Protection Clause forbids differences in treatment based on race, we would not be faced with this dilemma in 1978. We must remember, however, that the principle that the "Constitution is color-blind" appeared only in the opinion of the lone dissenter. The majority of the Court rejected the principle of color-blindness, and for the next 58 years, from *Plessy* to *Brown v. Board of Education,* ours was a Nation where, by law, an individual could be given "special" treatment based on the color of his skin.

It is because of a legacy of unequal treatment that we now must permit the institutions of this society to give consideration to race in making decisions about who will hold the positions of influence, affluence, and prestige in America. For far too long, the doors to those positions have been shut to Negroes. If we are ever to become a fully integrated society, one in which the color of a person's skin will not determine the opportunities available to him or her, we must be willing to take steps to open those doors. I do not believe that anyone can truly look into America's past and still find that a remedy for the effects of that past is impermissible. . . .

City of Richmond v. Croson (1989)

(*Source:* City of Richmond v. Croson 57 LW 4134 [1989]. *Most legal references have been omitted.*)

QUESTIONS FOR REFLECTION

1. Justice O'Connor doubts that it is possible to distinguish "benign" from pernicious racial classifications. Why? Do you agree?

2. Why, in Justice O'Connor's view, was the evidence of discrimination presented in the case inadequate?

3. Justice Scalia objects to racial quotas on several grounds not mentioned in Justice O'Connor's opinion. What are they?

4. What are Justice Marshall's arguments for his conclusion that Richmond's plan is acceptable?

5. Why does Justice Marshall object to the majority's application of "strict scrutiny" to this case?

Justice O'Connor announced the judgment of the Court and delivered the opinion of the Court with respect to Parts I, III-B, and IV, an opinion with respect to Part II, in which the Chief Justice and Justice White join, and an opinion with respect to Parts III-A and V, in which the Chief Justice, Justice White and Justice Kennedy join.

In this case, we confront once again the tension between the Fourteenth Amendment's guarantee of equal treatment to all citizens, and the use of race-based measures to ameliorate the effects of past discrimination on the opportunities enjoyed by members of minority groups in our society. In *Fullilove v. Klutznick* (1980), we held that a congressional program requiring that 10% of certain federal construction grants be awarded to minority contractors did not violate the equal protection principles embodied in the Due Process Clause of the Fifth Amendment. Relying largely on our decision in *Fullilove,* some lower federal courts have applied a similar standard of review in assessing the constitutionality of state and local minority set-aside provisions under the Equal Protection Clause of the Fourteenth Amendment. . . .

I

On April 11, 1983, the Richmond City Council adopted the Minority Business Utilization Plan (the Plan). The Plan required prime contractors to whom the city awarded construction contracts to subcontract at least 30% of the dollar amount of the contract to one or more Minority Business Enterprises (MBEs). The 30% setaside did not apply to city contracts awarded to minority-owned prime contractors.

The Plan defined an MBE as "[a] business at least fifty-one (51) percent of which is owned and controlled . . . by minority group members." "Minority group members" were defined as "[c]itizens of the United States who are Blacks, Spanish-speaking, Orientals, Indians, Eskimos, or Aleuts." There was no geographic limit to the Plan; an otherwise qualified MBE from anywhere in the United States could avail itself of the 30% set-aside. The Plan declared that it was "remedial" in nature, and enacted "for the purpose of promoting wider participation by minority business enterprises in the construction of public projects." The Plan expired on June 30, 1988, and was in effect for approximately five years. . . .

[II . . .]

III

A

The Equal Protection Clause of the Fourteenth Amendment provides that "[N]o State shall . . . deny to *any person* within its jurisdiction the equal protection of the laws" (emphasis added). As this Court has noted in the past, the "rights created by the first section of the Fourteenth Amendment are, by its terms, guaranteed to the individual. The rights established are personal rights." The Richmond Plan denies certain citizens the opportunity to compete for a fixed percentage of public contracts based solely upon their race. To whatever racial group these citizens belong, their "personal rights" to be treated with equal dignity and respect are implicated by a rigid rule erecting race as the sole criterion in an aspect of public decisionmaking.

Absent searching judicial inquiry into the justification for such race-based measures, there is simply no way of determining what classifications are "benign" or "remedial" and what classifications are in fact motivated by illegitimate notions of racial inferiority or simple racial politics. Indeed, the purpose of strict scrutiny is to "smoke out" illegitimate uses of race by assuring that the legislative body is pursuing a goal important enough to warrant use of a highly suspect tool. The test also ensures that the means chosen "fit" this compelling goal so closely that there is little or no possibility that the motive for the classification was illegitimate racial prejudice or stereotype.

Classifications based on race carry a danger of stigmatic harm. Unless they are strictly reserved for remedial settings, they may in fact promote notions of racial inferiority and lead to a politics of racial hostility. We thus reaffirm the view expressed by the plurality in *Wygant* that the standard of review under the Equal Protection Clause is not dependent on the race of those burdened or benefited by a particular classification.

Our continued adherence to the standard of review employed in *Wygant,* does not, as Justice Mar-

shall's dissent suggests, indicate that we view "racial discrimination as largely a phenomenon of the past" or that "government bodies need no longer preoccupy themselves with rectifying racial injustice." As we indicate below States and their local subdivisions have many legislative weapons at their disposal both to punish and prevent present discrimination and to remove arbitrary barriers to minority advancement. Rather, our interpretation of §1 stems from our agreement with the view expressed by Justice Powell in *Bakke,* that "[t]he guarantee of equal protection cannot mean one thing when applied to one individual and something else when applied to a person of another color."

Under the standard proposed by Justice Marshall's dissent, "[r]ace-conscious classifications designed to further remedial goals," are forthwith subject to a relaxed standard of review. How the dissent arrives at the legal conclusion that a racial classification is "designed to further remedial goals," without first engaging in an examination of the factual basis for its enactment and the nexus between its scope and that factual basis we are not told. However, once the "remedial" conclusion is reached, the dissent's standard is singularly deferential, and bears little resemblance to the close examination of legislative purpose we have engaged in when reviewing classifications based either on race or gender. The dissent's watered-down version of equal protection review effectively assures that race will always be relevant in American life, and that the "ultimate goal" of "eliminat[ing] entirely from governmental decisionmaking such irrelevant factors as a human being's race" will never be achieved.

Even were we to accept a reading of the guarantee of equal protection under which the level of scrutiny varies according to the ability of different groups to defend their interests in the representative process, heightened scrutiny would still be appropriate in the circumstances of this case. One of the central arguments for applying a less exacting standard to "benign" racial classifications is that such measures essentially involve a choice made by dominant racial groups to disadvantage themselves. If one aspect of the judiciary's role under the Equal Protection Clause is to protect "discrete and insular minorities" from majoritarian prejudice or indifference, some maintain that these concerns are not implicated when the "white majority" places burdens upon itself.

In this case, blacks comprise approximately 50% of the population of the city of Richmond. Five of the nine seats on the City Council are held by blacks. The concern that a political majority will more easily act to the disadvantage of a minority based on unwarranted assumptions or incomplete facts would seem to militate for, not against, the application of heightened judicial scrutiny in this case.

In *Bakke,* the Court confronted a racial quota employed by the University of California at Davis Medical School. Under the plan, 16 out of 100 seats in each entering class at the school were reserved exclusively for certain minority groups. Among the justifications offered in support of the plan were the desire to "reduc[e] the historic deficit of traditionally disfavored minorities in medical school and the medical profession" and the need to "counte[r] the effects of societal discrimination." Five Members of the Court determined that none of these interests could justify a plan that completely eliminated non-minorities from consideration for a specified percentage of opportunities.

Justice Powell's opinion applied heightened scrutiny under the Equal Protection Clause to the racial classification at issue. His opinion decisively rejected the first justification for the racially segregated admissions plan. The desire to have more black medical students or doctors, standing alone, was not merely insufficiently compelling to justify a racial classification, it was "discrimination for its own sake," forbidden by the Constitution. Nor could the second concern, the history of discrimination in society at large, justify a racial quota in medical school admissions. Justice Powell contrasted the "focused" goal of remedying "wrongs worked by specific instances of racial discrimination" with "the remedying of the effects of 'societal discrimination,' an amorphous concept of injury that may be ageless in its reach into the past." He indicated that for the governmental interest in remedying past discrimination to be triggered "judicial, legislative, or administrative findings of constitutional or statutory violations" must be made. Only then does the Government have a compelling interest in favoring one race over another.

In *Wygant* (1986), four Members of the Court applied heightened scrutiny to a race-based system of employee layoffs. Justice Powell, writing for the plurality, again drew the distinction between "societal discrimination" which is an inadequate basis for race-conscious classifications, and the type of identified discrimination that can support and define the scope of race-based relief. The challenged classification in that case tied the layoff of minority teachers to the percentage of minority students enrolled in the school district. The lower courts had upheld the scheme, based on the theory that minority students were in need of "role models" to alleviate the effects of prior discrimination in society. This Court reversed, with a plurality of four Justices reiterating the view expressed by Justice Powell in *Bakke* that "[s]ocietal discrimination, without more, is too amorphous a basis for imposing a racially classified remedy."

The role model theory employed by the lower courts failed for two reasons. First, the statistical disparity between students and teachers had no probative value in demonstrating the kind of prior discrimination in hiring or promotion that would justify race-based relief. Second, because the role model theory had no relation to some basis for believing a constitutional or statutory violation had occurred, it could be used to "justify" race-based decisionmaking essentially limitless in scope and duration.

III

B

We think it clear that the factual predicate offered in support of the Richmond Plan suffers from the same two defects identified as fatal in *Wygant.* The District Court found the city council's "findings sufficient to ensure that, in adopting the Plan, it was remedying the present effects of past discrimination in the *construction industry*" (emphasis added). Like the "role model" theory employed in *Wygant,* a generalized assertion that there has been past discrimination in an entire industry provides no guidance for a legislative body to determine the precise scope of the injury it seeks to remedy. It "has no logical stopping point." "Relief" for such an ill-defined wrong could extend until the percentage of public contracts awarded to MBEs in Richmond mirrored the percentage of minorities in the population as a whole.

Appellant argues that it is attempting to remedy various forms of past discrimination that are alleged to be responsible for the small number of minority businesses in the local contracting industry. Among these the city cites the exclusion of blacks from skilled construction trade unions and training programs. This past discrimination has prevented them "from following the traditional path from laborer to entrepreneur." The city also lists a host of nonracial factors which would seem to face a member of any racial group attempting to establish a new business enterprise, such as deficiencies in working capital, inability to meet bonding requirements, unfamiliarity with bidding procedures, and disability caused by an inadequate track record.

While there is no doubt that the sorry history of both private and public discrimination in this country has contributed to a lack of opportunities for black entrepreneurs, this observation, standing alone, cannot justify a rigid racial quota in the awarding of public contracts in Richmond, Virginia. Like the claim that discrimination in primary and secondary schooling justifies a rigid racial preference in medical school admissions, an amorphous claim that there has been past discrimination in a particular industry cannot justify the use of an unyielding racial quota.

It is sheer speculation how many minority firms there would be in Richmond absent past societal discrimination, just as it was sheer speculation how many minority medical students would have been admitted to the medical school at Davis absent past discrimination in educational opportunities. Defining these sorts of injuries as "identified discrimination" would give local governments license to create a patchwork of racial preferences based on statistical generalizations about any particular field of endeavor.

These defects are readily apparent in this case. The 30% quota cannot in any realistic sense be tied to any injury suffered by anyone. The District Court relied upon five predicate "facts" in reaching its conclusion that there was an adequate basis for the 30%

quota: (1) the ordinance declares itself to be remedial; (2) several proponents of the measure stated their views that there had been past discrimination in the construction industry; (3) minority businesses received .67% of prime contracts from the city while minorities constituted 50% of the city's population; (4) there were very few minority contractors in local and state contractors' associations; and (5) in 1977, Congress made a determination that the effects of past discrimination had stifled minority participation in the construction industry nationally.

None of these "findings," singly or together, provide the city of Richmond with a "strong basis in evidence for its conclusion that remedial action was necessary." There is nothing approaching a prima facie case of a constitutional or statutory violation by *anyone* in the Richmond construction industry.

The District Court accorded great weight to the fact that the city council designated the Plan as "remedial." But the mere recitation of a "benign" or legitimate purpose for a racial classification, is entitled to little or no weight. Racial classifications are suspect, and that means that simple legislative assurances of good intention cannot suffice.

The District Court also relied on the highly conclusionary statement of a proponent of the Plan that there was racial discrimination in the construction industry "in this area, and the State, and around the nation." It also noted that the city manager had related his view that racial discrimination still plagued the construction industry in his home city of Pittsburg. These statements are of little probative value in establishing identified discrimination in the Richmond construction industry. The factfinding process of legislative bodies is generally entitled to a presumption of regularity and deferential review by the judiciary. But when a legislative body chooses to employ a suspect classification, it cannot rest upon a generalized assertion as to the classification's relevance to its goals. A governmental actor cannot render race a legitimate proxy for a particular condition merely by declaring that the condition exists. The history of racial classifications in this country suggests that blind judicial deference to legislative or executive pronouncements of necessity has no place in equal protection analysis.

Reliance on the disparity between the number of

prime contracts awarded to minority firms and the minority population of the city of Richmond is similarly misplaced. There is no doubt that "[w]here gross statistical disparities can be shown, they alone in a proper case may constitute prima facie proof of a pattern or practice of discrimination" under Title VII. But it is equally clear that "[w]hen special qualifications are required to fill particular jobs, comparisons to the general population (rather than to the smaller group of individuals who possess the necessary qualifications) may have little probative value."

In the employment context, we have recognized that for certain entry level positions or positions requiring minimal training, statistical comparisons of the racial composition of an employer's workforce to the racial composition of the relevant population may be probative of a pattern of discrimination. But where special qualifications are necessary, the relevant statistical pool for purposes of demonstrating discriminatory exclusion must be the number of minorities qualified to undertake the particular task.

In this case, the city does not even know how many MBEs in the relevant market are qualified to undertake prime or subcontracting work in public construction projects. . . . Nor does the city know what percentage of total city construction dollars minority firms now receive as subcontractors on prime contracts let by the city.

To a large extent, the set-aside of subcontracting dollars seems to rest on the unsupported assumption that white prime contractors simply will not hire minority firms. Indeed, there is evidence in this record that overall minority participation in city contracts in Richmond is seven to eight percent, and that minority contractor participation in Community Block Development Grant *construction* projects is 17% to 22%. Without any information on minority participation in subcontracting, it is quite simply impossible to evaluate overall minority representation in the city's construction expenditures.

The city and the District Court also relied on evidence that MBE membership in local contractors' associations was extremely low. Again, standing alone this evidence is not probative of any discrimination in the local construction industry. There are numerous explanations for this dearth of minority participation, including past societal discrimination in education and economic opportunities as well as both black and white career and entrepreneurial choices. Blacks may be disproportionately attracted to industries other than construction. The mere fact that black membership in these trade organizations is low, standing alone, cannot establish a prima facie case of discrimination.

For low minority membership in these associations to be relevant, the city would have to link it to the number of local MBEs eligible for membership. If the statistical disparity between eligible MBEs and MBE membership were great enough, an inference of discriminatory exclusion could arise. In such a case, the city would have a compelling interest in preventing its tax dollars from assisting these organizations in maintaining a racially segregated construction market.

Finally, the city and the District Court relied on Congress' finding in connection with the set-aside approved in *Fullilove* that there had been nationwide discrimination in the construction industry. The probative value of these findings for demonstrating the existence of discrimination in Richmond is extremely limited. By its inclusion of a waiver procedure in the national program addressed in *Fullilove,* Congress explicitly recognized that the scope of the problem would vary from market area to market area. . . .

In sum, none of the evidence presented by the city points to any identified discrimination in the Richmond construction industry. We, therefore, hold that the city has failed to demonstrate a compelling interest in apportioning public contracting opportunities on the basis of race. To accept Richmond's claim that past societal discrimination alone can serve as the basis for rigid racial preferences would be to open the door to competing claims for "remedial relief" for every disadvantaged group. The dream of a Nation of equal citizens in a society where race is irrelevant to personal opportunity and achievement would be lost in a mosaic of shifting preferences based on inherently unmeasurable claims of past wrongs. "Courts would be asked to evaluate the extent of the prejudice and consequent harm suffered by various minority groups. Those whose societal injury is thought to exceed some arbitrary level of tolerability then would be entitled to preferential classifications. . . . " We think such a result would be contrary to both the letter and spirit of a constitutional provision whose central command is equality.

The foregoing analysis applies only to the inclusion of blacks within the Richmond set-aside program. There is *absolutely no evidence* of past discrimination against Spanish-speaking, Oriental, Indian, Eskimo, or Aleut persons in any aspect of the Richmond construction industry. The District Court took judicial notice of the fact that the vast majority of "minority" persons in Richmond were black. It may well be that Richmond has never had an Aleut or Eskimo citizen. The random inclusion of racial groups that, as a practical matter, may never have suffered from discrimination in the construction industry in Richmond, suggests that perhaps the city's purpose was not in fact to remedy past discrimination.

If a 30% set-aside was "narrowly tailored" to compensate black contractors for past discrimination, one may legitimately ask why they are forced to share this "remedial relief" with an Aleut citizen who moves to Richmond tomorrow? The gross overinclusiveness of Richmond's racial preference strongly impugns the city's claim of remedial motivation.

IV

As noted by the court below, it is almost impossible to assess whether the Richmond Plan is narrowly tailored to remedy prior discrimination since it is not linked to identified discrimination in any way. We limit ourselves to two observations in this regard.

First, there does not appear to have been any consideration of the use of race-neutral means to increase minority business participation in city contracting. Many of the barriers to minority participation in the construction industry relied upon by the city to justify a racial classification appear to be race neutral. If MBEs disproportionately lack capital or cannot meet bonding requirements, a race-neutral program of city financing for small firms would, *a fortiori,* lead to greater minority participation. The principal opinion in *Fullilove* found that Congress had carefully examined and rejected race-neutral alternatives before enacting the MBE set-aside. There

is no evidence in this record that the Richmond City Council has considered any alternatives to a race-based quota.

Second, the 30% quota cannot be said to be narrowly tailored to any goal, except perhaps outright racial balancing. It rests upon the "completely unrealistic" assumption that minorities will choose a particular trade in lockstep proportion to their representation in the local population.

Since the city must already consider bids and waivers on a case-by-case basis, it is difficult to see the need for a rigid numerical quota. As noted above, the congressional scheme upheld in *Fullilove* allowed for a waiver of the set-aside provision where an MBE's higher price was not attributable to the effects of past discrimination. Based upon proper findings, such programs are less problematic from an equal protection standpoint because they treat all candidates individually, rather than making the color of an applicant's skin the sole relevant consideration. Unlike the program upheld in *Fullilove,* the Richmond Plan's waiver system focuses solely on the availability of MBEs; there is no inquiry into whether or not the particular MBE seeking a racial preference has suffered from the effects of past discrimination by the city or prime contractors.

Given the existence of an individualized procedure, the city's only interest in maintaining a quota system rather than investigating the need for remedial action in particular cases would seem to be simple administrative convenience. But the interest in avoiding the bureaucratic effort necessary to tailor remedial relief to those who truly have suffered the effects of prior discrimination cannot justify a rigid line drawn on the basis of a suspect classification. Under Richmond's scheme, a successful black, Hispanic, or Oriental entrepreneur from anywhere in the country enjoys an absolute preference over other citizens based solely on their race. We think it obvious that such a program is not narrowly tailored to remedy the effects of prior discrimination. . . .

Justice Scalia, concurring in the judgment.

I agree with much of the Court's opinion, and, in particular, with its conclusion that strict scrutiny must be applied to all governmental classification by race, whether or not its asserted purpose is "remedial" or "benign." I do not agree, however, with the Court's dicta suggesting that, despite the Fourteenth Amendment, state and local governments may in some circumstances discriminate on the basis of race in order (in a broad sense) "to ameliorate the effects of past discrimination." The benign purpose of compensating for social disadvantages, whether they have been acquired by reason of prior discrimination or otherwise, can no more be pursued by the illegitimate means of racial discrimination than can other assertedly benign purposes we have repeatedly rejected. The difficulty of overcoming the effects of past discrimination is as nothing compared with the difficulty of eradicating from our society the source of those effects, which is the tendency—fatal to a nation such as ours—to classify and judge men and women on the basis of their country of origin or the color of their skin. A solution to the first problem that aggravates the second is no solution at all. I share the view expressed by Alexander Bickel that "[t]he lesson of the great decisions of the Supreme Court and the lesson of contemporary history have been the same for at least a generation: discrimination on the basis of race is illegal, immoral, unconstitutional, inherently wrong, and destructive of democratic society." At least where state or local action is at issue, only a social emergency rising to the level of imminent danger to life and limb—for example, a prison race riot, requiring temporary segregation of inmates—can justify an exception to the principle embodied in the Fourteenth Amendment that "[o]ur Constitution is colorblind, and neither knows nor tolerates classes among citizens." . . .

In my view there is only one circumstance in which the States may act by race to "undo the effects of past discrimination": where that is necessary to eliminate their own maintenance of a system of unlawful racial classification. If, for example, a state agency has a discriminatory pay scale compensating black employees in all positions at 20% less than their nonblack counterparts, it may assuredly promulgate an order raising the salaries of "all black employees" by 20%. This distinction explains our school desegregation cases, in which we have made plain that States and localities sometimes have an obligation to adopt race-conscious remedies. . . .

A State can, of course, act "to undo the effects of past discrimination" in many permissible ways that do not involve classification by race. In the particular field of state contracting, for example, it may adopt a preference for small businesses, or even for new businesses—which would make it easier for those previously excluded by discrimination to enter the field. Such programs may well have racially disproportionate impact, but they are not based on race. And, of course, a State may "undo the effects of past discrimination" in the sense of giving the identified victim of state discrimination that which it wrongfully denied him—for example, giving to a previously rejected black applicant the job that, by reason of discrimination, had been awarded to a white applicant, even if this means terminating the latter's employment. In such a context, the white job-holder is not being selected for disadvantageous treatment because of his race, but because he was wrongfully awarded a job to which another is entitled. That is worlds apart from the system here, in which those to be disadvantaged are identified solely by race.

I agree with the Court's dictum that a fundamental distinction must be drawn between the effects of "societal" discrimination and the effects of "identified" discrimination, and that the situation would be different if Richmond's plan were "tailored" to identify those particular bidders who "suffered from the effects of past discrimination by the city or prime contractors." In my view, however, the reason that would make a difference is not, as the Court states, that it would justify race-conscious action, but rather that it would enable race-neutral remediation. Nothing prevents Richmond from according a contracting preference to identified victims of discrimination. While most of the beneficiaries might be black, neither the beneficiaries nor those disadvantaged by the preference would be identified *on the basis of their race.* In other words, far from justifying racial classification, identification of actual victims of discrimination makes it less supportable than ever, because more obviously unneeded.

In his final book, Professor Bickel wrote:

"[A] racial quota derogates the human dignity and individuality of all to whom it is applied; it is invidious in principle as well as in practice. Moreover, it can easily be turned against those it purports to help. The history of the racial quota is a history of subjugation, not beneficence. Its evil lies not in its name, but in its effects: a quota is a divider of society, a creator of castes, and it is all the worse for its racial base, especially in a society desperately striving for an equality that will make race irrelevant."

Those statements are true and increasingly prophetic. Apart from their societal effects, however, which are "in the aggregate disastrous," it is important not to lose sight of the fact that even "benign" racial quotas have individual victims, whose very real injustice we ignore whenever we deny them enforcement of their right not to be disadvantaged on the basis of race. As Justice Douglas observed: "A DeFunis who is white is entitled to no advantage by virtue of that fact; nor is he subject to any disability, no matter what his race or color. Whatever his race, he had a constitutional right to have his application considered on its individual merits in a racially neutral manner." When we depart from this American principle we play with fire, and much more than an occasional De Funis, Johnson, or Croson burns.

It is plainly true that in our society blacks have suffered discrimination immeasurably greater than any directed at other racial groups. But those who believe that racial preferences can help to "even the score" display, and reinforce, a manner of thinking by race that was the source of the injustice and that will, if it endures within our society, be the source of more injustice still. The relevant proposition is not that it was blacks, or Jews, or Irish who were discriminated against, but that it was individual men and women, "created equal," who were discriminated against. And the relevant resolve is that that should never happen again. Racial preferences appear to "even the score" (in some small degree) only if one embraces the proposition that our society is appropriately viewed as divided into races, making it right that an injustice rendered in the past to a black man should be compensated for by discriminating against a white. Nothing is worth that embrace. Since blacks have been disproportionately disadvantaged by racial discrimination, any race-neutral remedial program aimed at the disadvantaged *as such* will have a disproportionately beneficial impact on blacks. Only such a program, and not one that operates on the basis of race, is in accord with the letter and the spirit of our Constitution. . . .

Justice Marshall, with whom Justice Brennan and Justice Blackmun join, dissenting.

It is a welcome symbol of racial progress when the former capital of the Confederacy acts forthrightly to confront the effects of racial discrimination in its midst. In my view, nothing in the Constitution can be construed to prevent Richmond, Virginia, from allocating a portion of its contracting dollars for businesses owned or controlled by members of minority groups. Indeed, Richmond's set-aside program is indistinguishable in all meaningful respects from—and in fact was patterned upon—the federal set-aside plan which this Court upheld in *Fullilove* v. *Klutznick* (1980).

A majority of this Court holds today, however, that the Equal Protection Clause of the Fourteenth Amendment blocks Richmond's initiative. The essence of the majority's position is that Richmond has failed to catalogue adequate findings to prove that past discrimination has impeded minorities from joining or participating fully in Richmond's construction contracting industry. I find deep irony in second-guessing Richmond's judgment on this point. As much as any municipality in the United States, Richmond knows what racial discrimination is; a century of decisions by this and other federal courts has richly documented the city's disgraceful history of public and private racial discrimination. In any event, the Richmond City Council *has* supported its determination that minorities have been wrongly excluded from local construction contracting. Its proof includes statistics showing that minority-owned businesses have received virtually no city contracting dollars and rarely if ever belonged to area trade associations; testimony by municipal officials that discrimination has been widespread in the local construction industry; and the same exhaustive and widely publicized federal studies relied on in *Fullilove,* studies which showed that pervasive discrimination in the Nation's tight-knit construction industry had operated to exclude minorities from public contracting. These are precisely the types of statistical and testimonial evidence which, until today, this Court had credited in cases approving of race-conscious measures designed to remedy past discrimination.

More fundamentally, today's decision marks a deliberate and giant step backward in this Court's affirmative action jurisprudence. Cynical of one municipality's attempt to redress the effects of past racial discrimination in a particular industry, the majority launches a grapeshot attack on race-conscious remedies in general. The majority's unnecessary pronouncements will inevitably discourage or prevent governmental entities, particularly States and localities, from acting to rectify the scourge of past discrimination. This is the harsh reality of the majority's decision, but it is not the Constitution's command.

[I . . .]

II

"Agreement upon a means for applying the Equal Protection Clause to an affirmative-action program has eluded this Court every time the issue has come before us." My view has long been that race-conscious classifications designed to further remedial goals "must serve important governmental objectives and must be substantially related to achievement of those objectives" in order to withstand constitutional scrutiny. Analyzed in terms of this two-prong standard, Richmond's set-aside, like the federal program on which it was modeled, is "plainly constitutional."

A

I

Turning first to the governmental interest inquiry, Richmond has two powerful interests in setting aside a portion of public contracting funds for minority-owned enterprises. The first is the city's interest in eradicating the effects of past racial discrimination. It is far too late in the day to doubt that remedying such discrimination is a compelling, let alone an important, interest. In *Fullilove*, six members of this Court deemed this interest sufficient to support a race-conscious set-aside program governing federal contract procurement. The decision, in holding that the federal set-aside provision satisfied the Equal Protection Clause under any level of scru-

tiny, recognized that the measure sought to remove "barriers to competititve access which had their roots in racial and ethnic discrimination, and which continue today, even absent any intentional discrimination or unlawful conduct." Indeed, we have repeatedly reaffirmed the government's interest in breaking down barriers erected by past racial discrimination, in cases involving access to public education, employment, and valuable government contracts.

Richmond has a second compelling interest in setting aside, where possible, a portion of its contracting dollars. That interest is the prospective one of preventing the city's own spending decisions from reinforcing and perpetuating the exclusionary effects of past discrimination.

The majority pays only lip service to this additional governmental interest. But our decisions have often emphasized the danger of the government tacitly adopting, encouraging, or furthering racial discrimination even by its own routine operations. In *Shelley* v. *Kraemer* (1948), this Court recognized this interest as a constitutional command, holding unanimously that the Equal Protection Clause forbids courts to enforce racially restrictive covenants even where such covenants satisfied all requirements of state law and where the State harbored no discriminatory intent. Similarly, in *Norwood* v. *Harrison* (1973), we invalidated a program in which a State purchased textbooks and loaned them to students in public and private schools, including private schools with racially discriminatory policies. We stated that the Constitution requires a State "to steer clear, not only of operating the old dual system of racially segregated schools, but also of giving significant aid to institutions that practice racial or other invidious discrimination."

The majority is wrong to trivialize the continuing impact of government acceptance or use of private institutions or structures once wrought by discrimination. When government channels all its contracting funds to a white-dominated community of established contractors whose racial homogeneity is the product of private discrimination, it does more than place its imprimatur on the practices which forged and which continue to define that community. It also provides a measurable boost to those economic entities that have thrived within it, while denying important economic benefits to those entities which, but for prior discrimination, might well be better qualified to receive valuable government contracts. In my view, the interest in ensuring that the government does not reflect and reinforce prior private discrimination in dispensing public contracts is every bit as strong as the interest in eliminating private discrimination—an interest which this Court has repeatedly deemed compelling. The more government bestows its rewards on those persons or businesses that were positioned to thrive during a period of private racial discrimination, the tighter the dead-hand grip of prior discrimination becomes on the present and future. Cities like Richmond may not be constitutionally required to adopt set-aside plans. But there can be no doubt that when Richmond acted affirmatively to stem the perpetuation of patterns of discrimination through its own decisionmaking, it served an interest of the highest order.

[2 . . .]

B

In my judgment, Richmond's set-aside plan also comports with the second prong of the equal protection inquiry, for it is substantially related to the interests it seeks to serve in remedying past discrimination and in ensuring that municipal contract procurement does not perpetuate that discrimination. The most striking aspect of the city's ordinance is the similarity it bears to the "appropriately limited" federal set-aside provision upheld in *Fullilove*. Like the federal provision, Richmond's is limited to five years in duration and was not renewed when it came up for reconsideration in 1988. Like the federal provision, Richmond's contains a waiver provision freeing from its subcontracting requirements those nonminority firms that demonstrate that they cannot comply with its provisions. Like the federal provision, Richmond's has a minimal impact on innocent third parties. While the measure affects 30% of *public* contracting dollars, that translates to only 3% of overall Richmond area contracting.

Finally, like the federal provision, Richmond's does not interfere with any vested right of a contractor to a particular contract; instead it operates en-

tirely prospectively. Richmond's initiative affects only future economic arrangements and imposes only a diffuse burden on nonminority competitors —here, businesses owned or controlled by nonminorities which seek subcontracting work on public construction projects. The plurality in *Wygant* emphasized the importance of this not disrupting the settled and legitimate expectations of innocent parties. "While hiring goals impose a diffuse burden, often foreclosing only one of several opportunities, layoffs impose the entire burden of achieving racial equality on particular individuals, often resulting in serious disruption of their lives. That burden is too intrusive."

These factors, far from "justify[ing] a preference of any size or duration," are precisely the factors to which this Court looked in *Fullilove*. The majority takes issue, however, with two aspects of Richmond's tailoring: the city's refusal to explore the use of race-neutral measures to increase minority business participation in contracting and the selection of a 30% set-aside figure. The majority's first criticism is flawed in two respects. First, the majority overlooks the fact that since 1975, Richmond has barred both discrimination by the city in awarding public contracts and discrimination by public contractors. The virtual absence of minority businesses from the city's contracting rolls, indicated by the fact that such businesses have received less than 1% of public contracting dollars, strongly suggests that this ban has not succeeded in redressing the impact of past discrimination or in preventing city contract procurement from reinforcing racial homogeneity. Second, the majority's suggestion that Richmond should have first undertaken such race-neutral measures as a program of city financing for small firms ignores the fact that such measures, while theoretically appealing, have been discredited by Congress as ineffectual in eradicating the effects of past discrimination in this very industry. For this reason, this Court in *Fullilove* refused to fault Congress for not undertaking race-neutral measures as precursors to its race-conscious set-aside. The Equal Protection Clause does not require Richmond to retrace Congress' steps when Congress has found that those steps lead nowhere. Given the well-exposed limitations of race-neutral measures, it was thus appropriate for a municipality like Richmond to conclude that, in the words of Justice Blackmun, "[i]n order to get beyond racism, we must first take account of race. There is no other way."

As for Richmond's 30% target, the majority states that this figure "cannot be said to be narrowly tailored to any goal, except perhaps outright racial balancing." The majority ignores two important facts. First, the set-aside measure affects only 3% of overall city contracting; thus, any imprecision in tailoring has far less impact than the majority suggests. But more important, the majority ignores the fact that Richmond's 30% figure was patterned directly on the *Fullilove* precedent. Congress' 10% figure fell "roughly halfway between the present percentage of minority contractors and the percentage of minority group members in the Nation." The Richmond City Council's 30% figure similarly falls roughly halfway between the present percentage of Richmond-based minority contractors (almost zero) and the percentage of minorities in Richmond (50%). In faulting Richmond for not presenting a different explanation for its choice of a set-aside figure, the majority honors *Fullilove* only in the breach.

III

I would ordinarily end my analysis at this point and conclude that Richmond's ordinance satisfies both the governmental interest and substantial relationship prongs of our Equal Protection Clause analysis. However, I am compelled to add more, for the majority has gone beyond the facts of this case to announce a set of principles which unnecessarily restrict the power of governmental entities to take race-conscious measures to redress the effects of prior discrimination.

A

Today, for the first time, a majority of this Court has adopted strict scrutiny as its standard of Equal Pro-

tection Clause review of race-conscious remedial measures. This is an unwelcome development. A profound difference separates governmental actions that themselves are racist, and governmental actions that seek to remedy the effects of prior racism or to prevent neutral governmental activity from perpetuating the effects of such racism.

Racial classifications "drawn on the presumption that one race is inferior to another or because they put the weight of government behind racial hatred and separatism" warrant the strictest judicial scrutiny because of the very irrelevance of these rationales. By contrast, racial classifications drawn for the purpose of remedying the effects of discrimination that itself was race-based have a highly pertinent basis: the tragic and indelible fact that discrimination against blacks and other racial minorities in this Nation has pervaded our Nation's history and continues to scar our society. As I stated in *Fullilove*: "Because the consideration of race is relevant to remedying the continuing effects of past racial discrimination, and because governmental programs employing racial classifications for remedial purposes can be crafted to avoid stigmatization, . . . such programs should not be subjected to conventional 'strict scrutiny'—scrutiny that is strict in theory, but fatal in fact."

In concluding that remedial classifications warrant no different standard of review under the Constitution than the most brute and repugnant forms of state-sponsored racism, a majority of this Court signals that it regards racial discrimination as largely a phenomenon of the past, and that government bodies need no longer preoccupy themselves with rectifying racial injustice. I, however, do not believe this Nation is anywhere close to eradicating racial discrimination or its vestiges. In constitutionalizing its wishful thinking, the majority today does a grave disservice not only to those victims of past and present racial discrimination in this Nation whom government has sought to assist, but also to this Court's long tradition of approaching issues of race with the utmost sensitivity.

MYRL L. DUNCAN

The Future of Affirmative Action:
A Jurisprudential/Legal Critique

(*Source: Reprinted from Myrl L. Duncan, "The Future of Affirmative Action: A Jurisprudential/Legal Critique,"* Harvard Civil Rights–Civil Liberties Law Review 17 [1982].)

QUESTIONS FOR REFLECTION

1. What is the compensatory argument for affirmative action? What criticisms have been offered against it? How does Duncan respond to these criticisms?

2. What is the distributive argument for affirmative action? On what conception of distributive justice does it rely?

3. What arguments from social utility support affirmative action? Are there utilitarian arguments against such programs?

4. Discuss the chief objections to affirmative action and Duncan's responses to them.

Introduction

The ultimate objective of affirmative action is to bring about a society in which " . . . persons will be regarded as persons and discrimination . . . will be an ugly feature of history that is instructive but that is behind us." While it is probably impossible to eliminate bigotry, affirmative action seeks to diminish its measurable effects. Affirmative action can be defined as a public or private program designed to equalize hiring and admissions opportunities for historically disadvantaged groups by taking into consideration those very characteristics which have been used to deny them equal treatment. Such explicit, systemic consideration of these characteristics in determining who obtains a job or a place in an entering class is and has historically been extremely controversial. . . .

I believe that our past failure fully to understand and articulate the goals and justifications for affirmative action is in large part responsible for this controversy. Therefore, this Article attempts to set out and evaluate the justifications for affirmative action, and to rebut the current arguments against it, through a philosophical inquiry. The analysis focuses on three major rationales underlying arguments for affirmative action: compensatory justice, distributive justice, and social utility. The discussion exemplifies its general points by reference to a specific minority group: blacks. . . .

I. Arguments in Support of Affirmative Action

Affirmative action has been justified on each of three ethical grounds: compensatory justice, distributive justice and social utility. These three rationales are developed by James Nickel in a seminal article, *Preferential Policies in Hiring and Admissions: A Jurisprudential Approach.* While Nickel's analysis will serve as the foundation for much of this discussion, he did not invent these ethical rationales. Aristotle articulated the principles of rectification (compensatory justice) and distributive justice, and utilitarianism was set out by Jeremy Bentham and John Stuart Mill. The discussion which follows examines each of these ethical grounds, and shows how they may be applied to the affirmative action controversy.

A. Compensatory Justice

Compensatory justice awards reparations for past injury. Its aim is to make whole those who were injured by putting them where they would have been "but for" the injustices suffered. Compensatory justice theory holds that past injury creates an entitlement to reparation in the injured party.

The compensatory justice rationale for affirmative action faces an initial hurdle: some of the injury for which compensation is sought was inflicted on persons long since dead. It is necessary to ask whether compensation is owing for these injuries.

If historical injuries such as the degradations of slavery, Jim Crow laws, and "inherently unequal" education could be separated from present effects of that history, the answer would clearly be that compensation is not required. By definition one is only entitled to compensation for injuries suffered. However, past and present injury are inseparable. Present day discrimination in hiring is a "but for" result of prior history; hiring discrimination greatly contributes to discriminatory housing patterns, which in turn result in *de facto* school segregation. Similar to the practices condemned by a significant body of thirteenth amendment law, present inequalities are in essence "badges of slavery."

Since the injuries sustained by blacks today cannot be disassociated from the facts of slavery and segregation, it is irrelevant whether a compensatory affirmative action system is viewed as making reparations for prior history, or as compensating for the present injurious effects of that history. The relevant inquiries are 1) who has been injured? and 2) how should compensation be determined?

Prior injustice or injury must be established for a remedy based on compensatory justice to be appropriate. It is therefore necessary to determine if all group members have been injured before reparations can be awarded solely on the basis of group membership. I conclude that in the racial discrimination context, because discrimination was and is

suffered by black individuals solely because of their membership in the group of blacks, compensation is due purely on the basis of membership in that group.

Race discrimination has been, and continues to be, directed not at individuals, but at blacks as a group. Chief Justice Taney's infamous and inaccurate opinion in *Dred Scott v. Sanford,* lumped together all blacks, freedmen as well as slaves, as a race fit only for slavery:

> They had for more than a century before [the adoption of the Declaration of Independence and the Constitution] been regarded as beings of an inferior order, and altogether unfit to associate with the white race, either in social or political relations; and so far inferior, that they had no rights which the white man was bound to respect; and that the negro might justly and lawfully be reduced to slavery for his benefit. He was bought and sold, and treated as an ordinary article of merchandise and traffic, whenever a profit could be made by it. This opinion was at that time fixed and universal in the civilized portion of the white race.

No less emphatically, Jim Crow laws stamped all blacks as inferior. As Professor Wasserstrom observes, "[t]he point of maintaining racially segregated bathrooms was not in any simple or direct sense to keep both whites and blacks from using each other's bathrooms; it was to make sure that blacks would not contaminate bathrooms used by whites." Likewise, it was the state's imprimatur of inferiority upon blacks as a group, not as individuals, which the Supreme Court found especially stigmatizing in *Brown.*

The direct descendant of these earlier attitudes, race discrimination in employment affects not only black individuals but blacks as a group. For example, because lower paying jobs were historically the only ones available to blacks, seniority systems which effectively lock blacks into these jobs perpetuate past discrimination against the entire group. Likewise, seniority systems based on the "last hired, first fired" principle work to the disadvantage of blacks as a group, since they have only recently enjoyed widespread employment opportunity. The use of subjective hiring and promotional criteria, evaluated by primarily white supervisory personnel, also hinders blacks by permitting consciously or unconsciously biased decisionmaking. More overtly, blacks are discriminated against by employers who harass them or who maintain segregated employee facilities such as restrooms, locker rooms and drinking fountains.

While these examples do not constitute an exhaustive list, they demonstrate, as Justice Marshall concluded in his separate opinion in *Bakke,* that "the relationship between [unemployment and poverty statistics] and the history of unequal treatment afforded to the Negro cannot be denied. At every point from birth to death the impact of the past is reflected in the still disfavored position of the Negro."

Despite these well-known, well-documented patterns and practices of blatant discrimination against blacks as a distinct group, one opponent of affirmative action, Professor Cowan, argues that "past or future discrimination and injustice done [to blacks] as a group and special advantages to them as a group are both out of the question, since in the moral context, there is no such group." Cowan asserts that the original discrimination was unjust in that it was based on "morally irrelevant" characteristics, such as race and that group-based affirmative action is likewise unjust because it considers the same "morally irrelevant" characteristics in granting benefits. Professor Cowan cannot, however, be correct when he suggests both that a social order which subjugated groups of persons on the basis of "morally irrelevant" characteristics like race was unjust, and that in trying to redefine that social order it is somehow unjust to fashion group remedies for group injuries. Perhaps the reason for his failure to understand why group remedies are the best solutions to the problem is his misleading use of the phrase "'morally irrelevant' characteristics." In our society race has *never* been an irrelevant characteristic, either morally or socially. Even a cursory reading of American racial history would lead the most unsympathetic participant in the affirmative action debate to conclude that our culture has made race count for more than a matter of "superficial physiology." To suggest the contrary is to ignore social reality.

Furthermore, Cowan's argument fails to recognize the all-encompassing nature of the discriminatory injury. Because race was made a "morally relevant" factor for purposes of discriminating against a group, it must be "morally relevant" for purposes of compensation. Paul Taylor supports this argument when he says: "[T]o ignore the fact that a person is [black] would be to ignore the fact that there had been a social practice in which unjust actions were directed toward [black] persons as such." Although Taylor assumes, I believe incorrectly, that some blacks may not have suffered injustice, he contends that because the original injury was inflicted on their group, they too are entitled to compensation. To disregard the collective injury is, Taylor feels, to ignore "morally speaking . . . the most hideous aspect of the injustices of human history: those carried out systematically and directed toward whole groups of men and woman *as* groups." Taylor and I agree that because past discrimination was aimed at minorities as groups, and not as individuals, compensatory justice is now due them as groups.

There still, however, remains the question whether some persons have evaded injury. If that were the case, group-based affirmative action would be over-inclusive, according to the principles of compensatory justice. Nickel answers the question in the affirmative, suggesting also that those who have overcome losses through their own efforts are undeserving of compensation. Nickel nonetheless concludes that affirmative action can be based solely on group membership for reasons of administrative convenience.

I disagree on both points. The all-encompassing nature of racial discrimination makes it almost inconceivable that individual group members did not suffer some kind of injury. The black child who attended an integrated school but was harrassed, or shunned, by classmates suffered humiliation. The fact that the child may later have earned a Ph.D. does not negate the fact that he or she encountered, and was required to overcome, a headwind of racial discrimination.

Even accepting *arguendo* the assertion that middle class blacks are unlikely to have endured certain injuries, they have nonetheless suffered humiliation. While they may not have suffered an "unequal" education if they attended high quality public or private schools, they have surely been labeled inferior by certain members of society. But our society's perception of black inferiority has been felt by even the most prominent blacks. Thus, in addition to any vicarious suffering they have experienced, they have suffered direct stigmatization and their own self-images may have been injured. In short, as Justice Marshall concluded in his separate opinion in *Bakke*,

> [I]t is unnecessary in 20th century America to have individual Negroes demonstrate that they have been victims of racial discrimination; the racism of our society has been so pervasive that none, regardless of wealth or position, has managed to escape its impact. . . .

Alan Goldman suggests that not all group members are entitled to reparations since, even though discrimination is widespread, not every black person has been denied a job or an educational benefit. Goldman's definition of discrimination is clearly too narrow. A minority group member may not have been directly denied a job and yet may have suffered injustice. For example, it is all too common for employers to rely on their white male work force to do word-of-mouth recruitment, thereby effectively excluding minority applicants. Discrimination likewise occurs when an individual, influenced by a company's reputation for not hiring blacks or for hiring them for only the lowest level jobs, does not even bother to apply. Thus, in Title VII cases, the Supreme Court recognizes this argument, refusing to deny relief on the ground that the claimant failed to formally apply for the job. To do so

> could exclude from the Act's coverage the victims of the most entrenched forms of discrimination. Victims of gross and pervasive discrimination could be denied relief precisely because the unlawful practices had been so successful as totally to deter job applications from members of minority groups. . . .

Similarly, job restrictions which disproportionately exclude minorities discourage "otherwise qualified people from applying because of a self-recognized inability to meet the . . . standards." Clearly, discrimination has injured many more individuals than is apparent at first glance.

In summary, the premise that not all group members have suffered discrimination cannot withstand closer analysis. It fails to acknowledge that because discrimination is all-encompassing, the compen-

sation required to correct it must likewise be all-encompassing. Both because discrimination was aimed at the group *qua* group and because all members of the group have been injured, each individual black is entitled to affirmative action under a compensatory justice theory.

B. Distributive Justice

Inquiries guided by distributive justice look not to the past but to the present and the future in determining how such societal benefits as education and income should be distributed. Distributive justice requires [as Nickel asserts] that "benefits and burdens be distributed in accordance with relevant considerations such as the rights, deserts, merits, contributions and needs of the recipients." However, "distributive justice does not require that all people have the same income or equally good jobs."

Statistical data reflecting disparate employment and income levels for blacks and whites suggest distributive injustice. Conspicuously underrepresented in the economy's upper level positions, blacks occupy a disproportionately large segment of lower level positions. But distributive injustice is not established solely by such statistics. Rather, distributive injustice is established by the demonstration that this income distribution cannot be correlated to any of the "relevant considerations" listed above, but only to systematic racism.

While distributive justice theory may recognize the same past injuries as does the compensatory justice theory, its goal is not to repay the past injury but rather to neutralize its present effect. Under a distributive justice theory an individual is entitled to affirmative action not because society is admitting and paying for past errors but because he or she deserves a greater share of community resources.

Opponents of affirmative action might argue that the distributive justice theory does not justify affirmative action programs directed at groups, since such programs benefit persons who they assert have not been injured. Thus, those opposed to affirmative action might argue that minority group members who have received quality educations are not entitled to preferential treatment; since those individuals have had a chance to develop their abilities and obtain good jobs and societal positions, they do not suffer from distributive injustice.

For a number of interrelated reasons, such an "over-inclusiveness" argument is as unpersuasive under a distributive justice theory as it is under one of compensatory justice. First, the fact that one has received a quality education does not necessarily mean that he or she is thereafter immune from discrimination: black professionals who have received quality educations continue to suffer discrimination in the employment setting. The mere fact that some minority group members have received quality education and perhaps "good jobs" as well does not destroy their entitlement to distributive justice.

Second, the correlation between race or sex and relative inequality of opportunity is sufficiently high that it justifies the use of such indicators for reasons of administrative convenience. To take such a position is not to argue, as Nickel fears, that all groups should be "represented at all levels of income and achievement in proportion to their numbers in the country's population," but rather to suggest that relative inequality of opportunity bears a significant enough relationship to minority status to support a group based affirmative action program.

Finally, there exist clear examples of unmistakable, large-scale inequality of opportunity. For example, in 1980 black men comprised 25.6% of the nation's male file clerks (up from 22% in 1972); 22.1% of all male textile operatives (up from 18%) and 32.8% of all male garbage collectors (down from 33.3%). In contrast, black men accounted for only 2.1% of male physicians, 3.3% of male university teachers (down from 3.6%) and 3.2% of the male managers and administrators (up from 2.6%). Similarly, black women comprise 40.4% of the nation's female clothing ironers and only 5.2% of the managers and administrators. Under the distributive justice theory, such pervasive inequality of opportunity requires the remedy of group based affirmative action programs.

C. Social Utility

Social utility theory supports affirmative action programs on the ground that they are necessary to promote maximum well-being for society as a whole. In contrast to the compensatory and distributive jus-

tice theories, which focus on individual entitlements, this theory looks only to the general welfare. Therefore, affirmative action is justified to the extent that it increases societal well-being, by making job and education opportunities available on a more equal basis to all members of society. Likewise, the general welfare is enhanced as minority access to medical and legal services increases.

In determining whether affirmative action is justified, social utility theory looks to empirically based standards of social welfare rather than to abstract notions of "justice" and "entitlement." Since neither past nor present discrimination need be shown, this theory presents fewer justification problems than the two theories outlined above; also, since the general welfare may be enhanced through a process of social experimentation, this theory allows for greater program flexibility.

In providing versatility, however, the social utility principle also allows for greater dispute. The maxims of compensatory and distributive justice dictate only one result from a given set of facts; thus, disputes framed in these terms either reject the maxim or dispute the facts. Social cost-balancing, by contrast, is inherently weighted by a multitude of subjective factors, so that no one group's calculus of "the greatest good" need be accepted by any other group.

Since entitlements are not at issue, the overinclusiveness arguments discussed with respect to the compensatory and distributive justice theories are inapposite. Affirmative action programs should be set up to aid minorities even if they cannot show that they were harmed or are being treated unequally, so long as such a program would redound to the benefit of the whole society. Considerations of administrative convenience must be factored into the social cost-balancing which would justify an affirmative action program on utilitarian grounds.

Arguments for affirmative action based on utilitarian theory focus on the various ways in which such programs will benefit the public at large. Widely-recognized advantages include the promotion of minority role models, increased student body diversity, and improved provision of services to the minority community.

The presence of minority group members in prominent positions in society—as professionals, governmental or business leaders—will, it is widely believed, exert a positive influence on other group members who will be encouraged to attain their own potential. The absence of such role models sends the contrary message—that the group is relegated to society's less desirable positions. The presence of minority individuals in such positions may also help break down the traditional stereotypical images of minority group members held by whites. From a societal perspective, it is clearly desirable that all persons be free to attain their full potential.

Minority groups add a valuable perspective to the educational experience:

> [Learning] occurs through interactions among students of both sexes, of different races, religions, and backgrounds . . . who are able, directly or indirectly, to learn from their differences and to stimulate one another to reexamine even their most deeply held assumptions about themselves and their world.

Focusing on law schools, for example, white students have learned that blacks may have a different perception of police conduct than theirs. Without exposure to those perspectives, attorneys will fail to fully appreciate many of the complexities of the society with which they will deal in the practice of law or as government officials. An analogous argument could be applied to work situations, which are themselves "learning experiences."

Finally, affirmative action programs may be established in professional schools as a means of combatting the shortage of vital services in black communities. Minority professionals may not only be more likely to serve the minority community but also more valuable to it. For example, commonality of background may be helpful to an attorney in understanding and developing a case or counseling a client. Also, black clients may benefit psychologically by being represented by an attorney of the same race in an otherwise white dominated courtroom.

It may be contended that minorities need the "best" doctors and lawyers, not just members of their own race. This argument, however, not only ignores the "identification" values outlined above, but also appears to be predicated on the questionable theory that students who score highest on admissions tests become the best practitioners. The argument would lose much of its weight if the data

were to show that the highest-scoring young attorneys are being hired by prestigious corporate law firms or that the top-ranking physicians are being accepted into highly specialized fellowship programs, making either group largely unavailable for service in the minority community.

On balance, since it is impossible to know with certainty which professionals will provide the most valuable service to minority communities, affirmative action programs can be defended under utilitarian theory on the grounds that blacks who become doctors or lawyers [according to Nickel] "are more likely to help meet [minority needs] than whites who become doctors or lawyers." Such programs can therefore be justified on the administrative convenience principle which, as noted above, is particularly compelling under social utility theory.

The improvements in the position of the minority community derived from role models, educational opportunity, and improved services, inure to the benefit of society as a whole. Affirmative action, by redistributing opportunity, will alleviate the underlying inequalities, and lessen undesirable social tensions. The general welfare would clearly be enhanced if, for example, the controversy over busing children to attend racially balanced schools could be avoided. Discord over school integration will continue to exist, however, so long as the large scale economic inequality which accounts for discrimination in housing, and hence for de facto school segregation, goes unrelieved.

Affirmative action also enhances the greater societal good by increasing the effectiveness of the economic sector. Assuming that the business community desires to hire the most talented personnel possible, it should look to the largest possible labor pool. Employers who find ways to avoid hiring minorities, or who place them only in non-decision making positions, ignore the potential of minorities and decrease their own profitability. Affirmative action, by broadening the talent base of a business, ultimately works to its advantage. If the business can then produce goods and services more efficiently, society at large also shares in the benefit.

The various social utility arguments for affirmative action analyzed in this subsection, are related to the justice arguments discussed earlier. It would not be necessary to improve the lot of minority groups

—as a matter of justice or of social welfare—except for past discrimination or present inequality. Under a compensatory justice theory, the all-encompassing and comprehensive nature of the injury due to past discrimination entitles minority groups to present compensation. Under a distributive justice rationale, continuing inequality of opportunity—both crude and subtle—entitles minority groups to programs that guarantee them equal job and educational opportunities. Utilitarian theory argues that the effects of group based discrimination have a serious adverse effect on the public welfare and must be eradicated through the use of systematic programs. Discrimination constitutes the core of all three rationales for affirmative action.

Affirmative action is morally justified on all three grounds discussed above: compensatory justice, distributive justice and social utility. The three rationales, however may not be equally acceptable to the American public, and thus are not equally useful in building the public support necessary for affirmative action programs. In order to ascertain whether a consensus of support might be achieved for one rationale more easily than for another, it is necessary to review the contentions of those opposed to affirmative action. . . .

THOMAS SOWELL

"Affirmative Action": A Worldwide Disaster

Thomas Sowell is Senior Research Fellow at the Hoover Institution at Stanford University. (Source: Reprinted from Commentary *[December 1989], by permission; all rights reserved.)*

QUESTIONS FOR REFLECTION

1. What patterns does Sowell find in affirmative-action programs around the world?

2. What are Sowell's responses to arguments from compensation? Do you find them convincing?

3. To what incentives do affirmative-action policies give rise, according to Sowell? How are these incentives harmful, in his view?

4. Some advocates of affirmative action believe that race is a good proxy for disadvantage in general. Sowell disagrees. Why? What evidence does he present?

Arguments for and against "affirmative action" have raged for about twenty years in the United States. Similar arguments have provoked controversy—and even bloodshed—for a longer or a shorter period, in the most disparate societies, scattered around the world. India, Nigeria, Australia, Guyana, Malaysia, Sri Lanka, Pakistan, and Indonesia are just some of the countries where some groups receive official, government-sanctioned preferences over others. While the American phrase "affirmative action" is used in Australia and Canada, other countries have used a variety of other phrases, such as "positive discrimination" (India), "sons of the soil" preferences (Indonesia, Malaysia), "standardization" (Sri Lanka), or "reflecting the federal character" of the country (Nigeria). The same general principle of government apportionment of coveted positions, to supersede the competition of the marketplace or of academia, was of course also embodied in the *numerus clausus* laws used to restrict the opportunities of Jews in pre-war Central and Eastern Europe.

The countries with preferential policies have varied enormously in cultural, political, economic, and other ways. The groups receiving preferences have likewise varied greatly, from locally or nationally dominant groups in some countries to the poorest and most abject groups, such as the untouchables of India. Such vast disparities in settings and people make it all the more striking that there are common patterns among these countries—patterns with serious implications for "affirmative-action" policies in the United States. Among these patterns are the following:

1. Preferential programs, even when explicitly and repeatedly defined as "temporary," have tended not only to persist but also to expand in scope, either embracing more groups or spreading to wider realms for the same groups, or both. Even preferential programs established with legally mandated cut-off dates, as in India and Pakistan, have continued far past those dates by subsequent extensions.

2. Within the groups designated by government as recipients of preferential treatment, the benefits have usually gone disproportionately to those members already more fortunate.

517

3. Group polarization has tended to increase in the wake of preferential programs, with nonpreferred groups reacting adversely, in ways ranging from political backlash to mob violence and civil war.

4. Fraudulent claims of belonging to the designated beneficiary groups have been widespread and have taken many forms in various countries.

In the United States, as in other countries around the world, the empirical consequences of preferential policies have received much less attention than the rationales and goals of such policies. Too often these rationales and goals have been sufficient unto themselves, both in the political arena and in courts of law. Without even an attempt at empirical assessment of costs versus benefits, with no attempt to pinpoint either losers or gainers, discussions of preferential policies are often exercises in assertion, counter-assertion, and accusation. Illusions flourish in such an atmosphere. So do the disappointments and bitterness to which illusions lead.

Foremost among these illusions is the belief that group "disparities" in "representation" are suspect anomalies that can be corrected by having the government temporarily apportion places on the basis of group membership. Every aspect of this belief fails the test of evidence, in country after country. The prime moral illusion is that preferential policies compensate for wrongs suffered. This belief has been supported only by a thin veneer of emotional rhetoric, seldom examined but often reiterated.

I. The Assumptions of "Affirmative Action"

"Temporary" Policies

When U.S. Supreme Court Justice William J. Brennan described the "affirmative-action" plan in the *Weber* case as "a temporary measure," he was echoing a view widely held, not only in the United States but also around the world. Britain's Lord Scarman likewise said:

> We can and for the present must accept the loading of the law in favor of one group at the expense of others,

defending it as a temporary expedient in the balancing process which has to be undertaken when and where there is social and economic inequality.

The rhetoric of transience and the reality of persistence and proliferation are both international features of preferential policies. "Affirmative-action" plans initially justified in the United States by the unique historic sufferings of blacks have been successively extended, over the years, to groups that now add up to several times as many people as the black population—and more than half of the total American population. These include not only American Indians, Hispanics, and Asians, but also women. A very similar pattern emerged in India, where official preferences were established more than forty years ago for untouchables, for some tribal groups, and for unspecified "other backward classes." Since then, so many groups have managed to get themselves included under "other backward classes" that they now outnumber the untouchables and the tribal peoples put together.

Even where no new groups are added to those legally entitled to official preferences, new occupations, institutions, and sectors of the society can fall under the coverage of preferential policies. Malays were granted preferential employment in government back in colonial Malaya under the British. After Malaya became independent Malaysia, and especially after the "New Economic Policy" announced in 1969, preferences spread to university admissions, government loans, occupational licenses, and employment in private businesses, both local and foreign-owned. The island nation of Sri Lanka has followed a pattern much like that of Malaysia. Preferences for the Sinhalese have not spread to other groups but have simply become more pronounced and more widespread over time.

Perhaps the classic example of preferences that spread far beyond their initial group and their original rationale have been the preferences in Pakistan. The desperately poor Bengalis of East Pakistan were "underrepresented" in the civil service, the military, business, and the professions. Even the administration of East Pakistan was filled with West Pakistanis. Preferential policies to correct this were advocated in 1949 as "temporary" expedients to be phased out in five to ten years. In reality, however, these policies have lasted decades beyond this time and in 1984 were extended to 1994 by the late President Zia. Not only did preferential quotas spread well beyond people from the East Pakistan region; they persisted long after East Pakistan broke away in 1971 to form the independent nation of Bangladesh. In other words, those who provided the initial rationale for preferential policies have now disappeared by secession but the policies themselves have acquired a political life of their own.

Despite such patterns in these and other countries, the word "temporary" continues to be used in discussions of preferential policies—judicial and scholarly, as well as popular and political. No argument seems to be considered necessary to show that this transience can be enforced, so that the word "temporary" will be something more than political decoration. Indeed, few seem to feel a need to specify whether the dimensions of "temporary" are to be measured in actual units of time or by the attainment of some preconceived social results. If the latter, then the distinction between "temporary" and "eternal" can be wholly illusory in practice. In short, the nebulousness of the concept of "temporary" preference has matched its futility.

Statistical Disparities

Equally nebulous are the assumptions about the statistical "disparities" and "imbalances" that preferential policies are supposed to correct.

The idea that large statistical disparities between groups are unusual—and therefore suspicious—is commonplace, but only among those who have not bothered to study the history of racial, ethnic, and other groups in countries around the world. Among leading scholars who have in fact devoted years of research to such matters, a radically different picture emerges. Donald L. Horowitz of Duke University, at the end of a massive and masterful international study of ethnic groups—a study highly praised in scholarly journals—examined the idea of a society where groups are "proportionately represented" at different levels and in different sectors. He concluded that "few, if any, societies have ever approximated this description."

A worldwide study of military forces and police forces by Cynthia Enloe of Clark University likewise concluded that "militaries fall far short of mirroring, even roughly, the multi-ethnic societies" from which they come. Moreover, just "as one is unlikely to find a police force or a military that mirrors its plural society, so one is unlikely to find a representative bureaucracy." One reason is that "it is common for different groups to rely on different mobility ladders." Some choose the military, some the bureaucracy, and some various parts of the private sector. Even within the military, different branches tend to have very different racial or ethnic compositions—the Afrikaners, for example, being slightly underrepresented in the South African navy and greatly overrepresented in the South African army, though their utter dominance in the government ensures that they cannot be discriminated against in either branch. Powerless minorities have likewise been greatly overrepresented or even dominant in particular branches of the military or the police—the Chinese in Malaysia's air force and among detectives in the police force, for example.

In the private sector as well, it is commonplace for minorities to be overrepresented, or even dominant, in competitive industries where they have no power to prevent others from establishing rival businesses. Jewish prominence in the clothing industry, not only in the United States, but in Argentina and Chile as well, did not reflect any ability to prevent other Americans, Argentines, or Chileans from manufacturing garments, but simply the advantages of the Jews' having brought needle-trade skills and experience with them from Eastern Europe. The fact that Jews owned more than half the clothing stores in mid-19th-century Melbourne likewise reflected that same advantage, rather than any ability to forbid other Australians from selling clothes. In a similar way, German minorities have been dominant as pioneers in piano manufacturing in colonial America, czarist Russia, Australia, France, and England. Italian fishermen, Japanese farmers, and Irish politicians have been among many other minority groups with special success in special fields in various countries, without any ability to keep out others.

Another distinguished scholar who has studied multi-ethnic societies around the world, Myron Weiner of MIT, refers to "the universality of ethnic inequality." He points out that those inequalities are multidimensional:

All multi-ethnic societies exhibit a tendency for ethnic groups to engage in different occupations, have different levels (and, often, types) of education, receive different incomes, and occupy a different place in the social hierarchy.

Yet the pattern Professor Weiner has seen, after years of research, as a "universality" is routinely assumed to be an *anomaly,* not only by preferential-policy advocates, but also by the intelligentsia, the media, legislators, and judges—all of whom tend to assume, as a *norm,* what Professor Horowitz has found to exist (or even to be approximated) in "few, if any, societies." That what exists widely across the planet is regarded as an anomaly, while what exists virtually nowhere is regarded as a norm, is a tribute to the effectiveness of sheer reiteration in establishing a vision—and of the difficulties of dispelling a prevailing vision by facts.

Some might try to salvage the statistical argument for discrimination by describing discrimination as also being universal. But, to repeat, groups who are in no position to discriminate against anybody have often been overrepresented in coveted positions—the Chinese in Malaysian universities, the Tamils in Sri Lankan universities, the southerners in Nigerian universities, all during the 1960's, and Asians in American universities today being just some of the minorities of whom this has been true. All sorts of other powerless minorities have dominated particular industries or sectors of the economy, the intellectual community, or government employment. Among businessmen, India's Gujaratis in East Africa, the Lebanese in West Africa, the Chinese in Southeast Asia, the Jews in Eastern Europe, and Koreans and Vietnamese in black ghettos across the United States are just some examples. Among high government officials, the Germans were greatly overrepresented in czarist Russia, as were Christians in the Ottoman empire. Among intellectuals, the Scots were as dominant in 18th- and 19th-century Britain as the Jews have been in other parts of Europe. In short, large statistical disparities have been commonplace, both in the presence of discrimination and in its absence. Indeed, large disparities have been commonplace in the utilization of preferential programs designed to reduce disparities.

The intellectual and political *coup* of those who promote the randomness assumption is to put the burden of proof entirely on others. It is not merely the individual employer, for example, who must disprove this assumption in his own particular case in order to escape a charge of discrimination. All who oppose the randomness assumption find themselves confronted with the task of disproving an elusive plausibility, for which no evidence is offered. As for counter-evidence, no enumeration of the myriad ways in which groups are grossly disparate—in age of marriage, alcohol consumption, immigration patterns, performance in sports, performance on tests—can ever be conclusive, even when extended past the point where the patience of the audience is exhausted.

Those viscerally convinced of the pervasiveness of discrimination and its potency as an explanation of social disparities—and convinced also of the effectiveness of preferential policies as a remedy—are little troubled by the logical shakiness of the statistical evidence. That is all the more reason for others to be doubly troubled—not simply because an incorrect policy may be followed but also, and more importantly, because actions ostensibly based on the rule of law are in substance based on visceral convictions, the essence of lynch law. . . .

Assumptions as Law

Flaws in logic or evidence are unfortunate in intellectual speculation but they are far more serious in courts of law, where major penalties may be inflicted on those whose employees or students, for example, do not have a racial or ethnic composition that meets the preconceptions of other people. Some U.S. Supreme Court Justices have repeatedly treated statistical disparities as tantamount to discrimination and assumed the task of restoring groups to where they would have been otherwise. Even where group disparities in "representation" reflect demonstrable performance disparities, these performance disparities themselves have been taken as proof of societal discrimination. Thus, in the *Weber* case, Justice Harry Blackmun declared that there could be "little doubt that any lack of skill" on the part of minority workers competing with Brian Weber "has its roots in purposeful discrimination of the past." In the *Bakke* case, four Justices declared that the failure of minority medical-school applicants to perform as well as Allan Bakke "was due principally to the effects of past discrimination." The Court's task, therefore, was one of "putting minority applicants in the position they would have been in if not for the evil of racial discrimination."

All this presupposes a range of knowledge that no one has ever possessed. Ironically, this sweeping assumption of knowledge has been combined with an apparent ignorance of vast disparities in performance, disparities favoring groups with no power to discriminate against anybody. From such judicial speculation it is only a short step to the idea of restoring groups to where they would have been—and *what* they would have been—but for the offending discrimination.

What would the average Englishman be like today "but for" the Norman conquest? What would the average Japanese be like "but for" the enforced isolation of Japan for two-and-a-half centuries under the Tokugawa shoguns? What would the Middle East be like "but for" the emergence of Islam? In any other context besides preferential-policy issues, the presumption of knowing the answers to such questions would be regarded as ridiculous, even as intellectual speculation, much less as a basis for serious legal action.

To know how one group's employment, education, or other pattern differs statistically from another's is usually easy. What is difficult to know are the many variables determining the interest, skill, and performance of those individuals from various groups who are being considered for particular jobs, roles, or institutions. What is virtually impossible to know are the patterns that would exist in a nondiscriminatory world—the deviations from which would indicate the existence and magnitude of discrimination.

Age distribution and geographic distribution are only two very simple factors which can play havoc with the assumption that groups would be evenly or randomly distributed in occupations and institutions, in the absence of discrimination. When one group's median age is a decade younger than another's—not at all uncommon—that alone may be enough to cause the younger group to be statistically "overrepresented" in sports, crime, and entry-level jobs, as well as in those kinds of diseases and acci-

dents that are more prevalent among the young, while the older group is overrepresented in homes for the elderly, in the kinds of jobs requiring long years of experience, and in the kinds of diseases and accidents especially prevalent among older people.

Another very simple factor operating against an even "representation" of groups is that many ethnic groups are distributed geographically in patterns differing from one another. It would be unlikely that American ethnic groups concentrated in cold states like Minnesota and Wisconsin would be as well represented among citrus growers and tennis players as they are on hockey teams and among skiers. It is also unlikely that groups concentrated in landlocked states would be equally represented in maritime activities, or that groups from regions lacking mineral deposits would be as well-represented among miners or in other occupations associated with extractive industries as groups located in Pennsylvania or West Virginia.

Differences in geographic concentrations among racial and ethnic groups are by no means confined to the U.S. In Brazil, people of German and Japanese ancestry are concentrated in the south. In Switzerland, whole regions are predominantly French, German, or Italian. In countries around the world, an overwhelming majority of the Chinese or the Jewish population is heavily concentrated in a few major cities—often in just one city in a given country. Group differences in geographical distribution can reach right down to the neighborhood level or even to particular streets. In Buenos Aires, people of Italian ancestry have concentrated in particular neighborhoods or on particular streets, according to the places of their own or their ancestral origins in Italy. In Bombay, people from different parts of India are likewise concentrated in particular neighborhoods or on particular streets.

Lest the point be misunderstood, while these two simple and obvious factors—age and location—are capable of disrupting the even "representation" that many assume to exist in the absence of discrimination, there are also innumerable other factors, of varying degrees of complexity and influence, that can do the same. Moreover, differences in age and location may play a significant role in explaining *some* socioeconomic differences between *some* groups but not other socioeconomic differences between those groups, or among other groups. The purpose here is not to pinpoint the reasons for intergroup differences—or even to assume that they can all be pinpointed—but rather to show how arbitrary and unfounded is the assumption that groups would be evenly "represented," in the absence of discrimination. Precisely because the known differences among groups are large and multidimensional, the presumption of weighing these differences so comprehensively and accurately as to know where some group would be "but for" discrimination approaches hubris.

Even the more modest goal of knowing the *general direction* of the deviation of a group's position from where it would have been without discrimination is by no means necessarily achievable. What are the "effects" of centuries of injustice, punctuated by recurring outbursts of lethal mass violence, against the overseas Chinese in Southeast Asia or against the Jews in Europe? Both groups are generally more prosperous than their persecutors. Would they have been still more prosperous in the absence of such adversity? Perhaps—but many peoples with a long history of peace, and with prosperity supplied by nature itself, have quietly stagnated. This is not to say that the Jews and the Chinese would have done so. It is only to say that *we do not know and cannot know.* No amount of good intentions will make us omniscient. No fervent invocation of "social justice" will supply the missing knowledge.

Incentives and Results

"Affirmative-action" policies assume not only a level of knowledge that no one has ever possessed but also a degree of control that no one has ever exercised. Proponents of preferential policies have tended to reason in terms of the rationales and goals of such policies—not in terms of the *incentives* these policies create. Yet these incentives acquire a life of their own, independent of—and often counter to—the avowed goals of preferential policies. Nor are these simply isolated "mistakes" that can be "corrected." They are the fruition of fundamental misconceptions of the degree of control that can be maintained over a whole galaxy of complex social interactions.

At the individual level, the potential beneficiary and the potential loser are not mere blocks of wood passively placed where the policy dictates. Nor are they automatons who continue acting as before, except for modifications specified for them by others. Rather, they respond in *their own ways* to preferential policies. One of these ways was exemplified by a question raised by a group activist seeking preferential hiring in India's city of Hyderabad: "Are we not entitled to jobs just because we are not as qualified?" A Nigerian wrote of "the tyranny of skills." The sense of entitlement—independent of skills or performance—has long been an accompaniment of preferential policies, for the most disparate groups in the most disparate societies.

The late South African economist W. H. Hutt pointed out long ago that the most "virulent" white supporters of early racial-preferential policies in the mines were "those who had not troubled to qualify themselves for promotion," and who therefore relied on being white instead. Today, in the Virgin Islands, even schoolchildren excuse their own substandard academic and behavioral performance by pointing out that government jobs will be waiting for them as U.S. citizens—jobs for which their better-behaved and better-performing West Indian classmates are ineligible. In Malaysia, likewise, "Malay students, who sense that their future is assured, feel less pressure to perform," according to a study there. A study of black colleges in the United States similarly noted that even students planning postgraduate study often showed no sense of urgency about needing to be prepared "because they believed that certain rules would simply be set aside for them." In India, even a fervent advocate of the untouchables, and of preferential policies for them, has urged untouchable students in medical and engineering schools to abandon their "indifference."

The disincentives created by group preferences apply to both preferred and non-preferred groups. As W. H. Hutt wrote of the South African "color bar," these racial preferences "have vitiated the efficiency of the non-whites by destroying incentives" and have also "weakened incentives to efficiency on the part of the whites who have been featherbedded." A very similar principle is found in the very different setting of Jamaica, after it became independent and black-run. There it was the whites who faced the disincentives of the non-preferred. Many withdrew from the competition for public office because they "felt that the day of the black man had come and questioned why they had to make the effort if the coveted job or the national honor would go to the blacks, despite their qualifications." The upshot is that preferential policies represent not simply a transfer of benefits from one group to another, but can also represent a net loss, as both groups perform less well as a result.

Those who initiate preferential policies cannot sufficiently control the reactions of either preferred or non-preferred groups to ensure that such policies will have the desired effect, or even move in the desired direction: Counterproductive reactions that reduce national prosperity or social tranquility adversely affect even members of the preferred group, who are also members of the general society. Whether their gains in one role exceed their losses in the other role is an empirical question whose answer depends on the specifics of each situation. One of the clearly undesired and uncontrolled consequences of preferential policies has been a backlash by non-preferred groups. This backlash has ranged from campus racial incidents in the United States to a bloody civil war in Sri Lanka.

Honors

Nowhere is control more illusory than in the awarding of honors, whose very meaning and effect depend upon other people's opinions. Preferential honors for members of particular groups can easily render suspect not only those particular honors but also honors fully merited and awarded after free and open competition. If one-fifth of the honors received by preferred groups are awarded under double standards, the other four-fifths are almost certain to fall under a cloud of suspicion as well, if only because some of those who lost out in the competition would prefer to believe that they were not bested fairly. It is by no means clear that more real honors—which are ultimately other people's opinions—will come to a group preferentially given awards. Preferential honors can in practice mean a moratorium on recognition of the group's achievements, which can be confounded with patronage or pay-offs. This need not inevitably be so. The point is that the matter is out of the control of those who decide award policy, and in the hands of others observing the outcomes and deciding what to make of them.

Honor is more than a sop to personal vanity. It is a powerful incentive which accomplishes many social tasks, including tasks that are too arduous and dangerous to be compensated by money—even inducing individuals in crisis situations to sacrifice their lives for the greater good of others. In more mundane matters, honor and respect from one's colleagues and subordinates are important and sometimes indispensable aids, without which even the most talented and conscientious individuals sometimes cannot fulfill their promise. To jeopardize the respect and recognition of individuals from preferred groups by rewarding "honors" tainted with double standards is not only to downgrade their own achievements but also to downgrade their chances of accomplishing those achievements in the first place. For example, minority faculty members have often complained about a lack of intellectual and research interaction with their colleagues, and of being thought of as "affirmative-action" professors. After the media revealed that black students were admitted to the Harvard Medical School with lower qualifications, white patients began to refuse to be examined by such students. The negative effects of tainted honors are by no means limited to academia.

Partial Preferences

The illusion of control includes the belief that preferential policies can be extended *partway* into a process while maintaining equal treatment in the remainder of the process. For example, in the early days of "affirmative action" in the United States, it was sometimes asserted that special efforts to recruit minority employees or minority students would be followed by equal treatment at the actual selection stage and afterward. Special concern for particular groups might also mean only special scrutiny to see that they were treated equally. President John F. Kennedy's Executive Order No. 10,925 required that employers who were government contractors "take affirmative action to ensure that the applicants are employed, and that employees are treated during employment without regard to race, creed, color, or national origin." That is virtually the antithesis of what "affirmative action" has come to mean today, either in the United States or in other countries where the term refers to statistical results viewed precisely *with regard* to race, color, creed, or national origin.

The concept of preferential concern stopping partway into a process is not confined to employment or to the United States. In India, a government minister has urged a small lowering of university-admissions standards for students from scheduled castes (untouchables) and scheduled tribes, with the proviso that "he was recommending relaxation for admission and not for passing or grading." Similar views were once expressed in the United States, where special recruitment programs for minority students quickly led to lower admission standards for them—and this in turn sometimes led to "affirmative grading," to prevent excessive failures by minority students. Double standards in grading may originate with the individual professor or be a result of administrative pressures. Halfway around the world—in Soviet Central Asia—professors are also pressured to give preferential grading to Central Asian students. In Malaysia, preferential grading is virtually institutionalized. As Gordon P. Means puts it:

> Although grading is supposed to be without reference to ethnicity, all grades must be submitted to an evaluation review committee having heavy Malay representation. Individual faculty members report various instances when grades were unilaterally raised, apparently for purposes of "ethnic balance."

Sometimes preferential grading takes the less direct form of creating special or easier subjects for particular groups, such as Maori Studies in New Zealand, Malay Studies in Singapore, or a variety of ethnic studies in the United States.

Whether in employment, education, or other areas, carefully limited or fine-tuned preferences have repeatedly proved to be illusory. Neither time limitations nor other limitations have in fact stopped their persistence and spread.

A wide variety of moral arguments has been used to justify preferential policies. Some of these arguments have little in common, except for being largely unexamined in the excitement of crusading zeal—and being successful politically. Among the reasons given for preferences are that (1) the group is indigenous; (2) the group has been historically wronged; and (3) the group happens to be less well represented in desirable institutions or occupations, for whatever reason, so that this "imbalance" must be "corrected."

Whatever the arguments for preferential policies, these preferences (as we have seen) can long outlive the validity of those arguments, whether the degree of validity be zero or 100 percent, or anywhere in between. A genuinely disadvantaged group can cling to preferences, or seek more, long after their disadvantages have been redressed. The moral question, therefore, is not simply whether particular groups deserve particular benefits for particular periods of time, or until particular social conditions are achieved. The real question is whether the *actual consequences of the particular processes* being initiated are likely to be justified, morally or otherwise. . . .

Historical Compensation

The wrongs of history have been invoked by many groups in many countries as a moral claim for contemporary compensation. Much emotional fervor goes into such claims but the question here is about their logic or morality. Assuming for the sake of argument that the historical claims are factually correct, which may not be the case in all countries, to transfer benefits between two groups of living contemporaries because of what happened between two sets of dead people is to raise the question whether any sufferer is in fact being compensated. Only where both wrongs and compensation are viewed as collectivized and inheritable does redressing the wrongs of history have a moral, or even a logical, basis.

The biological continuity of the generations lends plausibility to the notion of group compensation—but only if guilt can be inherited. Otherwise there are simply windfall gains and windfall losses among contemporaries, according to the accident of their antecedents. Moreover, few people would accept this as a general principle to be applied consistently, however much they may advocate it out of compassion (or guilt) over the fate of particular unfortunates. No one would advocate that today's Jews are morally entitled to put today's Germans in concentration camps, in compensation for the Nazi Holocaust. Most people would not only be horrified at any such suggestion but would also regard it as a second act of gross immorality, in no way compensating the first, but simply adding to the sum total of human sins.

Sometimes a more sociological, rather than moral, claim is made that living contemporaries are suffering from the *effects* of past wrongs and that it is these effects which must be offset by compensatory preferences. Tempting as it is to imagine that the contemporary troubles of historically wronged groups are due to those wrongs, this is confusing causation with morality. The contemporary socioeconomic position of groups in a given society often bears no relationship to the historic wrongs they have suffered. Both in Canada and in the United States, the Japanese have significantly higher incomes than the whites, who have a documented history of severe anti-Japanese discrimination in both countries. The same story could be told of the Chinese in Malaysia, Indonesia, and many other countries around the world, of the Jews in countries with virulent anti-Semitism, and a wide variety of other groups in a wide variety of other countries. Among poorer groups as well, the level of poverty often has little correlation with the degree of oppression. No one would claim that the historic wrongs suffered by Puerto Ricans in the United States exceed those suffered by blacks, but the average Puerto Rican income is lower than the average income of blacks.

None of this proves that historic wrongs have no contemporary effects. Rather, it is a statement about the limitations of our knowledge, which is grossly inadequate to the task undertaken and likely to remain so. To pretend to disentangle the innumerable sources of intergroup differences is an exercise in hubris rather than morality.

As one contemporary example of how easy it is to go astray in such efforts, it was repeated for years that the high rate of single-parent, teenage preg-

nancy among blacks were "a legacy of slavery." Evidence was neither asked nor given. But when serious scholarly research was finally done on this subject, the evidence devastated this widely held belief. The vast majority of black children grew up in two-parent homes, even under slavery itself, and for generations thereafter. The current levels of single-parent, teenage pregnancy are a phenomenon of the last half of the 20th century and are a disaster that has also struck groups with wholly different histories from that of blacks. Passionate commitment to "social justice" can never be a substitute for knowing what you are talking about.

Those who attribute any part of the socioeconomic fate of any group to factors internal to that group are often accused of "blaming the victim." This may sometimes be part of an attempt to salvage the historical-compensation principle but it deserves separate treatment.

"Blame" and "Victims"

The illusion of morality is often confused with the reality of causation. If group A originates in a country where certain scientific and technological skills are widespread and group B originates in a country where they are not, then when they immigrate to the same third country, they are likely to be statistically "represented" to very different degrees in occupations and institutions requiring such skills. There is nothing mysterious about this, in causal terms. But those who wish to attribute this disparity to institutional discrimination are quick to respond to any mention of group B's lesser scientfic-technological background as a case of "blaming the victim." By making the issue *who* is to blame, such arguments evade or preempt the more fundamental question—whether this is a matter of blame in the first place.

Clearly today's living generation—in any group—cannot be *blamed* for the centuries of cultural evolution that went on before they were born, often in lands that they have never seen. Nor can they be blamed for the fact that the accident of birth caused them to inherit one culture rather than another. In causal terms, it would be a staggering coincidence if cultures evolving in radically different historical circumstances were equally effective for all purposes when transplanted to a new society. Blame has nothing to do with it. . . .

"Underrepresentation" and "Life Chances"

Quite aside from claims of historic wrongs, the argument has often been made—on grounds of morality as well as political or social expediency—that the "underrepresentation" of particular groups in desirable roles is an "imbalance" to be "corrected." Majorities have pressed such claims as readily as minorities, in circumstances where their only disadvantages were their own lack of skills or interest, as well as where a plausible case could be made that imposed disabilities have handicapped them.

Among the many unexamined assumptions behind preferential policies is the belief that intergroup friction is a function of the magnitude of income gaps, so that more social harmony can be achieved by reducing these gaps. As with so much that has been said in this area, evidence has been neither asked nor given, while counter-evidence is plentiful, varied, and ignored.

In Bombay, the hosility of the Maharashtrians has been directed primarily at the South Indians, who are somewhat ahead of them economically, rather than against the Gujaratis, who are far ahead of them. Throughout sub-Saharan Africa, there has historically been far more hostility directed by Africans against Asians than against Europeans, who are economically far ahead of both. A similar pattern is found *within* African groups. In Nigeria, for example, the Yoruba were far ahead of the Ibo economically in 1940, while there was a much smaller gap at that time between the Hausa and the Ibo. Yet the hostility and violence between Hausa and Ibo in that era greatly exceeded any friction between either of these groups and the Yoruba. Later, as the Ibos rose, narrowing the gap between themselves and the Yoruba, it was precisely then that Ibo-Yoruba outbreaks of violence occurred.

Advocates of preferential policies often express a related belief, similarly unsupported by evidence, that an even distribution of groups across sectors of the economy tends to reduce social frictions and hostility. Much history suggests the opposite, that

(in the words of Professor Horowitz) "the ethnic division of labor is more a shield than a sword."

The utter dominance of particular sectors by particular minority groups has been quietly accepted for generations in many countries—until a specific, organized campaign has been whipped up against the minority, often by members of the majority who are seeking to enter the minority-dominated sector and are finding their competition very formidable. Often majority-group customers or suppliers actually prefer dealing with the minority-run entrepreneurs. Even in the midst of ethnic riots against other groups certain middleman minorities have been spared—the Greeks in the Sudan, Hindus in Burma, Marwaris in Assam. Organized boycotts of minority businessmen have been spearheaded by majority-group business rivals, from Uganda and Kenya to the Philippines and the United States. Contrary to what is widely (and lightly) assumed, neither an even representation of groups nor mass resentment at unevenness is "natural."

Repeatedly, in countries scattered around the world, it has been precisely the rise of newly emerging ethnic competitors—whether in business, government, or the professions—which has produced not only friction with groups already dominant in the sectors concerned but also, and much more importantly, has led the newcomers to whip up their whole group emotionally against the already established group. A Sri Lankan legislator noted this pattern early in that country's inter-ethnic troubles:

> University graduates and people like that are the cause of all the trouble—not the vast mass of the Sinhalese people. It is those men, these middle-class unemployed seeking employment, who are jealous of the fact that a few Tamils occupy seats of office in government—these are the people who have gone round the countryside, rousing the masses and creating this problem.

Halfway around the world a similar charge was made, that "the educated Nigerian is the worst peddler of tribalism." In the very different setting of Hungary in the 1880's, the promotion of anti-Semitism was largely the work of students, intellectuals, and sections of the middle classes, while the Hungarian peasant masses remained relatively unresponsive.

Advocates of preferential policies often see these policies as not only promoting social harmony by reducing gaps in income and "representation," but also as part of a more general attempt to "equalize life chances." Much effort is expended establishing the moral desirability of this goal and the extent to which we currently fall short of it, while little or no effort goes into establishing our *capability* to accomplish such a staggering task. One clue to the magnitude and difficulty of what is being attempted are the various ways in which first-born children excel their siblings. A completely disproportionate number of the famous individuals in history were either first-born or the only child. In more mundane achievements as well, the first-born tend to excel. A study of National Merit Scholarship finalists showed that, even in five-child families, the first-born became finalists more often than all the other siblings combined. The same was true in two-, three-, and four-child families. Such disparities, among people born of the same parents and raised under the same roof, mock presumptions of being able to equalize life chances across broader and deeper differences among people in a large, complex, and, especially, multi-ethnic society.

The abstract moral desirability of a goal cannot preempt the prior question of our capacity to achieve it. This is not even a question of falling short of all that might be hoped for. It is a question of risking counterproductive, disastrous, and even bloody results.

Beneficiaries and Losers

Part of the moral aura surrounding preferential policies is due to the belief that such policies benefit the less fortunate. The losers in this presumed redistribution are seldom specified, though the underlying assumption seems to be that they are the more fortunate.

Empirical evidence for such assumptions is largely lacking and the *a priori* case for believing them is unconvincing. For example, the effects of preferential policies depend on the costs of complementary factors required to use the preferences. These costs can obviously be borne more readily by those who are already more fortunate. Benefits set aside for businessmen of the preferred group are of no use to members of that group who do not happen to own a business, or possess the capital to start one. Preferential admission to medical school is a benefit only to those who have already gone to college. Because preferential benefits tend to be concentrated on more lucrative or prestigious things, they are often within striking distance only for the fortunate few who have already advanced well beyond most other members of the preferred group. In Third World countries, where the great demand is for clerical jobs in the government, the poorer groups in these countries often have difficulty reaching even the modest level of education required for such employment.

Preferential scholarships for Malays in Malaysia are a classic example. Students from families in the lower-income brackets—63 percent of the population—received 14 percent of the university scholarships, while students whose families were in the top 17 percent of the income distribution received more than half of the scholarships. In India, preferential programs for both untouchables and "other backward classes" show the same pattern. In the state of Haryana, 37 different untouchable castes were entitled to preferential scholarships but only 18 actually received any—and just one of these received 65 percent of the scholarships at the graduate levels and 80 percent at the undergraduate level. Similar patterns are found in other parts of the country. In the state of Tamil Nadu, the highest of the so-called "backward classes" (11 percent of the total) received nearly half of all jobs and all university admissions set aside for such classes. The bottom 12 percent received no more than 2 percent of the jobs and university admissions.

In some cases—including the United States—the less fortunate members of a preferred group may actually retrogress while the more fortunate advance under preferential policies. After "affirmative-action" policies took hold in the early 1970's, blacks with little education and little job experience fell further behind the general population—and indeed further behind whites with little education and little job experience. Meanwhile, blacks with college education or substantial job experience advanced economically, both absolutely and relative to whites with the same advantages. Yet another example of the benefits of "affirmative action" to those already more fortunate are the business "set-asides" that give minority entrepreneurs preferential access to government contracts under Section 8(a) of the Small Business Act. Minority businessmen who participate in this program have an average net worth of $160,000. This is not only far higher than the average net worth of the groups they come from, but also higher than the average net worth of Americans in general.

This pattern of simultaneous advance at the top and retrogression at the bottom is not confined to the United States. In India, the era of preferential policies has seen the proportion of untouchables increase significantly among high-level government officials, while the proportion of untouchables who work as landless agricultural laborers has also increased. In Malaysia, the representation of Malays on corporate boards of directors has increased significantly, while the proportion of Malays among the population living below the official poverty level has also increased.

Just as the advocates of preferential policies arbitrarily assume that such policies will benefit the "disadvantaged," so they arbitrarily assume that this will be at the expense of the "privileged." They neither offer evidence of this in advance nor are so impolitic as to collect data on this point after preferential programs have been inaugurated. Such evidence as exists points in the opposite direction. In Bombay, preferential policies to put Maharashtrians into the ranks of business executives had only minor effects on the Gujaratis who were dominant in that occupation, reducing the proportion of Gujarati executives from 52 percent to 44 percent. Among the South Indians, however, their 25-percent representation among Bombay executives was cut in half, to 12 percent. A similar pattern appeared in the very different setting of prewar Hungary, where policies favoring Gentiles had relatively little effect on the Jewish financial and industrial elite but imposed real hardships on the Jewish middle class and lower middle class. In the United States, despite voluminous official statistics on all sorts of racial and ethnic matters, no one seems to have collected data on the actual losers under "affirmative action." It may be significant, however, that those who have pro-

tested their losses all the way up to the U.S. Supreme Court have not been named Adams, Cabot, or Rockefeller, but DeFunis, Bakke, and Weber.

II. The Illusion of Compensation

What makes compensation an illusion is not only that sufferers are not in fact compensated, or the effects of historic wrongs redressed—or even accurately identified and separated from innumerable other social factors at work simultaneously. Both the principle of compensation and the particular form of compensation via preferential policies require careful examination.

The Principle of Compensation

Given the mortality of human beings, often the only compensation for historic wrongs that is within the scope of our knowledge and control is purely symbolic compensation—taking from individuals who inflicted no harm and giving to individuals who suffered none. In addition to the moral shakiness and social dangers of such a policy, it also promotes a kind of social irredentism, a set of *a priori* grievances against living people, whether or not they have ever inflicted harm on those who feel aggrieved. In view of the futile but bitter and bloody struggles engendered by territorial irredentism, there is little good to hope for by applying this same principle in a new field.

The factual reality that actual benefits from compensatory preferences tend to be concentrated in the already more fortunate elites among the preferred groups makes the moral case for such policies weaker and the social dangers greater. The more educated, articulate, and more politically sophisticated elites have every incentive to whip up group emotions in favor of more and better preferences, despite the increasing group polarization this may produce, and to be intransigent against any suggestion that any such preferences should ever be reduced or ended. This has been a common pattern in the most disparate countries.

In principle, compensation can take many forms, beginning with a simple transfer of money from one group to another. In practice, however, preferential policies are the form taken in many countries around the world. The implications of that particular form, and of its alternatives, raise still more troubling questions.

The Form of Compensation

If, notwithstanding all philosophic objections to the principle of group compensation, such a policy is in fact chosen, then the particular form of the compensation can make a major difference in the costs and the consequences of compensatory policies. When resources, or the benefits they create, are transferred from group A to group B, this is not necessarily—or even likely—a zero-sum process, in which the value of what is lost by one is the same as the value of what is gained by the other. What is transferred may be subjectively valued differently by the losers and the recipients. There may also be objectively discernible differences in the use of the same resources by the two groups.

Compensatory policies may, in theory, take place through transfers of money, transfers of in-kind benefits, or through differential applications of rules and standards. In Australia, for example, various money and in-kind transfers to the aborigines add up to more than $2,000 annually for every aboriginal man, woman, and child. Such transfers arouse relatively little political opposition or social backlash. Similarly, in the United States, monetary compensation for Japanese Americans interned during World War II aroused relatively little controversy—and even that little controversy quickly subsided, once the decision was made.

Such monetary transfers are less costly to individual members of the majority population the more the majority outnumbers the minority receiving the transfer. Obviously, if group A is 100 times as large as group B, each member of group B can receive $100 at a cost of only one dollar to each member of group A. However, even where the losses sustained by one group are significant, monetary transfers may still be efficient, in the narrowly economic sense that what is lost by one group as a whole is gained by another group, with no direct net loss to society as a whole. Whatever the merits or demerits of the particular transfer on other grounds, it is not inefficient. Politically and socially, the opposition to such transfers is therefore unlikely to be as great as opposition to the same net transfers in forms that cost more to the losers than is gained by the gainers. Preferential policies often cost the losers more than is gained by the gainers. Preferential policies, by definition, involve a differential application of rules and standards to individuals originating in different groups. Even where the preferences are not stated in terms of differential rules or standards, but rather in terms of numerical quotas, "goals," or "targets," differences in the qualifications of the respective pools of applicants can readily make numerical similarities amount to differences in standards. This is a very common result in countries around the world. In Nigeria, programs to have college-student populations reflect "the federal character" of the country—i.e., tribal quotas under regional names—led to a situation where cut-off scores for admission to the same college varied substantially between students from different tribes or regions. In Sri Lanka, demographic "standardization" policies led to similar disparities in qualification requirements for individuals from different regions of the country. In India, attempts to meet quotas for untouchable students led to drastic reductions in the qualifications they needed for admission to various institutions. Where applicant pools in different groups are different in qualifications, numerical quotas are equivalent to different standards. Therefore preferential policies in general, however phrased, are essentially an application of different rules or standards to individuals from different groups. The question then is: what are the effects of transfers between groups in this particular form?

There are many ways in which intergroup transfers through differential standards can become negative-sum processes, in which what is lost by one group exceeds what is gained by another, thus representing a direct loss to society as a whole—as well as causing indirect losses, due to a larger resistance or backlash than if the recipient group had obtained the same value or benefit in some other form. An obvious example is when a particular group, in which 90 percent of the students admitted to college succeed in graduating, loses places to another group in which only 30 percent of the students graduate. Group A must lose 900 gradu- ates, in order for group B to gain 300 graduates. It might be objected that this overstates the net loss, since there may be some marginal benefit simply from having attended college, even without graduat- ing. Offsetting this, however, is the fact that groups with lower qualifications tend to specialize in easier and less remunerative fields, whether in India, Ma- laysia, the Soviet Union, or the United States. There- fore group A may lose 900 graduates largely concen- trated in mathematics, science, and engineering, while group B gains 300 graduates largely concen- trated in sociology, education, and ethnic studies.

The *apparent* losses to one group under preferen- tial policies may also far exceed the real losses, thereby further raising the indirect social costs of backlash and turmoil. For example, an observer of India's preferential policies for untouchables (known offi- cially as "scheduled castes") has commented:

> . . . we hear innumerable tales of persons being de- prived of appointments in favor of people who ranked lower than they did in the relevant examinations. No doubt this does happen, but if all these people were, in fact, paying the price for appointments to Scheduled Castes, there would be many more SC persons ap- pointed than there actually are. To illustrate: suppos- ing that 300 people qualify for ten posts available. The top nine are appointed on merit but the tenth is reserved, so the authorities go down the list to find an SC applicant. They find one at 140 and he is appointed. Whereupon all 131 between him and the merit list feel aggrieved. He has not taken 131 posts; he has taken one, yet 131 people believe they have paid the price for it. Moreover, the remaining 159 often also resent the situation, believing that their chances were, somehow, lessened by the existence of SC reservations.

Where certain opportunities are rigidly "set aside" for particular groups, in the sense that mem- bers of other groups cannot have them, even if these opportunities remain unused, then there is the po- tential for a maximum of grievance for a minimum of benefit transfer. Admission to medical school in India's state of Gujarat operates on this principle— and has led repeatedly to bloody riots in which many people have died. Reservations or "set-asides" in general tend to provoke strong objections. The first major setback for "affirmative action" in the U.S.

Supreme Court was based on objections to reserved- admissions places for minority applicants in the 1978 *Bakke* case. A later major setback occurred in *City of Richmond v. Croson* (1989), where minority business set-asides were struck down by the Su- preme Court. Similarly, in India, an exhaustive, scholarly legal study of preferential policies found: "Virtually all of the litigation about compensatory discrimination has involved reservations, even though preferences in the form of provisions of facilities, resources, and protections directly affect a much larger number of recipients." This litigation has been initiated mostly by non-preferred individ- uals who complain of being adversely affected. In some ultimate sense, non-preferred individuals are just as much adversely affected by preferences in other forms that direct resources away from them and toward preferred groups. But it is preference in the specific form of "reservation" or "set-aside" that seems most to provoke both violence and litigation.

By contrast, resource transfers designed to enable disadvantaged groups to meet standards are ac- cepted while attempts to bring the standards down to them are overwhelmingly rejected. In the United States, preferential policies have repeatedly been rejected in public-opinion polls. However, the same American public has strongly supported "special educational or vocational courses, free of charge, to enable members of minority groups to do better on tests." More than three-fifths of all whites even sup- port "requiring large companies to set up special training programs for members of minority groups." The issue is not simply whether one is for or against the advancement of particular groups or is willing to see transfers of resources for their betterment. The method by which their betterment is attempted matters greatly in terms of whether such efforts have the support or the opposition of others.

III. Replacing Illusions

With all the empirical weaknesses, logical flaws, and social dangers of preferential policies, why have they become so popular and spread so rapidly around the world? One reason is that their *political* attractions are considerable. They offer an immedi- ate response—a quick fix—at relatively little government expense, to the demands of vocal, aroused, and often organized elites, speaking in the name of restive masses. This restiveness of the masses is by no means incidental. Violence has frequently preceded preferences, from the American ghetto riots of the 1960's to the Malay and Indonesian riots against the Chinese at about the same time, to terrorism in India, and massive mob violence against the Tamils in Sri Lanka. This violence by the masses is typically used politically to promote elite purposes via preferential policies. An international study of ethnic conflicts concluded:

> Preferences tend to respond to middle-class aspirations almost entirely. They do little or nothing about the resentments of those who do not aspire to attend secondary school or university, to enter the modern private sector or the bureaucracy, or to become businessmen. Although lower-class resentments are often profound—it is not, after all, the middle class that typically participates in ethnic violence—the resentments may have nothing to do with occupational mobility and preferences do not address them.

Preferential policies, then, are politically attractive as a response, however socially ineffective or counterproductive such policies may later prove to be in practice. At a sufficiently superficial level, the moral attractions of preferential policies are considerable as well. Even in South Africa, moral appeals were made on behalf of a "civilized labor policy"—protecting European workers' customary standard of living from being undercut by Africans and Indians accustomed to living on less—and clergy, intellectuals, and others not personally benefiting joined in support of these policies on that basis. Preferential policies allow intellectuals as well as politicians to be on the side of the angels (as locally defined at the time) at low cost—or rather, at a low down payment, for the real costs come later, and have sometimes been paid in blood.

The last refuge of a failed policy is "the long run," in which it will supposedly be a success. In other words, those who predicted the short run wrongly ask to be trusted with the much harder task of predicting the long run rightly. This argument, used to defend the counterproductive effects of preferential policies, is far less defensible in an international perspective where older preferential policies (as in

India or Sri Lanka) have progressed from intergroup political hostility to bloodshed in the streets and deaths by the thousands, while newer programs (as in the United States) are still in the process of increasing group polarization, and the even more recent preferential policies taking shape in Australia and New Zealand are still at the stage of optimistic predictions.

Even the most damning indictment of a policy is almost certain to be met with the response: "But what would you replace it with?" However effective as a political tactic, such a question confuses rather than clarifies. It is like an arbitrary prohibition against saying that the emperor has no clothes, until a complete wardrobe has been designed. The question misconceives policy, and human actions in general, in yet another way: no one who extinguishes a forest fire or removes a cancer has to "replace" it with anything. We are well rid of evils.

This is not to say that none of the aspects of social issues raised during "affirmative-action" controversies should ever be addressed by public policy. The case for public policy in general, or for a particular public policy, must be made on the individual merits of the particular issues raised—but not as a general "replacement" for some discredited policy.

What must be replaced are the social illusions and misconceptions underlying preferential policies, for any alternative policy based on the same illusions and misconceptions will have the same fatal weaknesses in its structure. In some countries and for some purposes social policy may wish to ameliorate the lot of the less fortunate or make it possible for individuals or groups to acquire the knowledge and skills necessary for their own advancement. It is infinitely more important that such efforts be based on facts and logic than that there be one particular scheme selected from innumerable possibilities as the uniquely designated "replacement" for existing policy.

We may or may not be able to agree on what the ideal, or even a viable, policy must be. What we can agree on is far more fundamental: We can agree to *talk sense*. That will mean abandoning a whole vocabulary of political rhetoric which preempts factual questions by arbitrarily calling statistical disparities "discrimination," "exclusion," "segregation," and the like. It will mean confronting issues instead of impugning motives. It will mean specifying goals and defending those specifics, rather than speaking in terms of seeking some nebulously unctuous "change" or "social justice." Perhaps more than anything else, talking sense will mean examining policies in terms of the incentives they create, and the results to which these incentives lead, rather than the hopes they embody. It will mean that evidence takes precedence over assertion and reiteration. . . .

VI. Politics versus Progress

. . . Could some judicious blend of preferential programs and programs designed to improve the performances of less educated groups work? Here the problem is that the two kinds of programs create incentives that work at cross-purposes, even if their goals are the same. Forcing students to meet higher standards—a painful process for them and their teachers alike—will be made all the more difficult if the students know that these standards are unnecessary for them to reach whatever educational or employment goals they have, or even to be promoted to the next grade. If group-representation statistics are the standard by which institutions will be judged, other standards will be sacrificed for the sake of body count. This is true not only of educational institutions but of other institutions as well.

Political feasibility is the greatest obstacle to new policies with an overriding goal of advancing the less fortunate because time is the key ingredient in such advancement on a large scale. Even in the extreme case of South Africa, where massive transfers of the nation's resources were focused on a small minority of its people, in *addition* to preferential policies pursued in utter disregard of the losses and even tragedies suffered by others as a result, it was decades before the Afrikaner "poor whites" became middle-class. Only in terms of political appearances are preferential policies a "quick fix." The dangers of an actual retrogression among the masses of the beneficiary group cannot be dismissed, either from an analytical or an empirical perspective. Even greater dangers have materialized in countries that have experienced bloodshed in the wake of group polarization brought on by preferential policies.

While current political feasibility may be the touchstone of the professional politician, it cannot be the last word for others. In many countries, what is most politically feasible are policies that further a continued drift in the direction of group polarization and the dangers and disasters this entails. Specific alternative policies will differ for different groups and different countries. What is crucial is that these alternatives be examined in terms of the incentives they create and the results to which such incentives can be expected to lead—regardless of the rationales, aspirations, or symbolism of these policies. Determining in this way what *should* be done is not an exercise in utopianism, for once there is a consensus on what needs to be done, that in itself changes what is politically feasible.

The starting point for rethinking and reform must be a recognition that "affirmative action" has been a failure in the United States and a disaster in other countries that have had such policies longer. Indeed, a growing polarization and increasing numbers of ugly racial incidents (especially on campuses that are strongholds of "affirmative action") may be early warnings that we too may be moving from the stage of mere failure to the stage of social disaster.

Index